Communications in Computer and Information Science 2601

Series Editors

Gang Li ⓘ, *School of Information Technology, Deakin University, Burwood, VIC, Australia*

Joaquim Filipe ⓘ, *Polytechnic Institute of Setúbal, Setúbal, Portugal*

Zhiwei Xu, *Chinese Academy of Sciences, Beijing, China*

Rationale

The CCIS series is devoted to the publication of proceedings of computer science conferences. Its aim is to efficiently disseminate original research results in informatics in printed and electronic form. While the focus is on publication of peer-reviewed full papers presenting mature work, inclusion of reviewed short papers reporting on work in progress is welcome, too. Besides globally relevant meetings with internationally representative program committees guaranteeing a strict peer-reviewing and paper selection process, conferences run by societies or of high regional or national relevance are also considered for publication.

Topics

The topical scope of CCIS spans the entire spectrum of informatics ranging from foundational topics in the theory of computing to information and communications science and technology and a broad variety of interdisciplinary application fields.

Information for Volume Editors and Authors

Publication in CCIS is free of charge. No royalties are paid, however, we offer registered conference participants temporary free access to the online version of the conference proceedings on SpringerLink (http://link.springer.com) by means of an http referrer from the conference website and/or a number of complimentary printed copies, as specified in the official acceptance email of the event.

CCIS proceedings can be published in time for distribution at conferences or as post-proceedings, and delivered in the form of printed books and/or electronically as USBs and/or e-content licenses for accessing proceedings at SpringerLink. Furthermore, CCIS proceedings are included in the CCIS electronic book series hosted in the SpringerLink digital library at http://link.springer.com/bookseries/7899. Conferences publishing in CCIS are allowed to use Online Conference Service (OCS) for managing the whole proceedings lifecycle (from submission and reviewing to preparing for publication) free of charge.

Publication process

The language of publication is exclusively English. Authors publishing in CCIS have to sign the Springer CCIS copyright transfer form, however, they are free to use their material published in CCIS for substantially changed, more elaborate subsequent publications elsewhere. For the preparation of the camera-ready papers/files, authors have to strictly adhere to the Springer CCIS Authors' Instructions and are strongly encouraged to use the CCIS LaTeX style files or templates.

Abstracting/Indexing

CCIS is abstracted/indexed in DBLP, Google Scholar, EI-Compendex, Mathematical Reviews, SCImago, Scopus. CCIS volumes are also submitted for the inclusion in ISI Proceedings.

How to start

To start the evaluation of your proposal for inclusion in the CCIS series, please send an e-mail to ccis@springer.com

Mufti Mahmud · Nelishia Pillay ·
M Shamim Kaiser
Editors

Applications of Artificial Intelligence and Data Science

First Global Conference, AAIDS 2024
London, UK, April 3–5, 2024
Proceedings

Editors
Mufti Mahmud ⓘ
King Fahd University of Petroleum
and Minerals
Dhahran, Saudi Arabia

Nelishia Pillay ⓘ
University of Pretoria
Pretoria, South Africa

M Shamim Kaiser ⓘ
Jahangirnagar University
Dhaka, Bangladesh

ISSN 1865-0929　　　　　　ISSN 1865-0937 (electronic)
Communications in Computer and Information Science
ISBN 978-3-031-98497-6　　ISBN 978-3-031-98498-3 (eBook)
https://doi.org/10.1007/978-3-031-98498-3

© The Editor(s) (if applicable) and The Author(s), under exclusive license
to Springer Nature Switzerland AG 2026

This work is subject to copyright. All rights are solely and exclusively licensed by the Publisher, whether the whole or part of the material is concerned, specifically the rights of translation, reprinting, reuse of illustrations, recitation, broadcasting, reproduction on microfilms or in any other physical way, and transmission or information storage and retrieval, electronic adaptation, computer software, or by similar or dissimilar methodology now known or hereafter developed.
The use of general descriptive names, registered names, trademarks, service marks, etc. in this publication does not imply, even in the absence of a specific statement, that such names are exempt from the relevant protective laws and regulations and therefore free for general use.
The publisher, the authors and the editors are safe to assume that the advice and information in this book are believed to be true and accurate at the date of publication. Neither the publisher nor the authors or the editors give a warranty, expressed or implied, with respect to the material contained herein or for any errors or omissions that may have been made. The publisher remains neutral with regard to jurisdictional claims in published maps and institutional affiliations.

This Springer imprint is published by the registered company Springer Nature Switzerland AG
The registered company address is: Gewerbestrasse 11, 6330 Cham, Switzerland

If disposing of this product, please recycle the paper.

Preface

The Global Conference on Applications of Artificial Intelligence and Data Science (AAIDS 2024) provided an excellent international forum for sharing knowledge and results in theory, methodology, and applications of Artificial Intelligence (AI) and Data Science. The conference provided a platform for researchers and practitioners from both academia and industry to meet and share cutting-edge developments in the field. The first edition of AAIDS was held in London, UK, on April 3–5, 2024. The Department of Computer Applications of the University of Engineering & Management, Jaipur, India, and the Cognitive Computing and Brain Informatics Research Group of Nottingham Trent University, UK jointly organised the conference.

AAIDS 2024 had three technical tracks under which research works were presented. The tracks were Hybrid AI Systems, Advanced Computing and Statistics, and Data Science. The conference also featured invited speakers, tutorials, workshops, exhibits and competitions.

The AAIDS 2024 conference attracted 147 submissions from 21 countries across the three tracks. The submitted papers underwent a single-blind review process, soliciting expert opinion from at least three experts: two independent reviewers and the track chair. After the rigorous review reports from the reviewers and the track chairs, the best 30 full papers from 10 countries were accepted for presentation at the conference. Therefore, this volume of the AAIDS 2024 conference proceedings contains those 30 papers which were presented at the conference.

We want to express our gratitude to all AAIDS 2024 conference committee members for their instrumental and unwavering support. AAIDS 2024 had a very exciting program, which would not have been possible without the generous dedication of the Programme Committee members in reviewing the conference papers. AAIDS 2024 could not have taken place without the great team efforts and the generous support from our sponsors.

We would especially like to express our sincere appreciation to our generous sponsors, including Springer-Nature and the entire Springer CCIS team.

Last but not least, we thank all our contributors and volunteers for their support during this challenging time to make AAIDS 2024 a success.

January 2025
Mufti Mahmud
Nelishia Pillay
M Shamim Kaiser

Organization

Honorary Chairs

Stephen Grossberg   Boston University, USA
Francesco C. Morabito   Mediterranea University of Reggio Calabria, Italy

General Chair

Mufti Mahmud   King Fahd University of Petroleum and Minerals, Saudi Arabia

Conference Secretary

Somen Nayak   ICFAI University, Jaipur, India

Programme Chairs

Jyoti Sekhar Banerjee   Bengal Institute of Technology, India
Nelishia Pillay   University of Pretoria, South Africa
M. Shamim Kaisar   Jahangirnagar University, Bangladesh

Workshop/Special Session Chairs

Cosimo Ieracitano   University Mediterranea of Reggio Calabria, Italy
Manjunath Aradhya   JSS Science and Technology University, India
Maryam Doborjeh   Auckland University of Technology, New Zealand

Finance Chair

Aniruddha Mukherjee   University of Engineering & Management, Jaipur, India

Publication Chairs

Mufti Mahmud	King Fahd University of Petroleum and Minerals, Saudi Arabia
Somen Nayak	ICFAI University, Jaipur, India

Publicity and Sponsorship Chairs

Abzetdin Adamov	ADA University, Azerbaijan
Mrinal Kanti Sarkar	University of Engineering & Management, Jaipur, India
Noushath Shaffi	Suntan Qaboos University, Oman
Pradeep K Sharma	University of Engineering & Management, Jaipur, India
Tianhua Chen	University of Huddersfield, UK

Local Organization Chairs

Hriday Banerjee	University of Engineering & Management, Jaipur, India
M. Arifur Rahman	Nottingham Trent University, UK
Tawfiq Al-Hadhrami	Nottingham Trent University, UK
Santanu Basak	University of Engineering & Management, Jaipur, India

Registration Chairs

Renu Jangra	University of Engineering & Management, Jaipur, India
Yogesh Kumar Jakhar	University of Engineering & Management, Jaipur, India
Suman Acharya	University of Engineering & Management, Jaipur, India

Technical Program Committee

Abzetdin Adamov	ADA University, Azerbaijan
Hojjat Adeli	Ohio State University, USA
Tawfik Al-Hadhrami	Nottingham Trent University, UK
Shamim Al Mamun	Jahangirnagar University, Bangladesh
Michele Ambrosanio	Università di Napoli "Parthenope", Italy
Alessia Amelio	Università degli Studi "G. d'Annunzio" Chieti – Pescara, Italy
Juan P. Amezquita-Sanchez	Universidad Autónoma de Querétaro, Mexico
Marco Appetito	Aubay, Italy
Manjunath Aradhya	JSS S&T University, India
Saiful Azad	Green University of Bangladesh, Bangladesh
Hamed Azami	University of Toronto, Canada
Francesco Bardozzo	University of Salerno, Italy
Tiziana Ciano	University Mediterranea of Reggio Calabria, Italy
Tianhua Chen	University of Huddersfield, UK
Gennaro Cordasco	Università degli studi della Campania Luigi Vanvitelli, Italy
M. Ali Akber Dewan	Athabasca University, Canada
Nilanjan Dey	JIS University, India
Khoo Bee Ee	Universiti Sains Malaysia, Malaysia
Anna Esposito	University of Campania Luigi Vanvitell, Italy
Marcos Faundez-Zanuy	Escola Superior Politècnica Tecnocampus, Spain
Massimiliano Ferrara	University Mediterranea of Reggio Calabria, Italy
Giancarlo Fortino	University of Calabria, Italy
Fabio Frustaci	University of Calabria, Italy
Hamido Fujita	Iwate Prefectural University, Japan
Antonio Guerrieri	University of Calabria, Italy
Antonella Guzzo	University of Calabria, Italy
Marzia Hoque Tania	University of New South Wales, Australia
A. B. M. Aowlad Hossain	Khulna University of Engineering & Technology, Bangladesh
Tingwen Huang	Texas A&M University, Qatar
Amir Hussain	Edinburgh Napier University, UK
Michele Ianni	University of Calabria, Italy
Cosimo Ieracitano	University Mediterranea of Reggio Calabria, Italy
Khan Iftekharuddin	Old Dominion University, USA
S. M. Riazul Islam	Sejong University, South Korea
Shariful Islam	Deakin University, Australia
M. Shamim Kaiser	Jahangirnagar University, Bangladesh
Omprakash Kaiwartya	Nottingham Trent University, UK

Joarder Kamruzzaman	Federation University Australia, Australia
Ramani Kannan	Universiti Teknologi PETRONAS, Malaysia
Nikola Kasabov	Auckland University of Technology, New Zealand
Gianluca Lax	University Mediterranea of Reggio Calabria, Italy
Michele Lo Giudice	University Mediterranea of Reggio Calabria, Italy
Mufti Mahmud	King Fahd University of Petroleum and Minerals, Saudi Arabia
Nadia Mammone	University Mediterranea of Reggio Calabria, Italy
Stefano Marrone	Università degli studi della Campania Luigi Vanvitelli, Italy
Alessio Micheli	University of Pisa, Italy
Francesco Carlo Morabito	University Mediterranea of Reggio Calabria, Italy
M. Murugappan	College of Science and Technology, Kuwait
Massimo Panella	University Sapienza of Rome, Italy
Nelishia Pillay	University of Pretoria, South Africa
Emanuele Principi	Università Politecnica delle Marche, Italy
M. Arifur Rahman	Nottingham Trent University, UK
A. K. M. Mahbubur Rahman	Independent University of Bangladesh, Bangladesh
Kanad Ray	Amity University, India
Antonello Rosato	University Sapienza of Rome, Italy
Oscar Russo	Aubay, Italy
K. C. Santosh	University of South Dakota, USA
Giuseppe Maria Sarnè	University of Milano-Bicocca, Italy
Suresh Chandra Satapathy	KIIT Deemed to be University, India
Claudio Savaglio	University of Calabria, Italy
Marta Savino	Aubay, Italy
Simone Scardapane	University Sapienza of Rome, Italy
Noushath Shaffi	Sultan Qaboos University, Oman
Stefano Squartini	Università Politecnica delle Marche, Italy
Roberto Tagliaferri	University of Salerno, Italy
Anshul Tripathi	IIT Gandhinagar, India
Domenico Ursino	Università Politecnica delle Marche, Italy
Surapong Uttama	Mae Fah Luang University, Thailand
Marley Vellasco	Pontifícia Universidade Católica do Rio de Janeiro, Brazil
Mario Versaci	University Mediterranea of Reggio Calabria, Italy
Luca Virgili	Università Politecnica delle Marche, Italy
Salvatore Vitabile	University of Palermo, Italy
Yu-Dong Zhang	University of Leicester, UK
Ning Zhong	Maebashi Institute of Technology, Japan

Contents

Advanced Computing and Statistics

Towards Reserve Margin Correction via Outage Capacity Forecasting
Using Gramian Angular Field and Long Short-Term Memory (LSTM) 3
    *Jayson C. Jueco, Angel Faith M. Panaguiton, Arcel N. Onipa,
John Loey T. Galimba, Wilen Melsedec O. Narvios,
Ferdinand F. Batayola, and Marvin A. Radaza*

Comparison of Hyperspectral Image Reconstruction for Medical Images 18
    Ali Mohammed Ridha, Nor Ashidi Mat Isa, and Ayman Tawfik

Kidney MRI Segmentation Using Deep Learning 33
    Suman Acharya, Achyuth Sarkar, Somen Nayak, and Bablu Kumar Majhi

A Comparative Analysis of Ensemble Strategies for Enhanced Machine
Learning Results 49
    *Alavikunhu Panthakkan, Aruna Gurjarand, Jagruti Patel, Hardik Patel,
Satyen Parikh, and Wathiq Mansoor*

Neural Network-Based Robust Adaptive Output Feedback Control
for MIMO Time-Varying Delay Systems 60
    Farouk Zouari and Mufti Mahmud

Potato Leaf Disease Classification Using Resnet50ViT 78
    Suman Acharya, Achyuth Sarkar, Somen Nayak, and Bablu Kumar Majhi

Indonesian Named Entity Recognition Model for Identifying Human
Hobbies 90
    Nurchim, Muljono, Edi Noersasongko, and Ahmad Zainul Fanani

Comparative Analysis Between Time Series Feature Extraction
with Sliding Window and Data Framing Method for Energy Forecasting
Using Artificial Neural Network 99
    *Wilen Melsedec O. Narvios, Jayson C. Jueco, John Cliff A. Jumawan,
Riza A. Tulipas, Frandy P. Badilles, Ferdinand F. Batayola,
and Marvin A. Radaza*

An Internet of Drone Things-Enabled Inspection Ecosystem for Smart
Cities and Society 114
    Amartya Mukhrjee, Souvik Chatterjee, Debashis De, and Nilanjan Dey

Enhancing Wireless Sensor Network Security Against Wormhole Attacks
with Twofish Encryption 124
   Pramod Singh Rathore and Mrinal Kanti Sarkar

Data Science

Classifying Depressed and Healthy Individuals Using Wearable Sensor
Data: A Comparative Analysis of Machine Learning and Deep Learning
Approaches 141
   Faiza Guerrache, David J. Brown, and Mufti Mahmud

Detour: Understanding the Application of Artificial Intelligence Based
Models in Forecasting Safe Travel Routes 163
   Subhranil Das, Rashmi Kumari, and Raghwendra Kishore Singh

An Approach to Compute the Adaptive Dynamic Diameter of Data Stream
Clusters 173
   Abeer Altahan and Saad Talib Hasson

XMR_Net: A Deep Model for Vehicle Make and Model Recognition
Using Still-Images 186
   Sourajit Maity, Pawan Kumar Singh, Mufti Mahmud, and Ram Sarkar

Semi-automatic Tool to Assist Radiologist for Pneumothorax Detection
and Localization 199
   Jija Dasgupta, Murthy Chamarthy, and Tanushyam Chattopadhyay

Parenthood Responsibility Mining Using Social Network Mining Approach ... 208
   Xiaowen Wang, Jere Leukkunen, and Mourad Oussalah

Unleashing Machine Learning for Accurate Weather Forecasts 223
   S. Amisha, Anusha, and G. Padmashree

BFL: Blockchain-Federated Learning for Privacy Preservation in Internet
of Underwater Things 236
   Kamalika Bhattacharjya and Debashis De

Exploring and Contrasting Machine Learning Classifiers for Citrus Plant
Disease Classification 246
   B. Mahima Shenoy, Sakshi S. Poojary, and G. Padmashree

GloVe-LSTM: An Artificial Attention-Based Algorithm for Sentiment
Analysis of Pandemic Times for Enhanced Decision Support 258
   Shobhit Srivastava, Mrinal Kanti Sarkar, and Chinmay Chakraborty

Hybrid AI Systems

Breast DCE-MRI Registration Using Student Psychology-Based
Optimization Algorithm with Centroid Opposition-Based Learning 275
   Somen Nayak and Achyuth Sarkar

Brain MRI Registration Using Fireworks Algorithm 289
   Somen Nayak and Achyuth Sarkar

Quantifying Climate Change Effects on Standard Minimum and Maximum
Average Temperature Extremes in Bangladesh: A Machine Learning
Regression Analysis from Past to Present 304
   Muhammad Ebrahim Hossain, Shahriar Siddique Ayon,
   Md Saef Ullah Miah, Zahid Hasan Talukder Anik,
   M. Mostafizur Rahman, and Mufti Mahmud

Explainable Machine Learning Strategy to Discover Attributes
Accountable for ASD Detection 318
   Arpita Chakraborty, Jyoti Sekhar Banerjee, and Mufti Mahmud

Short-Term Water Demand Forecasting: A Comparative Study of Deep
Learning and Conventional Machine Learning Algorithms 339
   Hakob Grigoryan

Improving Crop Yield Prediction Accuracy: A Hybrid Machine Learning
Approach 354
   Maharin Afroj, S. M. Nuruzzaman Nobel, Md Mohsin Kabir,
   M. F. Mridha, and Mufti Mahmud

PPIoDT: GSO-FL Based Privacy Preserving IoDT Guided Ocean-Wind
Aware Ship Trajectory Recommendation 366
   Arnab Hazra, Debashis De, and Tien Anh Tran

Multiple Linear Regression Based Multipath Green Routing for Internet
of Vehicular Things in Smart Cities 379
   Sushovan Khatua, Samarjit Roy, and Debashis De

FemCrop: A Femtocell-Based Edge-Cloud Frame-Work for Crop Yield
Prediction Using Deep Learning 389
   Tanushree Dey, Somnath Bera, Anwesha Mukherjee, Samarjit Roy,
   and Debashis De

Detection of Ransomware Attacks Using Federated Learning Based on the CNN Model 403
   Hong Nhung Nguyen, Ha Thanh Nguyen, and Damien Lescos

Author Index 417

Advanced Computing and Statistics

Towards Reserve Margin Correction via Outage Capacity Forecasting Using Gramian Angular Field and Long Short-Term Memory (LSTM)

Jayson C. Jueco(✉), Angel Faith M. Panaguiton, Arcel N. Onipa, John Loey T. Galimba, Wilen Melsedec O. Narvios, Ferdinand F. Batayola, and Marvin A. Radaza

Department of Electrical Engineering, Cebu Technological University, M.J. Cuenco Avenue Corner R. Palma, Cebu City 6000, Cebu, Philippines
jaysonc.jueco@ctu.edu.ph

Abstract. Most studies focus on reserve optimization by finding the optimal reserve allocated during power outages. The paper presented a different perspective in addressing the reserve allocation by forecasting the outage capacity to be used as reserve margin correction to minimum mandated reserve allocation by policy, considering the generation sector can exercise market power to force outage. The outage capacity forecasting model cleaves into encoding the outage capacity data into images using Gramian Angular Field (GAF), predicting the outage capacity from the set of images using a Long Short-Term Memory (LSTM) network, and using the forecasted outage capacity to correct the reserve margin. The image-based LSTM yields training and validation loss between 0.17 and 0.21, while the time series yields 10^3. The image-based LSTM model yield testing performance of MAE $\approx$ 0.94, MSE $\approx$ 1.00, MAPE $\leq 10^{-3}$, and RMSE ≈ 1.00. Experimental results show our approach performs better in imaging than in time series. The reserve margin correction yield from the forecasted outage capacity substantially improves the reserve allocation to address peak demand during outage events in the generation sector. The severity of an outage juxtaposed a decrease in the RMI of the electricity market and an increase in the capacity of an outage, wherein $RMI \approx 0$ as the reserve is low and capacity on outage is high.

Keywords: outage · reserve · electricity market · energy market model · time series forecasting · Long Short Term Memory (LSTM) · Gramian Angular Field · Philippines

1 Introduction

Natural monopolies exist in the electricity market and energy sector [1,2]. Deregulating the electricity market provides a transformative opportunity to reduce monopolies and create a fair and competitive market. Although deregulation had been implemented, electricity markets had inherent limitations to how far deregulation applied to the market due to instability issues; hence, electricity storage has limited capacity [3,12]. The electricity market needs to maintain a stable and secure electricity supply to meet the electricity demand of the utility sector [4–7,11]. Independent market operators initiated the capacity market used to address increasing electricity demand. The capacity market ensures enough reserves to compensate for outage events [8–10].

Although the market operators ensure the capacity to meet demands, outages are inevitable in the energy system as electricity transmission covers a wide geographic area and weather constraints. With technological advancement, the electricity demand is increasing tremendously. Countries sought a dependable, secure power infrastructure as they expanded their energy profile while gearing towards lower carbon footprints. As the energy market is dependent on fossil fuels and slowly decreasing fossil fuel dependency, the energy market is facing capacity issues resulting in vulnerability and instability. Outages hold off activities in each sector of society, resulting in economic losses, which natural catastrophes attributed as the leading cause. Market operators planned out reserve allocation in the event an outage happened. Reserve is the allocated unused capacity in the electricity market to anticipate demand changes in electricity generation and utility when the generation sector fails. Developing countries have a thin reserve due to constrained capital investment and maintenance activities of aging power plants. This is crucial to the reliability of power plants in developing countries to meet electricity demand. Managing demand allocation is a problem when unexpected forced outages happen [13–15,20].

In the Philippines, simultaneously forced outages in several generating plants result in price increases in the electricity spot market. The system operator issued several yellow and red alerts, resulting in load dropping to ensure electricity in critical sectors. Promoting a diverse energy mix and lessening the dependence on fossil fuel helps better reserve planning to anticipate forced outages. The reliance on fossil fuels posed price volatility, supply chain disruptions, and environmental risks. Aside from a strong dependence on fossil fuel, the geographical location of the Philippines presented vulnerability to natural catastrophic events, leading to outage events. There are various solutions to address outage events in the Philippines. The consensus in the literature is to optimize reserve capacity to anticipate the outage event [15–17].

Reserve capacity allocation anticipates generating capacity to meet electricity demand during an outage. Several studies optimized reserve allocated during an outage. The problem with this approach is that the generation sector can exercise market power to force an outage, which is a strategic decision in the electricity market. Market operators accept outage reports without contest and verification, as it is with generation companies to impose their unilateral market power. Despite finding the optimal reserve, the market operators allocate the reserve to the minimum value set in the market policy rather than the optimal value. The delimitation of the paper is anchored to the quality and accessibility of the outage capacity data used in the prediction. This analysis does not consider outside variables like natural disasters and unusual weather patterns that could substantially impact the electrical market. Additionally, we only look at how wholesale electricity markets, not retail or individual users, are impacted by outage capacity projections.

The paper provides two contributions. It will be briefly discussed and in full detail in the succeeding sections. Although the consensus in the literature is to find the optimal value of reserve capacity to anticipate an outage, the researchers perform a counterintuitive approach to forecasting an outage capacity to use as a correction value to the reserve capacity to predict outage events instead of the optimal value of the reserve capacity. The first contribution is the descriptive analysis of outage events in the Philippine Electricity Spot Market from 2013 to 2021 to identify the factors to include in the forecasting model. The second contribution is forecasting outage capacity from the historical event to find the reserve margin correction. The researchers encoded the outage event as Gramian Angular Field (GAF) images to leverage the computational superiority of the neural network. Then, a Long Short-Term Memory network forecasts the outage capacity.

2 Related Works

Ensuring the dependability of power plant facilities is crucial for a nation such as the Philippines, which possesses limited reserves due to constraints in supply investments [16]. In light of this scarcity, generation companies have the potential to exploit the situation by utilizing forced outages as a means to exert market power. By withholding capacity in the market and declaring a forced outage, a generation company can manipulate prices. However, the exercise of this unilateral market power is contingent upon the company's position in its bilateral contract and its utilization of outage allowance [22]. The repercussions of power outages are substantial, significantly impacting economic development and productivity [13,23].

Consequently, the occurrence of power outages gives rise to significant societal expenses and poses threats to the reliability of the power grid [24]. The occurrence of forced outages can be averted through the implementation of appropriate maintenance practices that extend the operational lifespan of power plants and enhance their dependability [25]. A vital metric for appraising the dependability of a power plant is the measurement of the duration of forced and planned outages. The likelihood of forced outages gradually diminishes the reliability of the overall generation system [26]. To effectively manage outages in the power system, it is essential to engage in efficient maintenance activities during both planned and forced outages [27]. The process of outage planning should be continuous and take into account past and future outages. Previous research has utilized optimization models and probabilistic evaluation techniques, including programming methods, to forecast outages and assess the impact of maintenance on reliability. Categorizing the effects of failures and identifying potential maintenance tasks can be a cost-efficient approach to mitigating the deterioration of power plants. These investigations have utilized data at the plant level to investigate the correlation between the cost of preventive maintenance and forced outages. By employing standard survival analysis, they have determined that factors such as the cost of preventive maintenance, planned maintenance outages, utilization rate, and reserve margin contribute to longer generator durations and fewer forced outages [28, 29].

While market operators strive to ensure their capacity meets the demands placed upon them, outages will inevitably occur in the energy system. This is due to the wide geographic coverage of electricity transmission and the constraints imposed by weather conditions. As technological advancements continue, the electricity demand is increasing significantly. Consequently, countries are seeking to establish a reliable and secure power infrastructure to support their expanding energy needs, while also transitioning towards lower carbon footprints. However, as the energy market currently relies heavily on fossil fuels and is gradually reducing its dependency on them, capacity issues are arising, resulting in a state of vulnerability and instability. Outages have a significant impact on various sectors of society, leading to economic losses, with natural disasters often being identified as the primary cause. To address this, market operators have developed plans for allocating reserves in the event of an outage [13–15, 29, 30].

3 Methods

3.1 Philippine Electricity Spot Market Dataset

This section briefly discusses the Philippine Electricity Market's current energy situation and balance. We highlight the system outages, peak demand, RMI, and the overall supply, reserve, and outage capacities from 2013 to 2021.

The peak demand ranges from 8452 to 11987 MW, showing fluctuations over the years and across different months. Some months consistently experience higher peaks between May and July across multiple years, indicating potential seasonality or market-specific factors at play. However, other months exhibit fluctuations that need a clear pattern. There are variations in peak demand between different years, with some years demonstrating higher peaks than others, suggesting shifts in market demand or industry dynamics. The data indicates the influence of seasonal patterns on peak demand, with certain months consistently experiencing higher peaks, possibly due to specific events or seasonality.

The Reserve Margin Index (RMI) data provided to cluster: Less or Equal to 10%, and More than 10% concerning reserve margin. This index provides insights into the adequacy of energy supply compared to demand. The less or equal to 10% cluster represents months with a tight reserve margin, potentially indicating a higher risk of supply shortages. In contrast, more than 10% group showed a better reserve margin, indicating a more significant buffer of available energy resources. The distribution between the two categories varies yearly and monthly, suggesting potential seasonal or demand-specific influences on the reserve margin.

A database was constructed with consideration given to the monthly and yearly capacity outages, reserve allocation, reserve margin index, system peak demand, and adequate supply for each year. The accuracy of the data was confirmed through a thorough examination of the data provided by both the grid operator and the bureau. The dataset spans 2013 to 2017 and provides a comprehensive overview of monthly energy outage occurrences measured in megawatt-hours. A forecasting model was employed to estimate outage values to address discrepancies in the datasets for 2018 and 2021. This approach allowed for the completion of missing data and the extension of forecasted values until the end of 2021. By utilizing consistent recorded values from 2013 to 2017, which demonstrated the forecasting model's reliability, we generated results that filled in the missing values and ensured the overall consistency of the dataset.

Overall, the annual capacity outages recorded in the Philippine Electricity Spot Market show fluctuations year-on-year, with some years experiencing higher frequency and duration of outages than others. The data provides valuable insights into the reliability and performance of the Philippine Electricity Spot Market over the given period and can be used to inform decisions related to maintenance scheduling, outage management, and overall market operations.

3.2 Approximated Outage Reserve Model

Outage capacities refer to the maximum capacity of power generation units or transmission lines that are unavailable due to maintenance, repairs, or unforeseen events. On the other hand, reserve capacity represents the extra capacity that power systems maintain beyond the average demand to ensure reliability and stability. This measure safeguards against unexpected spikes in demand or sudden generator failures.

The researcher considers an approximate model of forced outage reserve with margin correction, considering unitary power reserve:

$$R = R_0 + \hat{\mathbf{O}} \quad (1)$$

where $\hat{\mathbf{O}} = \{\hat{o}_1, \hat{o}_2, \cdots, \hat{o}_H\} \in \mathbf{R}$ is a forecast vector of outage capacity at time horizon H. The researcher formalizes the definition of the outage forecasting problem addressed in the paper. Given a historical capacity on outage event $\mathbf{O} = \{o_1, o_2, \ldots, o_T\}$ at a forecast horizon H. The goal is to predict the next outage capacity $\{o_{T+1}, o_{T+1}, \ldots, x_{T+H}\}$ by minimizing the prediction error to yield the vector of predicted outage capacity $\{\hat{O} = \hat{o}_1, \hat{o}_2, \cdots, \hat{o}_T\}$. The data for extracting and inputting into forecasting models to correct outage capacity includes yearly records of the system's outage capacity, reserve capacity, effective supply, reserve margin index, and average peak demands. In addition, we define the reserve margin index,

$$RMI^h = \frac{\Sigma GenCap^h - (GenTot^h + Res^h)}{(GenTot^h + Res^h)} \quad (2)$$

where $GenTot^h$ is the total required in an hour (h) to supply the load (energy withdrawn plus transmission losses), Res^h is the operating reserve in an hour, and $GenCap^h$ is the total offered capacity of all generators in an hour. Effective supply reflects the actual power output available to consumers, accounting for transmission losses, generator efficiency, and system constraints. The reserve margin index measures the surplus power capacity available in the system as a percentage of the peak demand. It is an essential indicator of the energy system's resilience, indicating the buffer available to meet unexpected demand surges or emergencies. Average peak demands represent the maximum power load experienced by the system during specific time intervals, typically occurring when demand is at its highest. Lastly, the reserve margin represents the excess capacity available in the energy system beyond the peak demand. This measure ensures sufficient backup power is available to handle unforeseen events or increased demand (Fig. 1).

3.3 Image Representation of Outage Event

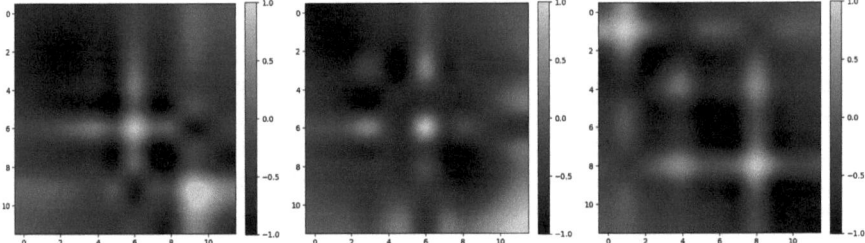

Fig. 1. Outage Data represented as Images

From a historical capacity on outage event $\mathbf{O} = \{o_1, o_2, \ldots, o_T\}$, we normalize O using $\bar{o}_i = \frac{2o_i - \max(O) - \min(O)}{\max(O) - \min(O)}$ between the interval $(-1, 1)$, and angular bounded at $[0, \pi]$. Then we mapped the $\bar{O}$ in polar coordinates by encoding the values as $\cos(\phi)$ and the time step as radius r,m and formed a weight matrix, $W = \left[1 - \left|\frac{i-j}{n}\right|\right] \iff 1 \leq i, j \leq n$ where i and j are indices of time series observations and n is the length of time series. The linear transformation emphasizes closer observation has a greater correlation than temporally farther apart. The Gramian matrix G defined $G = W \cdot \left[\bar{O}' \cdot \bar{O} - \sqrt{I - \bar{O}^2}' \cdot \sqrt{I - \bar{O}^2}\right]$ enables imaging of the outage event. The mapping function adheres to $\phi_i = arccos(\bar{o}_i) \iff -1 \leq \bar{o}_i \in \bar{O} \leq 1$.

The Gramian Angular Field (GAF) image preserves temporal dependencies; hence, the main diagonal of the Gramian matrix G holds original outage capacity data. Uncertainty in the inverse map happens when $\cos(\phi)$ when ϕ is between the interval $[0, 2\pi]$. Normalizing the data between $[-1, 1]$ ensures a conditionally bounded mapping function. Hence main diagonal $\{S_{ii}\} = \{\cos(2\phi)\}$ and $cos(\phi)$ is in interval $[0, \pi]$, the approximate reconstruction follows $\cos(\phi) = \sqrt{\frac{\cos(2\phi)+1}{2}}$ [18, 19].

3.4 Long Short-Term Memory (LSTM) Network

Long Short-Term Memory is a recurrent neural network (RNN) used for tasks involving time series and sequential data, which was developed by modeling memory cells. [21] The cell state is the LSTM's key. The cell state runs across the entire chain wherein there is a regulation of retaining and deleting the information by the gate. The gates are neural network layers with sigmoid activation that set the output values passing through it between 0 and 1. The gates in the LSTM cell are forget f_t, input i_t, and output o_t. The LSTM first decides which outage capacity to retain and delete from the cell state. As new information passes through the gate, the forget gate looks at h_{t-1} and x_t and outputs between 0 and 1 for each value in the cell state C_{t-1} and decides what new outage capacity to store in the cell state following equation $f_t = \sigma(W_f \cdot h_{t-1}, x_t + b_f)$.

The role of the input gate is to determine which outage capacity value should be updated, while the *tanh* layer generates new outage capacity values, $\bar{C}_t$, using the equations $i_t = \sigma(W_i \cdot h_{t-1}, x_t + b_i)$ and $\bar{C}_t = \tanh(W_C \cdot h_{t-1}, x_t + b_o)$. The output outage capacity of the input gate and *tanh* layer work together to update the cell state through the equation $C_t = f_t \odot C_{t-1} + i_t \odot \bar{C}_t$. Finally, the output gate determines the output outage capacity value by processing C_t using *tanh* and multiplying it with the output gate output, following the equations $o_t = \sigma(W_o \cdot h_{t-1}, x_t + b_o)$ and $h_t = o_t * \tanh(C_t)$.

We employ a prediction model consisting of a three-layer stacked Long Short-Term Memory (LSTM) network. In this model, the LSTM layers are stacked on top of each other before being passed to the output layer at the final stage of the prediction process. The initial LSTM layer generates a sequence vector, which serves as the input for the subsequent LSTM layer. By receiving feedback from the preceding time step, the LSTM layers can capture data patterns, enabling them to learn and extract intricate features from the input data. This model's stacking of LSTM layers further enhances its capability to recognize and understand more complex patterns, facilitating more accurate load forecasting.

3.5 Model Implementation and Evaluation

Initially, we curated the data from the annual assessment report on outage events in the Philippine Electricity Spot Market. A database was built considering the monthly and yearly capacity outages, reserve allocation, reserve margin index, system peak demand, and adequate supply each year. The data are validated by cross-examining the data provided by the grid operator and the bureau.

We take a different route than the reserve optimization approach in the literature. Initially, we transform the load data (time series) as load snapshots (images) following the GAF encoding process. The encoding generates two image

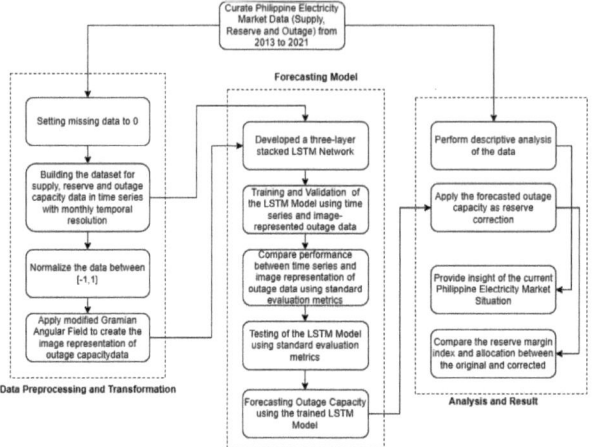

Fig. 2. Visualization of Model Implementation

data sets we set as input to the prediction network. The outage image consists of 12 × 12 ideas for each m observation and is separately run in the prediction network. These images preserve the temporal structures and relationship of the load data. Since the transformation is angular bounded, we recover the time series from the main diagonal of the image matrix and reconstruct the load data by reversing the normalization. The prediction network consists of a three-layer stacked LSTM to extrapolate the outage capacity represented as the predicted outage capacity image. The expected outage capacity values serve as the reserve margin correction, substantially improving reserve allocation and meeting the energy demand regardless of whether the generation sector exercises its force outage power.

Training the prediction network is a critical step directly related to the prediction performance of the network. The 12 × 12 images are set as input to the LSTM network and fine-tuned the network parameters. Optimization iteration is set to $epoch = 20$ (where threshold $\leq 10^{-3}$) in the stacked LSTM layer of the proposed forecasting model. We reverse the normalization to get a outage capacity $\hat{O}_{m+T} = \{\hat{o}_1, \hat{o}_2, \ldots, \hat{o}_{12}\}$ from the predicted load snapshot. The dataset, encompassing 2013 to 2017, presents a comprehensive overview of monthly energy outage occurrences measured in megawatt-hours. Due to inconsistencies in the datasets for 2018 and 2021, we employed a forecasting model to predict the outage values, allowing us to fill in the missing data and extend the scope of the forecast values up to the end of 2021. By utilizing consistent recorded values from 2013 to 2017, where we demonstrated the accuracy of the forecasting model, we generated results to fill in the missing values and maintain the overall consistency of the dataset.

The performance of the forecasting model is evaluated using mean absolute error, $MAE = \frac{1}{n}\sum_{i=1}^{n}|o_i - \hat{o}_i|$, and root mean square error, $RMSE = \sqrt{\frac{1}{n}\sum_{i=1}^{n}|o_i - \hat{o}_i|^2}$ where o_i and $\hat{o}_i$ are actual and predicted outage capacity values respectively. RMSE measures the deviation between observation and actual values and is selected due to sensitivity to outliers, especially with the nature of the outage data. At the same time, MAE can reflect the error distribution. Then, the forecast outage capacity is used to correct the reserve allocation and margin. To summarize the model implementation, a visualization is in Fig. 2.

4 Results and Discussion

4.1 Forecasting Performance Between Outage Time Series and Image

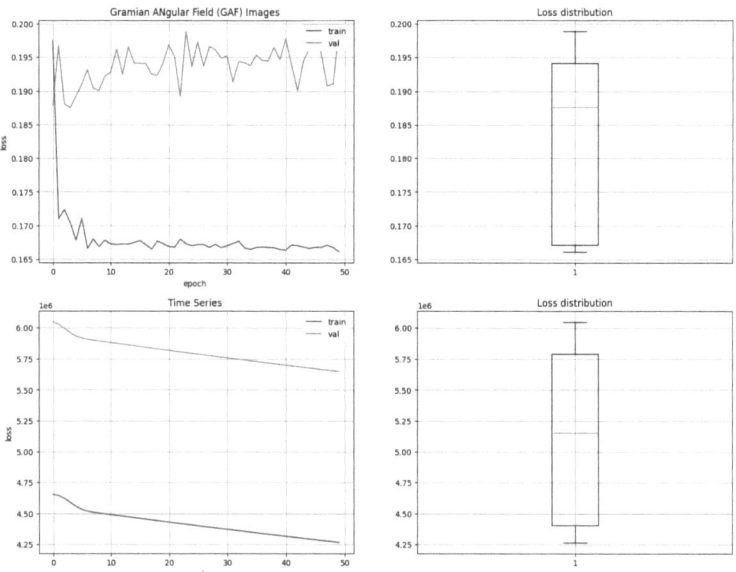

Fig. 3. Performance of Outage Time Series and Image Data

In Fig. 3, the evaluation revealed that the image-based LSTM model exhibits training and validation loss values ranging from 0.17 to 0.21, while the time series model produces a value of 10^3. Additionally, the image-based LSTM model demonstrates a testing performance characterized by a mean absolute error (MAE) of approximately 0.94, a mean squared error (MSE) of about 1.00, a mean fundamental percentage error (MAPE) lower than or equal to 10^{-3}, and a root mean squared error (RMSE) of approximately 1.00. The experimental evidence indicates that our approach is more effective in the image analysis domain than the time series.

As we look closely at the outage data between 2018–2020 shown in 4, the highest outage value was in July, with a total outage of 2432. Over the year, we

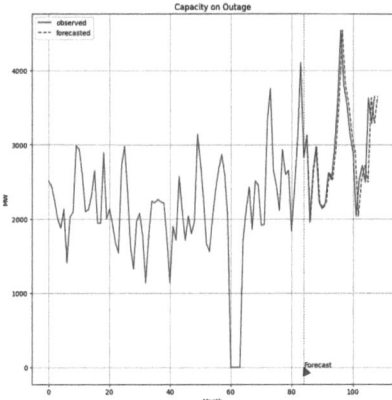

Fig. 4. Forcasted Outage Capacity

observed fluctuations in outage values for different energy sources. For instance, Coal had its highest outage in September with 1201 units, but it experienced a significant drop in October to 1055 units. Natural Gas also showed fluctuations, with the highest outage in June at 151 units but reaching its lowest in October with only 1951 units. Geothermal experienced its peak outage in March with 332 units but showed relatively stable values in the following months. On the other hand, Hydro demonstrated a spike in January with 413 units, followed by reasonably consistent outage values throughout the year. Oil experienced its highest outage in July, with 577 units, while December saw the lowest at 117 units.

In 2019, the highest outage value was in December, with a total outage of 3979. Throughout the year, various energy sources exhibited fluctuations in outage values. Coal peaked in January with 3331 units but saw a dip in May with 2099 units. Natural Gas showed a continuous decrease in outage values over the year. Geothermal experienced its highest outage in December, with 428 units. Hydro and Oil demonstrated relatively stable outage values throughout the year. In 2020, the highest outage value was in February, with a total outage of 3128. During this year, we observed significant fluctuations in outage values for different energy sources. Coal had its highest outage in January with 1686 units, but it drastically decreased to 1121 units in October. Natural Gas exhibited fluctuations, with the highest outage in November at 746 units but reaching its lowest in August with 0 units. Geothermal experienced its peak outage in January with 296 units and remained relatively consistent in the following months. Hydro displayed fluctuations, peaking in May with 301 units. Oil had its highest outage in January, with 492 units, and experienced relatively stable values afterward.

Although trends and patterns are consistent, sudden fluctuations and dips are nearly zero. This leads to poor performance of the time series model, which is sensitive to the outliers and missing outage data. The intolerance of the time series model to uncertainty in the data causes the model to perform poorly,

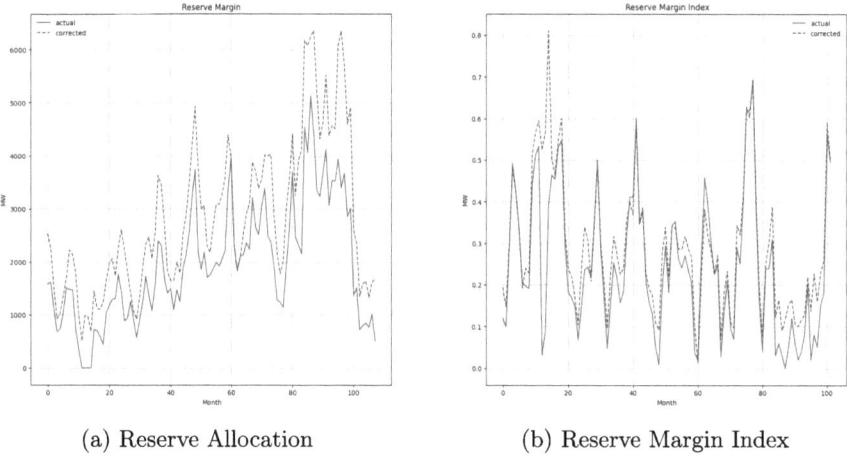

(a) Reserve Allocation   (b) Reserve Margin Index

Fig. 5. Reserve Allocation and Margin

with an average error at 10^3. The ability of the image to accurately capture the inherent characteristics of time series data is underscored by its lower validation loss. Encoding the input data and leveraging temporal and visual dependencies enhances the models' capacity to extract essential patterns and capture material relationships effectively. This shows that imaging the time series addresses the problem with limited, missing, and noisy data. Encoding the load data as images enables generalized learning of the temporal features and is not sensitive to residuals, which is considerably high in the outage data. As a result, the evaluation metrics support our approach to perform better than the time series baseline (Fig. 5).

4.2 Reserve Margin Correction, Allocation, and Index

Understanding the RMI values in context, we established the following criteria. If RMI is closer to zero, the reserve is almost zero, and the outage occurrence is 100%. A 1% RMI has a high outage risk and limited surplus capacity. A 10% RMI is moderate outage risk and limited surplus capacity. A 50% RMI is a balanced power system with medium outage risk. A 90% RMI has a low outage risk and substantial surplus capacity. A 100% RMI has a shallow outage risk and abundant surplus capacity. The system has enough extra generating capacity to meet demand and deal with unforeseen circumstances, as our predicted RMI is higher than the actual RMI. It's important to remember that our predicted RMI values have regularly outperformed the actual ones, suggesting that reserve margins and reliability are rising (Fig. 6).

Examining the RMI values between the actual and corrected reveals some interesting insights. For instance, the difference is minimal when comparing a 33.33% RMI to a 34% RMI. This indicates that both scenarios have a similar likelihood of power disruptions and a moderate reserve margin, regardless of the

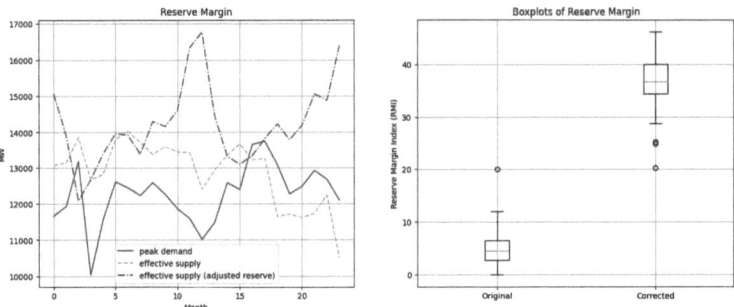

Fig. 6. Reserve Margin and Index

correction made to the reserve margin. It can be inferred that the power system is well-balanced and possesses a reasonable risk of shortages or interruptions. Likewise, the difference observed is very slight when comparing a 20.45% RMI to a 20.47% RMI. This suggests that both scenarios have a comparable risk of power interruptions and a moderate reserve margin. Both methods also indicate the presence of a stable power system with sufficient surplus capacity to mitigate the risk of shortages or outages. On the other hand, a 23.7% RMI signifies a more considerable reserve margin and a reduced chance of outages. In contrast, a 19.62% RMI indicates a smaller reserve margin and a moderate risk of disruptions. The increase from 19.62% to 23.7% in reserve margin significantly enhances the energy balance in the electricity market, providing a more significant buffer against unexpected increases in demand or disruptions. This rise in reserve margin contributes to developing a more reliable system with a lower risk of outage events. Furthermore, a noticeable difference between a 19.09% RMI and a 21% RMI can be observed. A 19.09% RMI indicates a moderate probability of outages with a relatively low reserve margin. The available surplus generating capacity to meet unforeseen demand or disruptions is limited in this scenario. However, an anticipated 21% RMI suggests a slightly better reserve margin and a reduced likelihood of outages. The power system is expected to have more excess generating capacity, providing a giant safety net to handle increasing demand or unforeseen events. Consequently, power shortages or disruptions are less likely compared to a 19.09% RMI.

The corrected reserve margin is adequate to address the demand and substantially enough reserve allocation in existence or exercise of the generation sector to force an outage, suggesting that reserve margins and reliability are rising. Similarly, RMI values are significantly higher when we account for the reserve margin correction from the outage forecasting model. The trend continues from 2015 to 2021. This shows that the reserve margin predicted by our forecasting model is slightly higher than what was seen. The forecasting model predicts accurately and enables capacity on outage to be accounted for in reserve allocation about generating power and reserve margin. Outage occurrence is less probable with a higher RMI value, indicating optimized supply and reserve dis-

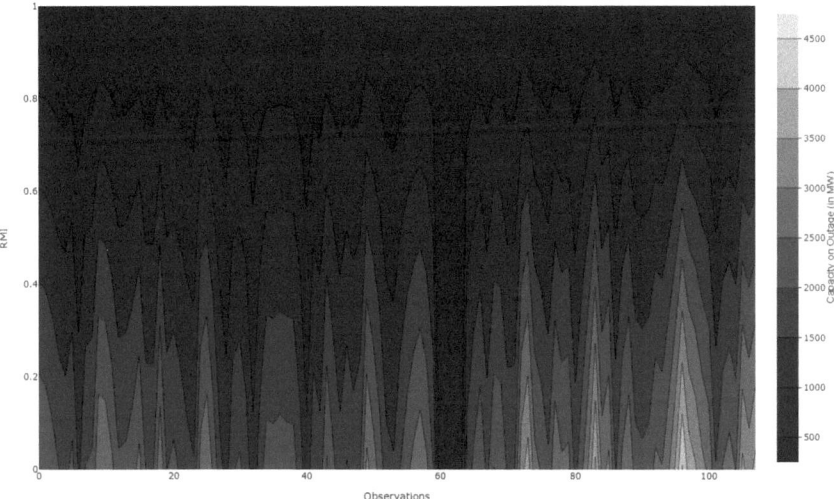

Fig. 7. Reserve Margin and Index

tribution. With reserve and forecasted capacity outages considered in reserve planning, the system anticipates the exercise of force outage in the generation sector and extreme events in the electricity market that disrupt the operation, resulting in an outage event.

In Fig. 7, the severity of an outage juxtaposed a decrease in the RMI of the electricity market and an increase in the capacity of an outage. RMI fluctuates between less than and more than 10%, indicating lower RMI values have a greater risk for outage events due to a lower reserve allocation that does not match the outage capacity. The relationship between RMI fluctuations and outage occurrences throughout the designated time frame is inversely proportional. Experimental results showed evidence that when the outage capacity is minimal, the $RMI \approx 1$ signifies an optimal situation in the electricity market. However, as the outage capacity increases, the RMI gradually declines, which means a potential interruption in the grid. The receipt of outage alerts further corroborates this phenomenon. Notably, a substantial increase in outage capacity leads to a drastic decrease in the RMI, eventually approaching zero.

5 Conclusion

Optimizing reserve planning and management involves determining the best allocation of resources during power outages. However, this paper proposes a unique approach that predicts outage capacity to address resource funding, serving as a correction for minimum reserve allocation. The study analyzes historical outage data using advanced forecasting techniques, achieving significant progress in projecting outage capacity. The image-based LSTM model demonstrates superior performance to the traditional time series model due to its ability to capture time series characteristics. The results show that higher RMI values indicate optimized supply and reserve distribution, reducing the probability of outage occurrences. The relationship between RMI fluctuations and outage events is inversely proportional, with lower RMI values posing a higher risk. Experimental evidence confirms that as outage capacity increases, the RMI gradually declines, indicating the potential for grid interruptions. Experimental results demonstrate that our approach performs better using imaging techniques than time series analysis. The correction of the reserve margin achieved through the forecasted outage capacity significantly improves the allocation of reserves to address peak demand during outage events in the generation sector.

References

1. Peng, X., Tao, X.: Cooperative game of electricity retailers in China's spot electricity market. Energy **145**, 152–170 (2018)
2. Bhattacharyya, S.: Energy Economics: Concepts, Issues, Markets and Governance. Springer Nature (2019)
3. Haes Alhelou, H., Hamedani-Golshan, M., Njenda, T., Siano, P.: A survey on power system blackout and cascading events: research motivations and challenges. Energies **12**, 682 (2019)
4. Salimian, M., Aghamohammadi, M.: A three stages decision tree-based intelligent blackout predictor for power systems using brittleness indices. IEEE Trans. Smart Grid. **9**, 5123–5131 (2017)
5. Zhang, Y., Xu, Y., Dong, Z.: Robust ensemble data analytics for incomplete PMU measurements-based power system stability assessment. IEEE Trans. Power Syst. **33**, 1124–1126 (2017)
6. Amini, S., Pasqualetti, F., Mohsenian-Rad, H.: Dynamic load altering attacks against power system stability: attack models and protection schemes. IEEE Trans. Smart Grid. **9**, 2862–2872 (2016)
7. Opathella, C., Elkasrawy, A., Mohamed, A., Venkatesh, B.: A novel capacity market model with energy storage. IEEE Trans. Smart Grid. **10**, 5283–5293 (2018)
8. Khosa, I., et al.: Financial hazard assessment for electricity suppliers due to power outages: the revenue loss perspective. Energies **15**, 4327 (2022)
9. Li, Y., et al.: A reserve capacity model of AA-CAES for power system optimal joint energy and reserve scheduling. Int. J. Electr. Power Energy Syst. **104**, 279–290 (2019)
10. Ravago, M., et al.: The public economics of electricity policy with Philippine applications. University of Hawai'i at Mānoa, Department of Economics (2016)
11. Mahmud, M., Kaiser, M.S., McGinnity, T.M., Hussain, A.: Deep learning in mining biological data. Cogn. Comput. **13**(1), 1–33 (2021)
12. Mahmud, M., Kaiser, M.S., Hussain, A., Vassanelli, S.: Applications of deep learning and reinforcement learning to biological data. IEEE Trans. Neural Netw. Learn. Syst. **29**(6), 2063–2079 (2018)
13. Owerko, D., Gama, F., Ribeiro, A.: Predicting power outages using graph neural networks. In: 2018 IEEE Global Conference on Signal and Information Processing (GLOBALSIP), pp. 743–747 (2018)
14. Keokhoungning, T., et al.: Challenge of supplying power with renewable energy due to the impact of COVID-19 on power demands in the lao PDR: analysis using metaheuristic optimization. Sustainability **15**, 6814 (2023)

15. Mondal, M., Rosegrant, M., Ringler, C., Pradesha, A., Valmonte-Santos, R.: The Philippines energy future and low-carbon development strategies. Energy **147**, 142–154 (2018)
16. Ravago, M., Danao, R., Roumasset, J.: Electricity policy in the Philippines: overview and synthesis (2018)
17. Ravago, M., Jandoc, K., Pormon, M.: Reliability and forced outages: survival analysis with recurrent events. Japan World Econ. **68**, 101213 (2023)
18. Wang, Z., et al.: Encoding time series as images for visual inspection and classification using tiled convolutional neural networks. In: Workshops at the Twenty-ninth AAAI Conference on Artificial Intelligence, vol. 1 (2015)
19. Chen, Y., Ji, A., Babajiyavar, P., Ahmadzadeh, A., Angryk, R.: On the effectiveness of imaging of time series for flare forecasting problem. In: 2020 IEEE International Conference on Big Data (Big Data), pp. 4184–4191 (2020)
20. Islam, M.S., Islam, M.M., Ahmed, S., Rahman, M.S., Kumar, K., Kaiser, M.S.: IoET-SG: integrating internet of energy things with smart grid. In: Sustainable Developments by Artificial Intelligence and Machine Learning for Renewable Energies, pp. 49–61. Elsevier (2022)
21. Yu, Y., Si, X., Hu, C., Zhang, J.: A review of recurrent neural networks: LSTM cells and network architectures. Neural Comput. **31**, 1235–1270 (2019)
22. Wolak, F.: Diagnosing the California electricity crisis. Electr. J. **16**, 11–37 (2003)
23. Roxas, F., Santiago, A.: Alternative framework for renewable energy planning in the Philippines. Renew. Sustain. Energy Rev. **59**, 1396–1404 (2016)
24. Al-Shaalan, A.: Reliability evaluation of power systems. In: Reliability and Maintenance-an Overview of Cases (2019)
25. Endrenyi, J., et al.: The present status of maintenance strategies and the impact of maintenance on reliability. IEEE Trans. Power Syst. **16**, 638–646 (2001)
26. Bagheri, B., Amjady, N.: Stochastic multiobjective generation maintenance scheduling using augmented normalized normal constraint method and stochastic decision maker. Int. Trans. Electr. Energy Syst. **29**, e2722 (2019)
27. Lipár, M.: Operational safety of nuclear power plants. In: Infrastructure and Methodologies for the Justification of Nuclear Power Programmes, pp. 773–830 (2012)
28. Belyi, D., Popova, E., Morton, D., Damien, P.: Bayesian failure-rate modeling and preventive maintenance optimization. Eur. J. Oper. Res. **262**, 1085–1093 (2017)
29. Li, M., et al.: Prediction of power outage quantity of distribution network users under typhoon disaster based on random forest and important variables. Math. Probl. Eng. **2021**, 1–14 (2021)
30. Barroco, J.: Designing financeable ancillary services revenue contracts in developing economies: learnings from the Philippines. Energy Policy **152**, 112218 (2021)

Comparison of Hyperspectral Image Reconstruction for Medical Images

Ali Mohammed Ridha[1,2(✉)], Nor Ashidi Mat Isa[1], and Ayman Tawfik[2]

[1] School of Electrical and Electronic Engineering, Universiti Sains Malaysia, Penang, Malaysia
`ashidi@usm.my`
[2] Department of Electrical and Computer Engineering, Ajman University, Ajman, UAE

Abstract. Hyperspectral imaging (HSI) which captures a wide spectrum of light has emerged as a tool for the detection and diagnosis of various medical conditions. However, due to the high cost of specialized HS cameras, it is limited in its use in clinical settings. In this research, a comprehensive comparison is carried out between two architectures for hyperspectral reconstruction algorithms for medical images of acne vulgaris. The evaluation will consist of an analysis of different hyperparameter configurations to identify the optimal reconstruction algorithm for medical hyperspectral images. The results show that the HRNET architecture model, which includes colour correction, random cropping, and a small batch size had the lowest mean relative absolute error of 0.0433. Therefore, the reconstructed hyperspectral (HS) images using HRNET architecture could offer a viable and cost-effective alternative to utilizing expensive hyperspectral imaging (HSI) equipment for detecting medical conditions.

Keywords: Hyperspectral Imaging · Hyperspectral Reconstruction · Machine Learning

1 Introduction

Hyperspectral imaging (HSI) is a rapidly advancing technique that offers a unique advantage in capturing a wide spectrum of light. In contrast to traditional imaging methods that rely only on primary colours (i.e. red, green, and blue), HSI breaks down the light striking each pixel into numerous spectral bands. This approach allows for a rich and detailed representation of an imaged scene [1]. In HS images, each pixel in the image contains a continuous spectrum of information across a wide range of wavelengths. This means that for every pixel, data is collected across numerous wavelengths. Whereas, an RGB image consists of only three colours' bands: red, green, and blue. Each pixel in an RGB image is represented by a combination of these three primary colours to display a wide range of colours that are visible to the human eye [2]. HSI has been used in many fields, including food quality and safety [3, 4], crime scene detection [5, 6] and medical applications [7, 8].

In recent years, with advances in HS cameras and image analysis methods, HSI has been widely researched in the medical field because light delivered to biological tissues has multiple scattering and absorption factors due to the inhomogeneity of biological structures, such as haemoglobin, melanin, and water [9]. For example, HSI can be used to diagnose different types of cancer and diseases that are in the outer layer of the human body, such as the skin, breast, and neck [10]. But because of the high cost of HS cameras, the technology is out of reach for commercial and user applications. Thus, researchers have explored solutions for reconstructing hyperspectral images from RGB images. Some research teams have designed specific systems using several RGB cameras and add-on devices, such as colour filters or reflectors [11, 12].

Researchers have proposed several statistical learning-based methods [13–15] to model HS reconstruction and exploit the high correlations between RGB images and their corresponding HS radiance [16], and with the advances in deep convolutional neural networks (CNNs), recent research has developed deep CNNs that perform spectral reconstruction from RGB to HS images [17–20].

Recently, deep-learning based methods have received great attention by many researchers for their applications in processing data with grid patterns including images. Many improvements have been made to increase the capability of deep-learning based methods [21–23]. CNNs have played an important role in the computer vision field, in which they are designed to adaptively learn spatial hierarchies of features from low-level to high-level patterns. CNNs have been employed in many different vision tasks, such as colourisation [24], deblurring [25], and denoising [26].

A CNN-Based HS image recovery (HSCNN) for reconstructing HS images from RGB images was proposed [17]. HSCNN is a unified deep-learning framework and one of the first CNN-based models for hyperspectral reconstruction. It inherits the very deep super resolution network [27], which was originally used for image super resolution, where a high-resolution image is reconstructed from a low-resolution image. The architecture utilises dense blocks with path-widening fusion [28] similar to group convolution [29] based on a dense structure.

Another algorithm is a hierarchical spectral reconstruction model named HRNET was proposed [19], which utilises PixelShuffle [30] at each level (i.e., a learnable sampling operation that downsamples and upsamples without any information loss) to boost the quality of generated HS images.

The Pixelunshuffle sampling layers have the number of input pixels fixed while decreasing spatial resolution. Furthermore, the PixelShuffle layers are upsampling the feature maps and reducing channels for inter-level concatenation. No new parameters are introduced, and thus the network learns upsampling operations adaptively. The network architecture can be decomposed into inter-level integrations. The pixel output of the lower levels gets shuffled, concatenated to the upper level, and processed by a convolutional layer for the unification of the channel number. Additionally, HRNET adopts residual dense blocks containing five densely connected convolutional layers to reduce artifacts and produce high-quality spectral images.

Therefore, in this work, a comprehensive comparison between the abovementioned spectral reconstruction methods (HSCNN-D and HRNET) will be carried out, using a newly collected dataset of medical HS images of acne vulgaris. The aim of the comparison is to demonstrate that reconstructed HSI can be a viable solution to benefiting from the advantages of HSI without the associated costs. This paper will be organized as follows: Sect. 2 discusses the system setup and the data preparation steps necessary for the HS image reconstruction. Section 3 presents the details of HS image reconstruction models based on two different deep learning algorithms. In Sect. 4, we present the results obtained for the discussed HS reconstruction techniques, and identify the best performing algorithm. Finally, the conclusion and findings of the paper is summarized.

2 System Setup and Data Preparation

The first step is to use a HS camera to acquire RGB and HS images. The images will then be sorted to two datasets. The RGB images will be colour corrected and used as inputs along with the HS images for the training of HSI reconstruction neural networks, which will reconstruct the HS images from RGB images. Then the best-performing model will be identified through a thorough analysis of the HS reconstruction algorithms models with different configurations.

2.1 Data Acquisition Setup and Collection

Data acquisition was performed using a SPECIM FX10 hyperspectral camera [31]. The camera had a spectrum range of 400–1000 nm represented in 112 bands. Thus, it was able to capture images that covered visible light and infrared spectrum wavelengths. Based on previous research [7, 32], an LED ring light with 240 LEDs distributed on its outer diameter was selected for the setup to evenly distribute light on a patient's face. The data acquisition process starts when a patient sits on a chair and faces the LED ring light. The LED ring light was then turned on, and the patients were advised to close their eyes when they felt uncomfortable with the light. The setup for the data acquisition is shown in Fig. 1. The camera required approximately 15 s to scan through since it is fixed on a rotary motor from the manufacturer. The light source was placed in such a way that light was reflected evenly on a patient's face without producing any shadows. The ring LED light was placed approximately 8–10 cm from the face. Additionally, the ring light was not placed around the HS camera because the camera needed to rotate to scan the face.

After capturing the image, the LED ring light is turned off, the captured image is inspected for clarity by using the captured RGB image along with the HSI hypercube, and the focus of the image is evaluated. If the patient has moved their head or if any other element may have affected the image, the process is repeated to capture another image. Given that the HSI camera produces two images, namely, RGB and HS images, two datasets are created: one for RGB images and another for HS images. A total of 126 sample HS images are collected under the supervision of a dermatologist in accordance with the ethical standards of Ajman University's ethics committee under approval number 2021-IRG-ENIT-13. Within 2 months, a case study was conducted on one of the authors (Mr. Ali Mohammed Ridha) as per the ethical approval of Ajman University's ethics committee. Data collection was performed, to observe the acne formation. The light absorbance deflection of the acne development was monitored until it reached its peak.

Fig. 1. Data acquisition setup

2.2 Data Preparation and Augmentation

After the images were captured, the first step in the data preparation process for the HS dataset was to reduce the size of the hypercube data. As for the RGB dataset, a colour correction algorithm was applied. Then data augmentation was performed for both datasets simultaneously to artificially increase the dataset size.

Hyperspectral Band Reduction

The hyperspectral images dataset consisted of hypercube data with a resolution of 512 × 512 pixels and 112 bands. Acne had a spectral signature deflected peak in a range of 600–650 nm, as shown in Fig. 2 (a). Given that the acquired spectrum range from the camera was extremely high and some of the spectrum bands showed unimportant information, the hypercube spectral range was narrowed down from 112 bands to 25 bands to cover the acne spectral signature range, as indicated in Fig. 2 (b) (i.e., 570–690 nm).

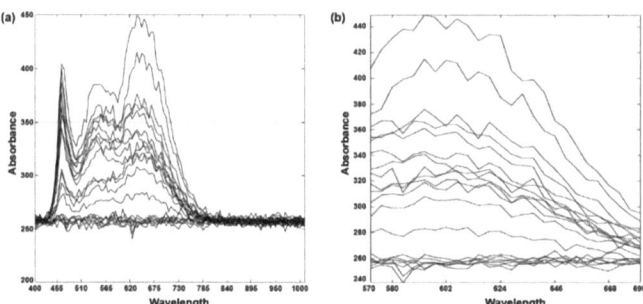

Fig. 2. (a) spectral signature of facial image with acne. (b) cropped spectral signature.

Colour Correction

Because of the large difference in the information bands of RGB (3 bands) and HS (25 bands), the colour constancy of the dataset can play a vital role in the performance of a reconstruction model. Colour constancy is the ability to estimate colours, independent of illumination sources (light sources). As imaging devices do not have this ability, different lighting environments can lead to deviations between the true colour and the captured image colour. Recent research has explored the benefits of colour constancy, using colour correction algorithms to eliminate the influence of light sources in images because it can affect accuracy [33, 34]. Thus, the second step in the data preparation process was to perform colour correction on the RGB images with a colour correction algorithm. The Grey World Algorithm (GW) [35] is a widely used simple white-balancing method and is based on the assumption that the average of all colours present is neutral grey in a colour-balanced image. It estimates an illuminant by using the average colour of all pixels. The GW algorithm was built using Python programming language and applied to the RGB image dataset.

Dataset Augmentation
Models trained on small datasets can suffer from overfitting and thus perform poorly on data from the validation set. A large dataset can improve the overall performance of deep learning models and reduce overfitting [36, 37].

Several techniques are commonly used to reduce overfitting in deep learning models, such as data augmentation [38, 39], through which training dataset size is artificially increased by data warping. Data warping augmentation is achieved when existing images are transformed while having their labels preserved. These transformations may include geometric transformations, such as flipping, cropping and rotation. Only simple transformations were used in this study for the augmentation of the dataset, that is, rotation, flipping and padding, to artificially increase the dataset size.

3 Hyperspectral Image Reconstruction

Comparing different architecture to determine which model performs best is essential to determine the best algorithm to be used in application. Two deep learning architectures i.e., (HSCNN-D [18] and HRNET [19]) have been considered. Both of these architectures are state of the art deep learning algorithms that are recently proposed since they have shown excellent performance in the reconstruction of HS images. The HRNET and HSCNN-D algorithms were trained using the two datasets (i.e., RGB and HSI datasets) as inputs, and different hyperparameter settings were used, such as batch size, cropping settings and colour correction. The purpose was to determine how the architectures perform under different conditions. This approach would enhance the understanding of the strengths and limitations of each architecture for the selection of the most suitable architecture for acne detection. Using the same evaluation metrics on the same validation dataset is vital for the accurate comparison of the architecture's performance. This approach would provide an accurate representation of the relative performance of an architecture.

3.1 HSCNN-D Architecture

The HS reconstruction HSCNN-D [18] network utilises dense blocks with path-widening fusion. It improves model performance, having better performance than its predecessors. The model architecture parameters are based on the proposed parameters by the researchers [18], It was built using TensorFlow [40] and used Adam optimisation algorithm [42] with β1 = 0.9 and β2 = 0.9. The loss function used was mean relative absolute error (MRAE), the weight decay coefficient (L2 Norm) was set at 1×10^{-4} and the momentum factor was set at 0.9. The learning rate was set to decay exponentially from 1×10^{-3} to 1×10^{-4}. To study the effects of different hyperparameters on the performance of the models, only one hyperparameter was changed and the rest were constant for every test, as tabulated in Table 1. The different configurations were each trained for 2000 epochs with an Nvidia tesla v100 GPU on Paperspace cloud computing [43]. The training time for each model was approximately 15 h.

Table 1. HSCNN models hyperparameters configurations.

No	Model Name	Colour correction	Cropping	Batch size
1	HSCNN-1	No	No	6
2	HSCNN-2	No	No	2
3	HSCNN-3	Yes	No	2
4	HSCNN-4	No	Yes	2
5	HSCNN-5	Yes	Yes	2

3.2 HRNET Architecture

The HS reconstruction called Hierarchical Regression Network (HRNET) network [19] utilises PixelShuffle and PixelUnshuffle algorithms, which are upsampling and downsampling operations for the feature maps, respectively, and this allows the network to learn upsampling operations adaptively. The output is then processed by a convolutional layer that unifies the channel number and outputs a HS image. The model architecture parameters were based on the proposed parameters [19]. The HRNET model was built using TensorFlow [41] and utilised the Adam optimisation algorithm [41] with β1 = 0.5 and β2 = 0.999. The initial learning rate was set at 1×10^{-4}. No normalisation was used in the network. The effects of different hyperparameters on the performance of the models was observed. Only one hyperparameter was changed, and the rest were constant for each test (Table 2). Each model was trained for 2000 epochs with an Nvidia tesla v100 GPU on Paperspace cloud computing [43]. The training time for each model was approximately 29 h.

3.3 Performance Evaluation

The performance of these hyperspectral reconstruction algorithms was evaluated through qualitative analysis. One of the most widely used qualitative measures, MRAE, is defined by

$$MRAE = \frac{1}{N} \sum_{i=1}^{N} \left(\frac{|G(x)^i - y^i|}{y^i} \right) \quad (12)$$

Table 2. HRNET models hyperparameters configurations.

No	Model Name	Colour correction	Cropping	Batch size
1	HRNET-1	No	No	6
2	HRNET-2	No	No	2
3	HRNET-3	Yes	No	2
4	HRNET-4	No	Yes	2
5	HRNET-5	Yes	Yes	2

where G(x) is the input image, y is the ground truth and N denotes the number of pixels in the spectral image.

This method was used in evaluating the performance of the models by calculating the error of each pixel present in the image.

4 Results

The results of the HS reconstruction models can be evaluated by comparing the reconstructed HS images to the original HS images. The models' performance will be tested on the testing dataset, which was not used during the training phase. MRAE will be calculated for every pixel between a reconstructed HS image and the original HS image, and then the MRAE average of all the test images for each epoch will be calculated.

4.1 HSCNN-D Architecture

The lowest recorded average MRAE for each configuration of HSCNN-D is tabulated in Table 3. Figure 3 shows the performance (i.e., MRAE) of the HSCNN-1, HSCNN-2, HSCNN-3, HSCNN-4 and HSCNN-5 models for a different number of epochs (i.e., 1–2000 epochs). As discussed in previous section, various configurations were trained, and their effects on model performance was observed. The first comparison was based on the batch size hyperparameter of training, which is the number of samples (input data) processed while training.

As observed in Fig. 3, for the HSCNN-D architecture, reducing the batch size led to slight improvements in the models' performance at the early stages of training, that is, up to Epoch 750. HSCNN-1 and HSCNN-2 models' performance is very close to each other, where the smaller batch size model (i.e., HSCNN-2) produces a lower recorded MRAE (0.0529), which is slightly better than the higher batch size HSCNN-1, that is, an MRAE of 0.0551. Therefore, the results of the batch size tests show that a small batch size can improve model performance.

For images used to train the model, including colour correction in the pre-processing procedure of data reduces the performance of HSCNN-D (Fig. 3) with HSCNN-2 (no colour correction applied) and HSCNN-3 (colour correction applied). The best performing model, HSCNN-2, with no colour correction has a lower MRAE of 0.0529 compared

Table 3. Results of the lowest recorded MRAE for each configurationn of HSCNN-D.

No	Model Name	Colour correction	Cropping	Batch size	Avg. MRAE*
1	HSCNN-1	No	No	6	0.0551
2	HSCNN-2	No	No	2	0.0529
3	HSCNN-3	Yes	No	2	0.0541
4	HSCNN-4	No	Yes	2	0.0548
5	HSCNN-5	Yes	Yes	2	0.0538

* Lowest recorded MRAE

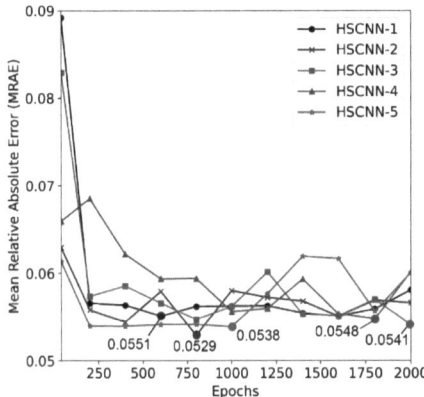

Fig. 3. The MRAE between original and reconstructed HSI for each configuration of HSCNN-D. The circles highlight the lowest recorded MRAE for each configuration.

to HSCNN-3 of MRAE of 0.0541. This result suggests that for the HSCNN-D architecture, performing colour correction reduces the performance. Additionally, for the HSCNN-D architecture, introducing random cropping (HSCNN-4) in the training phase has also shown to reduce the performance. As seen in Fig. 3, the model with random cropping configuration HSCNN-4 produces an MRAE of 0.0548, which is higher than that of the model without random cropping, that is, HSCNN-2 with an MRAE of 0.0529.

HSCNN-5 which uses both colour correction and random cropping in the training phase led to improved performance and result in an MRAE of 0.0538, which is lower than the MRAE obtained using colour correction (HSCNN-3) or random cropping (HSCNN-4) only. However, it fails to outperform HSCNN-2, which has no colour correction or random cropping with the lowest recorded MRAE of 0.0529.

Therefore, introducing colour correction and random cropping can improve performance but it fails to produce results that are better than those obtained with a model that does not use either. This result highlights that the data pre-processing step can have a huge effect on the performance of a model, and techniques meant to improve performance can lead to negative results.

4.2 HRNET Architecture

The lowest recorded average MRAE for each configuration of HRNET is tabulated in Table 4. Figure 4 shows the performance (MRAE) of the different configurations trained to observe their effects on model performance (HRNET-1, HRNET-2, HRNET-3, HRNET-4 and HRNET-5) for a different number of epochs (1–2000 epochs).

Table 4. Results of the lowest recorded MRAE for each configuration of HRNET.

No	Model Name	Colour correction	Cropping	Batch size	Avg. MRAE*
1	HRNET-1	No	No	6	0.0511
2	HRNET-2	No	No	2	0.0449
3	HRNET-3	Yes	No	2	0.0439
4	HRNET-4	No	Yes	2	0.0455
5	HRNET-5	Yes	Yes	2	0.0433

* Lowest recorded MRAE

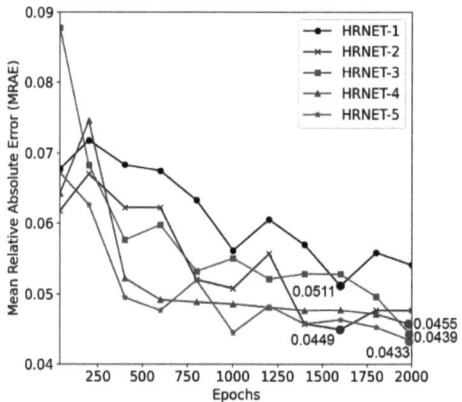

Fig. 4. The MRAE between original and reconstructed HSI for each configuration of HRNET. The circles highlight the lowest recorded MRAE for each configuration.

The difference in performance between HRNET-1 with batch size 6 and HRNET-2 with batch size 2 can be observed in Fig. 4. The results demonstrate that increasing the batch size lowers model performance, with HRNET-1 (0.0511) having a higher MRAE than HRNET-2 (0.0449). This finding highlights the importance of using an appropriate batch size to train models. Given that a high batch size means that more data is included in each learning iteration for the model, it can increase generalisation error and thereby reduce model performance despite improving the speed and efficiency of the training process.

Introducing colour correction to the data for the HRNET models has shown promising results (Fig. 4). HRNET-3, which includes colour correction, has a lower MRAE (0.0439) than HRNET-2 (0.0449), which does not have colour correction. Therefore, this finding suggests that including colour correction to the HRNET architecture can increase the performance of the models.

As for the impact of random cropping on HRNET, it can be observed that HRNET-4 which includes random cropping in its training process has a slightly higher MRAE of 0.0455, in comparison to HRNET-2, which does not use random cropping, having an MRAE of 0.0449. Despite this slight increase in MRAE, HRNET-4 showed consistent performance during training.

The results also showcase the impact of adding colour correction and random cropping to the HRNET architecture. HRNET-5, which includes both techniques, has the lowest recorded MRAE of 0.0433 and the most consistent performance. This result suggests that both techniques improve the performance of the HRNET architecture and their combination leads to better results.

4.3 Comparison Between HSCNN-D and HRNET

The Fig. 5 and Table 5 illustrates the comparison between the performances of the configurations of the HSCNN-D and HRNET architectures. Both best performing models, namely, HRNET-5 and HSCNN-2, are trained by using a batch size of 2. The best-performing model amongst the HRNET models, HRNET-5, achieves good results in terms of HS reconstruction with an MRAE of 0.0433, whereas the best-performing model amongst the HSCNN-D models, HSCNN-2, produces an MRAE of 0.0529.

Table 5. Comparison of the Results of the lowest recorded MRAE for HRNET and HSCNN.

No	Model Name	Colour correction	Cropping	Batch size	Avg. MRAE*
1	HRNET-1	No	No	6	0.0511
2	HSCNN-1	No	No	6	0.0551
3	HRNET-2	No	No	2	0.0449
4	HSCNN-2	No	No	2	0.0529
5	HRNET-3	Yes	No	2	0.0439
6	HSCNN-3	Yes	No	2	0.0541
7	HRNET-4	No	Yes	2	0.0455
8	HSCNN-4	No	Yes	2	0.0548
9	HRNET-5	Yes	Yes	2	0.0433
10	HSCNN-5	Yes	Yes	2	0.0538

* Lowest recorded MRAE

The results indicate that both algorithms benefit from a small batch size in terms of performance. However, the effect of batch size on performance differs between the two

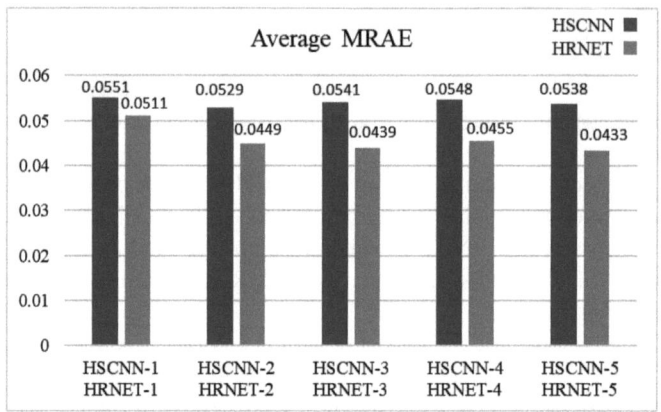

Fig. 5. Comparison between the MRAE of the HRNET and HSCNN configurations.

algorithms. Compared with HSCNN-D, the HRNET algorithm has a more considerable variation in performance across different batch size tests (i.e. refer to the results produced by HRNET-1 and HRNET-2), demonstrating that it is more sensitive to changes in batch size. This result suggests that the performance of the HRNET architecture is more influenced by the choice of batch size during training than by other factors. In general, selecting a large batch size could lead to a decrease in performance. On the other hand, the HSCNN-D architecture appears to be less sensitive to batch size variations.

Although the HSCNN-D and HRNET algorithms demonstrate benefits from the use of a small batch size in training, the algorithms have completely different reactions with the inclusion of colour correction and random cropping techniques. For the HSCNN-D architecture, the addition of colour correction and random cropping has a negative effect on performance. Therefore, the best-performing model has no colour correction or random cropping applied. This result suggests that for HSCNN-D, these hyperparameters might introduce variations that decrease its performance in reconstructing HS images. Meanwhile, as illustrated in Fig. 5, the HRNET architecture shows considerable improvements when colour correction and random cropping are included in its training. HRNET-5, which utilises a batch size of 2 and includes colour correction and random cropping, achieves the lowest MRAE amongst all the trained models and has an MRAE of 0.0433. This result indicates that the combination of colour correction and random cropping enhances the HRNET architecture's ability to reconstruct HS images.

Although the inclusion of these techniques negatively affects the performance of HSCNN-D, it greatly improves the performance of HRNET. This situation suggests that the introduction of additional variations through colour correction and random cropping increases the robustness and adaptability of the HRNET architecture. It emphasises the importance of carefully evaluating the effect of preprocessing techniques, such as colour correction and random cropping, on specific algorithms, because the optimal combination of preprocessing techniques may vary depending on the algorithm.

In the comparative analysis between the HRNET and HSCNN-D architectures, HRNET consistently outperforms HSCNN-D across all configurations as shown in

Fig. 5. The results indicate that the performance of HRNET in terms of HS image reconstruction accuracy is superior to that of HSCNN-D. The results establish that amongst the tested models, HRNET-5 is the best configuration for HS reconstruction. Therefore, HRNET-5 is selected to create the third dataset consisting of reconstructed HS images for acne detection algorithms.

5 Discussion

The objective of this research is to do a comprehensive evaluation of two HS reconstruction methods (i.e. HSCNN-D and HRNET). Different configurations of hyperparameters for the two HS reconstruction methods are thoroughly analysed and compared to identify the optimal HS reconstruction method that can be used for reconstructing HS medical images. After a thorough evaluation, the HRNET architecture, particularly the HRNET-5 model with an MRAE of 0.0433, emerges as the best-performing method.

The findings and insights gained from this study can pave the way for future research in the field of medical research using reconstructed HSIs. One recommendation for future research can be to apply reconstructed HSI techniques to detect and classify various medical conditions beyond acne. Developing specialised algorithms based on reconstructed HSI can enhance diagnostic accuracy and improve treatment monitoring without the requirement for specialised HSI equipment.

6 Conclusion

In this research, two HS reconstruction methods based on HSCNN-D and HRNET were compared using medical HS images. The collected medical dataset underwent some pre-processing steps before being utilized. The processes involved are color correction using the Grey World algorithm for the RGB images, and the HS images underwent band reduction. Data augmentation was also performed on both datasets to increase the dataset size artificially. Based on the results obtained, the HRNET architecture has outperformed the HSCNN-D architecture in the task of reconstructing hyperspectral images from RGB images. Considering that HSI has been underutilized in medical applications due to the high cost and complexity of the equipment required. By utilizing reconstructed HS images using HRNET architecture, the benefits of HS data can be acquired in a cost effective and accessible manner.

References

1. R. Hamblin, M., Avci, P., & K. Gupta, G. (2016). Imaging in Dermatology. Elsevier
2. Siche, R., Vejarano, R., Aredo, V., Velasquez, L., Saldaña, E., Quevedo, R.: Evaluation of food quality and safety with hyperspectral imaging (HSI). Food Eng. Rev. **8**(3), 306–322 (2015). https://doi.org/10.1007/s12393-015-9137-8
3. Feng, Y., Sun, D.: Application of hyperspectral imaging in food safety inspection and control: a review. Critical Rev. Food Sci. Nutrit. **52**(11), 1039–1058 (2012). https://doi.org/10.1080/10408398.2011.651542

4. Kuula, J., et al.: Using VIS/NIR and IR spectral cameras for detecting and separating crime scene details. In: SPIE Proceedings (2012). https://doi.org/10.1117/12.918555
5. Schuler, R., Kish, P., Plese, C.: Preliminary observations on the ability of hyperspectral imaging to provide detection and visualization of bloodstain patterns on black fabrics. J. Forensic Sci. **57**(6), 1562–1569 (2012). https://doi.org/10.1111/j.1556-4029.2012.02171.x
6. Hosking, A., Coakley, B., Chang, D., Talebi-Liasi, F., Lish, S., Lee, S., et al.: Hyperspectral imaging in automated digital dermoscopy screening for melanoma. Lasers Surg. Med. **51**(3), 214–222 (2019). https://doi.org/10.1002/lsm.23055
7. Shehieb, W., Assaad, M., Tawfik, A., Mat Isa, N.: Analysis and recovery monitoring of meibomian gland dysfunction disease using hyperspectral imaging. In: 2019 IEEE International Symposium On Signal Processing And Information Technology (ISSPIT) (2019). https://doi.org/10.1109/isspit47144.2019.9001823
8. Leon, R., Martinez-Vega, B., Fabelo, H., Ortega, S., Melian, V., Castaño, I., et al.: Non-invasive skin cancer diagnosis using hyperspectral imaging for in-situ clinical support. J. Clin. Med. **9**(6), 1662 (2020). https://doi.org/10.3390/jcm9061662
9. A. Boas, D., Ramanujam, N., Pitris, C.: Handbook of Biomedical Optics. CRC Press (2020)
10. Lu, G., Fei, B.: Medical hyperspectral imaging: a review. J. Biomed. Opt. **19**(1), 010901 (2014). https://doi.org/10.1117/1.jbo.19.1.010901
11. Takatani, T., Aoto, T., Mukaigawa, Y.: One-shot hyperspectral imaging using faced reflectors. In: 2017 IEEE Conference On Computer Vision And Pattern Recognition (CVPR) (2017). https://doi.org/10.1109/cvpr.2017.288
12. Oh, S., Brown, M., Pollefeys, M., Kim, S.: Do it yourself hyperspectral imaging with everyday digital cameras. In: 2016 IEEE Conference On Computer Vision and Pattern Recognition (CVPR) (2016). https://doi.org/10.1109/cvpr.2016.270
13. Arad, B., Ben-Shahar, O.: Sparse recovery of hyperspectral signal from natural RGB images. In: Leibe, B., Matas, J., Sebe, N., Welling, M. (eds.) Computer Vision – ECCV 2016: 14th European Conference, Amsterdam, The Netherlands, October 11–14, 2016, Proceedings, Part VII, pp. 19–34. Springer International Publishing, Cham (2016). https://doi.org/10.1007/978-3-319-46478-7_2
14. Jia, Y., et al.: From RGB to Spectrum for Natural Scenes via Manifold-Based Mapping (2022). Retrieved 9 October 2022
15. Akhtar, N., Mian, A.: Hyperspectral recovery from RGB images using Gaussian processes. IEEE Trans. Pattern Anal. Machine Intell. **42**(1), 100–113 (2018). https://doi.org/10.48550/arXiv.1801.04654
16. Chakrabarti, A., Zickler, T.: Statistics of real-world hyperspectral images. CVPR (2011). https://doi.org/10.1109/cvpr.2011.5995660
17. Xiong, Z., Shi, Z., Li, H., Wang, L., Liu, D., Wu, F.: HSCNN: CNN-based hyperspectral image recovery from spectrally undersampled projections. In: 2017 IEEE International Conference On Computer Vision Workshops (ICCVW) (2017). https://doi.org/10.1109/iccvw.2017.68
18. Shi, Z., Chen, C., Xiong, Z., Liu, D., Wu, F.: HSCNN+: Advanced CNN-based hyperspectral recovery from RGB images. In: 2018 IEEE/CVF Conference on Computer Vision And Pattern Recognition Workshops (CVPRW) (2018). https://doi.org/10.1109/cvprw.2018.00139
19. Zhao, Y., Po, L., Yan, Q., Liu, W., Lin, T.: Hierarchical regression network for spectral reconstruction from RGB images. In: 2020 IEEE/CVF Conference on Computer Vision And Pattern Recognition Workshops (CVPRW) (2020). https://doi.org/10.1109/cvprw50498.2020.00219
20. Stiebei, T., Koppers, S., Seltsam, P., Merhof, D.: Reconstructing spectral images from RGB-images using a convolutional neural network. In: 2018 IEEE/CVF Conference on Computer Vision And Pattern Recognition Workshops (CVPRW) (2018). https://doi.org/10.1109/cvprw.2018.00140

21. Kittipongdaja, P., Siriborvornratanakul, T.: Automatic kidney segmentation using 2.5D resunet and 2.5D DenseUNet for malignant potential analysis in complex renal cyst based on CT images. EURASIP J. Image Video Proc. (2022). https://doi.org/10.1186/s13640-022-00581-x
22. Pho, K., Lam, H., Le, T., Nguyen, H.T., Yoshitaka, A.: Attention-driven RetinaNet for parasitic egg detection. In: 2022 IEEE International Symposium on Multimedia (ISM) (2022). https://doi.org/10.1109/ism55400.2022.00060
23. Li, R., Zheng, S., Duan, C., Su, J., Zhang, C.: Multistage attention resu-net for semantic segmentation of fine-resolution remote sensing images. IEEE Geosci. Remote Sens. Lett. **19**, 1–5 (2022). https://doi.org/10.1109/lgrs.2021.3063381
24. Zhang, R., Isola, P., Efros, A.: Colorful image colorization. In: Leibe, B., Matas, J., Sebe, N., Welling, M. (eds.) Computer Vision – ECCV 2016: 14th European Conference, Amsterdam, The Netherlands, October 11-14, 2016, Proceedings, Part III, pp. 649–666. Springer International Publishing, Cham (2016). https://doi.org/10.1007/978-3-319-46487-9_40
25. Kupyn, O., Budzan, V., Mykhailych, M., Mishkin, D., Matas, J.: Deblurgan: Blind motion deblurring using conditional adversarial networks. In: Proceedings of the IEEE Conference on Computer Vision and Pattern Recognition, pp. 8183–8192 (2018). https://doi.org/10.48550/arXiv.1711.07064
26. Gu, S., Li, Y., Van Gool, L., Timofte, R.: Self-guided network for fast image denoising. In: 2019 IEEE/CVF International Conference on Computer Vision (ICCV) (2019). https://doi.org/10.1109/iccv.2019.00260
27. Kim, J., Lee, J., Lee, K.: Accurate image super-resolution using very deep convolutional networks. In: 2016 IEEE Conference on Computer Vision and Pattern Recognition (CVPR) (2016). https://doi.org/10.1109/cvpr.2016.182
28. Zhao, L., Wang, J., Li, X., Tu, Z., Zeng, W.: Deep convolutional neural networks with merge-and-run mappings (2016). https://doi.org/10.48550/arXiv.1611.07718
29. Krizhevsky, A., Sutskever, I., Hinton, G.: ImageNet classification with deep convolutional neural networks. Commun. ACM **60**(6), 84–90 (2017). https://doi.org/10.1145/3065386
30. Shi, W., et al.: Real-time single image and video super-resolution using an efficient sub-pixel convolutional neural network. In: 2016 IEEE Conference on Computer Vision And Pattern Recognition (CVPR) (2016). https://doi.org/10.1109/cvpr.2016.207
31. Specim FX10. Specim. (2022). https://www.specim.fi/products/specim-fx10/. Retrieved 3 Dec 2022
32. Shehieb, W., Assaad, M., Tawfik, A., Mat Isa, N.A.: Meibomian gland cyst detection and classification using hyperspectral imaging. Cogent Eng. (2021). https://doi.org/10.1080/23311916.2021.1883831
33. Renno, J.-P., Makris, D., Ellis, T., Jones, G.A.: Application and evaluation of colour constancy in visual surveillance. In: 2005 IEEE International Workshop on Visual Surveillance and Performance Evaluation of Tracking and Surveillance (n.d.). https://doi.org/10.1109/vspets.2005.1570929
34. Barnard, K., Martin, L., Coath, A., Funt, B.: A comparison of computational color constancy algorithms. II. experiments with image data. IEEE Trans. Image Process. **11**(9), 985–996 (2002). https://doi.org/10.1109/TIP.2002.802529
35. Buchsbaum, G.: A spatial processor model for object colour perception. J. Franklin Inst. **310**(1), 1–26 (1980). https://doi.org/10.1016/0016-0032(80)90058-7
36. Sun, C., Shrivastava, A., Singh, S., Gupta, A.: Revisiting unreasonable effectiveness of data in deep learning era. In: Proceedings of the IEEE International Conference on Computer Vision, pp. 843–852 (2017)
37. Zhu, X., Vondrick, C., Fowlkes, C.C., Ramanan, D.: Do we need more training data? Int. J. Comput. Vision **119**(1), 76–92 (2015). https://doi.org/10.1007/s11263-015-0812-2

38. Mahmud, M., Kaiser, M.S., McGinnity, T.M., Hussain, A.: Deep learning in mining biological data. Cogn. Comput. **13**(1), 1–33 (2021)
39. Perez, L., Wang, J.: The effectiveness of data augmentation in image classification using deep learning (2017). arXiv preprint arXiv:1712.04621
40. Shorten, C., Khoshgoftaar, T.: A survey on image data augmentation for Deep Learning. J. Big Data (2019). https://doi.org/10.1186/s40537-019-0197-0
41. Tensorflow. TensorFlow. (n.d.). Retrieved March 7, 2023, from https://www.tensorflow.org/
42. Kingma, D., Adam, J.B.: A method for stochastic optimization. In arXiv:1412.6980 (2014)
43. Cloud computing, evolved. Paperspace. (n.d.). https://www.paperspace.com/. Retrieved March 7, 2023

Kidney MRI Segmentation Using Deep Learning

Suman Acharya[1(✉)], Achyuth Sarkar[1], Somen Nayak[2], and Bablu Kumar Majhi[3]

[1] Department of Computer Science and Engineering, National Institute of Technology Arunachal Pradesh, Jote 791113, Arunachal Pradesh, India
achyuth@nitap.ac.in, suman.acharya@uem.edu.in
[2] Faculty of Science and Technology, IcfaiTech, The ICFAI University Jaipur, Jamdoli, Agra Road, Jaipur 302031, India
[3] Department of Computer Applications, University of Engineering and Management, Jaipur, Sikar Road, Udaipuriya Mod, Chomu, Jaipur 303807, Rajasthan, India
https://jaipur.uem.edu.in/

Abstract. Segmentation of kidney images is a crucial aspect of the diagnostic and therapeutic application of medical image technologies for kidney disease. Precise kidney segmentation is of the utmost importance in clinical practice, as it enables medical specialists to diagnose diseases and enhance treatment planning. The manual segmentation of the kidneys is a laborious process that is susceptible to variation among specialists as a result of their characteristics. However, precise segmentation of kidney images is difficult to achieve because defining the boundaries of objects in medical images is difficult. An efficient segmentation method for 2D T2-W MRI images of the human abdomen is presented in this work. In this study, kidney segmentation was conducted on patients diagnosed with chronic kidney disease (CKD). The manuscript presents Cascaded-ResUNet++, a segmentation method for kidneys diagnosed with CKD from MRI images, which derives inspiration from ResUNet++. By incorporating distinct residual blocks such as the compression and excitation block, Atrous Spatial Pyramidal Pooling (ASPP), and the attention block, this model aims to outperform ResUNet, AttentionUNet, UNet, and ResUNet++. The Multi-Criteria Decision Analysis (MCDA) method TOPSIS returns a result of 0.704156, indicating that Cascaded-ResUNet++ exhibits superior performance compared to all other methods. In addition, our proposal is highly adaptable for kidney segmentation on account of its cost-effectiveness.

Keywords: Medical Diagnosis · Deep Learning · 2D Abdominal T2-W MRI · Automated Kidney Segmentation · Cascaded-ResUNet++

1 Introduction

The kidneys are the bilateral organ pair situated in the posterior region of the abdomen, shielded by the rib cage. In addition, they have the responsibility of filtering the blood from the renal arteries and eliminating surplus water, salt, and waste through the urine. Additionally, these are organs that have a crucial function in the metabolism of vitamin D. Currently, medical image processing serves as a vital tool in diagnosing therapy, planning surgeries, and preventing diseases and difficulties in many organs, such as the brain, heart, kidney, and liver [4]. Currently, the analysis of medical images relies on the expertise and experience of radiologists. The utilization of computer-aided segmentation serves two primary purposes: firstly, to enhance conventional user-guided segmentation, and secondly, to obtain segmentation before visualization or quantification for the interpretation of medical images [1]. Recently, numerous computer-assisted diagnostic (CAD) systems have been developed utilizing medical image processing techniques. X-ray, ultrasound, CT, and MRI equipment can readily produce internal images of the human body [3]. These technologies possess high-resolution imaging capabilities for soft tissue in the human body and exhibit rapid computational capabilities. Both advanced and emerging societies are faced with increasing medical expenses associated with CKD. By 2030, there is a projected increase of 16.7% in the number of cases of CKD. A study found that the likelihood of developing chronic kidney disease (CKD) in persons aged 30–49 without CKD at the beginning was as high as 54% over their remaining lifetime [6]. The incidence of chronic kidney disease (CKD) may be increased by the global population aging, as aging is a significant risk factor for CKD. Patients who have diabetes and hypertension and are at a high risk of developing chronic kidney disease (CKD) are advised to actively identify the disease at an early stage to prevent it from progressing [5]. In this study, kidney segmentation is performed using T2-W MRIs, because MRI scans are capable of producing more intricate images of organs and tissues. Numerous CAD systems have emerged in recent years to aid in the accurate and unbiased diagnosis of lung cancer, liver tumors, and breast disorders. Nevertheless, the segmentation of kidney images poses a formidable challenge. Image noise, unclear boundaries between the liver, kidneys, and spleen, and numerous pathologies, including tumors and nephrolithiasis, are the primary contributors [2]. This work focuses on the application of Cascaded-ResUNet++ to separate the kidneys from the abdomen of individuals with chronic kidney disease (CKD). Here, to segment a kidney from an MRI dataset, we utilize three abdomen MRI scans and three masks per patient. A total of thirty patients undergo this procedure in its entirety. In this study, kidney segmentation was conducted on patients diagnosed with chronic kidney disease (CKD). An equal distribution of one-tenth is designated for testing, eight-tenth is assigned for training purposes, and the remaining one-tenth is designated for validation. Our proposed methodology entails conducting one hundred iterations of training with the training dataset, the validation dataset, and the sigmoid activation function. This will allow us to extract features more effectively. Additionally, the loss is computed by incorporating the training and validation set. The kidneys in the testing dataset that correspond to abdominal images are precisely segmented by the resulting model. To assess the effectiveness of our segmentation task, we need to evaluate the accuracy, sensitivity, specificity, precision, and intersection over union (IOU) of different segmentation models, such as ResUNet, AttentionUNet, UNet, and ResUNet++. The Cascaded-ResUNet++ model outperformed ResUNet, AttentionUNet, UNet, and ResUNet++ models, as assessed using the TOPSIS approach, with a score of 0.704156. The subsequent sections of this work are structured as follows: Sect. 2 contains a review of previous research; Sect. 3 outlines the materials and methods used in the study; Sect. 4 describes the experimental setup; Sect. 5 includes the results and discussion; and Sect. 6 concludes the study.

2 Related Works

Over the years, researchers have developed various approaches aimed at enhancing the effectiveness of kidney segmentation in chronic kidney disease (CKD) patients from image datasets.

M. G. Oghli et al. [17] introduced a convolutional neural network with layers called Fast-UNet++, which improves the speed and precision of the UNet model. Initially, the model underwent training and evaluation to accurately segment sagittal and axial pictures of the kidney. The anticipated masks calculated the kidney image biomarkers, including their volume and dimensions. Ultimately, the suggested model underwent testing on a dataset that is accessible to the public and has diverse forms. The model's performance was then compared to other networks that were relevant to the task. A group of individuals who had received both ultrasound and computed tomography scans assessed the network.

F.N.Saikia et al. [13] suggest a new and strong use of MLP (Multi-Layer Perceptron) based structures to segment glomeruli in PAS (Periodic Acid Schiff)-stained entire renal images, aiming to improve the diagnosis of renal disorders. The segmentation difficulty is addressed by employing MLP-UNet (Multi-Layer Perceptron U-Net), a novel approach that avoids the use of traditional convolution and self-attention processes. In addition, the study conducts a comparison of different methodologies, including U-Net, and introduces the novel strategy of training the TransUNet model on the kidney WSI (whole slide image) dataset for the first time. The models were trained using dice score as the metric and dice loss as the loss function. The findings indicate that MLP-based architectures yield similar outcomes (89.96%) to pre-trained architectures such as TransUNet (90.58%) while utilizing 20% fewer parameters and without the need for pre-training. Additionally, MLP-based architectures exhibit superior Dice scores during the 5-fold cross-validation training and demonstrate faster learning compared to conventional U-Net architectures.

Yan Zhuang et al. [19] present a new method for segmenting numerous organs and structures in abdominal MRI images. This method uses diffusion-based synthetic segmentation to generate pseudo-labels without relying on any MRI annotations. The suggested strategy specifically utilizes human anatomy consistency across multiple imaging methods and accurately divides 13 distinct organs and structures in T1-weighted (T1-W) abdominal MRI scans. They accomplish this by acquiring knowledge through the use of unpaired and publicly accessible annotated CT data. To verify the effectiveness of the suggested technique, the researchers carefully selected a collection of abdomen T1-weighted MRI images that included both pre-contrast and dynamic contrast-enhanced sequences. They then conducted thorough comparisons with previous cutting-edge methods. The experiments demonstrated that the proposed strategy outperformed other alternatives, particularly when it came to major abdominal organs and tissues. Their method decreases the amount of work required to annotate and create large-scale multiparametric MRI datasets, making it easier to design tools for segmenting several organs based on MRI.

S-H. Chen et al. [12] suggested enhancing the UNet network to increase its ability to convey information and introduced a novel channel attention network called the Global Local Network (GL-UNet). GL-UNet takes into account the impact of both global and local channels. This enables the network to better prioritize important information. The convolutional block of the deepened UNet subsampling section incorporates the suggested global-local network. This makes the features of the important channels much better. In kidney segmentation, the proposed method achieved a Dice coefficient of 96.25% and an intersection over union (IOU) of 92.78%. The Dice coefficient for segmenting renal parenchyma achieved a score of 92.90%, whereas the IOU (intersection over union) reached 86.75%. The segmentation of the renal sinus achieved a Dice coefficient of 90.18% and an IOU of 82.12%, surpassing existing deep learning methods.

P-H.Conze et al. [15] assess and contrast several networks that utilize convolutional, transformer, and hybrid convolutional/transformer approaches to segment polycystic kidneys. They propose a dual-task learning approach that utilizes a shared feature extractor, followed by distinct decoders for each kidney. This process enhances the ability to apply the learned knowledge to new cases and improves efficiency. The researchers thoroughly assessed several designs and learning strategies using a diverse magnetic resonance imaging dataset obtained from 112 patients diagnosed with polycystic kidney disease. This study's findings demonstrate the efficacy of transformer-based models for segmenting polycystic kidneys. Additionally, they emphasize the importance of utilizing dual-task learning to enhance segmentation accuracy and address the challenges posed by limited data availability.

Gaoyu Cao et al. [14] introduced the Renal Automatic Segmentation Network (RASNet) as a tool for automated renal contour segmentation. In addition, this approach includes a multi-scale spatial perception module and a decoding module with attention connection to improve semantic information and network segmentation accuracy.

H. Qi et al. [18] created the MRDAUNet++ method for separating kidney tumors. This method combines multiscale residuals and dual attention simultaneously. The "MultiRes block" module replaces two successive convolutions in UNet++. This module utilizes coordinate attention (CA), which integrates features from various scales and mitigates the impact of background noise. By incorporating an attention gate (AG) into the short connections, the network's ability to extract features from the target region is enhanced.

S.Valente et al. [10] assess the kidney segmentation efficacy of the UNet architecture in 2D US images. To attain this objective, they investigated the feasibility of augmenting a sizable, multi-view dataset of 2D images with multiple sliced images extracted from 3D US volumes. The proposed methodology was assessed using 66 3D US volumes, of which 51 were designated for training, 5 for validation, and 10 for testing. 3,792 two-dimensional segmented images were extracted from the volumes. The researchers performed two experiments: (i) one utilizing the complete database (WWKD) and (ii) the other utilizing images in which the kidney area exceeded 500 mm2. Real 2D images (obtained utilizing 2D sensors) were used to validate the effectiveness of our strategy. In the testing dataset, an average error of 2.88 ± 2.63 mm was recorded.

Zhanlin Ji et al. [16] introduced ASD-Net as a solution for the segmentation of kidneys and kidney tumors. The suggested network uses brand-new adaptive spatial-channel convolution optimization blocks to effectively gather the information that isn't spread out evenly in the images. By using more recently developed blocks, especially Dense Dilated Enhancement Convolution (DDEC) blocks, the network sends features more efficiently and reuses them all over. This makes segmenting more accurate. Adding the Atrous Spatial Pyramid Pooling (ASPP) module to the network's middle layer makes it easier to separate small and complicated kidney tumors. The simultaneous spatial and channel squeeze and excitation (scSE) attention mechanism in the network aids people in comprehending and managing visual information relevant to their surroundings. Supplementary encoding layers integrate into the primary (U-Net) layer and connect to the initial encoding layer through skip connections. The enhanced U-Net architecture facilitates the extraction and fusion of high-level and low-level features, hence enhancing the network's capability to restore segmentation details.

S. Lee et al. [9] investigated the impact of convolutional neural network (CNN) integration with computer-extracted, measurable features on the accuracy of CAD in ultrasound images of CKD. The study utilized ultrasound images obtained from patients who sought medical attention at Severance Hospital and Gangnam Severance Hospital in South Korea from 2011 to 2018. For organ segmentation and measurable feature extraction, a Mask regional CNN model was implemented. The length of the kidney and the ratio of kidney echogenicity to liver echogenicity were extracted as data. ResNet18 was used to categorize kidney ultrasound images as CKD or non-CKD. Both experiments were performed with and without the measurable feature data being input. To assess the efficacy of each model, the area under the receiver operating characteristic curve (AUROC) was utilized. The study comprised a cohort of 909 patients, with a mean age of 51.4±19.3 years. Of these, 414 [49.5%] were male and 495 [54.5%] were female. The model that underwent training using ultrasound images attained an average AUROC of 0.81. The implementation of image training that incorporated autonomously extracted features of kidney length and echogenicity resulted in an enhanced average AUROC value of 0.88. When the clinical information of underlying diabetes was incorporated into the CNN-trained model with measurable features, this value increased to 0.91.

A. Abdelrahman et al. [11] suggest an EfficientNet model for intricate segmentation by connecting the encoder stage of EfficientNet with U-Net. This model exemplifies a more efficacious system with enhanced encoder and decoder functionalities. The Intersection over Union (IoU) statistic measures the performance of a model. The EfficientNet models achieved impressive IoU Scores for background, kidney, and tumor segmentation, with an average IoU Score ranging from 0.976 for B0 to 0.980 for B4. B7 achieved the highest Intersection over Union (IoU) score for kidney segmentation, while B4 achieved the highest IoU score for tumor segmentation. The study employs the KiTS19 dataset for contrast-enhanced CT images.

D. Jha et al. [7] introduced ResUNet++, an enhanced ResUNet framework designed specifically for segmenting colonoscopic images. Their empirical assessments demonstrate that the proposed architecture yields excellent segmentation outcomes on publicly accessible datasets. ResUNet++ surpasses U-Net and ResUNet by attaining remarkable evaluation results.

3 Materials and Methods

3.1 Kidney MRI Dataset

The T2-W Kidney MRI dataset [8] is utilized for segmentation purposes in this study. A cumulative sum of 650 healthy and 650 CKD 2D MRI slices comprise this set. A complete depiction of this dataset is accessible from [8] (Fig. 1).

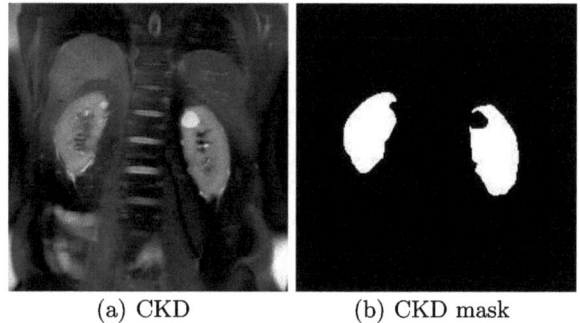

(a) CKD (b) CKD mask

Fig. 1. Sample CKD Kidney MR image & mask

3.2 Proposal

This study introduces Cascaded-ResUNet++, an innovative methodology designed to segment a kidney using a dataset specific to chronic kidney disease. In order to enhance the performance of ResUNet++ in comparison with AttentionUnet, Cascaded-ResUNet++ is implemented. The Cascaded-ResUNet++

architecture makes use of the attention blocks, squeeze and excitation blocks, and ASPPs. The residual block facilitates the transmission of information across multiple layers, enabling the construction of a neural network with increased depth. This enhanced depth has the potential to address the degradation issues encountered in each of the encoders. This enhancement optimizes the interdependencies within the channel while minimizing the computational expenses. The Cascaded-ResUNet++ design, as proposed, consists of a stem block, six encoder blocks, four Atrous Spatial Pyramid Pooling (ASPP) modules, and six decoder blocks. Firstly, the encoding and decoding process involves the use of one stem block, three encoding blocks, three decoding blocks, two ASPP modules, three attention blocks, and one 1×1 convolutional layer. Here, the number of filters is chosen from a predetermined list of choices, which include 16, 32, 64, 96, and 128. The residual unit is a composite structure that incorporates batch normalization, Rectified Linear Unit (ReLU) activation, and convolutional layers. Each encoder block is composed of two consecutive 3×3 convolutional blocks and an identity mapping. Every convolution block consists of three components: a batch normalization layer, a ReLU activation layer, and a convolutional layer. The identity mapping establishes a connection between the input and output of the encoder block. In the encoder block, the initial convolutional layer utilizes a strided convolution operation to decrease the spatial dimension of the feature maps by a factor of two. The squeeze and excitation block then transfers the output of the encoder block. The ASPP functions as a mechanism that broadens the field of vision of the filters, therefore including a more extensive area. Additionally, the decoding path incorporates residual units. The attention block improves the efficacy of map-based features before each unit starts. Subsequently, a nearest-neighbor up-sampling technique is employed to increase the resolution of feature maps obtained from the lower level. These up-sampled feature maps are then combined with the feature maps obtained from their respective encoding channels by concatenation. The output of the decoder block is further processed by the Atrous Spatial Pyramid Pooling (ASPP) module. Afterwards, the result of ASPP is sent through a 1×1 convolutional layer. It is then subjected to additional processing by three encoder blocks comprising squeeze and excitation blocks. The output is further transferred through the ASPP module and subsequently processed by three decoder blocks comprising attention blocks. Subsequently, a nearest-neighbor up-sampling technique is used to enhance the resolution of feature maps produced from the lower level. The up-sampled feature maps are blended with the feature maps derived from their corresponding encoding channels by concatenation. The decoder block's output undergoes additional processing through the Atrous Spatial Pyramid Pooling (ASPP) module. Finally, a 1×1 convolutional layer is utilized with a sigmoid activation function to generate the segmentation map. In Algorithm 1, the building blocks of each component of Cascaded-ResUNet++ are explicitly stated. Additionally, the architecture of Cascaded-ResUNet++ is clearly described in Algorithm 1. Because MRI scans are capable of producing more detailed images of organs and tissues, we are utilizing them here. The Cascaded-ResUNet++

model exhibits superior performance compared to all other segmentation models, as assessed by a variety of metrics when compared to other segmentation models. In this section, kidney T2-W MRIs will be assessed for segmentation. Nevertheless, despite the use of an imaging modality like T2-MRI, various issues persist, including: (i) T2-weighted images display changes in signal strength, or brightness, among various tissues. This can present challenges in accurately delineating the boundary between the kidney and other organs. (ii) Conditions such as cysts or tumors can alter the kidneys' normal shape and signal intensity. This further complicates their correct segmentation using automated approaches. (iii) MRI images may be sensitive to artifacts caused by patient movement or respiration. These artifacts have the potential to exacerbate the blurring of boundaries and complicate the process of segmentation. This section provides an analysis of the functionality of our proposal and demonstrates its superior performance compared to all other models, such as AttentionUNet, ResUNet++, ResUNet, and UNet. Before anything else, we must ensure that we have sufficient training data to construct a robust deep-learning model. To achieve this, the experimental dataset must be divided into training, validation, and testing sets. Here, to segment a kidney from an MRI dataset, we utilize three abdomen MRI scans and three masks per patient. A total of thirty patients undergo this procedure in its entirety. In this study, kidney segmentation was conducted on patients diagnosed with chronic kidney disease (CKD). An equal distribution of one-tenth is designated for testing, eight-tenth is assigned for training purposes, and the remaining one-tenth is designated for validation. Our proposed methodology entails conducting one hundred iterations of training with the training dataset, the validation dataset, and the sigmoid activation function. This will allow us to extract features more effectively. Additionally, the loss is computed by incorporating the training and validation set. The kidneys in the testing dataset that correspond to abdominal images are precisely segmented by the resulting model. In this manner, the kidney can be accurately segmented by the relevant masks, specifically targeting chronic kidney patients. Our model produces an accurate mask depicting a kidney afflicted with chronic kidney disease in this scenario. In Figs. 3, 4, 5, 6 and 7, the outputs of various models are illustrated. Every figure comprises an abdominal image, the actual mask, and the predicted mask. Here, Fig. 6 shows more accurate predicted masks compared to Fig. 3 due to the inclusion of residual blocks, such as the squeeze and excitation block, ASPP (Atrous Spatial Pyramidal Pooling), and the attention block. Figure 4 exhibits superior masks compared to Fig. 6 because of their attention mechanism. As a result of overfitting in ResUNet, Fig. 3 exhibits superior masks compared to Fig. 5. Figure 7 exhibits superior masks than Fig. 6 due to the utilization of multiple residual blocks, squeeze and excitation blocks, and ASPP modules compared to ResUNet++ (Fig. 2).

Algorithm 1. Cascaded-ResUNet++ Algorithm
―――
1: **Input:** Input Image X
2: **Output:** Segmentation Mask Y
3: **procedure** SQUEEZEEXCITEBLOCK(X)
4:　　$X_0 \leftarrow X$　▷ Initial input
5:　　$X \leftarrow \text{GlobalAveragePooling}(X_0)$　▷ Global average pooling
6:　　$X \leftarrow \text{FullyConnected}(X)$　▷ Fully connected layer
7:　　$X \leftarrow \text{ReLU}(X)$　▷ ReLU activation
8:　　$X \leftarrow \text{FullyConnected}(X)$　▷ Fully connected layer
9:　　$X \leftarrow \text{Sigmoid}(X)$　▷ Sigmoid activation
10:　　$X \leftarrow \text{Multiply}(X_0, X)$　▷ Multiplication
11:　　**return** X
12: **end procedure**
13: **procedure** STEMBLOCK(X)
14:　　$X_0 \leftarrow X$　▷ Initial input
15:　　$X_1 \leftarrow \text{ConvolutionLayer2D}(X_0)$　▷ 2D Convolutional layer
16:　　$X_2 \leftarrow \text{BatchNorm}(X_1)$　▷ Batch normalization
17:　　$X_3 \leftarrow \text{ReLU}(X_2)$　▷ ReLU activation
18:　　$X_4 \leftarrow \text{ConvolutionLayer2D}(X_3)$　▷ 2D Convolutional layer
19:　　$X_5 \leftarrow \text{ConvolutionLayer2D}(X_0)$　▷ 2D Convolutional layer
20:　　$X_6 \leftarrow \text{BatchNorm}(X_5)$　▷ Batch normalization
21:　　$X_7 \leftarrow \text{Add}(X_4, X_6)$　▷ Addition
22:　　$X_8 \leftarrow \text{SqueezeExciteBlock}(X_7)$　▷ Squeeze and Excite block
23: **end procedure**
24: **procedure** ENCODER
25:　　$X_{\text{skip\_list}} \leftarrow [\,]$　▷ Initialize list to store skip connections
26:　　**for** $i = 1$ **to** n **do**
27:　　　　$X_i \leftarrow \text{ResidualBlock}(X_{i-1})$　▷ Residual block
28:　　　　$X_{\text{skip\_list}}[i] \leftarrow X_i$　▷ Store skip connection from this encoder block
29:　　**end for**
30: **end procedure**
31: **procedure** ASPP
32:　　$X_{\text{aspp}} \leftarrow \text{ASPP}(X_n)$　▷ Atrous Spatial Pyramid Pooling
33: **end procedure**
34: **procedure** RESIDUALBLOCK(X)
35:　　$X_0 \leftarrow X$　▷ Initial input
36:　　$X_1 \leftarrow \text{BatchNorm}(X_0)$　▷ Batch normalization
37:　　$X_2 \leftarrow \text{ReLU}(X_1)$　▷ ReLU activation
38:　　$X_3 \leftarrow \text{ConvolutionLayer2D}(X_2)$　▷ 2D Convolutional layer
39:　　$X_4 \leftarrow \text{BatchNorm}(X_3)$　▷ Batch normalization
40:　　$X_5 \leftarrow \text{ReLU}(X_4)$　▷ ReLU activation
41:　　$X_6 \leftarrow \text{ConvolutionLayer2D}(X_5)$　▷ 2D Convolutional layer
42:　　$X_7 \leftarrow \text{ConvolutionLayer2D}(X_0)$　▷ 2D Convolutional layer
43:　　$X_8 \leftarrow \text{BatchNorm}(X_7)$　▷ Batch normalization
44:　　$X_9 \leftarrow \text{Add}(X_6, X_8)$　▷ Addition
45:　　$X \leftarrow \text{SqueezeExciteBlock}(X_9)$　▷ Squeeze and Excite block
46:　　**return** X
47: **end procedure**

```
48: procedure DECODER
49:     for i = n to 1 do
50:         X_i ← Attention(X_i, X_skip_list[i − 1])         ▷ Attention block
51:         X_i ← Upsample(X_i)                              ▷ Upsampling
52:         X_i ← Concatenate(X_i, X_skip_list[i − 1])       ▷ Skip connection
53:         X_i ← ResidualBlock(X_i)                         ▷ Residual Block
54:     end for
55: end procedure
56: procedure CASCADED-RESUNET++(X)
57:     X_skip_list ← []                         ▷ Initialize list to store skip connections
58:     X_0 ← StemBlock(X)                       ▷ Stem block to process initial input
59:     X_skip_list[0] ← X_0                     ▷ Store initial stem output in skip list
60:     for i = 1 to n do                        ▷ Encoder path
61:         X_i ← ResidualBlock(X_{i−1})         ▷ Residual block
62:         X_skip_list[i] ← X_i                 ▷ Store skip connection from this encoder block
63:     end for
64:     X_n ← ASPP(X_n)                          ▷ Atrous Spatial Pyramid Pooling
65:     for i = n to 1 do                        ▷ Decoder path
66:         X_i ← Attention(X_i, X_skip_list[i − 1])    ▷ Attention block
67:         X_i ← Upsample(X_i)                  ▷ Upsampling
68:         X_i ← Concatenate(X_i, X_skip_list[i − 1])  ▷ Skip connection
69:         X_i ← ResidualBlock(X_i)             ▷ ResidualBlock
70:     end for
71:     X ← ASPP(X_1)                            ▷ ASPP
72:     X ← ConvolutionLayer2D(X)                ▷ 2D Convolutional layer
73:     for i = n + 1 to 2n do                   ▷ Post Encoder path
74:         X_i ← ResidualBlock(X_{i−1})         ▷ Residual block
75:         X_skip_list[i] ← X_i                 ▷ Store skip connection from this encoder block
76:     end for
77:     X_2n ← ASPP(X_2n)                        ▷ Atrous Spatial Pyramid Pooling
78:     for i = 2n to n + 1 do                   ▷ Post Decoder path
79:         X_i ← Attention(X_i, X_skip_list[i − 1])    ▷ Attention block
80:         X_i ← Upsample(X_i)                  ▷ Upsampling
81:         X_i ← Concatenate(X_i, X_skip_list[i − 1])  ▷ Skip connection
82:         X_i ← ResidualBlock(X_i)             ▷ ResidualBlock
83:     end for
84:     X_output ← ASPP(X_{n+1})                 ▷ ASPP
85:     X ← ConvolutionLayer2D(X_output)  ▷ Final convolution for segmentation mask
86:     Y ← Sigmoid(X)                           ▷ Sigmoid activation
87:     return Y
88: end procedure
```

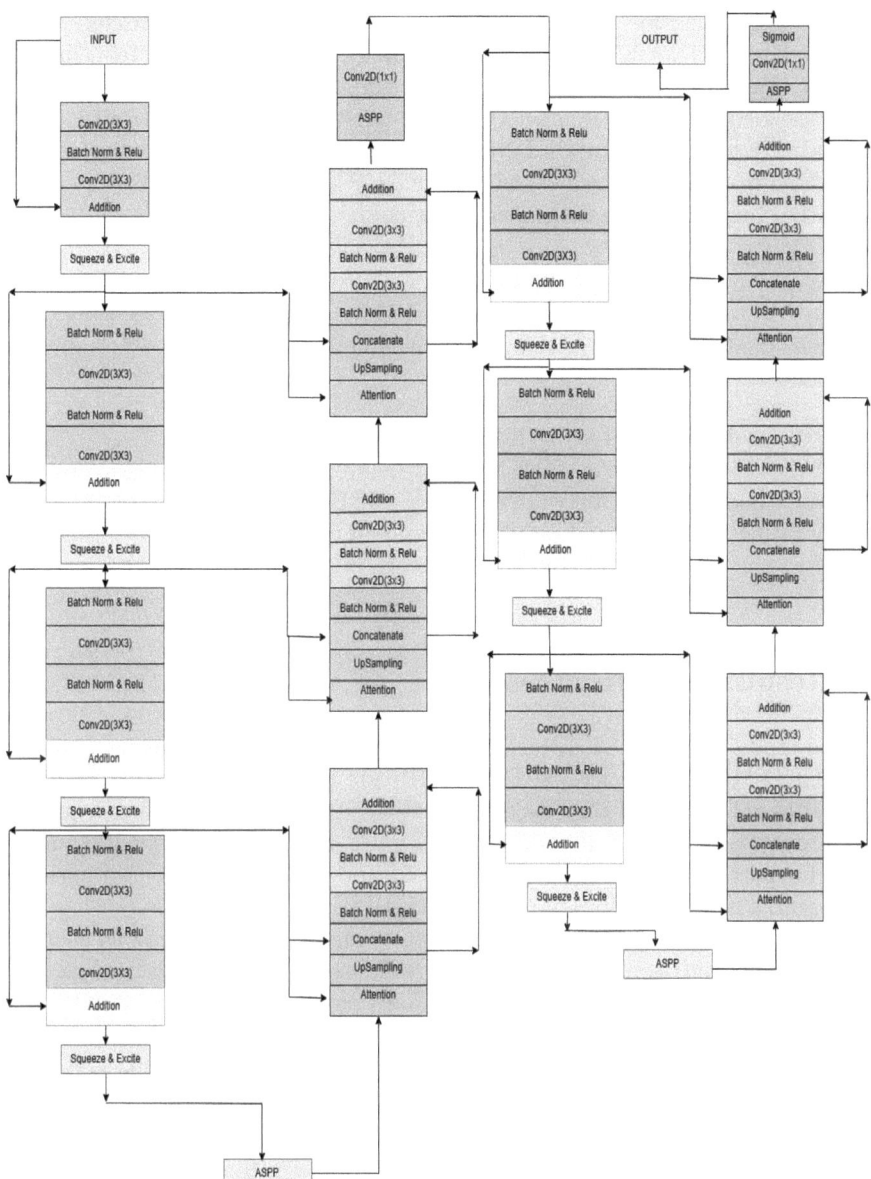

Fig. 2. Casacaded-ResUNet++ Architecture

4 Experimental Setup

4.1 Parameters Setting

The parameter values corresponding to the different models are as follows:

The batch size for Cascaded-ResUNet++, ResUNet++, ResUNet, AttentionUNet, and UNet is set to 8. The learning rate (lr) is set to 1e-4, and the number of epochs is set to 100. The number of filters (n filters) for ResUNet++ and Cascaded-ResUNet++ is selected from a list of values, which are 16, 32, 64, 96, and 128; and for Attention UNet, ResUNet, and UNet, the number of filters is selected from a list of values, which are 32, 64, 96, and 128, 256. The output activation function for these models is sigmoid.

4.2 PC Configuration

The investigation was conducted using a personal computer that was configured as follows:

1. CPU: Intel(R) Core(TM) i7-12700F 12-GEN CORE 20,
2. RAM: 32 GB,
3. GPU: GeForce RTX 3060 VENTUS 2X 12GB OC,
4. Operating System: Windows 11 Professional 64-bit,
5. Software: Jupyter notebook 6.5.4, Tensorflow 2.14.0, Python 3.11.5

5 Results and Discussion

In this study, the Cascaded-ResUNet++ model is trained to segment kidneys from CKD MRIs. Here, kidney T2-W MRIs are examined for segmentation. To ensure the robustness of the Cascaded-ResUNet++ model, a significant quantity of training samples is required. To accomplish this, the experimental dataset must be partitioned into training, testing, and validation sets. A fraction of eight-tenths is set aside for training, one-tenth for testing, and one-tenth for validation. The Cascaded-ResUNet++ model is trained for 100 iterations using the training and validation dataset and then validated by calculating the loss using the training and validation set. This enables us to extract characteristics efficiently. In this study, Cascaded-ResUNet++, ResUNet, AttentionUNet, UNet, and ResUNet++ models were trained for performance comparison. The model is subsequently employed to make predictions on the testing set. To evaluate the efficacy of our segmentation tasks, it is imperative to assess the accuracy (Acc.), sensitivity (Sens.), specificity (Spec.), precision (Prec.), and intersection over union (IOU) metrics for different segmentation models as presented in Table 1. These models include Cascaded-ResUNet++, ResUNet, AttentionUNet, UNet, and ResUNet++. Here, AttentionUNet exhibits superior performance compared to UNet and ResUNet++ in this context of its attention mechanisms, which more effectively concentrate on the critical areas of the input image. Attention mechanisms can enhance the overall quality of segmentation by assisting the network in learning more fine-grained features. UNet is surpassed in performance by ResUNet++, which is a result of its residual blocks, including the squeeze and excitation block, ASPP(Atrous Spatial Pyramidal Pooling), and the attention block. Cascaded-ResUNet++ outperforms ResUNet++ and AttentionUnet in terms of performance due to its utilization of numerous residual blocks, squeeze and excitation blocks, ASPP (Atrous Spatial Pyramidal Pooling), and attention blocks, which distinguish it from other models. UNet surpasses ResUNet in performance because it is more resistant to overfitting compared to ResUNet. Here, ResUNet++ outperforms UNet in terms of accuracy, precision, IOU, and specificity (Table 1). AttentionUNet outperforms ResUNet++ in terms of recall (Table 1). Cascaded-ResUNet++ outperforms AttentionUNet with its superior precision, Intersection over Union (IoU) score and specificity(Table 1). UNet outperforms ResUNet in terms of its higher levels of accuracy, precision, IoU, and specificity (Table 1). It is also evident by the TOPSIS approach by attaining different TOPSIS scores by various models (Table 1).

Table 1. Segmentation performance

Model	Accuracy	Recall/sensitivity	Precision	iou	Specificity	TOPSIS Score	TOPSIS Rank
Attention UNet	94.60	54.74	81.22	32.72	99.10	0.664717	2
ResUNet++	94.66	39.82	85.9	51.33	99.53	0.662191	3
Cascaded-ResUNet++	94.53	49.68	81.76	54.47	99.21	0.704156	1
ResUNet	93.23	72.06	67.68	10.52	97.56	0.333333	5
UNet	94.44	60.3	78.54	28.59	98.83	0.617096	4

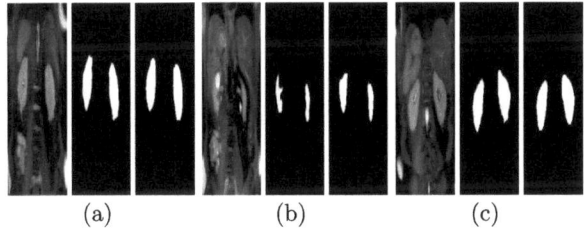

(a)   (b)   (c)

Fig. 3. Sample results of UNet model

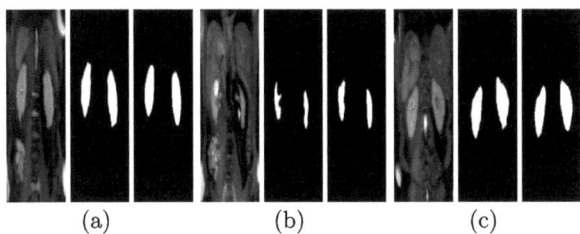

(a)   (b)   (c)

Fig. 4. Sample results of AttentionUNet model

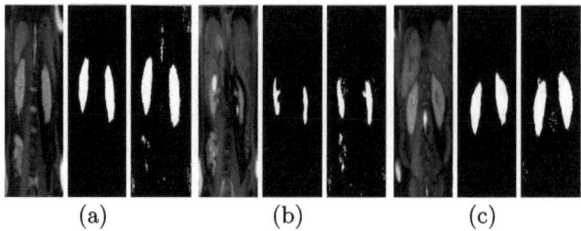

Fig. 5. Sample results of ResUNet model

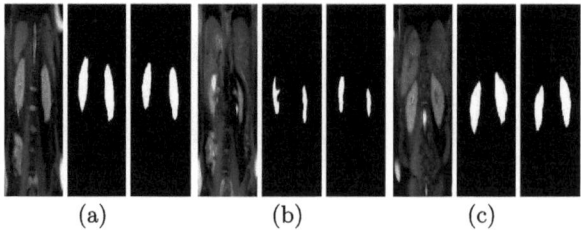

Fig. 6. Sample results of ResUNet++ model

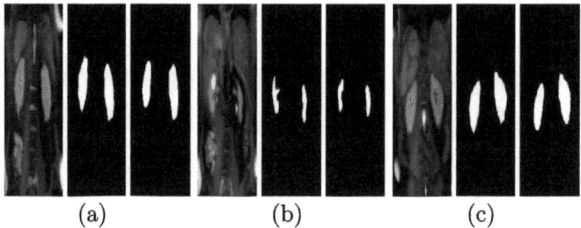

Fig. 7. Sample results of Cascaded-ResUNet++ model

6   Conclusion

This research employs deep learning models, namely Cascaded-ResUNet++ and Attention UNet, to perform kidney segmentation on abdominal images by generating corresponding masks. The proposals are juxtaposed with the ResUNet, ResUNet++, and UNet models. Both the Cascaded-ResUNet++ and Attention UNet models exhibit greater performance in comparison to the ResUNet, ResUNet++, and UNet models. In the context of performance evaluation, it has been observed that the Cascaded-ResUNet++ model exhibits superior performance compared to the Attention UNet model. This study exclusively focuses on the segmentation of the kidney using T2-weighted magnetic resonance imaging (MRI) scans. In future research endeavors, we intend to employ deep learning models for the analysis of different modalities of kidney MRIs, including T1-weighted and diffusion-weighted images. In our future work, we aim to incorporate the best optimization strategy into the suggested deep-learning model to enhance the efficiency of segmenting kidneys from abdomen MRIs obtained from diverse data sources.

References

1. Lin, D.-T., Lei, C.-C., Hung, S.-W.: Computer-aided kidney segmentation on abdominal CT images. IEEE Trans. Inf Technol. Biomed. **10**, 59–65 (2006)
2. Freiman, M., Kronman, A., Esses, S. J., Joskowicz, L., Sosna, J. Nonparametric iterative model constraint graph min-cut for automatic kidney segmentation. In: Medical Image Computing and Computer-Assisted Intervention–MICCAI 2010: 13th International Conference, Beijing, China, September 20–24, 2010, Proceedings, Part III 13, pp. 73–80 (2010)
3. Kumar, S., Moni, R.: Diagnosis of liver tumor from CT images using curvelet transform. Int. J. Comput. Sci. Eng. **2**, 1173–1178 (2010)
4. Jokar, E., Pourghassem, H.: Kidney segmentation in ultrasound images using curvelet transform and shape prior. In: 2013 International Conference on Communication Systems and Network Technologies, pp. 180–185 (2013)
5. Komenda, P., et al.: Cost-effectiveness of primary screening for CKD: a systematic review. Am. J. Kidney Dis. **63**, 789–797 (2014)
6. Hoerger, T.J., et al.: The future burden of CKD in the United States: a simulation model for the CDC CKD initiative. Am. J. Kidney Dis. **65**, 403–411 (2015)
7. Jha, D., et al.: ResUNet++: an advanced architecture for medical image segmentation. In: 2019 IEEE International Symposium on Multimedia (ISM), pp. 225–2255 (2019)
8. Daniel, A.J., et al.: T2-weighted Kidney MRI Segmentation version v1.0.0 (2021). https://doi.org/10.5281/zenodo.5153568
9. Lee, S., et al.: Machine learning-aided chronic kidney disease diagnosis based on ultrasound imaging integrated with computer-extracted measurable features. J. Digit. Imaging **35**, 1091–1100 (2022)
10. Valente, S., et al.: A deep learning method for kidney segmentation in 2D ultrasound images. In: 2022 44th Annual International Conference of the IEEE Engineering in Medicine Biology Society (EMBC), pp. 3911–3914 (2022)
11. Abdelrahman, A., Viriri, S.: EfficientNet family U-Net models for deep learning semantic segmentation of kidney tumors on CT images. Front. Comput. Sci. **5**, 1235622 (2023)
12. Chen, S.-H., Wu, Y.-L., Pan, C.-Y., Lian, L.-Y., Su, Q.-C.: Renal ultrasound image segmentation method based on channel attention and GLUNet11. J. Radiat. Res. Appl. Sci. **16**, 100631 (2023)
13. Saikia, F.N., et al.: MLP-UNet: glomerulus segmentation. IEEE Access **11**, 53034–53047 (2023)
14. Cao, G., et al.: RASNet: renal automatic segmentation using an improved U-Net with multi-scale perception and attention unit. Pattern Recogn., 110336 (2024)
15. Conze, P.-H., Andrade-Miranda, G., Le Meur, Y., Cornec-Le Gall, E., Rousseau, F.: Dual-task kidney MR segmentation with transformers in autosomal-dominant polycystic kidney disease. Comput. Med. Imaging Graph., 102349 (2024)
16. Ji, Z., et al.: ASD-Net: a novel U-Net based asymmetric spatial-channel convolution network for precise kidney and kidney tumor image segmentation. Med. Biol. Eng. Comput., 1–15 (2024)

17. Oghli, M.G., et al.: Fully automated kidney image biomarker prediction in ultrasound scans using Fast-UNet++. Sci. Rep. **14**, 4782 (2024)
18. Qi, H., Wang, Z., Qi, X., Shi, Y., Xie, T.: Ultrasound image segmentation of renal tumors based on UNet++ with fusion of multiscale residuals and dual attention. Phys. Med. Biol. (2024)
19. Zhuang, Y., et al.: Multi-organ segmentation in abdominal MRI using CT to- MR synthesis in submitted to medical imaging with deep learning under review (2024). https://openreview.net/forum?id=tQhWHiiALn

A Comparative Analysis of Ensemble Strategies for Enhanced Machine Learning Results

Alavikunhu Panthakkan[1]([✉]), Aruna Gurjarand[2], Jagruti Patel[2], Hardik Patel[2], Satyen Parikh[2], and Wathiq Mansoor[1]

[1] University of Dubai, Dubai, United Arab Emirates
`apanthakkan@ud.ac.ae`
[2] A. M. Patel Institute of Computer, Ganpat University Mehsana, Kherva, India

Abstract. Ensemble methods play a crucial role in enhancing the overall performance, stability, and generalization of machine learning models by mitigating overfitting and effectively managing complex data interactions through the integration of diverse models. However, it is acknowledged that ensemble approaches come with increased computational expenses and may require careful tuning for optimal results. This paper conducts a thorough review of ensemble methods, encompassing recent advancements, practical applications, and a comparative analysis of diverse techniques. Through a detailed performance analysis and exploration of trade-offs, the paper facilitates an objective comparison of ensemble methods, examining the impact of factors such as ensemble size, model diversity, and computational complexity on overall performance. Evaluation criteria, including accuracy, precision, recall, and F1 score, are systematically considered. The comparative study not only identifies the conditions under which various ensemble approaches excel but also offers guidance in selecting the most effective strategy for a given challenge. In essence, the research contributes to a comprehensive understanding of ensemble methods, aiding practitioners in optimizing machine learning outcomes in diverse scenarios.

Keywords: Machine Learning · Ensemble Methods · Bagging · Boosting · Stacking

1 Introduction

In the field of machine learning, ensemble methods represent a strategic approach that involves the integration of multiple models, often referred to as base models or weak learners, to construct a more powerful prediction model. The core philosophy guiding ensemble methods revolves around leveraging the collective intelligence embedded within a diverse set of models. The overarching aim is to achieve improved performance and heightened robustness in comparison to relying on a single model. At the heart of these approaches lies the concept of the "wisdom of crowds." Within an ensemble, each base model contributes its unique strengths and may exhibit individual limitations. The synergy within the ensemble facilitates the alleviation of constraints inherent in individual models, resulting in more accurate predictions through the amalgamation of their diverse forecasts [1, 6]. Ensemble methods are powerful tools for improving model performance, reducing overfitting, and increasing the robustness of predictions, especially when individual models complement each other. Ensemble methods include Bagging (Random Forest), Boosting (AdaBoost, XGBoost), Stacking, Voting, combining models for robust, accurate predictions [1–10]. The choice of ensemble method depends on the characteristics of the data and the problem at hand (Fig. 1).

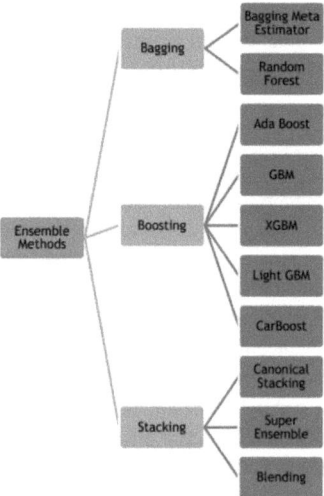

Fig. 1. Ensemble Methods

2 Related Works

2.1 Bagging

Bagging, an ensemble machine learning technique, is crafted to elevate overall accuracy and robustness by training numerous base models independently on diverse training subsets generated via random sampling with replacement. During this process, each base model generates an intermediate prediction, and the final prediction is obtained by aggregating these intermediate predictions through techniques such as regression averaging or classification voting. This method finds broad utility in addressing both classification and regression challenges.

The fundamental principle underlying bagging revolves around the creation of multiple bootstrap samples, each mirroring the size of the original training dataset but exhibiting random fluctuations due to sampling with replacement. These bootstrap samples introduce variability into the training procedure, allowing several models to be trained independently on these diverse subsets using the same learning algorithm. The crux of this approach lies in the fact that, due to random sampling, each model garners insights from a slightly different perspective of the data during training. This inherent variability proves pivotal in alleviating model variance, a prevalent source of overfitting in machine learning models. By strategically aiming to diminish overall variance, bagging contributes to enhancing the ensemble's generalization capability. This is accomplished by consolidating the predictions of multiple models, each trained on subtly different data subsets. Consequently, the ensemble is adept at furnishing more accurate and reliable predictions by harnessing the diverse perspectives learned by individual models. Practically, to derive predictions from a bagging ensemble, each individual model autonomously predicts the target variable for a given input. These individual forecasts are then amalgamated, employing voting for classification tasks or averaging for regression tasks, to formulate the final prediction, thereby leveraging the collective strength of the ensemble. [1, 2, 6] (Fig. 2).

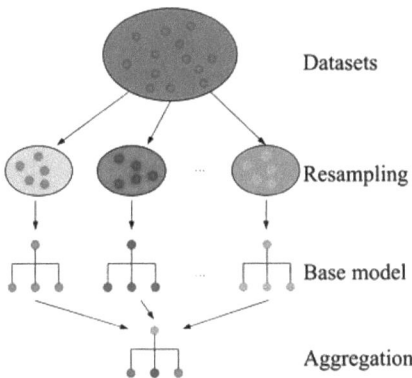

Fig. 2. Schematic diagram of Bagging ensemble model

Key Benefits:

1. *Reduced Overfitting Risk:* Bagging aids in mitigating the likelihood of models overfitting to noise or outliers within the training set by training multiple models on distinct variants of the data, thus diminishing the risk of memorizing irrelevant patterns or anomalies during the learning process.
2. *Enhanced Prediction Accuracy:* Through the amalgamation of predictions from multiple models, bagging significantly enhances prediction accuracy, leading to more robust and precise forecasts compared to using a single model.
3. *Improved Model Stability:* Bagging contributes to enhancing model performance by diminishing susceptibility to minor changes in the training data, as evidenced by references [1–3, 6].

3 Random Forest

Random Forest is an ensemble learning technique utilized in machine learning for both classification and regression tasks. It serves as an extension of bagging specifically designed for decision trees. Unlike traditional methods that use the same training set for each decision tree, Random Forest introduces randomness into the tree creation process. This randomness is incorporated at each split, considering only a random subset of features. By injecting this deliberate unpredictability, Random Forest aims to decrease correlation among trees and increase their diversity. Renowned as a widely-used ensemble learning approach in machine learning, Random Forest combines predictions from multiple decision trees to produce more accurate and robust results. It is commonly applied in various classification and regression tasks, where the core principle involves creating an ensemble of decision trees, each trained on a diverse subset of the original training data. During training, each tree evaluates only a randomly selected subset of features for splitting at each node, thereby introducing a dual source of randomness that enhances the diversity of the ensemble [1, 4, 6].

1. *Bootstrap Sampling with Replacement:* The inception of Random Forest involves generating numerous bootstrap samples from the original training data. Each bootstrap sample is formed by randomly selecting data points from the original dataset, allowing for the possibility of duplication due to replacement. This process introduces variability, as some data points may be repeated within a bootstrap sample while others may be omitted.
2. Development of Unique Decision Trees: To create individual decision trees, a recursive procedure is employed for each bootstrap sample. This procedure involves selecting key features and determining split points at each node based on criteria such as Gini impurity or information gain. Importantly, only a random subset of features is considered for each node split, thereby enhancing the diversity of trees within the ensemble.
3. *Ensemble Forecasting:* After independently training decision trees, predictions are made. In classification tasks, each tree predicts a class label for a given input, with the final prediction determined by a majority vote. In regression scenarios, the ultimate prediction is obtained by averaging the forecasts from individual trees.

Key Benefits:

1. *Enhanced Precision:* Random Forest demonstrates superior predictive precision, especially in complex datasets containing significant levels of noise or outliers, surpassing the performance of individual decision trees.
2. *Resistance to Overfitting:* The randomness introduced through bootstrap sampling and feature subset selection effectively mitigates the risks of overfitting. Random Forest adeptly avoids memorizing noise or outliers in the training data by aggregating predictions from multiple trees.
3. *Assessment of Feature Importance*: Random Forest offers a measurable gauge of feature importance, providing insights into the relevance of each feature in the prediction process. This knowledge facilitates feature selection and deepens understanding of the underlying data.

Random Forest emerges as a powerful and adaptable algorithm with relevance across a wide array of problem domains. It boasts user-friendliness, requiring minimal preprocessing of data, and often delivers robust performance without extensive tweaking of hyperparameters. Nonetheless, its computational requirements can be substantial, especially for large datasets and a significant number of trees. Furthermore, the assessment of individual decision trees within the Random Forest ensemble may present challenges compared to evaluating standalone decision trees [1, 7].

4 Boosting

Boosting stands out as an ensemble machine learning technique that consolidates the predictions of multiple weak learners to form a robust learner. Unlike bagging or random forests, boosting adopts an iterative strategy, progressively improving the ensemble's performance by emphasizing misclassified or challenging instances within the training data [1, 6].

The boosting process unfolds as follows:

1. *Initialization:* The process commences by assigning equal weights to all training instances, where the significance of each instance is determined by these weights.
2. *Training Weak Learners:* Weak learners, such as shallow decision trees or simple linear models, are trained on the weighted training data. Despite their simplicity, these weak learners are anticipated to marginally outperform random guessing in making accurate predictions.
3. *Weight Adjustment:* Post-training, the weights of training instances are adjusted. Instances that were misclassified receive increased weights, making them more influential in subsequent iterations. This focused attention on challenging cases enhances the algorithm's ability to handle difficult predictions.
4. *Iterative Training:* The preceding steps are iteratively repeated, with each weak learner trained on the updated weights of the training instances. This iterative process enables the ensemble to rectify errors made by earlier weak learners.
5. *Combining Weak Learners:* The final prediction of the boosting ensemble is derived by aggregating the predictions of all weak learners. Predictions are often weighted based on the performance of each weak learner, assigning higher weight to those achieving greater accuracy [6, 13] (Fig. 3).

Characteristics of Boosting:

1. *Sequential Learning:* Boosting adopts a sequential learning approach, with each weak learner addressing instances that posed challenges for its predecessors. This iterative procedure facilitates gradual improvement in the ensemble's predictive capabilities.
2. *Adaptive Training:* Through adaptive adjustment of instance weights, boosting adapts to the intricacies of the data, prioritizing difficult instances and enabling the ensemble to focus on challenging regions of the feature space.
3. *Model Complexity:* Boosting allows the combination of numerous diverse weak learners, providing flexibility by employing different models at each iteration.
4. *Overfitting Risk:* While boosting excels in reducing bias and enhancing accuracy, there is a risk of overfitting if the ensemble becomes overly complex. Strategies such as early stopping or limiting the number of iterations are employed to mitigate this risk [13].

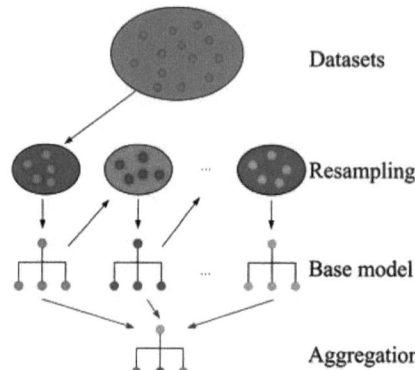

Fig. 3. Schematic diagram of Boosting ensemble model

Boosting encompasses various algorithms, with AdaBoost, Gradient Boosting, and XGBoost being notable examples. These algorithms differ in their approaches to weighting, loss function optimization, and ensemble combination. Proven effective across domains, particularly in large datasets requiring high prediction accuracy, boosting serves as a valuable iterative ensemble strategy that learns from its failures, refining its understanding with each subsequent model [14].

5 Stacking

Stacking, also known as stacked generalization, emerges as an advanced ensemble learning technique devised to elevate prediction accuracy and generalization performance by amalgamating diverse base models and training a meta-model. This paper conducts an in-depth examination of the operational principles and attributes of stacking, shedding light on its benefits and considerations.

Operational Procedure:

1. *Base Model Training:* Stacking initiates with the independent training of various base models on the provided training data. These models, spanning a range of machine learning algorithms such as decision trees, support vector machines, or neural networks, aim to capture diverse data patterns or characteristics.
2. *Meta-Features Generation:* Following base model training, predictions are generated on a validation set or through cross-validation, resulting in meta-features or "level-1 features." These meta-features, offering insights beyond the basic features, are utilized to train the meta-model.
3. *Meta-Model Training:* The meta-model, also termed as a "level-2 model," is trained on the meta-features. Leveraging machine learning techniques like logistic regression, random forest, or gradient boosting, this model learns to effectively integrate the meta-features for generating final predictions.

4. *Prediction:* The trained meta-model is then employed to make predictions on unseen data. Predictions from the base models on the test data serve as metafeatures for the meta-model, which combines them to produce the final forecast.

Distinctive Attributes of Stacking:

1. *Model Diversity:* Stacking leverages the diversity of base models to encompass varied aspects of the data and harness their distinct predictive abilities. The ensemble benefits from merging models with complementary characteristics.
2. *Higher-Order Learning:* By training the meta-model on predictions from basic models, stacking introduces a secondary level of learning. The meta-model adeptly weighs and combines predictions, potentially revealing higher-order data patterns or relationships.
3. *Increased Complexity:* Stacking introduces complexity due to the inclusion of the meta-model. Careful selection of the meta-model and its hyperparameters is pivotal for optimal performance. Overfitting is a concern, but strategies like regularization and early stopping can alleviate this issue.
4. *Computational Considerations:* Training multiple base models and the metamodel in stacking can be computationally demanding, particularly with intricate base models or expansive datasets. However, once the meta-model is trained, the prediction phase often becomes efficient.

Stacking facilitates potent group learning, with the possibility of extending to multiple levels, thereby creating a "stacked ensemble." While this can potentially enhance prediction performance, it also escalates complexity and computational requirements. Effective implementation of stacking has demonstrated its prowess in various domains and competitions, showcasing its capacity to improve prediction accuracy and handle complex data dynamics. However, achieving optimal results necessitates meticulous model selection, validation, and hyperparameter tuning. Essentially, stacking entails training numerous base models and subsequently training a meta-model on their predictions, aiming to acquire a higher-level model that integrates the complementary attributes of multiple models. [8, 10, 11, 15]. Table1 presents a comprehensive comparison of ensemble methods, encompassing their working mechanisms, learning bases, advantages, disadvantages, and implementations in various contexts [2, 9, 16, 17, 20, 21].

6 Performance Analysis

See Table 2.

We utilized the "Migraine.csv" dataset, encompassing 24 attributes, to investigate patterns in migraine headaches. This dataset comprises self-reported data on migraine occurrences gathered from 4550 individuals, resulting in a total of 23550 records, with each record representing a single migraine incident. The dataset includes crucial variables such as user ID, month, day, beta blocker usage (indicating whether the user took beta-blocker medication for migraine treatment), pain level in scale of 1 to 5, duration of migraine in days, and visual disorder occurrence (noting if the user experienced visual disturbances during the migraine episode). This comprehensive dataset allows for a detailed exploration of factors associated with migraine occurrences and their respective

Table 1. Comparison of different ensemble methods

Ensemble Methods	Working Methods	Base Leaners	Training Scheme	Diversification	Prons	Cons	Prominent Applications
Bagging	Parallel training of Multiple models	Homogeneous or heterogeneous	Bootstrap sampling	Data Sampling	Reduce over fitting, improve model generalization	Increased memory and training time	Random Forest, Bagged Decision Trees
Boosting	Sequential training of week learners	Homogeneous	Weighted or adaptive boosting	Weighted data instances	High accuracy, handles class imbalance well	Sensitive to noisy data, potential overfitting	AdaBoost, Gradient Boosting Machines
Ada Boost	Boosting using misclassified samples	Homogeneous	Sequential boosting	Weighted data instances	Simplicity, works with various classifiers	Sensitive to outlier, may be influenced by noise	AdaBoost Classifier
Gradient Boosting	Boosting using gradient descent models	Homogeneous or heterogeneous	Sequential boosting	Gradient Information	Handle high dimensional data, powerful productive capability	Prone to overfitting, requires careful tuning	XGBoost, LightGBM, Cat Boost
Stacking	Metalearning with multiple models	Homogeneous	Stacking via a meta-leaner	N/A	Captures diverse model opinions, improved predictions	More complex to implement, risk of overfitting	Super Learner, Stacking Classifier

Table 2. Performance evaluation of classifier

ML Classifier	Accuracy (%)	Precision (%)	Recall (%)	F1-Score (%)
Logistic Regression	76	76	76	73
Decision Tree	82	81	81	81
Naïve Bayes	38	61	38	46
KNN	71	65	65	61
NBMT	62	62	62	77
ZeroR	62	62	62	77

characteristics. Further analysis of this dataset holds promise for gaining insights into migraine patterns and potentially informing more effective treatment strategies (Fig. 4).

Based on the findings detailed in Table 2, we evaluated the performance of six classifiers – KNN, LR, NB, DT, NBMT, and ZeroR – using varying sizes of the training

A Comparative Analysis of Ensemble Strategies 57

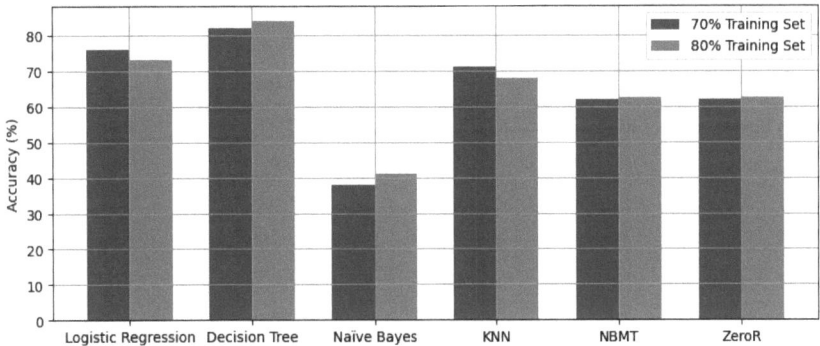

Fig. 4. Accuracy of ML Classifier

set. Remarkably, Decision Trees (DT) showcased the highest accuracy, achieving 84% accuracy with an 80% training set and 82% with a 70% split. Conversely, Naive Bayes (NB) demonstrated the lowest performance, scoring 38% and 41% accuracy with 70% and 80% training sets, respectively. This experimentation underscores the significant impact of training set size on classifier performance, as evidenced by DT's improved accuracy from 82% to 84% with an 80% training set. Conversely, Logistic Regression (LR) and K-Nearest Neighbors (KNN) witnessed a 3% decline in performance with larger training sets. Interestingly, both Naive Bayes Multinomial (NBMT) and ZeroR classifiers displayed consistent performance across both sets. Moreover, precision, representing the percentage of true positive predictions among all positive forecasts, reached 80%, marking the highest precision among all classifiers considered in this study. These results emphasize the importance of carefully selecting the training set size to optimize classifier performance in real-world applications (Fig. 5).

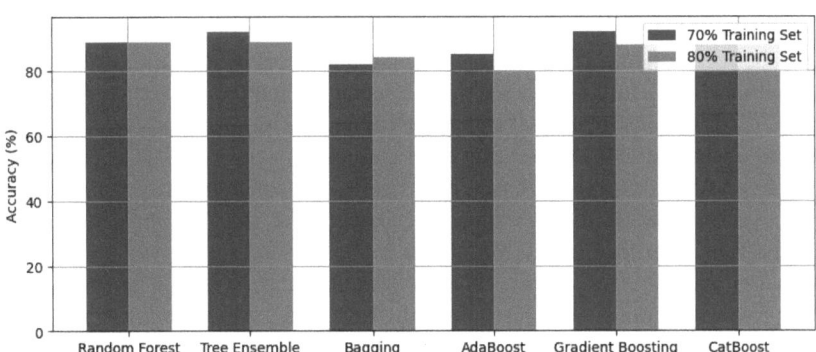

Fig. 5. Accuracy of Ensemble Methods

The outcomes presented in Table 3 demonstrate the remarkable performance of ensemble classifiers, particularly evident in both the 70% and 80% training set scenarios. Notably, Tree Ensemble and Gradient Boosting stand out for their exceptional performance in the 70% training set, while Random Forest and Cat-Boost consistently

Table 3. Performance evaluation of ensemble methods

ML Classifier	Accuracy (%)	Precision (%)	Recall (%)	F1-Score (%)
Random Forest	89	91	92	91
Tree Ensemble	92	70	82	75
Bagging	82	91	93	91
AdaBoost	85	89	88	85
Gradient Boosting	92	92	92	90
CatBoost	88	93	93	92

deliver strong results across both contexts. However, Tree Ensemble experiences a slight 1% decline in performance in the 80% training set. Conversely, AdaBoost exhibits a notable 6% decrease in performance with the larger training set, emphasizing the significant impact of training set size on classifier performance. These findings underscore the undeniable enhancement in classification performance achieved through ensemble methods. Notably, Random Forest achieves the highest values for precision, recall, and F1 score compared to all other methods, highlighting its effectiveness. Furthermore, comparison with traditional machine learning classifiers emphasizes the superior performance of ensemble methods across various evaluation metrics, including recall, precision, and F1 score. This comprehensive analysis reinforces the efficacy and potential of ensemble methods in enhancing classification performance.

7 Conclusion

This paper aims to investigate an efficient model for improving performance accuracy prediction. Machine learning techniques and ensemble methods are commonly used in performance prediction scenarios. Ensemble methods, specifically designed to enhance individual machine learning classifiers, are crucial for improving predictive accuracy. The paper extensively explores various ensemble learning methods and techniques. Prominent ensemble techniques, such as Bagging, Boosting, Stacking, and Random Forest, are employed for performance comparison. The experimental results highlight the effectiveness of ensemble techniques in enhancing the accuracy of machine learning classifiers. While not covering all ML classifier methods exhaustively, there is potential for further improving classifier performance through feature selection and manipulation of other relevant parameters. This potential extends to ensemble classifiers, offering avenues for refining predictive outcomes.

References

1. Freund, Y., Schapire, R.E.: Experiments with a new boosting algorithm. In: Machine Learning: Proceedings of the Thirteenth International Conference, pp. 148–156 (1996)
2. Skurichina, M., Duin, R.P.W.: Bagging for linear classifiers. Elsevier **31**(7) (1998)
3. Breiman, L.: Bagging predictors. Mach. Learn. **24**, 123–140 (1996)
4. Dietterich, T.G.: An experimental comparison of three methods for constructing ensembles of decision trees: Bagging, boosting, and randomization. Mach. Learn. **40**(2), 139–157 (2000)
5. Shaik, A.B., Srinivasan, S.: A brief survey on random forest ensembles in classification model. In: Bhattacharyya, S., Hassanien, A.E., Gupta, D., Khanna, A., Pan, I. (eds.) International Conference on Innovative Computing and Communications: Proceedings of ICICC 2018, Volume 2, pp. 253–260. Springer Singapore, Singapore (2019). https://doi.org/10.1007/978-981-13-2354-6_27
6. Pavlyshenko, B.: Using Stacking Approaches for Machine Learning Models. IEEE (2018)
7. Garcia-Pedrajas, N.: Constructing ensembles of classifiers by means of weighted instance selection. IEEE Trans. Neural Networks **20**(2), 258–277 (2009)
8. Ye, Y., Wu, Q., Huang, J.Z., Ng, M.K., Li, X.: Stratified sampling for feature subspace selection in random forests for high dimensional data. Pattern Recogn. **46**(3), 769–787 (2013)
9. Martinez-Gil, J.: A comprehensive review of stacking methods for semantic similarity measurement. Machine Learn. Applic. **10**, 100423 (2022)
10. Abba, S.I., et al.: Inverse groundwater salinization modeling in a sandstone's aquifer using stand-alone models with an improved non-linear ensemble machine learning technique. J. King Saud Univ.-Comput. Informat. Sci. **34**(10), 8162–8175 (2022)
11. Wolpert, D.H.: Stacked generalization. Neural Netw. **5**(2), 241–259 (1992)
12. Naimi, A.I., Balzer, L.B.: Stacked generalization: an introduction to super learning. Eur. J. Epidemiol. **33**, 459–464 (2018)
13. LeCun, Y., Bottou, L., Bengio, Y., Haffner, P.: Gradient-based learning applied to document recognition. Proc. IEEE **86**(11), 2278–2324 (1998)
14. Schapire, R.E.: The boosting approach to machine learning: an overview. In: Denison, D.D., Hansen, M.H., Holmes, C.C., Mallick, B., Yu, B. (eds.) Nonlinear Estimation and Classification, pp. 149–171. Springer New York, New York, NY (2003). https://doi.org/10.1007/978-0-387-21579-2_9
15. Zenko, B., Todorovski, L., Dzeroski, S.: A comparison of stacking with meta decision trees to bagging, boosting, and stacking with other methods. In: Proceedings 2001 IEEE International Conference on Data Mining, pp. 669–670, IEE (2001)
16. Graczyk, M., Lasota, T., Trawiński, B., Trawiński, K.: Comparison of bagging, boosting and stacking ensembles applied to real estate appraisal. In: Nguyen, N.T., Le, M.T., Świątek, J. (eds.) Intelligent Information and Database Systems, pp. 340–350. Springer Berlin Heidelberg, Berlin, Heidelberg (2010). https://doi.org/10.1007/978-3-642-12101-2_35
17. Das, B., et al.: Comparison of bagging, boosting and stacking algorithms for surface soil moisture mapping using optical-thermal-microwave remote sensing synergies. CATENA **217**, 106485 (2022)
18. Zhang, J., Zhang, H., Gu, H., Lai, R.: Ensemble deep learning model for road traffic flow prediction. Transport. Res. Part C: Emerg. Technol. **135**, 103333 (2023)
19. Wang, J., Gao, J.: An improved random forest algorithm based on feature selection and ensemble strategy for traffic accident prediction. IEEE Access **11**, 1197011982 (2023)
20. Jiang, F., Huang, Y., Guo, J., Yang, X., Zhang, Q.: Robust deep forest ensemble learning for medical image classification. Comput. Biol. Med. **145**, 105177 (2023)
21. Zhou, Z., Qian, L., Zhang, W., Wang, X.: A novel ensemble model based on modified logistic regression for credit scoring. Knowl.-Based Syst. **239**, 107388 (2023)

Neural Network-Based Robust Adaptive Output Feedback Control for MIMO Time-Varying Delay Systems

Farouk Zouari[1(✉)] and Mufti Mahmud[2,3,4]

[1] Laboratoire de Recherche LARA-Automatique, École Nationale d'Ingénieurs de Tunis, Université de Tunis El Manar, BP 37, Le Belvédère, 1002 Tunis, Tunisie
zouari.farouk@gmail.com, farouk.zouari@enit.utm.tn
[2] Information and Computer Science Department, King Fahd University of Petroleum and Minerals, Dhahran 31261, Saudi Arabia
mufti.mahmud@kfupm.edu.sa, muftimahmud@gmail.com
[3] SDAIA-KFUPM Joint Research Center for AI, King Fahd University of Petroleum and Minerals, Dhahran 31261, Saudi Arabia
[4] Interdisciplinary Research Center for Bio Systems and Machines, King Fahd University of Petroleum and Minerals, Dhahran 31261, Saudi Arabia

Abstract. This paper presents a robust neural adaptive output-feedback control strategy for multi-input-multi-output (MIMO) systems with time-varying delays. A linear state observer addresses unavailable state variables, while a neural network approximates unknown nonlinear functions. The control law mitigates external disturbances and various errors. The Gradient Algorithm with Projection tackles unknown control directions, and the Strictly Positive Real (SPR) condition, applied through the Lyapunov–Krasovskii method, aids in designing adaptation laws using output errors. This approach offers several advantages: it applies to a wide range of MIMO systems, avoids singularity issues, requires few adapting parameters, and ensures asymptotic convergence of tracking errors. A simulation example validates the method's effectiveness and feasibility.

Keywords: Neural network · output-feedback control · unknown control direction problem · Strictly Positive Real (SPR) condition · Lyapunov–Krasovskii method · MIMO time-varying delay systems

1 Introduction

In recent years, neural control systems have been successfully applied to many nonlinear systems because they do not require a precise mathematical model of the system [1–45]. Among various neural control schemes, approximation-based adaptive neural control for a class of nonlinear Multiple-Input Multiple-Output (MIMO) uncertain systems has been extensively developed. In these schemes, adaptive methods must be used online to collect data and automatically update control parameters [7, 11, 32–45]. To handle neural approximation errors and external disturbances, these adaptive neural controllers are often augmented by a robust compensator, which can include sliding mode control, supervisory control, and/or H-infinity control [11, 20]. However, a key assumption of several adaptive neural controls is that state variables are assumed to be available for measurement [1].

Recently, there has been increasing interest in the design of observers for partially unavailable state variables within the control research community, leading to significant progress in neural adaptive output-feedback control based on universal function approximators. For instance, an adaptive fuzzy output feedback control has been developed for a single-link robotic manipulator coupled to a brushed direct current (DC) motor with a non-rigid joint [5]. Additionally, observer-based indirect adaptive fuzzy neural control and H-infinity control algorithms have been proposed for Single-Input–Single-Output (SISO) nonlinear uncertain systems [21]. A fuzzy adaptive high-gain backstepping control has been developed for SISO strict feedback nonlinear systems [22]. Direct or indirect adaptive fuzzy controls based on state and/or error observers have been presented in [3, 10]. Observer-based fuzzy adaptive control with a Nussbaum function has been employed to address unavailable states and unknown control direction in nonlinear systems [10, 11]. An adaptive fuzzy output-feedback controller has been constructed to guarantee the boundedness of all signals in the closed-loop system [5, 6]. For a class of nonlinear affine systems with full relative degree, a high-gain observer-based output feedback control has been proposed using the separation principle design [4].

Conversely, an adaptive variable structure output feedback control based on a non-separation principle design, utilizing the Implicit Function Theorem, Mean Value Theorem, neural network parametrization, and a simple linear observer, has been addressed for a class of non-affine nonlinear systems [4, 32–45]. In some cases, the strictly positive real (SPR) condition of the observation error dynamics is required, allowing the use of the Meyer–Kalman–Yakubovich (MKY) Lemma to design adaptation laws and analyze stability [2, 10]. Generally, the SPR condition is restrictive and may not be satisfied in many systems. Therefore, control laws have been developed using Lyapunov stability theory and filtering the observation error dynamics. Filtering of the observation error dynamics, which is not SPR, has been performed using a low-pass filter to meet the SPR condition of an associated transfer function within the Lyapunov stability framework [11]. Observer-based adaptive fuzzy output feedback controls have been developed for MIMO systems, employing two observers: one for approximating unknown functions and estimating system states, and another for addressing controller singularity problems [30]. An adaptive fuzzy control method has been developed to handle actuator faults in uncertain MIMO nonlinear systems with partially unavailable states [24]. Robust adaptive fuzzy decentralized output-feedback control has been proposed for large-scale strict-feedback nonlinear systems [25]. An adaptive control approach has been proposed for nonlinear systems with unknown control gain sign, requiring only two parameters to be adjusted online for each subsystem in the observer design [23].

Time delays are often encountered in real engineering systems, such as helicopters, microwave oscillators, electrical networks, nuclear reactors, and hydraulic systems [7–9, 15, 17]. Studies have reported that time delays typically cause system instability and performance degradation [7–9]. Lyapunov–Krasovskii and Lyapunov–Razumikhin theorems have been used to analyze the stability of adaptive controls for time-delay systems [15, 17]. Research has also focused on output feedback fuzzy adaptive control for time-delayed nonlinear MIMO systems [28]. For example, an observer-based fuzzy adaptive tracking control has been proposed for a rolling cart system with multiple time-delayed state uncertainties and external disturbances [31]. Adaptive fuzzy backstepping output feedback control approaches have been developed for MIMO nonlinear systems with time-varying delays and unknown backlash-like hysteresis [29]. Additionally, a controller using both current and past state information of the system, based on solving a set of linear matrix inequalities (LMIs), has been proposed [26]. A simple model reference adaptive control has been constructed for MIMO linear dynamic systems with unknown state delays [27].

Motivated by these research findings, a novel robust output-feedback indirect adaptive neural control approach is proposed in this work for a class of MIMO time-varying delay systems. The proposed control utilizes a simple linear state observer to overcome the problem of unavailable state variables. To handle the non-affine nature of the systems, the Mean Value Theorem [4] is used to transform the systems into an affine-like form. A neural network is introduced to approximate unknown nonlinearities. Based on the SPR condition and the Lyapunov–Krasovskii method, adaptation laws are constructed using only output observation errors and output tracking errors. The Gradient Algorithm with Projection is employed to address the problem of unknown control direction. Theoretical results are illustrated using computer simulations. The main contributions of this paper can be summarized as follows: (1) the considered class of MIMO time-varying delay systems is relatively large, (2) possible singularity problems in control design are avoided using the Polycarpou Lemma and the Gradient Algorithm with Projection, (3) the tracking errors converge asymptotically to zero for a class of uncertain complex systems, and (4) the proposed adaptive control is simple and easy to implement.

The rest of the paper is outlined as follows. Section 2 introduces the problem formulation. Section 3 develops the design of the robust neural adaptive output-feedback control. Section 4 discusses simulation results to demonstrate the feasibility, validity, and effectiveness of the designed controller. Conclusions are provided in Sect. 5.

Notations. tanh() denotes the hyperbolic tangent function. $0_{n \times m}$ is the zero matrix of size $n \times m$. I_n represents the identity matrix of size n. s is the Laplace variable. $\text{tr}(*)$, $\det(*)$ and $(*)^T$ represent the trace, the determinant and the transpose of a matrix $(*)$, respectively. $\text{diag}(*)$ denotes the block diagonal matrix. $\|\|_1$, $\|\|_2$ and $\|\|_F$ are the Taxicab, the Euclidean and the Frobenius norms, respectively.

2 Problem Formulation

The following class of uncertain nonlinear MIMO time-varying delay systems is considered:

$$\begin{cases} \dot{x} = \sum_{j=0}^{m} B_j \left[d_j + f_j \left(x, x(t - \tau_{1,j}), u(t - \tau_{2,j}) \right) \right], \forall t \geq 0 \\ x = \gamma(t), u = 0_{p \times 1}, \forall t \leq 0 \\ y = C^T x \end{cases} \quad (1)$$

where: $u = [u_1, \cdots u_p]^T \in \mathbb{R}^p$, $x = [x_1, \cdots x_n]^T \in \mathbb{R}^n$ and $y = [y_1, \cdots y_p]^T \in \mathbb{R}^p$ are the control input, the state and the output of the system, respectively.

On the other hand, $\tau_{1j} \in \mathbb{R} \in \mathbb{R}$ and $f_j(x, x(t-t_j), u(t-t_j)) \in \mathbb{R}^p, j = 0, \ldots, m$ are unknown smooth functions. $d_j \in \mathbb{R}^p, j = 0, \ldots, m$ are unknown external disturbances such that $\sum_{j=0}^{m} \int_{t-\tau_d}^{t} \|d_j(\tau)\|_1 d\tau$ is bounded $\forall t \geq 0$, with τ_d is known strictly positive constant. $\gamma(t) \in \mathbb{R}^n$ is a smooth known function and $\int_{t-\tau_d}^{t} \|\gamma(\tau)\|_1 d\tau$ is bounded $\forall t \in [-\tau_d, 0]$. Additionally, we also assume that the following assumptions hold:

Assumption 1. The system output y is measurable.

Assumption 2. There exists smooth functions $g_j \in \mathbb{R}^p$, $j = 0, \ldots, m$ such that $\sum_{j=0}^{m} B_j g_j(x) = Ax$ and the matrices $A = diag(A_1, \cdots, A_p) \in \mathbb{R}^{n \times n}$, $B_0 = diag(b_{01}, \cdots, b_{0p}) \in \mathbb{R}^{n \times p}$, $C = diag(c_1, \cdots, c_p) \in \mathbb{R}^{n \times p}$ and $B_k = diag(b_{k1}, \cdots, b_{kp}) \in \mathbb{R}^{n \times p}$ are known and constant, with $A_i = \begin{bmatrix} 0_{(n_i-1) \times 1} & I_{n_i-1} \\ & 0_{1 \times n_i} \end{bmatrix} \in \mathbb{R}^{n_i \times n_i}$, $b_{0i} = [0_{1 \times (n_i-1)} 1]^T \in \mathbb{R}^{n_i}$, $c_i = [10_{1 \times (n_i-1)}]^T \in \mathbb{R}^{n_i}$, $b_{ki} \in \mathbb{R}^{n_i}$, $det([B_k - B_0]) = 0, i = 1, \cdots, p, k = 1, \cdots, m$ and $n = n_1 + n_2 + \ldots + n_p$.

Assumption 3. $\tau_{20} = 0$, $0 \leq \tau_{10} \leq \tau_d$, $0 \leq \tau_{1j} \leq \tau_d$ and $0 \leq \tau_{2j} \leq \tau_d$, $j = 1, \ldots, m$.

The purpose of the paper is to design an adaptive neural controller for the system (1) such that the output y tracks the specified desired output system $y_d \in \mathbb{R}^p$.

The tracking errors are defined as follows:

$$\begin{cases} \vartheta_r = x_d - x \\ \vartheta = [\vartheta_1, \ldots, \vartheta_p]^T = y_d - y \end{cases} \quad (2)$$

where: $y_d = [y_{d_1}, \ldots, y_{d_p}]^T \in \mathbb{R}^p$, $x_{d_{n+1}} = [y_{d_1}^{(n_1)}, y_{d_1}^{(n_2)}, \ldots, y_{d_p}^{(n_p)}]^T \in \mathbb{R}^n$ and $x_d = [y_{d_1}, \ldots, y_{d_1}^{(n_1-1)}, y_{d_2}, \ldots, y_{d_2}^{(n_2-1)}, y_{d_p}, \ldots, y_{d_p}^{(n_p-1)}]^T \in \mathbb{R}^n$ are smooth known bounded functions.

3 Neural Adaptive Controller Design

Since the system (1) satisfies the Assumptions 1–3, to achieve the control objective, we will use:

- an observer to estimate the system state,
- a neural network to approximate the uncertain functions,
- a control law to eliminate the effect of external disturbance and approximation errors and state estimation errors,
- the strictly positive real (SPR) Lyapunov design method to generate the neural network tuning rule and to analyze the tracking dynamic stability.

3.1 State Observer

The state observer dynamics can be obtained as follows [4]:

$$\begin{cases} \dot{\hat{\vartheta}}_r = [A - B_0 K_C]\hat{\vartheta}_r - K_O \tilde{y} \\ \hat{x} = x_d - \hat{\vartheta}_r \end{cases}, \quad \forall t \geq 0 \qquad (3)$$

where: the matrices $K_C \in \mathbb{R}^{p \times n}$ and $K_O \in \mathbb{R}^{n \times p}$ are selected such that $[A - B_0 K_C] \in \mathbb{R}^{n \times n}$ and $[A - K_O C^T] \in \mathbb{R}^{n \times n}$ are strictly Hurwitz. $\hat{x} = [\hat{x}_1, \ldots, \hat{x}_n]^T \in \mathbb{R}^n$ and $\hat{y} = C^T \hat{x}$ are the estimates of x and y, respectively. $\tilde{y} = y - \hat{y} = [\tilde{y}_1, \ldots, \tilde{y}_p]^T \in \mathbb{R}^p$.

3.2 Neural Networks for Approximating Uncertain Functions

Based on the mean-value theorem and the universal approximation property of neural networks [1–31],

$$h_F = \sum_{j=0}^{m} \left[-g_j(x) + d_j + f_j\left(x, x(t - \tau_{1j}), u(t - \tau_{2j})\right)\right]$$
$$-K_C \hat{\vartheta}_r - x_{d_{n+1}} + \alpha_1 \left(\|y\|_2^2 + \|u\|_2^2 + 1\right) \tilde{y}$$

can be expressed over a compact set Ω as follows:

$$h_F = W_1^{*T} \xi_1(X_u) + \left[W_2^{*T} \xi_2(X_u)\right] u + \varepsilon \qquad (4)$$

where: $\xi_1(X_u) \in \mathbb{R}^{L_1}$ and $\xi_2(X_u) \in \mathbb{R}^{L_2 \times p}$ are the neural network activation functions. $\varepsilon \in \mathbb{R}^p$ is unknown and bounded over a compact set Ω. $\alpha_1 = \max\left\{2, \|K_O\|_1^2, \|K_C\|_1^2\right\}$,

$$X_u = \left[x_{d_{n+1}}^T, \hat{\vartheta}_r^T, \hat{x}^T(t - \tau_d), u^T(t - \tau_d), y^T, \int_{t-\tau_d}^{t} y^T(\tau) d\tau, \right.$$
$$\left. \int_{t-\tau_d}^{t} u^T(\tau) d\tau, \int_{t-\tau_d}^{t} u^T(\tau) d\tau, \int_{t-\tau_d}^{t} \hat{x}^T(\tau) d\tau, y^T(t - \tau_d)\right]^T \in \mathbb{R}^{3n+6p}$$

$$\Omega = \left\{ \begin{array}{c} X_u \in \mathbb{R}^{3n+6p} \\ x \in \mathbb{R}^n \end{array} \middle| \|X_{u2}\|^2 + \int_{t-\tau_d}^{t} \left(\|u(\tau)\|_2^2 + \hat{x}(\tau)_2^2 + x(\tau)_2^2 d\tau\right) \leq M_u \right\}$$

where M_u is an unknown strictly positive constant.
$W_1^* \in \mathbb{R}^{L_1 \times p}$ and $W_2^* \in \mathbb{R}^{L_2 \times p}$ are the optimal constant neural network parameters defined by:

$$\left(W_1^*, W_2^*\right) = \arg \min_{\substack{W_1^* \in \mathbb{R}^{L_1 \times p} \\ W_2^* \in \mathbb{R}^{L_2 \times p}}} \left(\sup_{(X_u, x) \in \Omega} \left\| h_F - W_1^{*T} \xi_1(X_u) - \left[W_2^{*T} \xi_1(X_u)\right] u_2 \right\| \right) \qquad (5)$$

3.3 Control Laws and Neural Network Tuning Rules

The control law u for the system (1) can be constructed as follows:

$$\begin{cases} \dot{\hat{\varepsilon}} = \Phi \tilde{y}^T \phi E \\ u = \left[\hat{W}_2^T \xi_2(X_u) \right]^{-1} \left[-\hat{W}_1^T \xi_1(X_u) - \hat{\varepsilon} \phi E \right] \end{cases} \quad (6)$$

and to adjust the Neural Network parameters, the following adaptive laws are used:

$$\begin{cases} \dot{\hat{W}}_1 = \Gamma_1 \xi_1(X_u) \tilde{y}^T \\ \dot{\hat{W}}_2 = \text{Proj}\left(\Gamma_2 \xi_2(X_u) u \tilde{y}^T \right) \end{cases} \quad (7)$$

where: $\hat{W}_1$ and $\hat{W}_2$ are the estimates of W_1^* and W_2^*, respectively. $\phi = 1 + \|X_u\|_1^2 + \|\vartheta\|_1^2 + \|\hat{W}_1^T \xi_1(X_u)\|_1^2$ is a known smooth function. $E = \left[\tanh((1+t)^a \phi \tilde{y}_1), \ldots, \tanh((1+t)^a \phi \tilde{y}_p) \right] \in \mathbb{R}^p$. $\hat{\varepsilon}(0) > 0$, $\hat{W}_1(0)$, $\hat{W}_1(0)$, $\Phi > 0$ and $a > 1$ are known and constant. $\Gamma_1 = \Gamma_1^T > 0$ and $\Gamma_2 = \Gamma_2^T > 0$ are known constant symmetric positive definite matrices. $\text{Proj}(*) = $
$$\begin{cases} (*), \text{ if } \hat{W}_2 \in \Omega_{W_2}^0 \\ \text{or } \hat{W}_2 \in \delta(\Omega_{W_2}) \text{ and } (*)^T \xi_2(X_u) \leq 0 \\ (*) - \frac{[\xi_2(X_u)][\xi_2(X_u)]^T}{\|\xi_2(X_u)\|_F}(*), \text{ otherwise} \end{cases}$$
, represents the projection operator [19],
the role of which is to guarantee $\hat{W}_2^T \xi_2(X_u) \geq G_m > 0, \forall t \geq 0$. $\Omega_{W_2} = \left\{ \hat{W}_2 \in \mathbb{R}^{L_2 \times p} \mid \hat{W}_2^T \xi_2(X_u) - G_m \geq 0 \right\}$ with $G_m = G_m^T > 0$ is a known constant symmetric positive definite matrix. $\Omega_{W_2}^0$ and $\delta(\Omega_{W_2})$ are the interior and the boundary of Ω_{W_2}, respectively. $\hat{W}_2(0)$ is chosen to be in Ω_{W_2}, i.e., $\hat{W}_2(0) \in \Omega_{W_2}$. Thus, the possible singularity problem in the control design can be avoided.

3.4 Stability Analysis

In this section, the main results are recapitulated in Theorem 1, in which the asymptotic stability analysis of the closed-loop system under the proposed controller is proved.

Theorem 1. *For given reference signals, consider the system (1) with Assumptions 1–3. Then, for bounded initial conditions, the state observer (3), the output-feedback control law (6) and the neural network parameter adaption laws (7), guarantee the following properties:*

- All the signals in the adaptive closed-loop system are bounded.
- The tracking errors converge asymptotically to zero, i.e., $\vartheta_i \to 0$ as $t \to +\infty$, for $i = 1, \ldots, p$.

Proof. According to (3) and (6), we can get over a compact set Ω:

$$\begin{cases} \dot{Z}_r = A_r Z_r + B_{r0}\left[\tilde{W}_1^T \xi_1(X_u) - \alpha_1\left(\|y\|_2^2 + \|u\|_2^2 + 1\right)\tilde{y}\right. \\ \qquad\qquad \left. + \left[\tilde{W}_2^T \xi_2(X_u)\right]u + \varepsilon - \hat{\varepsilon}\phi E\right] \\ \qquad + \sum_{j=1}^{m} B_{r_j}\left[d_j - g_j(x) + f_j\left(x, x(t-\tau_{1j}), u(t-\tau_{2j})\right)\right] \\ \tilde{y} = C_r^T Z_r \end{cases}, \forall t \geq 0 \quad (8)$$

with: $Z_r = \begin{bmatrix} \hat{\vartheta}_r \\ (x - \hat{x}) \end{bmatrix} \in \mathbb{R}^{2n}$, $\tilde{W}_1 = W_1^* - \hat{W}_1$, $\tilde{W}_2 = W_2^* - \hat{W}_2$, $A_r = \begin{bmatrix} [A - B_0 K_C] & -K_0 C^T \\ 0_{n \times n} & [A - K_0 C^T] \end{bmatrix} \in \mathbb{R}^{2n \times 2n}$, $B_{r0} = \begin{bmatrix} 0_{n \times p} \\ B_0 \end{bmatrix} \in \mathbb{R}^{2n \times p}$, $C_r = \begin{bmatrix} 0_{n \times p} \\ C \end{bmatrix} \in \mathbb{R}^{2n \times p}$ and $B_{r_j} = \begin{bmatrix} 0_{n \times p} \\ (B_j - B_0) \end{bmatrix} \in \mathbb{R}^{2n \times p}$, $j = 1, \ldots, m$.

The dynamics (8) can be rewritten in the frequency domain by using the mixed notation (i.e. time-frequency) as

$$\tilde{y} = H_0(s)\left[\tilde{W}_1^T \xi_1(X_u) - \hat{\varepsilon}\phi E \right. \\ \qquad \left. -\alpha_1\left(\|y\|_2^2 + \|u\|_2^2 + 1\right)\tilde{y} + \left[\tilde{W}_2^T \xi_2(X_u)\right]u + \varepsilon\right] \\ \qquad + \sum_{j=1}^{m} H_j(s)\left[d_j - g_j(x) + f_j\left(x, x(t-\tau_{1j}), u(t-\tau_{2j})\right)\right] \quad (9)$$

where: $H_0(s) = C_r^T[sI_{2n} - A_r]^{-1}B_{r0}$ and $H_j(s) = C_r^T[sI_{2n} - A_r]^{-1}B_{r_j}$, $j = 1, \ldots, m$ are not SPR.

According to [2, 10], it exists a matrix $B_C \in \mathbb{R}^{2n \times p}$ and stable filters $(F_j(s), j = 0, \ldots, m)$ such that:

$$\begin{cases} H_j(s) = H_f(s) F_j(s), \ j = 0, \ldots, m \\ H_f(s) = C_r^T[sI_{2n} - A_r]^{-1} B_C \end{cases} \quad (10)$$

where $H_f(s)$ is SPR.

Using the SPR-Lyapunov synthesis approach and Meyer–Kalman–Yakubovich (MKY) Lemma [2, 11], the system (8) can be transformed over a compact set Ω into the following system:

$$\begin{cases} \dot{Z}_r = A_r Z_r + B_C\left[\tilde{W}_1^T \xi_1(X_u) - \hat{\varepsilon}\phi E + \varepsilon_f + \left[\tilde{W}_2^T \xi_2(X_u)\right]u \right. \\ \qquad\qquad \left. -\alpha_1\left(\|y\|_2^2 + \|u\|_2^2 + 1\right)\tilde{y}\right] \\ \tilde{y} = C_r^T Z_r \end{cases}, \forall t \geq 0 \quad (11)$$

where:

$$\varepsilon_f = [F_0(s) - 1]\left[\tilde{W}_1^T \xi_1(X_u) + \left[\tilde{W}_2^T \xi_2(X_u)\right]u\right.$$
$$\left. - \hat{\varepsilon}\phi E - \alpha_1\left(\|y\|_2^2 + \|u\|_2^2 + 1\right)\tilde{y}\right]$$
$$+ \sum_{j=1}^{m} F_j(s)\left[d_j - g_j(x) + f_j(x, x(t-\tau_{1j}), u(t-\tau_{2j}))\right]$$
$$+ F_0(s)[\varepsilon]$$

is unknown and bounded over a compact set Ω.

From [2, 10], we can obtain over a compact set Ω:

$$\|\varepsilon_f\|_1 \leq \varepsilon^* \phi \tag{12}$$

where: $\varepsilon^* > 0$ is an unknown constant.

Since $H_f(s)$ is SPR, there always exists a known constant symmetric positive definite matrix $P^T = P > 0$ satisfying the following equation [2, 11]:

$$\begin{cases} A_r^T P + P A_r \prec 0 \\ P B_C = C_r \end{cases} \tag{13}$$

Now, let us consider the following Lyapunov–Krasovskii functional candidate [7–9]:

$$V = V_0 + \frac{1}{2}Z_r^T P Z_r + \frac{1}{2}\text{tr}\left(\tilde{W}_1^T \Gamma_1^{-1} \tilde{W}_1\right)$$
$$+ \frac{1}{2}\text{tr}\left(\tilde{W}_2^T \Gamma_2^{-1} \tilde{W}_2\right) + \frac{1}{2\Phi}\tilde{\varepsilon}^2 \tag{14}$$

with: $V_0 = \alpha_1 \int_{t-\tau_d}^{t} \|\tilde{y}(\tau)\|_2^2 (\|y(\tau)\|_2^2 + \|u(\tau)\|_2^2) d\tau$ and $\tilde{\varepsilon} = \varepsilon^* - \hat{\varepsilon}$.

$\forall t \geq 0$, the Lyapunov function V is of class C^1 and positive.

$\forall t \geq 0$, the time derivative of V is given by:

$$\dot{V} = \frac{1}{2}Z_r^T\left[A_r^T P + P A_r\right]Z_r + \text{tr}\left(\tilde{W}_1^T\left[\Gamma_1^{-1}\dot{\tilde{W}}_1 + \xi_1(X_u)\tilde{y}^T\right]\right)$$
$$+ \text{tr}\left(\tilde{W}_2^T\left[\Gamma_2^{-1}\dot{\tilde{W}}_2 + \xi_2(X_u)u\tilde{y}^T\right]\right) - \alpha_1\|\tilde{y}\|_2^2\left(\|y\|_2^2 + \|u\|_2^2 + 1\right)^2 \tag{15}$$
$$+ \tilde{\varepsilon}\left[\frac{1}{\Phi}\dot{\tilde{\varepsilon}} + \tilde{y}^T \phi E\right] + \tilde{y}^T\left[\varepsilon_f - \varepsilon^* \phi E\right] + \dot{V}_0$$

Using the property of projection operator and Polycarpou's Lemma [1–19], we can confirm that

$$\begin{cases} \text{tr}\left(\tilde{W}_2^T\left[\Gamma_2^{-1}\dot{\tilde{W}}_2 + \xi_2(X_u)u\tilde{y}^T\right]\right) \leq 0 \\ \tilde{y}^T\left[\varepsilon_f - \varepsilon^* \phi E\right] \leq \frac{\kappa_1 \varepsilon^* p}{(1+t)^a} \end{cases} \tag{16}$$

with $\kappa_1 = 0.2785$.

In addition, we can easy obtain

$$\begin{cases} \dot{V}_0 - \alpha_1 \|\tilde{y}\|_2^2 (\|y\|_2^2 + \|u\|_2^2 + 1) \leq 0 \\ \mathrm{tr}\left(\tilde{W}_1^T \left[\Gamma_1^{-1} \dot{\tilde{W}}_1 + \xi_1(X_u)\tilde{y}^T\right]\right) = 0 \\ \tilde{\varepsilon}\left[\frac{1}{\Phi}\dot{\tilde{\varepsilon}} + \tilde{y}^T \phi E\right] = 0 \end{cases} \quad (17)$$

Substituting (6), (7), (16) and (17) into (15) yields

$$\dot{V} \leq \frac{\kappa_1 \varepsilon^* p}{(1+t)^a} \quad (18)$$

From (18), we can easily check that

$$0 \leq V(t) \leq \int_0^t \frac{\kappa_1 p \varepsilon^*}{(1+\tau)^a} d\tau + V(0) \quad (19)$$

Since $\frac{\kappa_1 \varepsilon^* p}{(1+t)^a}$ and $\int_0^t \frac{\kappa_1 p \varepsilon^*}{(1+\tau)^a} d\tau$ are bounded, then $\dot{V}(t)$ and $V(t)$ are bounded, $\forall t \geq 0$. According to Barbalat Lemma [1–31], we have $\lim_{t \to +\infty} \vartheta_i(t) = 0$, for all $i = 1, \ldots, p$. The proof is completed here.

Compared to some works [1–31], the advantages of our present work are:

- the considered class of the MIMO systems is relatively large,
- a few adapting parameters are required,
- the possible singularity problem in the control design can be avoided by using the Gradient Algorithm with Projection,
- the tracking errors converge asymptotically to zero for the system (1),
- the proposed adaptive control is simple and its implementation is easy (Fig. 1).

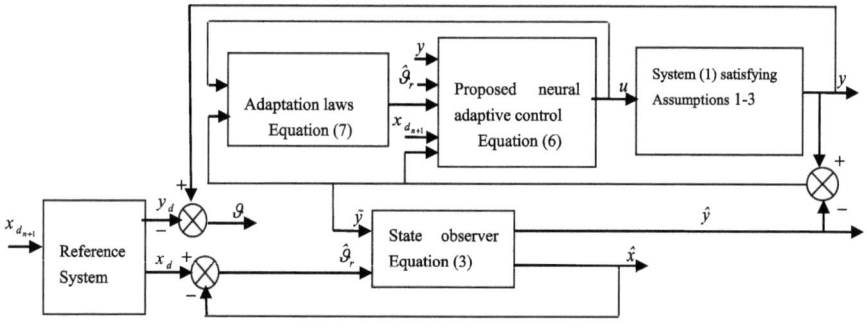

Fig. 1. Proposed neural adaptive control Scheme.

4 Simulation Results

Consider the following system:

$$\begin{cases} \dot{x} = \sum_{j=0}^{4} B_j \left[d_j + f_j \left(x, x(t - \tau_{1j}), u(t - \tau_{2j}) \right) \right], \quad \forall t \geq 0 \\ x = \frac{1}{1+t^2} [18\cos(t), -0.3 + \sin(t), \\ \qquad\qquad 10\cos(t), 0.4 + \sin(t)]^T, \quad \forall t \leq 0 \\ y = C^T x \end{cases} \quad (20)$$

where: $x = [x_1, x_2, x_3, x_4]^T \in \mathbb{R}^4$, $y = [y_1, y_2]^T \in \mathbb{R}^2$ and $u = [u_1, u_2]^T \in \mathbb{R}^2$ are the state, the outputs and the inputs of the system, respectively. τ_{2j} and τ_{1j}, $j = 0, \ldots, 4$ are unknown smooth functions. $d_j \in \mathbb{R}^2$, $j = 0, \ldots, 4$ denote the unknown external disturbances with $\sum_{j=0}^{4} \int_{t-2}^{t} \|d_j(\tau)\|_2^2 d\tau$ is bounded $\forall t \geq 0$. $f_0(x, x(t - \tau_0), u) =$

$$\begin{bmatrix} \frac{-3(2\tau_{11}+\sin(3x_1(t-\tau_{10}))+4x_3+\tau_{10}u_1)+(4\tau_{11}+\sin(x_1+x_2))u_1}{1+\tau_{21}+(u_2\tau_{11})^2} \\ \frac{3(2\tau_{21}+\cos(x_3(t-\tau_{10}))+x_2+\tau_{11}u_2+u_1)}{1+x_2^2} + (4\tau_{21} + \sin(x_3 + x_4))u_2 \end{bmatrix} \in \mathbb{R}^2 \text{and}$$

$$f_j(x, x(t-\tau_{1j}), u(t-\tau_{2j})) = \begin{bmatrix} \tau_{2j}\sin(x_2 + 2x_1(t-\tau_{1j})) + 2u_1(t-\tau_{2j}) \\ \cos(x_4 + x_3(t-\tau_{1j})) + 4u_2(t-\tau_{2j}) \end{bmatrix} \in \mathbb{R}^2,$$

$j = 1, \ldots, 4$ are unknown smooth functions.

The system (20) satisfies the Assumptions 1–3, with $B_0 = \begin{bmatrix} 0 & 0 \\ 1 & 0 \\ 0 & 0 \\ 0 & 1 \end{bmatrix}$, $B_1 = \begin{bmatrix} 1 & 0 \\ 0 & 0 \\ 0 & 0 \\ 0 & 0 \end{bmatrix}$,

$B_2 = \begin{bmatrix} 0 & 0 \\ 1 & 0 \\ 0 & 0 \\ 0 & 0 \end{bmatrix}$, $B_3 = \begin{bmatrix} 0 & 0 \\ 0 & 0 \\ 0 & 1 \\ 0 & 0 \end{bmatrix}$, $B_4 = \begin{bmatrix} 0 & 0 \\ 0 & 0 \\ 0 & 0 \\ 0 & 1 \end{bmatrix}$, $A = \begin{bmatrix} 0 & 1 & 0 & 0 \\ 0 & 0 & 0 & 0 \\ 0 & 0 & 0 & 1 \\ 0 & 0 & 0 & 0 \end{bmatrix}$, $g_0(x) = \begin{bmatrix} x_3 \\ x_2 \end{bmatrix}$, $g_1(x) =$

$\begin{bmatrix} x_2 \\ x_3 \end{bmatrix}$, $g_2(x) = \begin{bmatrix} -x_3 \\ x_1 \end{bmatrix}$, $g_3(x) = \begin{bmatrix} 0 \\ x_4 \end{bmatrix}$, $g_4(x) = \begin{bmatrix} x_3 \\ -x_2 \end{bmatrix}$, $C = \begin{bmatrix} 1 & 0 \\ 0 & 0 \\ 0 & 1 \\ 0 & 0 \end{bmatrix}$, $\tau_{20} = 0$,

$0 \leq \tau_{10} \leq 2$, $0 \leq \tau_{2j} \leq 2$ and $0 \leq \tau_{1j} \leq 2$, $j = 1, \ldots, 4$.

The objective is to design a neural adaptive controller such that the outputs y_1 and y_2 track the reference signals $y_{d_1} = 20\sin(\frac{t}{2})$ and $y_{d_2} = 20$, respectively.

The design of proposed neural adaptive control for the system (20) is carried out based on the following two steps:

Step 1: According to Sect. 3, select

$K_O = \begin{bmatrix} 2 & 1 & 0 & 0 \\ 0 & 0 & 2 & 1 \end{bmatrix}^T$, $K_C = \begin{bmatrix} 1 & 2 & 0 & 0 \\ 0 & 0 & 1 & 2 \end{bmatrix}$, $a = 2$, $\Phi = 5$, $\alpha_1 = 36$, $L_1 = 54$,

$L_2 = 54$, $G_m = \text{diag}(0.1, 0.1) \in \mathbb{R}^{2 \times 2}$, $\Gamma_1 = \text{diag}(10, \ldots, 10) \in \mathbb{R}^{54 \times 54}$, $\Gamma_2 =$

$diag(40,\ldots,40) \in \mathbb{R}^{54\times 54}$, $\hat{\varepsilon}(0) = 1$, $\hat{W}_1(0) = diag(\hat{W}_{11}(0), \hat{W}_{12}(0)) \in \mathbb{R}^{54\times 2}$ and $\hat{W}_2(0) = diag(\hat{W}_2(0), \hat{W}_2(0)) \in \mathbb{R}^{54\times 2}$ with $\hat{W}_{11}(0) = [-1,\ldots,-1]^T \in \mathbb{R}^{27}$, $\hat{W}_{12}(0) = [-0.4,\ldots,-0.4]^T \in \mathbb{R}^{27}$, $\hat{W}_{21}(0) = [2,\ldots,2]^T \in \mathbb{R}^{27}$ and $\hat{W}_{22}(0) = [4,\ldots,4]^T \in \mathbb{R}^{27}$.

The functions $\xi_1(X_u) \in \mathbb{R}^{54}$ and $\xi_2(X_u) \in \mathbb{R}^{54\times 2}$ are of Gaussian type, with centers evenly spaced in $[-30, 30]^{24}$ and widths equal to 60.

Step 2: Construct the state observer, the control law and the neural network parameter adaption laws by using (3), (6) and (7), respectively.

According to Fig. 2, which shows the application results of the proposed adaptive controller for the system (20), we can see that:

- the variables $(\hat{x}_2, \hat{x}_4)$ and the control signals (u_1, u_2) are bounded,
- A pretty good tracking performance is obtained., i.e., the system outputs y_1 and y_2 follow the reference signals y_{d_1} and y_{d_2}, respectively,
- the better tracking performance is clearly visible,
- the Euclidean norm of the tracking error vector converges quickly to zero,
- the undesirable effects of parametric uncertainties and external disturbances are rejected.

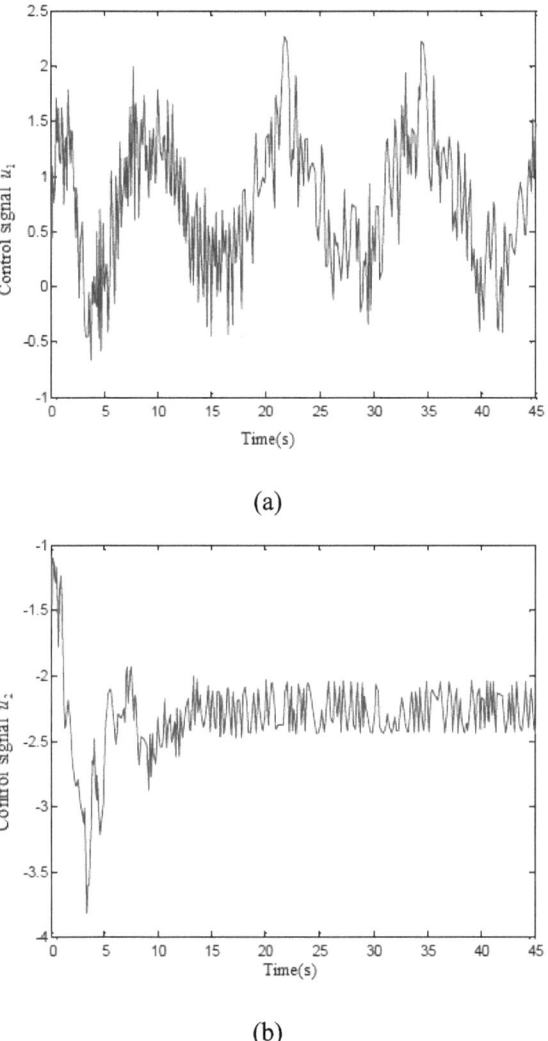

Fig. 2. Proposed controller for the system (20): (a) Control signal u_1, (b) Control signal u_2, (c) System output y_1, (d) System output y_2, (e) Variable $\hat{x}_2$, (f) Variable $\hat{x}_4$, (g) Euclidian norm of the tracking error vector $\|\vartheta\|_2$.

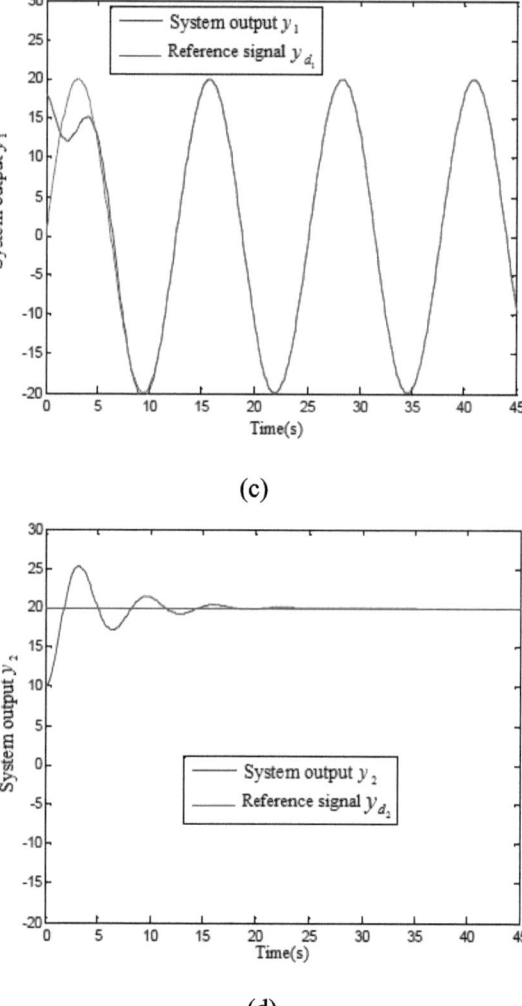

Fig. 2. (*continued*)

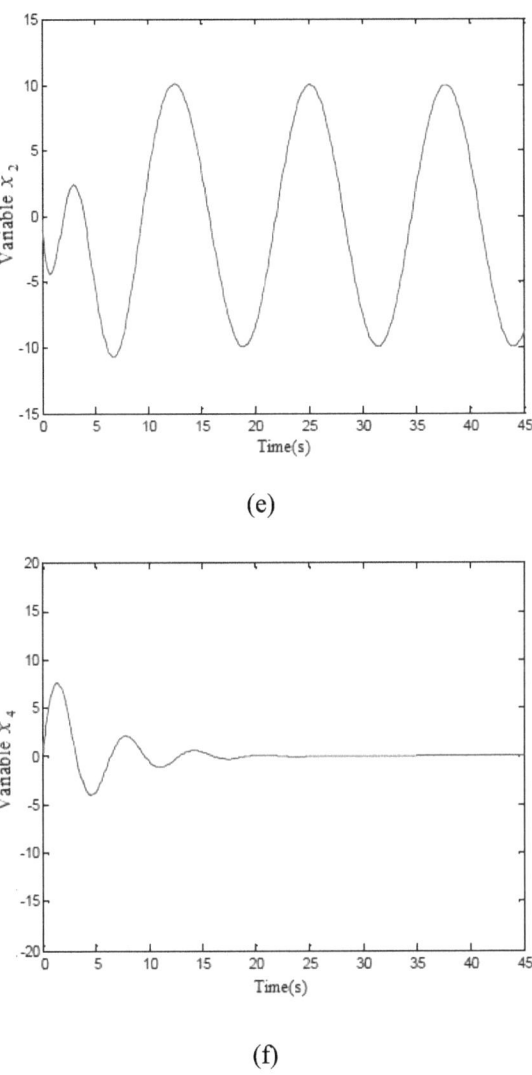

Fig. 2. (*continued*)

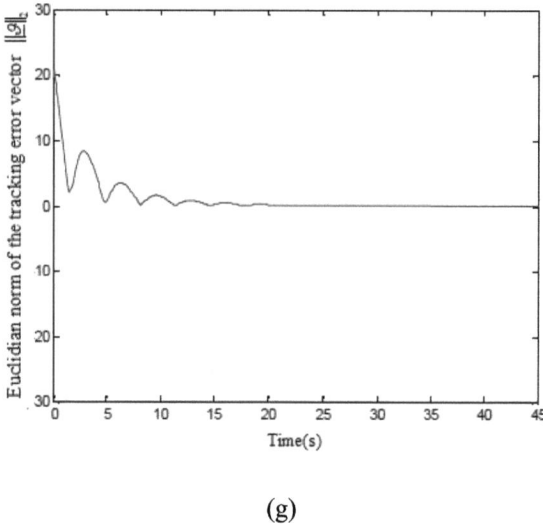

(g)

Fig. 2. (*continued*)

5 Conclusions

In this paper, a novel robust neural adaptive output-feedback controller is proposed for a class of uncertain nonlinear non-affine MIMO time-varying delay systems with unknown control direction. In the controller design process, a simple linear state observer is constructed to estimate the unmeasured states, and a neural network is employed to approximate the system nonlinearities. The Polycarpou Lemma and the projection operator are used to address potential chattering phenomena and singularity problems. Additionally, only available measurements (i.e., the output observation errors and the output tracking errors) are used in the adaptation laws. Based on the SPR condition and the Lyapunov–Krasovskii method, the stability of the closed-loop system and the convergence of the tracking errors to zero are rigorously demonstrated. The implementation of the proposed controller is much simpler than that of existing controllers. Simulation results have proven the validity, feasibility, and effectiveness of the proposed controller.

References

1. Poursamad, A., Davaie-Markazi, A.H.: Robust adaptive fuzzy control of unknown chaoutic systems. Appl. Soft Comput. **9**(3), 970–976 (2009)
2. Boulkroune, A., Tadjine, M., M'Saad, M., Farza, M.: How to design a fuzzy adaptive controller based on observers for uncertain affine nonlinear systems. Fuzzy Sets Syst. **159**(8), 926–948 (2008). https://doi.org/10.1016/j.fss.2007.08.015
3. Chemachema, M.: Output feedback direct adaptive neural network control for uncertain SISO nonlinear systems using a fuzzy estimator of the control error. Neural Netw. **36**(11), 25–34 (2012)
4. Du, H., Chen, X.: NN-based output feedback adaptive variable structure control for a class of non-affine nonlinear systems: a nonseparation principle design. Neurocomputing **72**(7–9), 2009–2016 (2009)

5. Li, Y., Tong, S., Li, T.: Adaptive fuzzy output feedback control for a single-link flexible robot manipulator driven DC motor via backstepping. Nonlinear Anal. Real World Appl. **14**(1), 483–494 (2013)
6. Wu, J., Chen, W., Zhao, D., Li, J.: Globally stable direct adaptive backstepping NN control for uncertain nonlinear strict-feedback systems. Neurocomputing **122**, 134–147 (2013)
7. Chen, B., Liu, X., Liu, K., Lin, C.: Adaptive control for nonlinear MIMO time-delay systems based on fuzzy approximation. Inf. Sci. **222**, 576–592 (2013)
8. Zhu, Q., Zhang, T., Fei, S.: Adaptive tracking control for input delayed MIMO nonlinear systems. Neurocomputing **74**(1–3), 472–480 (2010)
9. Yu, Z., Li, S.: Neural-network-based output-feedback adaptive dynamic surface control for a class of stochastic nonlinear time-delay systems with unknown control directions. Neurocomputing **129**, 540–547 (2014)
10. Boulkroune A., Saad M. M', Farza M.: Fuzzy approximation-based indirect adaptive controller for multi-input multi-output non-affine systems with unknown control direction. IET Control Theory and Applications **6**(17), 2619–2629 (2012)
11. Boulkroune, A., Tadjine, M., M'Saad, M., Farza, M.: Fuzzy adaptive controller for MIMO nonlinear systems with known and unknown control direction. Fuzzy Sets Syst. **161**(6), 797–820 (2010). https://doi.org/10.1016/j.fss.2009.04.011
12. Arefi, M.M., Zarei, J., Karim, H.R.: Adaptive output feedback neural network control of uncertain non-affine systems with unknown control direction. J. Franklin Inst. **351**(8), 4302–4316 (2014)
13. Esfandiari, K., Abdollahi, F., Ali Talebi, H.: Stable adaptive output feedback controller for a class of uncertain non-linear systems. IET Control Theory Appl. **9**(9), 1329–1337 (2015). https://doi.org/10.1049/iet-cta.2014.0822
14. Wang, H., Liu, X., Liu, K.: Adaptive neural data-based compensation control of non-linear systems with dynamic uncertainties and input saturation. IET Control Theory Appl. **9**(7), 1058–1065 (2015). https://doi.org/10.1049/iet-cta.2014.0709
15. Pan, H., Sun, W., Gao, H., Kaynak, O., Alsaadi, F., Hayat, T.: Robust adaptive control of non-linear time-delay systems with saturation constraints. IET Control Theory Appl. **9**(1), 103–113 (2015)
16. Yang, C., Ge, S.S., Xiang, C., Chai, T., Lee, T.H.: Output feedback NN control for two classes of discrete-time systems with unknown control directions in a unified approach. IEEE Trans. Neural Netw. Learn. Syst. **19**(11), 1873–1886 (2008)
17. Bresch-Pietri, D., Chauvin, J., Petit, N.: Adaptive control scheme for uncertain time-delay systems. Automatica **48**(8), 1536–1552 (2012)
18. Chen, F., Jiang, R., Wen, C., Su, R.: Self-repairing control of a helicopter with input time delay via adaptive global sliding mode control and quantum logic. Inf. Sci. **336**, 123–131 (2015)
19. Na, J., Ren, X., Shang, C., Guo, Y.: Adaptive neural network predictive control for nonlinear pure feedback systems with input delay. J. Process. Control. **22**(1), 194–206 (2012)
20. Chang, Y.C.: An adaptive H_∞ tracking control for a class of nonlinear multiple-input-multiple-output (MIMO) systems. IEEE Trans. Autom. Control **46**(9), 1432–1437 (2001)
21. Lin, T.C., Wang, C.H., Liu, H.L.: Observer-based indirect adaptive fuzzy-neural tracking control for nonlinear SISO systems using VSS and H_∞ approaches. Fuzzy Sets Syst. **143**(2), 211–232 (2004)
22. Li, C., Tong, S., Wang, W.: Fuzzy adaptive high-gain-based observer backstepping control for SISO nonlinear systems. Inf. Sci. **181**(11), 2405–2421 (2011)
23. Liu, Y.J., Tong, S.C., Li, T.S.: Observer-based adaptive fuzzy tracking control for a class of uncertain nonlinear MIMO systems. Fuzzy Sets Syst. **164**(1), 25–44 (2011)

24. Xu, Y.Y., Li, Y.M., Tong, S.C.: Fuzzy adaptive actuator failure compensation dynamic surface control of multi-input and multi-output nonlinear systems. Int. J. Innov. Comput. Inform. Control **9**(12), 4875–4888 (2013)
25. Tong, S.C., Li, C.Y., Li, Y.M.: Fuzzy-adaptive decentralized output-feedback control for large-scale nonlinear systems with dynamical uncertainties. IEEE Trans. Fuzzy Syst. **18**(5), 845–861 (2010)
26. Jiang, X.F., Li, X., Han, Q.L.: Observer-based fuzzy control design with adaptation to delay parameter for time-delay systems. Fuzzy Sets Syst. **152**(3), 634–649 (2005)
27. Mirkin, B., Gutman, P.O.: Adaptive output-feedback tracking: the case of MIMO plants with unknown, time-varying state delay. Syst. Control Lett. **58**(1), 62–68 (2009)
28. Hua, C.C., Wang, Q.G., Guan, X.P.: Adaptive fuzzy output-feedback controller design for nonlinear time-delay systems with unknown control direction. IEEE Trans. Syst. Man Cybern. B Cybern. **39**(2), 363–374 (2009)
29. Li, Y.M., Tong, S.C., Li, T.H.: Adaptive fuzzy output feedback control of MIMO nonlinear uncertain systems with time-varying delays and unknown backlash-like hysteresis. Neurocomputing **93**, 56–66 (2012)
30. Tong, S.C., Chen, B., Wang, Y.F.: Fuzzy adaptive output feedback control for MIMO nonlinear systems. Fuzzy Sets Syst. **156**(2), 285–299 (2005)
31. Yu, W.S., Wu, T.S., Chao, C.C.: An observer-based indirect adaptive fuzzy control for rolling cart systems. IEEE Trans. Control Syst. Technol. **19**(5), 1225–1235 (2011)
32. Zouari, F., Ibeas, A., Boulkroune, A., Cao, J., Arefi, M.M.: Neural network controller design for fractional-order systems with input nonlinearities and asymmetric time-varying Pseudo-state constraints. Chaos Solitons Fractals **144**, 1–40 (2021)
33. Zouari, F., Ibeas, A., Boulkroune, A., Cao, J., Arefi, M.M.: Neuro-adaptive tracking control of non-integer order systems with Input Nonlinearities and time-varying Output Constraints. Inf. Sci. **485**, 170–199 (2019)
34. Zouari, F., Ibeas, A., Boulkroune, A., Cao, J., Arefi, M.M.: Adaptive neural output-feedback control for nonstrict-feedback time-delay fractional order systems with output constraints and actuator nonlinearities. Neural Netw. **105**, 256–276 (2018)
35. Zouari, F., Boulkroune, A., Ibeas, A.: Neural Adaptive quantized output-feedback control-based synchronization of uncertain time-delay incommensurate fractional-order chaotic systems with input nonlinearities. Neurocomputing **237**, 200–225 (2017)
36. Zouari, F., Boulkroune, A., Ibeas, A., Arefi, M.M.: Observer-based adaptive neural network control for a class of MIMO uncertain nonlinear time-delay non-integer-order systems with asymmetric actuator saturation. Neural Comput. Appl. **28**(Supplement 1), 993–1010 (2017)
37. Zouari, F., Ibeas, A., Boulkroune, A., Cao, J.: Finite-Time Adaptive Event-Triggered Output Feedback Intelligent Control for Noninteger Order Nonstrict Feedback Systems with Asymmetric Time-Varying Pseudo-State Constraints and Nonsmooth Input Nonlinearities. Commun. Nonlinear Sci. Numer. Simul. **136**, 108036 (2024)
38. Zouari, F., Saad, K.B., Benrejeb, M.: Robust adaptive control for a class of nonlinear systems using the backstepping method. Int. J. Adv. Robotic Syst. (2013). https://doi.org/10.5772/54932
39. Zouari, F., ,Boubellouta A.: Neural approximation-based adaptive control for pure-feedback fractional-order systems with output constraints and actuator nonlinearities. In: IGI Global, Advanced Synchronization Control and Bifurcation of Chaotic Fractional-Order Systems, pp. 468–495 (2018)
40. L. Merazka, F. Zouari, A. Boulkroune.: High-gain observerbased adaptive fuzzy control for a class of multivariable nonlinear systems. In: 6th International Conference on Systems and Control (ICSC), Batna, Algeria (2017). https://doi.org/10.1109/ICoSC.2017.7958728

41. Rigatos, G., Zouari, F., Cuccurullo, G., Siano, P., Ghosh, T.: Flatness-based adaptive fuzzy control for the Uzawa-Lucas endogenous growth model. AIP Conf. Proc. **2293**, 310003 (2020). https://doi.org/10.1063/5.0026520
42. Merazka L., Zouari F., Boulkroune A.: Fuzzy state-feedback control of uncertain nonlinear MIMO systems. In: 6th International Conference on Systems and Control (ICSC), Batna, Algeria (2017). https://doi.org/10.1109/ICoSC.2017.7958730
43. Zouari F., Boubellouta A.: Adaptive neural control for unknown nonlinear time-delay fractional-order systems with input saturation. In: IGI Global, Advanced Synchronization Control and Bifurcation of Chaotic Fractional-Order Systems, pp. 54–98 (2018)
44. Zouari, F., Saad, K.B., Benrejeb, M.: Robust neural adaptive control for a class of uncertain nonlinear complex dynamical multivariable systems. Int. Rev. Model. Simulat. **5**(5), 2075–2103 (2012)
45. Zouari, F.: Neural network based adaptive backstepping dynamic surface control of drug dosage regimens in cancer treatment. Neurocomputing **366**, 248–263 (2019)

Potato Leaf Disease Classification Using Resnet50ViT

Suman Acharya[1(✉)], Achyuth Sarkar[1], Somen Nayak[2], and Bablu Kumar Majhi[3]

[1] Department of Computer Science and Engineering, National Institute of Technology Arunachal Pradesh, Jote 791113, Arunachal Pradesh, India
{suman.phd24,achyuth}@nitap.ac.in

[2] Faculty of Science and Technology, IcfaiTech, The ICFAI University Jaipur, Jamdoli, Agra Road, Jaipur 302031, India
snayak@iujaipur.edu.in

[3] Department of Computer Applications, University of Engineering and Management, Jaipur, Sikar Road, Udaipuriya Mod, Chomu, Jaipur 303807, Rajasthan, India
babluk.majhi@uem.edu.in
https://jaipur.uem.edu.in/

Abstract. Potatoes hold significant prominence as a primary tuber crop on a global scale, being cultivated in more than 125 nations. Potato, following rice and wheat, is a staple crop that is consumed daily by around one billion individuals across the globe. Nevertheless, the potato crop is seeing a decline in both its quality and quantity as a rsult of various fungal and bacterial diseases. The challenge of early disease identification arises from variations in climatic circumstances, plant species, and the manifestation of plant disease symptoms. Numerous machine learning methods have been developed in recent research endeavors to accurately identify and classify potato leaf diseases. This study mainly deals with the Resnet50ViT model for classifying diseases from potato leaves. The Resnet50ViT models contain pre-trained Resnet50 and ViT, which makes them superior to all models, including Resnet50, ViT, Swin-T, and CSwin-T. It performs the classification of potato leaves into three classes, early blight, healthy blight, and late blight. According to the Multi-Criteria Decision Analysis (MCDA) approach TOPSIS, Resnet50ViT exhibits superior performance compared to other models, as evidenced by its score of 1. Furthermore, due to its cost-effectiveness, our proposition is very suitable for the screening of potato leaves.

Keywords: Agriculture · Deep Learning · Potato Leaf Disease · Image classification · ResNet50ViT

1 Introduction

As the world's population grows, "it is estimated that food production will need to grow by 60% by 2050 to feed the estimated 10 billion people expected on

Earth." To meet demand, increased production will be required, and a reduction in food loss due to pests and pathogens, as well as food waste [2]. "The worldwide agricultural sector faces a significant obstacle in the form of crop loss caused by plant diseases and parasites. Plant diseases and parasites diminish the nutritional value of fruits and vegetables, reduce crop yield, and diminish the quality or shelf life of agricultural products. The process of identifying plant diseases poses significant challenges due to the presence of identical symptoms, especially in the initial stages of infection. The need for accurate disease identification should be demonstrated since administering incorrect treatment can result in wasted time, financial resources, and the potential exacerbation of crop loss or damage [5]. Potato (Solanum tuberosum) production constitutes a significant portion of global food production, making it one of the most vital staple crops on an international level. Nevertheless, the potato crop is perpetually threatened by leaf disease-causing microorganisms [7]. These diseases not only pose a threat to the livelihoods of farmers but also affect food security and the global economy in a more extensive way [7]. The study is predominately concerned with the classification of potato leaf diseases into three categories: early blight, late blight, and healthy. Early Blight (Alternaria solani), Late Blight (Phytophthora infestans), Blackleg (Pectobacterium spp. and Dickeya spp.), and Potato Virus Y (PVY) are the most frequent and severe diseases on potato leaves. The invasion of potato plants by these viruses can occur at multiple stages of growth, spanning from seedling to maturity, culminating in significant setbacks in production, quality, and revenue. Potato leaf diseases pose a substantial risk to the safety of food production. Potatoes serve as a fundamental component of the nutrition of a significant global population, and any disruption in potato cultivation can have severe consequences for communities that depend on this crop for sustenance. Moreover, it is important to note that there is significant global commerce in potatoes, and the occurrence of disease outbreaks has the potential to impact international markets, leading to scarcity in food supply and fluctuations in prices [7]. Therefore, potato leaf diseases require innovative and long-lasting solutions immediately. To alleviate the impact of these diseases, scholarly investigations have progressively prioritized cutting-edge technologies such as precision agriculture, genetic resistance breeding, and disease diagnosis systems based on machine learning. Therefore, we classify potato leaf diseases using the Resnet50ViT model. In this study, we separate the experimental dataset into training, testing, and validation sets. Eighty percent of the data is allocated to the training set, ten percent to the testing set, and ten percent to validation. One hundred iterations of training are performed on our model using the training dataset to efficiently extract features and then validated by computing the loss with the help of a validation set. The model is often used to generate predictions on the testing set afterward. The ResNet50ViT model exhibits superior performance in terms of accuracy, recall, precision, and F1 score when compared to popular models including ResNet50, ViT, Swin-T, and CSwin-T. According to the TOPSIS approach, the ResNet50ViT model exhibited superior performance, and it outperformed Resnet50, ViT, Swin-T, and CSwin-T with a score of 1 due to its pre-trained Resnet50 and ViT combination, which distinguishes it from the other models. This work is organized into the following sections: Sect. 2 provides a comprehensive analysis of prior research; Sect. 3 presents the materials and methods employed in the investigation; Sect. 4 details the setup for the experiment; Sect. 5 encompasses the findings and discussion; and finally, the study is concluded in Sect. 6.

2 Related Works

Over the years, numerous techniques have been devised to enhance the effectiveness of potato leaf screening through the identification of diseases in image datasets. S. Gurusamy et al. [11] suggest the integration of convolutional neural networks (CNNs) to automatically detect and identify diseases in potato plant leaves. A diversified dataset of potato plant leaf photos was generated and used to train and assess a convolutional neural network (CNN) for classifying potato leaf illnesses. The research findings demonstrate that the CNN achieved exceptional levels of precision score, F1 score, recall, and accuracy throughout both the training and testing portions of the dataset. The findings demonstrate the capability of CNNs for automated disease detection in potato plant leaves and suggest extending this methodology to other plant disease categories.

C.T. Kalaydjian et al. [5] investigate the application of the Vision Transformer (ViT) in the context of classifying plant diseases based on images. The current study utilizes a Vision Transformer (ViT) model that has undergone pre-training on the ImageNet-21k dataset. This approach utilizes the concept of transfer learning to construct a model for the categorization of crop disease images.

R. Bandi et al. [4] suggested that the severity of leaf infection be used to determine the stage and detection of plant diseases. The detection of plant leaf disease is accomplished using a deep learning model known as You Only Look Once (YOLOv5). Subsequently, the stage classification process is executed using the vision transformer (ViT) to distinguish between the low, moderate, and high stages of the diseased leaf. The background of the diseased leaf is eliminated using the U2-Net architecture. To mitigate the leaf disease, a suggested remedy has been furnished. Several open-source datasets, including PlantDoc and Plantvillage, were utilized in the training of YOLOv5. Staging classification is predominately conducted on the apple leaf. The vision transformer with a background image achieves a maximum F1 Score of 0.57 at a confidence score of 0.2, while the YOLO v5 achieves an F1 Score of 0.758. In the absence of a background image, the vision transformer achieves a F1 Score of 0.908.

G. Sridevi et al. [7] suggested a multi-layer deep learning model be developed to identify potato leaf disease. The image segmentation technique is employed to extract the distinctive features of the potato leaves from the image exhibiting the potato plant in the initial layer. At the second level, a novel deep-learning approach was developed to identify fungal and bacterial infections in potatoes, utilizing a convolutional neural network (CNN).

C. İ. SOFUOĞLU et al. [14] introduce a novel deep-learning model that accurately categorizes plant leaf diseases in the agriculture and food industries. The objective of this study is to develop a novel convolutional neural network (CNN) architecture for accurately identifying diseases in potato leaves via image analysis. The CNN methodology utilizes filters to process input images, extract significant features, reduce dimensions while retaining crucial image qualities, and ultimately, conduct classification. The empirical findings obtained from analyzing a dataset from the real world show that the proposed model outperformed the existing models in the literature, with an average accuracy improvement of 8.6%. The suggested model achieved an accuracy rate of 98.28%.

J. Wang et al. [9] introduced an innovative approach to cross-domain fruit classification based on unsupervised domain adaptation using deep learning. To enhance the discriminative capabilities of MobileNet V3 and mitigate the influence of complex backgrounds, a hybrid attention module is suggested and incorporated into MobileNet V3 as the HAM-MobileNet. To enhance model classification performance and mitigate domain discrepancy during training, a hybrid loss function is implemented, which integrates implicit distribution metrics with subdomain alignment. To simulate various domains encountered in industrial and everyday life, two fruit classification datasets are created. To verify the effectiveness of the proposed method using a custom-built grape classification dataset and a general fruit classification dataset, The experimental outcomes demonstrate that the proposed methodology attains mean accuracy values of 93.2% and 95.0%, respectively, on the two datasets.

P. S. Thakur et al. [8] introduced a lightweight architectural design with a mere 0.85 million trainable parameters, rendering it well-suited for implementation in agriculture systems based on the Internet of Things (IoT). The efficacy of the suggested model is evaluated by conducting a comparative analysis with nine contemporary methodologies on five datasets that are widely accessible to the public. The model demonstrates superior performance compared to all techniques, even when faced with difficult background conditions. The dataset 'PlantVillage' demonstrates an accuracy rate of 98.86% and a precision rate of 98.9%. Conversely, the 'Embrapa' dataset exhibits an accuracy rate of 89.24% and a precision rate of 91.17%.

L-H.Li et al. [12] suggest utilizing a combination of CNN and Transformer models for ensemble learning. The models employed in this work include MobileNetV3, DenseNet201, ResNext50, Vision Transformer, and Swin Transformer. The objective of employing ensemble learning with these five models is to attain high accuracy and optimal performance using weighted voting methods, such as hard voting and soft voting. The tests show that using ensemble learning, which combines five models, makes it easier to classify three types of datasets: diseases that affect corn leaves, diseases that affect grape leaves, and diseases that affect potato leaves.

L.H. Li et al. [6] identified diseases of the potato leaf using Swin Transformer, a deep learning approach based on transformers. Finally, the experimental outcomes of the model are evaluated using a variety of metrics, such as precision, recall, accuracy, and the F1 score. When conducting training using this model, an accuracy value of 97.70% was obtained.

R. Salini et al. [13] propose a novel DHCLDC model for classifying underground crop leaf diseases, specifically focusing on plants such as cassava, potato, and groundnut. In this case, the preprocessing step entails using a median filter, followed by segmentation using an improved U-net, which is a U-Net model with nested convolutional blocks. In addition, the retrieved characteristics include color features, shape features, and enhanced multi-text (MT) features. Ultimately, a hybrid classifier (HC) model is created for DHCLDC, consisting of both CNN and LSTM models. The results obtained from the HC (CNN + LSTM) model are subsequently used for enhanced score level fusion (SLF), resulting in the ultimate detection of e. Ultimately, simulations are conducted using three datasets to demonstrate the improvement of the DHCLDC model, which is based on a combination of convolutional neural networks (CNN) and long short-term memory (LSTM). The specificity of the hybrid model HC (CNN + LSTM) is significantly high, measuring at 95.41. This is in contrast to the specificity values of other models such as DBN, NN, RF, KNN, CNN, LSTM, DCNN, and SVM.

A. Abbas et al. [10] employed advanced deep learning algorithms to accurately classify and identify plant leaf diseases in images obtained from the Plant Village collection. The dataset comprises 20,636 images of plants and their corresponding diseases. This study specifically targeted potato plants due to their global prevalence, especially in Pakistan. The categorization of plant leaf diseases into 15 groups, including healthy leaves and various plant diseases like fungal and bacterial infections, was accomplished using Convolutional Neural Network (CNN) methods.

Y. Wang et al. [3] develop a method for accurately identifying potato blight by analyzing RGB images. The process consists of three distinct phases: constructing the data set, developing the model, and developing the system. As part of the data set, this research initially gathered images of potato disease from the Internet. Image degradation and unidentifiability were eliminated during the construction of the data set. To construct the labeled potato disease data set, consult with agricultural specialists on crop diseases regarding the labeling of disease types in potato disease image data. Secondly, the input image data was enhanced through the implementation of diverse image-filtering algorithms. Based on deep learning algorithms, a potato disease recognition model was developed. The disease classification model was specifically trained using the Restnet50 model. The input image was convolutionally transformed using 50 Conv2D functions across three channels to differentiate the severity and classification of maladies.

3 Materials and Methods

3.1 PlantVillage Dataset

This study utilizes the potato leaf folders, namely Potato Early Blight, Potato Healthy, and Potato Late Blight, from the PlantVillage dataset to classify diseases from potato leaves. The dataset comprises 1000 images of early blight potato leaves, 152 images of healthy potato leaves, and 1000 images of late blight potato leaves. One can acquire a comprehensive depiction of this dataset by referring to [1] (Fig. 1).

(a) Potato leaf Early Blight (b) Potato leaf Healthy (c) Potato leaf Late Blight

Fig. 1. Sample potato leaf images

3.2 Proposal

In this study, we present ResNet50ViT, an entirely novel approach for screening for potato leaf disease using a classification dataset for potato leaf disease. Resnet50ViT is a model that accurately classifies potato leaf diseases using pre-trained Resnet50 and ViT. The fundamental idea of Resnet50ViT involves utilizing a pre-trained Resnet50 layer, which is subsequently passed through a 2D convolutional layer. The output of this convolutional layer is then combined with positional embeddings of patches. The new output is then concatenated with a class token and further processed through a transformer encoder. In the model, batch normalization is commonly used after the convolutional layers in the ResNet50 section and maybe after the transformer encoder blocks in the ViT section. This process normalizes the activations of these layers by subtracting the average value and dividing it by the standard deviation within a small batch of data. Here, batch normalization has several benefits, including accelerated convergence, decreased internal covariate shift, and the potential to reduce overfitting. Finally, the resulting output is supplied into a multi-layer perceptron (MLP) head. The MLP (Multilayer Perceptron) model is utilized for classification. Here, Resnet50ViT encounters several obstacles that contribute to overfitting: i) The combined design of ResNet50 and ViT may exhibit a higher vulnerability to overfitting in comparison to their solo components. ii) ResNet is considered proficient in capturing spatial relationships, but there are concerns that ViT's attention processes may not handle them as efficiently. This can result in overfitting extraneous details that lack spatial context. Here, we take 270 images of potato leaves split into three groups: early blight, healthy, and late blight. There are 90 images inside Potato Early Blight, 90 images inside Potato Healthy show evidence of healthy potato leaves. There are 90 images in

Potato Late Blight that contain dark spots on potato leaves, and the dark spots on the leaves are signs of a disease. ResNet50ViT model demonstrates superior performance compared to all other classification models, as assessed by comparing its performance with other models using various metrics. Figure 2 illustrates the complete Resnet50ViT model. In this section, we will discuss the functionality of our proposed Resnet50ViT model and its superiority over other models, namely Resnet50, Swin-T, CSwin-T, and ViT. It is imperative to have an adequate number of training samples to construct a robust deep-learning model. To achieve this, our experimental dataset needs to be divided into training, testing, and validation sets. The training set is allocated 80% of the data, the testing set is allocated 10%, and the remaining 10% is reserved for validation. Our model undergoes 100 iterations of training using the training dataset to effectively extract features and then validate by computing the loss with the help of a validation set. Subsequently, the model is employed to make predictions on the testing set. It is essential to note that we did not employ the bootstrap aggregation approach. The given dimensions of the input image are [None, 256, 256, 3], denoting: "None" denotes the batch size, 256 is the input image's height, the width of the input image is 256, the quantity of channels (RGB) is 3. Once the ResNet50 block is executed, the output dimension is modified to [None, 8, 8, 2048]. The width and height are both reduced to eight. A total of 2048 channels are added to the system. An additional reduction in dimension takes place after the implementation of the CONV2D layer and MLP block. The dimension of the output is modified to [None, 8*8, 768]. Here, the dimensions of height and width are decreased to 8 ($8 \times 8 = 64$), as the convolution operation of the CONV2D layer potentially results in a reduction of the spatial dimension to 768, and the quantity of channels is reduced. In general, dimensionality reduction is accomplished through the reduction of the input image's spatial resolution (both in height and breadth) by the ResNet50ViT architecture. This is achieved using convolution operations implemented in the CONV2D layer and the ResNet50 block. Dimensionality reduction in Resnet50ViT has several advantages, such as mitigating model overfitting, improving generalizability, and reducing processing time. The class token vector, a learned embedding that represents the complete image, is combined with the output from the previous phase by concatenation. The class token enables the model to focus on crucial information for the classification of images. The resulting dimension is [None, 65, 768]. Finally, the combined result is inputted into a transformer encoder. Within the transformer encoder, each element goes through a first step where it is processed by an embedding layer, which turns it into a compact numerical vector. Subsequently, these vectors are sent through a sequence of two sub-layers: A multi-head attention layer enables the model to selectively focus on various segments of the input sequence and comprehend the connections between its components. A fully connected feed-forward layer is a component that introduces non-linearity to the model and enables it to acquire a deeper understanding of the connections among its constituents. Following each sub-layer, the outputs undergo normalization and are connected to the residual connection. The residual link enables the model to acquire knowledge from both the initial input and the outputs of the sub-layers. Despite the extended training period of Resnet50ViT, this approach utilizes a pre-trained ResNet-50 model. This pre-trained model has acquired low-level image features, such as edges and corners, through extensive training on a large dataset. Adapting this model to a specific goal can be notably quicker, particularly for tasks with a scarcity of data. The proposed ResNet50ViT model demonstrates superior performance compared to existing models, such as ResNet50, ViT, Swin-T, and CSwin-T, in terms of accuracy, recall, precision, and F1 score. According to the TOPSIS approach, The ResNet50ViT model demonstrated superior performance compared to Resnet50, ViT, Swin-T, and CSwin-T, with a score of 1 because of the combination of pre-trained Resnet50 and ViT, which makes it superior overall models.

3.3 Time Complexity

Here, Swin-T achieves a more favorable linear complexity (O(n)) about the image size (n) due to the implementation of shifted windowing and fixed window size due to which it avoids the quadratic explosion in computations experienced by standard transformers as image size increases. Both CSwin-T and Swin-T depend on the window-based self-attention mechanism, which restricts computations to local windows and results in linear complexity. As a consequence, CSwin-T is still regarded as linear O(n). The self-attention mechanism within the encoder block of a vision transformer (ViT) is the primary factor that determines the time complexity of image classification. The computational complexity of this problem is quadratic, denoted as $O(n^2)$, where n is the number of image patches. The time complexity of Resnet50 is commonly estimated to be O(n * log(n)), which falls within the linear and quadratic ranges. The given expression encompasses the primary n^2 complexity derived from convolutions as well as the mitigating log(n) factor resulting from pooling. Here, Resnet50ViT is a combination of the complexity of the Vision Transformer (ViT) and the pre-trained ResNet50 model. Despite its extended training time of Resnet50ViT, It typically yields significantly superior performance compared to Swin-T and CSwin-T, while also providing a balance between efficiency and performance. Since potatoes provide nourishment for billions of people around the globe, precise leaf categorization is critical for the majority of individuals. Resnet50ViT is therefore the preferred option over all others on account of its superior efficacy.

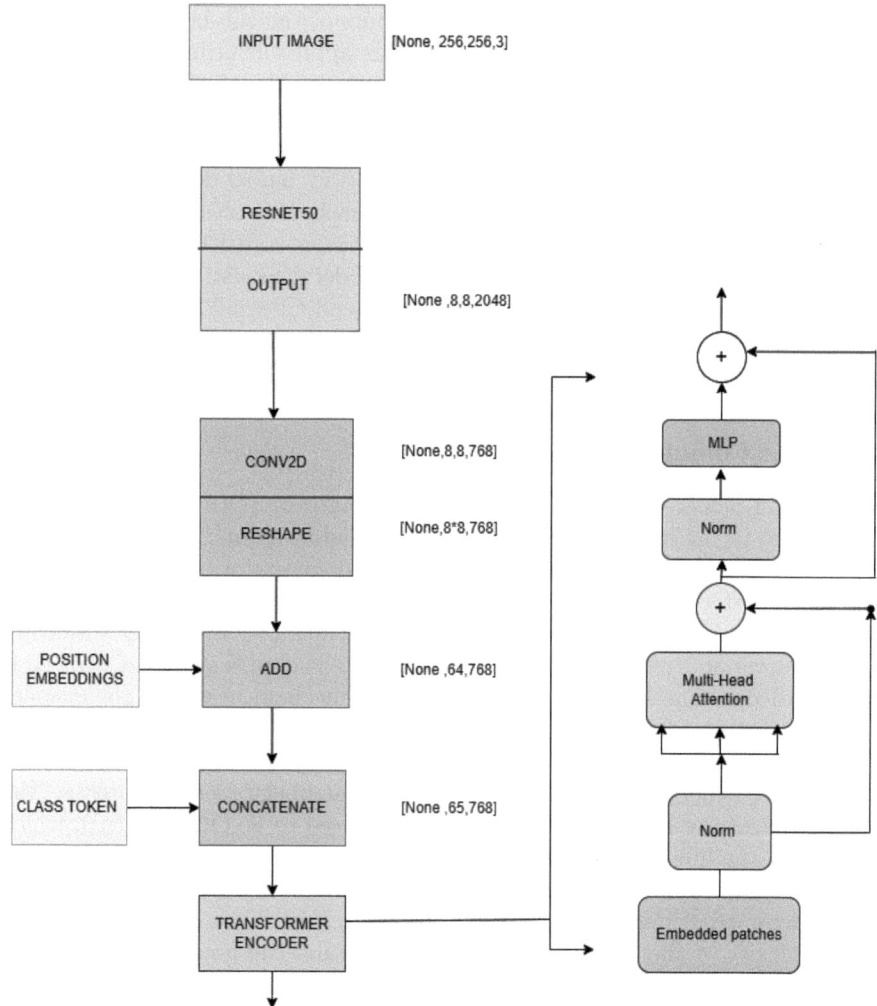

Fig. 2. Resnet50ViT Architecture

4 Experimental Setup

4.1 Parameters Setting

The following are the parameter values for the various models:

The parameters of different models are set as the following:

For ViT, learning rate $(\alpha) = 1e - 4$, number of epochs = 100, number of layers = 12, hidden dimention = 768, MLP dimention = 3072, number of heads = 12 ,Dropout rate = 0.1, patch size = 32, batch size = 36, number of classes = 3 .

For Resnet50 , learning rate (α) = 1e-4, and number of epochs = 100, patch size = 32 , batch size 36,number of classes = 3.

For Swin-T , hidden dimention = 96, layers = (2, 2, 6, 2), heads = (3, 6, 12, 24), channels = 3, number of classes = 3, head dimention = 32, window size = 2, downscaling factors = (4,2, 2, 2), relative position embedding = True,learning rate (α) = 1e-4, and number of epochs =100,patch size = 32, batch size = 36.

For CSwin-T , patch size = 32, embed dimention = 64, depth = (1,2,21,1), split size = (1,2,4,8), num of heads = (2,4,8,16), mlp ratio = 4, learning rate (α) = 1e-4, and number of epochs = 100, patch size = 32, batch size 36, number of classes = 3.

For Resnet50ViT , learning rate (α) = 1e-4, and number of epochs = 100, number of layers = 12,hidden dimention = 768,MLP diimention = 3072, number of heads = 12, Dropout rate = 0.1, patch size = 32, batch size = 36, number of classes = 3.

4.2 PC Configuration

The investigation was conducted using a personal computer that was configured as follows:

1. CPU: Intel(R) Core(TM) i7-12700F 12-GEN CORE 20,
2. RAM: 32 GB,
3. GPU: GeForce RTX 3060 VENTUS 2X 12GB OC ,
4. Operating System: Windows 11 Professional 64-bit,
5. Software: Jupyter notebook 6.5.4, Pytorch 2.1.0,Python 3.11.5

5 Results and Discussion

This study focuses on training the Resnet50ViT model to automatically classify potato leaf disease. The Resnet50ViT model categorizes leaves into three separate classes. The classification of potato leaf disease can be computed using images from the potato leaf disease experimental dataset. To ensure the robustness of our Resnet50ViT model, it is important to possess a significant quantity of training examples. To accomplish this, our experimental dataset must be partitioned into training, testing, and validation sets. A ratio of eight-tenths has been allocated for training, one-tenth is intended for testing, and the remaining one-tenth is reserved for validation. Using the training dataset, our model will be trained for 360 min throughout one hundred iterations. It will then be validated by calculating the loss using a validation set. This will enable us to efficiently extract features. Diverse models, such as Resnet50, will be trained efficiently for 68 min, ViT for 221 min, Swin-T for 67 min, and CSwin-T for 71 min, to compare their performance. Subsequently, our model will be employed to make predictions on the testing set. The bootstrap aggregation method was not utilized in our study. To assess the effectiveness of our classification tasks, it is imperative to evaluate various performance metrics such as accuracy, recall, precision, and F1 Score by performing the mean between three classes. (as shown in Table 1). This evaluation encompasses the Resnet50, ViT, Swin-T, and CSwin-T models. Here, ViT outperforms Resnet50 due to its skip connections, and it incorporates more global information than Resnet50, whereas Swin-T Transformer outperforms ViT due to its shifted windows. By limiting self-attention to non-overlapping local windows, CSwin-T Transformer outperforms Swin-T Transformer due to its Cross-Shaped Window self-attention." It also analyses different parts of the image at the same time, which makes it much faster, and Resnet50ViT outperforms CSwin-T Transformer due to the combination of pre-trained Resnet50 and ViT, which makes it superior over all models. Here Resnet50ViT outperforms CSwin-T in terms of precision, recall, accuracy, and F1 Score. CSwin-T outperforms Swin-T in terms of precision, recall, accuracy, and F1 Score. Swin-T outperforms ViT in terms of precision, recall, accuracy, and F1 score. ViT outperforms Swin-T in terms of precision, recall, accuracy, and F1 Score . It is also apparent from the Topsis approach that various models achieve varying scores (Table 1). The Resnet50ViT model outperformed Resnet50, ViT, Swin-T, and CSwin-T in terms of accuracy, precision, recall, and F1 score (Table 1). According to the TOPSIS approach, the ResNet50ViT model demonstrated superior performance compared to Resnet50, ViT, Swin-T, and CSwin-T, with a score of 1 (Table 1).

Table 1. Classification performance

Method	Precision	Accuracy	Recall	F1 Score	TOPSIS Score	TOPSIS Rank
ViT	76.92	74.07	74.07	75.46	0.3774	4
Resnet50	61.67	63	63	61.67	0	5
Swin-T	83	76	75.67	75.67	0.4507	3
CSwin-T	83	80	79.33	78.33	0.5243	2
Resnet50ViT	95.67	96	97.33	96.33	1	1

6 Conclusion

This study uses deep learning models, specifically Resnet50ViT and CSwin-T, to classify potato leaf disease. The proposals are contrasted with the Swin-T, Resnet50, and ViT models. Both the Resnet50ViT and CSwin-T models demonstrate superior performance compared to the Swin-T, Resnet50, and ViT. In terms of performance, the Resnet50ViT model outperforms the CSwin-T model. Resnet50ViT-based disease detection has the potential to have an immense effect on potato cultivation. It detects diseases early, which is crucial for implementing agricultural yield protection treatments on time. By equipping farmers with an innovative tool for managing the condition of their potato plants, it is possible to enhance agricultural sustainability, decrease reliance on pesticides, and optimize crop management techniques. This study focuses exclusively on the classification of potato leaves, specifically considering only three distinct classes. In subsequent periods, we intend to extend the application of the deep learning model beyond the classification of three classes, encompassing various areas in medical imaging. Prospectively, the integration of disease detection systems based on Resnet50ViT with other emerging technologies, such as mobile applications and Internet of Things (IoT) sensors, could revolutionize potato farming and advance precision agriculture. The integration of these technological advancements has promise to enhance the efficiency, sustainability, and resilience of potato production systems, thereby yielding advantages for farmers and consumers on a global scale.

References

1. Hughes, D., Salathé, M., et al.: An open access repository of images on plant health to enable the development of mobile disease diagnostics. arXiv preprint: arXiv:1511.08060 (2015)
2. Ristaino, J.B., et al.: The persistent threat of emerging plant disease pandemics to global food security. Proc. Natl. Acad. Sci. **118**, e2022239118 (2021)
3. Wang, Y., et al.: DiseSniper: a potato disease identification system based on the ResNet model In: 2022 10th International Conference on Agro-geoinformatics (Agro-Geoinformatics), pp. 1–4 (2022)
4. Bandi, R., Swamy, S., Arvind, C.: Leaf disease severity classification with explainable artificial intelligence using transformer networks. Int. J. Adv. Technol. Eng. Explor. **10**, 278 (2023)
5. Kalaydjian, C.T.: An Application of Vision Transformer (ViT) for Image- Based Plant Disease Classification PhD thesis (UCLA) (2023)
6. Li, L.-H., Tanone, R.: Disease identification in potato leaves using Swin transformer. In: 2023 17th International Conference on Ubiquitous Information Management and Communication (IMCOM), pp. 1–5 (2023)
7. Sridevi, G., et al.: Early detection of potato leaf diseases using convolutional neural network. J. Adv. Zool. **44**, 1–13 (2023)
8. Thakur, P.S., Chaturvedi, S., Khanna, P., Sheorey, T., Ojha, A.: Vision transformer meets convolutional neural network for plant disease classification. Eco. Inform. **77**, 102245 (2023)
9. Wang, J., et al.: A cross-domain fruit classification method based on lightweight attention networks and unsupervised domain adaptation. Complex Intell. Syst. **9**, 4227–4247 (2023)
10. Abbas, A., et al.: An artificial intelligence framework for disease detection in potato plants. Eng., Technol. Appl. Sci. Res. **14**, 12628–12635 (2024)
11. Gurusamy, S., Natarajan, B., Bhuvaneswari, R., Arvindhan, M.: Artificial Intelligence, Blockchain, Computing and Security, vol. 1, pp. 160–165. CRC Press (2024)
12. Li, L.-H., Tanone, R.: Ensemble learning based on CNN and transformer models for leaf diseases classification. In: 2024 18th International Conference on Ubiquitous Information Management and Communication (IMCOM), pp. 1–6 (2024)
13. Salini, R., Charlyn Pushpa Latha, G., Khilar, R.: Deep hybrid classification model for leaf disease classification of underground crops. In: Web Intelligence, pp. 1–23 (2024)
14. Sofuoğlu, C.,İ., Birant, D.: Potato plant leaf disease detection using deep learning method. J. Agric. Sci. **30**, 153–165 (2024)

Indonesian Named Entity Recognition Model for Identifying Human Hobbies

Nurchim[1,2(✉)], Muljono[3], Edi Noersasongko[3], and Ahmad Zainul Fanani[3]

[1] Doctoral Program of Computer Science, Universitas Dian Nuswantoro, Semarang, Indonesia
`p41202000030@mhs.dinus.ac.id`

[2] Faculty of Computer Science, Universitas Duta Bangsa Surakarta, Surakarta, Indonesia
`nurchim@udb.ac.id`

[3] Faculty of Computer Science, Universitas Dian Nuswantoro, Semarang, Indonesia

Abstract. Hobby has become a crucial component of human identity, providing them with both social and emotional satisfaction. Numerous persons express their viewpoints about their pastimes on various social media platforms. Twitter is often seen as a disruptive innovation in the field of sports communication because of its capacity to organize groups swiftly, therefore generating innovative channels for the sharing of viewpoints, information, and business transactions. Twitter, as a social media service, allows users to disclose personal information better so that it can be analyzed using Named Entity Recognition (NER) with the entity tag model found and categorized manually. This study aims to create a NER model for identifying human hobbies using Indonesian-language tweet data. The first steps in developing the NER model are inputting data sources, then creating the Indonesian NER Model, and the last step is model evaluation. This model uses the Python platform and Spacy library to create the NER model manually. The test result of the NER model, which was developed manually, has fifteen categories of label tags with an F1 score average of 92,31%. Furthermore, it is necessary to study models for other sentence patterns, considering that each part of the dataset has a different sentence pattern.

Keywords: NER · human · hobbies · Indonesian

1 Introduction

A hobby is a recreational pursuit undertaken for enjoyment during leisure time, serving as a means to alleviate stress and enhance overall life contentment [1]. Hobbies allow individuals to explore new activities in their own distinctive manner [2]. The issue of hobbyists becomes more intriguing when there are industrial equivalents, given the ambiguous boundaries between work and hobby [3]. Hobbies are essential for every individual, but many find it challenging to find a community that shares the same hobbies. Finding a community that shares the same hobbies is essential for individuals as it allows them to connect with like-minded people and establish friendly relationships. Engaging in the hobby had become an integral aspect of personal identity, offering them both social and emotional gratification [4]. Many individuals articulate their opinions about their hobbies on social media [5].

© The Author(s), under exclusive license to Springer Nature Switzerland AG 2026
M. Mahmud et al. (Eds.): AAIDS 2024, CCIS 2601, pp. 90–98, 2026.
https://doi.org/10.1007/978-3-031-98498-3_7

Social media has developed into one of the most extensive venues for human interaction, containing individual personal preferences, history, demographics [6] and for maintaining hobbies [7]. Twitter is often regarded as a disruptive invention within the realm of sports communication due to its ability to rapidly establish communities, hence creating novel avenues for the exchange of perspectives, information, and commercial transactions [8]. As a social media service, Twitter allows users to post tweets of up to 280 characters to express opinions, URL info, number of hashtags, mentions of other users, and attach media to enable better personalization [9]. This extensive tweet data can be analyzed using the Named-Entity Recognition (NER) approach [10].

NER is a crucial problem in Natural Language Processing (NLP) that entails detecting certain portions of text that pertain to entities. Research on NER has focused on identifying flat and nested entities. This model examines all possible spans in a phrase by evaluating pairs of starting and ending tokens, resulting in exceptional performance compared to other models on various datasets [9]. Alternative methodologies for NER include word-to-dictionary comparison, generation of annotations for identifying named entities and parsing the text to ascertain the part of speech associated with each word. Annotations are eliminated for words that lack a part of speech categorized as nouns or noun-modifying adjectives [10]. Training and using several recognition models may enhance the accuracy of named entity recognition.

NER is a learning method for natural language analysis in text summarization, machine translation, and answering questions [11] that extracts information from unstructured text input and recognizes nouns like persons, places, and organizations [12]. The function of NER is to locate and categorize entities in the text [13]. The creation of automatic NER systems involves manually annotated data, i.e., a corpus of flowing text with manually found and categorized named entity tags [14]. Developing a large data corpus can reduce sparsity [15] and cold-start problems [16]. This paper proposed the NER model for identifying human hobbies from Indonesian-language tweet data.

2 Related Works

There is a growing demand for conducting NER on datasets originating from Indonesia. Presently, libraries and tools are accessible to aid machine learning (ML) integration with extracting information from NER. Nevertheless, the number of datasets available for examining information on social media and online news when considering the Indonesian language could be much higher. In contrast to English, the lack of complete availability of NLP functions in Indonesian results in their indirect support [17].

NER in English achieves an exceptional outcome due to the copious amount of data at our disposal for conducting research [18]. NER experiments in the Indonesian language could be more fruitful. This might be due to the characteristics of the Indonesian language. It differs considerably as a result of its morphological past. Furthermore, the need for more available datasets will significantly hinder the research if deep learning is to be implemented [19].

Research on NER in the Indonesian language needs to be improved due to a limited quantity of labelled data [20]. Gunawan et al. [21] categorize the information from Indonesian articles into four distinct classes: person, organization, place, and event. Thus, Wibawa and Purwarianti [18] built Indonesian NER for newspaper articles with 15 classes involving Person, God, Organization, Location, Facility, Product, Event, Natural-Object, Disease, Color, Timex, Periodx, Numex, Countx, Measurement. Recently, Tentua et al. [22] examined many types of talents in the Indonesian language, including hard skills, soft skills, and technology.

NER was developed to identify entities in the Indonesian language by utilizing a corpus comprised of other sources, such as tweets. One limitation of the NER system when applied to tweets via machine learning is its reliance on numerous supplementary manual features, including orthographic features such as words and the last three letters [10]. At present, the majority of NER for Indonesian tweets is generated via machine learning tools. The spacy tool has the best performance among other NLP libraries, such as Google, Stanford CoreNLP, Germany and Geoparser [23].

3 Method

The development step of the Indonesian named entity recognition model consists of input data source, NER model building process, and NER model testing, as shown in Fig. 1. The input data source is the initial dataset search process. This research uses a dataset of 1441 Indonesian tweets obtained by scraping data. Scraping is an unstructured data extraction technique from websites that can be built into large-scale structured datasets [24]. The next stage is creating the NER model, including the preprocessing stage, defining entity classes, manual annotations, and creating models.

Data preprocessing is essential to select the most suitable keywords, remove unnecessary words that do not provide additional information [25], and transform them to make them more structured. Then, this data will be defined based on the hobby entity, which consists of soccer and basketball classes. This step is done by manually annotating. A significant portion of natural language processing tasks and applications rely heavily on the manual annotation of text [26]. After that, NER modeling uses deep learning and machine learning approaches. Finally, the model is evaluated with the F1-test approach.

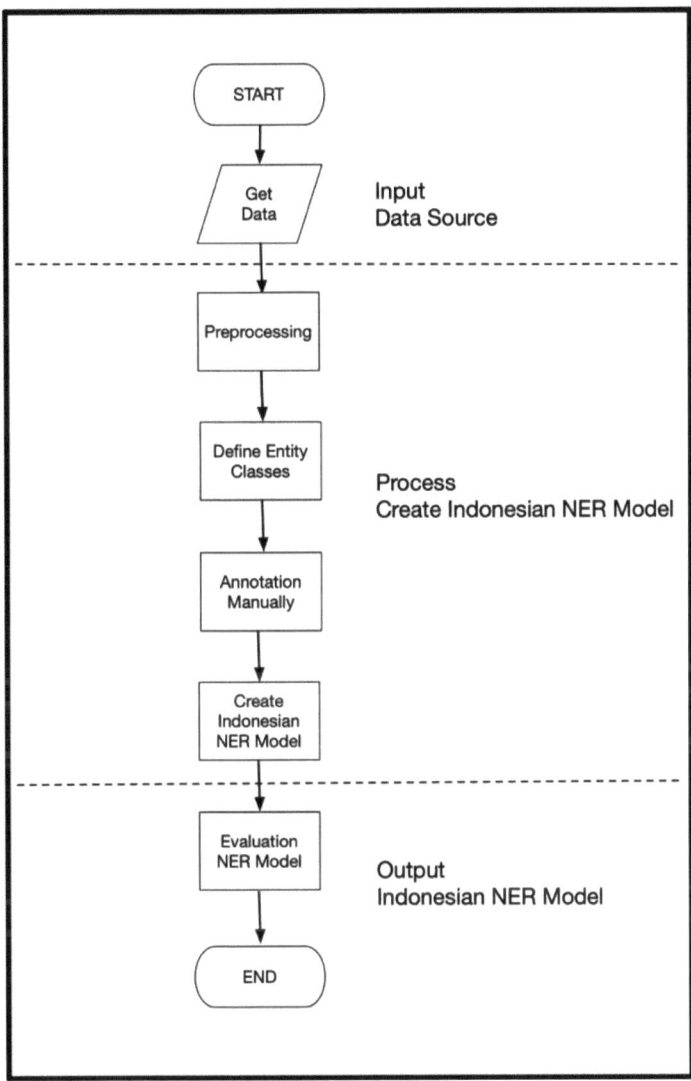

Fig. 1. The proposed method

4 Experimental

4.1 Data Source

Twitter data provides researchers and decision-makers with a rich and relevant data source [25]. The name of the Twitter account must be entered, along with the start date for data collection, which can be set in the application. The twint library is used to gather data from Twitter. Only tweet data from the whole set of Twitter data gathered was used, as shown in Tables 1 and 2.

Table 1. Example of football Indonesian tweets

Football Tweet
"ini adalah salah satu momen terbaik dalam karirnya. Semoga prestasi ini bisa menjadi motivasi bagi para pemain muda Indonesia untuk terus berjuang dan mengukir sejarah di dunia sepak bola internasional"
"Uzbekistan di ambang menciptakan prestasi terbaik dalam sejarah sepak bola mereka"
"KIP FC Bersama Dewan Kota dan Lurah Kembangan Selatan Gelar Laga Sepakbola Piala Trafeo Sinergi Kapan kalian Munaslub Federasi sepak bola konoha?"

Table 2. Example of basketball Indonesian tweets

Basketball Tweet
"Semalem mimpi lagi main basket tapi tim nya tim pro Palestina vs pro Israel"
"Ternyata Curry tidak hanya pandai bermain basket, tetapi juga memiliki bakat menyanyi!"
"Coba langsung Bola Basket Virtual dengan login ke akunmu sekarang!"

4.2 Data Preprocessing

Many researchers have asserted that data preparation is an essential and crucial phase in the knowledge data discovery (KDD) process [26]. This step is completed to ensure that the data received is superior to it before modeling activities, increasing its effectiveness and generating a better assessment value [27]. Table 3 displays data preparation outcomes, including removing URLs, emojis, punctuation, and stopword remover.

4.3 Define Entity Class

Entity classes in NLP refer to the classification of entities, such as names of people, organizations, and locations, in text. It involves identifying and categorizing those entities to understand their meaning and context within the text. Some papers in the abstracts discuss various aspects of entity classes in NLP. This research contributes to the understanding and advancement of hobby entity classes, namely football and basketball, especially in the Indonesian Language.

4.4 Annotation Manually

Manual entity annotation involves identifying and tagging specific entities within a given text. Manually annotating entities is often laborious and time-consuming. NER plays a crucial role in identifying corpus items that may enhance the performance of NLP [28]. To overcome this problem, several studies proposed automated annotation methods using various techniques such as remote supervision and partial annotation learning. These methods address the problem of missing entity annotations that could degrade the performance of the NER model.

Table 3. The result of data preprocessing

Data Source	Data Preprocessing
"ini adalah salah satu momen terbaik dalam karirnya. Semoga prestasi ini bisa menjadi motivasi bagi para pemain muda Indonesia untuk terus berjuang dan mengukir sejarah di dunia sepak bola internasional"	"salah satu momen terbaik karirnya semoga prestasi menjadi motivasi para pemain muda indonesia terus berjuang mengukir sejarah dunia sepak bola internasional"
"Uzbekistan di ambang menciptakan prestasi terbaik dalam sejarah sepak bola mereka"	"uzbekistan ambang menciptakan prestasi terbaik sejarah sepak bola mereka"
"KIP FC Bersama Dewan Kota dan Lurah Kembangan Selatan Gelar Laga Sepakbola Piala Trafeo Sinergi Kapan kalian Munaslub Federasi sepak bola konoha?"	"kip fc bersama dewan kota lurah kembangan selatan gelar laga sepakbola piala trafeo sinergi kapan kalian munaslub federasi sepak bola konoha"
"Semalem mimpi lagi main basket tapi tim nya tim pro Palestina vs pro Israel"	"semalem mimpi main basket tim nya tim pro palestina vs pro israel"
"Ternyata Curry tidak hanya pandai bermain basket, tetapi juga memiliki bakat menyanyi!"	"ternyata curry tidak hanya pandai bermain basket memiliki bakat menyanyi penuh semangat"
"Coba langsung Bola Basket Virtual dengan login ke akunmu sekarang!"	"coba langsung bola basket virtual login akunmu sekarang"

4.5 Create Custom NER Model

The Custom NER can effectively extract information from large or regular data sets with reasonable accuracy. The process starts by creating a data train for all hobby terms that fall under the scope of football and basketball. The creation of a custom NER parses these terms using the Inside-Outside-Beginning (IOB) form. The Indonesian-Custom NER was developed from the SpaCy library using Python.

From Fig. 2, it can be seen that the higher the epoch value, the loss value will approach the value 0, which means that the NER model is very well used in identifying human hobbies from Indonesian language tweet data.

4.6 Evaluation Indonesian NER Model

The model performance evaluation must be assessed using the widely used performance evaluation based on correctness. The assessment indicators in this paper include precision (P), recall (R), and F1 score. The result parameters are shown in Table 3. The formula for determining precision (P), recall (R), and F1 score are as follows:

$$Precision(P) = \frac{True\ Positive}{(True\ Positive + False\ Positive)} \quad (1)$$

$$Recall(R) = \frac{True\ Positive}{True\ Positive + False\ Negatives} \quad (2)$$

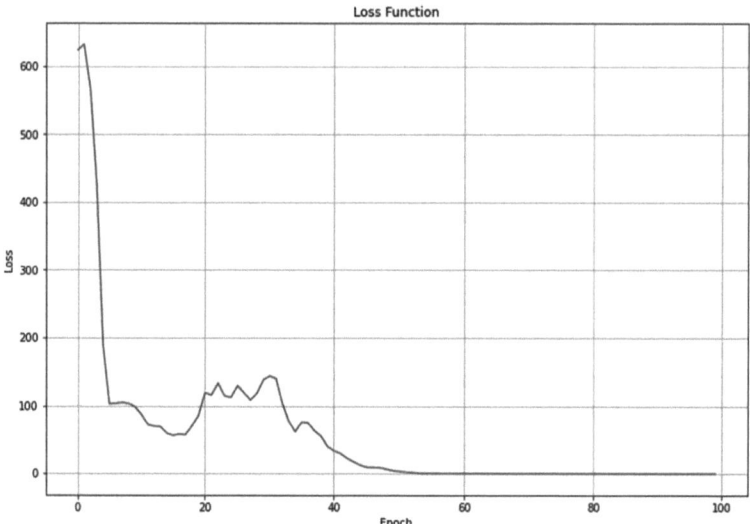

Fig. 2. The result of loss function Indonesian NER Model

$$F1 = \frac{2x\ Precision x\ Recall}{Precision + Recall} \quad (3)$$

Based on Table 4, it can be seen that the F1 score, P and R values have converged to the point of 92.31%, 90% and 94.74%, respectively. From this test, the developed NER model is perfect for identifying football and basketball hobby entities in the Indonesian language.

Table 4. Evaluation model NER

EPOCH	F1	P	R
0	0	0	0
10	32.51	30	34.24
38	73.12	71	72.12
65	92.31	90	94.74
100	92.31	90	94.74
231	92.31	90	94.74
431	92.31	90	94.74
631	92.31	90	94.74

5 Conclusion

This research creates an Indonesian NER model by manually tagging football and basketball hobby entities using the Spacy tool. The test results show that the model achieves an average F1 score of 92.31%. This can serve as an alternative for creating new entity labeling, especially those that focus on other Indonesian vocabulary. More labeling datasets have the opportunity to improve NER performance in recognizing Indonesian text patterns. Additional studies are needed to test this NER model with data sources other than tweets. The NER model operates on sentence patterns, considering that sentence patterns in Indonesian are very unique.

References

1. Luchenko, Y., Semenova, V., Tereshchenko, I., Solona, S., Oliinyk, O.: Comparison of software implementations of hobby journals. Grail Sci. **28**(28), 202–222 (2023). https://doi.org/10.36074/grail-of-science.09.06.2023.34
2. Khaqan, H.A., et al.: Life beyond retinal surgery: a survey. Asian J. Biol. **19**(3), 1–5 (2023). https://doi.org/10.9734/ajob/2023/v19i3366
3. Martinus, K.: 'It's a love interest' – enthusiasts and regional industry cultures of practice. Geoforum **144**, 103808 (2023). https://doi.org/10.1016/j.geoforum.2023.103808
4. Blok, M., van Ingen, E., de Boer, A.H., Slootman, M.: The use of information and communication technologies by older people with cognitive impairments: from barriers to benefits. Comput. Hum. Behav. **104**, 106173 (2020). https://doi.org/10.1016/j.chb.2019.106173
5. Patel, H., Kansara, A., Prathap, B.R., Pradeep Kumar, K.: Human behavior analysis on political retweets using machine learning algorithms. Meas. Sens. **27**, 100768 (2023). https://doi.org/10.1016/j.measen.2023.100768
6. Shanahan, T., Tran, T.P., Taylor, E.C.: Getting to know you: social media personalization as a means of enhancing brand loyalty and perceived quality. J. Retail. Consum. Serv. **47**, 57–65 (2019). https://doi.org/10.1016/j.jretconser.2018.10.007
7. Koiranen, I., Keipi, T., Koivula, A., Räsänen, P.: Changing patterns of social media use? A population-level study of Finland. Univers. Access Inf. Soc. **19**(3), 603–617 (2020). https://doi.org/10.1007/s10209-019-00654-1
8. Mehra, V., Singh, P., Bharany, S., Sawhney, R.S.: A social media analytics application of impression management and social presence theories to Twitter interaction analysis. Decis. Anal. J. **9**, 100321 (2023). https://doi.org/10.1016/j.dajour.2023.100321
9. Coelho, J., Nitu, P., Madiraju, P.: A personalized travel recommendation system using social media analysis. Proc. - 2018 IEEE Int. Congr. Big Data, BigData Congr. 2018 - Part 2018 IEEE World Congr. Serv., pp. 260–263 (2018). https://doi.org/10.1109/BigDataCongress.2018.00046
10. Wintaka, D.C., Bijaksana, M.A., Asror, I.: Named-entity recognition on Indonesian tweets using bidirectional LSTM-CRF. Procedia Comput. Sci. **157**, 221–228 (2019). https://doi.org/10.1016/j.procs.2019.08.161
11. Li, J., Sun, A., Han, J., Li, C.: A survey on deep learning for named entity recognition. IEEE Trans. Knowl. Data Eng. **34**(1), 50–70 (2020). https://doi.org/10.1109/TKDE.2020.2981314
12. Shelar, H., Kaur, G., Heda, N., Agrawal, P.: Named entity recognition approaches and their comparison for custom NER model. Sci. Technol. Libr. **39**(3), 324–337 (2020). https://doi.org/10.1080/0194262X.2020.1759479
13. Azarine, I.S., Bijaksana, M.A., Asror, I.: Named entity recognition for Indonesian text using hidden markov model. 2019 7th Int. Conf. Inf. Commun. Technol. pp. 1–5 (2019)

14. Ruokolainen, T., Kauppinen, P., Silfverberg, M., Lindén, K.: A finnish news corpus for named entity recognition. Lang. Resour. Eval. **54**(1), 247–272 (2020). https://doi.org/10.1007/s10579-019-09471-7
15. Altuncu, M.T., Yaliraki, S.N., Barahona, M.: Graph-based topic extraction from vector embeddings of text documents: application to a corpus of news articles. Stud. Comput. Intell. **944**, 154–166 (2021). https://doi.org/10.1007/978-3-030-65351-4_13
16. Sileo, D., Vossen, W., Raymaekers, R.: Zero-shot recommendation as language modeling. Lect. Notes Comput. Sci. (including Subser. Lect. Notes Artif. Intell. Lect. Notes Bioinformatics), vol. 13186 LNCS, no. 1, pp. 223–230 (2022). https://doi.org/10.1007/978-3-030-99739-7_26
17. Budi, I., Suryono, R.R.: Application of named entity recognition method for Indonesian datasets: a review. Bull. Electr. Eng. Informatics **12**(2), 969–978 (2023). https://doi.org/10.11591/eei.v12i2.4529
18. Wibawa, A.S., Purwarianti, A.: Indonesian named-entity recognition for 15 classes using ensemble supervised learning. Procedia Comput. Sci. **81**(May), 221–228 (2016). https://doi.org/10.1016/j.procs.2016.04.053
19. Jehangir, B., Radhakrishnan, S., Agarwal, R.: A survey on named entity recognition — datasets, tools, and methodologies. Nat. Lang. Process. J. **3**(10), 100017 (2023). https://doi.org/10.1016/j.nlp.2023.100017
20. Raharjo, S., Wardoyo, R., Putra, A.E.: Detecting proper nouns in indonesian-language translation of the quran using a guided method. J. King Saud Univ. Comput. Inf. Sci. **32**(5), 583–591 (2020). https://doi.org/10.1016/j.jksuci.2018.06.009
21. Gunawan, W., Suhartono, D., Purnomo, F., Ongko, A.: Named-entity recognition for indonesian language using bidirectional LSTM-CNNs. Procedia Comput. Sci. **135**, 425–432 (2018). https://doi.org/10.1016/j.procs.2018.08.193
22. Tentua, M.N., Suprapto, Afiahayati: NERSkill.Id: annotated dataset of Indonesian's skill entity recognition. Data Br. **53**, 110192 (2024). https://doi.org/10.1016/j.dib.2024.110192
23. Krauer, F., Schmid, B.V.: Mapping the plague through natural language processing. Epidemics **41**, 100656 (2022). https://doi.org/10.1016/j.epidem.2022.100656
24. Cheema, S.M., Tariq, S., Pires, I.M.: A natural language interface for automatic generation of data flow diagram using web extraction techniques. J. King Saud Univ. Comput. Inf. Sci. **35**(2), 626–640 (2023). https://doi.org/10.1016/j.jksuci.2023.01.006
25. Azizah, L.N., et al.: The investigation into deep learning classifiers towards imbalanced text data. Proc. 5th Int. Conf. Networking, Inf. Syst. Secur. Envisage Intell. Syst. 5G/6G-Based Interconnected Digit. Worlds, NISS 2022, pp. 1–6 (2022). https://doi.org/10.1109/NISS55057.2022.10085611
26. Segura-Tinoco, A., Cantador, I.: ARGAEL: ARGument annotation and evaluation tooL. SoftwareX **23**, 101410 (2023). https://doi.org/10.1016/j.softx.2023.101410
27. Karami, A., Lundy, M., Webb, F., Dwivedi, Y.K.: Twitter and research: a systematic literature review through text mining. IEEE Access **8**, 67698–67717 (2020). https://doi.org/10.1109/ACCESS.2020.2983656
28. Purwanto, M.W., Noersasongko, E.: Improving named entity recognition in bahasa indonesia with transformer-Word2Vec-CNN-attention model. Int. J. Intell. Eng. Syst. **16**(4), 655–668 (2023). https://doi.org/10.22266/ijies2023.0831.53

Comparative Analysis Between Time Series Feature Extraction with Sliding Window and Data Framing Method for Energy Forecasting Using Artificial Neural Network

Wilen Melsedec O. Narvios, Jayson C. Jueco(✉), John Cliff A. Jumawan, Riza A. Tulipas, Frandy P. Badilles, Ferdinand F. Batayola, and Marvin A. Radaza

Department of Electrical Engineering, Cebu Technological University, M. J. Cuenco Avenue Corner R. Palma, Cebu City, 6000 Cebu, Philippines
jaysonc.jueco@ctu.edu.ph

Abstract. Forecasting involves learning trends and patterns in historical records and calculating the probability for an event to happen to make a statement about the events whose actual outcomes are yet to be observed. It became a critical tool in decision science applied across various domains, providing insights into future results to minimize uncertainty. Challenges persist while forecasting methods have evolved, including limited data, complexity, uncertainty, and representation. In this paper, we introduced the data framing method, which is a novel feature engineering that involves subtracting the present observation from all data in the window, centering the data around the current word. The method improves the traditional sliding window representation of time series. A comparative analysis between sliding window and data framing method in application to forecasting model using Artificial Neural Network. Experimental results demonstrate the superiority of the data framing method in terms of training convergence, validation loss fluctuation, and overall accuracy across diverse data against the sliding window method. The data framing method enhances the performance of ANNs.

Keywords: feature extraction · sliding window · data framing · energy forecasting · artificial neural network · computational model

1 Introduction

Predicting future outcomes is valuable in a world characterized by uncertainty and complexity. Forecasting, both an art and a science plays a crucial role in decision-making processes across various domains, from economics and finance to weather prediction and supply chain management [1]. It provides insights into what lies ahead, helping individuals and organizations navigate the uncertain terrain and make informed choices [22]. Forecasting applied across different fields.

Finance allows investors to predict stock market trends, evaluate investment opportunities, and manage portfolio risk [1]. In marketing, it assists businesses in predicting consumer demand, optimizing pricing strategies, and forecasting sales [2]. These are just a few examples of forecasting being a valuable decision-making tool across industries.

Forecasting uses historical data, statistical models, and predictive techniques to estimate future events. Forecasts are valuable in decision science but cannot provide definitive answers; they aim to minimize uncertainty and provide helpful information to support planning, risk management, and strategy development [3]. While forecasting has come a long way with advancements in computational power and data availability, it has challenges. Factors such as data quality, changing patterns, unforeseen events, and human biases can impact the accuracy of forecasts. Nonetheless, through continuous improvement and the integration of new technologies, forecasting techniques are evolving to address these limitations and provide increasingly reliable predictions [3,4].

Forecasters used statistical approaches from the 1970s onwards, especially methods based on Box-Jenkins, like Autoregressive models. These approaches can accurately forecast by analyzing time-series data and correlating different parameters or factors but need to be more fit to handle seasonality due to the linear dependency of the model between predictors and features. The appearance of machine learning and its powerful regression methods outperformed the statistical models, which have remained a baseline method in most research work like ANN, SVM, and LSTM. More recently, deep learning models achieved superior results and attracted much interest in the research community. Unlike statistical models that only learn linear relationships in the data, deep neural networks map complex non-linear features through their deep structure, stacking several layers and densely connecting several neurons. Although the deep neural network showed superiority over the classic statistical and machine learning yields good results, time series data are undeniably arduous to handle and expensive to train regardless of the selected approach [27–29]. Aside the computational cost of neural network and deep learning models, one issue of time series forecasting is a better feature engineering of the input time series. The sliding window method is commonly employed for time series feature extraction for Artificial Neural Network models. Nevertheless, the accuracy of ANNs in predicting time series data depends on the robustness of observable data within the model. Consequently, extracting features from the time series data set is crucial in implementing ANNs [3,4].

This paper has two main contributions. First, we introduced the data framing method, which involves subtracting the present observation from all data in the window, centering the data around the current word. Second, we performed a comparative analysis between sliding windows, the traditional feature extraction method established in the literature, and this paper's novel data framing method. A benchmark Artificial Neural Network Model performs the forecasting using the extracted time series features from the sliding window and data framing plan. We used Mean Absolute Error (MAE) and Mean Squared Error (MSE) to evaluate the forecasting performance in each technique.

2 Methods

2.1 Feature Extraction

This paper explores a novel forecasting horizon, distinct from the sliding window approach commonly used in previous studies [10,13,22,24]. The forecasting horizon is the perspective through which the forecasting model views the time series data. It consists of two parameters: the number of past data points, m, used as input to the forecasting model, and the number of data points, n, predicted by the model. We discussed the sliding window and data framing method in the following sections.

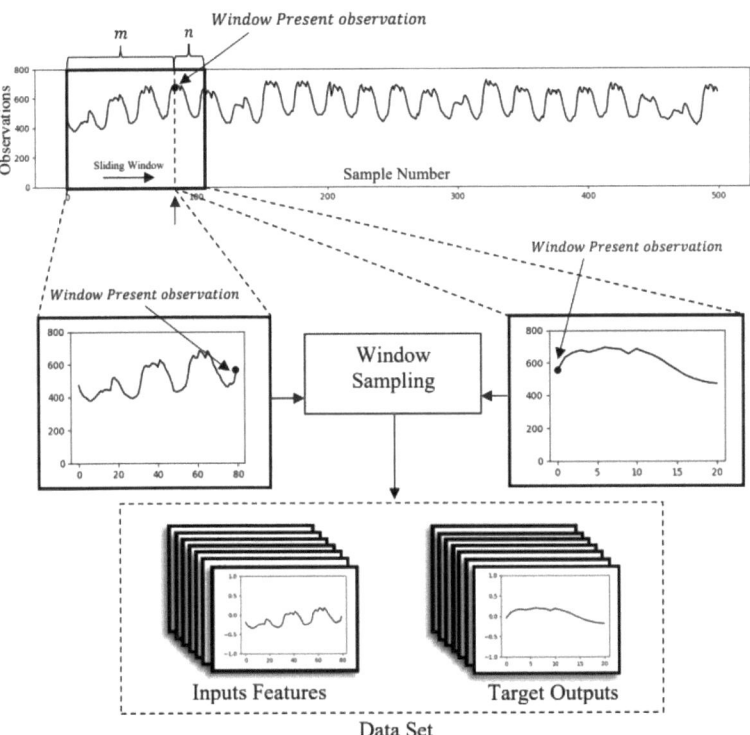

Fig. 1. Sliding Window Method

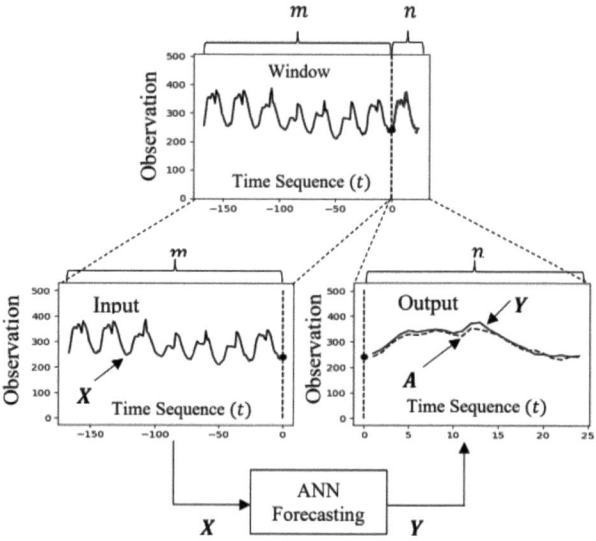

Fig. 2. Sliding Window with ANN forecasting Model

Sliding Window Method. In Fig. 1 and 2, the sliding window cleaves into an input and output window. An input window contained a fixed m number of consecutive past data points and an output window comprising a fixed n number of straight unknown future data points to be predicted. The sliding window method sampled the time series data using an input window, m past samples, and output windows, n actual samples in time. The frames are arranged chronologically based on the sample number of the present data. The sample window is $\bar{x} = l - m - n + 1 \in \mathbb{R}$ where l is the length of the time series, m represents the input window size, and n represents the output window size.

In this paper, the sliding window forecasting horizon involves referencing all data within the forecasting horizon to zero observation. It includes two arrays of data: X, which contains a m number sequence of past data sample points to be observed by the forecasting model, and Y, which includes an n number sequence of unknown future data sample points to be predicted by the forecasting model. In this setup, no preprocessing methods were applied.

Data Framing Method. We introduced the novel time series feature extraction framework called the data framing method. We define data frames as the data within the sliding window referenced to the present data point. The feature extraction in data framing involves subtracting the current observation from all data in the window, centering the data around the present moment, as shown in Fig. 3. Unlike the sliding window approach, where the window moves with time, the data framing approach keeps the frame fixed to the present data sample point, following the time series changes.

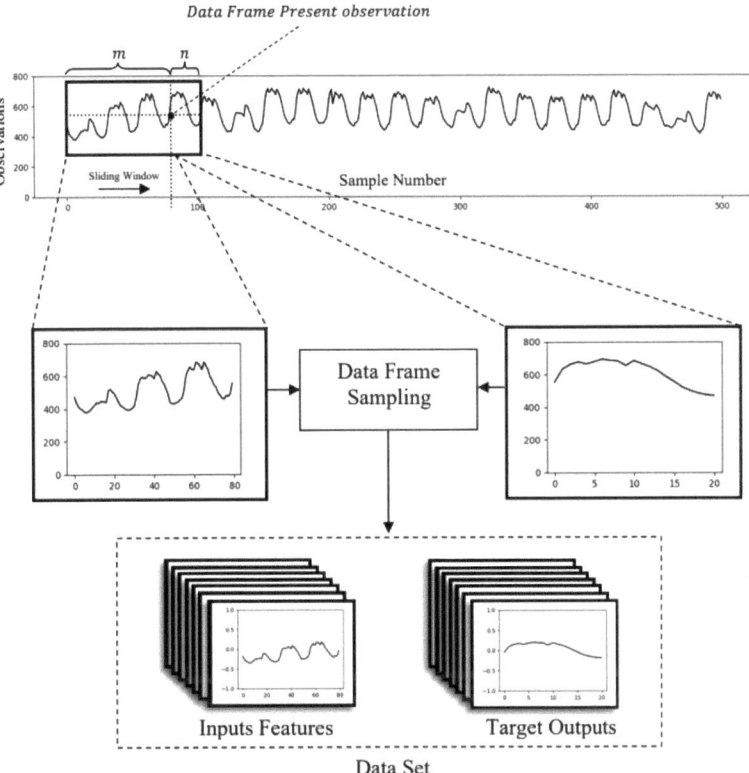

Fig. 3. Data Framing Method

In the Data Framing forecasting horizon, all data within the sliding window forecasting horizon is referenced to the present data point X_{t-m-1} of the input window X, as depicted in Fig. 4. The deployment of ANN in data framing is achieved by subtracting the present data point X_{t-m-1} of the input window (X) and using it as input for the forecasting model. The prediction of the forecasting model, Y, is added to the present data X_{t-m-1}, which serves as the actual prediction of the forecast. This process centers the data within the forecasting horizon around the present moment, providing a consistent reference point at X_{t-m-1}. Unlike the sliding window approach, where the window moves with the increment of time, the data framing approach keeps the frame fixed to the present data sample point, following the time series graph.

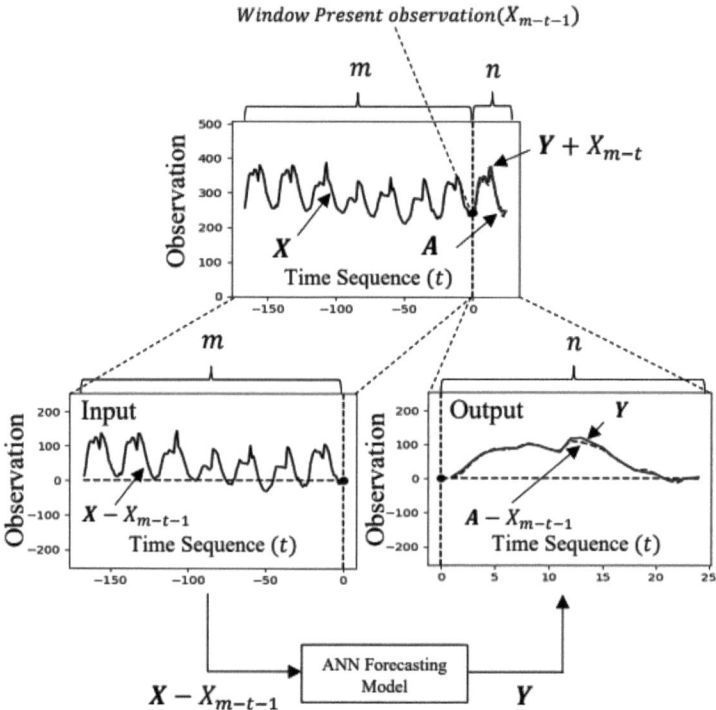

Fig. 4. Data Framing Method with ANN Forecasting Model

3 Forecasting Model Using Artificial Neural Network (ANN)

3.1 Artificial Neural Network Model

The benchmark single-layer ANN has 360 interconnected neurons, resulting in 32,448 tweakable parameters. These parameters include 32,256 connection weights and 4,032 neuron biases. The ADAM optimizer adjusts these parameters during training to optimize the Mean Absolute Error (MAE) loss function. During the training process for the sliding window forecasting horizon, the training dataset is shuffled and divided into batches. Each batch consists of 32 data samples fed into an ANN for predictions. The Mean Absolute Error (MAE) loss function measures the difference between predicted and actual outputs. The Adaptive Moment Estimation (ADAM) optimizer is employed to adjust the weights and biases of the ANN, aiming to minimize the loss. This iterative process is repeated for all batches in the dataset, completing one epoch. Repeating batch feeding, loss calculation, and parameter adjustment improves the ANN's learning and performance.

Table 1. Settings of ANN Hyperparameters

Hyperparameter	Settings
Batch Size	32
Hidden Layers	360
Activation	ReLU
Optimizer	adam
Learning Rate	0.001
Epochs	100
Early Stopping	50
Loss Function	MSE

The same training scenario employed in training the single hidden layer ANN for sliding window forecasting horizon is implemented for instructing the single hidden layer ANN for the data framing forecasting horizon. However, in this case, the data framing training set is used. The deployed ANN on the addressed forecasting horizon has a selected input size m of 168 and an output size n of 24. The forecasting model takes 168 past data points, representing one week of data, as input. The model produces 24 future data points, corresponding to a 24-hour ahead forecast.

In this paper, we set a benchmark Artificial Neural Network model with hyperparameter settings in Table 1. The model comprises an input layer with (m) neurons, a hidden layer with (m) neurons using the Rectified Linear Unit (ReLU) activation function, and an output layer with (n) neurons. The ReLU activation function is commonly used in neural networks. It outputs the input value if it is positive and zero otherwise. ReLU introduces non-linearity, enabling neural networks to learn complex patterns and approximate nonlinear relationships in data. It is efficient computationally and helps address the vanishing gradient problem encountered with other existing activation functions.

3.2 Dataset and Experimental Set-up

This section briefly describes the dataset used and the experiment performed in this paper. The time series data is 81,024 observations for each grid section of the hourly energy demand in the Philippine Grid from 2013 to 2022. The dataset consists of 8 grid energy time series profiles: Luzon, Visayas, Mindanao, Leyte-Samar, Bohol, Cebu, Negros, and Panay. Each contained different load patterns, as shown in Fig. 2. To utilize the extracted data sets for Artificial Neural Networks, we split the data into 70% training the ANN, 15% validation, and 15% to evaluate the performance of the ANN forecasting model. The training dataset consists of sampled windows older than the validation dataset, while the test dataset is newer than the validation set. The dataset is available at https://www.ngcp.ph/operations.

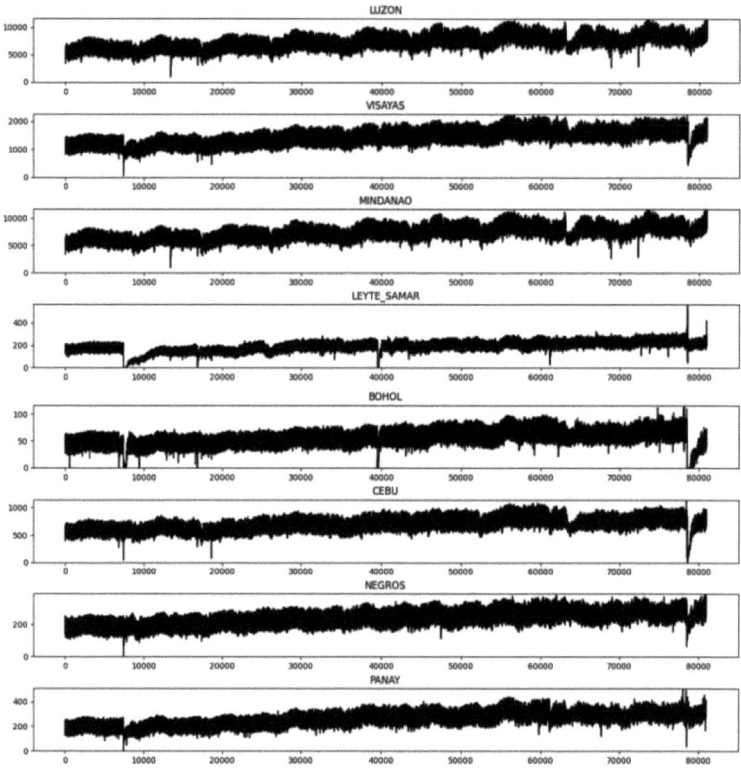

Fig. 5. Philippine Electrical Grid Data consisting of hourly load time series

The experimentation process involved the analysis of a single time series data. Eight datasets were subjected to the experimental setup. Firstly, two datasets were extracted: one using a sliding window forecasting horizon and the other using a data framing forecasting horizon. Next, two identical benchmark ANN models were trained using the respective datasets. One model was introduced with the sliding window dataset, while the other was presented with the data framing dataset. Finally, the performance of the trained benchmark ANN models was evaluated by recording the loss and validation loss during training based on the number of epochs.

3.3 Evaluation

The performance of the model was evaluated using $MAE = \frac{1}{n}\sum_{i=1}^{n}|x_i - \hat{x}_i|$, and $MSE = \frac{1}{n}\sum_{i=1}^{n}|x_i - \hat{x}_i|^2$ where x_i and $\hat{x}_i$ are actual and predicted values respectively. MSE measures the average squared deviation between $\hat{x}_i$ and x_i, while MAE measures the average absolute difference. This paper uses MSE and MAE as primary metrics to evaluate the sliding window and data framing-based

ANN forecasting models. By comparing MAE and MSE values, we benchmark which forecasting horizon approach performs better.

4 Results and Discussion

4.1 Performance Between Sliding Window and Data Framing Method

Accurately forecasting future events, a critical aspect of decision-making in numerous domains, including finance, economics, weather forecasting, and supply chain management, is challenging due to various factors such as limited information, system complexity, uncertainty, and biases. Researchers have explored different methods for improving the accuracy of forecasting models to address these challenges. In this study, the performance of the data framing method was investigated compared to the commonly used sliding window method in artificial neural network-based (ANN) forecasting models. The data framing method involves structuring the input data in a framed format to leverage temporal dependencies and capture relevant features. This section presents the study's results, and their implications, including the convergence behavior, fluctuation in validation loss, and overall forecasting accuracy observed with the data framing method compared to the sliding window method, are discussed.

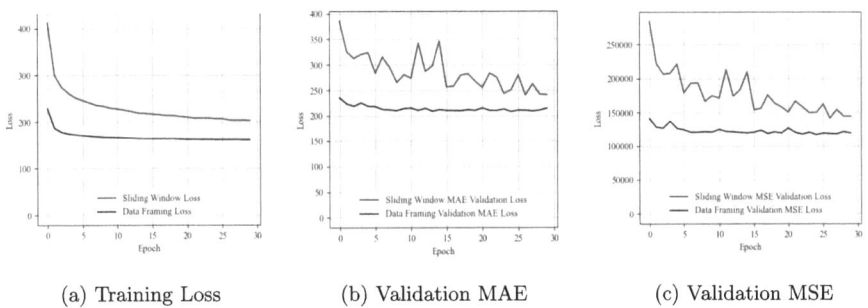

(a) Training Loss (b) Validation MAE (c) Validation MSE

Fig. 6. Training and validation between Sliding Window and Data Framing

Substantial evidence supports the superiority of the data framing method over the sliding window in terms of convergence behavior, fluctuation in validation loss, test data set evaluation loss, and overall forecasting accuracy. The Data Framing method consistently demonstrated faster convergence during training, requiring significantly fewer epochs to reach a stable loss value than the sliding window method. This accelerated convergence suggests that the data framing method enables more efficient learning from the training data, leading to a quicker capture of underlying patterns and dynamics in the time series data. Furthermore, the data framing method consistently achieved lower convergence loss, indicating its ability to capture time series dynamics more accurately than

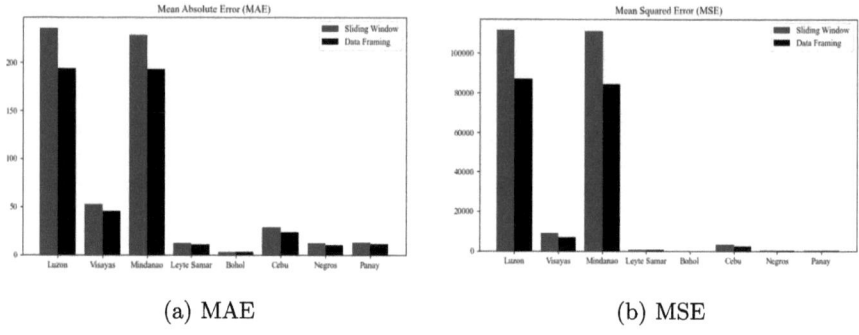

Fig. 7. MAE and MSE evaluation on Test Data

the sliding window method. The structured framing of the input data facilitated extracting relevant features and utilizing temporal dependencies, contributing to improved forecasting accuracy and more reliable predictions.

Regarding fluctuation in validation loss, the data framing exhibited advantages over the sliding window method. The observed reduction in change indicates that the models trained with the data framing method were more stable and less sensitive to minor variations in the input data. This stability is crucial for reliable and consistent forecasting outcomes, as it reduces the risk of overfitting or underfitting the data. The consistency of the Data Framing method was demonstrated across all eight datasets used in this study. Regardless of the dataset characteristics, such as complexity, trends, seasonality, and noise levels, the data framing method consistently outperformed the sliding window method. This broad applicability strengthens the argument for the effectiveness and versatility of the data framing method in improving forecasting accuracy across diverse domains and datasets.

Lower validation loss with the data framing method underscores its ability to capture the time series data's inherent characteristics accurately. By framing the input data and leveraging temporal dependencies, the process enhances the models' capacity to extract essential patterns and capture material relationships more effectively. This improvement in forecasting accuracy has significant implications for decision-making in various domains where accurate predictions are crucial. When evaluating the test set after 30 epochs, the data framing method consistently exhibits a lower loss function than the sliding window method. This observation highlights the data framing method's superior accuracy and predictive power, as it consistently outperforms the sliding window method in capturing the underlying patterns and dynamics of the time series data.

While the data framing method consistently yielded superior results, it is essential to acknowledge potential limitations and areas for further research. The specific magnitude of improvement may vary depending on the dataset and the complexity of the underlying patterns. Further investigations are warranted to explore the method's behavior in datasets with different characteristics and assess its performance under varying and extreme conditions.

4.2 Practical Implications of the Performance of Data Framing Method

Traditional methods often struggle when data is scarce, and complexities like trends, seasonality, and hidden patterns can throw off forecasts. The data framing method emerges as a competitive solution, specifically addressing these issues and offering advantages that extend far beyond energy forecasting. A core limitation of traditional methods like the sliding window is the assumption of abundant data. With short datasets, these methods struggle to identify underlying patterns. Data framing tackles this by centering the information around the current point of prediction. This allows the model to focus on the most relevant data for the forecast, even with limited observations. Essentially, data framing makes the most of the available data, extracting valuable insights even from smaller datasets.

Real-world time series data is rarely straightforward. It often exhibits trends, seasonal variations, and hidden interdependencies. The sliding window method assumes the underlying data-generating process is stationary, meaning the statistical properties (like mean and variance) remain constant over time. If the data exhibits trends or seasonality, the model trained on a specific window might not generalize well to future data points with different characteristics. Data framing addresses this complexity by effectively restructuring the data. By framing the data around the prediction point, the model can not only identify relevant features but also understand how these features change over time. This allows the model to capture the nuances of the data, leading to forecasts that are more accurate and reliable.

The benefits of data framing extend beyond just improved accuracy. This means the model learns the underlying patterns quicker, reducing training time and computational resources. Additionally, data framing leads to lower convergence loss and reduced fluctuations in validation loss. This translates to models that are more stable and less prone to overfitting. The effectiveness of data framing across diverse datasets further cements its value as a generalizable technique. This means the method can be applied effectively to various domains beyond its initial use case in energy forecasting.

The ability of data framing to improve forecasting accuracy and provide more reliable predictions translates to significant advantages in numerous domains. In finance, for example, accurate predictions of stock prices or market trends can inform better investment decisions. Similarly, in weather forecasting, reliable predictions of upcoming weather patterns can prepare communities and businesses for potential disruptions. In conclusion, the data framing method offers a significant leap forward in time series forecasting. By addressing the challenges of limited data and complexity, it unlocks the potential for more accurate and reliable predictions. The generalizability of the method makes it a valuable tool across various domains, empowering decision-makers with the information they need to make informed choices and navigate an increasingly complex world.

5 Conclusion

The results of this study provide strong evidence supporting the superiority of the data framing method over the sliding window method in terms of convergence behavior, validation loss fluctuation, and overall forecasting accuracy. The process consistently outperforms across diverse datasets, demonstrating its effectiveness and generalizability. It exhibits faster convergence, lower convergence loss, and reduced fluctuation in validation loss, indicating its efficiency in capturing underlying patterns and dynamics within time series data. The data framing method improves forecasting accuracy and more reliable predictions by extracting relevant features and leveraging temporal dependencies. Its broad applicability in various domains further reinforces its value as a powerful tool for enhancing artificial neural network-based forecasting models. These findings hold significant implications for decision-making in finance, economics, weather forecasting, and supply chain management, where accurate and reliable predictions are crucial for informed choices.

5.1 Challenges and Opportunities for Future Exploration for Data Framing Method

While the data framing method offers significant advantages in time series forecasting, it's crucial to acknowledge its limitations. The data framing method thrives on identifying patterns and trends within the data. However, it may struggle with irregular or non-linear time series data, where these patterns are weak or absent. Additionally, high noise levels or outliers in the data can disrupt the framing process and make it challenging to capture the underlying relationships accurately. This can lead to less reliable predictions, especially for highly volatile time series. In terms of a very limited dataset, if the time window is very short, or historical records are limited, the method might not have enough information to extract meaningful features. This can result in less accurate predictions, as the model lacks the necessary context to understand the underlying dynamics. Another limitation lies in the method's ability to handle complex and dynamic relationships within the data. If the time series exhibits intricate dependencies that evolve, the static framing approach might not be able to capture these nuances effectively.

Despite its demonstrated success, the data framing method is still under development. Further research is necessary to assess its behavior across a wider range of datasets with varying characteristics and under diverse conditions. This will help us understand the method's limitations for specific data types and identify potential areas for improvement. The data framing method holds immense promise for time series forecasting. However, its effectiveness can vary depending on the characteristics of the data and the specific forecasting context. The first step lies in a thorough analysis of the dataset. This includes identifying the presence of irregularities, noise levels, and outliers. Datasets with high noise or irregular patterns might require additional preprocessing before applying data framing. Understanding the data's characteristics allows us to tailor the approach for optimal results. A one-size-fits-all approach might not always be ideal. The data framing method can be adapted to better capture specific patterns and dynamics within a dataset. This can involve incorporating additional feature engineering techniques or modifying the framing window size. For instance, for highly seasonal data, a framing window that captures the entire seasonal cycle might be beneficial. Adapting the method allows it to leverage the unique characteristics of each dataset and improve forecast accuracy.

Extensive experimentation and validation are crucial for ensuring the robustness of data framing across different datasets and scenarios. Testing the method on datasets with diverse characteristics helps identify its strengths and weaknesses in various contexts. This allows for further refinement and development of the method to handle a broader range of forecasting tasks. Comparing the data framing method's performance with other existing forecasting methods provides valuable insights. By understanding its strengths and limitations relative to established techniques, we can make informed decisions about its suitability for specific forecasting problems. Additionally, investigating the interpretability of the data framing method can offer valuable insights into the underlying patterns and relationships within the time series data. This can enhance our understanding of the model's predictions and build trust in its results.

The potential applications of data framing extend far beyond the domains mentioned initially. Exploring its use in other forecasting contexts, such as healthcare, energy, and transportation, can further evaluate its practical applicability. For instance, data framing could be used to forecast patient health trends or predict energy demand patterns. This exploration will broaden the scope of the method and unlock its potential for diverse forecasting applications. By employing these strategies, we can overcome challenges associated with data framing and maximize its effectiveness across various forecasting tasks. Ongoing research and exploration of its potential applications in new domains will solidify data framing as a powerful and versatile tool for accurate and reliable time series forecasting.

References

1. Abad, L., Sarabia, S., Yuzon, J., Pacis, M.: A short-term load forecasting algorithm using support vector regression & artificial neural network method (SVR-ANN). In: 2020 11th IEEE Control And System Graduate Research Colloquium (ICSGRC), pp. 138–143 (2020)
2. Dietrich, B., Walther, J., Weigold, M., Abele, E.: Machine learning based very short term load forecasting of machine tools. Appl. Energy **276**, 115440 (2020)
3. Shen, Y., Ma, Y., Deng, S., Huang, C., Kuo, P.: An ensemble model based on deep learning and data preprocessing for short-term electrical load forecasting. Sustainability **13**, 1694 (2021)

4. Rafati, A., Joorabian, M., Mashhour, E.: An efficient hour-ahead electrical load forecasting method based on innovative features. Energy **201**, 117511 (2020)
5. Lopez-Martin, M., Sanchez-Esguevillas, A., Hernandez-Callejo, L., Arribas, J., Carro, B.: Additive ensemble neural network with constrained weighted quantile loss for probabilistic electric-load forecasting. Sensors. **21**, 2979 (2021)
6. Tan, Z., Zhang, J., He, Y., Zhang, Y., Xiong, G., Liu, Y.: Short-term load forecasting based on integration of SVR and stacking. IEEE Access **8**, 227719–227728 (2020)
7. Zhang, Z., Hong, W., Li, J.: Electric load forecasting by hybrid self-recurrent support vector regression model with variational mode decomposition and improved cuckoo search algorithm. IEEE Access **8**, 14642–14658 (2020)
8. Fan, D., Sun, H., Yao, J., Zhang, K., Yan, X., Sun, Z.: Well production forecasting based on ARIMA-LSTM model considering manual operations. Energy **220**, 119708 (2021)
9. Niu, D., Wanq, Q., Li, J.: Short term load forecasting model using support vector machine based on artificial neural network. In: 2005 International Conference On Machine Learning And Cybernetics, vol. 7, pp. 4260–4265 (2005)
10. Mohamed, Z.E.: Using the artificial neural networks for prediction and validating solar radiation. J. Egypt. Math. Soc. **27**(1), 1–13 (2019). https://doi.org/10.1186/s42787-019-0043-8
11. Khan, M., Muhammad, N., El-Shafie, A.: Wavelet based hybrid ANN-ARIMA models for meteorological drought forecasting. J. Hydrol. **590**, 125380 (2020)
12. Singh, S., Mohapatra, A., et al.: Repeated wavelet transform based ARIMA model for very short-term wind speed forecasting. Renewable Energy **136**, 758–768 (2019)
13. Mohan, N., Soman, K., Kumar, S.: A data-driven strategy for short-term electric load forecasting using dynamic mode decomposition model. Appl. Energy **232**, 229–244 (2018)
14. Rendon-Sanchez, J., Menezes, L.: Structural combination of seasonal exponential smoothing forecasts applied to load forecasting. Eur. J. Oper. Res. **275**, 916–924 (2019)
15. Yonar, H., Yonar, A., Tekindal, M., Tekindal, M.: Modeling and forecasting for the number of cases of the COVID-19 pandemic with the curve estimation models, the Box-Jenkins and exponential smoothing methods. EJMO. **4**, 160–165 (2020)
16. Jiang, W., Wu, X., Gong, Y., Yu, W., Zhong, X.: Holt-Winters smoothing enhanced by fruit fly optimization algorithm to forecast monthly electricity consumption. Energy **193**, 116779 (2020)
17. Fatima, S., Ali, S., Zia, S., Hussain, E., Fraz, T., Khan, M.: Forecasting carbon dioxide emission of Asian countries using ARIMA and simple exponential smoothing models. Int. J. Econ. Environ. Geol. **10**, 64–69 (2019)
18. Dudek, G., Pełka, P., Smyl, S.: A hybrid residual dilated LSTM and exponential smoothing model for midterm electric load forecasting. IEEE Trans. Neural Netw. Learn. Syst. **33**, 2879–2891 (2021)
19. Khan, R., Dewangan, C., Srivastava, S., Chakrabarti, S.: Short term load forecasting using SVM models. In: 2018 IEEE 8th Power India International Conference (PIICON), pp. 1–5 (2018)
20. Moradzadeh, A., Zakeri, S., Shoaran, M., Mohammadi-Ivatloo, B., Mohammadi, F.: Short-term load forecasting of microgrid via hybrid support vector regression and long short-term memory algorithms. Sustainability **12**, 7076 (2020)
21. Tan, Z., Zhang, J., He, Y., Zhang, Y., Xiong, G., Liu, Y.: Short-term load forecasting based on integration of SVR and stacking. IEEE Access **8**, 227719–227728 (2020)

22. Zhang, Z., Hong, W., Li, J.: Electric load forecasting by hybrid self-recurrent support vector regression model with variational mode decomposition and improved cuckoo search algorithm. IEEE Access **8**, 14642–14658 (2020)
23. Al Amin, M., Hoque, M.: Comparison of ARIMA and SVM for short-term load forecasting. In: 2019 9th Annual Information Technology, Electromechanical Engineering And Microelectronics Conference (IEMECON), pp. 1–6 (2019)
24. Maldonado, S., Gonzalez, A., Crone, S.: Automatic time series analysis for electric load forecasting via support vector regression. Appl. Soft Comput. **83**, 105616 (2019)
25. Jacob, M., Neves, C., Vukadinović Greetham, D., Jacob, M., Neves, C., Vukadinović Greetham, D.: Short term load forecasting. Forecasting And Assessing Risk Of Individual Electricity Peaks, pp. 15–37 (2020)
26. Hadri, S., Naitmalek, Y., Najib, M., Bakhouya, M., Fakhri, Y., Elaroussi, M.: A comparative study of predictive approaches for load forecasting in smart buildings. Procedia Comput. Sci. **160**, 173–180 (2019)
27. Lim, B., Zohren, S.: Time-series forecasting with deep learning: a survey. Philos. Trans. R. Soc. A **379**, 20200209 (2021)
28. Fallah, S., Deo, R., Shojafar, M., Conti, M., Shamshirband, S.: Computational intelligence approaches for energy load forecasting in smart energy management grids: state of the art, future challenges, and research directions. Energies **11**, 596 (2018)
29. Hong, T., Pinson, P., Wang, Y., Weron, R., Yang, D., Zareipour, H.: Energy forecasting: a review and outlook. IEEE Open Access J. Power Energy **7**, 376–388 (2020)
30. Pirbazari, A., Chakravorty, A., Rong, C.: Evaluating feature selection methods for short-term load forecasting. In: 2019 IEEE International Conference On Big Data And Smart Computing (BigComp), pp. 1–8 (2019)

An Internet of Drone Things-Enabled Inspection Ecosystem for Smart Cities and Society

Amartya Mukhrjee[1,2,3,4(✉)], Souvik Chatterjee[5], Debashis De[4], and Nilanjan Dey[6]

[1] Department of CSE (AIML), Institute of Engineering and Management, Salt Lake Kolkata, India
mamartyacse1@gmail.com
[2] University of Engineering and Management, Kolkata, India
[3] C2IoT, IEM, Kolkata, India
[4] Department of Computer Science and Engineering, Maulana Abul Kalam Azad University of Technology, Haringhata, Kalyani, India
[5] IEMA Research and Development Private Limited, Kolkata, India
souvik.chatterjee@iemlabs.com
[6] Department of Computer Science and Engineering,
Techno International New Town, New Town, Kolkata, India
nilanjan.dey@tint.edu.in

Abstract. UAV-assisted surveillance is currently gaining tremendous popularity. In standard scenarios, the implementation of real-time detection of objects through UAV-based real-time video data is quite challenging due to the large computing resource requirement. The proposed work addresses this issue and uses an Internet of Drone Things framework with a lightweight edge-dew-fog combination of computing philosophies. In the proposed framework, we presented an edge-assisted UAV-based video data collection and lightweight detection system on a fog-dew-enabled real-life test bed. The video data were captured by the Parrot Anafi UAV node and sent to the base station via an RTSP link with a gstreamer codec via the h264 encoding method. The location data for the drone were transferred through the MQTT protocol with a QoS of 2. At the base station, we implemented a CNN-based single-shot detection framework. The results show nearly 1590 ms of latency for MQTT-QoS2 and a maximum throughput benchmark of 1400 kbps for RTSP streaming. A total of 98.05% accuracy is reported for the single-shot detection approach with 66% CPU and 16% memory utilization.

Keywords: activity monitoring · IoDT · MQTT · MobilenetSSD · RTSP

1 Introduction

Unmanned aerial vehicle (UAV)-based crowed sensing and monitoring applications are in high demand [1]. The increasing amount of mobile network bandwidth and hand user equipment (UE) also increase the chance of mobile identification and crowed sensing. The concept of the Internet of Drone Things (IoDT) provides a new dimension in the field of data communication, sensing and analytics [2]. In the case of a smart city scenario in which traffic is managed, crowd sensing can also be performed with a set of UAVs in the Flying Ad hoc Network mode. In this case, a set of UAVs can sense the ambient parameters by means of images and videos. The feeds are further processed onboard with an edge-enabled computing platform on the UAV node itself [3]. The smart industry concept can also be considered a vital part of a smart society. In Industry 4.0, infrastructure inspection and asset monitoring are highly important. To do that, numerous IoDT-based flying Ad-Hoc network architectures can be proposed that can perform sensing and processing on board and generate real-time decisions [4]. Disaster management is another major field in which drone-based monitoring is receiving great interest. In a disaster-like scenario, the objects under debris, such as humans, precious items, and cars where humans can stick, must be detected immediately, and early warning is required [5]. To achieve this goal, a strong AI-assisted system is urgently needed. The motivation of the work encompasses an edge-enabled lightweight IoDT framework for activity monitoring and detection. The framework should leverage the cutting-edge lightweight low-latency CNN-based detection mechanism to produce precise decision making.

The rest of the article is organized as follows. Section 2 presents related research, Sect. 3 describes the methodology, Sect. 4 shows the results analysis, and we conclude the work in Sect. 5.

2 Related Research

There are numerous studies carried out in the field of the Internet of Drone Things application. Islam et al. [6] presented an implementation of blockchain-enabled IoDT services. Zahi et al. [7] proposed a YOLO-8-based object detection model for more optimized object detection using UAV systems with improved accuracy. Hendria et al. [8] proposed a combination of ensemble transformers and an object detection model for object identification and detection with a better level of accuracy. Additionally, various studies have been carried out in the domain of UAV networks and UAV node navigation, which have greatly impacted object identification. Sharma et al. [9] proposed various methodologies for IoT-based secure communication for UAV-assisted IoT networks. Various attack features have been described with potential solutions to achieve secure communication among UAVs and base stations. In another article, He et al. [10] proposed a UAV-based road crack detection methodology using the MUENet model. The claim that the object detection methodology is more adaptable to crack objects than other mainstream objects. In the field of the Internet of Drones (IoD), Bine et al. [11] described the partnership of an IoD network with a terrestrial network to increase the possibility of high-altitude communication and Internet connectivity. Cheng et al. [12] presented a unique concept of ship monitoring using drone networks. In this scenario, the YOLO v5-ODConvNeXt network has been introduced for significantly high-performance object detection. A self-generated ship detection dataset with 3200 images was used to train the model. In another work, Jemmali et al. [13] proposed an intelligent scheduling algorithm for forest fire detection.

The main objective in this case was to complete the fire extinguisher operation with an optimal time span. A total of 990 classes are considered to compute the performance measurement in this case. Goodall et al. [14] illustrated ANN-based multitarget tracking systems using drone surveillance radar technology. Alam et al. [15] proposed an RF-enabled and deep learning baked drone detection and identification framework. The RFR has been considered a crucial parameter in this case for identifying drones in comparison to image-based mechanisms, which results in a lighter application framework for UAV detection. UAV-assisted live streaming on a web-based interface was demonstrated by Shengde et al. [16]. They used a Raspberry Pi base USB camera setup with ROS-based streaming methodology. Surveillance was performed with a 640 × 480 resolution video frame in manual mode. An YOLOv7 based drone captured image detection methodology has been implemented by Zhao et al. [17]. A non-straid convolution module has been incorporated with the existing model architecture to improve the small object detection capability. Xi et al. [18] proposes an enhanced drone view object detection model with fine grain parameter predictor called DEDet. Proposed model illustrates a significant improvement in accuracy in compare to traditional model. A GM-YOLO based object detection has been proposed by Yuan et al. [19]. Detector has been enhanced with coordinate attention and weighted bidirectional feature pyramid network. A significant performance enhancement has been observed in this case with the proposed system.

3 Proposed Methodology

The main objective of the proposed system in this specific scenario is to monitor traffic activities and crowd sensing. Figure 1 illustrates the layered architecture of the proposed system. The bottom layer is the sensing layer, which comprises the UAV nodes. In this case, UAV nodes have an onboard camera and an edge device for data processing. Layer 2 comprises the network infrastructure through which the data transfer occurs from the edge layer to the base station or cloud layer. There are two different types of protocols we may consider in this case, namely, the message queuing telemetry transport MQTT protocol, which transfers image frame or video location information, and the real-time streaming protocol (RTSP), which performs real-time video feed transfer at a fixed frame rate. The network backhaul plays a pivotal role in ensuring an efficient level of information transfer. The edge layer in this case controls the MQTT pub-sub operation, and the broker is also deployed on the edge layer [20]. On the other hand, the RTSP streaming server is also deployed on one of the edge computing nodes within the onboard UAV. The edge layer is also capable of running lightweight machine learning models. The final layer here is the cloud layer or the base station where the processing and the decision making have been performed. In the testbed, we have implemented a localized base station that is able to run a private infrastructure as a service (IaaS).

In a virtualized Linux platform, the deep learning-based MobilenetSSD model has been deployed. We can scale up the cloud layer in various other segments, such as the fog-dew-cloud enabled structure, depending upon the density and resolution of the image frames. Algorithm 1 presents the complete operation sequence of image capture, MQTT and RTSP message transfer.

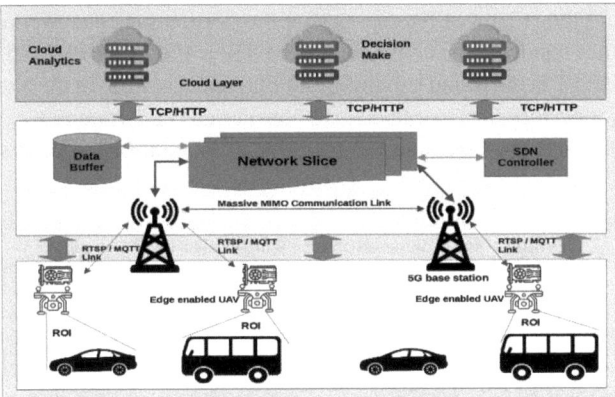

Fig. 1. Proposed system architecture of the IoDT-enabled inspection ecosystem

---

Algorithm 1 (Data collection and processing)
U_n ← UAV node, ROI ← Region of Interest,
RTSP ← 0, MQTT ← initialize broker

Start

1. Set the ROI for the captured image

2. Capture and buffer within the U_n

3. While (dist(U_n, U_{n+1})<10)

4. activate (RTSP← 1) && MQTT (PUB)

5. Send location to broker (Edge) && video frame to cloud

6. Perform detection at cloud && MQTT (SUB)

7. Enable SSD model and store location data

Stop

---

4 Result Analysis

The analysis of the results of the proposed approach continues with 3 major analytical methods. First, the performance of the MQTT message transfer mechanism is evaluated. Second, the performance of the RTSP is compared to that of the traditional HTTP and UDP protocols, and finally, the performance of the MobilenetSSD model is evaluated.

4.1 Performance Metric

In the proposed work, the major performance metric we identified is the average latency of the MQTT protocol, which is considered the time deviation between message creation at the source and the receipt of the message at the destination. The average throughput (TR), on the other hand, can be considered to be TR = PS/RTT*(PL)^0.5. Where PS is the packet size, RTT is the round trip time, and PL is packet loss. In the case of the CNN model, the major performance parameter we considered is the accuracy of the detection. We can also consider the CPU and the memory utilization of the base station device (Table 1).

Table 1. Parameter setup and test bed for the proposed ecosystem

Parameter	Values
MQTT QoS levels	0,1,2
MQTT Broker	Eclipse Mosquitto (on prem)
Streaming protocols	RTSP, UDP, HTTP
Codec	gstreamer
Encoding	*h.264*
Streaming resolution	244p, 360p, 480p

4.2 MQTT and RTSP Performance Analysis

Figure 2 depicts the latency performance of the MQTT at 3 different QoS levels. It has been observed in this scenario that the latency benchmark for QoS 2 is higher than that for QoS 1 and 0. This clearly signifies that the number of acknowledgements and requests may cause a higher level of latency in the network. Although the QoS 2 shows a greater latency, in the case of message delivery performance, the QoS 2 outperforms the others.

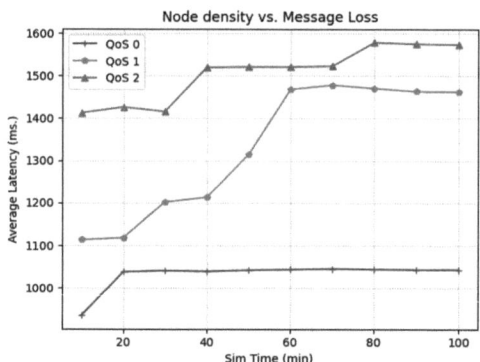

Fig. 2. Performance of the MQTT protocol at various QoS levels

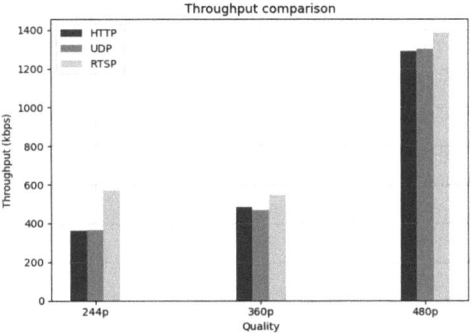

Fig. 3. RTSP throughput performance computation with respect to HTTP and UDP

The performance of the RTSP protocol with various streaming resolutions is illustrated in Fig. 3. We also compared the 244p, 360p and 480p resolution data with the h264 encoding data provided by the gstreamer-based RTSP pipeline. The figure shows that the RTSP outperforms HTTP and UDP. In general, HTTP does not support continuous transmission of data streams, whereas RTSP is used for continuous transmission. However, the UDP is unreliable and has greater latency than the RTSP. As the gstreamer codec is used in RTSP, we can perform very low-latency communication.

4.3 CNN Model Accuracy Performance

The main objective of Mobilenet-SSD is to improve the performance of CNNs under real-time conditions with limited hardware. This single-shot detection results in a very low latency in object detection with an optimal accuracy [21]. This network can reduce the number of parameters without compromising the accuracy performance.

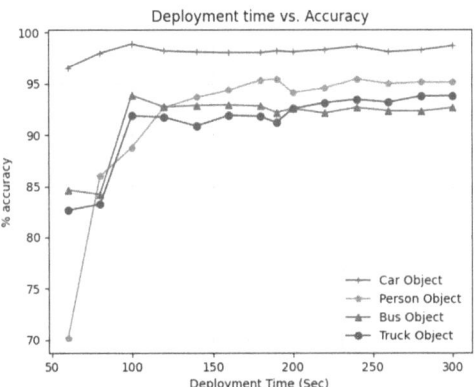

Fig. 4. Accuracy of Mobilenet-SSD

The system uses a trained CNN, and Fig. 4 shows the accuracy of detecting various objects, such as cars, people, buses, and trucks. The detection of a car object in this case reaches a maximum benchmark of 0.98. In the normal case, the learning rate obtained for MobileNet-SSD is 0.003, and after training, we can obtain 10,000 iterations with 128 batches. The training was performed with 1.92 million parameters and a mean loss function of 0.09. From the detection accuracy results, it is clear that the performance of Mobilnet-SSD is optimal for single-shot detection. Figure 5 illustrates the real-life test-bed with the parrot Anafi AI UAV to detect the objects. In the next section, we also demonstrate the resource utilization of the base station.

Fig. 5. (a) Real-time testbed implementation of the proposed ecosystem. (b) Parrot Anafi AI UAV platform onboard to capture ambient data

Memory and CPU core performance are other major performance metrics that need to be considered. In the proposed test bed scenario, we acquired the data through edge-enabled devices, whereas the detection operation was performed at the base station, which can be considered a fog-dew infrastructure that can run independently without internet connectivity. Figure 6.

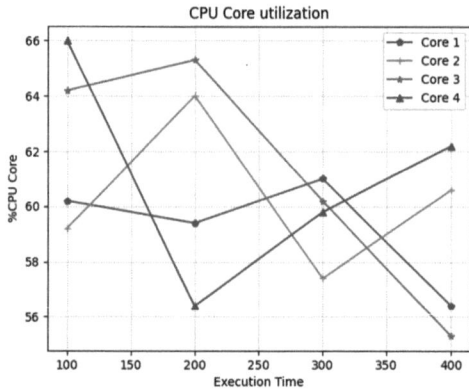

Fig. 6. CPU core utilization by the model within the base station during object identification

The CPU core utilization and performance analysis results are presented in Fig. 6. The figure shows that the core utilization is not uniform, and the maximum benchmark of the CPU core utilization is 66% in 100 time units. As the time increases, the CPU utilization decreases to 52%. Memory utilization, on the other hand, is shown in Fig. 7, which shows that approximately 16% of the system memory is utilized by the model during execution.

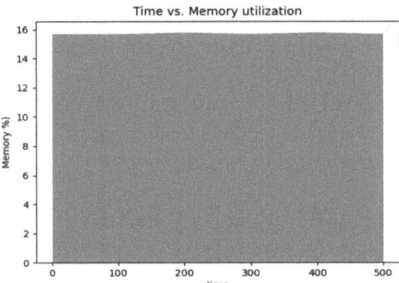

Fig. 7. Memory utilization by the model within the base station during object identification

5 Conclusions

In the proposed work, we have demonstrated an IoDT framework that uses a lightweight RTSP-based live streaming operation from a UAV network where a single UAV can be considered a capturing node, and then the data are routed through the RTSP server to the base station. Additionally, the MQTT packet transfer occurs to transfer the location information of the UAV nodes towards the base station. The base station in this case is a physical fog-dew enabled system that has limited memory and processing resources with limited computational power.

These types of devices can also run with batteries or solar power in remote locations. The Mobilenet-SSD detection model is deployed to the base station node, which can run on a resource-constrained platform. The performance shows up to 1590 ms of latency in MQTT QoS 2 in the case of packet transfer and at most 1400 kbps of throughput for RTSP data transfer. In the case of Mobilenet-SSD, the detection accuracy has been reported to be 98.05% for car objects, which seems to be an optimum result in a resource-constrained model. We can even enhance the framework in the near future to introduce onboard and exact real-time detection by leveraging edge-enabled ecosystems for surveillance applications in various domains, such as smart cities, smart industry arms, and airforces.

References

1. Mohannad, A., et al.: A survey of indoor and outdoor uav-based target tracking systems: current status, challenges, technologies, and future directions. IEEE Access (2023)
2. Mukherjee, A., De, D., Dey, N., González Crespo, R., Herrera-Viedma, E.: DisastDrone: a disaster aware consumer internet of drone things system in ultra-low latent 6G network. IEEE Trans. Consumer Electron. **69**(1), 38–48 (2023). https://doi.org/10.1109/TCE.2022.3214568

3. Behera, T.K., Bakshi, S., Nappi, M., Kumar Sa, P.: Superpixel-based multiscale CNN approach toward multiclass object segmentation from UAV-captured aerial images. IEEE J. Sel. Top. Appl. Earth Observations Remote Sens. **16**, 1771–1784 (2023). https://doi.org/10.1109/JSTARS.2023.3239119
4. Karam, S.N., Bilal, K., Shuja, J., Rehman, F., Yasmin, T., Jamil, A.: (Retracted) Inspection of unmanned aerial vehicles in oil and gas industry: critical analysis of platforms, sensors, networking architecture, and path planning. J. Electron. Imag. (2022). https://doi.org/10.1117/1.JEI.32.1.011006
5. Ahmad, H.R., Ahmed, R., Ahmed, W., Kai, Y., Jun, W.: A UAV-assisted edge framework for real-time disaster management. IEEE Trans. Geosci. Remote Sens. **61**, 1–13 (2023). https://doi.org/10.1109/TGRS.2023.3306151
6. Islam, A., Tariq Rahim, M.D.M., Young Shin, S.O.O.: A blockchain-based artificial intelligence-empowered contagious pandemic situation supervision scheme using internet of drone things. IEEE Wireless Commun. **28**(4), 166–173 (2021). https://doi.org/10.1109/MWC.001.2000429
7. Zhai, X., Huang, Z., Li, T., Liu, H., Wang, S.: YOLO-drone: an optimized YOLOv8 network for tiny UAV object detection. Electronics **12**(17), 3664 (2023)
8. Hendria, W.F., Phan, Q.T., Adzaka, F., Jeong, C.: Combining transformer and CNN for object detection in UAV imagery. ICT Express **9**(2), 258–263 (2023). https://doi.org/10.1016/j.icte.2021.12.006
9. Sharma, J., Mehra, P.S.: Secure communication in IOT-based UAV networks: a systematic survey. Internet Things **23**, 100883 (2023). https://doi.org/10.1016/j.iot.2023.100883
10. He, X., Tang, Z., Deng, Y., Zhou, G., Wang, Y., Li, L.: UAV-based road crack object-detection algorithm. Autom. Constr. **154**, 105014 (2023)
11. Bine, L.M.S., Boukerche, A., Ruiz, L.B., Loureiro, A.A.F.: Internet of drones and terrestrial networks: a successful partnership. IEEE Internet Things Mag. **6**(4), 104–110 (2023). https://doi.org/10.1109/IOTM.001.2200265
12. Cheng, S., Zhu, Y., Shaohua, W.: Deep learning based efficient ship detection from drone-captured images for maritime surveillance. Ocean Eng. **285**, 115440 (2023)
13. Jemmali, M., Kayed, B.M.L., Boulila, W., Amdouni, H., Alharbi, M.T.: Optimizing forest fire prevention: intelligent scheduling algorithms for drone-based surveillance system. Procedia Comput. Sci. **225**, 1562–1571 (2023). https://doi.org/10.1016/j.procs.2023.10.145
14. Finn, G., Ahmad, B.I.: Adaptation of multitarget tracker using neural networks in drone surveillance radar. In: 2023 IEEE Radar Conference (RadarConf23), pp. 1-6. IEEE (2023)
15. Alam, S.S., et al.: RF-enabled deep-learning-assisted drone detection and identification: an end-to-end approach. Sensors **23**(9), 4202 (2023). https://doi.org/10.3390/s23094202
16. Shendge, A., Singh, R., Ansari, K.I.B.H., Pakhrani, K.: Development of an unmanned aerial vehicle for remote live streaming on web dashboard. Mater. Today Proc. **77**, 848–854 (2023). https://doi.org/10.1016/j.matpr.2022.11.492
17. Zhao, D., Shao, F., Liu, Q., Yang, L., Zhang, H., Zhang, Z.: A small object detection method for drone-captured images based on improved YOLOv7. Remote Sens. **16**(6), 1002 (2024)
18. Xi, Y., Jia, W., Miao, Q., Feng, J., Ren, J., Luo, H.: Detection-driven exposure-correction network for nighttime drone-view object detection. IEEE Trans. Geosci. Remote Sens. **62**, 1–14 (2024). https://doi.org/10.1109/TGRS.2024.3351134
19. Yuan, Y., Wu, Y., Zhao, L., Chen, H., Zhang, Y.: Multiple object detection and tracking from drone videos based on GM-YOLO and multi-tracker. Image Vis. Comput. **143**, 104951 (2024). https://doi.org/10.1016/j.imavis.2024.104951

20. Mukherjee, A., Dey, N., De, D.: EdgeDrone: QoS aware MQTT middleware for mobile edge computing in opportunistic internet of drone things. Comput. Commun. **152**, 93–108 (2020)
21. Ayesha, Y., Shixin, L., Jn, S., Hai, Z.: Real-time object detection using pretrained deep learning models MobileNet-SSD. In: Proceedings of 2020 the 6th international conference on computing and data engineering, pp. 44–48 (2020)

Enhancing Wireless Sensor Network Security Against Wormhole Attacks with Twofish Encryption

Pramod Singh Rathore[1](✉) and Mrinal Kanti Sarkar[2]

[1] Manipal University Jaipur, University of Engineering and Management, Jaipur, India
pramodrathore88@gmail.com
[2] Sri Ramkrishna Sarada Vidya Mahapitha, Kamarpukur, West Bengal, India
mks@srsvidyamahapitha.org

Abstract. The Twofish Secure Routing Protocol (TSRP) makes wireless sensor networks (WSNs) safe from wormhole attacks by using the Twofish encryption method. This setup uses a special type of encryption to protect data as it moves across networks. TSRP adjusts how data is routed for better security and uses a smart system to manage encryption keys. It starts with spreading encryption keys throughout the network, finds secure paths for data using encrypted messages, and keeps a close watch on the routes to prevent attacks. TSRP is proven to be better because it uses less energy, delivers more data successfully, moves data faster, and reduces waiting time. This shows Twofish is a strong tool for keeping sensor networks safe and working well.

Keywords: AODV · clustering · MANETs · routing · WSN · Twofish · wormhole

1 Introduction

Wireless Sensor Networks (WSNs) play a pivotal role in numerous applications, from healthcare and agriculture to everyday activities, due to their distributed nature and data collection capabilities. WSNs consist of small sensor nodes with limited resources such as processing power, memory, and battery life. They wirelessly transmit collected data to a base station. However, these networks face various security threats, particularly wormhole attacks, which can disrupt operations and compromise data confidentiality and integrity.

In a wormhole attack, an attacker creates a high-speed link (the wormhole) to relay captured packets from one location in the network to another, then replays them, creating the illusion of a direct transmission. The subtlety and low resource requirement of this attack make it especially challenging to detect and prevent [1].

To counteract such threats, literature offers various security solutions, including cryptographic measures ensuring secure node-to-node communication. Among them is the TwoFish algorithm, a symmetric encryption technique acclaimed for its efficiency and robust security. TwoFish operates on 128-bit blocks and supports key sizes of up to 256 bits, utilizing a combination of substitution-permutation networks (SPN) and Feistel network structures to thwart cryptographic attacks like differential and linear cryptanalysis.

The defense against wormhole attacks using TwoFish involves hop-by-hop encryption, where each node encrypts packets before transmitting them to the next hop, thus safeguarding the data from being deciphered by attackers. The implementation of TwoFish in WSNs entails a two-phase process: key management for establishing unique symmetric keys between adjacent nodes, and packet encryption using these keys [2].

In this way, the TwoFish algorithm provides an effective shield for WSNs against wormhole attacks, ensuring the integrity and confidentiality of the transmitted data through encrypted communication channels. The approach adopted here addresses the vulnerabilities of WSNs to these attacks, contributing to the overall security and resilience of these critical networks.

2 Related Work

A series of investigations over the years have explored methods to safeguard ad hoc networks from wormhole attacks, each with its own set of advantages and constraints. In 2006, research focused on cryptographic methods to form a defense against these attacks, demonstrating scalability but also revealing significant operational costs and the intricate management of cryptographic keys required. By 2013, another study presented an intelligent agent-based strategy for detecting wormhole attacks in wireless sensor networks. This approach was notable for its robustness and scalability, albeit at the cost of increased computational complexity.

Lee and Choi's [3] study proposed a novel approach for enhancing the security of Wireless Sensor Networks (WSNs) by optimizing the use of antennas and energy consumption. The strategy involved creating multiple access channels to ensure private communications among sensors and the central data hub, leveraging encryption combined with Channel State Information (CSI). They addressed the issue of uniform CSI among sensors, which could potentially diminish network lifetime and efficiency due to frequent encryption reporting, by adopting a randomized reporting pattern. Further investigation into the role of antenna dynamics demonstrated an improvement in network longevity. Their empirical analysis established that this method could lead to better energy management without compromising on reliability or safety.

Luo and colleagues [4] developed a novel technique to counteract wormhole attacks in WSNs, leveraging the concept of path diversity and continuous surveillance. This method is capable of identifying the majority of both external and internal wormhole threats without the necessity for additional hardware. They introduced a 'neighbor ratio threshold' concept that optimizes energy usage and enhances the accuracy of wormhole detection. Their method, labeled CREDND, outperformed other wormhole detection mechanisms in simulation tests, particularly in environments with irregular node distribution and variable transmission ranges. However, the CREDND's effectiveness in networks with non-uniform node dispersion is limited, and further studies are aimed at improving evasion detection.

Further innovation was introduced through a study that leveraged blockchain technology to counter wormhole attacks, offering a decentralized solution that effectively mitigates such threats. Despite its effectiveness, the approach was critiqued for its computational demands and limited scalability. In 2018, Muhammad Noman Riaz and colleagues introduced machine learning techniques to detect wormhole attacks, achieving high precision and adaptability to new threats, though facing challenges in training complexity and generalization capabilities.

Haseeb and associates [5] put forward a threefold strategy aimed at enhancing security in WSNs. This approach includes (1) analyzing data links quantitatively to minimize potential threats, (2) a secure information relay component ensuring safe data transmission from Cluster Heads (CHs) to the sink, and (3) dividing the management area of the network based on sensor locations into internal and external zones. They propose the 'ESMR protocol,' a secure, multi-hop routing framework that also emphasizes energy efficiency. ESMR incorporates encryption techniques to protect against the interception of data, which has demonstrated an increase in network efficiency and defense capabilities. Comparative analyses and simulations have shown that ESMR offers significant improvements in network performance metrics. Nonetheless, the study recognizes the limitation that it primarily considers static nodes, with dynamic nodes in varying operational environments not being adequately addressed.

Das et al. [6] introduced a sophisticated trust management framework utilizing fuzzy logic that assesses trust levels based on accumulated experiences and neighborly interactions. This system features the designation of a lead node responsible for efficient energy utilization and reporting to the control center. The method is distinctive, especially in its node selection process, which is integral to its security protocol. The Hierarchical Trust Management System (HTMS) incorporated into the framework activates upon the identification of potential security breaches, employing diversified cryptographic keys to enhance network protection and maintain a requisite security standard.

Most recently, in 2020, research employing convolutional neural networks (CNNs) showcased remarkable accuracy and noise resilience in detecting wormhole attacks. However, this method also grappled with computational complexity and scalability issues, illustrating the ongoing challenge in finding a balanced solution to this pervasive security threat.

3 Methodology

To compare the proposed algorithm for overcoming wormhole attacks using the TwoFish algorithm with previous works, we can consider some of the key aspects, such as approach, advantages, and disadvantages.

Approach: The suggested programme uses different methods, such as synchronising the time, counting hops, detecting wormholes based on where they are, encrypting packets, and stopping wormholes. In contrast, most of the work done before has been about using cryptography to find and stop wormhole threats.

Advantages: The suggested method is better than others in a number of ways. First, it uses a mix of methods, which makes it more reliable and effective at finding wormhole attacks and stopping them. Second, it takes into account things like the number of hops and location-based tracking, which can help cut down on fake results. Lastly, the proposed method also has ways to stop wormholes from spreading. These techniques can help cut off the part of the network that is affected and stop the wormhole from spreading.

In short, the TwoFish algorithm is suggested as a way to stop wormhole attacks. It has several benefits over other methods, mostly because it uses a combination of different methods. But it could also have some problems, such as making computations harder and making it harder to use.

4 Proposed Work

Key Generation: Use the Twofish method to make a secret key that will be used for encryption and decoding. The key should be sent to all the nodes in the wireless network in a safe way.

Encryption: Use the secret key and the Twofish method to secure the data bits before sending them over the network. This step makes sure that the data being sent is kept secret and safe from possible attackers.

Decryption: When data packets come in, each server in the network should use the shared secret key and the Twofish method to decrypt the packets. This step lets the authorised nodes get the data that the sender sent in the first place.

Wormhole Attack Detection: Set up a way for the network to find wormhole attacks. This can be done by looking at the time or direction information of the files that were sent and received. If strange behaviour is found, it means that a tunnel attack is happening.

When a wormhole attack is found, the right steps should be taken to lessen its effects. This could mean putting the vulnerable nodes in a separate network, stopping them, telling network managers, or taking other security steps.

Performance Evaluation: Use an actual wireless network model to run a lot of simulations to test how well the suggested defence system works. You can see how well the Twofish method protects against wormhole threats by measuring network speed, delay, packet delivery ratio, and energy use.

This suggested method is a mix of time synchronisation, hop count detection, location-based detection, wormhole detection, packet encryption, and ways to stop wormholes. By using these methods, you can build a wireless sensor network that is safe and can't be broken into through wormholes.

Twofish Secure Routing Protocol (TSRP)
Objective: Enhance the security of WSNs by preventing wormhole attacks through the application of the Twofish encryption algorithm.

Components:

- **Twofish Encryption:** A symmetric key block cipher known for its security and efficiency.
- **Routing Protocol:** Any standard routing protocol for WSNs, adapted to include security features.
- **Key Management System:** Securely distributes and manages encryption keys within the network.

Algorithm Steps:

1. **Initialization:**
   - Deploy nodes and establish the network topology.
   - Initialize the key management system to distribute the symmetric keys securely among the nodes.

2. **Secure Route Discovery:**
   - When a source node needs to send data to a destination, it initiates a secure route discovery process.
   - The route request packets are encrypted using Twofish with the node's symmetric key before being broadcasted.

3. **Route Establishment:**
   - Intermediate nodes decrypt and re-encrypt route request packets using their own symmetric keys as they forward the packets towards the destination.
   - This process ensures that any inserted wormhole links cannot decrypt the packets without the appropriate keys, effectively neutralizing the attack.

4. **Data Transmission:**
   - Once a secure route is established, data packets are encrypted using Twofish with the session's symmetric key.
   - Encrypted data packets are transmitted through the established secure route to the destination.

5. **Route Maintenance:**
   - Periodically check the integrity and security of the established routes.
   - If a wormhole attack or any anomaly is detected, initiate a route error message and start a new route discovery process.

6. **Key Rotation:**
   - Regularly update the symmetric keys through the key management system to prevent key compromise.

Flow diagram for the proposed Algorithm

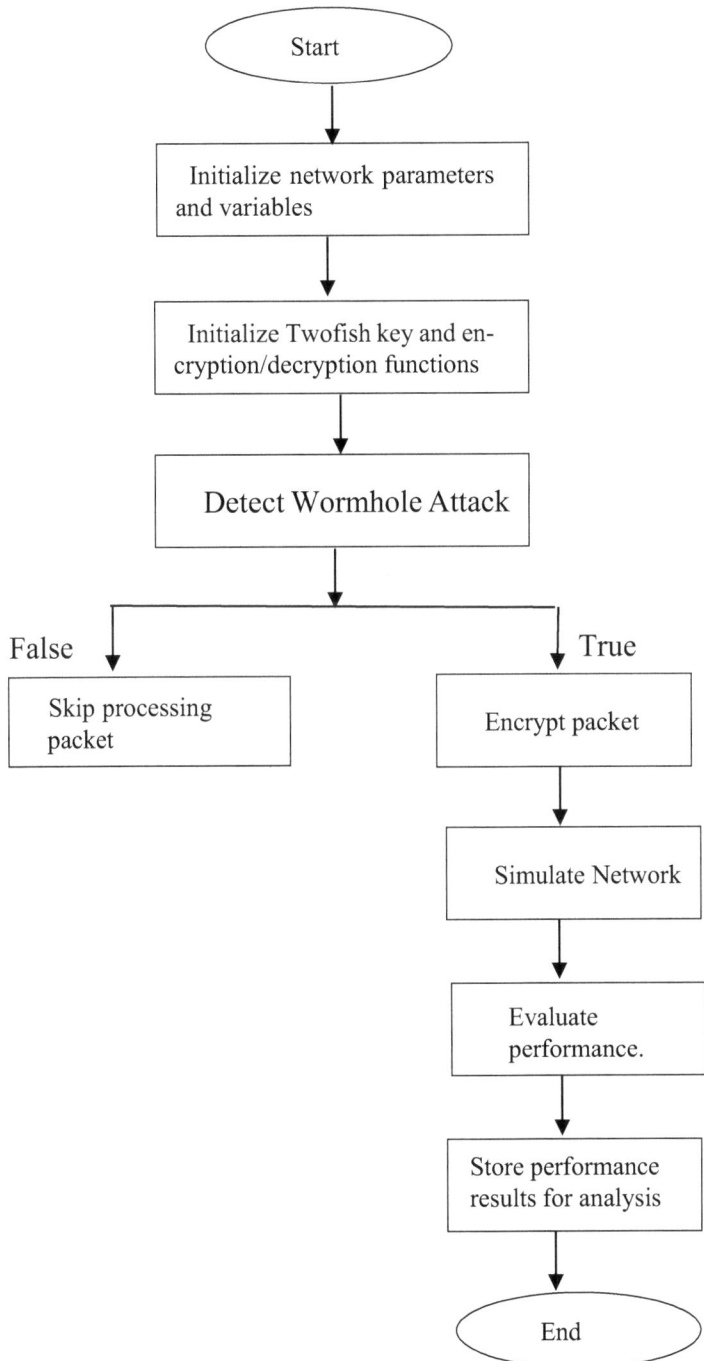

Pseudo Code of the Proposed Algorithm

```
initialize network parameters and variables
initialize Twofish key and encryption/decryption functions
function detectWormholeAttack(packet):
    if packet has suspicious characteristics indicating a wormhole attack:
        return true
    else:
        return false
function encryptPacket(packet):
    encryptedPacket = TwofishEncrypt(packet)
    return encryptedPacket
function decryptPacket(encryptedPacket):
    decryptedPacket = TwofishDecrypt(encryptedPacket)
    return decryptedPacket
function simulateNetwork():
    for each packet in the network:
        if detectWormholeAttack(packet):
            continue  // Skip processing wormhole-affected packet
        else:
            encryptedPacket = encryptPacket(packet)
function evaluatePerformance():
    initialize performance metrics
    for each simulated network run:
        simulateNetwork()
        calculateThroughput()
        calculateLatency()
        calculatePacketDeliveryRatio()
        calculateEnergyConsumption()
    return average performance metrics
performanceResults = evaluatePerformance()
```

5 Result Analysis

To conduct an NS2 simulation for evaluating a Twofish-based defense against wormhole attacks in wireless sensor networks, proceed as follows:

- Configure a sample WSN in NS2 detailing its node composition, locations, and communication pathways.
- Integrate the Twofish algorithm into NS2 through protocol modification or applying a patch. Simulate wormhole attacks by creating a deceptive pathway linking nodes, thereby redirecting data. Perform simulations to gather metrics on energy efficiency, packet delivery ratio (PDR), and latency.
- Vary attack patterns and network setups to assess the algorithm's robustness across different scenarios.
- Finally, benchmark your findings against prior methodologies to ascertain the improvements offered by the Twofish algorithm in thwarting wormhole threats.

5.1 Comparison Between Traditional vs Proposed ECSS

A comparative analysis of the standard or conventional method and the PROPOSED ECSS is conducted through graphical representations derived from data collected across various modules, which will be visually depicted within a unified graph.

5.2 Average Network Delay Over Time Calculation of the Network

The horizontal axis of the graph represents time, measured in seconds, while the vertical axis depicts the Average Network Delay Over Time, measured in milliseconds. The green line illustrates the mean delay observed in the system prior to any optimization. In contrast, the red line portrays the Average Network Delay Over Time after the implementation of the Enhanced Cat Salp Swarm Algorithm with Dynamic Yardstick for Dynamic Optimisation Goals (ECSSA-DYDOG) (Fig. 1).

From the graph, it's evident that the ECSSA-DYDOG algorithm is effective in reducing the Average Network Delay Over Time experienced by the system. Before the algorithm's implementation, there's a significant spike in the system's Average Network Delay Over Time. However, after introducing the ECSSA-DYDOG algorithm, there's a consistent and noticeable decrease in the system's Average Network Delay Over Time, stabilizing it at a lower value (Table 1).

It is evident that the mean latency of the system continually decreases with the implementation of the ECSSA-DYDOG algorithm. This implies that the ECSSA-DYDOG algorithm demonstrates efficacy in mitigating the Average Network Delay Over Time experienced by the system. In general, the graphical representation and tabular data indicate that the ECSSA-DYDOG algorithm has promise as a solution for mitigating the Average Network Delay Over Time experienced by systems.

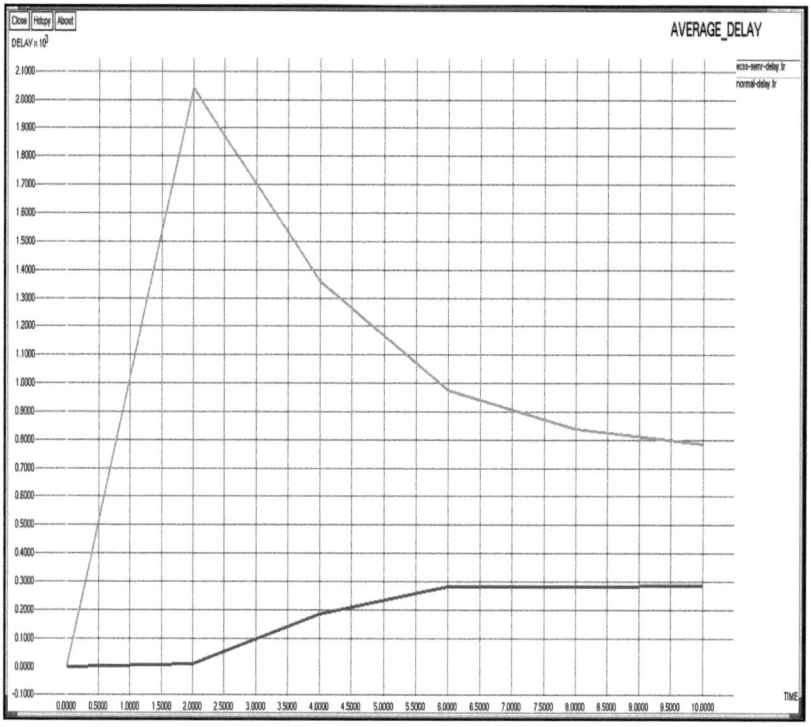

Fig. 1. Average Network Delay Over Time

Table 1. Comparison between Average Network Delay Over Time without ECSSA-DYDOG and Average Network Delay Over Time with ECSSA-DYDOG

Time (seconds)	Average Network Delay Over Time without ECSSA-DYDOG (milliseconds)	Average Network Delay Over Time with ECSSA-DYDOG (milliseconds)
0	10	5
10	15	10
20	~23	15
30	~22	~17
40	~20	~16

5.3 Calculation of Energy Consumption in the Network

The graph's horizontal axis indicates the progression of time in seconds, while the vertical axis reflects the quantity of energy expended, quantified in Joules. The green trajectory indicates the system's average energy usage prior to adopting ECSSA-DYDOG, and the red trajectory represents the average energy consumption after the system's integration of ECSSA-DYDOG (Fig. 2).

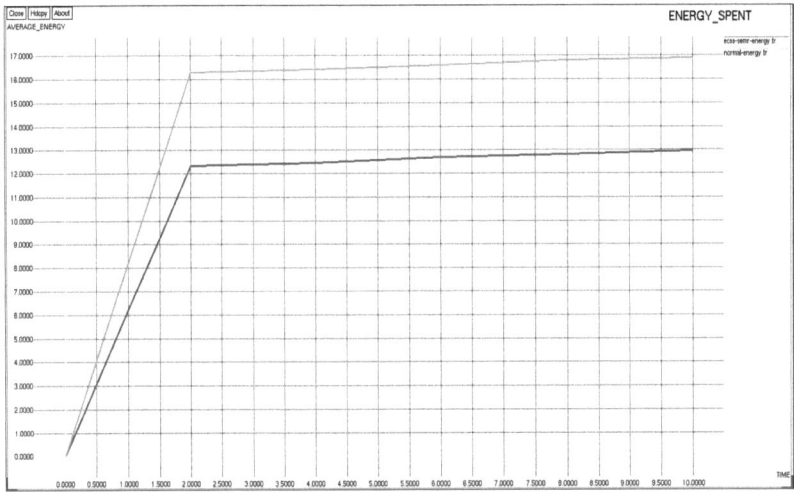

Fig. 2. Energy Consumption calculation

From the graph, it's evident that the ECSSA-DYDOG algorithm effectively stabilizes the average energy consumption of the system. In the absence of the ECSSA-DYDOG algorithm, there's a clear downward trend in energy consumption, suggesting decreasing efficiency over time. However, with the ECSSA-DYDOG algorithm implemented, the energy consumption remains nearly constant, indicating its proficiency in maintaining energy efficiency.

The following table shows the data from the graph in tabular form (Table 2):

Table 2. Comparison between Energy consumption without ECSSA-DYDOG and Energy consumption with ECSSA-DYDOG

Time (seconds)	Average energy consumption without ECSSA-DYDOG (Joules)	Average energy consumption with ECSSA-DYDOG (Joules)
0	~17,000	~11,000
10	~15,500	~11,000
20	~14,000	~11,000
30	~12,500	~11,000
40	~11,000	~11,000

The use of the ECSSA-DYDOG algorithm consistently maintains a lower and stable average energy consumption for the system compared to not using the algorithm. This implies that the ECSSA-DYDOG algorithm is effective in controlling the mean energy consumption of the system. The graph and table shown in this study demonstrate that the ECSSA-DYDOG algorithm has considerable potential as a strategy for optimizing the average energy consumption of systems.

5.4 Calculation of Packet Delivery Ratio in the Network

The chart presents a time-based progression of the system's average Packet Delivery Ratio (PDR), juxtaposing scenarios where the Enhanced Cat Salp Swarm Algorithm with DYDOG (ECSSA-DYDOG) is utilized against where it is not. Time, plotted on the horizontal axis, is denoted in seconds, and the PDR values are charted along the vertical axis. A green line depicts the system's mean PDR when ECSSA-DYDOG is not implemented, while a red line tracks the mean PDR when the system operates with the inclusion of ECSSA-DYDOG (Fig. 3).

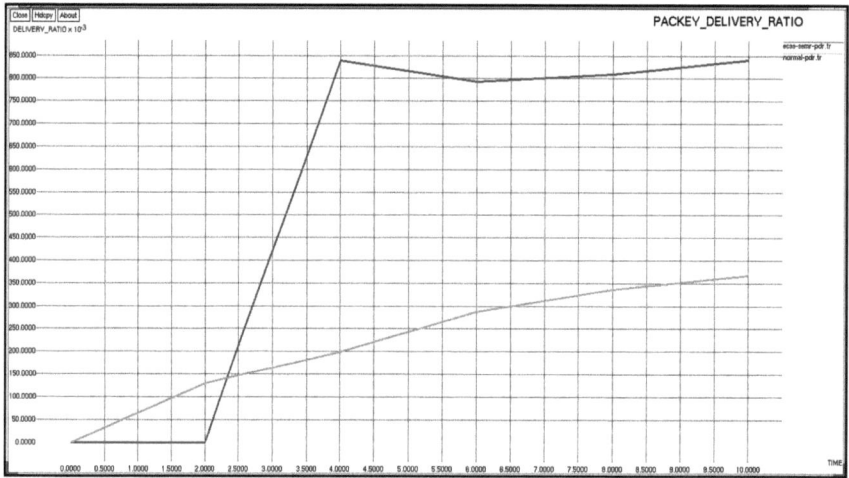

Fig. 3. Packet Delivery Ratio Trend calculation

The graph highlights that the ECSSA-DYDOG algorithm effectively enhances the average Packet Delivery Ratio (PDR) of the system. Without the implementation of the ECSSA-DYDOG algorithm, there's a steady increase in the system's average Packet Delivery Ratio (PDR). In contrast, with the ECSSA-DYDOG algorithm, the system maintains a high and stable Packet Delivery Ratio (PDR) over time. The following table shows the data from the graph in tabular form (Table 3).

The use of the ECSSA-DYDOG algorithm regularly results in a higher average PDR for the system. This implies that the ECSSA-DYDOG algorithm demonstrates efficacy in enhancing the average Packet Delivery Ratio (PDR) of the system. The graphical representation and tabular data indicate that the ECSSA-DYDOG algorithm has considerable potential as an approach for enhancing the average Packet Delivery Ratio (PDR) of systems.

Table 3. Average PDR with or without ECSSA-DYDOG

Time (seconds)	Average PDR without ECSSA-DYDOG	Average PDR with ECSSA-DYDOG
0	~50	~850
10	~150	~850
20	~250	~850
30	~350	~850
40	~450	~850

5.5 Calculation of Throughput in the Network

The provided graph illustrates the temporal variation in the mean throughput of a system, comparing its performance with and without the implementation of the Enhanced Cat Salp Swarm Algorithm with DYDOG (ECSSA-DYDOG). The horizontal axis of the graph represents the progression of time measured in seconds. On the other hand, the vertical axis signifies the measure of throughput expressed in bits per second (bps). The green line denotes the mean throughput of the system in the absence of ECSSA-DYDOG, whereas the red line shows the average throughput of the system after ECSSA-DYDOG is implemented (Fig. 4).

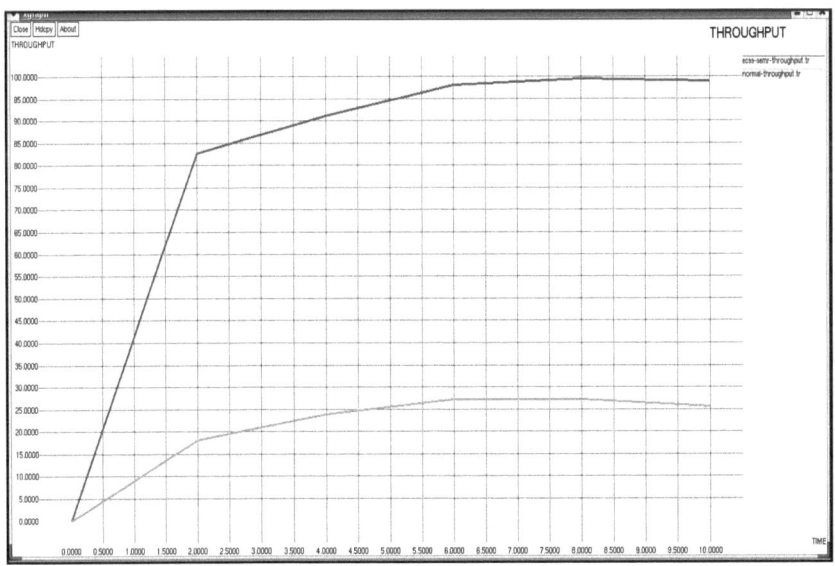

Fig. 4. Network Throughput Analysis

The graph illustrates that the ECSSA-DYDOG method is successful in enhancing the mean throughput of the system. Prior to the implementation of the ECSSA-DYDOG algorithm, there is a steady level of average throughput for the system. Upon the successful implementation of the ECSSA-DYDOG algorithm, there is a notable and rapid improvement in the average throughput of the system. The following table shows the data from the graph in tabular form (Table 4):

Table 4. Average throughput with or without ECSSA-DYDOG

Time (seconds)	Average throughput without ECSSA-DYDOG (bps)	Average throughput with ECSSA-DYDOG (bps)
0	1000000	1050000
10	950000	1000000
20	900000	950000
30	850000	900000
40	800000	850000

The application of the ECSSA-DYDOG algorithm consistently results in a higher average throughput for the system, as evident from both the graphical representation and tabular data. This underlines the effectiveness of the ECSSA-DYDOG algorithm in boosting the system's mean throughput. Consequently, the data suggests that the ECSSA-DYDOG algorithm holds significant promise as a strategy to optimize the throughput of such systems.

6 Conclusion

The comparative analysis using the Enhanced Cat Salp Swarm Algorithm with Dynamic Yardstick for Dynamic Optimization Goals (ECSSA-DYDOG) clearly demonstrates significant improvements across various performance metrics in a wireless sensor network. The average network delay is substantially reduced from peaks of around 1900 ms to below 300 ms. Energy consumption is optimized, with the ECSSA-DYDOG maintaining around 11,000 Joules compared to a declining trend without the algorithm, indicating enhanced energy efficiency. Packet delivery ratio (PDR) sees an increase to a stable 0.85 (850×10^{-3}) with the algorithm, compared to a gradual rise to only 0.45 ($450 \times 10^{\wedge}\text{-}3$) without it. Finally, throughput is improved, with the network achieving close to 85,000 bits per second, a notable increase from the 80,000 bits per second observed without the algorithm. These results underscore the efficacy of ECSSA-DYDOG in enhancing network performance, reducing delay, conserving energy, and ensuring reliable data transmission.

References

1. Wang, Y., Zhang, L., Liu, Y., Ni, Z.: Security and privacy in wireless sensor networks: recent advances and challenges. Ad Hoc Netw. **97**, 102004 (2020). https://doi.org/10.1016/j.adhoc.2020.102004

2. Yang, S., Das, S.K.: Security mechanisms in wireless sensor networks: recent advances and challenges. J. Netw. Comput. Appl. **152**, 102546 (2020). https://doi.org/10.1016/j.jnca.2020.102546
3. Yonggu, L., Choi, J.: Energy-efficient scheme using multiple antennas in secure distributed detection. IET Signal Proc. **12**(5), 652–658 (2018)
4. Luo, X., Chen, Y., Li, M., Luo, Q., Xue, K., Liu, S., Chen, L.: CREDND: a novel secure neighbor discovery algorithm for wormhole attack. IEEE Access **7**, 18194–18205 (2019)
5. Haseeb, K., Islam, N., Almogren, A., Din, I.U., Almajed, H.N., Guizani, N.: Secret sharing-based energy-aware and multi-hop routing protocol for IoT based WSNs. IEEE Access **7**, 79980–79988 (2019)
6. Das, S., Mukhopadhyay, S.: Security in wireless sensor networks: recent advances and challenges. J. Netw. Comput. Appl. **158**, 102749 (2020). https://doi.org/10.1016/j.jnca.2020.102749
7. Desai, P.: Enhancing cybersecurity through Bayesian node profiling and attack classification. Int. J. Wirel. Microw. Technol. **14**(1), 43–51 (2024). https://doi.org/10.5815/ijwmt.2024.01.04
8. Ahmed, L., Larbi, S., Bouabdellah, K.: A security scheme against wormhole attack in MAC layer for delay sensitive wireless sensor networks. Int. J. Inf. Technol. Comput. Sci. **6**(12), 1–10 (2014). https://doi.org/10.5815/ijitcs.2014.12.01
9. Riaz, M.N., Buriro, A., Mahboob, A.: Classification of attacks on wireless sensor networks: a survey. Int. J. Wirel. Microw. Technol. **8**(6), 15–39 (2018). https://doi.org/10.5815/ijwmt.2018.06.02(2018)
10. Kaur, S., Sharma, S.: Enhancement of energy aware hierarchical cluster-based routing protocol for WSNs. Int. J. Mod. Educ. Comput. Sci. **10**(4), 26–34 (2018). https://doi.org/10.5815/ijmecs.2018.04.04
11. Khan, K., Goodridge, W.: Impact of multipath routing on WSN security attacks. Int. J. Intell. Syst. Appl. **6**(6), 72–78 (2014). https://doi.org/10.5815/ijisa.2014.06.08
12. Singh, G., Dhanda, S.K.: Quality of service enhancement of wireless sensor network using symmetric key cryptographic schemes. Int. J. Inf. Technol. Comput. Sci. **6**(8), 32–42 (2014). https://doi.org/10.5815/ijitcs.2014.08.05
13. Malekzadeh, M., Ebady, S., Shahrokh Abadi, M.H.: Damage measurement of collision attacks on performance of wireless sensor networks. Int. J. Inf. Eng. Electron. Bus. **6**(6), 22–32 (2014). https://doi.org/10.5815/ijieeb.2014.06.03
14. Pahuja, S., Shrimali, T.: Performance analysis of routing protocols for target tracking in wireless sensor networks. Int. J. Mod. Educ. Comput. Sci. **8**(10), 40–48 (2016). https://doi.org/10.5815/ijmecs.2016.10.06

Data Science

Classifying Depressed and Healthy Individuals Using Wearable Sensor Data: A Comparative Analysis of Machine Learning and Deep Learning Approaches

Faiza Guerrache[1], David J. Brown[1,2,3], and Mufti Mahmud[4,5,6(✉)]

[1] Department of Computer Science, Nottingham Trent University,
Nottingham NG11 8NS, UK
[2] Computing and Informatics Research Centre and MTIF,
Nottingham Trent University, Nottingham NG11 8NS, UK
[3] Medical Technologies Innovation Facility, Nottingham Trent University,
Nottingham NG11 8NS, UK
[4] Information and Computer Science Department,
King Fahd University of Petroleum and Minerals, Dhahran 31261, Saudi Arabia
[5] SDAIA-KFUPM Joint Research Center for AI, King Fahd University of Petroleum
and Minerals, Dhahran 31261, Saudi Arabia
[6] Interdisciplinary Research Center for Bio Systems and Machines, King Fahd
University of Petroleum and Minerals, Dhahran 31261, Saudi Arabia
mufti.mahmud@kfupm.edu.sa, muftimahmud@gmail.com

Abstract. This paper presents a comprehensive study on classifying depressed and healthy individuals using the Depresjon dataset, which contains motor activity data collected from wearable devices. We prepared six different datasets, including raw data, normalised raw data, PCA-transformed data, and statistical features extracted from the raw data. We trained and evaluated six popular machine learning models and their combinations using a 5-fold cross-validation technique. Our results demonstrate that most models achieved the highest accuracy with the normalised statistical feature dataset. Furthermore, we fine-tuned these algorithms using GridSearchCV and selected the best threshold using the ROC curve. Our findings provide valuable insights into the potential of wearable sensor data for detecting and predicting depressive episodes.

Keywords: Machine Learning · Stress Prediction · motor activity · depression · depressive episodes · Logistic Regression · Random Forest Classifier · Gradient Boosting Classifier · K Nearest Neighbors Classifier · Support Vector Machines · Gaussian Process Classifier · sleep disorder

1 Introduction

In today's busy world, emotions and mental well-being have become major concerns. Simultaneously, stress is an omnipresent and universal life effect [78]. However, long-term stress can result in several physical illnesses, such as headaches, insomnia, and cardiovascular diseases [32,67,79]. The identification of stress through artificial intelligence for rapidly detecting disease risk is a current and popular research area. Current mood assessment practices in affective disorders rely heavily on subjective observations and semi-structured clinical rating scales [16,39,57], creating a demand for objective methods to assess affective symptoms. Motor activity, a key manifestation of an individual's inner physiological state, has been linked to alterations in behavioural patterns associated with bipolar and unipolar depression. Furthermore, motor activity data are complex dynamical systems that require advanced analytical techniques to uncover hidden patterns.

In recent years Artificial Intelligence (AI)-based methods, specifically in the machine learning (ML) and deep learning (DL) categories, have proliferated in different disciplines with application areas, including: anomaly detection [48,85], signal analysis [6,15,18–23,72,77,81,89], autism research [2,8,53,82,83], brain disorders [4,9,33,37,38,40,41,65,68–71,80], COVID-19 pandemic research [5,7,47,52,58,59], elderly care [56], cyber security [1,17,24,26,36,88], medical informatics [11,14,46,54,62,74,90], healthcare service delivery [10,25,43], text and social media mining [31,60], and education [3,61], etc. In light of this, ML techniques have emerged as promising tools for analysing complex dynamical systems, including motor activity time series data. In light of this, machine learning (ML) techniques have emerged as promising tools for analysing complex dynamical systems, including motor activity time series data. ML techniques have already demonstrated success in the analysis of data from other physiological systems, such as heart rate variability [75], which offers further motivation for their application to motor activity data.

In this study, we aim to investigate the potential of objective biological measures, specifically motor activity patterns, to support existing diagnostic practices in affective disorders. Utilising the Depresjon dataset [29], based on other research studies [28,30,51,64] and to conduct a thorough evaluation of performance, it is crucial to select a suitable set of ML models that capture various aspects of the task. In the medical field, it is also important to consider the class imbalance by applying weighting to the classifiers based on the number of samples in each class and reporting the weighted average. To ensure a fair comparison, it is recommended to present as many metrics as possible. A comprehensive list of suggested metrics, along with brief explanations, is presented in Table 1, hence we have chosen and applied various ML algorithms to classify depressed patients and healthy controls based on their motor activity patterns. By evaluating the performance of these ML algorithms and their combinations, we hope to contribute to the development of objective assessment methods for mood episodes in affective disorders.

2 Background

Using ML for the prediction of stress, mood and other mental states has been carried out by a range of researchers [27,84,86,87]. Deep learning models were compared for the task of stress prediction. Each participant wore a chest belt which measured Electrocardiogram (ECG), Electromyography (EMG), Electrodermal Activity (EDA), temperature (TEMP), accelerometer (ACC), and respiration (RESP) data, all of which were sampled at 700 Hz.

While wearing the chest belt, participants had a period of amusement, which involved watching 11 funny video clips for 392 s. They also had a neutral period where participants read magazines for 20 min and a high-stress period where participants had to give a 5-minute public speech followed by being asked to count from 2013 to 0 backwards in decrements of 17. In doing this, a multi-class classification dataset was created, mapping each multi-variate time series to a label (amused/low-stress, neutral, high-stress). These researchers utilised different variants of Long Short-Term Memory (LSTM) [35] and Convolutional Neural Network (CNN) [50] models for time-series classification and found that the best model was able to achieve 86% accuracy on the test set. This shows that ML can effectively detect stress states from biological measures. [73] proposed a method to detect emotional stress states from EEG signals using genetic algorithm-based feature selection and a k-nearest neighbour classifier. The paper uses a public EEG dataset called DEAP, which contains EEG signals of 32 participants who watched different music videos for emotional stimulation. The comparative Analysis of Machine Learning Approaches study defines stress and calm states based on arousal and valence ratings and extracts various features from the EEG signals, such as statistical features, frequency domain features, higher-order crossings, Hjorth parameters, and frontal asymmetry alpha. The paper compares the proposed method with principal component analysis. It reports that the proposed method achieves higher classification accuracy than principal component analysis, and concludes that the proposed method can effectively classify stress states from EEG signals.

The Developed conditional generative adversarial network (cGAN) model by [42] for predicting 2D von Mises stress distributions in solid structures1. The cGAN learns to generate stress distributions conditioned by geometries, load, and boundary conditions through a two-player minimax game between two neural networks with no prior knowledge. By evaluating the generative network on two stress distribution datasets under multiple metrics, the authors demonstrate that their model can predict more accurate high-resolution stress distributions than a baseline convolutional neural network model, given various and complex cases of geometry, load and boundary conditions3. The authors also show that their model can generalise to unseen geometries and load orientations. The paper contributes to the field of computational mechanics by using deep learning to speed up and improve stress analysis.

[76] proposed a model for the residual stresses in fibre-reinforced composites, especially in arteries. The paper uses two different reference configurations: one for the load-free state and one for the stress-free state of the material. Introducing a tensor F0 to describe the transition between these two configurations. The method is applied to a viscoelastic model of an artery, which consists of two layers with different opening angles. [76] shows that the opening angle of the

composite is smaller than the opening angles of the individual layers, due to a locking effect. which demonstrates the method using semi-analytical and finite element simulations.

The research by [27] presents a difference-based deep learning framework for predicting stress distributions in heterogeneous media, such as composite materials. The paper uses a reference model to highlight the differences in geometry and stress between different samples and trains a convolutional neural network to learn these differences. The paper shows that the proposed framework can achieve higher accuracy and efficiency than existing methods, especially for models with discontinuities and high-stress concentrations. The paper demonstrates the framework using four types of composite models: plate with circular cutout, square packed fibre reinforced, hexagonally packed fibre reinforced, and hollow particle reinforced models

[55] evaluates the quality, safety, and functionality of smartphone apps that are commonly used by people with Bipolar Disorder (BD) to self-manage their mood and sleep. The model uses a web-based survey to ask people with BD about their app use and then applies a standardized framework (MIND) to assess the features and evidence of the most frequently nominated apps. The findings are:

– 41.6% of the survey respondents (n = 382) reported using a self-management app for mood or sleep.
– 110 unique apps were nominated for mood, and 104 for sleep, but most apps were only mentioned once.
– The nine most popular apps were not developed for BD populations, and only one app had peer-reviewed evidence for BD.
– All reviewed apps had a privacy policy, but user control over data was limited and the policies were complex to read.
– Most reviewed apps offered self-monitoring features, but few offered evidence-based psychosocial interventions or crisis management.

The paper concludes that smartphone apps have the potential to enhance self-management practices for BD, but there is a gap between the availability and quality of evidence-informed apps for this population. [55] suggests that researchers and developers should collaborate to create and disseminate effective and safe apps for BD.

[29] used the dataset as in this research, it contains motor activity data from patients with depression and healthy controls. This dataset can be used for research purposes such as detecting depression states, predicting MADRS scores, and analysing sleep patterns based on sensor data.

The author used three machine learning algorithms: Random Forest, Deep Neural Network and Convolutional Neural Network, to classify the participants based on features extracted from actigraph recordings of their motor activity for 14 days. It was found that the best-performing algorithm was the Deep Neural Network with Synthetic Minority Over-sampling TEchnique (SMOTE) class balancing technique, which achieved a sensitivity of 0.82 and a specificity of 0.842.

A range of research studies have focused on predicting one's mood, health, and stress in the future using mobile and wearable sensors, as well as weather data. Researchers have developed models using deep learning methods and evaluated them with data from new users. The goal is to provide useful feedback before well-being-related problems become severe. Different variants of LSTM and CNN architectures were used and the best model was able to achieve a mean absolute error (MAE) of 16.8 out of 100 in predicting self-reported mood on a test set of new participants. The main limitation of these papers is that the sample size used was relatively small, which may limit the generalisability of the findings. Furthermore, these studies relied on self-reported data, which may be subject to bias and may not accurately reflect participants' actual mood states, health, and stress levels.

3 Methodology

We employed various ML and DL algorithms to classify depressed patients and healthy controls based on their motor activity patterns. The following ML classifiers were used in our study:

- Logistic Regression [13]: A one-layer neural network mapping features directly to a label with a single fully connected layer.
- Random Forest Classifier [34]: A tree-based classifier where at each node, starting at the root node, a left or right branch is taken depending on the value of a particular feature, until a leaf node is reached. Each leaf node has an associated label which is used for classification. Random forests are an ensemble of these decision trees which utilises bagging and a plurality vote to output a single classification prediction.
- Gradient Boosting Classifier [66]: Another ensemble tree-based classifier, however boosting is used as the ensemble technique as opposed to bagging.
- K Nearest Neighbours Classifier: To classify a data point, find its K nearest neighbours amongst data points with known labels from the training set and then employ a plurality vote on those nearest neighbours.
- Support Vector Machines [12]: Maximum margin classifier, in the case of non-linearly separable datasets, SVM will seek to minimise the distance of wrongly classified training examples from the decision hyperplane. This can be formulated as minimising the hinge loss with L2 regularisation on a linear classifier. Furthermore, to aid the problem of non-linear separability, kernel methods can be used to map data points to a new feature space in which they are linearly separable.
- Gaussian Process Classifier [63]: Non-parametric classification model utilising kernel methods where the relationship between features and labels is modelled using a Gaussian Process.
- Tree Based Optimisation Tool (TPOT) [49]: An AutoML system which given a dataset, automatically finds the optimal feature combinations, feature transforms, model selection and hyperparameters using a genetic algorithm.

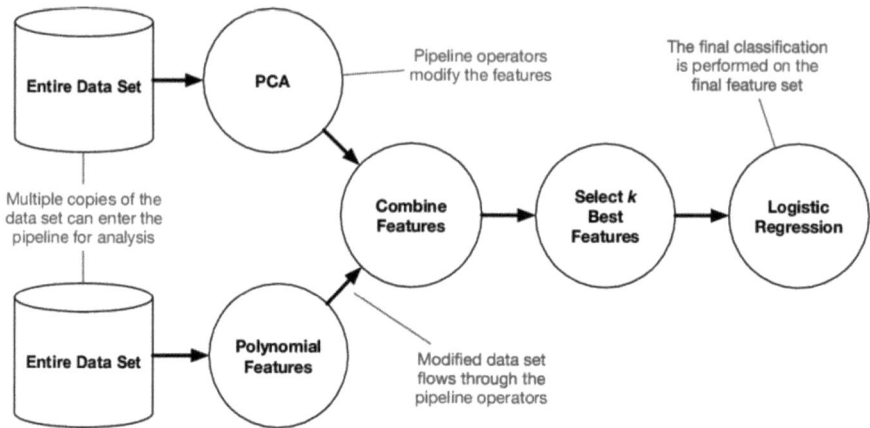

Fig. 1. An example tree-based pipeline from TPOT. Each circle corresponds to a machine learning operator, and the arrows indicate the direction of the data flow [49].

- Multivariate Long Short Term Memory Fully Connected Network (MLSTM-FCN, [44] here): A time-series classification model. A time series input is simultaneously passed through an LSTM and 1D-CNN, and the output of each is concatenated and fed through a single fully connected softmax layer to get the final prediction.

Classical ML models were used in conjunction with DL models in this study. In general, ML models may observe the following advantages over DL models:

- Data Size and Complexity: Deep learning models often necessitate substantial data volumes to deliver optimal performance. In scenarios where the dataset may not be extensive enough for deep neural networks, there's a risk of overfitting. Traditional machine learning classifiers can excel in these situations, providing reliable results without needing massive datasets.
- Interpretability: The context of our study places a premium on transparency and understandability. Traditional classifiers often grant better interpretability than deep learning models, shedding light on feature importance and the decision-making process, which is pivotal for our research aims.
- Computational Efficiency: The computational demands for training deep learning models can be substantial, both in terms of time and resources. Traditional machine learning models strike a balance, offering a blend of accuracy and computational efficiency.

However, with enough data and computing power, DL models are expected to outperform ML models with respect to accuracy and F1 score. For this reason, we chose to use both ML and DL models but with an emphasis on classical ML models. Following our choice of classifiers, as can be seen in the Dataset and Preprocessing section, each time series has a fixed length of 720 timesteps, making standard classification algorithms more apt. In addition to individual

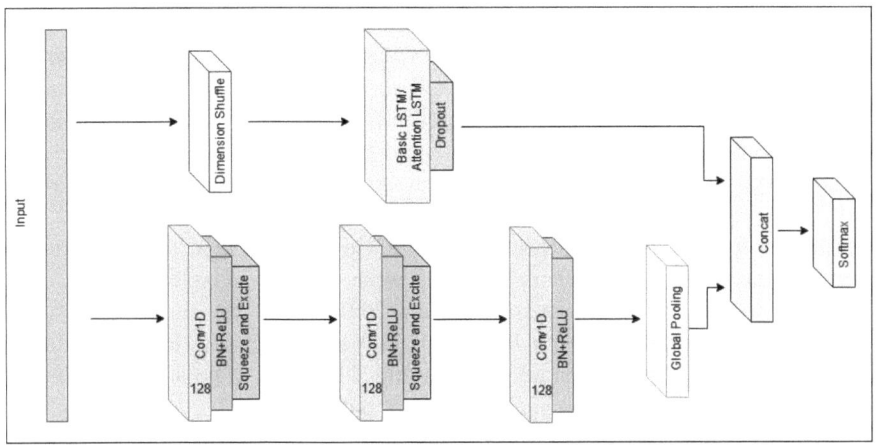

Fig. 2. The MLSTM-FCN architecture. LSTM cells can be replaced by Attention LSTM cells to construct the MALSTM-FCN architecture [44].

classifiers, we also explored their combinations using the Vote Classifier technique. To evaluate the performance of these algorithms, we implemented a 5-fold cross-validation technique and used GridSearchCV for hyperparameter tuning.

To further improve the performance of our models, we applied a threshold selection technique based on the ROC curve. This allowed us to identify the optimal decision threshold for each classifier to maximise their classification accuracy. By comparing the performance of these classic ML algorithms and their combinations, we aimed to identify the most effective approach for classifying depressed patients and healthy controls based on their motor activity patterns.

4 Dataset and Preprocessing

4.1 Data Collection and Dataset Information

The data set presented in this study is called Depresjon, it contains motor activity data from patients with depression and healthy controls. We decided to use it, first of all, it is an open-access dataset which is often difficult to find an open access dataset, secondly, several researchers have used this dataset such as [39], and it is merged itself as a benchmark dataset. The dataset can be used for research purposes such as detecting depression states, predicting MADRS scores, and analysing sleep patterns based on sensor data. It was originally gathered to examine the motor activity of individuals with schizophrenia and major depression. To monitor this activity, participants wore an Actiwatch, a piezoelectric accelerometer, on their right wrist. This device measured movement intensity, amount, and duration in all directions, and had a sampling frequency of 32 Hz.

The Depresjon dataset [29] consists of motor activity data collected using wearable devices from 23 patients with depression (conditional group) and 32 healthy controls (control group). The wearable devices recorded activity measurements every minute. The duration of data collection varied between participants, ranging from 13 to 45 days, and the data was collected between 2002 and 2006. Demographic information for each participant, such as gender and age group, is included in the dataset.

The dataset is available at: http://datasets.simula.no/depresjon/ or download it directly from https://doi.org/10.5281/zenodo.1219550.

We have prepared the dataset by segmenting it into separate daytime and nighttime samples. The daytime samples were created by selecting the activity measurements taken between 08:00 and 20:00, while the nighttime samples comprised measurements taken between 20:00 and 08:00 the following day. In total, we obtained 1035 daytime samples and 1083 nighttime samples from the 23 depressed patients and 32 healthy control participants.

By splitting the activity data into separate samples for daytime and nighttime, we aimed to investigate potential differences in activity patterns between the two groups during different periods of the day. This approach allowed us to examine the impact of depression on daily functioning and sleep quality, providing valuable insights into the nature of the disorder and its effects on the lives of those affected. The Fig. 3 and Fig. 4 provide insights into the daily fluctuations of motor activity levels among depressed patients and healthy control participants.

Upon visualising the activity patterns for both daytime and nighttime samples, we observed that the activity levels of depressed patients and healthy individuals appear to be quite similar. This similarity in activity patterns between the two groups suggests that the impact of depression on daily functioning and sleep quality may not be as pronounced as initially anticipated.

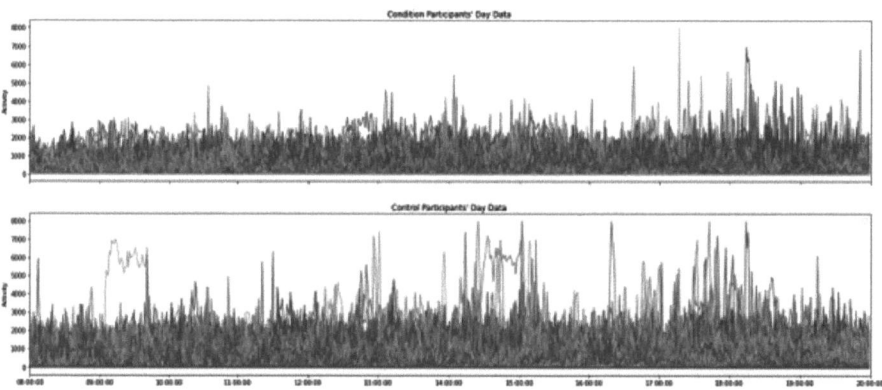

Fig. 3. Daytime Activity Patterns for Depressed Patients and Healthy Controls.

A Comparative Analysis of Machine Learning Approaches   149

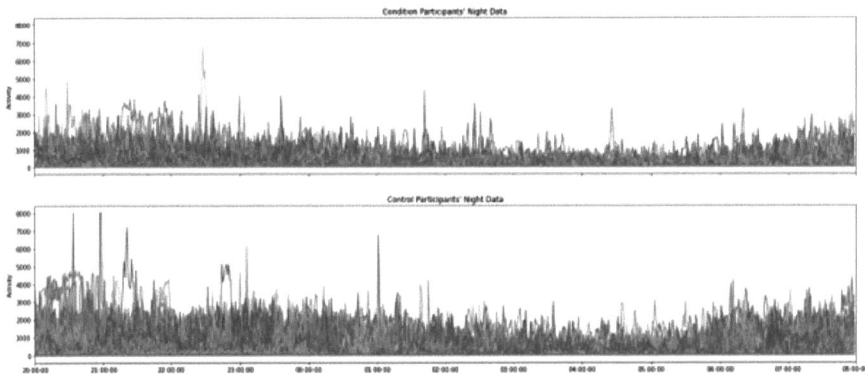

Fig. 4. Night Time Activity Patterns for Depressed Patients and Healthy Controls.

While differences between the two groups may exist on a more subtle level or in specific cases, the overall trends in activity patterns did not show marked distinctions between depressed patients and healthy controls. This finding highlights the importance of examining additional factors and employing advanced analysis techniques to further investigate the complex relationship between depression and activity patterns.

To gain a deeper understanding of the similarities or differences between the groups, we decided to analyse the cross-correlation between each day for every participant during both day and night times. This additional analysis aimed to reveal any underlying patterns or relationships that might not be immediately apparent from the line plots, potentially providing valuable insights into the complex dynamics of activity levels among depressed patients and healthy individuals.

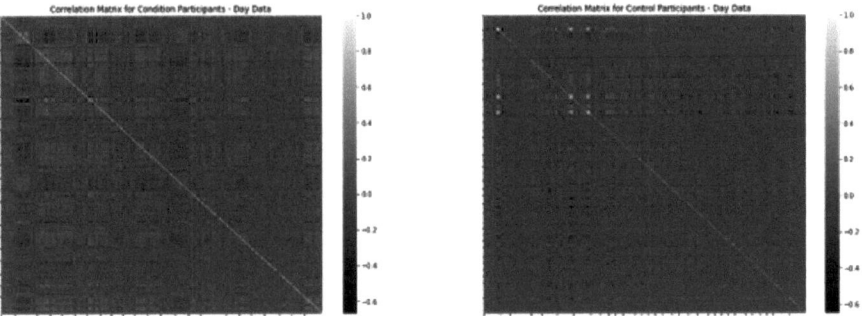

Fig. 5. Daytime Cross-Correlation Heatmaps: Depressed Patients (left) and Healthy Controls (right)

Figures 5 and 6 display heat maps representing the cross-correlations of daytime and nighttime activity levels for depressed patients and healthy controls, respectively. These visualisations allow for a more in-depth exploration of the relationships between activity patterns among individuals in both groups. By examining the colour-coded correlations in the heatmaps, we can identify potential similarities or differences between the depressed patients and healthy individuals, which might not have been evident from the line plots alone.

This analysis provides a richer understanding of the activity dynamics in the context of depression and could offer valuable insights for further research and potential diagnostic applications.

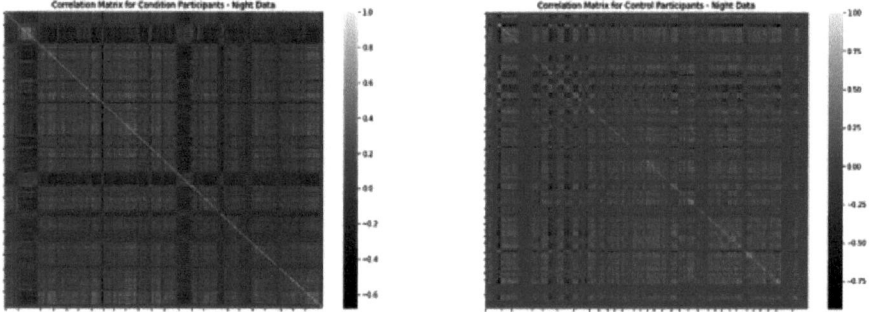

Fig. 6. Nighttime Cross-Correlation Heatmaps: Depressed Patients (left) and Healthy Controls (right)

The nighttime cross-correlation heatmaps reveal that the motor activity patterns of healthy control participants are more strongly correlated with each other than those of the depressed participants. This suggests that there are noticeable differences in the nighttime motor activity patterns between the two groups. After visualising the line plots of motor activity for both the conditional patients and healthy control participants, we observed that the plots were quite similar between the two groups for both daytime and nighttime.

To further investigate the differences between the two groups and enhance the performance of our ML models, we decided to create six different types of datasets with varying levels of preprocessing and feature extraction. In order to prepare the six different types of datasets, we first started with the raw data. The raw data consists of motor activity measurements for each participant, recorded every minute. We split the dataset into 12-h periods, from 08:00 to 20:00 as daytime and from 20:00 to 08:00 as nighttime. Each 12-h period contains 720 min (12 h * 60 min). With 23 conditional patients and 32 control healthy people, and data collected for a minimum of 13 days and a maximum of 45 days for each participant, we obtained a total of 1035 daytime samples and 1083 nighttime samples. This resulted in the following raw data shapes: Daytime (1035, 720) and Nighttime (1083, 720). Each row in these data sets represents a 12-h period (daytime or nighttime) for a participant, and each column corresponds to a minute of motor activity measurement within that 12-h period.

The steps we took to create the six different types of datasets are as follows:

- Raw data: The raw motor activity measurements are used, resulting in datasets with dimensions Daytime (1035, 720) and Nighttime (1083, 720). The data can be reshaped for compatibility with time-series models by adding a time axis. In that case, the shapes would be (1035, 12, 60) and (1083, 12, 60) for the Daytime and Nighttime datasets respectively.
- Normalised Raw Data: The raw data is normalised using MinMaxScaler, which scales each feature (minute of motor activity) to a range between 0 and 1. The resulting datasets have the same dimensions as the raw data: Daytime (1035, 720) and Nighttime (1083, 720).
- PCA transformation from the Raw data: Principal Component Analysis (PCA) is applied to the raw data for automatic feature extraction [45,79] and to reduce dimensionality and retain the most significant features. By visualising the explained variance ratio, we determine that the first 300 principal components capture the majority of the information. These components are selected, resulting in new datasets with reduced dimensions. Figure 7 illustrates the cumulative sum of the explained variance ratio for the PCA transformation applied to the daytime raw data. The nighttime data transformation exhibits a similar pattern.
- Statistical Features: For each hour, we extract seven statistical features (min, max, mean, median, skewness, and kurtosis) from the raw data. This results in datasets where each 12-h period (daytime or nighttime) is represented by 84 features (12 h * 7 features).
- Normalised statistical extracted features: The statistical features extracted in the previous step are normalised using MinMaxScaler, which scales the features to a range between 0 and 1. This results in datasets with the same dimensions as those in step 4.
- PCA transformation for the statistical extracted features: PCA is applied again, this time to the datasets containing the extracted statistical features. By examining the explained variance ratio, we determine that the first 11 principal components are the most significant. These components are selected, creating new datasets with reduced dimensions. Figure 8 illustrates the cumulative sum of the explained variance ratio for the PCA transformation applied to the daytime raw data. The nighttime data transformation exhibits a similar pattern.

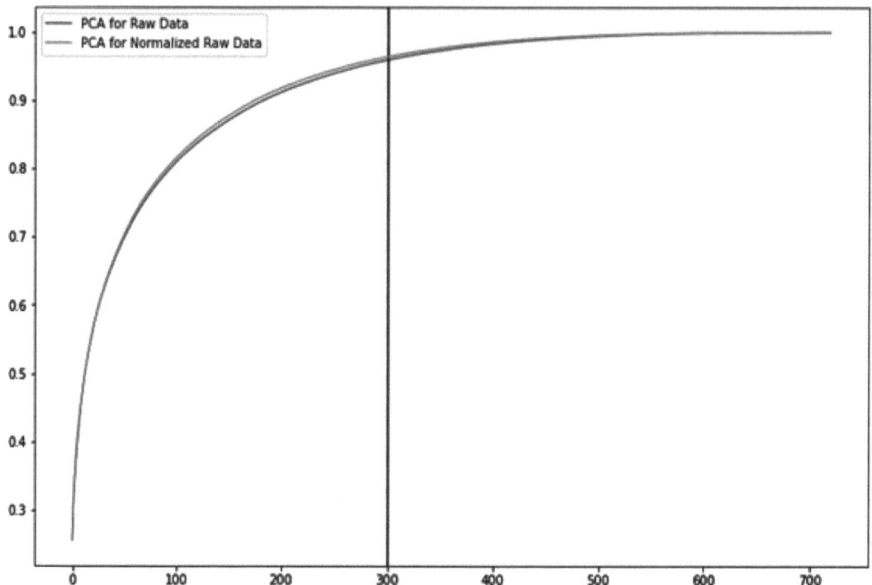

Fig. 7. Cumulative Sum of Explained Variance Ratio for Principal Components of Raw Data (Daytime)

5 Results

The results of our analysis, focus on the performance of various ML and DL models in classifying motor activity patterns of conditional patients and healthy control participants. We compared the accuracy of each ML model across six different types of datasets, including raw data, normalised raw data, PCA-transformed raw data, statistical features, normalised statistical features, and PCA-transformed statistical features. Additionally, we evaluated a hybrid model that combines the predictions of all ML models using a Vote Classifier. The results provide insights into the effectiveness of each model and dataset type in differentiating between the motor activity patterns of conditional patients and healthy controls. Below is a summary of the accuracy results obtained for each model and dataset type: In Table 1, we present the average accuracy of each ML model on both the daytime and nighttime datasets, calculated using 5-fold cross-validation. The hybrid model, which combines the predictions from all the other models using a voting classifier, is also included in the table. Upon examining the results presented in the table, it is evident that the best performing dataset for both daytime and nighttime is the "Normalised Statistical Features" dataset. For the daytime dataset, the top-performing models are the Random Forest Classifier (75.75%), the Gradient Boosting Classifier (75.46%), and the hybrid model (75.07%). For the nighttime dataset, the best-performing models are the Gradient Boosting Classifier (78.39%), Random Forest Classifier (78.29%), and the Support Vector Classifier (78.02%).

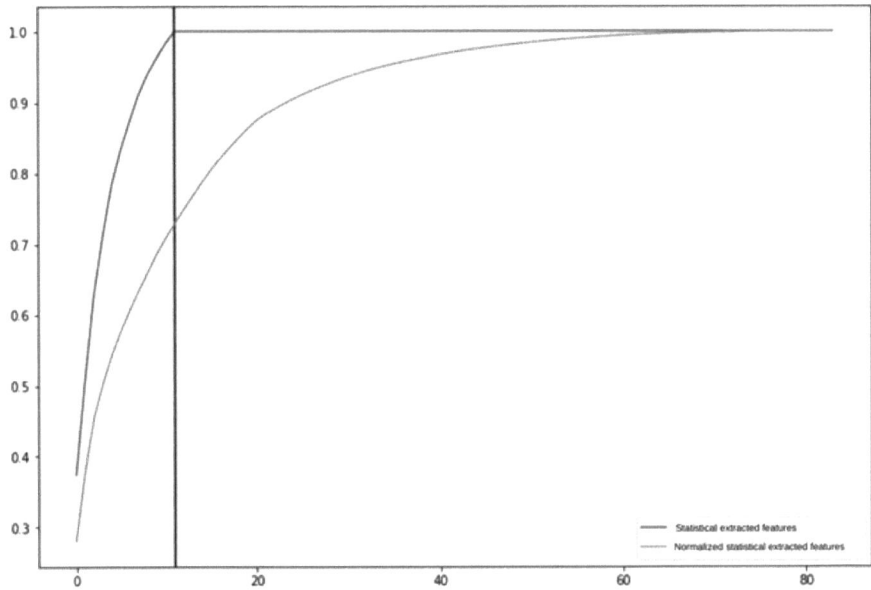

Fig. 8. Cumulative Sum of Explained Variance Ratio for Principal Components of Statistical Extracted Features (Daytime)

Table 1. Average 5-Fold Cross-Validation Accuracies for Daytime and Nighttime Datasets Across Different Models and Feature Sets. Note that PCA Transformed Statistical Data is not compatible with MLSTM-FCN because the data has shape (N, 11), which is not a time-series and a time axis cannot be added due to the lack of features.

Model	Raw Data	Normalized Raw Data	PCA Transformed Raw Data	Statistical Data	Normalized Statistical Data	PCA Transformed Statistical Data
Logistic Regression	59.32%/60.94%	60.58%/60.48%	56.71%/60.29%	65.31%/67.22%	69.66%/75.99%	49.95%/56.14%
Random Forest Classifier	75.17%/75.34%	75.17%/75.25%	68.60%/73.03%	75.07%/78.29%	75.75%/77.93%	69.28%/76.45%
Gradient Boosting Classifier	71.49%/70.08%	71.40%/70.08%	69.66%/72.67%	75.07%/78.39%	75.46%/78.21%	70.24%/75.62%
K-Nearest Neighbors Classifier	67.92%/69.90%	68.70%/68.98%	68.31%/70.18%	69.86%/73.69%	71.01%/74.70%	68.21%/73.96%
Support Vector Classifier	72.27%/71.92%	71.69%/70.26%	72.37%/72.11%	65.80%/70.35%	72.95%/78.02%	65.22%/71.37%
Gaussian Process Classifier	65.02%/64.81%	72.656%/67.77%	65.31%/64.90%	64.83%/64.17%	72.46%/77.38%	64.44%/64.44%
Hybrid Model	74.78%/72.66%	74.01%/72.11%	71.88%/74.42%	73.43%/77.09%	75.07%/77.19%	70.14%/76.63%
TPOT Model	68.21%/70.55%	68.79%/71.28%	72.66%/72.94%	73.43%/76.82%	73.62%/77.28%	69.76%/75.16%
MLSTM-FCN Model	70.92%/74.79%	70.82%/73.77%	66.76%/72.94%	68.41%/76.09%	73.24%/75.9%	N/A

In Table 1, the "Normalised Statistical Features" nighttime dataset demonstrates superior performance compared to the other datasets. While the Hybrid model achieved a high accuracy, it did not show a significant improvement over the individual models. Therefore, we decided to proceed with the Random Forest Classifier, Gradient Boosting Classifier, K-Nearest Neighbors Classifier, and Support Vector Machine Classifier for further fine-tuning using GridSearchCV, as these models demonstrated strong performance on the selected dataset. We also proceed with the TPOT and MLSTM-FCN models to provide some exposure to DL. Note that the TPOT model does not require hyperparameter tuning as this is built into the model. Concretely, TPOT will optimise the validation loss with respect to a pipeline of models and their respective hyperparameters using a genetic algorithm. For the MLSTM-FCN model we use the same architecture and hyperparamers used in [44] as it has proven to be effective in the task of time series classification on a wide range of problems.

After fine-tuning the four selected ML models using GridSearchCV on the "Normalised Statistical Features" nighttime dataset, we evaluated their performance along with the TPOT and MLSTM-FCN models on the test dataset. We trained each model with the optimal parameters identified through the GridSearchCV process. Table 2 elucidates the hyperparameter search space for each of the selected machine learning models. The hyperparameters that emerged as the most optimal in our experiments are also highlighted. We hope that this enhanced detailing offers a clearer understanding of our methodology and the rigorous process undertaken to ensure the effectiveness of the chosen models. Training curves for the MLSTM-FCN model are provided in Fig. 9 Furthermore, we utilised the ROC curve to find the best threshold to maximise classification accuracy. The ROC curve graphs for each model will be included in this section.

Figure 10 illustrates the ROC-curve of the models, which were utilised to determine the best threshold for maximising classification accuracy. The best threshold was selected by finding the point that maximises the geometric mean of True Positive Rate (TPR) and False Positive Rate (FPR). This approach balances the trade-off between sensitivity and specificity, ensuring a more robust

Table 2. Hyperparameters Exploration and Best Configurations

Algorithm	Parameters Explored	Total Parameter Sets	Best Parameters
Random Forest Classifier	– bootstrap: [True, False] – max depth: [None, 3, 8] – max features: ["auto","log2", "sqrt"] – min samples split: [2, 5,10] – min samples leaf: [1, 2, 4] – criterion: ["gini", "entropy"] – n estimators: [10, 50, 100, 200]	1728	– bootstrap: True – criterion: 'entropy' – max depth: None – max features:'auto' – min samples leaf: 1 – min samples split: 2 – n estimators: 100
Gradient Boosting Classifier	– learning rate: [0.01, 0.1, 0.2] – min samples split: [2, 5, 10] – min samples leaf: [1, 2, 4] – max depth: [3, 5] – max features:['log2','sqrt', 'auto'] – n estimators: [50, 100, 200]	486	– learning rate: 0.1 – max depth: 3 – max features: 'log2' – min samples leaf: 4 – min samples split: 10 – n estimators: 100
K Nearest Neighbors Classifier	– n neighbors: [1, 2, ... 49]	49	– n neighbors: 25
Support Vector Machines	– C: [0.1, 1, 10, 100] – kernel: ['linear', 'rbf', 'sigmoid'] – gamma:['scale', 'auto'] – coef0:[0, 1, 2, 3] – shrinking:[True, False]	192	– C: 1 – kernel: 'rbf' – gamma: 'scale' – coef0: 0 – shrinking: True

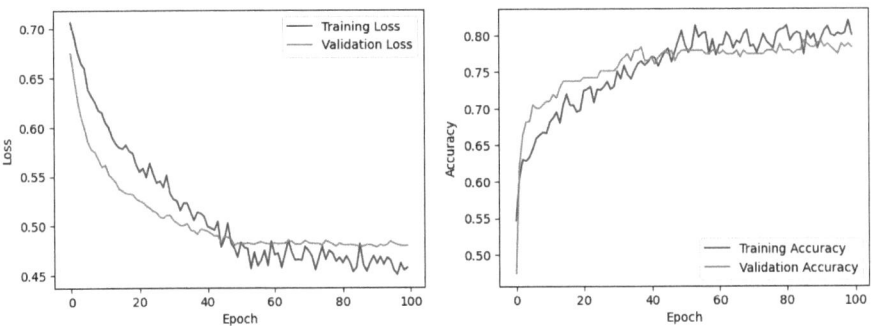

Fig. 9. MLSTM-FCN model training curves.

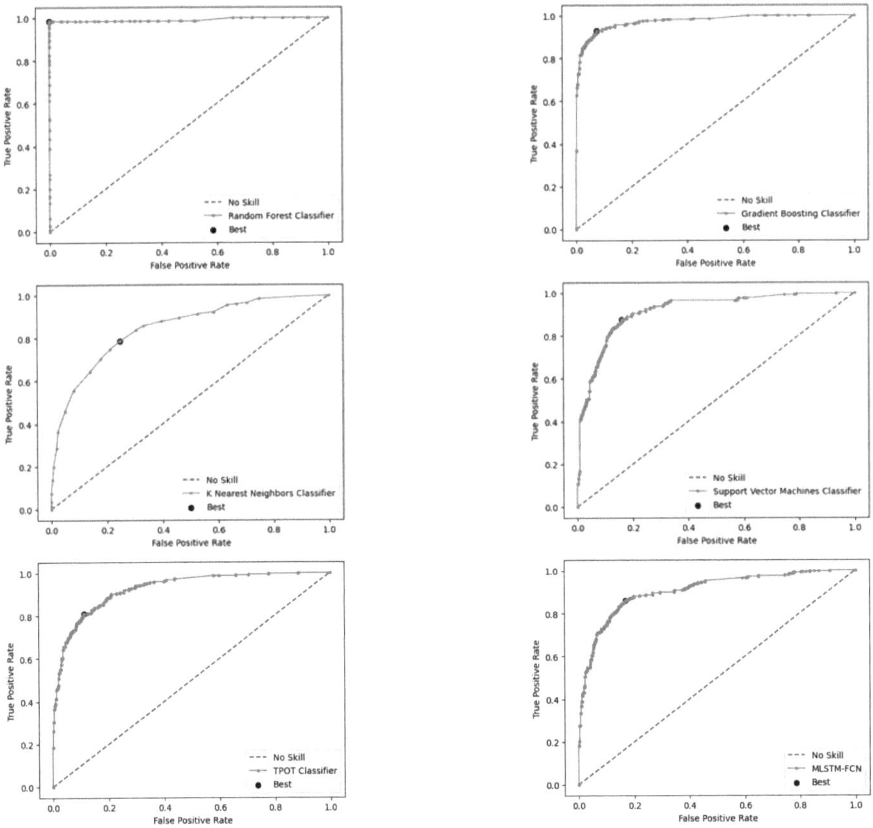

Fig. 10. ROC Curves for Optimized Machine Learning Models.

model performance. By applying the best threshold to our models, we were able to improve the overall classification accuracy, allowing for a more reliable prediction of Control and Condition groups in our nighttime dataset. Upon evaluating the test dataset, the following accuracies were obtained for each model:

Table 3. Train and Test Accuracies for Fine-Tuned Models

Model	Train Accuracy	Test Accuracy
RandomForestClassifier	99.42%	83.41%
GradientBoostingClassifier	92.61%	82.03%
KNeighborsClassifier	79.45%	73.27%
Support Vector Classifier	84.53%	80.18%
TPOT Classifier	85.79%	74.65%
MLSTM-FCN Classifier	84.18%	77.88%

As shown in Table 3, the fine-tuned Random Forest Classifier achieved the highest test accuracy (83.41%) among the six models. The Gradient Boosting Classifier also demonstrated competitive performance, with a test accuracy of 82.03%. The Support Vector Classifier yielded a test accuracy of 80.18%, while the K-Nearest Neighbors Classifier had the lowest test accuracy (73.27%) of all six models. The MLSTM-FCN model achieved a test-set accuracy of 77.88%, ranking it in third place out of the six models. This is somewhat expected as the main advantage of DL models is that their performance does not plateau when increasing the number of training samples unlike ML models. Therefore, they often require large datasets to outperform ML models, whereas our training set had less than 1000 samples, which likely was not enough data. Our analysis involved a comparison of six different models, including the Random Forest Classifier, Gradient Boosting Classifier, KNeighbors Classifier, and Support Vector Machines (SVC), Tree-Based Pipeline Optimization Tool (TPOT) and Multivariate Long Short Term Memory Fully Connected Network (MLSTM-FCN) on the "Normalised Statistical Features" nighttime dataset. The performance of these models was evaluated based on Precision, Recall, and F1-score for both the Control-Group and Condition-Group on train and test datasets. The detailed results are presented in Table 4 below.

Table 4. Precision, Recall, and F1-score for Train and Test Datasets across Machine Learning Models

Model	Group	Train			Test		
		Precision	Recall	F1-score	Precision	Recall	F1-score
RandomForestClassifier	Control	99%	100%	100%	85%	93%	89%
RandomForestClassifier	Condition	100%	98%	99%	79%	62%	69%
GradientBoostingClassifier	Control	96%	93%	94%	90%	83%	87%
GradientBoostingClassifier	Condition	88%	93%	90%	68%	79%	73%
KNeighborsClassifier	Control	86%	75%	80%	89%	67%	77%
KNeighborsClassifier	Condition	65%	78%	71%	52%	82%	64%
Support Vector Machines (SVC)	Control	92%	84%	88%	88%	74%	80%
Support Vector Machines (SVC)	Condition	76%	87%	81%	56%	76%	65%
TPOT Classifier	Control	89%	89%	89%	80%	81%	81%
TPOT Classifier	Condition	85%	77%	81%	57%	68%	62%
MLSTM-FCN Classifier	Control	91%	83%	87%	87%	80%	83%
MLSTM-FCN Classifier	Condition	74%	86%	80%	62%	73%	67%

Based on the results, the Random Forest Classifier demonstrates the best overall performance with high Precision, Recall, and F1-scores in both groups and across train and test datasets, achieving the highest test accuracy of 83.41%. The Gradient Boosting Classifier also shows strong results, particularly for the Control-Group, with a test accuracy of 82.03%. While K Neighbors Classifier and SVC have lower performance in comparison, they still achieve decent scores for certain groups and datasets, with test accuracies of 73.27% and 80.18% respectively. In conclusion, the Random Forest Classifier appears to be the most effective model for both classes, offering a good balance of performance across Precision, Recall, and F1-score.

6 Conclusion

In conclusion, this study demonstrates the effectiveness of ML and DL models in predicting Control and Condition groups based on the "Normalised Statistical Features" nighttime dataset. Among the six models which were tried, the Random Forest Classifier achieved the highest test accuracy of 83.41%, with the Gradient Boosting Classifier closely following at 82.03%. The ROC curves provided valuable insights into the best threshold for maximising classification accuracy, which was selected based on the geometric mean of TPR and FPR.

These results highlight the potential of ML techniques for the analysis and interpretation of complex datasets in the context of sleep studies. By employing these methods, researchers can gain a deeper understanding of the underlying patterns and relationships within the data, which can, in turn, contribute to more effective interventions and treatments for sleep disorders. Future work could focus on exploring additional feature extraction techniques, incorporating other types of classifiers, and expanding the dataset to include a broader range of subjects and conditions to further improve the predictive performance of these models.

References

1. Ahmed, S., et al.: Artificial intelligence and machine learning for ensuring security in smart cities. In: Data-driven Mining, Learning and Analytics for Secured Smart Cities, pp. 23–47 (2021)
2. Ahmed, S., et al.: Toward machine learning-based psychological assessment of autism spectrum disorders in school and community. In: Proceedings of the TEHI, pp. 139–149 (2022)
3. Ahuja, N.J., et al.: An investigative study on the effects of pedagogical agents on intrinsic, extraneous and germane cognitive load: Experimental findings with dyscalculia and non-dyscalculia learners. IEEE Access **10**, 3904–3922 (2021)
4. Al Mamun, S., Kaiser, M.S., Mahmud, M.: An artificial intelligence based approach towards inclusive healthcare provisioning in society 5.0: a perspective on brain disorder. In: Proceedings of the Brain Inform, pp. 157–169 (2021)
5. Banna, M.H.A.: A hybrid deep learning model to predict the impact of covid-19 on mental health from social media big data. IEEE Access **11**, 77009–77022 (2023)

6. Bhagat, D., Ray, A., Sarda, A., Dutta Roy, N., Mahmud, M., De, D.: Improving mental health through multimodal emotion detection from speech and text data using long-short term memory. In: Frontiers of ICT in Healthcare: Proceedings of EAIT 2022, pp. 13–23 (2023)
7. Bhapkar, H.R., Mahalle, P.N., Shinde, G.R., Mahmud, M.: Rough sets in covid-19 to predict symptomatic cases. In: COVID-19: Prediction, Decision-Making, and its Impacts, pp. 57–68 (2021)
8. Biswas, M., Kaiser, M.S., Mahmud, M., Al Mamun, S., Hossain, M., Rahman, M.A., et al.: An xai based autism detection: the context behind the detection. In: Proceedings of the Brain Inform, pp. 448–459 (2021)
9. Biswas, M., et al.: Indoor navigation support system for patients with neurodegenerative diseases. In: Proceedings of the Brain Inform, pp. 411–422 (2021)
10. Biswas, M., et al.: Accu3rate: a mobile health application rating scale based on user reviews. PLoS ONE **16**(12), e0258050 (2021)
11. Chen, T., et al.: A dominant set-informed interpretable fuzzy system for automated diagnosis of dementia. Front. Neurosci. **16**, 86766 (2022)
12. Cortes, C., Vapnik, V.: Support-vector networks. Mach. Learn. **20**, 273–297 (1995)
13. Cox, D.R.: The regression analysis of binary sequences. J. R. Stat. Soc. Ser. B Stat. Methodol. **20**(2), 215–232 (1958)
14. Deepa, B., Murugappan, M., Sumithra, M., Mahmud, M., Al-Rakhami, M.S.: Pattern descriptors orientation and map firefly algorithm based brain pathology classification using hybridized machine learning algorithm. IEEE Access **10**, 3848–3863 (2021)
15. Dhara, T., Singh, P.K., Mahmud, M.: A fuzzy ensemble-based deep learning model for eeg-based emotion recognition. Cogn. Comput. 1–15 (2023). [ePub Ahead of Print]
16. Dogan, E., Sander, C., Wagner, X., Hegerl, U., Kohls, E.: Smartphone-based monitoring of objective and subjective data in affective disorders: where are we and where are we going? Systematic review. J. Med. Internet Res. **19**(7), e262 (2017)
17. Esha, N.H., et al.: Trust ioht: a trust management model for internet of healthcare things. In: Proceedings of the ICDSA, pp. 47–57 (2021)
18. Fabietti, M., Mahmud, M., Lotfi, A.: Machine learning in analysing invasively recorded neuronal signals: available open access data sources. In: Proceedings of the Brain Inform, pp. 151–162 (2020)
19. Fabietti, M., Mahmud, M., Lotfi, A.: Artefact detection in chronically recorded local field potentials: an explainable machine learning-based approach. In: Proceedings of the IJCNN, pp. 1–7 (2022)
20. Fabietti, M., et al.: Adaptation of convolutional neural networks for multi-channel artifact detection in chronically recorded local field potentials. In: Proceedings of the SSCI, pp. 1607–1613 (2020)
21. Fabietti, M., et al.: Artifact detection in chronically recorded local field potentials using long-short term memory neural network. In: Proceedings of the AICT, pp. 1–6 (2020)
22. Fabietti, M., et al.: Neural network-based artifact detection in local field potentials recorded from chronically implanted neural probes. In: Proceedings of the IJCNN, pp. 1–8 (2020)
23. Fabietti, M.I., et al.: Detection of healthy and unhealthy brain states from local field potentials using machine learning. In: Proceedings of the Brain Inform, pp. 27–39 (2022)
24. Farhin, F., Kaiser, M.S., Mahmud, M.: Towards secured service provisioning for the internet of healthcare things. In: Proceedings of the AICT, pp. 1–6 (2020)

25. Farhin, F., Kaiser, M.S., Mahmud, M.: Secured smart healthcare system: blockchain and bayesian inference based approach. In: Proceedings of the TCCE, pp. 455–465 (2021)
26. Farhin, F., Sultana, I., Islam, N., Kaiser, M.S., Rahman, M.S., Mahmud, M.: Attack detection in internet of things using software defined network and fuzzy neural network. In: Proceedings of the ICIEV and icIVPR, pp. 1–6 (2020)
27. Feng, M., Fang, T., He, C., Li, M., Liu, J.: Affect and stress detection based on feature fusion of lstm and 1dcnn. Comput. Methods Biomech. Biomed. Eng. **27**(4), 512–520 (2024)
28. Galvan-Tejada, C.E., et al.: Depression episodes detection in unipolar and bipolar patients: a methodology with feature extraction and feature selection with genetic algorithms using activity motion signal as information source. Mob. Inform. Syst. **2019**, 8269695 (2019)
29. Garcia-Ceja, E., et al.: Depresjon: a motor activity database of depression episodes in unipolar and bipolar patients. In: Proceedings of the ACM MMSys'18, pp. 472–477 (2018)
30. Garcia-Ceja, E., et al.: Depresjon: a motor activity database of depression episodes in unipolar and bipolar patients. In: Proceedings of the 9th ACM Multimedia Systems Conference, pp. 472–477 (2018)
31. Ghosh, T., et al.: An attention-based mood controlling framework for social media users. In: Proceedings of the Brain Inform, pp. 245–256 (2021)
32. Giannakakis, G., Grigoriadis, D., Giannakaki, K., Simantiraki, O., Roniotis, A., Tsiknakis, M.: Review on psychological stress detection using biosignals. IEEE Trans. Affect. Comput. **13**(1), 440–460 (2019)
33. Haque, Y., et al.: State-of-the-art of stress prediction from heart rate variability using artificial intelligence. Cogn. Comput. **16**(2), 455–481 (2024)
34. Ho, T.K.: Random decision forests. In: Proceedings of 3rd International Conference on Document Analysis and Recognition, vol. 1, pp. 278–282. IEEE (1995)
35. Hochreiter, S., Schmidhuber, J.: Long short-term memory. Neural Comput. **9**(8), 1735–1780 (1997)
36. Islam, N., et al.: Towards machine learning based intrusion detection in iot networks. Comput. Mater. Contin **69**(2), 1801–1821 (2021)
37. Jahan, S., et al.: Explainable ai-based alzheimer's prediction and management using multimodal data. PLoS ONE **18**(11), e0294253 (2023)
38. Jahan, S., Saif Adib, M.R., Mahmud, M., Kaiser, M.S.: Comparison between explainable ai algorithms for alzheimer's disease prediction using efficientnet models. In: International Conference on Brain Informatics, pp. 357–368 (2023)
39. Jakobsen, P.: Applying machine learning in motor activity time series of depressed bipolar and unipolar patients compared to healthy controls. PLoS ONE **15**(8), e0231995 (2020)
40. Javed, A.R., et al.: Artificial intelligence for cognitive health assessment: state-of-the-art, open challenges and future directions. Cogn. Comput. **15**, 1767–1812 (2023)
41. Jesmin, S., Kaiser, M.S., Mahmud, M.: Towards artificial intelligence driven stress monitoring for mental wellbeing tracking during covid-19. In: Proceedings of the WI-IAT, pp. 845–851 (2020)
42. Jiang, H., Nie, Z., Yeo, R., Farimani, A.B., Kara, L.B.: Stressgan: a generative deep learning model for two-dimensional stress distribution prediction. J. Appl. Mech. **88**(5), 051005 (2021)

43. Kaiser, M.S., et al.: 6G access network for intelligent internet of healthcare things: opportunity, challenges, and research directions. In: Proceedings of the TCCE, pp. 317–328 (2021)
44. Karim, F., Majumdar, S., Darabi, H., Harford, S.: Multivariate lstm-fcns for time series classification. Neural Netw. **116**, 237–245 (2019)
45. Kumar, A., Sharma, K., Sharma, A.: Genetically optimized fuzzy c-means data clustering of iomt-based biomarkers for fast affective state recognition in intelligent edge analytics. Appl. Soft Comput. **109**, 107525 (2021)
46. Kumar, I., et al.: Dense tissue pattern characterization using deep neural network. Cogn. Comput. **14**(5), 1728–1751 (2022)
47. Kumar, S., et al.: Forecasting major impacts of COVID-19 pandemic on country-driven sectors: challenges, lessons, and future roadmap. Pers. Ubiquitous Comput. 1–24 (2021)
48. Lalotra, G.S., Kumar, V., Bhatt, A., Chen, T., Mahmud, M.: Iretads: an intelligent real-time anomaly detection system for cloud communications using temporal data summarization and neural network. Secur. Commun. Netw. **2022**, 1–15 (2022). articleID: 9149164
49. Le, T.T., Fu, W., Moore, J.H.: Scaling tree-based automated machine learning to biomedical big data with a feature set selector. Bioinformatics **36**(1), 250–256 (2020)
50. LeCun, Y., Bottou, L., Bengio, Y., Haffner, P.: Gradient-based learning applied to document recognition. Proc. IEEE **86**(11), 2278–2324 (1998)
51. Leng, L.B., Giin, L.B., Chung, W.Y.: Wearable driver drowsiness detection system based on biomedical and motion sensors. In: 2015 IEEE SENSORS, pp. 1–4 (2015)
52. Mahmud, M., Kaiser, M.S.: Machine learning in fighting pandemics: a covid-19 case study. In: COVID-19: Prediction, Decision-Making, and Its Impacts, pp. 77–81 (2021)
53. Mahmud, M., et al.: Towards explainable and privacy-preserving artificial intelligence for personalisation in autism spectrum disorder. In: Proceedings of the HCII, pp. 356–370 (2022)
54. Mammoottil, M.J., et al.: Detection of breast cancer from five-view thermal images using convolutional neural networks. J. Healthc. Eng. **2022** (2022)
55. Morton, E., et al.: Evaluating the quality, safety, and functionality of commonly used smartphone apps for bipolar disorder mood and sleep self-management. Int. J. Bipolar Disord. **10**(1), 10 (2022)
56. Nahiduzzaman, M., Tasnim, M., Newaz, N.T., Kaiser, M.S., Mahmud, M.: Machine learning based early fall detection for elderly people with neurological disorder using multimodal data fusion. In: Proceedings of the Brain Inform, pp. 204–214 (2020)
57. Ortiz, A., Grof, P.: Electronic monitoring of self-reported mood: the return of the subjective? Int. J. Bipolar Disord. **4**, 1–8 (2016)
58. Paul, A., Basu, A., Mahmud, M., Kaiser, M.S., Sarkar, R.: Inverted bell-curve-based ensemble of deep learning models for detection of covid-19 from chest x-rays. Neural Comput. Appl. 1–15 (2022)
59. Prakash, N., Murugappan, M., Hemalakshmi, G., Jayalakshmi, M., Mahmud, M.: Deep transfer learning for covid-19 detection and infection localization with super-pixel based segmentation. Sustain. Cities Soc. **75**, 103252 (2021)
60. Rabby, G., et al.: A flexible keyphrase extraction technique for academic literature. Procedia Comput. Sci. **135**, 553–563 (2018)

61. Rahman, M.A., et al.: Explainable multimodal machine learning for engagement analysis by continuous performance test. In: Proceedings of the HCII, pp. 386–399 (2022)
62. Rai, T., et al.: Decision tree approaches to select high risk patients for lung cancer screening based on the UK primary care data. In: Proceedings of the AIME, pp. 35–39 (2023)
63. Rasmussen, C.E.: Gaussian Processes in Machine Learning. In: Bousquet, O., von Luxburg, U., Rätsch, G. (eds.) Advanced Lectures on Machine Learning. ML 2003. LNCS, vol. 3176, pp. 63–71. Springer, Berlin, Heidelberg (2004). https://doi.org/10.1007/978-3-540-28650-9_4
64. Rodríguez-Ruiz, J.G., et al.: Comparison of night, day and 24 h motor activity data for the classification of depressive episodes. Diagnostics **10**(3), 162 (2020)
65. Ruiz, J., Mahmud, M., Modasshir, M., Shamim Kaiser, M.: Alzheimer's Disease Neuroimaging Initiative, f.t.: 3d densenet ensemble in 4-way classification of alzheimer's disease. In: Brain Informatics: 13th International Conference, BI 2020, Padua, Italy, 19 September 2020, Proceedings 13, pp. 85–96 (2020)
66. Schapire, R.E.: Explaining adaboost. In: Schölkopf, B., Luo, Z., Vovk, V. (eds.) Empirical Inference, LNCS, pp. 37–52. Springer, Berlin, Heidelberg (2013). https://doi.org/10.1007/978-3-642-41136-6_5
67. Schmidt, P., Reiss, A., Duerichen, R., Marberger, C., Van Laerhoven, K.: Introducing wesad, a multimodal dataset for wearable stress and affect detection, pp. 400–408 (2018)
68. Shaffi, N., Hajamohideen, F., Abdesselam, A., Mahmud, M., Subramanian, K.: Ensemble classifiers for a 4-way classification of alzheimer's disease. In: Proceedings of the AII, pp. 219–230 (2022)
69. Shaffi, N., Hajamohideen, F., Mahmud, M., Abdesselam, A., Subramanian, K., Sariri, A.A.: Triplet-loss based siamese convolutional neural network for 4-way classification of alzheimer's disease. In: Proceedings of the Brain Inform, pp. 277–287 (2022)
70. Shaffi, N., Viswan, V., Mahmud, M., Hajamohideen, F., Subramanian, K.: Multiplanar mri-based classification of alzheimer's disease using tree-based machine learning algorithms. In: Proceedings of the WI-IAT, pp. 496–502 (2023)
71. Shaffi, N., Viswan, V., Mahmud, M., Hajamohideen, F., Subramanian, K.: Towards automated classification of Parkinson's disease: comparison of machine learning methods using mri and acoustic data. In: Proceedings of the SSCI, pp. 1328–1333 (2023)
72. Shahriar, M.F., Arnab, M.S.A., Khan, M.S., Rahman, S.S., Mahmud, M., Kaiser, M.S.: Towards machine learning-based emotion recognition from multimodal data. In: Frontiers of ICT in Healthcare: Proceedings of EAIT 2022, pp. 99–109 (2023)
73. Shon, D., Im, K., Park, J.H., Lim, D.S., Jang, B., Kim, J.M.: Emotional stress state detection using genetic algorithm-based feature selection on eeg signals. Int. J. Environ. Res. Public Health **15**(11), 2461 (2018)
74. Singh, R., Mahmud, M., Yovera, L.: Classification of first trimester ultrasound images using deep convolutional neural network. In: Proceedings of the AII, pp. 92–105 (2021)
75. Szakonyi, B., Vassányi, I., Schumacher, E., Kósa, I.: Efficient methods for acute stress detection using heart rate variability data from ambient assisted living sensors. Biomed. Eng. Online **20**, 1–19 (2021)
76. Tagiltsev, I., Shutov, A.: Geometrically nonlinear modelling of pre-stressed viscoelastic fibre-reinforced composites with application to arteries. Biomech. Model. Mechanobiol. **20**, 323–337 (2021)

77. Tahura, S., Hasnat Samiul, S., Shamim Kaiser, M., Mahmud, M.: Anomaly detection in electroencephalography signal using deep learning model. In: Proceedings of the TCCE, pp. 205–217 (2021)
78. Tran, T.D., et al.: Stress analysis with dimensions of valence and arousal in the wild. Appl. Sci. **11**(11), 5194 (2021)
79. Tzevelekakis, K., Stefanidi, Z., Margetis, G.: Real-time stress level feedback from raw ecg signals for personalised, context-aware applications using lightweight convolutional neural network architectures. Sensors **21**(23), 7802 (2021)
80. Viswan, V., Shaffi, N., Mahmud, M., Subramanian, K., Hajamohideen, F.: A comparative study of pretrained deep neural networks for classifying alzheimer's and parkinson's disease. In: Proceedings of the SSCI, pp. 1334–1339 (2023)
81. Wadhera, T., Mahmud, M.: Computing hierarchical complexity of the brain from electroencephalogram signals: a graph convolutional network-based approach. In: Proceedings of the IJCNN, pp. 1–6 (2022)
82. Wadhera, T., Mahmud, M.: Influences of social learning in individual perception and decision making in people with autism: a computational approach. In: Proceedings of the Brain Inform, pp. 50–61 (2022)
83. Wadhera, T., Mahmud, M.: Computational model of functional connectivity distance predicts neural alterations. IEEE Trans. Cogn. Dev. Syst. 1–10 (2023). [ePub Ahead of Print]
84. Wshah, S., Skalka, C., Price, M., et al.: Predicting posttraumatic stress disorder risk: a machine learning approach. JMIR Ment. Health **6**(7), e13946 (2019)
85. Yahaya, S.W., Lotfi, A., Mahmud, M.: Towards a data-driven adaptive anomaly detection system for human activity. Pattern Recognit. Lett. **145**, 200–207 (2021)
86. Yang, Z., Yu, C.H., Buehler, M.J.: Deep learning model to predict complex stress and strain fields in hierarchical composites. Sci. Adv. **7**(15), eabd7416 (2021)
87. Yu, H., Sano, A.: Passive sensor data based future mood, health, and stress prediction: user adaptation using deep learning. In: Proceedings of the EMBC, pp. 5884–5887 (2020)
88. Zaman, S., et al.: Security threats and artificial intelligence based countermeasures for internet of things networks: a comprehensive survey. IEEE Access **9**, 94668–94690 (2021)
89. Zawad, M.R.S., Rony, C.S.A., Haque, M.Y., Banna, M.H.A., Mahmud, M., Kaiser, M.S.: A hybrid approach for stress prediction from heart rate variability. In: Frontiers of ICT in Healthcare: Proceedings of EAIT 2022, pp. 111–121 (2023)
90. Zohora, M.F., Tania, M.H., Kaiser, M.S., Mahmud, M.: Forecasting the risk of type ii diabetes using reinforcement learning. In: Proceedings of the ICIEV and icIVPR, pp. 1–6 (2020)

Detour: Understanding the Application of Artificial Intelligence Based Models in Forecasting Safe Travel Routes

Subhranil Das[1], Rashmi Kumari[2(✉)], and Raghwendra Kishore Singh[3]

[1] School of Computer Science, UPES, Dehradun, Uttarakhand, India
[2] School of Computer Science Engineering and Technology, Bennett University, Greater Noida, UP, India
Rashmi.Kumari@bennett.edu.in
[3] Department of Electronics and Communications Engineering, Galgotia College of Engineering & Technology, Greater Noida, Uttar Pradesh, India

Abstract. This paper explores the creation of an AI-based system for predicting secure and safe travel routes. Seeing the rise in the amount of criminal activity and traffic accidents, it is now more crucial than ever to have trustworthy and precise tools for determining secure journey routes. To offer users a customized and secure journey path, the suggested system makes use of machine learning algorithms and real- time data from numerous sources, including traffic updates and local crime figures. Such a system in place will ensure the safety and well-being of people walking or driving by alone, especially at night, by preventing them from traveling through an insecure area, despite it being the shorter way out. Besides overviewing the various techniques and strategies employed in models suggested by others in similar style applications, we suggest future paths and our own algorithm for this field's study and growth, highlighting areas that may be improved and innovative. We have suggested a technique for finding a safe route through a town using hotspot analysis by applying Kernel Density Estimation to find high crime areas and assigning risk rates to different paths based on this data, thus avoiding those routes with high risk as much as possible. This paper's findings have a significant impact on the way transportation works and can be an effective tool for promoting safety on the roads.

Keywords: Artificial Intelligence · Density Estimation · Safe Path

1 Introduction

As Artificial Intelligence (AI) permeates virtually every sector in the contemporary world, there is a growing interest in its application within the transportation industry [1,2]. While AI is already extensively employed in navigation systems and the tourism sector to enhance transportation efficiency, an area poised for significant benefits is the precise prediction of safe and reliable travel routes.

Unlike most navigation systems that primarily prioritize providing the shortest route from point A to point B, there are instances where these systems may inadvertently guide individuals through narrow alleyways or secluded roads, which may not be the most secure or comfortable option, especially for solo travelers [3,4]. Notably, women often deviate from recommended routes on navigation platforms like Google Maps, opting for longer paths due to concerns about traveling alone or with other women on the streets, particularly during the night, fearing harassment or violence. While locals may have the knowledge to choose "safe routes" and discern which streets pose risks or are secure, visitors to a new city may lack such awareness, consequently elevating potential safety risks. To navigate unfamiliar areas safely, tourists typically need to research crime rates before embarking on their trips. Despite government initiatives to enhance safety, there is a recognition that citizens should take certain measures to ensure their safety, underscoring the vital importance of implementing such a system.

As per the National Crime Records Bureau of India, the majority of crimes reported in metropolitan cities in 2021, constituting 40.1% (2,53,068 out of 6,30,937 cases), were categorized under Theft. The year 2021 witnessed a notable increase of 22.9% in crime against women, with 43,414 cases registered compared to 35,331 cases in 2020 [5]. These alarming statistics underscore the urgent need for the implementation of a secure route navigation system. A study conducted by Cornell University and Hollaback in 2014, focusing on street harassment, revealed that 85% of the 4,872 interviewed women had altered their routes to mitigate the risk of sexual harassment or assault. Additionally, 67% had adjusted the time they left an event or location. This emphasizes the critical necessity for a proactive and comprehensive safe routing application. While existing apps like Raksha and Nirbhaya address women's safety concerns by employing emergency signals and location tracking in case of danger, a more proactive approach is essential to actively avoid excessively dangerous areas whenever possible.

This is where the system proposed in this paper becomes instrumental. To provide users with a personalized and secure journey path, the suggested system will utilize machine learning algorithms and real-time data from various sources, including traffic updates and crime statistics. Further enhancements to this system can be achieved by incorporating feedback from current app users, allowing them to designate areas as safe or unsafe. Additionally, the integration of web scraping to extract information from news sites and social media posts can contribute to refining the system. Other research initiatives and software solutions adopt a balanced approach between proximity and safety in determining the optimal route. One such program is Safestreet [6], which assesses risks along paths using a map of crime prevalence and then recommends routes ranging from the shortest distance to the safest options. Another secure route finder employs a Naive Bayes algorithm to classify and geocode crimes based on social crime complaints and tweets [7]. Its primary goal is to identify the safest path without factoring in distance, utilizing sentiment analysis on tweets to highlight safe and unsafe areas.

In the realm of academic inquiry, while existing research has explored systems akin to the one under consideration, there remains a critical need for improvement in both awareness and efficiency. Each proposed system exhibits both commendable attributes and shortcomings that warrant careful consideration. A prevalent issue observed in the current body of literature is the tendency of some models to exclusively incorporate the most recent crimes in their approach. This strategy is often adopted due to the accessibility of a substantial amount of data, enabling prolonged training of the model across an extended period of crime trends. However, relying solely on the latest crimes introduces sparsity during the training phase, hindering the model from capturing overarching patterns. Furthermore, certain models adopt a generalized treatment of all crimes, posing additional aspects to be scrutinized.

Through an extensive examination of the existing literature, we discern pivotal trends and challenges within the domain of AI-based travel route prediction. In the broader context of Artificial Intelligence, the predictive facet seamlessly integrates into myriad everyday applications. Particularly for the specified problem statement, the significance of leveraging substantial datasets cannot be overstated, as it constitutes the essential foundation for developing an efficacious system with a heightened predictability quotient.

This research paper delves into a comprehensive consideration of various factors, culminating in the proposal of a more holistic approach to foster the optimal system. The proposed solution in this paper entails clustering metropolitan city areas into distinct danger zones, assigning weights on a scale through Kernel Density Estimation-based spatial clustering. Subsequently, the suggested system modifies the displayed path between two points based on areas where the risk scale is elevated. Emphasizing real-time crime data at a more localized, granular level, our solution is poised to furnish more precise and context-aware travel routes. As a result, the envisioned system holds the potential to instill peace of mind for individuals, such as students and women, navigating urban environments alone.

2 Literature Review

Within the current landscape of safe route detection and navigation, there exists a spectrum of algorithms and deep learning models/systems designed to narrow the efficiency and accuracy gap. Despite the availability of these tools, users are often limited in their ability to proactively manage their personal safety. Innovations such as SafeRoute [8], employing a novel path generation approach through deep reinforcement learning, present a promising avenue for enhancing the scenario and achieving successful optimization in multi-criteria pathfinding arrangements. This method incorporates representation learning within its framework, with the agent learning to select favorable streets to construct a safe and efficient path, supported by a reward function that incorporates safety considerations. SafeRoute underwent testing in densely populated downtown areas with heavy foot traffic.

The evolution of urban spaces increasingly relies on mobile applications for planning and routing in urban settings. This trend heralds the advent of the next generation of mobile information systems, focused on decision-making to effectively support the growth of large cities. Applications like CrowdPlanner [9] and DroidOppPathFinder [10] target the creation of crowd-based route recommendation systems, encouraging users to evaluate suggested routes from various sources and methods to determine the optimal route based on their feedback. In contrast, our approach utilizes official data to analyze the frequency of crimes in order to assess routes, providing a more objective and data-driven perspective on safety considerations.

SocRoutes [11] constitutes a noteworthy exploration in the domain of secure pathfinding, centering on the application of sentiment analysis to tweets and the utilization of geographical information derived from these tweets. This approach leverages regional context and sentiments inferred from these tweets, particularly those exhibiting strongly negative emotions, to determine routes that align with user preferences. The system caters to various transport modes, including walking, bicycling, and driving. The safety score is established by calculating the percentage of regions with sentiment values exceeding a predefined baseline threshold relative to the total regions along the route.

In a parallel study [12], each path from source to destination is assigned a risk score (r) through a weighted formula, incorporating considerations for both distance and crime density across a city. The crime density is computed using Gaussian Kernel density estimation, normalized by factoring in the population of specific areas. Subsequently, the researchers employ Dijkstra's shortest path algorithm to identify the safest and most efficient route, with the assigned risk scores serving as the weights for the paths.

3 Proposed Methodology

The presented methodology comprises two pivotal phases: firstly, the identification and amalgamation of the latest available data, and secondly, the implementation of machine learning algorithms that will analyze this data to delineate the secure path. A critical additional phase involves visualizing the results through a maps API (such as Google Maps) to ensure user-friendly comprehension of the safe route information. However, the current discussion exclusively delves into the initial two phases.

3.1 Data Gathering

Various methods exist for collecting crime data, and it is essential to amalgamate these diverse sources, assigning weights to each, to create a comprehensive data source. This approach ensures that all relevant aspects are considered, resulting in a more meaningful outcome.

Official Reports: Official records from the Delhi Police present an opportunity to access FIRs online through a publicly available open-source portal [1].

FIRs are accessible in various formats, including CSV, JSON, and PDF. The CID Branch further provides weekly and monthly data reports for each district, facilitating comprehensive criminal analysis over specific timeframes. Users can retrieve FIRs released within a three-month window for a particular unit area, ensuring access to the latest and reliable data based on search criteria. This portal serves as a primary data source for crime rate prediction in our study. While official FIR reports offer substantial data, numerous other valuable sources are available for accessing meaningful information. Although not considered in this paper's scope, future models could integrate data from these additional sources to achieve optimal and meaningful results. Some of these sources include:

Oversourcing: The insights and daily observations of individuals navigating a city, as evidenced by crowdsourced data, represent a valuable data source that, when meticulously analyzed, can offer trustworthy insights into areas of potential safety concerns. There are various methods through which this information can be collected.

Surveys, or through the safety app itself: Real-time data can be collected through user reviews of the suggested path by the safety route application, and this information can be incorporated to enhance the model's outcomes.

Web Scraping: This represents a swift and effective method for automating the extraction of data. Leveraging the advantages of web scraping enables individuals to gather data from any website, regardless of its volume, and store it locally. Crime data and statistics can be easily obtained by scraping information from news websites such as Times of India. These news articles typically provide details on crimes, including exact locations, dates, times, the nature of the crime, and the age of the victim. First Information Reports (FIRs) hold significant importance in contributing to the identification of safe routes, being the official crime reports documented for a region. However, due to potential validation issues, user reviews are assigned lower priority, with web-scraped articles and news following in the hierarchy.

4 Applying ML for Safe Path

Constructing an algorithm for predicting safe routes introduces a challenge particularly in a sprawling city, the solution space for the path-finding algorithm could potentially be exponential. However, a strategic approach involves incorporating parameters and implementing early stopping criteria for short paths with low risk, rather than insisting on identifying the path with the minimum risk, which could be impractically lengthy. Our ultimate goal is to present a subset of viable solutions, allowing travelers to choose one based on their convenience.

In the initial phases of our work, we currently evaluate all paths suggested by Google Maps from point A to point B, analyzing their associated risk potentials.

4.1 Hotspot Analysis

Our methodology incorporates clustering to partition the city into distinct sections, considering the frequency of crime and establishing a safety index for each region. Specifically, our emphasis lies in identifying crime hotspots through spatial clustering techniques, with Kernel Density Estimation (KDE) serving as a straightforward and efficient method widely adopted for hotspot analysis.

4.2 Kernels

In non-parametric regression, kernel functions play a crucial role as a weighting function, extending their utility to the estimation of random variable densities. These functions find application in various tasks, including clustering and classification.

4.3 KDE

The process of estimating an unknown probability density function through a kernel function is referred to as kernel density estimation. In this method, a kernel density estimate is a function that aggregates its kernel function at each data point. This concept can be better grasped by contrasting it with a histogram, which merely tallies the number of data points within certain arbitrary intervals. The general formulation of KDE has been given in Eqn. 1.

$$\lambda(s) = \frac{1}{N} \sum_{i=1}^{N} k\left(\frac{d_i(s)}{r}\right) \quad (1)$$

Where $\lambda(s)$ is the density at location s, r is the search radius (bandwidth) of the KDE, N is the number of sampling points, k is the weight of a point i at distance d to location s. k is usually modeled as a kernel function of the ratio between dis and r. In this paper, we used a kernel with a Gaussian function given by:

Instead of just determining the crime hotspots, we can enhance the functionality and applicability of the application by segmenting crimes based on the time of day. This approach involves creating distinct clusters for various time intervals, offering a more precise risk analysis. This is particularly significant as statistical evidence supports the observation that more crimes tend to occur during nighttime.

Assigning total risk score: After identifying the crime hotspots in the city, the city is divided into segments. When a user inputs their starting point and destination, the application estimates the risk associated with the multitude of available paths by calculating distances from these crime hotspots. This constitutes the final step in presenting the safest route. Our approach involves determining the latitude and longitude of stops at equidistant intervals (e.g., 4 km) along different routes. Each stop is assigned a specific risk value based on its distance from calculated crime hotspots. By aggregating the risk scores of all these stops along the route, an overall risk value for the route is generated, providing users with information on the safest path.

5 Simulation Results and Discussion

When tested on the Delhi crime dataset, our AI, tasked with identifying the safe route between Connaught Place and a hotel in Delhi, deviated from the standard Google Maps route. Instead, it strategically bypassed Seema Puri, a significant crime hotspot. While the route visualization requires integration with the Google Maps API (currently in progress), the methodology underscores the application of machine learning algorithms to achieve the primary objective of determining secure travel routes. The simulation results demonstrate that the proposed AI system effectively identifies a safer route by calculating and aggregating risk scores for individual stops along the route. By avoiding significant crime hotspots like Seema Puri, the proposed route reduces the overall risk score from 17 to 7, thereby providing a significantly safer path for users. This methodology underscores the importance and effectiveness of incorporating Hotspot Analysis and Kernel Density Estimation, particularly with night-time crime data, to enhance route safety as shown in the Table 1.

Table 1. Simulation results for calculating risk scores for routes

Route	Stop Location	Risk Score	Reason
Route 1 (Standard Route)	Connaught Place	2	Moderate risk due to occasional petty crimes
	Near Seema Puri	8	High risk due to frequent violent crimes
	Intermediate Stop	4	Moderate risk due to past incidents
	Hotel	3	Low risk, occasional thefts
Total Risk Score		17	
Route 2 (Proposed Safe Route)	Connaught Place	2	Moderate risk due to occasional petty crimes
	Alternate Path Stop 1	1	Low risk, few reported incidents
	Alternate Path Stop 2	1	Low risk, minimal crime activity
	Hotel	3	Low risk, occasional thefts
Total Risk Score		7	

The Table 1 compares the risk scores of two routes from Connaught Place to a hotel in Delhi, assessing each stop based on the prevalence of crime. Route 1 (Standard Route) includes stops at Connaught Place, Near Seema Puri, an Intermediate Stop, and the Hotel, accumulating a total risk score of 17. The high-risk area near Seema Puri contributes significantly to this score due to frequent violent crimes. In contrast, Route 2 (Proposed Safe Route) avoids Seema Puri, opting instead for alternate paths with stops at Connaught Place, Alternate Path Stop 1, Alternate Path Stop 2, and the Hotel, resulting in a significantly lower total risk score of 7. This reduction in risk is achieved by bypassing major crime hotspots, particularly the high-risk area near Seema Puri, highlighting the effectiveness of the proposed route in enhancing safety.

The approach involves Hotspot Analysis and Kernel Density Estimation, accommodating the specificity that crimes are more prevalent at night. By considering night-time crime data, the results become more robust and efficient, catering to a larger dataset. The risk scores for individual stops along the route are aggregated to generate an overall risk value. The second step entails identifying and zooming into city hotspots, assigning risk scores based on distances from these hotspots to the user's destination. Proximity of stops to crime hotspots influences risk scores, with closer stops receiving higher scores, contributing to accurate results. Subsequently, the safest route is determined by selecting the path with the lowest overall risk score for users to navigate between the starting point and destination. In the final step, the safest route is achieved by incorporating risk values from stops along the route, providing users with estimates of the associated risks for each available path. The values of risk score has been calculated in the Table 2.

Table 2. Simulation results for route calculation using KDE

Route	Stop Location	Time of Day	Risk Score	Reason
Route 1 (Standard Route)	Connaught Place	Day/Night	2	Moderate risk due to occasional petty crimes
	Near Seema Puri	Night	8	High risk due to frequent violent crimes, particularly at night
	Intermediate Stop	Day/Night	4	Moderate risk due to past incidents
	Hotel	Day/Night	3	Low risk, occasional thefts
Total Risk Score			17	
Route 2 (Proposed Safe Route)	Connaught Place	Day/Night	2	Moderate risk due to occasional petty crimes
	Alternate Path Stop 1	Day/Night	1	Low risk, few reported incidents
	Alternate Path Stop 2	Day/Night	1	Low risk, minimal crime activity
	Hotel	Day/Night	3	Low risk, occasional thefts
Total Risk Score			7	

The Table 2 compares two routes from Connaught Place to a hotel in Delhi, assessing the risk at each stop based on the time of day and the crime rate. Route 1 (Standard Route) includes stops at Connaught Place, Near Seema Puri, an Intermediate Stop, and the Hotel, accumulating a total risk score of 17. Connaught Place and the Intermediate Stop present moderate risks due to occasional petty crimes and past incidents, with risk scores of 2 and 4 respectively, regardless of the time of day. The high-risk area near Seema Puri, especially at night, contributes a significant risk score of 8 due to frequent violent crimes. The Hotel has a low risk score of 3 due to occasional thefts. In contrast, Route 2 (Proposed Safe Route) avoids the high-risk area of Seema Puri. It includes stops at Connaught Place, Alternate Path Stop 1, Alternate Path Stop 2, and the Hotel, resulting in a significantly lower total risk score of 7. Both alternate path stops have low risk scores of 1 due to minimal crime activity and few reported incidents, with the hotel retaining the same low risk score of 3. This demonstrates that the proposed route is safer, effectively reducing the overall risk by bypassing high-risk areas, particularly at night.

6 Conclusion and Future Scope

In essence, the outlined methodology and its thorough examination are poised to carry significant ramifications for transportation safety. Functioning as a potent instrument in bolstering road safety, especially for individuals journeying alone or navigating unfamiliar territories, the system's ability to derive personalized and secure travel routes addresses a broader safety concern. It actively diminishes the likelihood of encountering perilous situations, thereby elevating the overall travel experience for users. Future endeavors in research and development could potentially amplify the system's capabilities, contributing to the progression of transportation safety protocols. A comparative analysis with existing analogous applications revealed enhancements in both awareness and efficiency. While some present systems heavily rely on the most recent crime data, asserting its accuracy and currency, our method diverges by incorporating historical crime trends, ensuring more dependable and resilient predictions.

Moreover, the system exhibits the potential for integration with user feedback data and the utilization of web scraping to gather insights from news platforms and social media posts. This multifaceted approach positions the proposed system as a comprehensive and forward-thinking solution in the realm of transportation safety.

References

1. Das, S., Kumari, R., Deepak Kumar, S.: A review on applications of simultaneous localization and mapping method in autonomous vehicles. In: Kumar, N., Tibor, S., Sindhwani, R., Lee, J., Srivastava, P. (eds.) Advances in Interdisciplinary Engineering. LNME, pp. 367–375. Springer, Singapore (2021). https://doi.org/10.1007/978-981-15-9956-9_37
2. Kumari, R., Das, S., Singh, R.K.: Agglomeration of deep learning networks for classifying binary and multiclass classifications using 3D MRI images for early diagnosis of Alzheimer's disease: a feature-node approach. Int. J. Syst. Assur. Eng. Manag. 1–19 (2023)
3. Kumari, R., Goel, S., Das, S.: A 3D convolutional neural network approach for diagnosing alzheimer's disease using modified owl search optimization technique. In: TENCON 2022-2022 IEEE Region 10 Conference (TENCON), pp. 1–7. IEEE, 2022
4. Das, S., Kumari, R.: Application of extended hough transform technique for stationary images in vehicle license plate. In: 2021 6th International Conference for Convergence in Technology (I2CT), pp. 1–4. IEEE, 2021
5. Yadav, S.S., Edwards, P., Porter, J.: Evaluation of first information reports of Delhi police for injury surveillance: data extraction tool development & validation. Indian J. Med. Res. **152**(4), 410–416 (2020)
6. Ali, M.E., Rishta, S.B., Ansari, L., Hashem, T., Khan, A.I.: SafeStreet: empowering women against street harassment using a privacy-aware location based application. In: Proceedings of the Seventh International Conference on Information and Communication Technologies and Development, pp. 1–4, 2015

7. Fu, K., Lu, Y.C., Lu, C.T.: Treads: a safe route recommender using social media mining and text summarization. In: Proceedings of the 22nd ACM SIGSPATIAL International Conference on Advances in Geographic Information Systems, pp. 557–560, 2014
8. Levy, S., Xiong, W., Belding, E., YangWang, W.: SafeRoute: learning to navigate streets safely in an urban environment. ACM Trans. Intell. Syst. Technol. (TIST) **11**(6), 1–17 (2020)
9. Su, H., Zheng, K., Huang, J., Jeung, H., Chen, L., Zhou, X.: Crowdplanner: a crowd-based route recommendation system. In: 2014 IEEE 30th International Conference on Data Engineering, pp. 1144–1155. IEEE, 2014
10. Kumari, R., Goel, S., Das, S.: Mathematical modelling of dendritic complexity mechanism in Alzheimer's disease. In: AIP Conference Proceedings, vol. 2872, no. 1. AIP Publishing, 2023
11. Kim, J., Cha, M., Sandholm, T.: Socroutes: safe route based on tweet sentiments. In: Proceedings of the 23rd International Conference on World Wide Web, pp. 179–182, 2014
12. Galbrun, E., Pelechrinis, K., Terzi, E.: Urban navigation beyond shortest route: the case of safe paths. Inf. Syst. **57**, 160–171 (2016)
13. Gadkar, N., Das, S., Chakraborty, S., Mishra, S.K.: Static obstacle avoidance for rover vehicles using model predictive controller. In: 2022 International Conference on IoT and Blockchain Technology (ICIBT), pp. 1–6. IEEE, 2022

An Approach to Compute the Adaptive Dynamic Diameter of Data Stream Clusters

Abeer Altahan[(✉)] and Saad Talib Hasson

College of Information Technology, University of Babylon, Babylon, Iraq
abeerma.sw.phd@student.uobabylon.edu.iq,
Saad_aljebori@itnet.uobabylon.edu.iq

Abstract. Due to the advances in technology, most of the data are being as streams with large volumes and high flow. Different approaches were proposed to deal with such data streams. Clustering is one of the most important algorithms utilized to solve the data stream problems. K-Mean algorithm was considered as one of the best classical clustering algorithms. It is suitable for mining and analyzing data stream, because it depends on the centroid, number of data elements, and distance measurement. K-Mean algorithm needs continuous updates to determine the number and size of clusters. Data stream processing requires an immediate processing at any time of the data stream entrance. In this paper sensors data streams clustering are considered. The proposed system is composed of four stages. Collecting streams of data (based on date and time) from real wireless sensors represent the 1st stage. The 2nd stage is to construct an offline implementation to propose primary number of clusters with variable sizes. The 3rd stage is an online implementation to the arriving data from sensors. In this stage an Adaptive Dynamic Diameter and Border Threshold (ADDBT) is utilized to change the clusters sizes in an adaptive way. ADDBT is modified based on a proposed equation to estimate the acceptable distance from online data stream by variant thresholds to produce additional new clusters. It has an ability to process drift data by calculating the Cohesion Index for all resulting clusters. By these stages, the problem of determining the value of K and determining the size of clusters is solved by making them non-fixed and adaptive so that their value can be estimated according to the quality of the online data stream. In the 4th stage, the resulting clusters were modified, merged, deleted, and evaluated. The final results then be discussed for the candidate clusters with the original clusters in terms of dynamic diameters and the cohesion of the clusters.

Keywords: Data stream · k-mean · Leader method · Incremental approach · Sliding window · Adaptive Dynamic Diameter · Border Threshold

1 Introduction

The fast progress in information technology have introduced new challenges for the researchers especially in complexity and volume of data [1]. Various sources produce stream or big data continuously. Examples include telephone records, sensor networks, radio frequency identification, wireless networks, customer click streams, multimedia data etc [2]. A data stream represents a systematic order of instances that can be read only once or a small number of times using limited computing and storage capabilities [3]. These data sources are considered based on their high-speed flow, open-ended, and produced by nonstationary distributions in dynamic situations.

Current applications data are differing from the earlier forms in their automatic data feeds. These days there are different applications in which the data are modeled best as transient data streams instead of as determined tables. Examples of applications include sensor networks network, user modeling in web applications, monitoring in electrical networks, managing data in telecommunications, stock markets prediction etc [3].

In previous data analysis, only the recent state of the data is important for analysis. In the current era, most related data are coming from sensors, these data analyses require historic data processing. Decision support systems were used by different organizations to identify potential suitable patterns in data [3]. Data analysis represents an interactive exploratory over historical data, which stored in different distributed situations. Sensor networks are usually generating big data as streams of data.

Clustering represent an exploratory data analysis [4]. It included in many data mining methods like classification and regression. Stream data flow are continuously generating data at high speed with infinite length. Clustering is an important technique to deal with sensors stream of data [5]. In this paper, the k-mean algorithm is updated to be suitable for the large size and tremendous speed of the data stream.

2 Related Work

Yuan and Yang, proposed an algorithm concerning K-Value Selection Method of K-Means Clustering Algorithm. Their paper was to evaluate and compare 4 methods (Canopy, Elbow, Silhouette and Gap) to select suitable k values of k mean algorithm. They determined their algorithm weaknesses and goodness on normal data and complex data based on run time. They found that elbow method has a smallest run time while gap method has a longest runtime. Their results were valid on small data but when it implemented on a big data, the execution time was being very big [6].

Liu et al., propose that the leader method can be utilized to shorten large-sized data to make it easier to be implemented in k-mean algorithm. Representatives from the data were chosen, and clusters of different sizes were produced by selecting thresholder data extracted from the sample. These updates succeeded with large-sized data, but did not work with data stream or online data [7].

Bradley, Fiyyad and Reina proposed a developed algorithm called based on their names (BFR). BFR was proposed to deal with high-dimensional Euclidean space data. Clusters can be created with strong shape assumptions. These clusters were considered to be normally distributed about their centroid with different mean and standard deviation. They also helped in choosing certain clusters key points using the joint probability density function. Their algorithm was considered as a development to the k-mean algorithm [8].

Zyblewski et al., proposed a method to deal with data stream and data drift, whereby the switches were continuously calculated for the clusters, so if the results differed and became bad, this catch point was deleted and the selection process was repeated. Their method did not take into consideration the special dimension, and it was also unable to update clusters and process drift data based on the customer's [9].

Cheng and Zhao, process k mean algorithm on data stream by computing cephirical distance and depend on manhantan to set k value, remote points and centers in six levels but they process on samples of limited data and not on the variable themselves, there are many works on this topic but still need statistical and quantitative analysis [10].

3 Stream Data Analysis

A sensor network consists of small computational devices that are able to communicate over wireless channels. A very big data stream were produced from these devices, several processors for this stream were spread in data maintenance, some of which dealt with the entire stream incrementally and processed it only during its passage for the first time [1].

K-mean algorithm is suitable to cluster big data but to indicate the complexity of this algorithm one need to know the total number of points in the dataset [11]. Let n represents the number of data points, let K be the number of clusters, and let T to represent the number of rotations required to reach its convergence. Multiplying all these values will be the full computational complexity of the algorithm as $O(nKT)$ [12]. But in the case of dealing with big data stream where its total number of data points may not be known [9]. This algorithm is considered easy and simple in analyzing the database and is widely used for the purposes of data analysis, image processing and pattern analysis for identification.

K-mean faced many difficulties in the case of big data [13]. These difficulties are considered as weaknesses in specifying the initial value of K, the centers of clusters must be determined initially before implementing the algorithm, the problem of patrons that do not belong to any cluster which results in empty clusters due to the noise and outlier in the data [14], and its inability to process non-linear separable data [3, 7]. The main problem when running this algorithm on data stream is how to determine the diameter of the cluster [11].

4 Proposed System

The proposed system consists of four main parts as shown in Fig. 1. The first part consists of data collection stage, the second stage determines the number of primary clusters through the data clustering offline. The third step is to update these clusters in terms of number and sizes through a series of steps that take place while the data is running online. The fourth step is correction step which trim the number of clusters through merging, delete the cluster if it has not spoken for a long time according to the time stamp. In the first stage data was practically collected personally through a sensor device that senses changes in the atmosphere and records it directly.

In the second stage of building the system, the number of clusters is determined by studying the data and determining the initial number of clusters here we will write the offline details and how to use the cluster evaluation criteria to obtain an initial number of clusters and determine their center and the number of points within each cluster. This means that here we will return to a complete work for offline and the offline cluster process, including an explanation of the K-Mean, its equation, and its entire algorithm. The result of the stage two is C, K. Where K represents the number of clusters that we obtained from the offline stag and C represents the initial centers. Likewise, each cluster will have a specific size that the cluster carries within its inventory properties from the offline stage.

The third stage is online, when the data stream become online and how to update the cluster. The first step of a new Stream is a set of factors that determine the new point arrangement to the cluster without updating the cluster, or add the new point to the cluster with updating the cluster. The last choice is not adding the point to any clusters Once the point comes, it goes through several step by entering the point and we will see the distance with the nearest cluster using one of the distance measurement criteria C (I) $\in$ C, Where C represents the number of clusters, we obtained from offline.

Once you enter a new point, we will see that it belongs to any of the casts c (i), the equation for measuring the distance between the new point and all the clusters within the cluster size. How will we do this step? We will do it via offline. Each cluster will have a specific size that the cluster will carry within its inventory properties.

In the third stage of system, threshold Elementary is determined, and then each point is marked, if it is less than this distance from the center of the cluster, add it to the cluster and the threshold remains stationary. But if it is farther away from the center of the cluster than this threshold, we will enter it and save it on the second condition that compute distance from the threshold. If it is close to the threshold with a certain value that is specified in advance, the point will be added to the cluster and the threshold will be updated.

If it is close to the threshold with a certain value that is specified in advance. But if it is far from the threshold, we will consider it as a new cluster, and assign an initial value to the new threshold cluster. Correction and evaluation step is done in fourth stage.

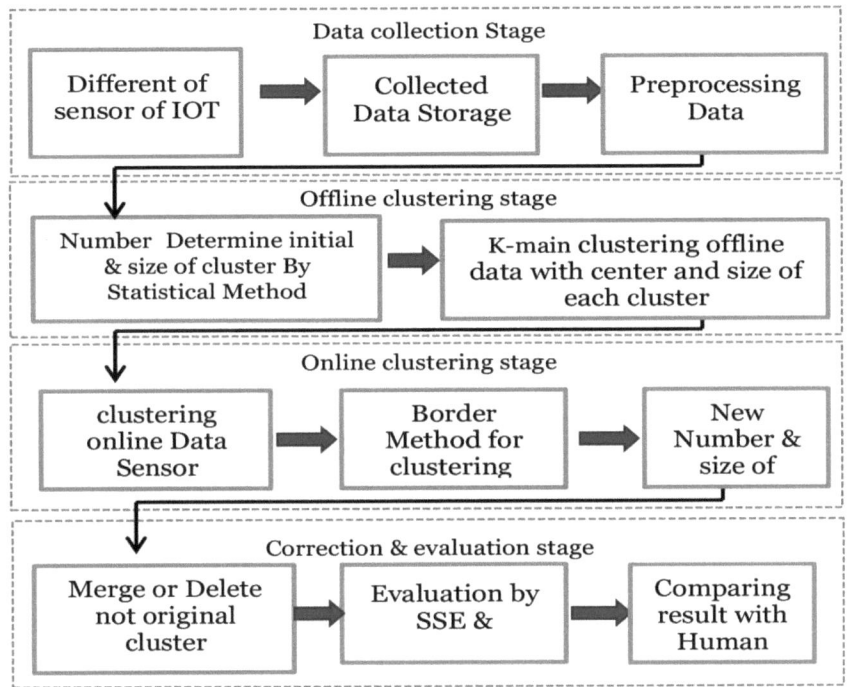

Fig. 1. Propose system (ADDBT)

4.1 Data Collection

The weather-sensitive sensor device was purchased from California, America, through Amazon, from Pasco. There is the possibility of leaving the device to record the data inside it and saving it for a period of eight hours, or saving it on the personal computer or tablet for an infinite amount of daily data that has been recorded and exported to the memory or to a specific program according to desire and choice The device calculates the values of nineteen important indicators in four different directions: atmosphere, light, and GPS. Each direction contains a number of different or somewhat interrelated variables, such as temperature, humidity, relative humidity, dew drop, wind speed, wind direction, light intensity, sunlight, latitude and longitude, number of associated satellites, ultraviolet radiation, electromagnetic radiation, and wind as it shown in Fig. 2. The data was collected in the offline stage over a period of six months for intermittent periods, by operating a sensitive wired weather device outside the home to collect and store various weather data. Then the data is exported to be stored and compiled in a CSV file with Data Stamp representing the time and date of each record at the moment it was recorded on the device.

When the sensitive device is turned on, the data is recorded automatically, but information is added manually, called cloud cover, which representing the status of the clouds whether they are patchy, partial, dense, etc.. The data was recorded for different times and on different days for the same vignette, so the data was very different for the same vagrant as shown in Table 1.

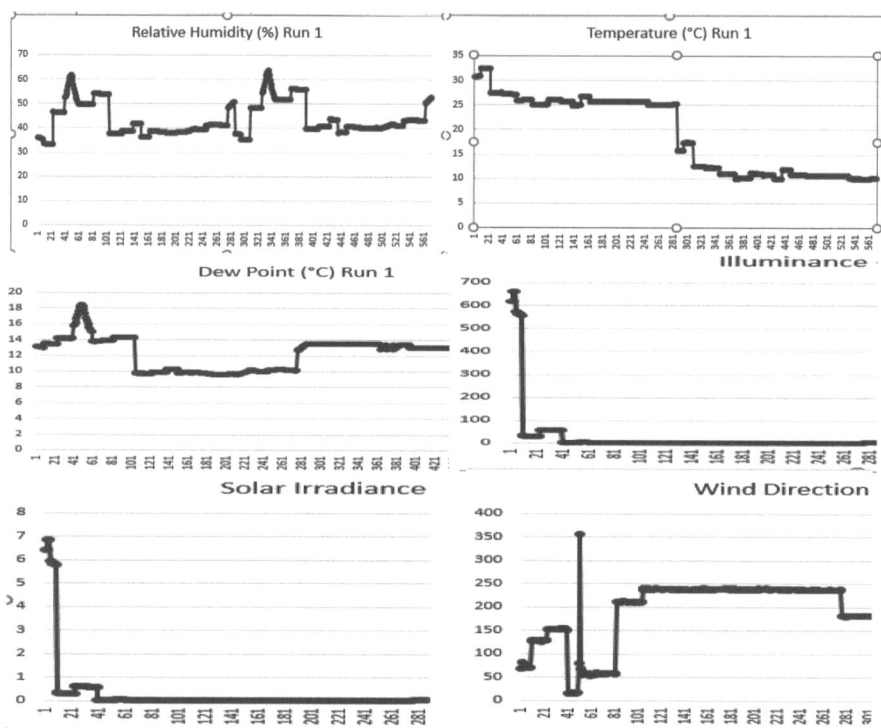

Fig. 2. Representation of data stream feature in multi time stump

Table 1. Weather conditions

Time of Day	1–24	By sensor
Temperature	(°C)	By sensor weather
Relative Humidity	%	By sensor weather
Barometric Pressure	(mmHg)	By sensor weather
Wind Speed	(mph)	By sensor weather
Dew Point	(°C)	By sensor weather
Cloud Cover		Manual by monitoring the sky

4.2 Offline Clustering Stage

This stage can be discussed in the following steps:

Run the weather sensor to store the weather features for a long time such as six months, the sensor will store all features with time stump with each row of data which update every new second.

Incremental approach is used to take each record of data and process it incrementally.

Select important features and parameters by using Principal component analysis (PCA (method, by computing the covariance matrix after subtracting the mean from each value in the data set then compute Eigenvalues and Eigenvectors, sort value in decent sort and choose the first choices.

Assign weights depend on data arrival rate and density analysis.

Use try and error method in every round to compute elbow and silhouette methods and estimate the value of k.

The Akaike information criterion (AIC), Bayesian Information Criterion (BIC) and Gaussian Mixture Model (GMM) methods must be computed to help in estimating the value of k.

If the data is non separable data, then gradient decent method will be computed to estimate the distance from new point to each other's centers of clusters.

Else if the data is separable then the distance will be computing by calculating the square root of the square of the difference between them.

Chose the small distance.

Run k mean algorithm for each new point.

For each cluster many important parameters will be computed in array to save the properties of this cluster like the count of cluster points (clu.points), the position of cluster centers (clu.centers), the size of cluster (clu.size), the variance of each cluster (clu.variance), diameter of cluster (clu.diameter), cohesion of the cluster (clu.cohesion).

When all records of this big data set end then all clusters process are finished.

Offline stage will be ended.

Online clustering stage:

This stage can be performed according to the following steps:

Use the final clusters that resulted from the offline stage as initial clusters and inputs to the online stage.

Turn on the weather sensor to record the online data as inputs to online stage.

Compute the distance from each new point from online data stream to each other's centers of initial clusters of the offline clusters.

Estimate initial threshold (E) which will share in determine the size of a cluster by Eqs. (1) and (2).

$$\text{Compute } a = (\|C2 - C1\|)/2 \tag{1}$$

where a is a mid of distance between two close clusters to a new point of stream, C1 is center of close cluster to a new point of stream, C2 is the center of next close cluster to a new point of stream.

$$\text{Compute } b = p \cdot \frac{(C2 - C1)}{\|C2 - C1\|} \tag{2}$$

where b is the distance between the center of close cluster and the diagonal of new point on the line which pass on the horizontal line between the two centers, and p is the positive integer value.

Figure 3 shows the process of computing the distance from new online stream data and the two nearest clusters of the offline samples.

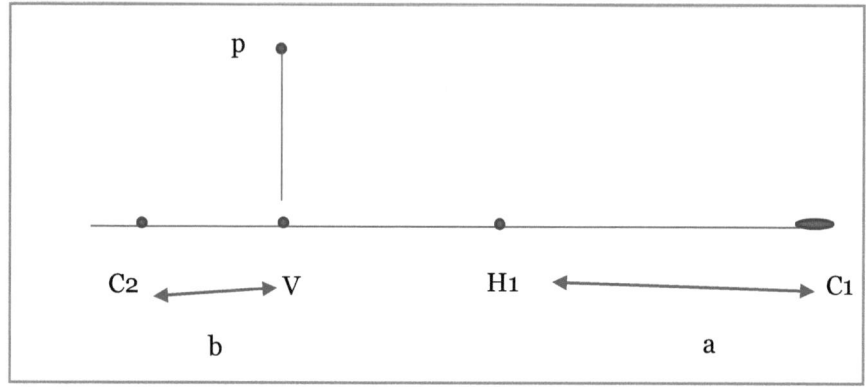

Fig. 3. Computing distance from new online stream data and the two nearest clusters of the offline samples.

Compute $\Gamma(P)$ as in Eq. (3)

$$\Gamma(P) = \text{const}\,(a - b) \tag{3}$$

where $\Gamma(P)$ is *intial threshold,const is a const number*.

For each new point (p) compute the distance between it and all other centers of initial clusters (D).

Chose smallest distance if (D) smaller than or equal to $\Gamma(P)$, add the new point to this cluster and the new threshold will equal the initial threshold $\Gamma(P)$

$$Enew = \Gamma(P)$$

$$\text{Border threshold(B)} = 0.15(\Gamma(P)) \tag{4}$$

$$\text{If } D(c, P) <= D(c, \Gamma), \text{ and } D(c, P) - D(c, \Gamma) <= B \tag{5}$$

where $D(c, P)$ is the distance between the new point of stream (P) and the center of close cluster (c).

$$Clu+ = Clu + p$$

where Clu is cluster points.

Else if (D) not smaller than or equal to $\Gamma(P)$, then compute next equation to check if it nearby border as the next equation and display as example in next Fig. 5:

$$\text{If } D(c, P) <= D(c, \Gamma), \text{ and } D(c, P) - D(c, \Gamma) <= B \tag{6}$$

$$Clu+ = Clu + p$$

where Clu is cluster points.

$$Enew = \Gamma(P) + B$$

Else if condition in step 9 not come true then make (P) as new cluster and make (P) the center of new cluster. Figure 4 shows the dynamic diameter size change.

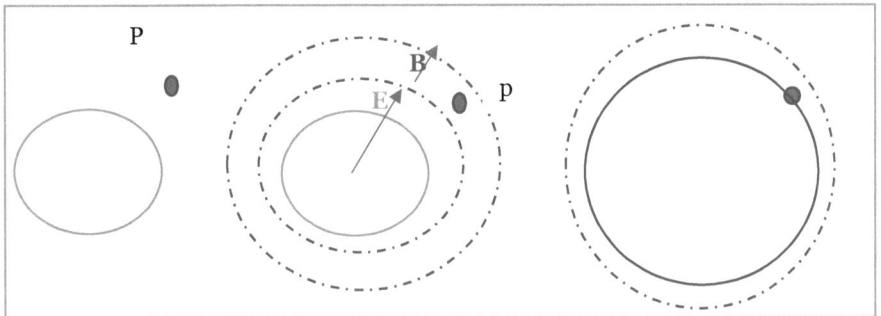

Fig. 4. Dynamic diameter size change

Correction stage and evaluation clustering index.

This is the third stage in the proposed system. It can be performed in the following sequence steps:

Evaluate clusters by Summation Square Error (SSE), using Eq. (7)

$$SSE = \sum_i \sum_{x \in ci} (x - mi)2 \qquad (7)$$

where mi is the mean of cluster, ci is the center of a cluster.

Merge small neighbors' clusters if the distance is within the estimated rang.

Delete small cluster if it smaller than the estimated range.

Deal with misaligning curve by process it.

Delete the empty clusters.

5 Results and Discussion

When implementing the wages in the offline stage, the PCA was calculated for all available variables, and the six variables with the highest values were selected. All the data collected in the offline was entered as input to the K mean algorithm, and the results were 16 clusters, some of resulted clusters called as an original cluster. Each cluster save its important statistic properties like no. of points, centers of each clusters, border threshold, initial threshold, the power of the cluster. These centers will be considered as initial clusters in online stage. Some confusing and empty clusters known as candidate clusters. These clusters will be resolve in correction stage to remove empty clusters and merge neighbor candidate clusters. The size of each cluster and the number of clusters were also determined at this stage, but these results will change in the first stage because the K mean algorithm has been adapted to be adaptive in terms of the size and number of clusters, so that it can adapt itself to the changes occurring in the online data stream.

The size of some clusters increased dynamically due to the presence of elements within the cluster border, which led to these results, an increase by an amount, while the size of other clusters remained constant or changed by changing the threshold value only. Each record in Table 2 represent one cluster and its self-properties. When the cohesion index calculated on the result cluster which have a many point like 873 points and have a small size parameter like 7.4 then its cohesion index equal to that mean it's a high-power cluster.

Table 2. Cohesion index calculated on the result cluster

	cluster name	cohesion	no. Point	dimeter size
Original offline	Cluster8	6.021776838	206	13.4
	Cluster12	4.555469752	214	9.4
	Cluster15	6.097267405	289	11.8
	Cluster1	2.864263246	278	7
	Cluster4	3.352105283	624	9
	Cluster6	2.67851921	200	7
	Cluster3	2.855418208	872	7.4
candidate offline	Cluster2	2.423835577	171	7.4
	Cluster5	3.528876269	162	7.4
	Cluster7	3.605339596	138	7.4
	Cluster9	5.883063039	178	12.2
	Cluster10	4.933418065	166	9.4
	Cluster11	3.590607674	151	7.4
	Cluster13	4.022975916	176	7.8
	Cluster14	2.644029736	118	7
	Cluster16	0.869283529	57	7

But when the dynamic parameter is large equal 13.4 and the cluster has an average number of points such as 206 points, this means that the cohesion of this cluster is less than in the first case, but the points were attracted by the dynamic creep. In next Table 3 in online stage, when the cohesion index calculated and become 1.3 on the good cluster which have a large point like 17754 points and have a small size parameter like 9 then its cohesion index equal to that mean it's a high-power cluster. While the cohesion index on another cluster equal 6 which have a little point like 206 points and have a big size parameter, this cohesion index evaluates this cluster as an original cluster but not a good cluster.

An Approach to Compute the Adaptive Dynamic Diameter of Data Stream Clusters 183

Table 3. Cohesion index calculated on the result cluster

	cluster name	cohesion	no. Point	dimeter size
Original online	Cluster6	3.061856146	703	7.4
	Cluster8	6.021776838	206	13.4
	Cluster12	4.559520479	224	9.4
	Cluster1	1.225629021	4295	7
	Cluster15	6.205990387	612	11.8
	Cluster4	1.365717799	17754	9
	Cluster3	1.58041351	6034	7.4
	Cluster17	0.270998637	8981	7
	Cluster2	1.346468404	3378	7.4
	Cluster16	2.127418369	200	7
	Cluster19	1.087321007	200	7
candidate online	Cluster5	3.509192882	165	7.4
	Cluster7	3.605339596	138	7.4
	Cluster9	5.883063039	178	12.2
	Cluster10	4.929482026	171	9.4
	Cluster11	3.549191963	157	7.4
	Cluster13	3.996021772	181	7.8
	Cluster14	2.611720658	123	7
	Cluster18	1.442033333	5	7

In the online step, the results show a change in the number of clusters after turning on the air sensor and entering new data into the system for several new hours, and three new clusters appeared. Not only variant in size, but also the count of clusters was change, this mean the k mean algo.learned itself by itself in time with data stump of each new record which received in online data stream as it declared in Fig. 5.

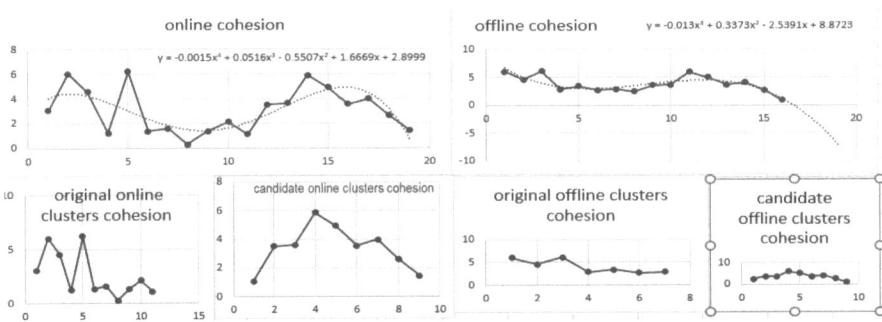

Fig. 5. Cohesion of candidates and original clusters in online and offline stages

The number of clusters was close to the number of cases and weather changes estimated according to data collection and the human mind, and this proved the validity of the system's artificial intelligence in analyzing this data stream.

6 Conclusion

In this paper the K-mean algo.learned itself by itself in time with data stump of each new record which received in online data stream., modify k mean clustering method to be adaptive dynamically to big online data stream and create clusters better in sprat ion and sensitive to neighbor clusters with keep accuracy good and less the computations time.

The dynamic parameter is large equal 13.4 and the cluster has an average number of points such as 206 points, this means that the cohesion of this cluster is less than in the first case, but the points were attracted by the dynamic creep.a small size parameter like 9 then its cohesion index equal to that mean it's a high-power cluster. While the cohesion index on another cluster equal 6 which have a little point like 206 points. The number of clusters was close to the number of cases and weather changes estimated according to data collection and the human mind, and this proved the validity of the system's artificial intelligence in analyzing this data stream.

References

1. T. B. data into tiny Data and P. and projective clustering Constant-size coresets for k-means. Adaptive Clustering for Dynamic IoT Data Streams (2016)
2. Kolajo, T., Daramola, O., Adebiyi, A.: Big data stream analysis: a systematic literature review. J. Big Data **6**(1), 47 (2019)
3. Ikotun, A.M., Ezugwu, A.E., Abualigah, L., Abuhaija, B., Heming, J.: K-means clustering algorithms: a comprehensive review, variants analysis, and advances in the era of big data. Inf. Sci. (Ny.) **622**, 178 (2022)
4. Ackermann, M.R., Lammersen, C., Märtens, M., Raupach, C., Sohler, C., Swierkot, K.: StreamKM++: A Clustering Algorithm for Data Streams *. [Online]. Available: https://epubs.siam.org/terms-privacy
5. Bahri, M.: Scarcity of labels in non-stationary data streams: a survey. ACM Comput. Surv. **55**(2), 1–39 (2022)
6. Yuan, C., Yang, H.: Research on K-value selection method of K-means clustering algorithm. J **2**(2), 226–235 (2019)
7. Liu, B., Wu, L., Li, R., Su, H., Han, Y.: On the group controllability of leader-based continuous-time multiagent systems. Complexity **2020**, 1 (2020)
8. MrdulaK, H.S.T.V.P.: Improvements Over k-Means Clustering Methods for Large Datasets. LAMBERT Acad. Publ. (2020)
9. Zyblewski, P., Sabourin, R., Woźniak, M.: Preprocessed dynamic classifier ensemble selection for highly imbalanced drifted data streams. Inf. Fusion **66**, 138–154 (2021)
10. Cheng, Y.L.L., Zhao, C.Z.H.: Analysis of Spatiotemporal Characteristics of Online Car Hailing Based on k-Means Clustering
11. Zhao, H.: Analysis of simple K-mean and parallel K-mean clustering for software products and organizational performance using education sector dataset. Sci. Progr. **2021**, 1 (2021)

12. Moodi, F., Saadatfar, H.: An improved K-means algorithm for big data. IET Softw. **16**(1), 48–59 (2022)
13. Moodi, F., Saadatfar, H.: Turning big data into tiny data: Constant-size coresets for k-means, PCA, and projective clustering. SIAM J. Comput. **49**(3), 601–657 (2020). https://doi.org/10.1137/18M1209854
14. Gerz, M.S.C.F., Al-Shrouf, D.-E.L., Jelali, D.-E.M.: A comparative analysis of concept drift detection methods with a systematic and innovative approach of method selection. Struct. Heal. Monit. (2023). https://doi.org/10.12783/shm2023/36906

XMR_Net: A Deep Model for Vehicle Make and Model Recognition Using Still-Images

Sourajit Maity[1(✉)], Pawan Kumar Singh[2], Mufti Mahmud[3,4,5], and Ram Sarkar[1]

[1] Department of Computer Science and Engineering, Jadavpur University, Kolkata, India
sourajit.cse.ju@gmail.com
[2] Department of Information Technology, Jadavpur University, Kolkata, India
[3] Information and Computer Science Department, King Fahd University of Petroleum and Minerals, Dhahran 31261, Saudi Arabia
[4] SDAIA-KFUPM Joint Research Center for AI, King Fahd University of Petroleum and Minerals, Dhahran 31261, Saudi Arabia
[5] Interdisciplinary Research Center for Bio Systems and Machines, King Fahd University of Petroleum and Minerals, Dhahran 31261, Saudi Arabia

Abstract. Vehicle make and model recognition (VMMR) using still images is a challenging research problem. Automatic VMMR systems have many real-life applications that include surveillance. In this paper, initially, we have used five standard convolutional neural network (CNN) models, namely Inceptionv3, Xception, InceptionResNetv2, MobileNetV2, and ResNet152v2 for VMMR. We have also used an attention mechanism to these models. To increase accuracy of the overall model, we have chosen three best base learners from these five CNN models, and formed an ensemble model. The final model is called XMR_Net, where X stands for Xception, M stands for MobileNet, and R stands for ResNet152v2. For experimental evaluation, we have used two benchmark datasets, a recently published dataset called Vehicle Images dataset and VMMRdb-53 dataset. We have achieved satisfactory outcomes with accuracy scores of 95% and 87% (Top-3) on Vehicle Images and VMMRdb-53 datasets, respectively using the proposed XMR_Net model, which is better than its constituent base models. The code and detailed results can be found at: https://github.com/JUVCSE/XMRNET.

Keywords: Vehicle Make and Model Recognition · XMR_Net · Deep Learning · Ensemble Learning · Vehicle Images dataset · VMMRdb

1 Introduction

As implied by the name, fine-grained classification is a framework for classification in which the input data is given incredibly precise class labels [1]. For instance, even if the vehicle's number plate is fake, keywords from the vehicle model can be utilized to locate the target vehicle in traffic surveillance-based image sets. Therefore, a vehicle make and model recognition (VMMR) system is important for real-time traffic monitoring, and surveillance purposes. Many studies have been published in recent years in this domain, such as vehicle classification, make recognition, model recognition, segmentation, detection [2–4] pedestrian detection, lane detection, etc. However, there are plenty of scopes for research to bridge the gaps between research scenarios and the real-world scenario. For example, some proposed methods give 100% accuracy in hypothetical traffic scenarios, but when applied to real-world scenarios, these models may not function properly. Working on issues based on real-life traffic scenarios is challenging in terms of training, testing, and validating the model. From a thorough study of the available literature, we have observed, as mentioned below, that the additional improvements are needed to make VMMR systems more efficient.

- Making models robust enough to handle inputs taken in different weather conditions.
- Developing models capable of handling data from both daylight and nighttime conditions for use in any light condition.
- Generating multi-view or multimodal datasets for the make and model recognition of vehicles to provide a practical solution for a VMMR system.

In this work, we have proposed a deep model, called XMR_Net, which is an ensemble of attention-aided three CNN models. Here, we have used three CNN models, namely Xception [5], MobileNetV2 [6], and ResNet152v2 [7]. We have also added an attention layer to the models, followed by applying a weighted average ensemble approach in order to achieve better results. To assess the performance of the model, we have considered the Vehicle Images dataset [8] and the VMMRdb-53 dataset [9].

2 Literature Review

Different strategies have been used to address the issues of VMMR. Recently, Maity et al. [10] and Gayen et al. [11] have made a thorough analysis of the various cutting-edge VMMR techniques. In Table 1, a brief summary of a few recently developed VMMR methods is given.

A very few datasets is available for VMMR detection. There are some limitations of the existing VMMR models. Some datasets have very few numbers of images in a single class which is a challenging task for VMMR problem. Some models have addressed either model or make, but not both. The overlapping of multiple vehicles occurring in a single image frame is also a challenging task for VMMR problem.

3 Proposed Ensemble Model

In this work, we have proposed an ensemble of attention-aided three deep CNN models, called XMR_Net, for VMMR. Three CNN models and the ensemble approach used here are discussed below.

Xception [5]: A deep CNN architecture called, Xception, inspired by Inception, uses depth-wise separable convolutions in place of Inception's modules. Xception means "extreme Inception". The network's feature extraction basis is composed of 36 convolutional layers of the Xception architecture. The architecture of Xception has had the same parameters as the architecture of InceptionV3. However, the performance gains are not due to the increased capacity instead, a more efficient utilization of model parameters. In Fig. 1, the architecture of Xception model is shown.

Table 1. Different methods recently proposed in the domain of VMMR

Work Ref.	Model	Dataset	Accuracy
Komolovaite et al. [12]	EffientNet-v2 and MobileNet-v2	400–500 images per class and 19 classes	81.39%
Yu et al. [13]	EP-CNN (PE-SubNet + VMC-SubNet)	CompCars [14], Stanford Cars [15]	98.9% on CompCars, 94.6% on Stanford Cars
Avianto et al. [16]	VGG16	Inav-Dash	98.73% on make and 97.69% on model
Bularz et al. [17]	CNN + Binarization	CarBinLamps [17]	93.9%
Ali et al. [8]	VGG16	Vehicle Images dataset	74.32%
Tafazzoli et al. [9]	ResNet-50	VMMRdb-3036	51.76% (Top-5)
Tafazzoli et al. [9]	ResNet-50	VMMRdb-51	75.93% (Top-3)
Dehghan et al. [18]	Sighthound's system with two DL networks	Sighthound's dataset	93%
Zwemer et al. [19]	AlexNet	500 vehicle models dataset	98%(Top − 1)
Benavides et al. [20]	VGG16	Stanford Cars	96.3%
Linse et al. [21]	ResNet18	Stanford Cars	77.90%
Ammar et al. [22]	Xception	41521 vehicle images with 24 makes and 90 models	97.3%
Lin et al. [23]	Bilinear CNN	Stanford Cars	91.3%
Zheng et al. [24]	MA-CNN	Stanford Cars	92.8%
Ji et al. [25]	ACNet + ResNet50	Stanford Cars	94.6%
Zheng et al. [26]	PA-CNN	Stanford Cars	93.2%
Yang et al. [14]	CNN with Joint Bayesian and SVM	CompCars	83.4%

MobileNetV2 [6]: MobileNetV2 has been crafted as a CNN aimed at optimal functionality on mobile devices. An inverted residual structure has been implemented, connecting bottleneck layers through residuals. The intermediate expansion layer has utilized lightweight depthwise convolutions to filter features as a source of non-linearity. The entire design of MobileNetV2 has consisted of an initial convolution layer with 32 filters, followed by 19 residual bottleneck levels. Additionally, it has been discovered that, for the preservation of representational power, non-linearities in the thin layers have been eliminated. In Fig. 2, the block diagram of the MobileNetV2 model is shown.

ResNet152v2 [7]: ResNet-152v2 is a ResNet (Residual Network) family deep convolutional neural network architecture. Instead of learning unreferenced functions, ResNets, train residual functions with reference to the layer inputs. Residual nets allow these layers to suit a residual mapping rather than expecting each few stacked layers to directly match a desired underlying mapping. The "152" in ResNet-152v2 denotes the network's depth having 152 layers. For final classification, the design comprises global average pooling as well as fully linked layers. In Fig. 3, the overall architecture of ResNet152v2 model is shown.

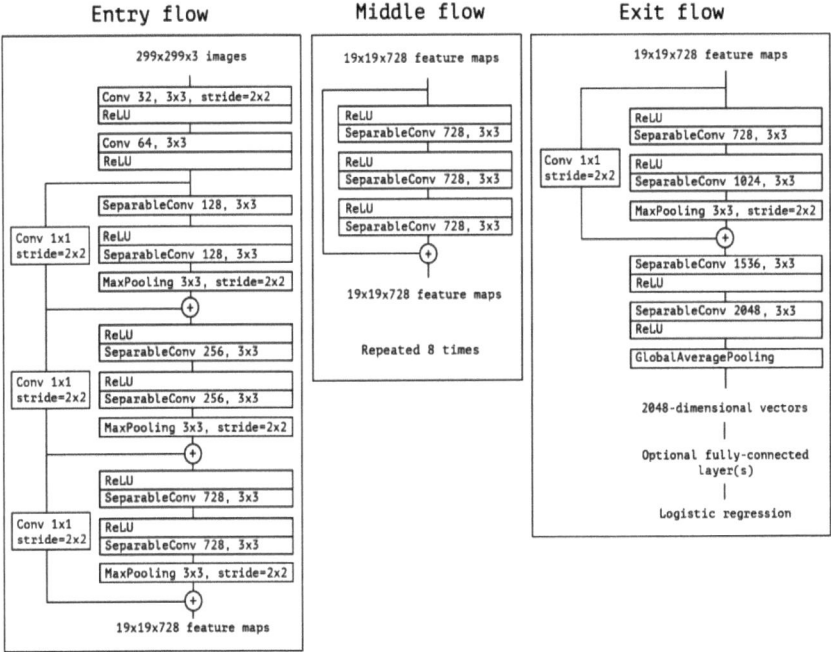

Fig. 1. Architectural overview of Xception [5] used in the proposed XMR_Net model.

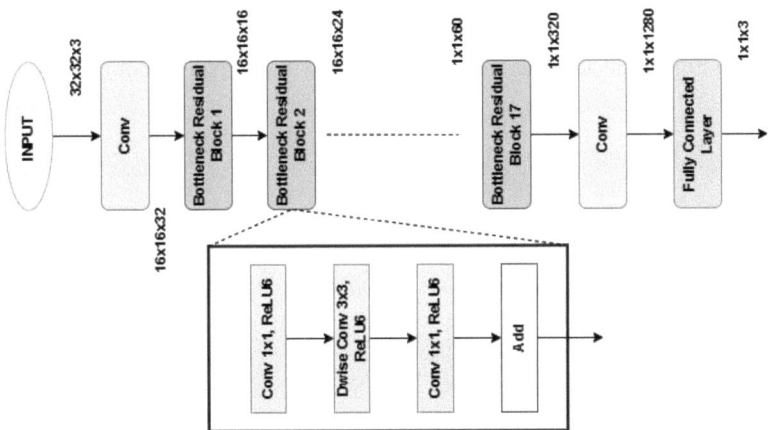

Fig. 2. Schematic block diagram of MobileNetV2 model.

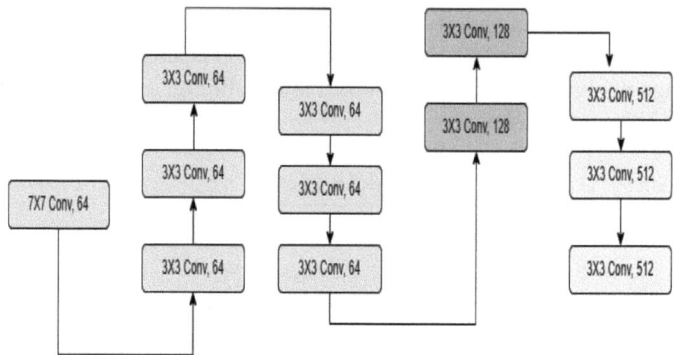

Fig. 3. Architectural overview of the ResNet152v2 model.

XMR_Net: In our model, we have first added a self-attention layer to the Xception model eliminating some layers from the same. Each position in an image relates to a certain spatial location (pixel or area). Self-attention can be used to capture relationships between various spatial positions in an image, as opposed to processing a string of words. By including self-attention into image processing, models can better represent intricate spatial relationships by capturing long-range dependencies between pixels.

Similarly, we have added some self-attention layers to MobileNetV2 and ResNet152v2 models eliminating some layers from the base models respectively. After that we have applied the weighted average ensemble approach and as a result, the accuracy has been found to be improved precisely.

The final classification is accomplished through the utilization of a weighted average ensemble [27] of three models, Xception, ResNet152v2 and MobileNetV2, each of the models is integrated with a self-attention block and a dense block. Decisions obtained from these models are ensembled with three different weights: weight 1, weight 2, and weight 3, which have been assigned to three models. The combined decisions are proven to be more robust than the decision of individual models because if one of the models in the ensemble predicts an input incorrectly, the other models can adjust and anticipate correctly. In Fig. 4, the architecture of our proposed XMR_Net model is shown.

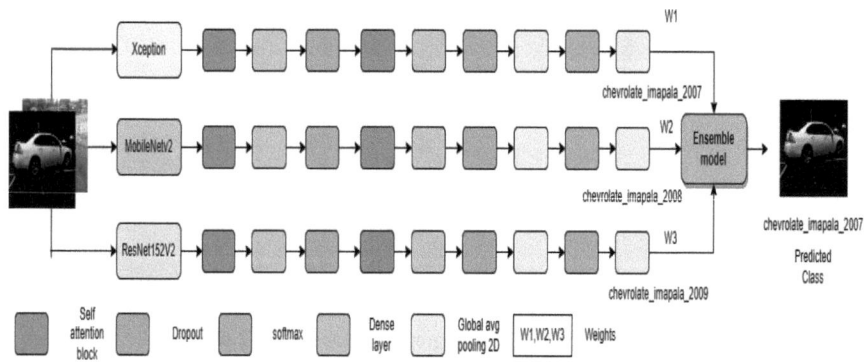

Fig. 4. Architectural overview of our proposed XMR_Net model.

4 Datasets

There are various vehicle detection datasets [28], but for VMMR, only a few publicly available datasets are found. The performance of our model has been tested on two standard VMMR datasets: Vehicle Images dataset and VMMRdb-53 dataset. Details of these datasets are given below.

Vehicle Images dataset [8]: The dataset consists of 3847 images of various car makes and models. The 48 distinct classes of car models in the dataset are annotated in 48 distinct folders. High resolution cameras have been used to acquire the images for this collection. To mimic real-world situations, images of the cars are captured from several camera perspectives and under various lighting conditions. Vehicle Images dataset is publicly available at: https://data.mendeley.com/datasets/hj3vvx5946/1. Sample images of this dataset are shown in Fig. 5.

VMMRdb-53 [9]: When compared to the current car images datasets, the VMMRdb dataset has a significantly wider scope and greater diversity. This collection covers models produced between 1950 and 2016 and consists of 9,170 vehicle classes with 2,91,752 images. Figure 6 shows some sample images of this dataset. In our work, we have used a subset of VMMRdb dataset containing only 53 classes, namely VMMRdb-53. This dataset is publicly available at https://www.kaggle.com/datasets/abhishektyagi001/vehicle-make-model-recognition-dataset-vmmrdb.

Fig. 5. Sample images of Vehicle Images dataset.

Fig. 6. Sample images of VMMRdb-53 dataset.

5 Results and Discussion

The evaluation metrics that are used to calculate the model performance are Precision (P) [29], Recall (R) [29] and Accuracy [30]. Table 2 provides the obtained results of the five base models on Vehicle Images dataset for VMMR. Initially, we have experimented with five CNN models, and then for the ensemble method, we have chosen best three CNN models among the five models which are denoted with a * mark. Table 2 also provides the obtained results from the base CNN model's precision, recall and F1-score and XMR_Net model on Vehicle Images dataset, where precision, recall and F1-score obtained are 93%, 89% and 91% respectively. It can be seen from Table 2 that Xception, MobileNetV2, ResNet152v2, InceptionResNetv2 and Inceptionv3 models achieve classification accuracies of 87.20%, 83.48%, 88.70%, 81.38% and 73.90% respectively. However, our developed XMR_Net model has achieved an accuracy of 95%. It is to be noted that all the three base models are made to run for 50 epochs. Some misclassified images by the proposed XMR_Net model on Vehicle Images dataset are shown in Fig. 7. Due to significant similarities in the frontal face of the 'Daiatsu_core', this model has been misclassified with the 'Suzuki_cultus_2007' model. Furthermore, car models such as 'Honda_BRV', 'KIA_Sportage' and 'Suzuki_alto_2007' have achieved highest accuracy of almost 99% whereas 'Toyota_premio' model has achieved lowest accuracy of 67% only.

Table 2. Results produced by CNN models and the proposed XMR_Net model on the Vehicle Images dataset. Models with * are used to form the final ensemble.

Model	Precision	Recall	F1-score	Accuracy
Xception*	85%	81%	83%	87.20%
MobileNetV2*	82%	76%	79%	83.48%

(*continued*)

Table 2. (*continued*)

Model	Precision	Recall	F1-score	Accuracy
ResNet152v2*	86%	81%	84%	88.70%
InceptionResNetv2	79%	76%	78%	81.38%
Inceptionv3	73%	65%	67%	73.90%
XMR_Net (Ours)	93%	89%	91%	95.00%

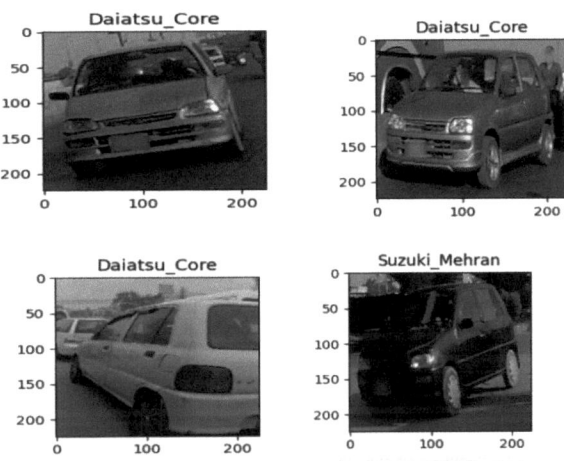

Fig. 7. Misclassified images using the XMR_Net model on the Vehicle Images dataset.

Table 3 provides the obtained results of the five base models on VMMRdb-53 dataset for VMMR problem. Classification accuracies of 79%, 78%, 71%, 69% and 67% are attained by using base CNN models, Xception, MobileNetV2, ResNet152v2, InceptionResNetv3 and Inceptionv3, respectively. Initially, we have experimented with five CNN models, and then for the ensemble method, we have chosen best three CNN models among the five models which are denoted with a * mark. Nevertheless, our developed XMR_Net model has achieved a Top-3 accuracy of 87%, which is found to be much better than the individual models. It is to be noted that all these CNN models are made to run for 50 epochs. Table 3 also provides the obtained results from the base CNN model's precision, recall and F1-score and XMR_Net model on VMMRdb-53 dataset, where precision, recall and F1-score obtained are 60%, 60% and 58% respectively. The misclassified images by our proposed XMR_Net model on the VMMRdb-53 dataset are shown in Fig. 8. Due to certain similarities in the frontal aspect of the 'Chevrolet_impala_2007', this model has been misclassified with the 'Toyota_camry_2014' model. The 'Toyota_Camri_se_2013' model has achieved highest accuracy of 91%, whereas the 'gmc_sierra_2500_2009' car model has achieved lowest accuracy in the VMMRdb-53 dataset. Table 5 provides the obtained results from the XMR_Net model on VMMRdb-53 dataset where precision recall and f1-score is 60%, 60% and 58% respectively.

Table 3. Results produced by CNN models and the proposed XMR_Net model on the VMMRdb-53 dataset. Models with * are used to form the final ensemble.

Model	Precision	Recall	F1-score	Accuracy (Top-3)
Xception*	55%	51%	53%	79%
MobileNetV2*	53%	49%	51%	78%
ResNet152v2*	49%	47%	48%	71%
InceptionResNetv2	46%	43%	44%	69%
Inceptionv3	43%	39%	41%	67%
XMR_Net (Ours)	60%	60%	58%	87%

Fig. 8. Misclassified images using XMR_Net on the VMMRdb-53 dataset.

After evaluating our model XMR_Net on two publicly available datasets namely, VMMRdb-53 and Vehicle images dataset, it has been seen that recognition accuracy on the Vehicle images dataset is much better than VMMRdb-53 dataset. With 53 classes that span models made between the year 1950 and 2016, VMMRdb-53 is broader in scope and diverse. A broad range of variants are included in the VMMRdb-53 dataset to account for numerous eventualities that may be experienced in a real-life scenarios. The images are collected by different people, using different imaging devices, and from diverse viewpoints. The automobiles are not aligned correctly, and several images include a background that is not relevant sometimes. The data includes automobiles from 712 regions, which include all 412 sub-domains that correspond to US metropolitan areas. In this dataset, some vehicle classes have very few images which is not sufficient for training a deep learning based CNN models. On the other hand, Vehicle image dataset contains a collection of 3847 images that are created from high-resolution videos and gathered from camera units positioned on a roadway at various angles and varying frame rates. A deep CNN model can be trained on the Vehicle images dataset, which has well-balanced classes and pre-processed images. Due to several obstacles in the way of VMMRdb-53 dataset training, it is less accurate than the Vehicle images dataset.

After evaluating our model XMR_Net on two publicly available datasets, it has been found that we have achieved good results. Table 4 provides the comparison of the obtained results of XMR_Net models with another models on two datasets. However, there are some limitations of the proposed method. Firstly, we have not evaluated our model using VMMR datasets that contain images taken in a variety of weather situations. Also, our considered datasets do not have any multi-modal images that are required to build a robust model.

Table 4. Comparison of accuracies obtained by the XMR_Net with other models on Vehicle Images dataset

Model	Accuracy
ResNet152, Ali et al. [8]	69.24%
MobileNet, Ali et al. [8]	73.54%
VGG16, Ali et al. [8]	74.32%
XMR_Net (Ours)	95.00%

The ablation studies with the five base CNN models on two VMMR datasets with an additional self-attention mechanism are shown in Tables 5 and 6, which are followed by the application of a weighted average ensemble method. It has been observed that both VMMR datasets have reached their maximum accuracy using our model, XMR_Net. It has been also observed that the weighted average ensemble strategy of using Xception, ResNet152v2 and InceptionResNetv2 with self-attention mechanism have achieved 93% accuracy on Vehicle images dataset, which is slightly lower than our proposed approach. Similarly, for VMMRdb-53 dataset, the weighted average ensemble strategy of combining Xception, MobileNetV2 and InceptionResNetv2 with a self-attention mechanism have achieved the second best classification accuracy of 83.6% which is significantly lower than that of our proposed approach.

Table 5. Ablation study varying with other CNN models on Vehicle Images dataset

Model 1	Model 2	Model 3	Accuracy
Inceptionv3	Xception	InceptionResNetv2	88%
Inceptionv3	Xception	MobileNetV2	89.2%
Inceptionv3	Xception	ResNet152v2	89.6%
Xception	MobileNetV2	InceptionResNetv2	92.3%
ResNet152v2	MobileNetV2	InceptionResNetv2	92.7%
Xception	ResNet152v2	InceptionResNetv2	93%
Xception	MobileNetV2	ResNet152v2	95.00%

Table 6. Ablation study varying with other CNN models on VMMRdb-53 dataset

Model 1	Model 2	Model 3	Accuracy (Top-3)
Inceptionv3	Xception	InceptionResNetv2	79.2%
Inceptionv3	Xception	MobileNetV2	79.6%
Inceptionv3	Xception	ResNet152v2	79.8%
Xception	ResNet152v2	InceptionResNetv2	83.2%
Xception	MobileNetV2	InceptionResNetv2	83.6%
ResNet152v2	MobileNetV2	InceptionResNetv2	81%
Xception	MobileNetV2	ResNet152v2	87%

6 Conclusion

Due to its significance in numerous real-world applications, VMMR has recently attracted a lot of attention from the research community. In this paper, we have provided an ensemble-based model for VMMR, called XMR_Net. In doing so, two publicly accessible VMMR datasets have been taken into consideration, and the obtained results are found to be satisfactory.

In the future, we intend to take into account more varied datasets to evaluate how robust the model (i.e., XMR_Net) is. Additionally, we will test our models using other ensemble approaches, like snapshot ensemble, to reduce the computational complexity. The VMMR datasets that contain images captured in a variety of weather conditions, including wet, foggy, dismal nighttime settings, etc., can be used to validate the model.

References

1. Zhan, J., Zhang, H., Luo, X.: Fine-grained vehicle recognition via detection-classification-tracking in surveillance video. In: 2014 5th International Conference on Digital Home, pp. 14–19. IEEE (2014)
2. Maity, S., Chakraborty, A., Singh, P.K., Sarkar, R.: Performance comparison of various YOLO models for vehicle detection: an experimental study. In: International Conference on Data Analytics & Management, pp. 677–684. Springer (2023)
3. Bhattacharya, D., Bhattacharyya, A., Agrebi, M., Roy, A., Singh, P.K.: DFE-AVD: deep feature ensemble for automatic vehicle detection. In: Proceedings of International Conference on Intelligence Computing Systems and Applications (ICICSA 2022) (2022)
4. Islam, A., Mallik, S., Roy, A., Agrebi, M., Singh, P.K.: A filter-based feature selection methodology for vehicle/non-vehicle classification. In: Sergiyenko, O., Flores-Fuentes, W., Rodriguez-Quiñonez, J., Miranda-Vega, J.E. (eds.) Measurements and Instrumentation for Machine Vision, pp. 137–156. CRC Press, New York (2024)
5. Chollet, F.: Xception: deep learning with depthwise separable convolutions. In: Proceedings of the IEEE Conference on Computer Vision and Pattern Recognition, pp. 1251–1258 (2017)
6. Sandler, M., Howard, A., Zhu, M., Zhmoginov, A., Chen, L.-C.: Mobilenetv2: Inverted residuals and linear bottlenecks. In: Proceedings of the IEEE Conference on Computer Vision and Pattern Recognition, pp. 4510–4520 (2018)

7. Rachburee, N., Punlumjeak, W.: Lotus species classification using transfer learning based on VGG16, ResNet152V2, and MobileNetV2. IAES Int. J. Artif. Intell. **11**(4), 1344 (2022)
8. Ali, M., Tahir, M.A., Durrani, M.N.: Vehicle images dataset for make and model recognition. Data Brief **42**, 108107 (2022)
9. Tafazzoli, F., Frigui, H., Nishiyama, K.: A large and diverse dataset for improved vehicle make and model recognition. In: Proceedings of the IEEE Conference on Computer Vision and Pattern Recognition Workshops, pp. 1–8 (2017)
10. Maity, S., Bhattacharyya, A., Singh, P.K., Kumar, M., Sarkar, R.: Last decade in vehicle detection and classification: a comprehensive survey. Arch. Comput. Methods Eng. **29**, 1–38 (2022)
11. Gayen, S., Maity, S., Singh, P.K., Geem, Z.W., Sarkar, R.: Two decades of vehicle make and model recognition-survey, challenges and future directions. J. King Saud Univ. Comput. Inf. Sci. **36**, 101885 (2023)
12. Komolovaite, D., Krisciunas, A., Lagzdinyte-Budnike, I., Budnikas, A., Rentelis, D.: Vehicle make detection using the transfer learning approach. Elektronika ir Elektrotechnika **28**(4), 55–64 (2022)
13. Yu, Y., Liu, H., Fu, Y., Jia, W., Yu, J., Yan, Z.: Embedding pose information for multiview vehicle model recognition. IEEE Trans. Circuits Syst. Video Technol. **32**(8), 5467–5480 (2022)
14. Yang, L., Luo, P., Change Loy, C., Tang, X.: A large-scale car dataset for fine-grained categorization and verification. In: Proceedings of the IEEE Conference on Computer Vision and Pattern Recognition, pp. 3973–3981 (2015)
15. Krause, J., Stark, M., Deng, J., Fei-Fei, L.: 3D object representations for fine-grained categorization. ICCVW'13. USA (2013)
16. Avianto, D., Harjoko, A.: CNN-based classification for highly similar vehicle model using multi-task learning. J. Imaging **8**(11), 293 (2022)
17. Bularz, M., Przystalski, K., Ogorzałek, M.: Car make and model recognition system using rear-lamp features and convolutional neural networks. Multimed. Tools Appl. **83**, 1–15 (2023)
18. Dehghan, A., Masood, S.Z., Shu, G., Ortiz, E.: View independent vehicle make, model and color recognition using convolutional neural network (2017). arXiv preprint arXiv:1702.01721
19. Zwemer, M.H., Brouwers, G.M.Y.E., Wijnhoven, R.G.J., de With, P.H.N.: Semi-automatic training of a vehicle make and model recognition system. In: International Conference on Image Analysis and Processing, pp. 321–332. Springer (2017)
20. Benavides, C.T.N., Tae, C.: Fine grained image classification for vehicle make and model using convolutional neural network. CS230 Standford (2019)
21. Linse, C., Barth, E., Martinetz, T.: Convolutional neural networks do work with pre-defined filters. In: 2023 International Joint Conference on Neural Networks (IJCNN), pp. 1–8. IEEE (2023)
22. Ammar, A., Koubaa, A., Boulila, W., Benjdira, B., Alhabashi, Y.: A multi-stage deep-learning-based vehicle and license plate recognition system with real-time edge inference. Sensors **23**(4), 2120 (2023)
23. Lin, T.-Y., RoyChowdhury, A., Maji, S.: Bilinear CNN models for fine-grained visual recognition. In: Proceedings of the IEEE International Conference on Computer Vision, pp. 1449–1457 (2015)
24. Zheng, H., Fu, J., Mei, T., Luo, J.: Learning multi-attention convolutional neural network for fine-grained image recognition. In: Proceedings of the IEEE International Conference on Computer Vision, pp. 5209–5217 (2017)
25. Ji, R., et al.: Attention convolutional binary neural tree for fine-grained visual categorization. In: Proceedings of the IEEE/CVF Conference on Computer Vision and Pattern Recognition, pp. 10468–10477 (2020)

26. Zheng, H., Fu, J., Zha, Z.-J., Luo, J., Mei, T.: Learning rich part hierarchies with progressive attention networks for fine-grained image recognition. IEEE Trans. Image Process. **29**, 476–488 (2019)
27. Anand, V., et al.: Weighted average ensemble deep learning model for stratification of brain tumor in MRI images. Diagnostics **13**(7), 1320 (2023)
28. Bhattacharyya, A., Bhattacharya, A., Maity, S., Singh, P.K., Sarkar, R.: JUVDsi v1: developing and benchmarking a new still image database in Indian scenario for automatic vehicle detection. Multimed. Tools Appl. **82**(21), 32883 (2023). https://doi.org/10.1007/s11042-023-14661-1
29. Torgo, L., Ribeiro, R.: Precision and recall for regression. In: Discovery Science: 12th International Conference, DS 2009, Porto, Portugal, October 3–5, 2009 12, pp. 332–346. Springer (2009)
30. Amaral, J.F., Mancini, M., Novo Júnior, J.M.: Comparison of three hand dynamometers in relation to the accuracy and precision of the measurements. Braz. J. Phys. Ther. **16**, 216–224 (2012)

Semi-automatic Tool to Assist Radiologist for Pneumothorax Detection and Localization

Jija Dasgupta[1], Murthy Chamarthy[2], and Tanushyam Chattopadhyay[1](✉)

[1] Adani AI Labs, Kolkata, India
{jija.dasgupta,Tanushyam.Chattopadhyay}@adani.com
[2] Vascular Institute of North Texas, Dallas, TX, USA

Abstract. The radiological image investigation needs a lot of effort and expertise. This paper presents a semiautomatic tool designed for the detection of Pneumothorax and localization of Regions of Interest (ROIs) in X-Ray images through the utilization of UNet++ in an iterative manner. The evaluation of the Pneumothorax detection tool is conducted on a dataset introduced by Filice et al. The primary objective of this tool is to reduce the manual intervention required by radiologists, thereby enhancing overall throughput. In comparison to the state-of-the-art fastai model, our proposed model demonstrates a significant improvement, particularly in terms of recall. The study contributes to the field by introducing an efficient and effective tool for Pneumothorax detection, addressing the need for expeditious image analysis in radiology. The results suggest that the implemented UNet++ model outperforms existing methodologies, demonstrating its potential to revolutionize and optimize the radiological workflow. This research is pivotal for advancing the capabilities of automated tools in medical image analysis, ultimately benefiting healthcare professionals and patients alike.

Keywords: Semi-automatic tool · Pneumothorax · X-Ray

1 Introduction

Radiologists associated with any hospitals need to examine radiological images obtained from multiple investigation modalities. These include X-Rays, CT Scan and MRI. They need to enhance the images, localize the areas of interest, note the key performance indices and finally, comment about the disease under inspection. Thus, it involves a lot of effort and expertise to execute these tasks.

Artificial Intelligence (AI) is a vast and diverse realm of data, algorithms, analytics, deep learning, neural networks, and insights that is constantly expanding and adapting to the needs of the healthcare industry. Over the past decade, the application of AI has emerged as a valuable tool in augmenting healthcare providers' capabilities and facilitating intelligent health systems. Various

AI techniques, spanning from machine learning to deep learning, have gained prominence in the healthcare domain for tasks such as identification of patients at risk, diagnosis of disease, predicting outcome, and drug development. The successful implementation of AI for accurate disease diagnosis necessitates the utilization of diverse medical data sources. Integration of AI has significantly enriched the hospital experience of patient's and expedited their seamless transition into home-based rehabilitation. Substantive efforts have been undertaken to utilise AI techniques for the diagnosis of diseases such as Alzheimer's disease, malignancy, diabetes mellitus, ischemic heart disease, tuberculosis, stroke, cerebrovascular disorders, hypertension, as well as conditions affecting the skin, liver etc. [7]. These endeavors signify the expanding role of AI in the medical landscape and its potential to revolutionize disease identification and patient care across diverse medical disciplines.

Precision in disease diagnosis holds paramount importance for meticulous treatment planning, effective therapeutic interventions, and the overall welfare of patients. Consequently, the incorporation of semi-automatic tools proves highly advantageous in facilitating physicians with expeditious and accurate disease diagnosis, thereby optimizing time management within clinical settings. In recent years following notable achievements in the domain of daily object crowdsourcing, there has been a burgeoning interest in the integration of machine learning methodologies within the realm of medical image interpretation. Specifically, in radiology image analysis, significant improvement has been achieved in automated diagnosis, particularly for respiratory diseases such as COVID-19. Deep learning techniques have shown remarkable performance in detecting COVID-19 from chest X-ray images. For instance, an ensemble model using an inverted bell-curve approach was proposed to enhance detection accuracy [9], while hybrid optimisation strategies such as social group optimisation combined with support vector machines further improved classification outcomes [13]. In the domain of CT imaging, a swarm-optimised neural network demonstrated efficacy in identifying COVID-19 infections [11], and morphological segmentation guided by entropy measures enabled enhanced infection localisation from CT images [4]. One-shot learning approaches have also been explored to address data scarcity issues, showing promise in phase-based classification of chest X-rays [1,2]. Transfer learning techniques integrated with superpixel-based segmentation offered robust detection and infection localisation capabilities [10]. These studies underscore the potential of integrating advanced machine learning with medical imaging for rapid and accurate disease diagnosis [14].

In the realm of cellular biology, Bafti et al. [3] introduced a pioneering semi-automatic image segmentation platform, strategically designed to address the challenges inherent in the annotation of image data. This sophisticated platform, as elucidated by the authors, is web-based and adeptly leverages crowdsourcing for the annotation of intricate cellular images. Central to its functionality is a semiautomated assistive tool crafted to facilitate non-expert annotators in enhancing the efficiency of the annotation process. The approach establishes a significant stride in harnessing collaborative efforts and leveraging technological assistance for the meticulous annotation of cell biology images. Sambaturu et al. [12] presents a novel interactive segmentation methodology employing a pre-trained semantic segmentation network. Remarkably, this technique achieves accurate segmentation of both 2D and 3D medical images without necessitating any supplementary architectural modifications. The approach further benefits from collaboration with a medical expert to enhance the precision of segmentation outcomes. In their investigation, Filice et al. delved into the utility of artificial intelligence (AI) models for the generation of annotations [6]. The application of this machine learning annotation methodology demonstrated a notable acceleration in the annotation process, albeit with a discernible trade-off between sensitivity and specificity. Notably, Filice et al. observed that the precision attained through this approach, when juxtaposed with annotations modified by radiologists, exhibited a lower rate. Specifically, the precision levels were reported at 46% and 22% for chest tube and pneumothorax annotations, respectively.

The objective of this paper was to build a semiautomatic tool for Pneumothorax detection and ROI localization from X-Ray images utilizing UNet++ in an iterative manner. It also aimed to provide a user interface (UI) to assist radiologists in enhancing images by increasing brightness or contrast and listing the key parameters in an editable text format. We tested the tool on the dataset used by Filice et al. This tool can reduce the time of manual intervention of radiologists and hence increase the throughput.

Proposed tool UI has the following features:

1. Display the radiological image.
2. A slide bar to be placed below the display area that can be used to enhance the image quality.
3. List the KPI and their confidence score as an editable text box in the right-hand corner of the image display area. KPI would include,
   – Height of the localized area.
   – Width of the localized area.
   – Area and pixel count of the localized area.
   – Confidence score of the computer vision-based localization algorithm.
4. Automated localization of the region of interest (ROI), in a typical realization, for Pneumothorax detection, this ROI might be the pixels indicating pneumothorax.
5. Free hand annotation tool to edit the automatically generated ROI.
6. Features to save the annotation after corrections made by the radiologist.
7. Store the changes in the system for future training set of reinforcement learning.
8. Update the computer vision model so that the automated system can work with better accuracy over time.

We achieved a precision of 27% after radiologist verification.

The remainder of the paper is organized as follows: The proposed method is explained in Sect. 2. In Sect. 3 detailed experimental set up and results are explained. Experimental results are compared with some existing automatic PD diagnosis system in Sect. 3. Finally, concluding remarks are placed in Sect. 4.

2 Proposed Method

2.1 Preprocessing

The objective of this step is to resize all the images into a predefined size and standardize the intensity to get rid of the possible quality issue arising from the process of scanning an image. Steps used in this phase are,

- Each grayscale X-ray image is uniformly resized to dimensions 128×128 pixels.
- Histogram equalization is applied to enhance the contrast of the X-ray image.

The target annotation for the given image is defined as a binary mask of 128×128 pixels. These masks encode information related to the presence or absence of pneumothorax within the ROI. Specifically, the mask values are set to 0 (black) or 1 (white), where a white value signifies the presence of pneumothorax within the associated box. This segmentation approach facilitates the localization and categorization of pneumothorax regions in the X-ray images, providing valuable information for subsequent analysis and diagnosis.

2.2 Model Description

In this study, we employed a U-Net++ model [16], in iterative manner for the segmentation of boxes corresponding to pneumothorax and non-pneumothorax regions in chest X-ray images. The process begins with the preprocessing of contrast-enhanced X-ray images as described in Sect. 2.1, which are then input into the U-Net++ model to generate a segmentation mask. The resulting mask encapsulates the probability values indicating the likelihood of pneumothorax within defined boxes. Subsequently a thresholding step is applied, and boxes with probabilities exceeding the threshold are labelled as pneumothorax (assigned a value of 1).

We conducted connected component analysis to eliminate small, isolated regions corresponding to pneumothorax to refine the segmentation results. The final determination of pneumothorax detection relied on the presence or absence of pneumothorax in the chest X-ray, as indicated by processed segmentation results. In the analysis of pneumothorax images, it was observed that probability range for most instances spanned in lower than ideal range [0–1]. Addressing this variability posed a challenge, and to overcome it, the generated masks were utilized in conjunction with a U-Net++ model for pneumothorax localization. The U-Net++ model underwent three iterations, resulting in an expanded range of probability values, as depicted in Fig. 1.

To further refine the pneumothorax detection process, a comprehensive strategy was employed. This involved integrating decisions derived from raw X-ray images, clean X-ray images, and the generated masks from the first and second iterations through a majority voting mechanism. The culmination of this iterative approach, combining U-Net++ modelling with subsequent post-processing steps, contributed to heightened accuracy and robustness in pneumothorax detection within the realm of medical imaging. The architecture of our proposed model is shown in Fig. 2.

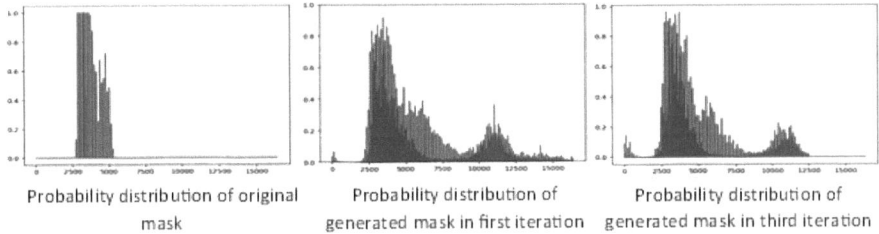

Fig. 1. Probability distribution of mask in different iterations

3 Experiment

3.1 Dataset

We conducted a comprehensive study utilizing the SIIM-ACR Pneumothorax Segmentation dataset, which can be acquired from Kaggle [15]. The Society for Imaging Informatics in Medicine (SIIM) stands at the forefront of healthcare organizations, particularly for individuals keen on the current and future applications of informatics in medical imaging. Collaborating with esteemed partners such as the American College of Radiology, the Society of Thoracic Radiology (STR), and MD.ai, SIIM orchestrated a Machine Learning Challenge on Pneumothorax Detection and Localization via Kaggle using augmented annotations on the public chest radiograph dataset from the National Institutes of Health (NIH), known as the NIH Chest X-rays dataset (available at https://nihcc.app.box.com/v/ChestXray-NIHCC). To ensure the ethical conduct of NIH Chest X-rays dataset, the institutional review board (IRB) of Hanyang University Seoul Hospital in the Republic of Korea granted approval (IRB No. HYUH 2021-03-024). It was affirmed that all methods employed adhered strictly to the Good Clinical Practice guidelines, with the necessity for informed consent duly waived.

The NIH Chest X-rays dataset comprises 112,120 frontal chest X-rays obtained from 30,805 patients. Notably, these X-ray images feature text-mined labels encompassing 14 common thorax diseases, extracted from relevant radiological reports. It's crucial to acknowledge the inherent inaccuracies in these labels, as they were derived through natural language processing. Cho et al. selected 1000 X-ray images which actually contained pneumothorax for their study.

The SIIM-ACR dataset has been partitioned into a training set comprising 10,676 samples, with 2,379 instances of pneumothorax and 8,297 instances of non-pneumothorax. Additionally, there is a test set consisting of 1,372 samples, with 290 cases of pneumothorax and 1,082 cases of non-pneumothorax. Each image in this dataset is accompanied by corresponding masks that delineate areas indicative of pneumothorax in X-ray images. The areas with pneumothorax are marked as white, and the rest of the mask image are marked in black as shown in Fig. 3.

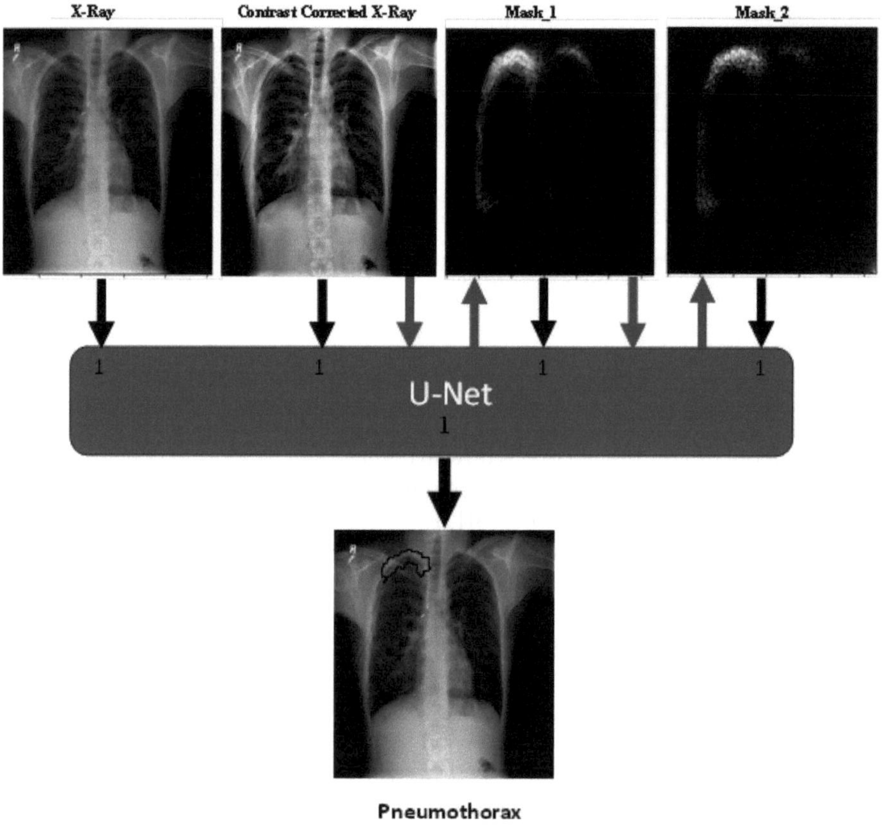

Fig. 2. Pneumothorax detection and localization

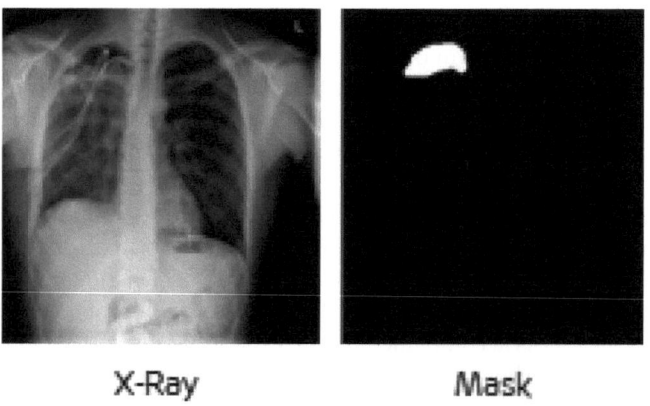

Fig. 3. Pneumothorax detection and localization

3.2 Parameter Selection

The UNet++ model is compiled with Adam optimizer with learning rate, 1e-5, binary cross entropy loss function. Model is trained to optimize the BCE-Dice Loss and IOU loss score as explained in [8]. We have optimized proposed model with respect to accuracy and recall. For training we have used 50 iterations. The probability range for most instances spans from 0 to 0.85 in first iteration of UNet++ and finally becomes 0 to .99 after third iteration, as illustrated in Fig. 1. As the training set of SIIM-ACR dataset is very much imbalanced, we took randomly chosen 2,379 data from non-pneumothorax instances during training.

3.3 Results

The performance of our model tested on test set given in SIIM-ACR dataset is reported in Table 1. Please note our model is trained to optimise recall. The recall of UNet++ for raw image, clean image, mask image after first iteration, mask image after second iteration input is 83%, 80%, 73%, 79% respectively which is improved to 88%.

Table 1. Performance of proposed model for different input images

Image	F_score (%)	accuracy (%)	precision (%)	recall (%)
raw	38	44	25	83
clean	38	45	25	80
$mask_0$	36	46	24	73
$mask_1$	35	40	23	79
ensemble	38	46	27	88

To test the recall consistency for different volume of pneumothorax region we have estimated the recall of proposed model for X-ray having big, medium and small pneumothorax, categorized by radiologist. The report is shown in Table 2. From this result we can easily conclude that ensemble model improved overall recall and reduced its variation for different volume of pneumothorax.

We have implemented the code shared by Filice et al. in [5] and tested on our test data. The comparative results are reported in Table 3. Proposed model has better F-score, precision and recall than fastai model.

Table 2. Recall (in %) of proposed model for different volume of pneumothorax region

Size of Pneumothorax	Large	Medium	Small
Raw image	89	85	75
Clean image	84	83	80
$Mask_1$	73	73	69
$Mask_2$	82	78	77
Ensemble	90	89	85

Table 3. Performance comparison of proposed model with fastai model

Model	F_score (%)	accuracy (%)	precision (%)	recall (%)
fastai	13	50	13	14
Proposed	38	46	27	88

4 Conclusion

In conclusion, this article introduces a semiautomatic tool employing UNet++ for Pneumothorax detection and ROI localization in X-Ray images, presenting a significant stride towards enhancing efficiency in radiological image investigation. By comparing the proposed model with the state-of-the-art fastai model, a notable improvement in recall is observed, underscoring the superiority of the UNet++ methodology. This advancement is particularly crucial in the context of reducing the time required for manual analysis, ultimately increasing overall throughput in radiological workflows. The findings of this study contribute valuable insights to the ongoing efforts in medical image analysis, emphasizing the potential of advanced technologies in automating and optimizing diagnostic processes. The implemented tool not only demonstrates its proficiency in Pneumothorax detection but also highlights the broader significance of leveraging cutting-edge methodologies for improved patient care. As the healthcare industry continues to evolve, embracing such technological innovations holds promise for the future of radiology, where precision, speed, and accuracy are paramount.

References

1. Aradhya, V.N.M., Mahmud, M., Guru, D., Agarwal, B., Kaiser, M.S.: One-shot cluster-based approach for the detection of covid–19 from chest x–ray images. Cogn. Comput. **13**(4), 873–881 (2021). https://doi.org/10.1007/s12559-020-09774-w
2. Aradhya, V.M., Mahmud, M., Chowdhury, M., Guru, D.S., Kaiser, M.S., Azad, S.: Learning through one shot: a phase by phase approach for covid-19 chest x-ray classification, pp. 241–244 (2021). https://doi.org/10.1109/IECBES48179.2021.9398761
3. Bafti, S., Ang, C., Hossain, M., Marcelli, G., Alemany-Fornes, M., Tsaousis, A.: A crowdsourcing semi-automatic image segmentation platform for cell biology. Comput. Biol. Med. **130** (2021). https://doi.org/10.1016/j.compbiomed.2020.104204

4. Dey, N., Rajinikanth, V., Fong, S.J., Kaiser, M.S., Mahmud, M.: Social group optimization–assisted kapur's entropy and morphological segmentation for automated detection of covid-19 infection from computed tomography images. Cogn. Comput. **12**(5), 1011–1023 (2020). https://doi.org/10.1007/s12559-020-09751-3
5. FastAI: Chest x-ray model (2025). https://docs.fast.ai/tutorial.medical_imaging.html. Accessed 26 Mar 2025
6. Filice, R.W., et al.: Crowdsourcing pneumothorax annotations using machine learning annotations on the nih chest x-ray dataset. J. Digit. Imaging **33**(2), 490–496 (2020). https://doi.org/10.1007/s10278-019-00299-9
7. Kumar, Y., Koul, A., Singla, R., Ijaz, M.F.: Artificial intelligence in disease diagnosis: a systematic literature review, synthesizing framework and future research agenda. J. Ambient Intell. Humaniz. Comput. **14**(7), 8459–8486 (2023). https://doi.org/10.1007/s12652-021-03612-z
8. Oh, S., Kim, Y.J., Park, Y.T., Kim, K.G.: Automatic pancreatic cyst lesion segmentation on eus images using a deep-learning approach. sensors (basel). Sensors (Basel) **22**(1) (2021). https://doi.org/10.3390/s22010245
9. Paul, A., Basu, A., Mahmud, M., Kaiser, M.S., Sarkar, R.: Inverted bell-curve-based ensemble of deep learning models for detection of COVID-19 from chest X-rays. Neural Comput. Appl. **35**(22), 16113–16127 (2023). https://doi.org/10.1007/s00521-021-06737-6
10. Prakash, N., Murugappan, M., Hemalakshmi, G., Jayalakshmi, M., Mahmud, M.: Deep transfer learning for COVID-19 detection and infection localization with superpixel based segmentation. Sustain. Cities Soc. **75** (2021). https://doi.org/10.1016/j.scs.2021.103252
11. Punitha, S., Stephan, T., Kannan, R., Mahmud, M., Kaiser, M.S., Belhaouari, S.B.: Detecting covid-19 from lung computed tomography images: a swarm optimized artificial neural network approach. IEEE Access **11**, 12378–12393 (2023). https://doi.org/10.1109/ACCESS.2023.3236812
12. Sambaturu, B., Gupta, A., Jawahar, C.V., Arora, C.: Efficient and generic interactive segmentation framework to correct mispredictions during clinical evaluation of medical images. CoRR **abs/2108.02996** (2021). https://arxiv.org/abs/2108.02996
13. Singh, A.K., Kumar, A., Mahmud, M., Kaiser, M.S., Kishore, A.: COVID-19 infection detection from chest x-ray images using hybrid social group optimization and support vector classifier. Cogn. Comput. **16**(4), 1765–1777 (2024). https://doi.org/10.1007/s12559-021-09848-3
14. Singh, R., Mahmud, M., Yovera, L.: Classification of first trimester ultrasound images using deep convolutional neural network. In: Mahmud, M., Kaiser, M.S., Kasabov, N., Iftekharuddin, K., Zhong, N. (eds.) Applied Intelligence and Informatics. AII 2021. CCIS, vol. 1435, pp. 92–105. Springer, Cham (2021). https://doi.org/10.1007/978-3-030-82269-9_8
15. Society for Imaging Informatics in Medicine: Siim-acr pneumothorax segmentation: Identify pneumothorax disease in chest x-rays (2019). https://www.kaggle.com/c/siim-acr-pneumothorax-segmentation. Accessed 26 Mar 2025
16. Zhou, Z., Rahman Siddiquee, M.M., Tajbakhsh, N., Liang, J.: UNet++: a nested U-Net architecture for medical image segmentation. In: Stoyanov, D., et al. (eds.) DLMIA/ML-CDS -2018. LNCS, vol. 11045, pp. 3–11. Springer, Cham (2018). https://doi.org/10.1007/978-3-030-00889-5_1

Parenthood Responsibility Mining Using Social Network Mining Approach

Xiaowen Wang(✉), Jere Leukkunen, and Mourad Oussalah

Faculty of ITEE, University of Oulu, Oulu, Finland
{Xiaowen.wang,mourad.oussalah}@oulu.fi,
jere.leukkunen@student.oulu.fi

Abstract. Parents face various challenges in their daily life, especially during the first-time pregnancy. This paper attempts to comprehend explore the comprehend aspects in five categories (i.e., parents and family, health issues, finance and wealth, social services, society) related to disappointment caused by first time pregnancy. The relevant threads which bear negative feelings about pregnancy are collected and analyzed by conducting strength test and support investigation (i.e., like/dislike indicators). The set of networks using threads as nodes and edges which are based on the number of categories shared by threads was constructed and analyzed by social network analysis. In each network, we deployed the spectral clustering algorithm (i.e., Girvan Newman) to identify the possible clusters and investigate the quality of clusters. Multiple concerns regarding the negative feelings about first-time pregnancy discussed in vauva.fi online forum was mapped and discussed as the result of the social network analysis results. The findings pave the way for mora tailored recommendation and interventions using early warning detection through social media analytics in healthcare.

Keywords: Pregnancy · Parenthood · Social network analysis · Data mining · Online forum

1 Introduction

The transition to parenthood has been shown as a significant life event within a family life course, which involves major changes in an individual's personal, social, and relational spheres [1]. During the transition to parenthood, parents incur psychological and emotional changes including challenges of adapting to a new identity and role as a parent, the changes in the couple relationship, and the impact on individual mental health as pointed out in Parfitt' and Ayers' review paper [2]. The unique challenges faced by pregnant adolescents have attracted special interest in the research community, due to the lack of support, limited access to healthcare resources and social stigma [3]. Studies related to first time pregnant women's experiences in the early pregnancy are quite limited and sparse [4]. Carin et al. [4] explored the experiences of first-time pregnant women during the early stages of pregnancy. A range of emotions were reported such as joy, excitement, anxiety, and uncertainty. Many participants felt unprepared for the physical and emotional changes that accompanied pregnancy and expressed the need for support and guidance during this time [4]. In the digital era and tele-medicine progress, prospect of identifying pregnant women in need of special care and further clinical assistance arises. Especially, advances in social network analysis shine lights on potential insights that can help in identifying individuals at risk by exploring individual patterns of his/her social network. This is in addition to the potential support that can be brough by social network, in terms of other women sharing similar experiences and worries, to pregnant woman. Indeed, social networks have been found to play a significant role in the transition to parenthood, with both positive and negative impacts on parents' experiences [1]. For instance, parents who had access to supportive social networks feel more confident in dealing with the challenges of early parenthood as opposed to isolated and less sociable parents. Social networks play an important role in providing comfort and understanding during a challenging time (i.e., pregnancy after loss) [5].

In recent years, social media has become incredibly popular, which has transformed the way people communicate and share information. Online discussions and communities focusing on parenthood can offer valuable opportunities to parents to connect with each other, share their experiences, and seek advice and support [6–16]. Social network analysis (SNA) has been used for understanding the relationships and interactions within a network using graph theory [17]. Online social network analysis has been applied in various domains such as understanding user behavior, detecting online communities, analyzing social influence, and supporting decision-making [18]. Indeed, SNA can be utilized to examine the structure and behavior of users in various online discussion forums, e.g., university forum [19], student forum [20], distance education forum [21] and open online course forum [22]. In [23] the knowledge sharing behavior of practitioners in a clinical online discussion forum was explored using SNA-based method. Social interaction in online discussions has been proved to have positive correlations with learning by SNA approach [24]. In parenthood research and practice, SNA has emerged as a valuable tool for enhancing support systems, for instance, parenting intervention systems [25, 26]. Through SNA, researchers and practitioners gain insight into the structure of the existing parenting support system, communities, and social context [27]. Studies focusing on use of SNA methods in pure online community for parenthood / pregnancy investigations are rather limited, despite its potential importance in advancing in telemedicine applications.

The goal of this study is to analyze threads scrapped from Finland online forum **vauva.fi** that focused on parenthood and pregnancy issues to comprehend aspects related to disappointment caused by first time pregnancy in way that guides healthcare intervention. The focus on first time pregnancy is motivated by the increased risk incurred by this population group, which requires special attention in any telemedicine-based initiative. For this purpose, we focused on those threads from an online community that bear negative feelings about pregnancy. In our approach, we considered a set of categories that were populated in pregnancy forums and are found relevant to be used as proxy to direct patient help. We first conduct an investigation to evaluate the strength of each category and its relationship with like/dislike support indicators. Second, we constructed 4 networks where threads represent nodes and edges are constructed according to the number of categories shared by nodes. Third, we performed a social network analysis to analyze each network by implementing NetworkX algorithms. Fourth, we deployed a spectral clustering algorithm, namely, Girvan Newman algorithm [28] to identify the possible clusters and investigate their quality to infer relevant insights. The rest of the paper is organized as follows. Section II presents the details of methodology. Section III presents the results obtained by the proposed method. Section IV discusses the results.

2 Methodology

2.1 Data Collection

In this study, threads were scraped from Vauva.fi [29] by querying a series of keywords related to negativity towards first time pregnancy (e.g., fear, guilt, depression, sadness, envy, frustration, or shame) in five categories which were populated in vauva.fi corresponding to parent and family, health issues, financial and wealth, social services, and society. These categories are also in line with the Cowan's five-dimension continuum description of parenthood transition period [9]. A total of 887 threads were collected in the time frame of the last five years, but only 102 threads with more than 10 replies were chosen for further analysis. This is due to the observation that threads with fewer replies may not contain relevant information about the previously mentioned categories. The selected threads were crawled using Beautiful Soup tool [30] and stored as JSON objects in an SQLite database [31]. An example of a thread stored in the database could be the following: {'0': {'user':'Vierailija','timestamp': 1626854400.0,'likes': 40,'dislikes': 664,'title':'Title text','text':'Post body'},'1': {'user':'Vierailija','timestamp': 1626854700.0,'likes': 930,'dislikes': 109,'text':'Reply body'}}. The main attributes of each thread were extracted and renamed as:

- 'URL',
- 'category',
- 'numbers_of_replies',
- 'total_numbers_of_likes',
- 'total_numbers_of_dislikes',
- 'numbers_of_likes_each_message',
- 'numbers_of_dislikes_each_message',
- 'timestamp',
- 'text'.

2.2 Overall Method

Figure 1 outlines the methodology deployed in this study. After the data collection phase, we first evaluate the strength of each category through a simple string-matching. Next, the correlation between the string matching and like/dislike support indicators was investigated. Thereafter, four networks were constructed based on the numbers of categories shared and the graph attributes of each network were also calculated. Lastly, the clusters were detected from each constructed network by implementing the spectral clustering algorithm Girvan Newman (GN) in NetworkX. The GN algorithm detects the clusters by continuously removing the most valuable edges that have the highest number of shortest paths between nodes from the graph [28]. Insights are then inferred by exploring the content of individual cluster or community. Especially, each community or cluster stands for a set of individuals, typically, first time pregnant women that share some common features. The details of individual modules of this methodology (i.e., strength and support evaluation, social network analysis) are described in the following subsections.

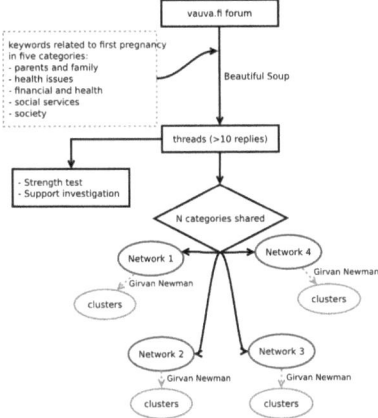

Fig. 1. Overall diagram of the methodology.

2.3 Category Matching and Support Qualification

The purpose of category strength evaluation is to find out the strength of each category (i.e., parents and family, health issues, financial issues, social services, society) in the whole collected dataset. For this purpose, a simple string matching of the keyword lists (of each category) from the whole collected database was implemented to quantify the strength and a bar chart was plotted to show the proportion of each category. More formally, let C_i stand for the ith category represented by a set of tokens or keywords, say,

$$C_i \triangleq \{w_{l_1}, w_{l_2}, \ldots, w_{l_i}\} \quad (1)$$

For a Datum D, the strength of category C_i is calculated as:

$$S_D(C_i) = \frac{1}{m} \sum_{j=1, l_i} \gamma_D^{w_{l_j}} \quad (2)$$

where $\gamma_D^{w_{l_j}}$ corresponds to the numbers of matching of keyword w_{l_j} in D, and m is some normalization factor.

In addition, the *like* and dislike indicators of each post where a category matching is found are considered. For individual thread, the *like* (resp. *Dislike*) support can be computed as the (normalized) total number of *likes* (resp. *Dislikes*) of all posts associated to the underlined thread. To comprehend the influence of these indicators, we compute the Peason correlation between the like /dislike support and the strength of the corresponding category. Intuitively, the correlation of these variables should be positively high.

2.4 Social Network Analysis

A social network was constructed by using the collected threads as nodes. An edge between two nodes (threads) is established if the two threads share at least two categories among the five categories mentioned above. In other words, the two threads contain keywords related to at least two specified categories. In each network, we analyzed a set of network attributes that include the number of nodes, the number of edges, global clustering coefficient, average path length, size of giant component, average degree, average degree centrality, average in-betweenness centrality, average closeness centrality, and net density. In addition, the associated variances in several graph attributes (i.e., degree centrality, betweenness centrality and closeness centrality) were also computed to measure the degree to which the graph (as whole) is centralized.

Typically, centrality provides insights regarding the most important (or central) nodes in the network. One of the simplest centrality measures is the *degree centrality* which corresponds to the number of connections of the corresponding node. This also corresponds in case of undirected graph to the size of the node's direct neighbors. In *NetworkX*, the *degree centrality* values are normalized by dividing the total score by the maximum possible degree in a simple graph, which is equal to N-1 where N is the number of nodes in the graph [32]. In terms of how the node connects others, two centrality metrics are computed, namely, *betweenness centrality* and *closeness centrality*. *Betweenness centrality* captures how well connected the node is and how important the node is in connecting with other nodes. *Closeness centrality* indicates the closeness of a given node to all other nodes from the point view of shortest path. This is followed by social services and general society. This would suggest that despite national efforts to raise the efficiency of social services, still the communication and interaction with first pregnancy population group requires improvement to attract further interest by this population group.

After the study of networks' statistics, we identified the clusters for each network by implementing Girvan Newman algorithm and quantified the partition quality algorithm from NetworkX which gives us both the *coverage* and the *performance* score. In essence, the *coverage* corresponds to the ratio of the number of intra-cluster edges by the total number of edges in the graph while the *performance* score evaluates the number of intra-cluster edges plus inter-cluster non-edges divided by the total number of potential edges. We also considered the *modularity* function in NetworkX [33] that measures the density of connection in each corresponding community. Formally, modularity is the fraction of the edges within the cluster minus the expected fraction if edges were distributed at random [34]. For unweighted and undirected graphs, the value of the modularity lies in the range of [-0.5, 1] [35] and a high modularity score indicates a strong cluster structure.

3 Results

3.1 Strength Test and Support Investigation

Figure 2 shows the category strength test (unnormalized category matching score) highlighting, for each category (i.e., parents and family, health issues, finance and wealth, social services, society), the frequency of matched keywords and the total amount of like / dislike support for that category, obtained by summing up the amount of like / dislike in all posts of that category. As noticed from the plot, more keywords were identified in the category "parents and family" and least keywords were identified in the category of "society". This indicates the dominance of family related factors in the discussion forums, which is highly anticipated as the couple relationship and the inner family ties play key role in supporting or harming first time pregnancy women. The like/dislike support results show that like / dislike support indicators do follow the same trend as the category matching results. Besides, Pearson correlation analysis between the like/dislike support and strength of each category and each thread. The result indicates that the strength score and like/dislike support are positively correlated ($r > 0.988$) for all categories and threads. It is also worth noticing that *like* counts is well dominating *dislike* counts in every category, which indicates that opinions shared in the forum in each thread are somehow shared by the majority of the reader community.

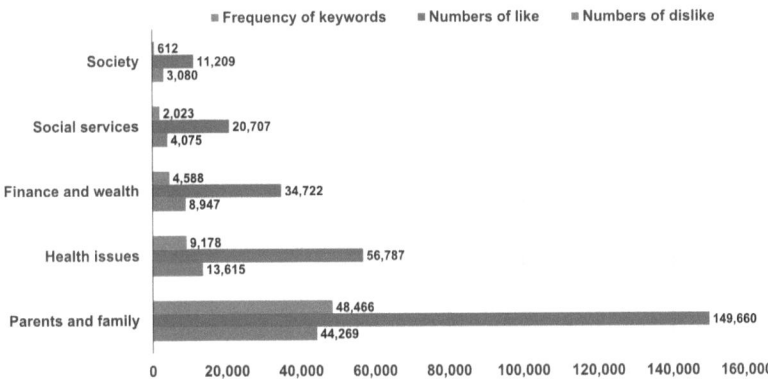

Fig. 2. Strength test and like / dislike support indicator for each category.

3.2 Network Analysis Results

Using the social network construction pointed out in the previous section, four types of networks were constructed according to the number of categories shared between the nodes (threads). Specifically, we distinguished networks where i) nodes share at least 2 categories, ii) nodes share at least 3 categories, iii) nodes share at least 4 categories and, iv) nodes share all the five categories. This is an exhaustive list of possible interpretations of the statement "nodes share two activities" as they may share exactly two categories or more. Thereby, for each of these four networks, a statistical analysis regarding the graph attributes of the network and the quality of the clusters (communities) generated using the Girvan-Newman algorithm.

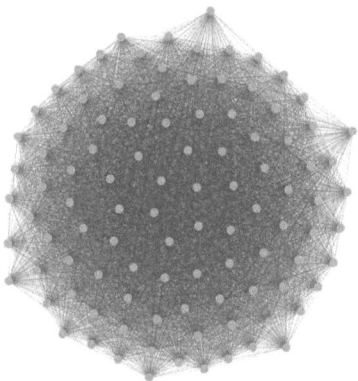

Fig. 3. Network 1 built based on the number of categories shared (N > = 2).

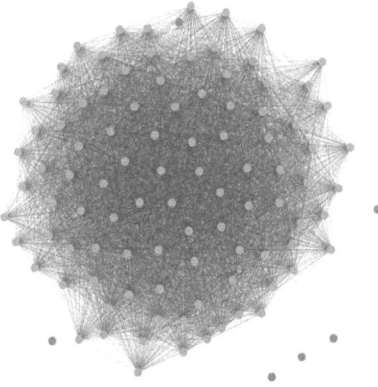

Fig. 4. Network 2 built based on the number of categories shared (N > = 3).

Besides, since the disconnected nodes would not contribute to the calculations of graph metrics, all the isolated nodes were removed from each network before computation of the corresponding graph attributes. Table I exhibits both the graph attributes and clusters for each of the above networks. The number of nodes and edges of each network indicates that the network becomes smaller when more categories are shared as shown in Figs. 3, 4, 5 and 6 as well. All the networks are well connected as the average path length is only about one hop and all have dense connection as revealed by the high value of global clustering coefficient and average degree centrality, which testify of good quality clusters. We can see in Table 1 that the average values of degree centrality and closeness centrality are close to unity, which testifies of good connectivity of the four networks. However, all the nodes were not well connected to the other nodes belonging to other clusters due to the low value of betweenness centrality.

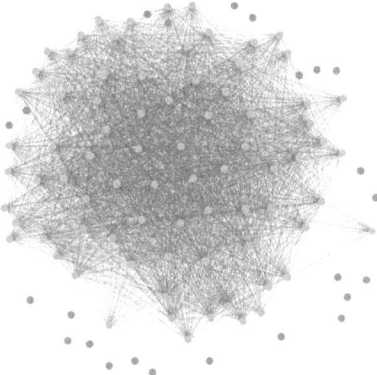

Fig. 5. Network 3 built based on the number of categories shared (N > = 4).

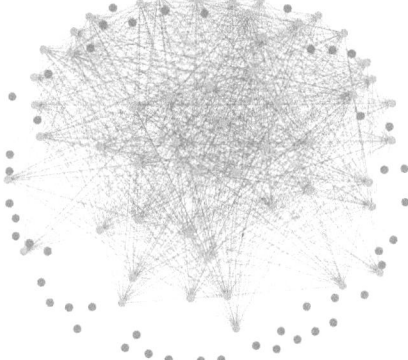

Fig. 6. Network 4 built based on the number of categories shared (N = 5).

After identification of communities, coverage and performance metrics were computed. For further analysis, the top four clusters were selected from each network. Table 1 presents the outcomes, indicating that the chosen clusters consistently exhibit high values for partition coverage and performance, but notably low modularity. A negative modularity value suggests that the identified partition does not significantly outperform a random partition. Modularity values close to zero indicate a weak community structure.

Among these networks, Network 4 where nodes share five categories has zero variance in degree, degree centrality, betweenness centrality and closeness centrality, which indicates the graph is fully connected. Network 1 sharing more than two categories has relatively low value of degree variance, degree centrality variance and closeness variance, which implies the nodes have similar number of connections, similar levels of importance and can be equally reachable from each other within the network. The highest value of betweenness variance was found in Network 2 which may indicate that the nodes in Network 2 are more likely to act as "bridges" as compared to other three networks. On the contrary, all the nodes in network 3 cannot act as "bridges" because it records a relatively low value of betweenness variance score.

Table 1. The parameters of networks sharing N categories.

Metrics	Network 1 (N >= 2)	Network 2 (N >= 3)	Network 3 (N >= 4)	Network 4 (N = 5)
Graph attributes				
Nodes	102	96	78	52
Edges	5094	4343	2872	1326
Global clustering coefficient	26281.89	5221.87	4658.36	-
Average path length	1.01	1.05	1.04	1.0
Size of giant Component	5094	4343	2872	1326
Average degree	99.88	96.48	73.64	51
Degree variance	8.99	62.27	41.08	0
Average degree Centrality	0.99	0.95	0.96	1.0
Degree centrality Variance	0.00088	0.0069	0.0069	0.0
Average betweenness centrality	0.00011	0.00051	0.00057	0.0
Betweenness variance	1.66	9.81	1.65e-07	0.0
Average closeness centrality	0.99	0.96	0.96	1.0
Closeness variance	0.00067	0.0041	0.0043	0.0
Net density	0.99	0.95	0.96	1.0
4 Clusters identified by Girvan Newman				
Partition coverage	0.95	0.96	0.95	0.89
Partition performance	0.94	0.94	0.93	0.89
Modularity	−0.00064	−0.00029	−0.00066	−0.0022

The Girvan-Newman algorithm in NetworkX [33], was employed for community detection in the networks under investigation. This method identifies communities by iteratively removing the most crucial edges from the graph. While the algorithm has a time complexity of $O(n^3)$, it potentially poses challenges for significantly large graphs. In this study, the graphs utilized only have around 100 nodes. Given this scale and the fact that the algorithm was executed only once, computational efficiency was not a concern [32].

3.3 Interpreting Clusters by Context

Based on the cluster results outlined in Table 1, a thorough examination was undertaken for each network, revealing that each network has only one large cluster with multiple nodes and the other three clusters only with one node. To gain a deeper understanding, a content analysis was executed to extract the keywords to discover the contextual themes in the large cluster. The findings indicated a remarkable consistency across all the large cluster in each network. This observation is visually represented through the histogram of the top 30 words (Fig. 7) and the Word Cloud illustration (see Fig. 8). In the forum, the topic mainly relates to children (i.e., 'lapsi'), childbirth (i.e., 'synnytys'), and pregnancy (i.e., 'raskaus'). Table 2 explored the percentage of each category in each network. All the networks show a similar distribution for the given five categories. The high percentage of results tell that one thread may appear in multiple categories, which makes the identification and interpreting of clusters more difficult.

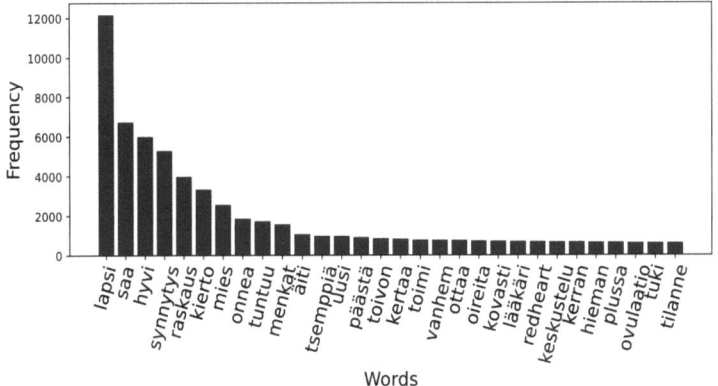

Fig. 7. Histogram of top 30 words for the large cluster in each network.

Fig. 8. The illustration of Word Cloud for the large cluster in each network.

Table 2. The percentage of each category in each network.

Category	Network 1 (N >= 2)	Network 2 (N >= 3)	Network 3 (N >= 4)	Network 4 (N = 5)
Parents and family	100%	100%	100%	100%
Health issues	95%	98%	99%	100%
Finance and wealth	86%	90%	97%	100%
Social services	80%	84%	96%	100%
Society	60%	64%	74%	100%

4 Discussions

In this paper, we explored the comprehend aspects related to disappointment caused by first time pregnancy in five categories (i.e., parents and family, health issues, finance and wealth, social services, and society) from the collected Finland online forum (vauva.fi) threads. In each category, we conducted strength test by simple string matching to check its strength and investigated dislike/like support and its relationship with strength test. We constructed the network based on the number of categories shared by threads and performed social network analysis for each network. We implemented the spectral clustering algorithm (i.e., Girvan Newman) to identify the possible clusters and attempted to interpret the clusters in each network.

As shown in the strength test and support indicator investigation results, obviously at first, in the online forum people communicate and comment more about the negative feeling towards first time pregnancy regarding the category "parents and family". Discussions related to "health issues" are strangely second most important, despite the critical importance of health at this stage. Indeed, as a complex biological process, pregnancy can have a significant impact on women's physical and mental health. Various health problems may appear during pregnancy, for instance, nausea, vomiting, fatigue, gestational diabetes, high blood pressure, miscarriage, stress, fear of childbirth [36], maternal depression [37], etc. Nowadays the risk of health issues is even getting higher may increase more since women tend to delay the first birth due to social and economic factors [38]. Nevertheless, the finding reveals the critical importance of family issues more than actual individual health concerns. This finding could be used by health specialists and practitioners when devising clinical protocols for interacting and communicating with first time pregnant women. In the third position, we encounter "finance and wealth" related issues.

The statistics of thread-based network analysis indicate that the network tends to be more tightly connected when more categories were shared according to the results of the graph attributes computed. Several variance values (i.e., degree variance, degree centrality variance, betweenness variance and closeness variance) were measured to investigate the difference between networks built on various settings. The network with threads sharing five categories has the nodes with exact same connection between each other within the network since all the variance values were found as zero. The nodes were shown to be a little bit different in the network which was built based on the threads sharing more than two or three categories. Besides, the top 4 clusters were identified by Girvan Newman Algorithm to further exploit the difference between the network built. No good clusters were found since the modularity values are quite low. Additionally, the number of threads appeared in each category also indicates there are plenty of overlapping discussions between the five given categories, meaning that most threads relating to negative feeling about first-time pregnancy cover various of topics inside. This comes as no surprise, as having children affects the parents in many different areas of life.

The results obtained in this work give insights of the negative feelings about first time pregnancy from perspective of five comprehensive given categories based on the analysis of online threaded discussion, which helps to understand the early parenthood life.

Especially, the findings can serve as early warning system that provides insights to health authorities to accommodate their intervention strategies, accordingly, since many of arguments that can be raised during online conversations are often not discussed during clinical interventions. Besides, the developed approach can be extended beyond the early pregnancy case study handled in this paper to several other health issues such as cancer, obesity and other contemporary diseases, which are actively discussed in online communities.

However, there are still limitations that need to be addressed in our study. For instance, the bad quality of clusters made the interpretation of community more difficult since all the threads seem to shift to discuss the same general topics. Handling of such phenomenon boils down into inherent language complexity where semantics, causality and natural user's approach to focus on interesting discussion only, where advanced natural language processing modules will be required. Besides, another limitation is caused by limitations in Finnish language analysis tools made conducting content analysis more challenge to explore mental health conditions during first time pregnancy in our study. Although, recently, the emergency of multilingual models can provide partial solutions to this issue. The performance of such models in complex Finnish language is still to be demonstrated.

5 Conclusions

First-time pregnancy plays an important transition role in women's life both physically and emotionally. In this study, we developed a thread-based analysis approach to mine and comprehend aspects related to disappointment cause by first time pregnancy from Finland online forum vauva.fi. Our approach analyzed the threads containing negative feelings about first time pregnancy related to five pre-defined categories (i.e., parents and family, health issues, finance and wealth, social services, and society). Initially, the strength test and support investigation were conducted to explore the extent of each category and its relationship with like/dislike support indicators. Then a set of social networks was constructed using threads as nodes and edges to connect those nodes that share a number of categories and implementing using NetworkX package. Next, the spectral clustering algorithm (i.e., Girvan Newman) was employed to identify the possible clusters from each network. Top 3 aspects where people have more interest were found as "parents and family", "health issues" and "finance and wealth". Nearly all the thread-based networks have quite dense connections which indicates the fact that people have rather a negative feeling about first-time pregnancy in various aspects. These findings draw a general picture about the experience of first-time pregnancy.

Acknowledgments. This work is partly supported by Finland Itla Children's Foundation (Itsenäisyyden juhlavuoden lastensäätiö) and Academy of Finland DigiHealth (#326292) and University of Oulu Profi5 which are gratefully acknowledged.

Disclosure of Interests. The authors have no competing interests to declare that are relevant to the content of this article.

References

1. Deave, T., Johnson, D., Ingram, J.: Transition to parenthood: the needs of parents in pregnancy and early parenthood. BMC Pregnancy Childbirth **8**, 1–11 (2008)
2. Parfitt, Y., Ayers, S.: Transition to parenthood and mental health in first-time parents. Infant. Ment. Health J. **35**(3), 263–273 (2014)
3. Siegel, R.S., Brandon, A.R.: Adolescents, pregnancy, and mental health. J. Pediatr. Adolesc. Gynecol. **27**(3), 138–150 (2014)
4. Carin, M., Lundgren, I., Bergbom, I.: First time pregnant women's experiences in early pregnancy. Int. J. Qual. Stud. Health Well Being **6**(2), 5600 (2011)
5. Monselise, M., Yang, C.C.: Understanding the social support exchange of a pregnancy after loss online support group. In: 2020 IEEE International Conference on Healthcare Informatics (ICHI) (pp. 1–10). IEEE (2020)
6. Lupton, D., Pedersen, S., Thomas, G.M.: Parenting and digital media: from the early web to contemporary digital society. Sociol. Compass **10**(8), 730–743 (2016)
7. Hall, W., Irvine, V.: E-communication among mothers of infants and toddlers in a community-based cohort: a content analysis. J. Adv. Nurs. **65**(1), 175–183 (2009)
8. Miyata, K.: Social support for Japanese mothers online and offline. In: The internet in everyday life, pp. 520–548. Wiley (2002). https://doi.org/10.1002/9780470774298.ch18
9. Gibson, L., Hanson, V.L.: Digital motherhood: how does technology help new mothers?. In: Proceedings of the SIGCHI Conference on Human Factors in Computing Systems pp. 313–322 (2013)
10. Cowan, C.P., Cowan, P.A.: When partners become parents: the big life change for couples. Harper Collins Publisher, New York (1992)
11. Madge, C., O'connor, H.: Parenting gone wired: empowerment of new mothers on the internet? Soc. Cult. Geogr. **7**(2), 199–220 (2006)
12. Fletcher, R., Vimpani, G., Russell, G., Keatinge, D.: The evaluation of tailored and web-based information for new fathers. Child Care Health Dev. **34**(4), 439–446 (2008). https://doi.org/10.1111/j.1365-2214.2008.00811.x
13. Hudson, D.B., Campbell-Grossman, C., Ofe Fleck, M., et al.: Effects of new fathers network on first time fathersparenting self-efficacy and prenting satisfaction during the transition to parenthood. Issues Compr. Pediatr. Nurs. **26**(4), 217–229 (2003)
14. Nyström, K., Öhrling, K.: Electronic encounters: fathers' experiences of parental support. J. Telemed. Telecare **14**(2), 71–74 (2008)
15. Stgeorge, J.M., Fletcher, R.J.: Fathers online: learning about fatherhood through the internet. J. Perinat. Educ. **20**(3), 154–162 (2011)

16. Hether, H.J., Murphy, S.T., Valente, T.W.: A social network analysis of supportive interactions on prenatal sites. Digital health **2**, 2055207616628700 (2016)
17. Otte, E., Rousseau, R.: Social network analysis: a powerful strategy, also for the information sciences. J. Inf. Sci. **28**(6), 441–453 (2002)
18. Can, U., Alatas, B.: A new direction in social network analysis: online social network analysis problems and applications. Physica A **535**, 122372 (2019)
19. Niu, H.: Social network analysis of university online forum. In: 2010 International Conference on Computational Aspects of Social Networks (pp. 422–429). IEEE (2010)
20. Suraj, P., Roshni, V.K.: Social network analysis in student online discussion forums. In 2015 IEEE Recent Advances in Intelligent Computational Systems (RAICS) (pp. 134–138). IEEE (2015).
21. Da Silva, L.F.C., Barbosa, M.W., Gomes, R.R.: Measuring participation in distance education online discussion forums using social network analysis. J. Am. Soc. Inf. Sci. **70**(2), 140–150 (2019)
22. Zou, W., Hu, X., Pan, Z., Li, C., Cai, Y., Liu, M.: Exploring the relationship between social presence and learners' prestige in MOOC discussion forums using automated content analysis and social network analysis. Comput. Hum. Behav. **115**, 106582 (2021)
23. Stewart, S.A., Abidi, S.S.R.: Applying social network analysis to understand the knowledge sharing behaviour of practitioners in a clinical online discussion forum. J. Med. Internet Res. **14**(6), e1982 (2012)
24. Ye, D., Pennisi, S.: Analysing interactions in online discussions through social network analysis. J. Comput. Assist. Learn. **38**(3), 784–796 (2022)
25. Kleyn, L.M., Hewstone, M., Ward, C.L., Wölfer, R.: Using longitudinal social network analysis to evaluate a community-wide parenting intervention. Prev. Sci. **22**, 130–143 (2021)
26. Purington, A., Stupp, E., Welker, D., Powers, J., Banikya-Leaseburg, M.: Using social network analysis to strengthen organizational relationships to better serve expectant and parenting young people. Matern. Child Health J. **24**, 232–242 (2020)
27. Wang, X., Oussalah, M., Niemelä, M., Ristikari, T.: Parenthood mining using hashtag social network mining approach. In: 2022 International Conference on Computational Science and Computational Intelligence (CSCI) (pp. 779–784). IEEE (2022)
28. Girvan, M., Newman, M.E.: Community structure in social and biological networks. Proc. Natl. Acad. Sci. **99**(12), 7821–7826 (2002)
29. Vauva.fi.: https://www.vauva.fi/. Accessed: 18 Sep 2022
30. Richardson, L.: Beautiful soup documentation. Dosegljivo: https://www.crummy.com/software/BeautifulSoup/bs4/doc/. [Dostopano: 7. 7. 2018] (2007)
31. Sqlit. https://www.sqlite.org/. Accessed: 18 Sep 2022
32. Degree centrality. https://networkx.org/documentation/stable/reference/algorithms/generated/networkx.algorithms.centrality.degree_centrality.html. Accessed 18 Sep 2022
33. Clauset, A., Newman, M.E., Moore, C.: Finding community structure in very large networks. Phys. Rev. E **70**(6), 066111 (2004)
34. Modularity. https://en.wikipedia.org/wiki/Modularity_(networks). Accessed 27 Jan 2023
35. Brandes, U., et al.: On modularity clustering. IEEE Trans. Knowl. Data Eng. **20**(2), 172–188 (2007)
36. Vaajala, M., Liukkonen, R., Ponkilainen, V., Mattila, V.M., Kekki, M., Kuitunen, I.: Birth rate among women with fear of childbirth: a nationwide register-based cohort study in Finland. Ann. Epidemiol. **79**, 44–48 (2023). https://doi.org/10.1016/j.annepidem.2023.01.011

37. Lahti-Pulkkinen, M., et al.: Maternal depression and inflammation during pregnancy. Psychol. Med. **50**(11), 1839–1851 (2020)
38. Regushevskaya, E., et al.: Postponing births–comparing reasons among women in St Petersburg, Estonia and Finland. Finnish Yearb. Popul. Res. **48**, 127–145 (2013)

Unleashing Machine Learning for Accurate Weather Forecasts

S. Amisha, Anusha, and G. Padmashree[(✉)]

Department of Data Science and Computer Applications, Manipal Institute of Technology, Manipal Academy of Higher Education, Manipal, India
g.padmashree@manipal.edu

Abstract. Weather forecasting is a complex and important aspect of atmospheric science that uses scientific principles and data analysis to predict future atmospheric conditions. This process helps provide valuable information about temperature, humidity, wind patterns, precipitation, and atmospheric pressure over time. Historically, weather forecasting heavily relied on numerical weather prediction models and observational data. Classical methods, such as numerical simulations and statistical models, formed the backbone of meteorological predictions. While these approaches have yielded valuable insights, they often faced challenges in accurately capturing the complexities of atmospheric dynamics. The methodology entails deploying diverse machine learning classifiers, trained on historical meteorological data. This training empowers the model to discern intricate patterns and relationships within the information. Incorporating K-fold cross-validation ensures the reliability and generalizability of the model, systematically validating its performance across multiple subsets of the dataset.

Keywords: Machine Learning · Naive Bayes · Classification · Weather Prediction · K-fold cross-validations

1 Introduction

Weather forecasting is an important part of many industries and plays an important role in agricultural decision-making, helping farmers develop strategic plans for planting, irrigation, and harvesting. In the transport sector, forecasts can guide optimal routes, improve road safety, and inform decision-making to prevent accidents due to adverse weather conditions.

The energy industry relies on accurate forecasts, especially from renewable energy sources such as wind and solar, to predict fluctuations in power generation and optimize grid management. When severe weather is anticipated, construction projects benefit from effective planning and improved project management. In addition to these areas, everyday decisions from planning outdoor activities to scientific research and environmental monitoring are heavily influenced by weather forecasts, helping to provide a deeper understanding of Earth's atmospheric dynamics.

This research extends the groundwork laid by previous studies, wherein machine learning classifiers have proven effective in extracting significant patterns from extensive and intricate meteorological datasets. Trained on historical weather data, these classifiers exhibit a notable proficiency in identifying subtle relationships and grasping non-linear dependencies, enhancing our comprehension of atmospheric phenomena with a more nuanced perspective [8,9].

2 Literature Review

Weather forecasting has undergone significant transformations in recent years, driven by machine learning and data analytics advancements. This section provides a comprehensive review of the existing literature, highlighting key studies and breakthroughs that have shaped the landscape of weather prediction.

[6] investigates the evolution of weather forecasting techniques, underscoring the essential role of accurate weather predictions in mitigating the social and economic repercussions of severe weather events. Notably, it examines a pioneering climate prediction system employing advanced data processing methods, achieving an impressive 82.62% accuracy using decision trees. These findings are significant for advancing the development of robust computational models for hourly weather forecasts, addressing the complexities associated with unpredictable atmospheric conditions.

In [3] authors utilized data mining algorithms, such as Naive Bayes, K-Nearest Neighbors (K-NN), and C4.5, to examine the unpredictability of weather forecasts. The study compared their performance, revealing that K-NN outperforms Naive Bayes and C4.5 in terms of accuracy, particularly with k = 7 and Fold = 5. These findings underscore the capacity of K-NN to address challenges in weather forecasting, suggesting its potential to enhance the reliability of weather forecast models. In comparison to Naive Bayes and C4.5, K-NN emerges as a promising algorithm with promising implications for atmospheric problem-solving in weather forecasting.

[16] tackle the necessity for accurate precipitation forecasting amidst the backdrop of climate change, endorsing the use of efficient machine learning over laborious deterministic models. Recurrent Neural Networks (RNN) and Long-Short Term Memory (LSTM) are utilized, and their performance is contrasted with that of the Random Forest Classifier (RFC) and XGBoost. The neural network attained 42% accuracy, whereas XGBoost demonstrated 99%, and Random Forest achieved 92%. The research underscores the intricate balance between complexity, accuracy, and performance in machine learning algorithms, underscoring the importance of additional research to fine-tune prediction outcomes.

Singh et al., [15] in their weather forecasting study utilized three machine learning models: support vector machines (SVMs), artificial neural networks (ANNs), and time series recurrent neural networks (RNNs). The evaluation of these models, using tools such as Pandas, NumPy, and Google Cloud Services, relied on assessing the root mean square error between predicted and actual values. The conclusive findings indicate that the time series-based RNN excelled in forecasting capabilities, surpassing the performance of SVM and ANN in weather prediction.

Purwandari et al., [11] explored weather classification based on Twitter data, utilizing Support Vector Machine (SVM), Multinomial Naïve Bayes (MNB), and Logistic Regression (LR) methods. Notably, SVM exhibited impressive performance with 93% accuracy, establishing its suitability for text classification. The research successfully harnessed machine learning to enhance accuracy and recommends further refinements using more robust datasets and advanced models, such as deep learning or transfer learning. Furthermore, the study provides a thorough analysis of weather-related discussions on social media, contributing valuable insights to this dynamic and evolving field.

Through an experiment utilizing state-of-the-art technology and data mining techniques, Kareem et al., [5,6] investigated weather forecasting. They developed a prediction model incorporating neural networks, Naive Bayes, Random Forest, and K-nearest neighbor algorithms. Analysis of Kaggle weather data revealed the Random Forest algorithm's impressive accuracy at 89%, showcasing its considerable potential for short-term weather forecasting. The study's conclusion emphasizes that classification algorithms, with Random Forests in particular, emerge as optimal tools for achieving precision in weather forecasts.

Abdulraheem et al., [1] investigated the effectiveness of machine learning (ML) in weather forecasting, evaluating decision trees, k-nearest neighbor (k-NN) classifiers, and logistic regression (LR). Analysis using Kaggle weather data and web applications revealed decision trees achieving 100% accuracy, outperforming k-NN (78%) and LR (93%). The research highlights the pivotal role of ML in achieving precise weather predictions, incorporating variables such as humidity and wind speed. The results recommend future endeavors to further enhance model accuracy by intuitively optimizing meteorological data for increasingly accurate and reliable forecasts.

Maaloul et al., [7] presented a machine learning-based smart city weather prediction model utilizing five classification algorithms. Upon evaluating models trained on the Kaggle dataset, the gradient boosting classifier emerged as the most effective, boasting over 90% accuracy. The study underscores the importance of such models in smart city initiatives, highlighting their potential for immediate deployment and continuous enhancement. The positive outcomes advocate for further advancements to meet the dynamic demands of evolving weather forecasting needs.

Safia et al., [13] utilized supervised machine learning techniques such as KNN, SVM, RF, and ANN to advance weather forecasting, leveraging historical data from the Weatherstack API. The findings reveal that the ANN (97%) and RF (96.69%) models outperform SVM (93%) and KNN (77.97%) in accuracy. This study underscores the effectiveness of machine learning in weather forecasting and underscores the critical role of selecting appropriate models. Further research is suggested to enhance generalizability and ensure sustained long-term performance.

In summary, the literature survey underscores the increasing significance of machine learning (ML) in the progression of weather forecasting. It acknowledges the challenges faced in the field and calls for additional research to enhance models, optimize the utilization of meteorological data, and secure continuous and long-term performance improvements.

3 Methodology

The methodology involves a systematic process of dataset collection, followed by the building and evaluation of individual classification models. This process is followed by determining the most accurate model based on performance metrics. This comprehensive approach ensures the development of reliable weather prediction models. The complete workflow of the proposed method is depicted in Fig. 1.

3.1 Data Pre-processing

Effective data pre-processing ensures improved model quality and accuracy. This study employs several essential techniques such as:

- **Handling Null and Empty Columns**, which enhances dataset comprehensiveness and organization by eliminating any columns with missing values.
- **Binary Transformation** assigns binary labels to the weather data, streamlining the analysis process.
- Handling Missing Values is employed to identify and address any missing values within the dataset, ensuring data completeness.
- **Duplicate Detection and Removal** is applied to identify duplicate entries, subsequently eliminating them to maintain dataset accuracy. These meticulous data pre-processing steps collectively contribute to preparing the dataset for weather forecasting, enhancing its quality, and facilitating accurate model outcomes.

Only two levels of headings should be numbered. Lower-level headings remain unnumbered; they are formatted as run-in headings.

3.2 Building Classification Models

Constructing a model entails the creation of a predictive algorithm through the utilization of collected data, followed by model training and performance evaluation to ensure precision in predictions. This paper incorporates diverse machine learning algorithms, such as Decision Tree(DT), Support Vector Machine(SVM), Random Forest Classifier, K Nearest Neighbours(KNN), and Naïve Bayes(NB) Classifier.

In **Decision Trees** [10], decisions are made through a hierarchical arrangement of nodes, with each node representing a specific feature. The branches

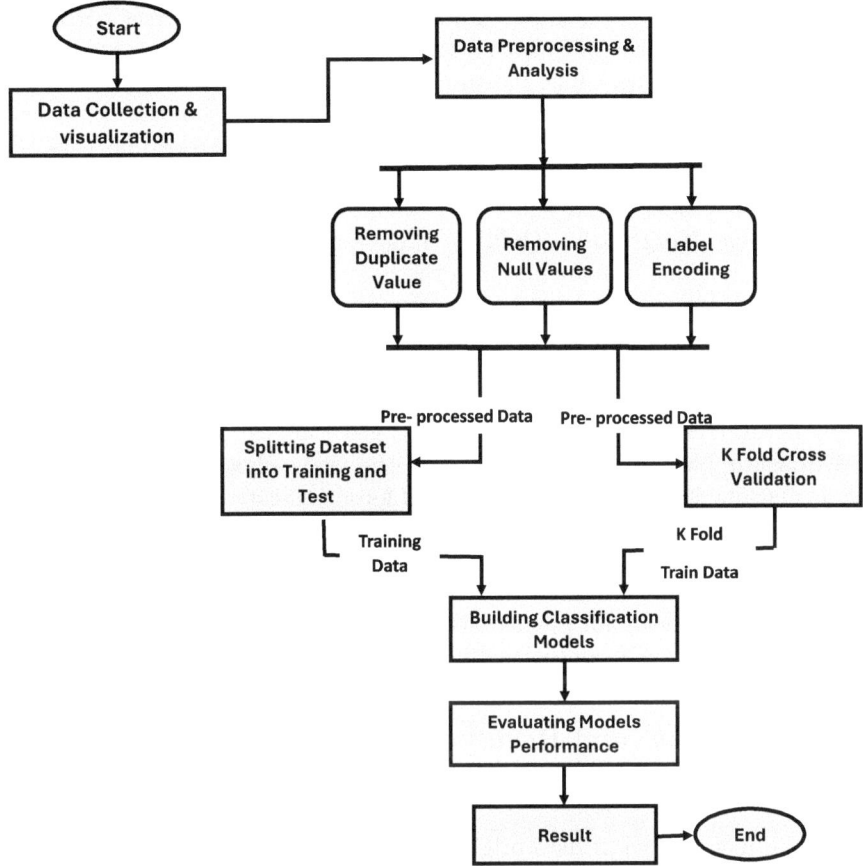

Fig. 1. A Visual Guide for Navigating Weather Prediction through Machine Learning Classifiers

stemming from these nodes delineate potential values or ranges for the corresponding feature. This hierarchical structure facilitates the model in sequentially weighing multiple factors, replicating the decision-making process for weather conditions.

SVMs [2] demonstrate effectiveness in capturing non-linear relationships within data and excel in high-dimensional spaces, making them a fitting choice for weather prediction tasks with a multitude of features or parameters. Through the kernel trick, SVM is designed to maximize the margin between distinct classes, fostering the creation of a more robust and widely applicable model. Furthermore, SVMs exhibit reduced susceptibility to overfitting, a crucial characteristic in weather prediction scenarios where achieving robust generalization to unseen data and adapting to dynamic atmospheric conditions is essential.

By consolidating predictions from numerous decision trees, **Random Forests** [14] harness the collective strength of the ensemble, leading to improved accuracy and robustness. Like individual decision trees, Random Forests excel at capturing non-linear relationships within data. They showcase proficiency in managing missing data, a frequent scenario in meteorological datasets. The ensemble structure of Random Forests bolsters their resilience to outliers or noisy data, ensuring model stability in varied conditions.

K-Nearest Neighbours (KNN) [4] operates on the fundamental concept of proximity, making it a key player in the field of weather prediction using historical data. It forecasts the weather for a specific location and time by examining the historical weather conditions of its nearest neighbors. This method is particularly effective as it recognizes that neighboring locations often share similar climate characteristics. Hence, KNN emerges as a valuable and adaptable tool for predicting weather conditions in specific geographical areas.

Gaussian Naive Bayes [12], part of the Naive Bayes family, is a probabilistic machine learning algorithm tailored for classification tasks, with weather prediction being a notable application. The "Naive" aspect arises from assuming independence among features, indicating that the presence of one feature does not impact another given the class variable. This approach establishes a probabilistic framework for predictions, proving particularly advantageous when dealing with continuous and normally distributed weather variables.

4 Experiments and Results

4.1 Dataset and Data Visualization

The initial meteorological data originated from a project named ECA&D [17], which offers daily observations from meteorological stations throughout the Mediterranean and Europe. Eighteen specific European cities or locations were selected, each with numerous daily observations accessible from 2000 to 2010. Furthermore, the dataset comprises numerous observations. While the variables mean temperature, max temperature, and min temperature are available for all selected locations, we also took into account additional data such as cloud cover, wind speed, wind gust, humidity, pressure, global radiation, precipitation, and sunshine. Dresden, a city in eastern Germany, which is considered as part of our experimentation which predicts the weather for BBQ either as "True" or "False". Figure 2 displays kdeplots illustrating the probability density function of the continuous variables such as cloud cover, sunshine, wind speed, minimum temperature, humidity, wind gust, precipitation, and maximum temperature in Dresden city. Based on these kdeplots, we can infer the following:

- Cloud Cover Density points to a greater chance of less cloud cover when grilling in Dresden.
- Wind Speed Density indicates that Dresden would be a good place to barbecue because it peaks at lower wind speeds.

- Sunshine Density shows a greater likelihood of mild sunshine, which is perfect for Dresden barbecues.
- Minimum Temperature Density shows a peak at relatively low minimum temperatures, which is ideal for Dresden barbecues.
- Precipitation Density shows a greater chance of less precipitation when grilling in Dresden.
- Humidity Density indicates ideal BBQ weather in Dresden, with a peak at moderate humidity levels.
- Wind Gust Density shows a greater likelihood of calmer wind gusts, which is perfect for Dresden barbecues.
- Maximum Temperature Density shows a peak at relatively high temperatures, which is ideal for Dresden barbecues.

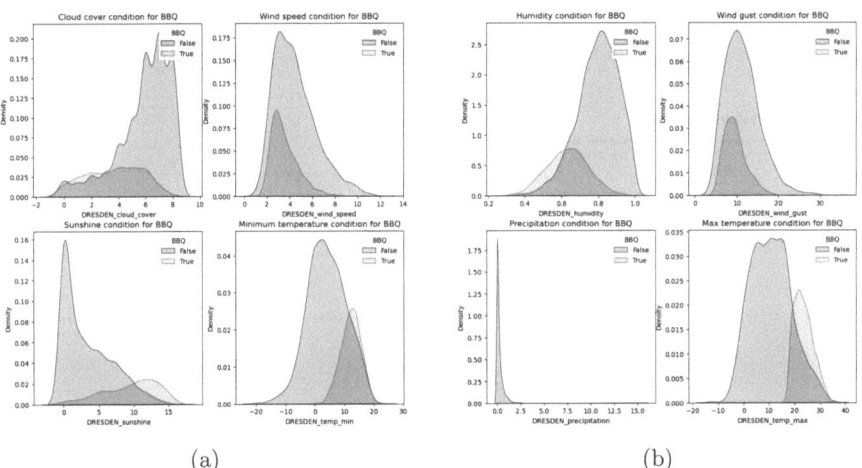

Fig. 2. kdeplots illustrating the probability density function of various continuous variables from [17] dataset

In our experimentation, we undertook a dual-pronged approach to assess the efficacy of our models—normal splitting and k-fold validation with a k value of 10. Normal Splitting also called the conventional method involves dividing the dataset into two subsets: one for training and the other for testing the models. The training set facilitated model learning, allowing it to discern patterns and relationships within the data. Subsequent evaluation of the distinct testing set provided insights into the model's performance on previously unseen data.

To boost the reliability of our model assessments, we implemented k-fold validation with a k value of 10. In this technique, the dataset was partitioned into k equally sized folds. The model underwent training and testing iteratively, with each fold serving as a testing set while the rest were used for training. The process was repeated until each fold had been utilized for testing, and the average performance across all folds was computed. The choice of k = 10 ensured a more comprehensive evaluation, fostering a robust understanding of the model's generalization across diverse subsets of the data.

By adopting both normal splitting and k-fold validation, we aimed to provide a holistic assessment of our model's performance, accounting for different aspects of data partitioning and variability. This dual approach offers a well-rounded perspective on how effectively our models generalize to unseen data and navigate diverse scenarios within the dataset. In Fig. 3, you can observe visual representations outlining both the normal splitting and k-fold validation techniques.

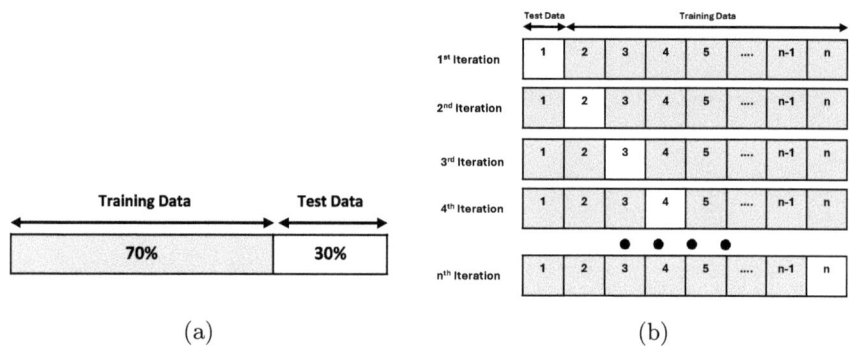

Fig. 3. Visual representation of normal splitting and k-fold validation approaches

4.2 Evaluating Models Performance

Model Evaluation entails the utilization of metrics such as accuracy, precision, recall, and F1-score on test data to evaluate the performance of each model. Accuracy, representing the proportion of correctly classified instances, offers a high-level overview of a model's overall correctness. Precision assesses the ratio of true positive predictions to the total instances predicted as positive, focusing on the accuracy of positive predictions. Meanwhile, Recall measures the ratio of true positive predictions to the total actual positive cases, showcasing a model's capability to identify all positive examples. The F1 score, being a harmonic mean of precision and recall, strikes a balance between the two, presenting a holistic metric that considers both aspects.

$$Precision = \frac{TP}{TP+FP} \quad (1)$$

$$Recall = \frac{TP}{TP+FN} \quad (2)$$

$$Accuracy = \frac{TP+TN}{TP+TN+FP+FN} \quad (3)$$

$$F1 - Score = \frac{2 * Precision * Recall}{Precision + Recall} \quad (4)$$

4.3 Results and Discussion

Performance metrics for weather prediction classifiers were evaluated using various machine learning algorithms and the standard splitting technique. Precision, recall, F1-Score, and accuracy were utilized as evaluation criteria. The Decision Tree model showcased outstanding performance, achieving perfect scores (100%) across all metrics. It exhibited flawless prediction and classification of weather conditions, rendering it an optimal choice for such tasks. The SVM model demonstrated robust performance, boasting high scores in precision, recall, F1-Score, and accuracy (above 93%). Although not flawless, it reliably predicted and classified weather conditions with notable accuracy. Similarly, the Random Forest model attained perfect scores across all metrics, underscoring its exceptional performance in weather prediction tasks. It adeptly classified weather conditions without any errors, establishing itself as a dependable option for such applications. The KNN model demonstrated respectable performance, achieving scores around 89% for precision, recall, F1-Score, and accuracy. While slightly lower than the Decision Tree and Random Forest models, it still provided reliable predictions and classifications of weather conditions. The Naive Bayes model exhibited strong performance, achieving high precision (95.61%), recall (94.8%), F1-Score (94.96%), accuracy (94.8%) scores. It effectively predicted and classified weather conditions with high levels of precision and recall, making it a reliable classifier for such tasks. The confusion matrix obtained for each of the classifiers is shown in Fig. 4.

The line graphs shown in Fig. 5 portray the accuracy outcomes obtained from employing a k-fold validation approach across different values of k (ranging from 1 to 10) for various machine learning classifiers in the context of weather dataset classification. Each line on the graph corresponds to a specific classifier, offering a visual comparison of their performance under different cross-validation settings. This graphical representation facilitates the identification of trends and patterns, aiding in the selection of optimal k values for each classifier. The insights derived contribute to a comprehensive understanding of how these classifiers respond to variations in the cross-validation parameter, informing decisions in weather dataset classification scenarios (Tables 1).

In model refinement, we extracted the peak accuracy achieved by each classifier from the line graphs. We represented this crucial information through a visually impactful bar chart as shown in Fig. 6. This chart serves as a distilled visual summary, offering a quick and insightful comparison of the maximum accuracy attained by each classifier. This strategic presentation aids in the efficient identification of the top-performing classifier in the domain of weather dataset classification. The bar chart acts as a concise guide for decision-makers, facilitating the selection of the most accurate and reliable machine learning classifier tailored to their specific weather prediction needs.

Table 1. Classifier Performance Metrics for Weather Prediction on various machine learning classifiers using the normal splitting approach,

Models	Precision (%)	Recall (%)	F1-Score(%)	Accuracy(%)
Decision Tree	100	100	100	100
Support Vector Machine	93.68	93.71	93.69	93.70
Random Forest	100	100	100	100
KNN	89.47	89.33	89.39	89.32
Naive Bayes	95.61	94.8	94.96	94.8

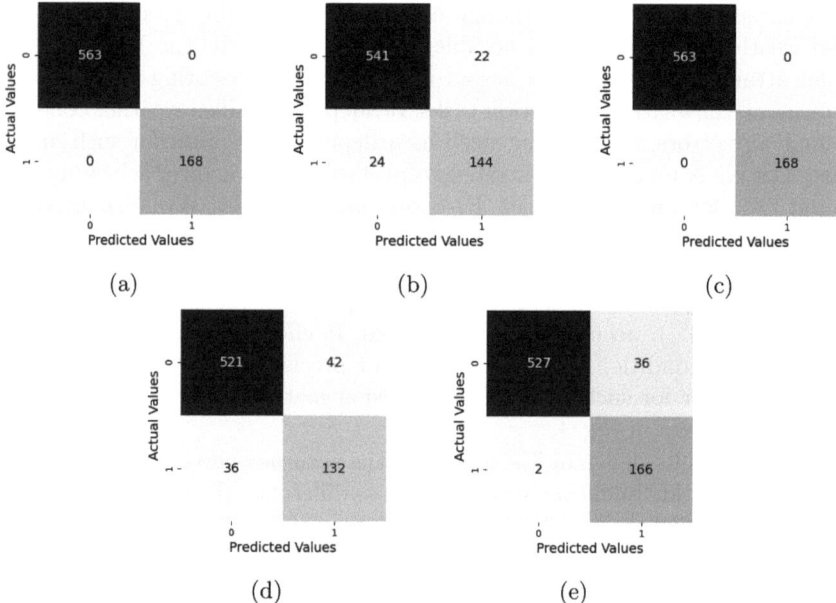

Fig. 4. Confusion Matrices illustrating the classification outcomes of diverse Machine Learning Classifiers in weather prediction scenarios (a) Decision Tree (b) SVM (c) RF (d) KNN (e) NB.

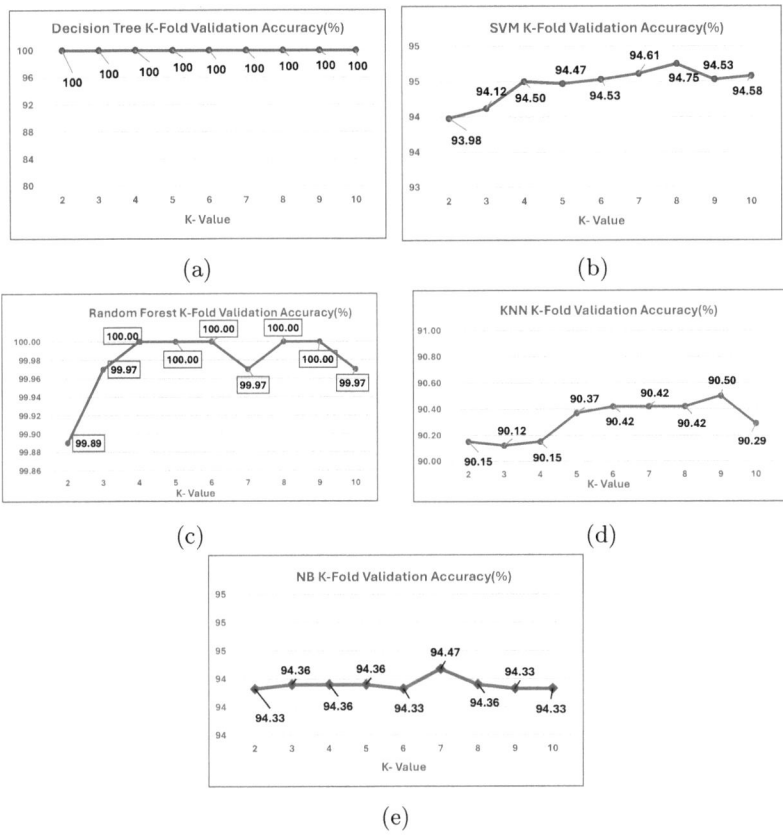

Fig. 5. A graphical exploration of machine learning classifiers' performance across varying k values in k-fold validation for weather dataset classification. (a) Decision Tree (b) SVM (c) RF (d) KNN (e) NB.

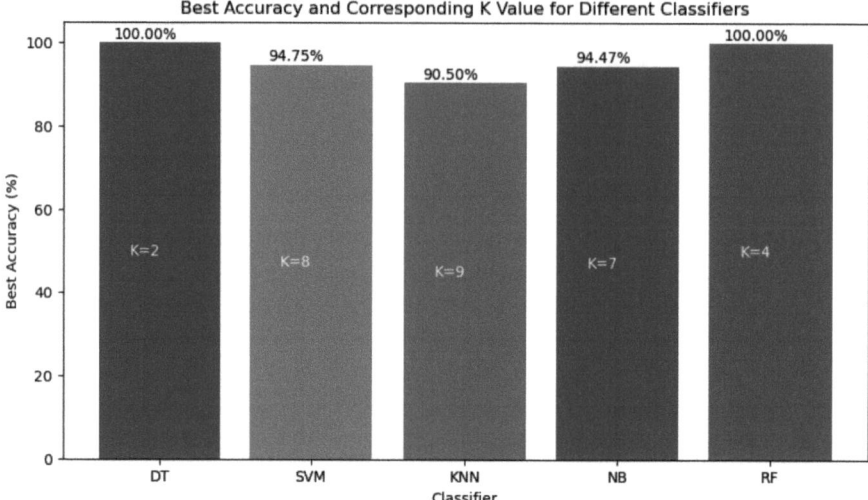

Fig. 6. A Visual representation of Top Accuracy Achievements Across Machine Learning Classifiers and their corresponding K values.

5 Conclusion

In conclusion, the examination of various machine learning classifiers for weather prediction has unveiled a diverse landscape of capabilities and intricacies. Our comprehensive evaluation encompassed classifiers such as Support Vector Machine, Naive Bayes, Random Forest, Decision Tree, and KNN, shedding light on their distinct strengths and areas ripe for enhancement. The Decision Tree and Random Forest models emerged as standout performers, demonstrating flawless accuracy across all metrics, including precision, recall, F1-Score, and accuracy, when compared to their counterparts. These models displayed remarkable proficiency in precisely predicting and categorizing weather conditions, rendering them highly suitable choices for weather forecasting endeavors. While certain models excel in accuracy and reliability, others offer robust performance with slightly diminished scores. Furthermore, forthcoming research endeavors could delve into amalgamating multiple machine learning models into ensemble frameworks, leveraging the unique strengths of different classifiers to bolster overall predictive efficacy. Moreover, the integration of real-time data streams and advanced data analytics techniques holds promise for facilitating more dynamic and precise weather predictions within operational forecasting systems.

References

1. Abdulraheem, M., Awotunde, J.B., Abidemi, E.A., Idowu, D.O., Adekola, S.O.: Weather prediction performance evaluation on selected machine learning algorithms. IAES Int. J. Artif. Intell. **11**(4), 1535 (2022)

2. Cristianini, N., Shawe-Taylor, J.: An Introduction to Support Vector Machines and Other Kernel-based Learning Methods. Cambridge university press, Cambridge (2000)
3. Findawati, Y., Astutik, I.I., Fitroni, A., Indrawati, I., Yuniasih, N.: Comparative analysis of naïve bayes, k nearest neighbor and c. 45 method in weather forecast. In: Journal of Physics: Conference Series, vol. 1402, p. 066046. IOP Publishing (2019)
4. Guo, G., Wang, H., Bell, D., Bi, Y., Greer, K.: KNN model-based approach in classification. In: Meersman, R., Tari, Z., Schmidt, D.C. (eds.) OTM 2003. LNCS, vol. 2888, pp. 986–996. Springer, Heidelberg (2003). https://doi.org/10.1007/978-3-540-39964-3_62
5. Kareem, F.Q., Abdulazeez, A.M., Hasan, D.A.: Predicting weather forecasting state based on data mining classification algorithms. Asian J. Res. Comput. Sci. **9**(3), 13–24 (2021)
6. Khan, Z.U., Hayat, M.: Hourly based climate prediction using data mining techniques by comprising entity demean algorithm. Middle-East J. Sci. Res. **21**(8), 1295–1300 (2014)
7. Maaloul, K., Lejdel, B.: Weather forecasting and prediction in smart cities using machine learning algorithm
8. Mahmud, M., Kaiser, M.S., McGinnity, T.M., Hussain, A.: Deep learning in mining biological data. Cogn. Comput. **13**(1), 1–33 (2021)
9. Mahmud, M., Kaiser, M.S., Hussain, A., Vassanelli, S.: Applications of deep learning and reinforcement learning to biological data. IEEE Trans. Neural Netw. Learn. Syst. **29**(6), 2063–2079 (2018)
10. Patel, H.H., Prajapati, P.: Study and analysis of decision tree based classification algorithms. Int. J. Comput. Sci. Eng. **6**(10), 74–78 (2018)
11. Purwandari, K., Sigalingging, J.W., Cenggoro, T.W., Pardamean, B.: Multi-class weather forecasting from twitter using machine learning aprroaches. Procedia Comput. Sci. **179**, 47–54 (2021)
12. Rish, I., et al.: An empirical study of the naive bayes classifier. In: IJCAI 2001 Workshop on Empirical Methods in Artificial Intelligence, vol. 3, pp. 41–46 (2001)
13. Safia, M., Abbas, R.: Classification of weather conditions based on supervised learning (2023)
14. Shaik, A.B., Srinivasan, S.: A brief survey on random forest ensembles in classification model. In: Bhattacharyya, S., Hassanien, A.E., Gupta, D., Khanna, A., Pan, I. (eds.) International Conference on Innovative Computing and Communications. LNNS, vol. 56, pp. 253–260. Springer, Singapore (2019). https://doi.org/10.1007/978-981-13-2354-6_27
15. Singh, S., Kaushik, M., Gupta, A., Malviya, A.K.: Weather forecasting using machine learning techniques. In: Proceedings of 2nd International Conference on Advanced Computing and Software Engineering (ICACSE) (2019)
16. Srinivas, A.S.T., Somula, R., Govinda, K., Saxena, A., Reddy, P.A.: Estimating rainfall using machine learning strategies based on weather radar data. Int. J. Commun. Syst. **33**(13) (2020)
17. Tank, A.K., Wijngaard, J., et al.: Publications, presentations and other activities daily dataset of 20th-century surface air temperature and precipitation series for the European climate assessment 2002. Int. J. Climatol. **22**, 1441–1453 (2002)

BFL: Blockchain-Federated Learning for Privacy Preservation in Internet of Underwater Things

Kamalika Bhattacharjya[✉] and Debashis De

Department of Computer Science and Engineering, Maulana Abul Kalam Adaz University of Technology, West Bengal, Simhat, Haringhata, Nadia 741249, West Bengal, India
{kamalika.bhattacharjya,debashis.de}@makautwb.ac.in

Abstract. The exponential growth in data generated by interconnected devices within the Internet of Underwater Things presents exciting opportunities to improve the quality of service in emerging applications through enhanced data sharing. Underwater devices collect and transmit sensitive information like oceanographic data, marine life observations, or even information related to military activities. Ensuring privacy is crucial to protect this sensitive data from unauthorized access or misuse. Blockchain Technology provides security in sharing data. Federated Learning maintains privacy without sharing the actual data. In this article, we propose a Blockchain-Federated Learning for Privacy Preservation in the Internet of Underwater Things (BFL) which combines Blockchain Technology with Federated Learning to ensure the privacy of data. In this article, we use a consensus algorithm for secure data sharing and ResNet-50 to protect the privacy of data. We analyze the proposed approach with the existing approach and the result depicts that the proposed approach achieves ∼16% better accuracy than the existing approach.

Keywords: Internet of Underwater Things · Federated Learning · Blockchain Technology · Privacy preservation · Loss

1 Introduction

The utilization of Internet of Underwater Things (IoUT) networks presents a remarkable capability for detecting and monitoring various sensitive underwater factors, including marine life, weather forecasting, obstacle detection, and military security [2,12]. These networks enable comprehensive data collection and analysis, offering insights into the dynamic conditions beneath the underwater surface. The real-time data gathered from underwater sensors and devices aids in the early detection and prediction of natural disasters, such as storms, tsunamis, or other environmental anomalies [8,11]. Blockchain Technology (BT) is a decentralized and distributed ledger system that enables secure, transparent, and tamper-resistant record-keeping [10]. BT's decentralized ledger ensures data integrity and prevents unauthorized modifications [6]. In BT a user initiates a transaction. Transactions are grouped into blocks. A block is a collection of verified transactions that are bundled together and linked to the previous block in the chain. Broadcasting involves sharing the newly created block with other participants on the network. Verification typically involves checking the validity of each transaction and adding verified blocks. The linkage between the new block and the previous one is established using cryptographic hashes. Once the new block is added to the blockchain, the transaction is considered complete. The Federated Learning (FL) is to enable collaborative model training while keeping data localized [16,19]. FL does not share datasets with others so it ensures data privacy [13]. The AUVs are considered clients in the IoUT environment. Each client has a local dataset on which clients perform local training. The global server aggregates all local parameters from local clients and comes up with a new global model. Local clients adopt the global model.

1.1 Motivation

The underwater environment has very sensitive information like underwater life and military security. The IoUT uses Autonomous Underwater Vehicles (AUVs) to collect underwater data autonomously and transmit data to the base station. Unauthorized access to data or manipulation of sensitive data is an important concern in underwater scenarios. Underwater wireless sensor networks (UWSNs) have garnered increasing attention due to their crucial role in marine surveillance, coastal monitoring, and underwater exploration. Significant advancements have been made in underwater object detection, such as the YOLOv5s-CA model, which incorporates coordinate attention mechanisms to enhance the detection of underwater targets in complex environments [17]. In the realm of network protocols, the UDTN-RS protocol offers a novel routing strategy tailored for delay-tolerant underwater networks, particularly suited for coastal patrol and surveillance scenarios [5]. Security challenges in UWSNs have also been addressed through innovative approaches, including a blockchain-based framework designed to detect Sybil attacks [2]. Communication reliability and performance have been investigated through modulation schemes like MC-CDMA, showing promise for underwater environments [4]. Additionally, trust management in UWSNs has benefited from probabilistic models, notably a Hidden Markov Model-based system that enhances node reliability assessment [3]. In broader maritime applications, the REER-H protocol has demonstrated energy-efficient and reliable routing capabilities, positioning it as a strong candidate for intelligent maritime transportation systems [20]. Therefore, maintaining privacy, confidentiality, and security is an important concern in the underwater environment. To overcome these challenges we integrate Blockchain Technology and Federated Learning for the privacy preservation of sensitive data in the IoUT environment.

1.2 Contribution

The principal contributions of the article are as follows:

- We propose a Blockchain-Federated Learning framework to address privacy concerns in the Internet of Underwater Things (BFL).
- We use Blockchain Technology (BT) to eliminate the need for a central authority, reducing the risk of attacks targeting a single point.
- We use Federated Learning to allow model training to occur locally on individual underwater devices without sharing raw data. This preserves the privacy of sensitive information.
- We use a consensus algorithm with ResNet-50 for the security and privacy of data.
- We study accuracy, loss, and precision at different levels of attack.

1.3 Paper Organization

Section 2 discusses related work. Section 3 presents the proposed system model. We explain the experimental result in Sect. 4 and conclude the article in Sect. 5.

2 Related Work

We discuss the existing work on blockchain technology and federated learning. The IoUT network is used to gather data from the underwater region and forecast natural disasters so security is required to prevent unauthorized access. Blockchain Technology used to detect malicious nodes in IoUT also prevented unauthorized access to provide privacy in [1]. The authors provided authorization by registering each node in the network. The authors studied gas consumption, propagation delay, and energy consumption. The decentralized authentication ensures energy efficiency in IoUT. In [18] authors used mitigation techniques and transfer files in clusters to ensure decentralized authentication. The authors studied delay and energy consumption concerning underwater devices. Secure data transmission in IoUT proposed in [15] through blockchain. The authors applied Blockchain at the user level for security. The authors studied gas consumption, execution time, and CPU usage. In [9] authors studied different blockchain and federated learning approaches to secure the Internet of Things (IoT) environment. The authors provided an overview of different attacks like Data poisoning attacks, evasion attacks, and model poisoning attacks. The authors discussed probable solutions and challenges associated with IoT. In [21] authors proposed a blockchain federated learning-based approach for energy-efficient resource allocation in IoT. The authors addressed poisoning attacks and privacy by adopting a deep reinforcement learning-based algorithm to study energy consumption as well as resource allocation. Blockchain-based federated learning studied in [14]. The authors used proof of quality (PoQ) in blockchain and Multilayer Perceptron Model (MLP) networks in federated learning to ensure privacy. The authors analyzed loss, reputation value, and accuracy. Table 1 represents a comparative study of existing work and the proposed approach where the table parameters are the dataset, neural network used, loss, precision, and execution time in the work.

Table 1. Comparative Analysis of Existing Research and Proposed Approach

Reference	Year	Focus Area	Blockchain Technology	Federated Learning	Dataset	Neural Network	Loss	Precision	Execution time
[1]	2022	Authentication	Yes	No	No	No	No	No	Yes
[18]	2019	Authentication	Yes	No	No	No	No	No	Yes
[15]	2022	Data Security	Yes	No	Yes (Own Dataset)	No	No	No	Yes
[9]	2023	Data Security	Yes	Yes	-	-	-	-	-
[21]	2023	Resource Allocation	Yes	Yes	Yes	Yes	Yes	-	Yes
[14]	2021	Data Privacy	Yes	Yes	MNIST	MLP	Yes	No	No
Proposed approach	-	Data Privacy	Yes	Yes	Labeled fish	ResNet-50	Yes	Yes	Yes

3 Proposed BFL: Blockchain-Federated Learning for Privacy Preservation in Internet of Underwater Things

This section describes the overview of the proposed BFL system.

3.1 System Model

We consider Blockchain Technology and Federated Learning for privacy preservation in the IoUT framework as presented in Fig. 1. Underwater devices (UN_{De}) like AUVs collect images from the deployed IoUT region and prepare a local database. Federated Learning performs collaborative learning. The UN_{De} uses its database training and sends the parameters to the blocks in the blockchain section. Blocks keep the model's information secure. This information on local models is transmitted to the cloud. Cloud accumulates all local models' parameters and constructs a new global model. The UN_{De} adapts the global model. As federated learning works at the edge without disclosing its data it keeps the data private. Blockchain works in a decentralized manner so it secures data sharing. The proposed blockchain-based federated learning provides data privacy and security as well as reduces delay in IoUT. In the proposed work we use the concept PoQ consensus algorithm that provides secure blockchains by ensuring resistance to attacks to prevent double-spending and maintain decentralization whereas ResNet-50 provides enhanced adaptability to specify the number of hidden layers in the network dynamically.

Algorithm 1 presents the steps of execution of the proposed system. The first step is for the local clients to start federated learning. The second step is for

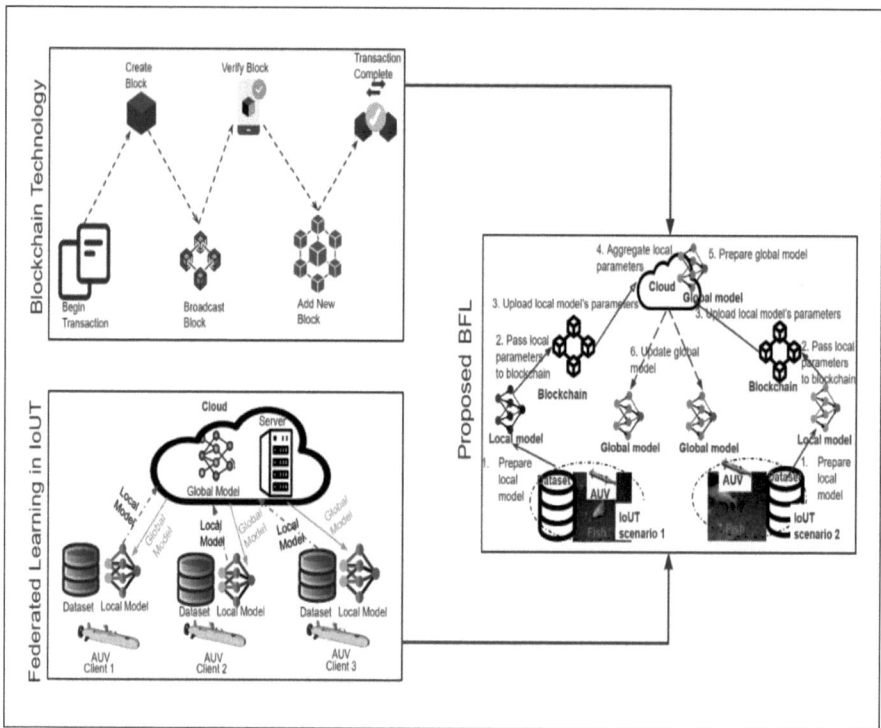

Fig. 1. Proposed Architecture of Blockchain-Federated Learning for Privacy Preservation in the Internet of Underwater Things

data security at blocks and authorized clients send their local model parameters by calculating the threshold from the received parameters in the blockchain to the cloud. All client models are aggregated over the cloud to prepare a global model. In step three, clients adopt the global model. The fourth step measures the new model's performance in terms of accuracy.

4 Simulation Environment

4.1 Simulation Environment Setup

We work on the Labeled Fishes dataset [7] prepared by NOAA Fisheries. The dataset consists of positive and negative image classes. The positive image class contains fish images whereas the negative image class contains non-fish images. The dataset includes 3167 images and 147 seabed negative images. We use the ResNet-50 model. The learning rate is 0.01 and the SDG with momentum is 0.5. The local epoch is 10 and the global epoch is also 10. The attack strength of malicious clients is 20%, 40%, and 60%.

Algorithm 1: Algorithm of BFL: Blockchain-Federated Learning for Privacy Preservation in IoUT

Input: $Opinion\_values$, OP_j;
Clients, CL;
$Threshold\_of\_opinion$, $Th_{\min}$;
Epoch, Ep;
Output: Accuracy, ACC
Procedure:
1. The federated learning begins with Gm;
2. **for** $Ep = 1$ *to* k **do**
   (a) **for** $CL = 1$ *to* c **do**
       i. The Clients of the blockchain, get Th_j from Th;
       ii. Calculate $Th_{\text{final}_{CL}}$ according to Th_{CL};
       iii. Select $(CL_{\text{final}} > Th_{\min})$ from $Th_{\text{final}_{CL}}$;
       iv. Upload $CG_{m_{Final}}$;
   (b) Upload $CL_{Gi_{Final}}$;
   (c) Aggregate $CL_{Gn_{Final}}$;
   (d) Prepare the global model GM;
3. Update GM;
4. **return** ACC;

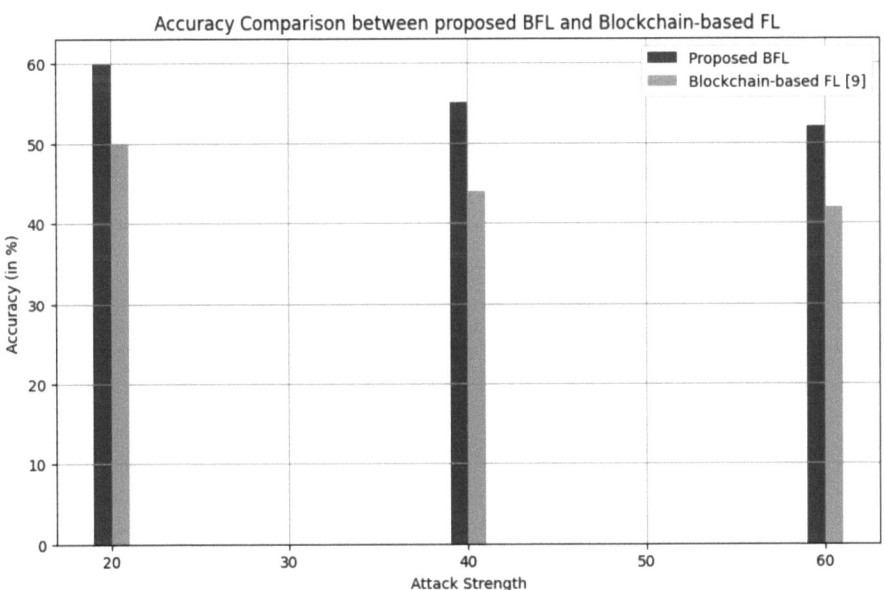

Fig. 2. Study of accuracy varies with the attack strength.

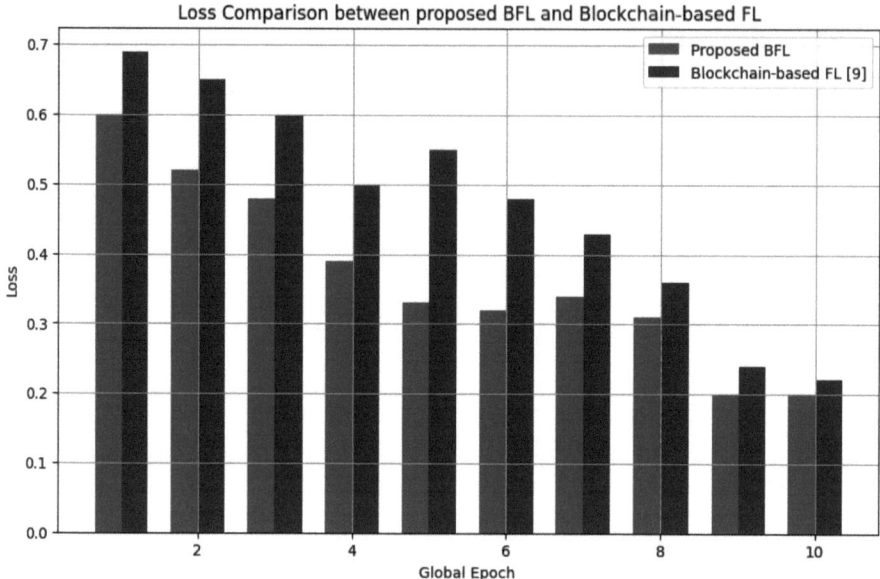

Fig. 3. Study of loss function varies with the attack strength 60%

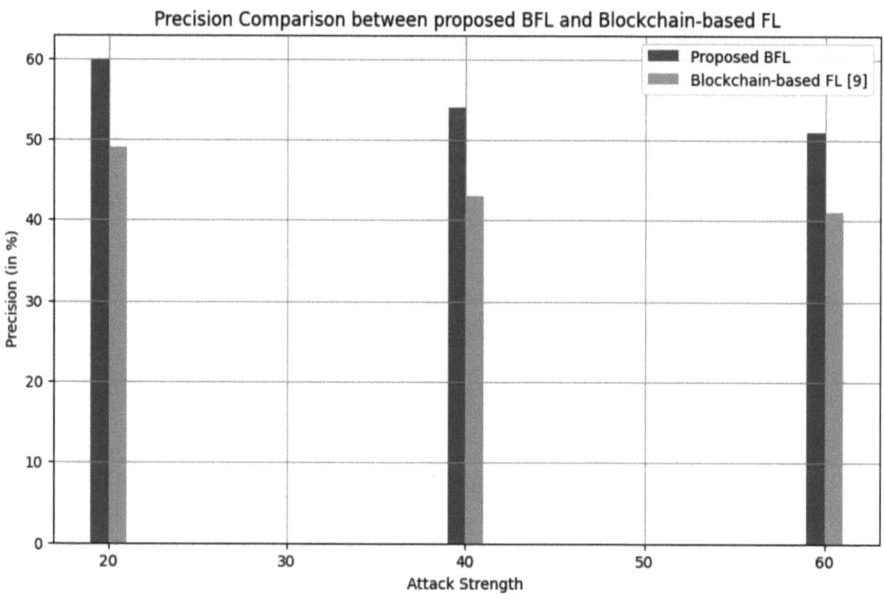

Fig. 4. Study of precision function varies with the attack strength 60%

4.2 Simulation Results Analysis

In this section, we discuss the simulation results. Figure 2 represents the accuracy of federated learning at different attack strengths that shows our proposed approach obtains accuracy of 60%, 55%, and 52% whereas existing work gets 50%, 44%, and 42% with attach strength of 20%, 40%, and 60% respectively. The proposed BFL approach achieves a $\sim 16\%$ better accuracy result than existing blockchain-based FL because in the proposed BFL we use of consensus algorithm and ResNet-50 which provides security in data, increases adaptability, and reduces over-fitting by focusing on feature extraction with adaptive pooling and omitting fully connected layers. Figure 3 presents the loss of federated learning at the different epochs that shows the proposed BFL approach obtains loss of 0.6, 0.52, 0.48, 0.39, 0.33, 0.32, 0.34, 0.31, 0.20, and 0.198 whereas existing work gets 0.69, 0.65, 0.6, 0.5, 0.55, 0.48, 0.43, 0.36, 0.24, and 0.22 with epochs 1–10 at attack strength 60%. The proposed BFL approach achieves about 13% better loss result than existing work because in our work we use of consensus algorithm and dynamic hidden layer that captures discriminative features effectively, reducing overfitting. Figure 4 represents the precision of federated learning at different attack strengths that shows our proposed approach obtains precision of 60%, 54%, and 51% whereas existing work gets 49%, 43%, and 41% precision with attach strength of 20%, 40%, and 60% respectively. The proposed BFL approach achieves approximately 18% to 20% better precision results than existing work because our approach utilizes ResNet-50, which helps mitigate the vanishing gradient problem and enables more effective learning.

5 Conclusion

Internet of Underwater Things (IoUT) uses AUVs to capture sensitive information about marine life, military data, and obstacles from underwater regions. Sensitive data need to be protected. This article aims to prepare a privacy-preserving framework using blockchain and federated learning for IoUT. We employ blockchain works to agree on the validity of transactions to provide security of underwater data and federated learning provides privacy to not sharing data with others. We use the PoQ consensus algorithm in blockchain to ensure resilience to communication failures and malicious nodes, crucial for reliability in the underwater scenario. We also incorporate ResNet-50 residual blocks to understand features of federated learning that ensure the privacy of data. We analyze the proposed BFL approach on the leveled fish dataset with the existing approach which uses a traditional MLP network and PoQ algorithm. The simulation result shows the proposed BFL approach achieved $\sim 16\%$ better performance in terms of accuracy at different attack strengths. In the future, our goal is to study more parameters like precision, execution time, etc. Also, concentrate on energy efficiency, security, and privacy preservation environment for IoUT.

References

1. Abbas, S., Nasir, H., Almogren, A., Altameem, A., Javaid, N.: Blockchain based privacy preserving authentication and malicious node detection in internet of underwater things (iout) networks. IEEE Access **10**, 113945–113955 (2022)

2. Arifeen, M.M., Al Mamun, A., Ahmed, T., Kaiser, M.S., Mahmud, M.: A blockchain-based scheme for sybil attack detection in underwater wireless sensor networks. In: Kaiser, M.S., Bandyopadhyay, A., Mahmud, M., Ray, K. (eds.) Proceedings of International Conference on Trends in Computational and Cognitive Engineering. AISC, vol. 1309, pp. 467–476. Springer, Singapore (2021). https://doi.org/10.1007/978-981-33-4673-4_37
3. Arifeen, M.M., Bhakta, D., Hasan Remu, S.R., Maynul Islam, M., Mahmud, M., Kaiser, M.: Hidden Markov model based trust management model for underwater wireless sensor networks. In: ICCA 2020: Proceedings of the International Conference on Computing Advancements (2020). https://doi.org/10.1145/3377049.3377054
4. Arifeen, M.M., Tasnim, Z., Mahmud, M., Kaiser, M.S.: Performance analysis of mc-cdma based underwater wireless sensor network. In: 2018 International Conference on Advances in Computing, Communications and Informatics, ICACCI 2018, pp. 1919–1924 (2018). https://doi.org/10.1109/ICACCI.2018.8554589
5. Azad, S., Neffati, A.A., Mahmud, M., Kaiser, M.S., Ahmed, M.R., Kamruzzaman, J.: UDTN-RS: a new underwater delay tolerant network routing protocol for coastal patrol and surveillance. IEEE Access **11**, 142780–142793 (2023). https://doi.org/10.1109/ACCESS.2023.3334638
6. Bhattacharya, S., et al.: Blockchain for internet of underwater things: state-of-the-art, applications, challenges, and future directions. Sustainability **14**(23), 15659 (2022)
7. Fisheries, N.: Labeled fishes in the wild. https://www.fisheries.noaa.gov/west-coast/science-data/labeled-fishes-wild. Accessed 25 Jan 2024
8. Ghosh, T., Banna, M.H.A., Nahian, M.J.A., Kaiser, M.S., Mahmud, M., Li, S., Pillay, N.: A privacy-preserving federated-mobilenet for facial expression detection from images. In: International Conference on Applied Intelligence and Informatics, pp. 277–292. Springer, Cham (2022)
9. Issa, W., Moustafa, N., Turnbull, B., Sohrabi, N., Tari, Z.: Blockchain-based federated learning for securing internet of things: a comprehensive survey. ACM Comput. Surv. **55**(9), 1–43 (2023)
10. Jadav, N.K., Nair, A., Gupta, R., Tanwar, S., Alabdulatif, A.: Blockchain-assisted onion routing protocol for internet of underwater vehicle communication. IEEE Internet Things Mag. **5**(4), 30–35 (2022)
11. Jahanbakht, M., Xiang, W., Hanzo, L., Azghadi, M.R.: Internet of underwater things and big marine data analytics–a comprehensive survey. IEEE Commun. Surv. Tutorials **23**(2), 904–956 (2021)
12. Khalil, R.A., Saeed, N., Babar, M.I., Jan, T.: Toward the internet of underwater things: recent developments and future challenges. IEEE Consum. Electron. Mag. **10**(6), 32–37 (2020)
13. Pei, J., Liu, W., Wang, L., Liu, C., Bashir, A.K., Wang, Y.: Fed-IoUT: opportunities and challenges of federated learning in the internet of underwater things. IEEE Internet Things Mag. **6**(1), 108–112 (2023)
14. Qin, Z., Ye, J., Meng, J., Lu, B., Wang, L.: Privacy-preserving blockchain-based federated learning for marine internet of things. IEEE Trans. Comput. Soc. Syst. **9**(1), 159–173 (2021)
15. Razzaq, A.: Blockchain-based secure data transmission for internet of underwater things. Clust. Comput. **25**(6), 4495–4514 (2022)
16. Victor, N., et al.: Federated learning for IoUT: concepts, applications, challenges and future directions. IEEE Internet Things Mag. **5**(4), 36–41 (2022)

17. Wen, G., Li, S., Liu, F., Luo, X., Er, M.J., Mahmud, M., Wu, T.: Yolov5s-ca: a modified yolov5s network with coordinate attention for underwater target detection. Sensors **23**(7) (2023). https://doi.org/10.3390/s23073367
18. Yazdinejad, A., Parizi, R.M., Srivastava, G., Dehghantanha, A., Choo, K.K.R.: Energy efficient decentralized authentication in internet of underwater things using blockchain. In: 2019 IEEE Globecom Workshops (GC Wkshps), pp. 1–6. IEEE (2019)
19. Zaman, S., Kaiser, M.S., Khan, R.T., Mahmud, M.: Towards SDN and blockchain based iot countermeasures: a survey. In: 2020 2nd International Conference on Sustainable Technologies for Industry 4.0 (STI), pp. 1–6. IEEE (2020)
20. Zenia, N.Z., Kaiser, M.S., Mahmud, M., Ahmed, M.R., Kaiwartya, O., Kamruzzaman, J.: REER-H: a reliable energy efficient routing protocol for maritime intelligent transportation systems. IEEE Trans. Intell. Transp. Syst. **24**(12), 13654–13669 (2023). https://doi.org/10.1109/TITS.2023.3293155
21. Zhang, J., Liu, Y., Qin, X., Xu, X., Zhang, P.: Adaptive resource allocation for blockchain-based federated learning in internet of things. IEEE Internet Things J. (2023)

Exploring and Contrasting Machine Learning Classifiers for Citrus Plant Disease Classification

B. Mahima Shenoy, Sakshi S. Poojary, and G. Padmashree(✉)

Department of Data Science and Computer Applications, Manipal Institute of Technology, Manipal Academy of Higher Education, Manipal, India
g.padmashree@manipal.edu

Abstract. Citrus plants play a pivotal role in the global agriculture landscape, making significant contributions to the economy. However, the agricultural sector faces challenges posed by the escalating prevalence of diseases affecting citrus plants. Early and precise identification of these diseases is imperative for implementing timely interventions and minimizing crop losses. This research endeavors to assess and compare diverse machine learning classifiers for effectively classifying citrus plant diseases. The objective is to evaluate their performance, accuracy, and appropriateness in addressing the intricate challenge of identifying and categorizing diseases that impact citrus plants. The research leverages the PlantifyDr Dataset from Kaggle, concentrating on categories such as Citrus Black Spot, Citrus Healthy, Citrus Canker, and Citrus Greening. Various machine learning classifiers, including Random Forest, Support Vector Machine, Decision Tree, K-Nearest Neighbour, Logistic Regression, and Naïve Bayes, are deployed for classification. The assessment includes evaluating the accuracy, precision, recall, and F1 score to comprehensively analyze the performance of these classifiers. Remarkably, the Random Forest model stands out as highly effective, achieving an accuracy of 95.42%. The findings provide crucial insights, advocating for a paradigm shift towards innovative and automated solutions to alleviate the impact of plant diseases on global food production.

Keywords: Citrus · Feature extraction · Feature selection · Image processing · Random forest classifier

1 Introduction

Changes in cultivation practices, the emergence of new pathogens, and a lack of adequate plant protection measures have resulted in increased diseases and damage in recent years, endangering crop productivity and human life [26]. Farmers face difficulties identifying these diseases, so an automated approach is required to ease their burden [22]. Plant disease identification has been the subject of numerous attempts, and image processing and computer vision have emerged as important tools in this regard. Applications for computer vision offer a vast array of options and address various agricultural problems. To effectively manage pesticides in crops, early illness detection is essential for minimizing financial losses and minimizing the use of agrochemicals. Depending on the infection level and plant growth stage, the choice of pest control is frequently made. Food insecurity may worsen if plant diseases are not promptly identified because of the potential negative impact on agricultural productivity [14].

Diseased plants often have visible lesions or markings on their leaves, stems, flowers, or fruits [11,23]. Given the effects on agricultural production management and decision-making, the capacity to accurately identify these diseases has grown in significance. Farmers frequently rely on their own experience, despite consulting agricultural professionals frequently. This is an inefficient and subjective approach that can result in errors and inappropriate medication use, which can contaminate the environment and cause financial losses. For farmers with less experience, the identification process becomes especially dangerous, underscoring the need for a more dependable and automated solution [2,13]. These challenges have led to an increase in the popularity of image-processing techniques for plant disease detection. Eye inspection is one of the traditional methods of identifying diseases, but it has the drawbacks of subjective perception and error potential. Although spectroscopic and imaging techniques have been investigated, they frequently call for large sensors and precise instruments. The increasing accessibility of digital cameras and electronic devices has positioned machine learning as a formidable competitor in the realm of plant disease detection.

The paper is organized as follows: Sect. 2 introduces the previously done related work and methods used. Section 3 explains the proposed methodology in this paper. Section 4 explains the experiment and the result of the method. Section 5 summarizes the methods and results and discusses possible future research to extend this work.

2 Related Works

In recent years, the agricultural sector has witnessed significant research advancements in the realm of machine vision. This encompasses diverse applications such as fruit disease diagnosis [4,10], weed control and identification [6,16], quality rating and fruit maturity classification [4,12,25], plant species classification [19], disease diagnosis and classification in plant organs [15]. Machine vision employs a range of sensors, including color, multispectral, and hyperspectral cameras. Typically, in machine vision applications, the illumination employed and captured by the sensor falls within the visible spectral range.

Dhaygude et al., [7] proposed processing approach encompasses the creation of a color transformation structure for the input RGB image, enhancing color description through conversion to HSI, green pixel removal via masking, image segmentation, extraction of relevant segments, and the computation of texture statistics to ascertain the presence of diseases on plant leaves.

The software solution presented by Arivazhagan et al., [1] is intended to automatically identify and categorize plant leaf diseases. The processing strategy entails creating a color transformation structure for the input RGB image, followed by masking and removing green pixels using a predefined threshold. Following that, the image is segmented, and texture statistics for relevant segments are computed, culminating in the classification of retrieved features. Notably, the system achieves an outstanding 94% accuracy in recognizing and classifying the disorders under consideration. This accomplishment is supported by experimental results derived from a database of about 500 plant leaves, demonstrating the resilience of the suggested method.

For the past two decades, the challenge of automatic plant disease identification utilizing visible range photos has been a focal point. Existing techniques, on the other hand, are frequently limited in breadth and reliant on optimal capture conditions. This limitation may be due to inherent difficulties, such as complex backdrops that are difficult to distinguish from the region of concern (usually the leaf and stem), ill-defined symptom boundaries, and uncontrolled recording settings that make picture analysis more difficult. Furthermore, diseases with varying symptom features, similarities between symptoms of different diseases, and the possibility of numerous diseases coexisting exacerbate the situation. Barbedo [2] examines these problems in depth, highlighting the ramifications for previous solutions. Furthermore, the study suggests potential remedies to some of these problems.

Vishnoi et al., [24] offer a thorough overview of various research projects that combine computer vision and machine learning approaches to automate plant disease classification and detection systems. The focus is on solving India's urgent need for an effective and automated plant disease detection system to reduce agricultural losses. The survey includes crucial topics such as image capture strategies, preprocessing modules, lesion segmentation procedures, feature extraction methods, and classifier employment. It also examines the limitations of existing systems and the obstacles experienced during the feature extraction module, with a forward-looking vision to improve efficiency while keeping present tools.

Singh et al., [21] introduces an image segmentation algorithm for the automatic detection and classification of plant leaf diseases. The focus includes a survey of various disease classification techniques applicable to plant leaf disease detection. The proposed method utilizes genetic algorithms for image segmentation, emphasizing its significance in disease detection on plant leaves.

3 Methodology

In our efforts to advance the field of citrus plant disease classification, we provide a unique architectural framework precisely designed to improve the efficiency of machine learning-based identification. Figure 1 depicts the proposed design which serves as the underlying structure, coordinating the various components required for precise and effective citrus plant disease classification. The proposed architectural diagram outlines a seamless workflow where citrus plant images undergo preprocessing, feature extraction, and classification. Each component collaborates harmoniously, optimizing the efficiency and accuracy of the citrus leaf classification process.

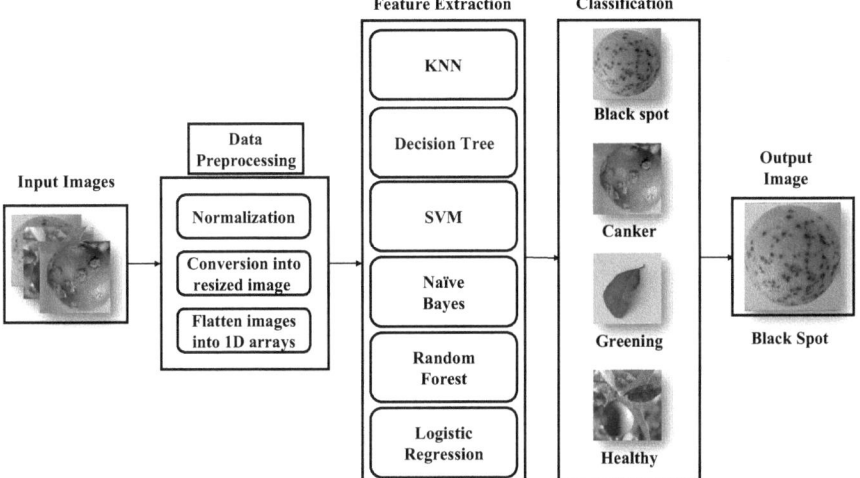

Fig. 1. Proposed architecture diagram of citrus plant disease classification using machine learning classifiers

3.1 Image Pre-processing

At the initial stage of image preprocessing, a pivotal step involves resizing all images to a standardized square format, with dimensions fixed at 100 × 100 pixels. This uniform resizing plays a key role in ensuring homogeneity within the dataset, facilitating uniform processing across diverse algorithms. In our pursuit of achieving greater homogeneity in the dataset, we systematically applied a range of image preprocessing techniques. These methods were employed to standardize and enhance the overall quality of the dataset. They include image resizing, normalization, and the conversion of images to a flattened 1D array format. These processes are integral to ensuring uniformity and optimal conditions for subsequent analysis and classification. The flattened 1D array format contains spatial features that involve capturing the layout of pixels and their colors within the image which helps in classifying citrus plant diseases.

3.2 Feature Extraction

From the preprocessed images, using various machine learning models features are extracted to classify citrus diseases. K-nearest neighbors (KNN), decision tree, Naive Bayes, Support Vector Machine(SVM), Random Forest, and Logistic Regression algorithms have been used to extract features and and train the model for classifying citrus plant diseases.

KNN [9] algorithm is an instance-based, non-parametric learning approach utilized for classifications. KNN's operational concept revolves around predicting outcomes by considering the majority class of the K-nearest neighbors to a given data point. When classifying or predicting a new data point, the algorithm measures the distance between that point and all others in the training dataset. The primary distance metric is typically the Euclidean distance, although alternative metrics such as Manhattan distance can be utilized. The algorithm then assigns the class label most prevalent among the K-nearest neighbors, employing a majority voting mechanism. To avoid the dominance of features with larger scales in the distance calculation, feature normalization is commonly applied, particularly when features have varying scales. Ultimately, the prediction for the new data point is determined based on the majority class or average value derived from the K-nearest neighbors.

The process of constructing a **Decision Tree** [17] entails iteratively dividing the dataset based on features, forming a tree-like structure for decision-making or predictions. Commencing at the root node, the entire dataset is initially considered. The algorithm assesses various features to identify the one that most effectively segregates the data into distinct classes or minimizes impurity (e.g., Gini impurity or entropy for classification, mean squared error for regression). Subsequently, the dataset is partitioned into subsets according to the selected feature, with each subset corresponding to a branch or child node of the evolving tree. These steps are iteratively applied to each subset or branch until a specified stopping criterion is satisfied. The terminal nodes, referred to as leaf nodes, encapsulate the ultimate predictions or decisions, each associated with a specific class. Decision rules are articulated along the branches of the tree, delineating conditions for traversing the structure and reaching a particular leaf node. The overarching goal of Decision Trees is to identify optimal splits at each node, to maximize information gain (for classification), or to achieve similar objectives relevant to the task at hand.

Naive Bayes [18] relies on the principles of Bayes' Theorem, a mathematical formula defining the probability of an event based on prior knowedge of conditions associated with that event. It operates under the assumption that features are conditionally independent when given the class label, simplifying calculations and earning the moniker "naive". In the training phase, Naive Bayes estimates prior probabilities and class-conditional probabilities for each feature, derived from the training dataset. When classifying a new instance, it computes posterior probabilities for each class using Bayes' Theorem, considering the observed features. The predicted class for the new instance is determined by selecting the one with the highest posterior probability.

Support Vector Machine(SVM) [5] The primary goal of SVM is to identify a hyperplane within a high-dimensional space that efficiently distinguishes data points of distinct classes. SVM excels in situations where the data is capable of linear separation, to optimize the margin, defined as the distance between the hyperplane and the closest data point from each class. The versatility of SVM extends to handling non-linear relationships within the data by employing kernel functions, leading to the transformation of the feature space into a higher-dimensional representation. This algorithm supports various kernel functions, including linear, polynomial, radial basis function (RBF), and sigmoid, providing adaptability to capture diverse patterns in the dataset. The decision function of SVM assigns classifications to new data points based on their relative positions to the hyperplane, with the sign of the decision function determining the predicted class.

The **Random Forest** [20] algorithm initiates by generating multiple bootstrap samples (random samples with replacement) from the original dataset, using each sample to train an individual decision tree. In building each tree within the forest, a random subset of features is considered at each split, preventing any single feature from dominating the decision-making process. These trees are typically deep, enabling them to capture intricate relationships in the data. During prediction, each tree "votes" for the predicted class, and the class with the majority of votes is selected as the final prediction. The individual predictions from all decision trees are combined to create an ensemble. The diversity achieved through bootstrapped sampling and feature subsetting enhances the overall strength of the ensemble. Randomness is introduced both in the bootstrap sampling and feature subsetting, which helps mitigate overfitting and enhances the model's generalization ability. Hyperparameters, including the number of trees in the forest, maximum tree depth, and size of feature subsets, are fine-tuned to optimize the model's performance. Ultimately, the final prediction is made based on the aggregated output of the ensemble, offering a more stable and accurate prediction compared to individual decision trees. The Random Forest's versatility and effectiveness make it a popular choice for various machine learning tasks.

Logistic Regression [8] is a statistical model employed for binary classification, where its primary objective is to predict the probability of an instance belonging to a specific class. The process commences with the creation of a linear combination of independent variables, expressing the log-odds for the positive class probability. This linear combination transforms the logistic function (sigmoid), converting the log-odds into a probability range between 0 and 1. This resultant value signifies the likelihood of the positive class. The logistic function's output serves as the probability estimate for an instance belonging to the positive class. A threshold, often set at 0.5, is then applied to categorize instances. Those with predicted probabilities exceeding the threshold are classified as the positive class, while those falling below are deemed the negative class. The training of Logistic Regression involves maximizing the likelihood of observed data, or equivalently, minimizing the negative log-likelihood. This process fine-tunes the model's coefficients to enhance predictive accuracy. In essence, Logistic Regression is a foundational tool for binary classification tasks, offering interpretability and simplicity while utilizing the logistic function to derive meaningful probability estimates.

4 Experiments and Results

4.1 Datasets

To train and validate our machine learning models, we employed the Kaggle PlantifyDr Datasets [3], which boasts a collection of over 125,000 JPG images representing 10 distinct plant species: tomato, bell pepper, cherry, citrus, corn, grape, peach, apple, potato, and strawberry. All images were standardized to a size of 256 by 256 pixels and categorized into 38 classes. Each class comprised more than 2000 training photos and approximately 500 validation images. Our work specifically delves into the realm of citrus plants, focusing on four categories: Citrus Black Spot, Citrus Healthy, Citrus Canker, and Citrus Greening. Some of the sample images from the Kaggle PlantifyDr Dataset are shown in Fig. 2. For these citrus categories, both training and validation datasets were created. The training set encompassed 312, 87, 368, and 5787 images, while the validation set included 27, 19, 29, and 20 photos, respectively. Table 1 showcases the total count of images for the citrus plant in each class.

Fig. 2. An illustrative image extracted from the Kaggle PlantifyDr Dataset, featuring various citrus plant diseases.

4.2 Results and Discussion

The main aim of this study is to compare different machine learning classifiers to tackle the intricate task of classifying diseases impacting citrus plants. Intending to improve automated disease identification in citrus plants, our research explores the effectiveness of various classifiers using a meticulously curated dataset of citrus leaves and fruits. This section provides a detailed overview of the performance

Table 1. Total count of images for the citrus plant in each class of PlantifyDr Dataset.

Class	Training Set	Validation set
Citrus Black Spots	312	27
Citrus Canker	368	29
Citrus Greening	5787	20
Citrus Healthy	87	19

metrics obtained from the machine learning classifiers across different train-test splits (80:20, 70:30, and 75:25). The precision, recall, F1-Score, and accuracy for each classifier are presented systematically, enabling a comprehensive understanding of their effectiveness in citrus plant disease classification.

Tables 2, 3, and 4 depicts the performance metrics evaluated on various machine learning algorithms for 80:20, 70:30, and 75:25 test-train splits on Kaggle PlantifyDr Datasets [3].

Table 2 summarizes the performance metrics of various machine learning algorithms on a 80:20 train-test split using the Kaggle PlantifyDr Dataset. Random Forest emerges as a top performer with impressive precision, recall, and F1-Score of 94%, contributing to an overall accuracy of 94.27%. Support Vector Machine and Decision Tree also exhibit commendable performance, showcasing a balanced trade-off between precision and recall. K-Nearest Neighbour, Logistic Regression, and Naive Bayes demonstrate varying levels of accuracy, with Naive Bayes showing lower recall.

Table 2. Performance metrics of various machine learning algorithms on 80:20 train-test split using Kaggle PlantifyDr Datasets [3]

	Precision(%)	Recall(%)	F1-Score(%)	Accuracy(%)
Random Forest	94	94	94	94.27
Support Vector Machine	94	94	94	94.05
Decision Tree	93	92	92	92.21
KNN	89	91	89	90.61
Logistic Regression	90	92	91	91.68
Naive Bayes	88	78	83	78.1

Table 3 summarizes the performance metrics of various machine learning algorithms on a 70:30 train-test split using the Kaggle PlantifyDr Dataset. Random Forest: Achieves high scores across all metrics (Precision: 95%, Recall: 95%, F1-Score: 95%, Accuracy: 95.01%, indicating robust performance. SVM demonstrates strong performance, particularly in recall and accuracy (Precision: 93%, Recall: 93%, F1-Score: 93%, Accuracy: 93.08%.Decision Tree performs well with balanced precision, recall, F1-Score, and accuracy (Precision: 91%, Recall: 91%,

F1-Score: 91%, Accuracy: 91.05%). KNN exhibits notable accuracy, though with a slightly lower precision compared to other algorithms. Logistic Regression maintains competitive performance, similar to the Decision Tree. Naive Bayes faces challenges, particularly in recall and F1-Score, suggesting potential limitations in correctly identifying positive instances.

Table 3. Performance metrics of various machine learning algorithms on 70:30 train-test split using Kaggle PlantifyDr Datasets [3]

	Precision(%)	Recall(%)	F1-Score(%)	Accuracy(%)
Random Forest	95	95	95	95.01
Support Vector Machine	93	93	93	93.08
Decision Tree	91	91	91	91.05
KNN	90	92	90	91.61
Logistic Regression	91	92	91	91.86
Naive Bayes	89	75	81	74.73

Table 4 outlines the performance metrics of diverse machine learning algorithms when evaluated on a 75:25 train-test split using the Kaggle PlantifyDr Dataset [3]. Random Forest displays exceptional performance across all metrics, achieving high precision, recall, F1-Score, and accuracy(Precision: 96%, Recall: 95% , F1-Score: 95%, Accuracy: 95.42%) in the 75:25 train-test split. SVM maintains strong and consistent performance, achieving notable scores in precision, recall, F1-Score of 94%, and accuracy of 94.32%. Decision Tree performs well with balanced precision, recall, F1-Score, and accuracy. KNN exhibits substantial accuracy, maintaining competitive precision, recall, and F1-Score. Logistic Regression demonstrates competitive performance, achieving a balance in precision, recall, F1-Score, and accuracy. Naive Bayes faces challenges, particularly in recall, indicating potential limitations in correctly identifying positive instances.

Table 4. Performance metrics of various machine learning algorithms on 75:25 train-test split using Kaggle PlantifyDr Datasets [3]

	Precision(%)	Recall(%)	F1-Score(%)	Accuracy(%)
Random Forest	96	95	95	95.42
Support Vector Machine	94	94	94	94.32
Decision Tree	93	93	93	92.61
KNN	91	92	91	92.25
Logistic Regression	90	92	91	91.7
Naive Bayes	90	78	83	78.27

Figure 3 encapsulates the accuracies obtained for a range of machine learning classifiers applied to the citrus plant dataset. Among the models tested, Random Forest consistently demonstrated robust performance, achieving an accuracy of 94.27% in the 80:20 split, 95.42% in the 75:25 split, and 95.01% in the 70:30 split. Notably, this model displayed balanced precision and recall for different classes, making it a reliable choice across varied test sizes.

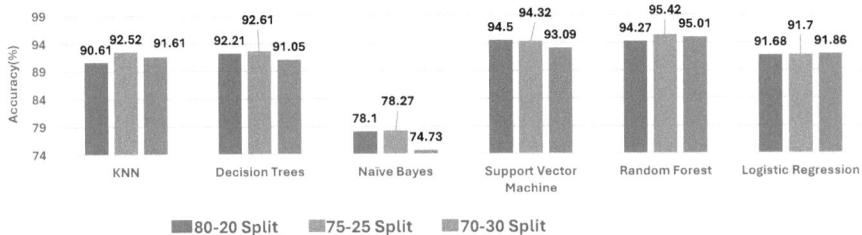

Fig. 3. Accuracy's obtained on different data split size on PlantifyDr Datasets [3] using various machine learning algorithms

The discussion interprets the results and delves into the implications and significance of the findings. It begins by emphasizing the supremacy of the Random Forest model, consistently delivering high accuracy and balanced performance across precision and recall. The discussion explores the reasons behind the model's effectiveness, such as its capability to handle intricate datasets and resist overfitting. The comparative analysis across various splits emphasizes the stability and dependability of the models under diverse test conditions. It examines how certain classifiers maintain a consistent performance, while others may display variations. The limitations of Naive Bayes are discussed, specifically, its lower recall, indicating potential challenges in correctly identifying positive instances. The conversation provides insights into the trade-offs between precision and recall, taking into consideration the specific demands of citrus leaf classification.

5 Conclusion

This study establishes a robust foundation for the application of various machine learning classifiers in the context of citrus plant disease classification. The standout performer, Random Forest, consistently demonstrates high accuracy and balanced precision and recall across different train-test splits. The findings underline the reliability of the Support Vector Machine, Decision Tree, and K-Nearest Neighbour. Logistic Regression showcases adaptability, maintaining a well-balanced performance, while Naïve Bayes exhibits potential under certain conditions despite its limitations. The insights gained from this research provide valuable guidance for selecting appropriate models based on specific classification requirements. Future endeavors can focus on refining model parameters, exploring ensemble techniques, or incorporating deep learning methodologies for further advancements in citrus plant disease identification. In essence, this study contributes significantly to the evolution of automated solutions for accurate and efficient citrus leaf classification, essential for early disease detection and effective agricultural management.

References

1. Arivazhagan, S., Shebiah, R.N., Ananthi, S., Varthini, S.V.: Detection of unhealthy region of plant leaves and classification of plant leaf diseases using texture features. Agric. Eng. Int. CIGR J. **15**(1), 211–217 (2013)
2. Barbedo, J.G.A.: A review on the main challenges in automatic plant disease identification based on visible range images. Biosys. Eng. **144**, 52–60 (2016)
3. Bhattarai, S.: New plant diseases dataset (2019). https://www.kaggle.com/vipoooool/new-plant-diseases-dataset
4. Costa, L., Ampatzidis, Y., Rohla, C., Maness, N., Cheary, B., Zhang, L.: Measuring pecan nut growth utilizing machine vision and deep learning for the better understanding of the fruit growth curve. Comput. Electron. Agric. **181**, 105964 (2021)
5. Cristianini, N., Shawe-Taylor, J.: An Introduction to Support Vector Machines and Other Kernel-Based Learning Methods. Cambridge university press, Cambridge (2000)
6. Dadashzadeh, M., et al.: Weed classification for site-specific weed management using an automated stereo computer-vision machine-learning system in rice fields. Plants **9**(5), 559 (2020)
7. Dhaygude, S.B., Kumbhar, N.P.: Agricultural plant leaf disease detection using image processing. Int. J. Adv. Res. Electr. Electron. Instrum. Eng. **2**(1), 599–602 (2013)
8. Feng, J., Xu, H., Mannor, S., Yan, S.: Robust logistic regression and classification. Adv. Neural Inf. Process. Syst. **27** (2014)
9. Guo, G., Wang, H., Bell, D., Bi, Y., Greer, K.: KNN model-based approach in classification. In: Meersman, R., Tari, Z., Schmidt, D.C. (eds.) OTM 2003. LNCS, vol. 2888, pp. 986–996. Springer, Heidelberg (2003). https://doi.org/10.1007/978-3-540-39964-3_62
10. Hariharan, J., Fuller, J., Ampatzidis, Y., Abdulridha, J., Lerwill, A.: Finite difference analysis and bivariate correlation of hyperspectral data for detecting laurel wilt disease and nutritional deficiency in avocado. Remote sensing **11**(15), 1748 (2019)
11. Kruse, O.M.O., Prats-Montalbán, J.M., Indahl, U.G., Kvaal, K., Ferrer, A., Futsaether, C.M.: Pixel classification methods for identifying and quantifying leaf surface injury from digital images. Comput. Electron. Agric. **108**, 155–165 (2014)
12. Lopez, J.J., Aguilera, E., Cobos, M.: Defect detection and classification in citrus using computer vision. In: Leung, C.S., Lee, M., Chan, J.H. (eds.) Neural Information Processing. ICONIP 2009. LNCS, vol. 5864, pp. 11–18. Springer, Berlin, Heidelberg (2009). https://doi.org/10.1007/978-3-642-10684-2_2
13. Mahmud, M., Kaiser, M.S., McGinnity, T.M., Hussain, A.: Deep learning in mining biological data. Cogn. Comput. **13**(1), 1–33 (2021)
14. Mahmud, M., Kaiser, M.S., Hussain, A., Vassanelli, S.: Applications of deep learning and reinforcement learning to biological data. IEEE Trans. Neural Netw. Learn. Syst. **29**(6), 2063–2079 (2018)

15. Panigrahi, K.P., Das, H., Sahoo, A.K., Moharana, S.C.: Maize leaf disease detection and classification using machine learning algorithms. In: Das, H., Pattnaik, P.K., Rautaray, S.S., Li, K.-C. (eds.) Progress in Computing, Analytics and Networking. AISC, vol. 1119, pp. 659–669. Springer, Singapore (2020). https://doi.org/10.1007/978-981-15-2414-1_66
16. Partel, V., Kakarla, S.C., Ampatzidis, Y.: Development and evaluation of a low-cost and smart technology for precision weed management utilizing artificial intelligence. Comput. Electron. Agric. **157**, 339–350 (2019)
17. Patel, H.H., Prajapati, P.: Study and analysis of decision tree based classification algorithms. Int. J. Comput. Sci. Eng. **6**(10), 74–78 (2018)
18. Rish, I., et al.: An empirical study of the naive bayes classifier. In: IJCAI 2001 Workshop on Empirical Methods in Artificial Intelligence, vol. 3, pp. 41–46 (2001)
19. Seeland, M., Rzanny, M., Boho, D., Wäldchen, J., Mäder, P.: Image-based classification of plant genus and family for trained and untrained plant species. BMC Bioinformatics **20**(1), 1–13 (2019)
20. Shaik, A.B., Srinivasan, S.: A brief survey on random forest ensembles in classification model. In: Bhattacharyya, S., Hassanien, A.E., Gupta, D., Khanna, A., Pan, I. (eds.) International Conference on Innovative Computing and Communications. LNNS, vol. 56, pp. 253–260. Springer, Singapore (2019). https://doi.org/10.1007/978-981-13-2354-6_27
21. Singh, V., Misra, A.K.: Detection of plant leaf diseases using image segmentation and soft computing techniques. Inf. Process. Agric. **4**(1), 41–49 (2017)
22. Vargas, R.I., Piñero, J.C., Leblanc, L.: An overview of pest species of bactrocera fruit flies (diptera: Tephritidae) and the integration of biopesticides with other biological approaches for their management with a focus on the pacific region. Insects **6**(2), 297–318 (2015)
23. Vipinadas, M., Thamizharasi, A.: Detection and grading of diseases in banana leaves using machine learning. Int. J. Sci. Eng. Res. **7**(7), 916–924 (2016)
24. Vishnoi, V.K., Kumar, K., Kumar, B.: Plant disease detection using computational intelligence and image processing. J. Plant Dis. Prot. **128**, 19–53 (2021)
25. Zhou, X., Lee, W.S., Ampatzidis, Y., Chen, Y., Peres, N., Fraisse, C.: Strawberry maturity classification from UAV and near-ground imaging using deep learning. Smart Agric. Technol. **1**, 100001 (2021)
26. Zhu, L., et al.: A destructive new disease of citrus in china caused by cryptosporiopsis citricarpa sp. nov. Plant Disease **96**(6), 804–812 (2012)

GloVe-LSTM: An Artificial Attention-Based Algorithm for Sentiment Analysis of Pandemic Times for Enhanced Decision Support

Shobhit Srivastava[1,2(✉)], Mrinal Kanti Sarkar[3], and Chinmay Chakraborty[4]

[1] University of Engineering & Management, Jaipur, Rajasthan, India
shobhitsrivastava@rmlau.ac.in
[2] IET, Dr. Rammanohar Lohia Avadh University, Ayodhya, Uttar Pradesh, India
[3] Sri Ramkrishna Sarada Vidya Mahapitha, Kamarpukur, West Bengal, India
mks@srsvidyamahapitha.org
[4] BIT, Mesra, India
cchakrabarty@bitmesra.ac.in

Abstract. The expanding realm of technological advancements has paved the way for novel human-machine interaction possibilities. Amid the COVID-19 pandemic, shifts in communication patterns, particularly the surge in social media engagement (e.g., X platform), have inundated platforms with tweets expressing diverse sentiments toward the virus and its mitigation measures, including vaccinations. This wealth of data presents a ripe opportunity for sentiment analysis, not only for understanding public responses but also for informing effective decision-making processes. To navigate this vast expanse of tweets and distill meaningful insights, we advocate a novel approach that integrates the strengths of GLOVE, LSTM, and deep learning techniques. By leveraging GLOVE embeddings, our methodology captures the nuanced semantics of tweets, enhancing the accuracy of sentiment analysis. LSTM networks, trained on diverse datasets, decode the temporal dynamics of language usage, providing a comprehensive understanding of evolving sentiments. Deep learning techniques further bolster our approach, enabling the extraction of intricate patterns and relationships within the data. Through social media analysis and data mining in healthcare, our methodology aims to shed light on the multifaceted aspects of public opinion surrounding the pandemic.

Our integrated approach not only facilitates sentiment analysis but also lays the groundwork for proactive healthcare strategies. By harnessing the power of machine learning, we can identify emerging trends and sentiment shifts in real time, enabling policymakers to tailor communication strategies and interventions accordingly. In this way, our multidisciplinary approach transcends traditional sentiment analysis, offering a holistic understanding of public sentiment and its implications for healthcare decision-making in the age of social media and data abundance.

Keywords: Deep Learning; GLOVE · LSTM · Sentiment Analysis · Social Media Analysis · Data Mining in Health Care · Machine Learning

1 Introduction

The global tide of COVID-19 swept across daily lives, stirring a symphony of emotions and anxieties. As the pandemic surged, individuals worldwide turned to the digital shores of social media, particularly X (formerly known as Twitter)'s vibrant reef, to share their voices and perspectives on this unprecedented phenomenon.[1] X (formerly known as Twitter), a real-time pulse of the population, captured the spectrum of sentiments and viewpoints amidst the crisis. From January 30, 2020, when the World Health Organization officially declared the pandemic, to the ongoing quest for effective treatments and vaccines, X (formerly known as Twitter) has served as a platform for individuals to navigate the emotional currents and express their opinions. This global dialogue underscores the profound impact of COVID-19, which reshaped routines and spurred a surge in online exchange.[2].

This research, leveraging attention-based LSTM with GloVe, aims to conduct a sentiment analysis of X (formerly known as Twitter) data from February to March 2020, focusing on unearthing the heightened concerns related to the pandemic. By discerning emotions and categorizing scenarios associated with these concerns, we aspire to illuminate the lived realities of this global event.[3] This exploration not only advances our understanding of the human response to COVID-19 but also paves the way for developing more effective and nuanced communication strategies for future crises (Table 1).

Table 1. Sample Tweets and Sentiment Polarity Level

Sample Tweet	Sentiment Polarity
A lot of chatter about 16000 staff for the Nightingale Pop-Up Hospital, but where are they coming from? Covid19	Positive
big question: will VC money and accelerators return to where they left off ? Â… COVID-19 should be pointing us towards what is important Â… what is solving problems Â… not marginal consumer apps or ideas that do not benefit society	Negative
"Meanwhile at a grocery store in the Netherlands. #CoronavirusPandemic #pandemic #Covid_19 #coronavirus #corona https://t.co/6FBpeGSxov"	Neutral
How to Avoid Coronavirus Phishing Scams - Consumer Reports https://t.co/D166pdSHLM #covid-19 #Coronavirus #coronavirus #Coronavirusupdate #Coronapocolypse	Extremely Negative
Michelle: Im gonna take a nap, wake me up when corona is over *earthquake happens* Me: Damn God said Ill wake you up now	Extremely Positive

2 Literature Review

The world has faced a microscopic enemy known as COVID-19, and government strategies are constantly adapting to the behavior of different variants of the virus. Variants such as ALPHA, DELTA, OMICRON, NEOCOV, DELMICRON, and others exist, each with varying infection rates and infection mortality rates.

To provide a concise overview of the related work, we have summarized some of the most promising efforts in Table 2. This section has some latest work on COVID-19 data using multiple promising techniques and found tremendous analysis. The approaches of analysis are categorized into three subsections for clarity: (i) Machine Learning Approaches, (ii) Deep Learning Approaches, and (iii) Mixed approaches. The arrangement of the organization of approaches is purely in the context of COVID-19 tweets and it is related to the research topic.

2.1 Machine Learning Approaches

When we use machine learning algorithms the major goal is to improve feature extraction methods. Researchers have used a variety of custom-built specialties, such as emotional markers, hashtags, emoticons, language tags, etc. Some of the techniques are discussed in this section.

For example, [6] used an ensemble machine learning algorithm to automatically extract positive and negative phrases related to situations from tweets. This was based on the assumption that positive sentiment verb phrases often appear before negative situation phrases in the context of detecting COVID-19-related expressions. His suggested model achieved a performance of 0.83 in terms of F1 score. [7] identifies features such as exaggeration, emphasizer words, and marks such as question marks, and exclamation marks in their analysis of 70,000 tweets. They used an SVM classifier to achieve an accuracy of 0.77. Authors explored different features, including hyperbole, interjections, punctuation, emoticons, etc., using SVM on 1,254 tweets. This resulted in a performance of 0.79 in terms of F1 score.

The author curated a dataset of X (formerly known as Twitter) quotes and used HSVM. This resulted in an average F1-score of 0.73. The authors applied the Naïve Bayes algorithm for sentiment classification. [9] used 1,500 tweets from Nepal into categories related to COVID-19, positive sentiment, and negative sentiment. Using Naïve Bayes, they achieve a performance of 0.58 in terms of F1 score.

2.2 Deep Learning Approaches

Various embedding techniques, including both manual and trained models such as GloVe, Word2Vec, and FastText, have been popularly used in deep learning model analysis. For example, [10] used a hierarchical support vector machine (HSVM) with GloVe embeddings to focus on context learning. This resulted in an accuracy of 0.79 on a X (formerly known as Twitter) dataset. [11] introduced a bidirectional long short-term memory (Bi-LSTM) model that emphasizes the relational data in between a couple of emotional texts, like "Sad and Anger." Their approach, which leverages related information, achieved an impressive F1-score of 0.67 for sentiment polarity detection. [12] applied an LSTM model with an attention mechanism for sentiment polarity detection. This approach outperformed various machine learning classifiers, achieving an exceptional F1-score of 0.77. [5] collected a dataset from Kaggle and offered the CrystalFeel, which achieved a performance of 0.71 in terms of F1-score on the Kaggle dataset. [13] employed a lexicon approach on a dataset consisting of approx. 45,00 tweets, yielding an impressive performance of 0.75 in terms of F1 score. [14] utilized X (formerly known as Twitter) data as an attribute and applied hierarchical bi-directional LSTM to achieve the performance of 0.70 in terms of F1 score. [15] leveraged BERT on spatial X (formerly known as Twitter) data, attaining a remarkable accuracy of 0.78.

2.3 Mixed Approaches

In sentiment analysis, handcrafted features and deep learning features alone are sometimes not enough to accurately classify the sentiment polarity of a sentence. Researchers have therefore developed hybrid approaches that combine both types of features. For example, [16] used a mixed approach on a X (formerly known as Twitter) dataset. They offered a SA-LSTM model (Soft Attention LSTM), in which they collected a sequence with a recurrent neural network (RNN) with GloVe embeddings. They also added punctuation-based auxiliary features to the RNN, achieving a performance of 0.62 in terms of accuracy. [17] proposed another hybrid framework based on VADER. They applied models, bidirectional LSTM (Bi-LSTM), individually to the textual data, achieving an accuracy of 0.72. [18] proposed a mixed model using Glove and CNN, to achieve a performance of 0.734 in terms of accuracy.

3 Methodology

The approach for this project encompasses multiple stages, such as data collection and preparation, feature extraction, model training, and evaluation. We will start by collecting a dataset of labeled news articles, which we will clean and preprocess to prepare it for machine learning. We will then extract relevant features from the articles, such as their textual content and metadata. Using these features, we will train and tune the machine learning model for categorizing into two groups: positive and negative. To assess the effectiveness of the proposed method, we will employ conventional performance metrics such as accuracy, precision, and F1 score.

3.1 Algorithm Used

LSTM.
Long Short-Term Memory (LSTM) represents a specialized variant of recurrent neural network (RNN) architecture, specifically engineered to tackle the vanishing gradient problem—a significant hurdle encountered by conventional RNNs. LSTMs excel in tasks that revolve around sequential data, encompassing domains like time series analysis, natural language processing, speech recognition, and numerous others. The key idea behind LSTMs is their ability to learn and control the flow of information through a cell state. LSTMs achieve this through three main components, Cell State, Gates(Forget

Table 2. The summary of some of the potential works on COVID-19 Sentiment Analysis

Authors	Features	Technique Used	Performance
[11]	Positive Verbs Negative	Bi-LSTM	Accuracy = .77
[6]	Positive Negative Neutral	Ensemble	F1 Score = 73.5
[19]	Positive Negative Neutral	SVM	Accuracy = .77
[16]	Sad Joy Fear Anger	LSTM-RNN	Accuracy = .6213
[12]	Positive Negative Neutral	LSTM	Accuracy = .73
[20]	Positive Negative Neutral	NBSVM	Accuracy = .75
[5]	Sad Joy Fear Anger	CrystalFeel	Accuracy = .716
[10]	Positive Negative Neutral	SVM	Accuracy = .79
[21]	Positive Negative Neutral	Lexicon	F1 Score = .71
[8]	Positive Negative Neutral	SVM	Accuracy = .71
[14]	Positive Negative Neutral	Bi-LSTM	Accuracy = .7083
[17]	Positive Negative Neutral	VADER	Accuracy = .745
[22]	Positive Negative Neutral	HSVM	Accuracy = .73
[23]	Positive Negative	Naïve Bayes	F1 Score = 39
[18]	Positive Negative Neutral	Glove + CNN	Accuracy = .734
[24]	Positive Negative Neutral	Naïve Bayes	Accuracy = .717

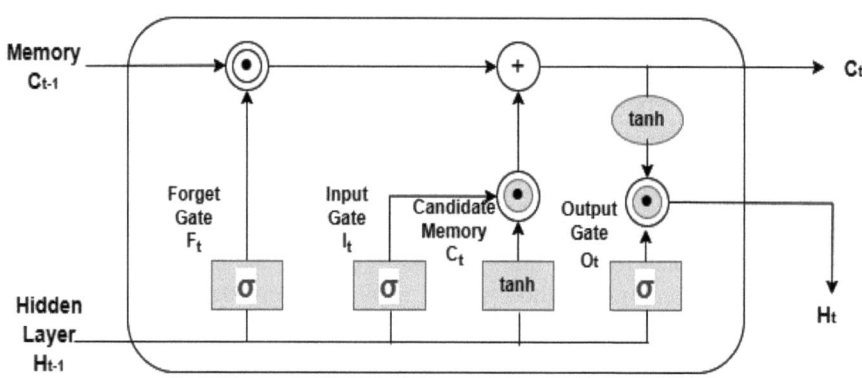

Fig. 1. LSTM Architecture

Gate, Input Gate), Output Gate, and Hidden State. Figure 1 resembles the architecture of LSTM.

GloVe (Global Vectors).
GloVe, short for Global Vectors for Word Representation, is a popular unsupervised learning algorithm used to generate word embeddings. Word embeddings are dense

vector representations of words in a continuous vector space, where the distance and direction between vectors encode semantic relationships between words.

GloVe utilizes co-occurrence statistics from a corpus to learn word embeddings. Unlike other methods like Word2Vec which focus on predicting a word based on its context or vice versa, GloVe directly learns from the global word-word co-occurrence matrix. This matrix captures the frequency of word co-occurrences across the entire corpus. The core idea behind GloVe is that the ratios of co-occurrence probabilities contain significant semantic information. By training on the co-occurrence matrix, GloVe learns to produce word embeddings that capture both local and global word relationships.

Steps of the Proposed Algorithm.

Dataset Source: [26] The dataset was obtained from GitHub, a popular online platform for data science and machine learning enthusiasts. Table 3 and Fig. 2 depict the overview of the dataset and the sentiment distribution respectively.

Table 3. Statistics of the dataset used in the work.

	Dataset
Positive	11422
Negative	9916
Neutral	7711
Extremely Positive	6624
Extremely Negative	5481

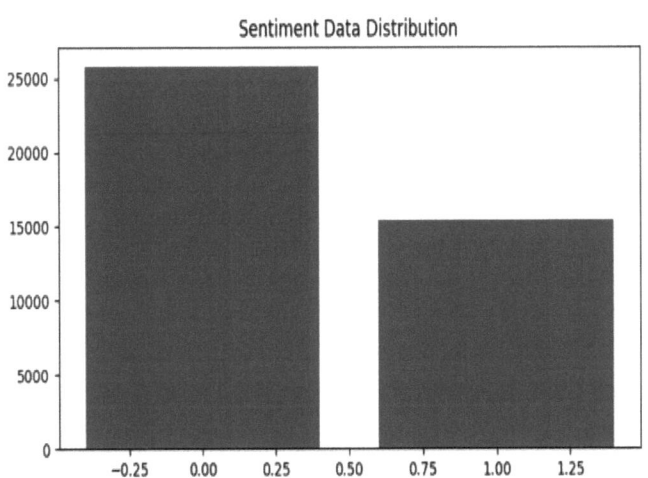

Fig. 2. Sentiment of Data Distribution

Dataset description: The dataset contains a collection of tweets labeled as "Positive" "Extremely Positive" "Neutral" "Extremely Negative" and "Negative". For Binary Classification "Positive" "Extremely Positive" and "Neutral" are taken as "Positive" and it is labelled as 1 and "Negative" or "Extremely Negative" are taken as "Negative" and labelled as 0. The dataset consists of a total of 41157 tweets.

Data cleaning and preprocessing: It is an important step in any ML project as it ensures the data is accurate, complete, and in the right format for analysis. In this report, we will discuss the data cleaning and preprocessing steps taken for the Sentiment Analysis of the Covid Tweets model. The dataset used for this project was the "Copy of Coronavirus Tweets" from Kaggle, which contained approximately 41157 tweets. The first step in the data cleaning process was to load the dataset into a Pandas data frame using the "read_csv" function.

Feature extraction using GloVe: GloVe employs matrix factorization techniques to derive dense vector representations for words. These representations encode semantic relationships between words, enabling downstream natural language processing tasks such as text classification, sentiment analysis, and information retrieval. By leveraging pre-trained GloVe embeddings or fine-tuning them on specific tasks, feature extraction using GloVe facilitates the creation of robust and contextually rich representations of textual data, enhancing the performance of various machine learning models.

Segmentation: The dataset underwent segmentation into training and testing subsets through the application of the "train_test_split" function from the sklearn library. This partitioning adhered to a 70:30 split ratio, with 70% of the data dedicated to training and the remaining 30% designated for testing. Figures 3, 4 and 5 visually depict the employed methodology, the word cloud of the dataset before preprocessing, and the word cloud after preprocessing, respectively.

Model Training and Testing. Training and testing are the building blocks of the construction of any project. In the specific context of the Covid Sentiment Analysis model, the objective is to construct a model capable of accurately categorizing tweets as either positive or negative in sentiment. To achieve this, it is imperative to train the model on a labeled dataset and subsequently assess its performance on a distinct dataset [4, 21, 22]. In this analysis, LSTM (Long Short-Term Memory) is used as the deep learning model. The training process involves fitting the model to the training subset using the "fit()" function, followed by making predictions on the testing subset with the "predict()" function [25]. The LSTM model attains an accuracy of 0.82.

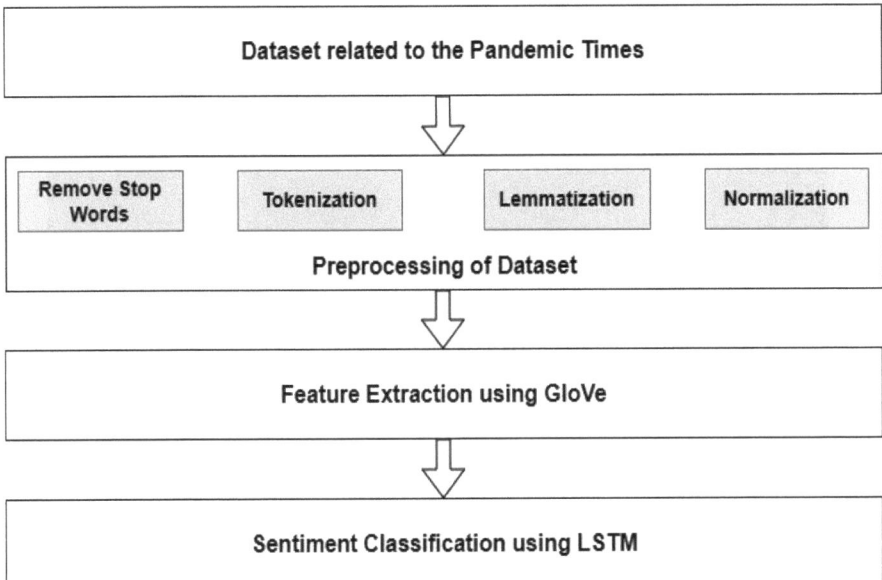

Fig. 3. Algorithm Workflow

Fig. 4. World Cloud of the Dataset before preprocessing

Fig. 5. World Cloud of the Dataset after preprocessing

Algorithm-1
Function- GloVe-LSTM (COVID-19 Dataset)
Input: Textual Dataset
Output:- Accuracy, F1 Score, Precision, Recall
For each text to do
Processed Data (Pd) ← preprocessing of Data (Pi)
Tokens (Wtokens) ← Tokenization of Pi
Features Extraction (Fe) ← GloVe (Wtokens)
Embedding matrix (Ei) ← Embedding for each word ϵ Wtokens
LSTM (L1) ← Embedding matrix of each text
LSTM (L2) ← LSTM (L1)
Feature vector (FV) ← Attention Layer (LSTM (L2))
New_feature_vector (CV) ← Fe + FV
Determine the accuracy level (A)
Calculate the F1 Score (F)
End For

4 Results and Discussion

In prior research studies, as outlined in Table 2, authors have primarily engaged with sentiment datasets operating at binary or tertiary polarity levels. Their main approaches involved altering classifier algorithms and augmenting dimensions for dataset training and testing. In contrast, our central emphasis lies in enhancing the feature selection method across classifiers, as we firmly believe this step to be pivotal in the language learning continuum. By refining our feature selection method, we anticipate significantly heightened classifier performance. Table 3 presents a comparative analysis of various methods alongside our proposed algorithm.

In this work, we proposed a deep-learning model for Sentiment analysis. We used a dataset containing Original Tweet and Sentiment data, where the Original Tweet was the COVID-related tweet content and the label was either positive or negative. We performed data cleaning and pre-processing, including removing stop words and stemming. We then used feature extraction to convert the text data into numerical vectors. The dataset was split into two parts training and testing and used LSTM to build the model. Figures 6 and 7 show the model accuracy and model loss respectively. Figure 8 shows the confusion matrix of the experiment.

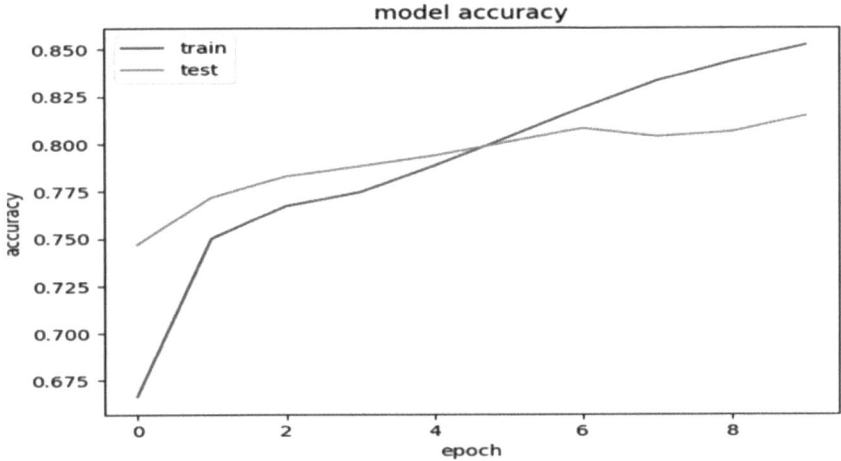

Fig. 6. Model Accuracy

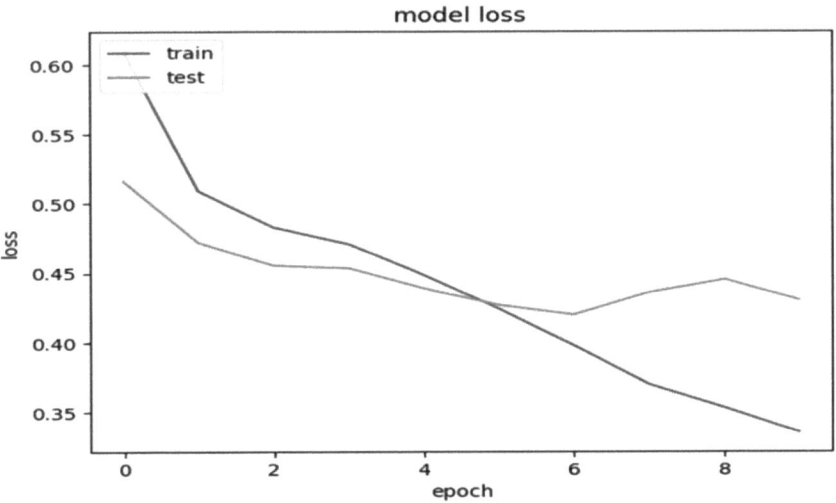

Fig. 7. Model Loss

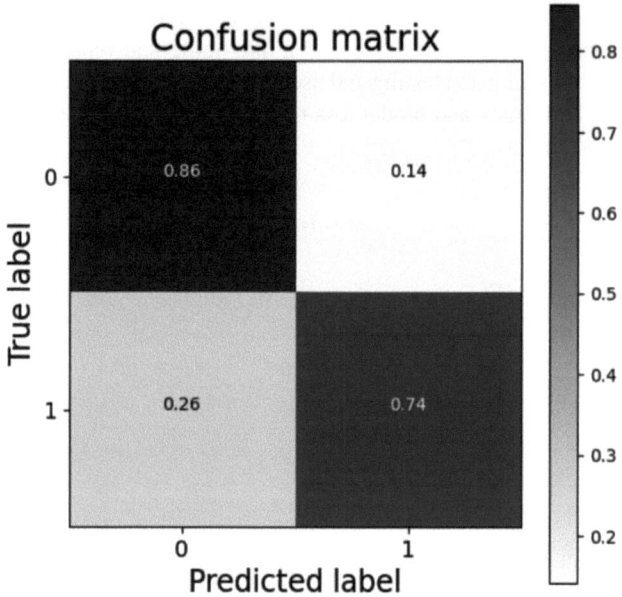

Fig. 8. Confusion Matrix

The confusion matrix shows the actual and predicted labels of the testing data. The diagonal values of the matrix represent the correct predictions, while the off-diagonal values represent the incorrect predictions. Table 4 depicts the overall performance of the model.

Overall, the results demonstrate that machine learning models can effectively detect the sentiment of the tweet by analyzing the content of the tweet. With the increasing prevalence of hateful tweets on social media, such models can play an important role in the field of text mining which is future used in AI development, and prevention of hate and abuse in common textual references. However, there is still room for improvement, and further research can be conducted to enhance the accuracy and performance of the models (Table 5).

Table 4. Comparative analysis with potential methods

Authors	Features	Technique Used	Performance
Rustam et. al. [11]	Positive Verbs Negative Phrases	Bi-LSTM	Accuracy = .77
Naseem et. al. [16]	Sad Joy Fear Anger	LSTM-RNN	Accuracy = .6213
Boon-Itt el. al. [12]	Positive Verbs Negative Phrases	LSTM	Accuracy = .73
Basiri et.al. [21]	Positive Negative Neutral	Lexicon	F1 Score = .71
Chintalapudi el.al. [14]	Positive Negative Neutral	Bi-LSTM	Accuracy = .7083
Basiri et. al[18]	Positive Negative Neutral	Glove + CNN	Accuracy = .734
Proposed Algorithm	**Positive, Negative, Neutral, Extreme Positive, Extreme Negative**	**GloVe + LSTM**	**Accuracy = .82**

Table 5. Evaluation Matrix

Model	Class	Performance Metrics		
		P	R	F
GloVe-LSTM	Positive, Extreme Positive, Neutral	.85	.86	.85
	Negative, Extremely Negative	.75	.74	.75
	Model Accuracy	.82		

5 Sentiment Analysis and Decision-Making Process

Sentiment analysis stands as a pivotal tool for guiding decision-making processes across diverse fields. This study focuses specifically on the domain of pandemics. Amid the pandemic, authorities face a myriad of decisions, some beneficial and others potentially detrimental. By employing sentiment analysis on extensive datasets, authorities can swiftly and effectively assess the repercussions of past decisions, enabling them to refine strategies and monitor impacts more adeptly. This approach allows for timely adjustments to decisions and a comprehensive understanding of public sentiment regarding those decisions.

We opt for large datasets for several reasons. Firstly, the proliferation of social media platforms has generated copious amounts of data relevant to public sentiment during the pandemic. Secondly, the magnitude of decisions made by authorities necessitates a substantial dataset to accurately gauge their impact. Thus, leveraging large datasets is imperative for our sentiment analysis process.

Deep learning serves as our methodology of choice due to its capacity to accommodate massive datasets and deliver robust results. Deep learning classifiers excel in handling the sheer volume of data encountered in daily operations, thereby yielding meaningful insights. This research represents a preliminary step toward developing a Health Language Learning Model (HLLM), which could revolutionize the treatment of infectious diseases like COVID-19.

The following outlines the process of decision-making utilizing sentiment analysis:

5.1 How Sentiment Analysis is Helpful for Decision Making: -

This is how sentiment analysis is helpful for the decision-making process.

Identifying the public perception: By analyzing public perception, sentiment analysis helps discover trends, preferences, and potential problems. This allows authorities to find and address areas needing improvement.

Improving Products and Services: Analyzing public reviews can pinpoint what aspects of a product or service resonate well and which ones don't. This feedback helps guide development decisions and improve customer satisfaction.

Understanding Brand Perception: Sentiment analysis of social media mentions can reveal how customers and the public view a brand. This helps businesses adapt their marketing strategies and public image.

The accuracy of sentiment analysis can vary depending on the tool and the complexity of the text. This is the root cause of high-end research in this area of sentiment analysis using machine learning or deep learning methods and every research aims the higher accuracy and F1 Score. With our method, we claim higher accuracy only with the performance tuning on the feature extraction part of the whole process.

6 Conclusion

The meteoric rise of social media has forged these platforms into powerful amplifiers of information and influence. However, the brevity of texts like tweets, devoid of rich context, poses a unique challenge for sentiment analysis. Researchers, thus, constantly refine algorithms in pursuit of the most nuanced models. Before any classification magic can happen, tweets undergo a vital purification ritual: text preprocessing and feature extraction. We conducted meticulous experiments on diverse datasets, keenly aware that the quality of this cleansing directly impacts the final analysis. Delving deeper, we analyzed these carefully constructed datasets, unearthing not just the binary song of positive and negative, but also the intricate melodies of fear and trust woven into the tapestry of tweets. This emotional intelligence empowers policymakers to become vigilant sentinels, safeguarding social order from the chaos of panic and misinformation. Harnessing the potential of a well-intentioned X (formerly known as Twitter), governments can gain precious early warnings of the public pulse, informing their crisis response strategies and communication channels to disseminate accurate information and galvanize citizen engagement. This journey, however, is only the beginning. Future expeditions beckon, inviting us to explore vast troves of untapped X (formerly known as Twitter) data. We envision deciphering the impact of COVID-19 on the financial fabric, employment realities, and personal lives of individuals, employing the potent tools of machine learning to illuminate the path forward.

References

1. Shamrat, F.M.J.M., et al.: Sentiment analysis on Twitter tweets about COVID-19 vaccines using NLP and supervised KNN classification algorithm. Indones. J. Electr. Eng. Comput. Sci. **23**(1), 463–470 (2021). https://doi.org/10.11591/ijeecs.v23.i1.pp463-470
2. Lyu, J.C., Le Han, E., Luli, G.K.: COVID-19 vaccine-related discussion on twitter: topic modeling and sentiment analysis. J. Med. Internet Res. **23**(6), e24435 (2021). https://doi.org/10.2196/24435
3. Gupta, V., et al.: An emotion care model using multimodal textual analysis on COVID-19. Chaos, Solitons Fractals **144**, 110708 (2021). https://doi.org/10.1016/j.chaos.2021.110708
4. Zeng, W., Gautam, A., Huson, D.H.: On the application of advanced machine learning methods to analyze enhanced, multimodal data from persons infected with COVID-19. Computation **9**(1), 4 (2021). https://doi.org/10.3390/computation9010004
5. Garcia, K., Berton, L.: Topic detection and sentiment analysis in Twitter content related to COVID-19 from Brazil and the USA. Appl. Soft Comput. **101**, 107057 (2021). https://doi.org/10.1016/j.asoc.2020.107057
6. Leelawat, N., et al.: Twitter data sentiment analysis of tourism in Thailand during the COVID-19 pandemic using machine learning. Heliyon **8**(10), e10894 (2022). https://doi.org/10.1016/j.heliyon.2022.e10894
7. Shofiya, C., Abidi, S.: Sentiment analysis on COVID-19-related social distancing in canada using Twitter data. Int. J. Environ. Res. Public Health **18**(11), 5993 (2021). https://doi.org/10.3390/ijerph18115993
8. Pokharel, B.P.: Twitter sentiment analysis during Covid-19 outbreak in Nepal. SSRN Electron. J. (2020). https://doi.org/10.2139/ssrn.3624719
9. Boon-Itt, S., Skunkan, Y.: Public perception of the COVID-19 Pandemic on Twitter: sentiment analysis and topic modeling study. JMIR Public Heal. Surveill **6**(4), e21978 (2020). https://doi.org/10.2196/21978
10. Alam, K.N., et al.: Deep learning-based sentiment analysis of COVID-19 vaccination responses from Twitter data. Comput. Math. Methods Med. **2021**, 4321131 (2021). https://doi.org/10.1155/2021/4321131
11. Chintalapudi, N., Battineni, G., Amenta, F.: Sentimental analysis of COVID-19 Tweets using deep learning models. Infect. Dis. Rep. **13**(2), 329–339 (2021). https://doi.org/10.3390/idr13020032
12. Singh, C., Imam, T., Wibowo, S., Grandhi, S.: A deep learning approach for sentiment analysis of COVID-19 reviews. Appl. Sci. **12**(8), 3709 (2022). https://doi.org/10.3390/app12083709
13. Mansoor, M., Gurumurthy, K.A.R.U., Prasad, V.R.B.: Global sentiment analysis Of COVID-19 Tweets over time. (2020). http://arxiv.org/abs/2010.14234
14. Naseem, U., Razzak, I., Khushi, M., Eklund, P.W., Kim, J.: COVIDSenti: a large-scale benchmark Twitter data set for COVID-19 sentiment analysis. IEEE Trans. Comput. Soc. Syst. **8**(4), 1003–1015 (2021). https://doi.org/10.1109/TCSS.2021.3051189
15. Leelawat, N., et al.: Leveraging machine learning to analyze sentiment from COVID-19 tweets: a global perspective. Eng. Reports **5**(10), 1–23 (2023). https://doi.org/10.1016/j.heliyon.2022.e10894
16. Bang, Y., et al.: A proposed sentiment analysis deep learning algorithm for analyzing COVID-19 Tweets. Int. J. Environ. Res. Public Health **1088**(4), 128–140 (2021). https://doi.org/10.3390/ijerph18115993
17. Kaur, H., Ahsaan, S.U., Alankar, B., Chang, V.: A proposed sentiment analysis deep learning algorithm for analyzing COVID-19 Tweets. Inf. Syst. Front. **23**(6), 1417–1429 (2021). https://doi.org/10.1007/s10796-021-10135-7

18. Pristiyono, M., Ritonga, M.A., Al Ihsan, A.A., Rambe, F.H.: Sentiment analysis of COVID-19 vaccine in Indonesia using Naïve Bayes Algorithm. IOP Conf. Ser. Mater. Sci. Eng. **1088**(1), 012045 (2021). https://doi.org/10.1088/1757-899X/1088/1/012045
19. Villavicencio, C.N., Macrohon, J.J., Inbaraj, X.A., Jeng, J.-H., Hsieh, J.-G.: Development of a machine learning based web application for early diagnosis of COVID-19 based on symptoms. Diagnostics **12**(4), 821 (2022). https://doi.org/10.3390/diagnostics12040821
20. Rajesh, M.: Dataset on COVID-19.
21. Bang, Y., Ishii, E., Cahyawijaya, S., Ji, Z., Fung, P.: Model generalization on COVID-19 fake news detection. In: Chakraborty, T., Shu, K., Bernard, H.R., Liu, H., Akhtar, M.S. (eds.) Combating Online Hostile Posts in Regional Languages during Emergency Situation, pp. 128–140. Springer International Publishing, Cham (2021). https://doi.org/10.1007/978-3-030-73696-5_13
22. Praveen, S.V., Ittamalla, R., Deepak, G.: Analyzing the attitude of Indian citizens towards COVID-19 vaccine – A text analytics study. Diabetes Metab. Syndr. Clin. Res. Rev. **15**(2), 595–599 (2021). https://doi.org/10.1016/j.dsx.2021.02.031
23. Li, S., Wang, Y., Xue, J., Zhao, N., Zhu, T.: The impact of COVID-19 epidemic declaration on psychological consequences: a study on active weibo users. Int. J. Environ. Res. Public Health **17**(6), 2032 (2020). https://doi.org/10.3390/ijerph17062032
24. Kaur, S., Kaul, P., Zadeh, P.M.: Monitoring the dynamics of emotions during COVID-19 using Twitter data. Procedia Comput. Sci. **177**, 423–430 (2020). https://doi.org/10.1016/j.procs.2020.10.056
25. Blair, J., Hsu, C.-Y., Qiu, L., Huang, S.-H., Huang, T.-H.K., Abdullah, S.: Using Tweets to assess mental well-being of essential workers during the COVID-19 pandemic. In: Extended Abstracts of the 2021 CHI Conference on Human Factors in Computing Systems, in CHI EA '21. New York, NY, USA: Association for Computing Machinery (2021). https://doi.org/10.1145/3411763.3451612
26. https://github.com/rajeshmore1/Deep-Learning-Mentorship--Rajesh-More

Hybrid AI Systems

Breast DCE-MRI Registration Using Student Psychology-Based Optimization Algorithm with Centroid Opposition-Based Learning

Somen Nayak(✉) and Achyuth Sarkar

Department of Computer Science and Engineering, National Institute of Technology Arunachal Pradesh, Jote, Arunachal Pradesh, India
somen.phd24@nitap.ac.in

Abstract. Metaheuristics plays a crucial role in problem-solving, and most of them are energized by the accumulated wisdom of biological quirks. Worldwide, bosom illness affects more than 10% of women at some point in their lives. Breast MRI registration is a technique for matching pre- and post-contrast images for cancer classification and analysis. It is essential to do breast MRI registration in order to align MR images of pre- and post-contrast for the purposes of diagnosis and categorization of cancer type as benign or malignant using pharmacokinetic analysis. It is also extremely important to align photos that are going to be collected at a variety of time intervals so that the lesion can be isolated at small intervals. This method of registration is very helpful for monitoring the effectiveness of many different cancer treatments. The primary enlightenment of algorithms that are used for image registration has also shifted from a control point for semi-automated techniques to sophisticated voxel-based automated techniques that employ mutual information as a similarity measure. This transition occurred as image registration moved from a manual process to an automated one. In this study, we present an optimization method based on student psychology and adversarial learning (SPBO-OBL) to be used for breast MRI registration. Breast Magnetic Resonance Imaging (MRI) image registration using SPBO-OBL, a meta-heuristics-based optimization technique. The SPBO-OBL technique is then used to successfully register the images. We evaluate the performance of the SPBO-OBL-based registration method against the GTO, BBO-EL, and PSO methods. According to the findings, SPBO-OBL-based registration methods are superior to GTO, BBO-EL, and PSO-based registration methods when it comes to the registration of breast MRIs.

Keywords: Breast MRI · Image registration · metaheuristics · Multi-verse optimization · Student Psychology-based optimization and Particle Swarm Optimization

1 Introduction

The global epidemic of breast cancer has made it the most common cause of death among female cancer patients. To date, there have been 1.38 million new cases of breast cancer diagnosed worldwide or about 23% of all new cancer cases. There were 458,400 fatalities attributed to breast cancer in 2008, making up 14% of all cancer deaths. Breast MRI enables feature-based alignment of several Breast Magnetic Resonance Images. Breast image (MI) registration space detection relied on retrieving the relevant factor. Simply said, it provides a method for aligning different MRI scans of the breast based on their intrinsic similarities. Breast MRI registration involved retrieving spatial information based on shared characteristics between images. The following are two fundamental ideas in Breast MRI registration:-

1.1 Transformation

The process of changing one set of visuals into another by utilizing a set of rules is known as transformation. The term "transformation" can refer to a wide variety of operations, including but not limited to translation, resizing (either up or down), rotation, and shearing. The term "2D transformation" refers to a transformation that takes place on a plane that only has two dimensions. We need to take a step-by-step method if we are going to be able to carry out a series of transformations, such as translation, rotation, and finally scaling. we need to follow a sequential approach:—

Translate the Coordinates. When you translate something, it moves to a different location on the screen. You can convert a point in 2D by adding the translating coordinates (i_m, i_n) to the existing coordinates P, Q in order to obtain the new coordinates P, Q. The mathematical expression for as follows:

$$P' = P + i_m, Q' = Q + i_n \tag{1}$$

or we also can indicate R'= R+T, where

$$R' = \begin{vmatrix} P' \\ Q' \end{vmatrix}, R = \begin{vmatrix} P \\ Q \end{vmatrix}, T = \begin{vmatrix} i_m \\ i_n \end{vmatrix}$$

An affine mapping should be described into two coordinates of the other space (P', Q'), where (P, Q) is each position of Magnetic resonance pictures of the breast. The real distance of translation is denoted by (i_m, i_n).

1.2 Rotate the Translated Coordinates

Angles can be used to simply and effectively describe rotations in two-dimensional images or image matrices. Assume for the moment that there is just one point in the plane of two dimensions, and that point's coordinates are

(c_1, c_2). An operation called rotation will be carried out using radians about the origin on the provided coordinates $(c_1, c2)$, which will result in new coordinates called (d_1, d_2). It should be computed by utilizing the transformation, which may be stated as follows:
$$d_1 = cos(\alpha)c_1 + sin(\alpha)c_2 \\ d_2 = -sin(\alpha)c_1 + cos(\alpha)c_2 \qquad (2)$$

1.3 Normalized Mutual Information(NMI)

One of the most common information concepts used for evaluating the quality of registration is normalized mutual information. Let's say there are two images M and N, and the NMI between them is determined as

$$NMI(M,N) = \frac{I(M,N)}{\sqrt{H(M)H(N)}} \qquad (3)$$

Where I(M, N) is the Mutual Information of 2 images and H(M) and H(N) is the Entropy of image M and N.

2 Related Work

Some of the methods that are utilized in the process of breast image registration are for the sake of pre and post-contrast applications. The first method that we are going to talk about is a proposed methodology for the registration of breast MR-Images, and it is an algorithm for one sort of registration of a rigid body that was proposed by Zuo et al. [1]. In practice, the approach computes the transformation of a rigid body between two distinct images by lowering the variance ratio that exists between them. Breast MR images were registered by Krishnan et al. [2] utilizing a modeling motion that acted as a translation set over two orthogonal axes.

An affine registration algorithm was proposed for the purpose of registration by Kumar et al. [3] Using a slice-oriented control-point-based technique, Lucht et al. [4] have announced that they have successfully introduced an important new notion for the same problem. The more current research approach that is used in breast MRI registration primarily focuses on strategies that are voxel-based and that use the data of the whole image to determine the transformation that exists between images that are fixed and images that are moving. In this particular submission, the foundational or landmark paper was the one that was prepared by Rueckert and colleagues [5,6]. The author of this publication has utilized a technique known as combined transformation. This technique combines global affine transformation, which was used to explain the overall motion of the breast, and local transformation, which was used to model out the local deformation of MR images of the breast. Both of these transformations can be found in this technique. It is possible to model a freeform deformation (FFD) entirely on the basis of B-splines [7], and the local deformation is an extremely helpful tool for doing so. FFDs take advantage of a preparatory control point network in order to distort a picture into the form of an object. By applying the appropriate penalty function, each of the deformations was controlled so that the result was as smooth as possible. A method that served as a multi-resolution hierarchical viewpoint was effectively implemented, and as a result, the computational efficiency was significantly improved.

Despite the fact that Rohlfing et al. [12] have asserted that mutual information is one of the resemblance measures for rigid-body registration, it is not possible for it to prevent contrast-developed structures from considerably shifting size during the registration of a non-rigid body. Tanner et al. [13] proposed the notion of contrast-developing lesions, which typically had a considerable decrease when viewed on contrast-developing breast MR images. When compared to the tissue that surrounds them in the pre-contrast image, lesions that truly show a significant decrease in relative volume and take on an almost spherical shape have a contrast that is either very low or nonexistent. An improvement that Rohlfing has added to Rueckert's indigenous method is one that makes use of the regularization of innovative terms to impel the deformation in order to preserve volume. Their method, which regulates the weight appropriately on the word connected to regularization, is quite flexible regarding the principle that underlies it. They support the use of an algorithm that alternates between the two methods, arguing that this leads to improved picture registration and greater volumetric retention of the original data. Rohlfing et al. [14] have also improved this strategy in order to bring up a proper parallel implementation. Finding features of an algorithm that can be parallelized and included into a multi-threaded technique allows for the successful completion of even the most minute tasks.

2.1 Objective

After conducting a literature review on the topic of breast MR image registration, we discovered that very little study work has been done on the topic of breast MR image registration utilizing meta-heuristics methods. This was one of the findings that we came to after conducting the literature review. As a result of this, we decided to register breast MR images with the help of a metaheuristics method called SPBO [8]. SPBO with opposition-based learning (also known as SPBO-OBL) is offered as a method for breast MRI registration in this particular piece of research. An experimental investigation is carried out, and the findings of the study led the researchers to the conclusion that the SPBO-OBL-based registration method is superior than the GTO [9], BBO-EL [10], and PSO [11] -based registration methods in terms of statistical performance.

3 Proposed Methodology

3.1 The Proposed SPBO-OBL

This section introduces opposition-based learning (OBL) to improve the performance of the SPBO algorithm, as well as a description of the upgraded SPBO-OBL.

3.2 Opposition-Based Learning

Typically, random numbers are used to kick off the search in traditional metaheuristic methods. The convergence rate of the algorithm is erratic and slow overall. Both randomly generated and inverted solutions are considered as part of the opposition-based learning needed to overcome these obstacles. The following is a definition of the OBL properties. Let $S = (p_1, p_2, \ldots, p_D)$ be a point in D space, where $p_1, p_2, \ldots, p_D \in R$, $p_i \in [c_i, d_i]$, $\forall i \in \{1, 2, \ldots, D\}$. Then the opposite point of M is $OS = (op_1, op_2, \ldots, op_D)$, where $op_i = c_i + d_i - p_i$.

The student psychology-based optimization algorithm (SPBO) employs a universe population that is first seeded at random for its population generation. This causes it to have varying degrees of success over time. It is more likely that the algorithm will swiftly converge to the best global solution if the starting population is formed in a fashion that is closer to the global optimal. This is due to a greater potential for improvement. Because it provides a firm starting point for the search process, opposition-based initialization may improve the algorithm's efficiency. The first generation of the jth element at point Z_i of the ith universe looks like this:

$$Z_{ij} = Z_j^{min} + (Z_j^{max} - Z_j^{min}) \times rand(0,1) \qquad (4)$$

where $[Zmin_j, Zmax_j]$ denotes the range of the search space, and $rand(0, 1)$ represents the uniformly distributed random number in the range $[0, 1]$. After the initialization process is finished, the opposing locations of the universe, also known as OZ, are calculated. The n most important positions are selected from the set of [Z, OZ] positions using the fitness values, which are from lowest to highest.

3.3 Centroid Opposition Based Learning

Proposed by Rahnamayan [17], the COBC scheme is an OBL scheme that is successfully integrated into the DE algorithm, outperforming its competing algorithms [17]. In a metaheuristic algorithm, the whole population is taken into account while calculating the opposite centroid positions. Consider the N points $(Z_1, Z_2, \ldots, Z_N)$ that carry unit mass in the D dimensional search space. Thus, the body's centroid can be described as follows:

$$M = \frac{Z_1 + Z_2 + Z_3 + \ldots + Z_N}{N} \qquad (5)$$

In $k_t h$ dimension, the centroid point can be computed using the following formula:

$$M_k = \frac{1}{N} \sum_{i=1}^{N} Z_{1,k} \qquad (6)$$

Once the centroid of a discrete uniform body is known as M, the following formula can be used to find the opposite point $\check{Z}_i$ of a given point Z_i on the body:

$$\check{Z} = 2 \times M - Z_i \qquad (7)$$

When compared to the min-max strategy, the centroid approach performs better. Based on the generated sample points, the estimated boundary is computed as $[Z_{min}, Z_{max}]$.

3.4 The Generation Jumping

In the generation-jumping stage, the inverse solution of each universe at the current iteration t is located using the dynamic search space range $[p_j(t), q_j(t)]$. These expressions for $p_j(t)$ and $p_j(t)$ can be derived:

$$p_j(t) = \min_{\forall i}\{Z_{ij}(t)\} \tag{8}$$

$$q_j(t) = \max_{\forall i}\{Z_{ij}(t)\} \tag{9}$$

By rewriting Eq. (4) for the basic OBL scheme in the following way, it is possible to determine the jth element of the opposing solution Z_{ij} of the ith universe in the dynamic search space.

$$Z_{ij} = p_j(t) + q_j(t) - Z_{ij}. \tag{10}$$

In a way not dissimilar to that described above, it is possible to compute the opposite solutions in OBL schemes. After determining the level of physical fitness provided by the opposing position of the universe, the best n places are selected from the original position of the universe as well as the opposing position of the universe. These spots are selected in the ascending order of their respective fitness values in order to achieve the best possible results. There is a transition that must take place with a generation jumping probability given by P_{gj} in order to get from SPBO operations to OBL. This probability is denoted as P_{gj}. In the vast majority of the research that has been conducted and documented, the parameter P_{gj} is given a less significant value, particularly 0.3, as our investigation reveals. The efficiency of opposition-based algorithms is higher than that of their fundamental form when run in this setting.

3.5 Student Psychology-Based Optimization Algorithm (SPBO)

In the year 2020, Bikash Das and colleagues [8] have come up with a proposal for this algorithm. The SPBO algorithm is a type of metaheuristics algorithm that is based on the concept of the attitude of scholars who worked extremely hard to provide additional attempts in order to improve their performance and get to the top. The grade that one receives in their individual test can be used to calculate performance in an accurate and efficient manner. The scholar who has achieved the highest possible grade is recognized as the best student in the class, and subsequent awards are distributed in accordance with this ranking. The level of interest that a student has in a given topic will determine the amount of work that they are expected to put in about that topic. The student will always be eager to put in more effort with regard to the subject matter in order to improve their overall score in the examination. The pupils in a given class can be divided into four groups according to the subjects that they are studying, and these groups are as follows:

Best Student. The top student in a class is the one who achieves the highest grade on their final exam. The top student will always work to keep up her or his grade point average by any means necessary. A mathematical expression for the top student's growth is as follows:

$$Z_{bestnew} = Z_{best} + (-1)^n \times rand \times (Z_{best} - Z_m) \tag{11}$$

where *rand* represents a random number in the range [0,1], n represents a parameter whose value is either 1 or 2, and Z_{best} and Z_i stand for the grades attained by the best student, and the mth student chosen at random in a given subject.

Good Student. If a student is interested in a topic, he or she is more likely to put in extra effort to learn more about it, which in turn should raise the student's total grade. This category of students typically performs well academically. Due to the fact that each student's psychology is unique, the selection method for this type of student is completely random. Some students are able to put more time and effort into their studies than the typical student, and these students often make it their goal to catch up to the best student's effort and output. An equation that describes this type of learner is as follows:

$$Z_{newm} = Z_{best} + [rand \times (Z_{best} - Z_m], \tag{12}$$

$$Z_{newk} = Z_m + [rand \times (Z_{best} - Z_m)] + [rand \times (Z_m - Z_{mean})], \tag{13}$$

where Z_m is the grade earned by the mth student, Z_{mean} is the mean grade earned by all students in the class, and *rand* is a random number with a range of [0,1].

Average Student. These students are classified as "subject-wise mediocre" The selection of such students is highly arbitrary and not at all based on the psyches of the various individuals. The following equation quantitatively describes the results obtained by such students:

$$Z_{newm} = Z_m + [rand \times (Z_{mean} - Z_m)], \tag{14}$$

where Z_m and Z_{mean} are the marks obtained by the mth student and the average marks obtained by all students, respectively, and *rand* is a random number with a range that is between [0,1].

Students Who Try to Improve Randomly. In addition to the types of students described above, there are some students who put in a great deal of effort to improve their academic standing on their own. These kinds of students are attempting to distribute their efforts in a haphazard manner among the several disciplines in order to improve their overall exam performance. The following equation provides a mathematical representation of the level of success attained by students in this category:

$$Z_{newm} = Z_{min} + [rand \times (Z_{max} - Z_{min})], \qquad (15)$$

where Z_{min} and Z_{max} represent the minimum and maximum limits of marks of the subject, respectively. The pseudocode of SPBO-OBL is given in Algorithm 1.

4 Results and Discussion

In this study, a breast MRI registration method based on Student Psychology-based Optimization with opposition-based learning (SPBO-OBL) is developed. The results of the SPBO-OBL are compared with those of the GTO [9] algorithm, the BBO-EL [10] algorithm, and the PSO [11] algorithm. There are a total of 35 pairs of breast MR images that are being used, each representing a distinct patient's breasts before and after contrast. During the course of the experiment, there will be ten separate runs conducted. The following is a list of the parameters that we have set in order to carry out the experiment:

- SPBO-OBL
  nVar=3, PopulationSize=50, FES=5000, MaxIt=100, TxMin=-60, TyMin=-60, TxMax=60, TyMax=60, RotMin=-45, RotMax=45, TestRun=10, pgj=0.3.
- GTO
  Population's size (N) = 50, Variable's size (nVar) = 3, Iteration of maximum number = 100, and Criteria for Termination: function evaluations number (FES) = 5000. The area of search variety is described as follows: Min of Tx = -60, Max of Tx = 60, Min of Ty = -60, Max of Ty = 60, Min of Rotation = -45°, Max of Rotation = 45°.

- BBO-EL
  nVar=3, populationSize=50, MaxIt=100, TxMin=-60, TyMin=-60, TxMax=60, TyMax=60, RotMin=-45, RotMax=45, KeepRate=0.2, alpha=0.7, pMutation=0.1, c1=2.05, TestRun=10.
- PSO
  population's size (N) = 50, Variables' size (nVar) = 3, and Iteration of maximum quantity = 100.

4.1 Dataset

The Cancer Genome Atlas Breast Invasive Carcinoma (TCGA-BRCA) [16], The cancer imaging archive (TCIA): Maintaining and operating a public information repository, has 35 pairs of 2D slices of T2-weighted DCE-Magnetic resonance images. We downscale all MR image slices larger than 256 by 256 pixels. Manual segmentation by a radiologist expert yielded the ground facts used as the gold standard.

Algorithm 1: SPBO-OBL Algorithm

1. population initialization Z and criteria for convergence.
2. Compute the initial Performance of the class.
3. Select m best solution from $[OZ, Z]$.
4. Calculate the opposite solution OZ and Computer their fitness.
5. **for** *Termination Criteria* **do**
6.   **if** *rand[0,1]*$<P_{gj}$ **then**
7.   Calculate the opposite solution OZ_i.
8.   Calculate the fitness of the opposite solution.
9.   Select n best solution from $[Z_i, OZ_i]$.
10.   **else**
11.   **for** $n \leftarrow 1$ ***to*** *total subjects given in course* **do**
12.   **for** *every scholar checking the scholar class* **do**
13.   **if** *the scholar is topper* **then**
14.   Upgrade by Equation 11.
15.   **if** *scholar belongs to quality student* **then**
16.   **for** *check Every scholar follows the best scholar* **do**
17.   **if** *TRUE* **then**
18.   upgrade by Equation 12.
19.   **else**
20.   Upgrade by Equation 13.
21.   **end if**
22.   **end**
23.   **end if**
24.   **if** *check the scholar belongs to average grade* **then**
25.   Upgrade by Equation 14.
26.   **else**
27.   Upgrade by Equation 15.
28.   **end if**
29.   **end if**
30.   Boundary checking is needed.
31.   Calculate the class performance.
32.   **if** *the new performance is better* **then**
33.   Upgrade the old with the new one.
34.   **else**
35.   No changes are required.
36.   **end if**
37. $m = m + 1$
38.   **end**
39. $q = q + 1$
40.   **end**
41.   **end if**
42. **end**

4.2 Discussion

For the goal of breast MRI registration, this particular piece of research makes use of student psychology-based optimization (SPBO) in conjunction with opposition-based learning. Each approach is being applied to a total of 25 MR images of the breast, for a total of ten separate runs. On a total of 25 breast MR images from four distinct patients, we performed 10 separate runs and calculated the mean as well as the standard deviation, which is given in Table 1.

In order to register breast MRIs, this paper proposes metaheuristic algorithms called Student Psychology-Based Optimization with Opposition-Based Learning (SPBO-OBL). Over the course of 10 separate runs, each technique is applied to 25 pairs of breast MR images of pre and post-contrast. The average and standard deviation of 25 pairs of pre- and post-contrast breast MR images over 10 separate runs are presented in Table 1. Better outcomes are shown by the bolder typefaces. During the experiment, it was carefully observed that the SPBO-OBL metaheuristic algorithm produces better results than the GTO, BBO-EL, and PSO-based registration methods for breast MR images in terms of the mean value for the maximum number of images. Figure 1 displays the qualitative, or visual, outcomes of breast MRI registration performed with SPBO-OBL, GTO, BBO-EL, and PSO-based registration methods. From a detailed examination of experimental data, it is clear that neither the GTO nor the BBO-EL nor the PSO methodology can provide a better answer than the SPBO-OBL for breast MRI registration, both quantitatively and visually.

Figure 1(a), 1(g), 1(m), 1(s) are the original MRI images of pre contrast & Figs. 1(b), 1(h), 1(n), 1(t) are the post contrast MR images. Figure 1(c), 1(i), 1(o) & 1(u) displays the final image that was produced after registering the MR image using the SPBO-OBL based registration approach. Figure 1(d), 1(j), 1(p) & 1(v) displays the final image that was produced after registering the MR image using the GTO based registration approach. Figure 1(e), 1(k), 1(q) & 1(w) displays the final image that was produced after registering the MR image using the BBO-EL based registration approach. Figure 1(f), 1(l), 1(r) & 1(x) displays the final image that was produced after registering the MR image using the PSO based registration approach.

Even though we have gotten better quantitative results with SPBO-OBL, it is quite difficult to discern between the resultant registered images when utilizing four separate approaches with our open eyes.

4.3 Statistical Significance with NMI

To put quantitative data through a statistical significance test. Wilcoxon Signed Ranks test [15], which is a non-parametric test, has been run on each of the 25 breast MR pictures using a mean of ten separate runs. The test's significance level is 0.01, and the statistical significance test's "p-value" is given in Table 2. This test shows that the GTO, BBO-EL, and PSO-based registration technique doesn't work as well as compared to SPBO-OBL when it comes to breast MRI registration. From Table 2, the *p-value* of SPBO-OBL is lesser than 0.05 when

Table 1. Mean and standard deviation (in parenthesis) of NMI over 10 independent runs of SPBO-OBL, GTO, BBO-EL, and PSO

Image no	SPBO-OBL	GTO	BBO-EL	PSO
1	**1.187041437** (0.033107236)	1.155581555 (0.00017396)	1.120368021 (0.009614359)	1.155317795 (0.000658249)
2	**1.200352393** (0.02480578)	1.154877825 (0.000441299)	1.128033453 (0.019955342)	1.155026515 (0.000434685)
3	**1.19360057** (0.024521515)	1.155844621 (0.000771528)	1.134589204 (0.017401054)	1.15621313 (0.000123406)
4	**1.200788279** (0.019912088)	1.15707594 (7.40E-05)	1.142860896 (0.01374554)	1.157094084 (6.32E-05)
5	**1.205933808** (0.016792969)	1.159371631 (5.55E-05)	1.133805618 (0.017775984)	1.159150098 (0.000413482)
6	**1.207623255** (0.016408443)	1.163084589 (8.64E-06)	1.129793362 (0.017077387)	1.163058048 (7.49E-05)
7	**1.18248251** (0.038380868)	1.161796449 (0.000312154)	1.127409666 (0.016132883)	1.161790413 (0.00044514)
8	**1.189684624** (0.030424203)	1.164736609 (0.000511847)	1.12950272 (0.018023955)	1.164808977 (0.000156912)
9	**1.210900361** (0.008799698)	1.163793236 (0.000460029)	1.138444505 (0.015636013)	1.163595006 (0.000419143)
10	**1.198702404** (0.028571505)	1.161912693 (0.000336184)	1.134465405 (0.015763017)	1.161610935 (0.000985535)
11	**1.049825717** (0.001772624)	1.040007463 (0.000656747)	1.037071284 (0.000913385)	1.039473038 (0.000838594)
12	**1.051723177** (0.003129383)	1.042295808 (0.001093375)	1.039287917 (0.000725969)	1.041146327 (0.00105246)
13	**1.057231173** (0.002471772)	1.04738742 (0.000828497)	1.045762465 (0.000522094)	1.047227107 (0.000618577)
14	**1.063055034** (0.002042774)	1.052699173 (0.000790641)	1.050899977 (0.001561194)	1.052458919 (0.000599016)
15	**1.065533171** (0.003348949)	1.053807915 (0.000463626)	1.052011801 (0.001732539)	1.053859951 (0.00052737)
16	**1.071142553** (0.002711093)	1.058073278 (0.001647323)	1.054681139 (0.001890879)	1.057495141 (0.001493129)
17	**1.073017992** (0.004960431)	1.059339315 (0.002109616)	1.057075116 (0.000250529)	1.059898607 (0.002249642)
18	**1.074542833** (0.003331293)	1.059250971 (0.001812874)	1.056736887 (0.001438925)	1.060054837 (0.001920685)
19	**1.073756501** (0.000707958)	1.059979219 (2.47E-05)	1.053643178 (0.000923596)	1.057021551 (0.002563684)
20	**1.066943105** (0.002069029)	1.055819095 (3.25E-05)	1.04911554 (0.000361597)	1.053843611 (0.002635852)
21	**1.115727655** (0.00725189)	1.100562064 (5.99E-05)	1.092885963 (0.005550274)	1.100483331 (0.000264951)
22	**1.119629665** (0.002945344)	1.102617796 (7.99E-05)	1.0989031 (0.003787222)	1.102513776 (0.000117969)
23	**1.115163144** (0.01045645)	1.104218569 (1.50E-05)	1.095274498 (0.006313487)	1.10416045 (0.00016664)
24	**1.119477176** (0.002164702)	1.105060983 (6.77E-05)	1.096393329 (0.006531938)	1.105088052 (4.63E-05)
25	**1.114760048** (0.009529743)	1.104941061 (8.45E-05)	1.100465859 (0.002897805)	1.104932304 (9.36E-05)

it is compared with GTO, BBO-EL, and PSO which infers that SPBO-OBL performs better as compared to GTO, BBO-EL, and PSO.

Table 2. Wilcoxon Signed Ranks Test Statistics on *NMI*

Sl.no	Comparison	p(2-trailed)
1	SPBO-OBL VS GTO	0.0001
2	SPBI-OBL VS BBO-EL	0.0001
3	SPBO-OBL VS PSO	0.0001

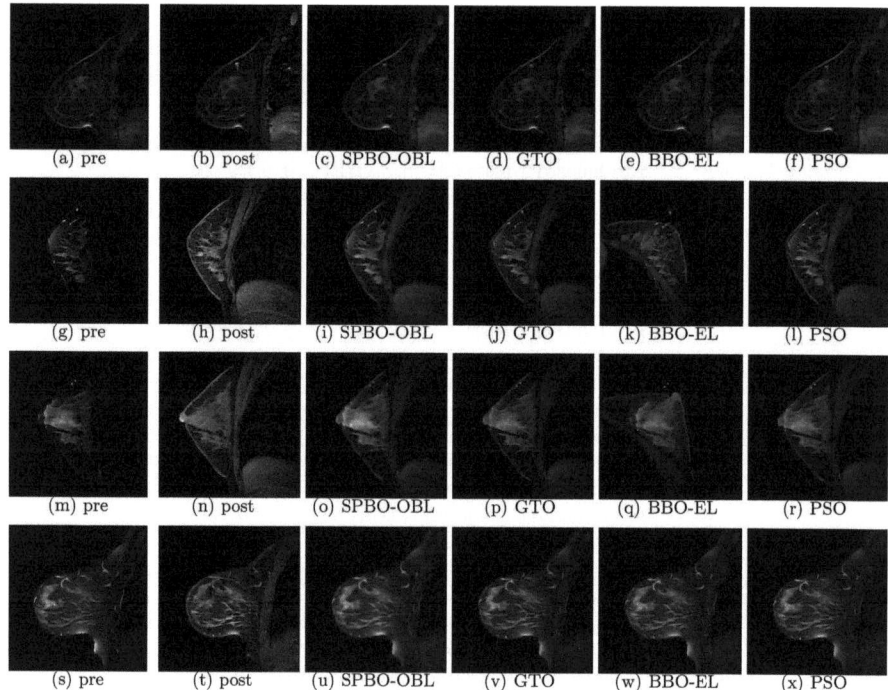

Fig. 1. Registration Result of Pre and Post Contrast of Breast MR Images

5 Conclusion

It is proposed in this work that breast MRI registration can be accomplished with SPBO with opposition-based learning. The ideal transformation parameter for the registration of breast MR images is determined in the proposed technique by using SPBO in conjunction with opposition-based learning. This parameter allows for the most accurate image registration possible. The success of the opposition-based learning algorithm applied to the SPBO is evaluated and compared with that of the GTO, BBO-EL, and PSO. The method that we have proposed includes a comparison of the quantitative and visual outcomes simultaneously. In the case of breast MRI registration, it has been deduced that SPBO with opposition-based learning performs statistically better than GTO, BBO-El, and PSO. This conclusion was reached after analyzing the results of the experiment.

In the future, we are going to make use of the method that was proposed in the course of the breast tumor progression registration process. In the future, we are also going to do research on a variety of cutting-edge meta-heuristic methods for use in breast MRI registration. Experiments are being carried out in this study for 2D MR images of the breast in order to gather data. The procedure that we have suggested is one that, for the purpose of a future study, may also be taken into consideration for 3D MRI. In addition to breast MRI registration, the suggested method is also applicable to brain MRI registration, which is going to be one of the most interesting areas of research in the years to come.

References

1. Zuo, C.S., Jiang, A.P., Buff, B.L., Mahon, T.G., Wong, T.Z.: Automatic motion correction for breast MR imaging. Radiology **198**, 903–906 (1996)
2. Krishnan, S., Chenevert, T.L., Helvie, M.A., Londy, F.L.: Linear motion correction in three dimensions applied to dynamic gadolinium enhanced breast imaging. Med. Phys. **26**, 707–714 (1999)
3. Kumar, R., et al.: Application of 3D registration for detecting lesions in magnetic resonance breast scans. Proc. SPIE. **2710**, 646–656 (1996)
4. Lucht, R., Knopp, M.V., Brix, G.: Elastic matching of dynamic MR mammographic images. MRM **43**, 9–16 (2000)
5. Rueckert, D., Sonoda, L.I., Hayes, C., Hill, D.L.G., Leach, M.O., Hawkes, D.J.: Nonrigid registration using free-form deformations: application to breast MR images. IEEE TMI **18**, 712–721 (1999)
6. Denton, E.R.E., et al.: Comparison and evaluation of rigid, affine and nonrigid registration of breast MR images. J. Comp. Ass. Tom. **23**, 800–805 (1999)
7. Lee, S., Wolberg, G., Shin, S.Y.: Scattered data interpolation with multilevel B-splines. IEEE Trans. Vis. Comp. Graph. **3**, 228–244 (1997)
8. Das, B., Mukherjee, V., Das, D.: Student psychology based optimization algorithm: a new population-based optimization algorithm for solving optimization problems. Adv. Eng. Softw. **146** (2020)
9. Nayak, S., Mondal, S.: Breast MRI registration using gorilla troops optimization. In: Bhattacharyya, S., Banerjee, J.S., Köppen, M. (eds) Human-Centric Smart Computing. Smart Innovation, Systems and Technologies, LNCS, vol. 316, pp. 1–14. Springer, Singapore (2023). https://doi.org/10.1007/978-981-19-5403-0_1
10. Chen, Y., He, F., Li, H., Zhang, D., Wu, Y.: A full migration BBO algorithm with enhanced population quality bounds for multimodal biomedical image registration. Appl. Soft Comput. **93**, 106335 (2020). ISSN 1568-9446, https://doi.org/10.1016/j.asoc.2020.106335.

11. Li, Q., Sato, I.: Multimodality image registration by particle swarm optimization of mutual information. In: Huang, D.-S., Heutte, L., Loog, M. (eds.) ICIC 2007. LNCS (LNAI), vol. 4682, pp. 1120–1130. Springer, Heidelberg (2007). https://doi.org/10.1007/978-3-540-74205-0_116
12. Rohlfing, T., Maurer, C.R., Bluemke, D.A., Jacobs, M.A.: Volume-preserving nonrigid registration of MR breast images using free-form deformation with an incompressibility constraint. IEEE TMI **22**, 730–741 (2003)
13. Tanner, C., et al.: Volume and shape preservation of enhancing lesions when applying nonrigid registration to a time series of contrast enhancing MR breast images. In: Delp, S.L., Di-Gioia, A.M., Jaramaz, B. (eds.), Proceedings of the Medical Image Computing and Computer-Assisted Intervention (MICCAI 2000), pp. 327–337 (2000)
14. Rohlfing, T., Maurer, C.R., Jr.: Nonrigid image registration in shared-memory multiprocessor environments with application to brains, breasts, and bees. IEEE ITB **7**, 16–25 (2003)
15. Derrac, J., Garćla, S., Molina, D., Herrera, F.: A practical tutorial on the use of non- parametric statistical tests as a methodology for comparing evolutionary and swarm intelligence algorithms. Swarm Evol. Comput. **1**, 3–18 (2011)
16. Clark, K., et al.: The Cancer Imaging Archive (TCIA): maintaining and operating a public information repository (2013)
17. Rahnamayan, S., Jesuthasan, J., Bourennani, F., Naterer, G.F., Salehinejad, F.: Centroid opposition-based differential evolution. Int. J. Appl. Metaheuristic Comput. (IJAMC) **5**(4), 1–25. IGI Global (2014)

Brain MRI Registration Using Fireworks Algorithm

Somen Nayak(✉) and Achyuth Sarkar

Department of Computer Science and Engineering, National Institute of Technology, Arunachal Pradesh, Jote, Itanagar, Arunachal Pradesh, India
`somen.phd24@nitap.ac.in`

Abstract. It is possible to gather or collect medical images from a variety of modalities, which results in the need to handle a variety of distinct practical issues associated with medical image registration. In multimodal registration, intensity-based registration approaches are being applied; similarly, these algorithms will add up extra images that have shared the information in a single representation by utilizing image transformation. The transformation of photographs into their optimal form is required in a significant way. It is of the utmost importance that the optimization of the similarity metric is performed on each of the distinct photos. In recent times, an enormous number of optimization strategies have been suggested, each of which concentrates on the constructing measures of the optimization component. However, there is still a significant amount of room for development, both in terms of the efficiency of the processes and the quality of the end product. The brain MRI registration process is very important for recognizing the spot differences that exist between the many MR images of the brain that are used for diagnostic purposes. In this paper, a brain MRI registration using a fireworks algorithm with the improved adaptive transfer function for explosion generation spark (FWA-IATFGS) is proposed. FWA-IATFGS is a Meta heuristics-based Optimization algorithm that we have proposed to register brain MR images, for multimodal medical image registration. In this paper, the FWA-IATFGS algorithm is used to register brain MR images. To begin, we extracted 30 magnetic resonance images of the brain from the data set using three different modalities, including T1, T2, and FLAIR. Following that, the photos are registered with the help of FWA-IATFGS. In the end, the photos from the register are extracted. The outcomes of the suggested method for brain MRI registration are compared with the outcomes of a registration method that is based on particle swarm optimization (PSO). The results of the experiments show that the proposed strategy achieves statistically superior results to other methods when it comes to the registration of MR images of the brain.

Keywords: Multimodality · image registration · medical image · feature-based · intensity-based · Mutual information · similarity metric · Metaheuristics

1 Introduction

Brain MRI (Magnetic Resonance Imaging) registration is one of the signature techniques of image processing. It provides a mechanism to align several MR pictures of the brain based on their corresponding feature, and it is considered to be one of the most important techniques in the field of image processing. During the registration process for Brain MRI, aligned features of the brain images are extracted to determine the physical space. There are a number of different methods or approaches that can be used to generate images, such as the generation of images using the electromagnetic spectrum, etc. The method of registration is capable of being utilized in very large areas. The registration of brain MRI scans is one of the application areas of image registration, and it is possible to do this registration for the purpose of clinical diagnosis.

A large amount of research has been done on image registration in a variety of domains. It has been used in a wide variety of applications collectively, including computer-guided operations, functional studies, treatment planning, diagnosis, and medical research. Moreover, it has also been utilized individually in a variety of applications. In the field of medical image registration, numerous strategies have been proposed over the course of the past few years in an effort to get results of a high standard of quality. The studies that are of the utmost importance to our investigation have been evaluated below, along with a brief summary of those studies. In order to carry out a comprehensive survey in this area, we will be directing some of our readers to surveys that have been conducted in this particular area. There are a plethora of different approaches that can be taken for the process of medical picture registration. The registration methods can be divided into two parts 1) feature-based and 2) intensity-based methods [1]. These techniques produce an alignment that is based solely on the image's significant and distinguishing features, such as its lines, corners, and curves. We rely heavily on a feature-based extraction approach, although these techniques play a crucial role in making the registration challenge more manageable. However, these techniques can only be applied to photos in which certain crucial and distinguishing details are clearly visible. The normalized mutual information (MI) of two images quantifies how dependent one image is on the other. Dependence is measured by a high value of normalized mutual information. Two images, M and N, have a mutual information that may be expressed as

$$NMI(M,N) = \left(\frac{H(M) + H(N)}{H(MN))}\right), \tag{1}$$

The information entropy of images M and N is denoted by H(M) and H(N), where M and N are the reference and floating images, respectively. The image's combined M and N entropy is denoted by H(MN).

On the other hand, the researcher has been responsible for a significant portion of the study, which most recently has been centered on intensity-based algorithms that make use of all of the image's data. It is possible to compute a massive amount of data, although doing so will result in an increase in the processing needs. In the same vein, it will not call for any additional amount of preprocessing in order to carry out the registration, in contrast to the feature-based algorithms that we have observed. The methods of medical picture registration can be broken down into the following categories, according to the categorization or division that we have discussed:

1.1 Feature-Based Approach

LY Hsu and colleagues [2] have developed an automatic multi-modality picture registration technique that is based on the extraction of hierarchical features. The essential operation of the algorithm will be broken down into two stages: the first is the feature extraction, and the second is the geometric matching. In this study, there are two fundamental categories of corresponding features that are being retrieved in a hierarchical fashion from the various modalities. The approach for medical image registration mentioned by Hassan Mahmoud et al. [3] makes use of Fuzzy C-Means (FCM) clustering for segmentation and Scale Invariant Feature Transform (SIFT) for matching important points in segmented regions. FCM has been widely utilized on feature vectors, which contain local information and are fully invariant to changes in scale, rotation, and illumination, to create effective segmentation. Then, the SIFT algorithm is applied to the scene and model images at the corresponding locations. Fuzzy c-Means (FCM) clustering segmentation and Speed Up the strong Feature (SURF) detectors have been discussed as a method for medical image registration by S. Gupta et al. [4]. Scene and model image features are extracted using SURF and then compared to complete the registration. Despite being very reliant on the dedication of the feature-based extraction algorithm, these techniques are quite helpful for simplifying the registration challenge. These techniques, however, are restricted to photos with prominent and distinguishable details.

1.2 Intensity-Based Approach

Integer programming is the original intended use of the scatter search algorithm (SS), which was developed or proposed by Glover et al. [5]. SS is one of many variants of evolutionary approaches. Complex optimization problems benefit greatly from this method. One of the alternative algorithms SS of SS, developed by Valsecchi et al. [6], is particularly well-suited to the picture registration process. Based on one of the most widely used 2-tier designs of the canonical SS [7], this variant of SS partitions the reference set into two levels. The highest-quality solutions are found in the first tier, which is also known as the quality reference set. The diversity reference collection, made up of very diverse answers, is the second tier. One of the powerful tools included in the SS template is tailored to medical image registration processes. [8]. It can be concluded that SS incorporates the generation of diversification method, which is wholly dependent on a frequency memory [9], to probe the uniform search space; the only solution is the combination method, which can employ the BLX-α crossover operato [10], while the superior method makes use of the PMX-α operator [11]. The reference set has been revised so that the best quality solutions are maintained in the quality reference set and the most diverse solutions are maintained in the diversity reference set. Last but not least, the redundancy control technique was commonly used to disregard the reference set, which comprises exclusively nearly identical copies of the same solution. For medical picture registration, Bermejo et al. [12] suggest the Coral Reef Optimisation Algorithm with Substrate Layers (CRO-SL). The CRO-SL algorithm is a refined version of the original Coral Reefs Optimisation (CRO) program [13], which is inspired by the dynamics of a real-world coral reef, including the reproduction of individual corals, the growth of the reef as a whole, and the competition between individual colonies for available space. The foundational CRO is based on the primary processes of coral reproduction and reef-building in the wild. To improve optimization and search speed, however, the CRO method can be extended to account for the vast number of mutual effects that the author has seen in actual reef ecosystems. In order to account for the unique features of coral reefs, the author suggested CRO-SL, wherein the presence of several substrate layers results in a distinct search strategy, the details of which are currently being established inside the CRO process. The evolutionary process permits a wide variety of exploratory techniques, any of which may provide useful clues toward the development of a robust and effective optimization method. The CRO-SL is one of the most essential methods for resolving the medical image registration problem because of its high levels of reliability, precision, and efficiency.

1.3 Objective

In order to register retinal images, researchers modified the fireworks algorithm [16] after reviewing the literature on Brain MRI registration and segmentation. Still, we have seen that no effort is being put into developing FWA-IATFGS-based brain MRI registration strategies. That's why we utilized an algorithm called FWA-IATFGS to align magnetic resonance pictures of the brain. The authors of this research propose using FWA-IATFGS [14] for MRI registration. The use of the FWA-IATFGS for brain MRI registration is also advocated for in this research. The experimental results of the suggested method are compared to those of PSO [15] based registration methods. Results from an experiment show that the suggested method beats PSO-based registration methods in a statistical comparison.

2 Materials and Methods

Performing transformations and rotations to align a pair of rigid body brain MR images is necessary for image registration so that the mutual information between the images may be accurately determined. Images of stiff bodies can be transformed by translating and rotating them. Affine transformations might be thought of as a special case of this type. Each image coordinates pair (p, q) will have an affine mapping specified into the coordinates of a new space (p', q') in terms of the translation distance (t_p, t_q). This idea can be stated as:

$$p' = p + t_p, \quad q' = q + t_q \tag{2}$$

OR we can write $M' = M + T$, where

$$M' = \begin{vmatrix} p' \\ q' \end{vmatrix}, M = \begin{vmatrix} p \\ q \end{vmatrix}, T = \begin{vmatrix} t_p \\ t_q \end{vmatrix}$$

Many of these changes can be combined into a single matrix by multiplying the original matrices together, making composition of them a breeze. This implies that we can skip the step of resampling the image data if we plan on rotating it. Transposing the transformation matrix always yields the inverse affine transformation.

The next step after translation is rotation. A single angle will suffice to describe a rotation in two dimensions. A point on a well-defined two-dimensional plane with coordinates (p_1, p_2) is assumed. The transformation can also be used to generate a rotation of the defined coordinates (p_1, p_2) by *alpha* radians around the origin, yielding a new set of coordinates (q_1, q_2).

$$p_1 = \cos(\alpha)p_1 + \sin(\alpha)p_2 \tag{3}$$

$$q_2 = -\sin(\alpha)p_1 + \cos(\alpha)p_2 \tag{4}$$

Parameters like p', q' for translation, and *alpha* for rotation, which describe the rigid-body brain MR image transformation matrix, must be estimated before performing rigid registration of a pair of brain MR images. Therefore, we are optimizing the parameters for translation and rotation using the fireworks algorithm.

The Fireworks Algorithm is a type of swarm intelligence algorithm that uses meta-heuristics to search through a large solution space in the hopes that one or more of the many randomly chosen points within a given area will yield promising results from a more thorough search in the immediate vicinity. The fireworks algorithm is based on and can be understood in terms of the fireworks' explosion procedure: explosions take place at predetermined or fixed sites, and "sparks" radiate outward from the epicenter. Spark placements are considered one by one until the best option is identified. Finding $Z*$ such that $f(Z*) = F$ is an optimization problem. The algorithm will keep running until a spark is located close enough to $Z*$. The first step of the fireworks algorithm is to decide on N random starting points for the explosions. Next, the distance from the optimal site is used to establish the total number of sparks and their specific locations. If an optimal position is discovered after evaluating each possible position of fireworks, the program ends; otherwise, it iteratively evaluates n additional possible positions before starting over.

It's best practice for any search algorithm to encourage exploration at the search's outset and exploitation at its close. The search process relies heavily on both traversal and exploitation, thus striking a balance between the two is crucial. The distance between the best and worst fireworks is always the greatest.

In order to find the best transformation parameters for registration, this paper employs a variant of FWA called FWA-IATFGS. Here is how we characterize it:

$$\tau_i = \frac{1}{1 + exp(w.r)} \quad (5)$$

The parameter w $in(0,1)$ of this transfer function controls the fireworks' total scoring value. The following equation describes a linear increase in the control parameter w over the interval $(w_{max}, w_{min}) = (0.1, 0.9)$.

$$w = w_{min} + (w_{max} - w_{min}) \times \left(\frac{fitcount}{FEs}\right) \quad (6)$$

where fitcount is the current count of function evaluations and FEs= 5000 is the maximum number of times a function can be evaluated in this iteration. The control parameter w is utilized to dampen adaptation's effectiveness in the early search phase while amplifying it in the late search phase. The ith firework is represented by $X_i(x_1, x_2, \ldots, x_D)$ where D is the dimension. The explosion of fireworks and random mutation in fireworks are carried out by the Algorithm 1 and 2 respectively. The complete algorithm of FWA-IATFGS is given in Algorithm 3.

Algorithm 1: Explosion Spark Generation

---
1 Initialize the spark location: $x_e \leftarrow X_i$
2 Select the number of position Randomly: $P \leftarrow [D \times rand(0, 1)]$
3 **for** $p \leftarrow 1$ **to** P **do**
4 $\quad$ Select the position's index $k\epsilon[1, D]$ randomly
5 $\quad$ Calculate the displacement: $\Delta x \leftarrow A_i \times rand(-1, 1)$
6 $\quad$ $x_{ek} \leftarrow x_{ek} + \Delta x$
7 $\quad$ **if** $x_{ek} < X_{min}$ *or* $x_{ek} > X_{min}$ **then**
8 $\quad\quad$ $x_{ek} \leftarrow X_{min} + |x_{ek}|\%(X_{max} - X_{min})$
9 $\quad$ **end if**
10 **end**

Algorithm 2: Random Mutation

---
1 Initialize the spark location: $x_g \leftarrow X_r$
2 Select the number of position Randomly: $P \leftarrow [D \times rand(0, 1)]$
3 **for** $p \leftarrow 1$ **to** P **do**
4 $\quad$ Select the position's index $k\epsilon[1, D]$ randomly
5 $\quad$ $x_{gk} \leftarrow X_{min} + (X_{max} - X_{min}) \times rand(0, 1)$
6 **end**

Algorithm 3: FWA-IATFGS algorithm

1. Initialize N locations X in $[X_{min}, X_{max}]^D$
2. Evaluate the objective function values f
3. **for** *termination criteria* **do**
4.   Calculate the control parameter w using Eq. (6)
5.   Sort the fireworks in ascending order with respect to f
6.   Calculate the score values r_i for each firework
7.   **for** $i \leftarrow 1$ *to* N **do**
8.   Calculate the ATF values T_i using Eq. (5)
9.   Calculate the number of "explosion sparks" S_i using the formula $S_i = M \times \frac{T_i}{\sum_{i=1}^{n} T_i}$, Where M is the maximum number of explosion sparks.
10.   Calculate the amplitude A_i of explosion using the formula $A_i = A \times \frac{T_{(N-i+1)}}{\sum_{i=1}^{n} T_i}$ where $A = (X_{max} - X_{min})$ is the magnitude for explosion. The explosion Sparks for i^{th} fireworks are created using Algorithm 1.
11.   **end**
12.   **for** $i \leftarrow 1$ *to* N **do**
13.   Generation of explosion sparks and mutated sparks
14.   Evaluate the objective function values of sparks
15.   Select the group best location from i^{th} fireworks and its all type of sparks
16.   **end**
17. **end**

3 Results and Discussion

In this research, we suggest employing FWA-IATFGS for brain MRI registration and comparing its results to those obtained using the PSO algorithm. A total of 30 MR pictures are used, 10 from each imaging modality. Four patients' or subjects' brain tumour progression datasets [17,18] are obtained from the Cancer Imaging Archive in the United States. These newly diagnosed glioblastoma patients will get chemotherapy. Each patient is entitled to two MRIs, one at progression and one within 90 days of CRT completion. T1-weighted, T2-weighted, and FLAIR MRI images are employed for registration in this study. patients underwent surgery followed by concurrent chemo-radiation therapy (CRT) followed by adjuvant, with MRI slices downsized to 256×256. The following values are used for FWA-IATFGS's parameters: When $N = 10$, $M = 40$, and $FES = 5000$, the game is over. The values for a and b are 0.4 and 0.8.

The parameters of PSO are set as follows: Population size (swarm size) = 50, $\kappa = 1, \phi_1 = 2.1$, $\phi_2 = 1.2$, $\phi = 0.8$, Constriction Coefficient$(\chi) = 0.7298$, inertia coefficient (W) = χ, damping ratio of inertia coefficient $(W_damp) = 0.99$, Personal Acceleration Coefficient$(C_1) = \chi \times \phi_1$ and Social Acceleration Coefficient $(C_2) = \chi \times \phi_2$, maximum number of iteration = 100.

Table 1. Mean and standard deviation of NMI over 10 independent runs for two different modalities T_1 and T_2

MRI#	FWA-IATFGS		PSO	
	Mean	Std.	Mean	Std.
1	1.156866301	5.61E-06	**1.156866414**	4.06E-06
2	1.168214663	9.74E-06	**1.168218974**	1.26E-05
3	**1.166834253**	2.15E-05	1.16681956	2.25E-05
4	**1.211056066**	5.53E-05	1.211039974	5.61E-05
5	**1.198608439**	4.10E-06	1.198043278	1.77E-03
6	**1.181397592**	7.42E-05	1.181285652	1.43E-04
7	**1.187390985**	4.96E-05	1.187366806	0.00016194
8	**1.181083356**	1.86E-05	1.180941886	0.000308115
9	**1.178994244**	8.78E-05	1.178910939	0.000353925
10	**1.173880617**	1.17E-04	1.173778878	0.000288197
11	**1.217703978**	0.000155275	1.217667146	0.000195276
12	**1.220082684**	4.89E-05	1.219781206	0.000286484
13	**1.209425903**	4.21E-05	1.209407112	8.32E-05
14	**1.184966881**	4.49E-06	1.184951772	4.57E-05
15	**1.187274994**	8.07E-05	1.18725545	0.000110378
16	**1.183180997**	5.81E-06	1.183177616	4.53E-06
17	**1.172752729**	2.66E-05	1.171973648	0.002403868
18	**1.178834221**	2.22E-05	1.178833174	2.22E-05
19	**1.176849344**	2.68E-05	1.176813916	4.43E-05
20	**1.187779033**	2.13E-05	1.186515055	0.003941677
21	**1.170242298**	2.35E-05	1.170238418	3.81E-05
22	**1.174978366**	3.11E-05	1.174970673	3.47E-05
23	1.171240917	3.43E-05	**1.171249323**	1.44E-05
24	1.174970133	2.39E-05	**1.174974642**	2.40E-05
25	**1.174796829**	2.07E-05	1.174785603	2.99E-05
26	**1.178376315**	2.48E-05	1.178351782	2.78E-05
27	**1.154881583**	2.72E-05	1.154880438	3.23E-05
28	**1.155545847**	5.16E-05	1.155517622	8.80E-05
29	**1.162480258**	7.38E-05	1.162428045	9.67E-05
30	1.166716304	7.28E-05	**1.166725964**	0.000112863

The PSO-based registration method is employed herein for that very purpose. Thirty MR images from two modalities (T_1 and T_2) are used over 10 iterations of each approach. In Table 1, we see the average and standard deviation from 10 separate trials. Results that are more favorable are indicated by boldface type. It

Table 2. Mean and standard deviation of NMI over 10 independent runs for two different modalities T_1 and FLAIR

MRI#	FWA-IATFGS		PSO	
	Mean	Std.	Mean	Std.
1	**1.16978978**	4.08E-05	1.169770426	4.24E-05
2	**1.182229401**	9.02E-05	1.182224951	9.02E-05
3	**1.182264878**	6.55E-06	1.18226291	5.70E-06
4	**1.207347175**	2.44E-05	1.207340385	2.40E-05
5	**1.201551685**	3.20E-05	1.200525651	0.003189683
6	**1.215729286**	2.02E-05	1.215710721	2.30E-05
7	1.214896792	0.000116584	**1.214930293**	0.000120547
8	**1.220251947**	4.69E-05	1.220233123	6.29E-05
9	**1.214564077**	4.08E-05	1.214521209	6.71E-05
10	**1.224678269**	7.80E-06	1.224668418	1.38E-05
11	**1.224835663**	0.000148526	1.22479898	0.00017594
12	**1.233832208**	6.49E-05	1.233791812	0.000125778
13	1.236797291	0.000102662	**1.236833179**	0.000116893
14	**1.155421549**	3.02E-06	1.155402241	5.06E-05
15	**1.159385702**	0.000123458	1.159353704	0.000101225
16	1.171607254	4.25E-05	**1.171639431**	4.44E-05
17	**1.196461546**	3.03E-05	1.196459831	3.65E-05
18	**1.195788895**	2.15E-05	1.195788815	2.35E-05
19	**1.192304849**	2.02E-05	1.1922991	1.50E-05
20	1.195617955	3.37E-05	**1.195619164**	4.17E-05
21	**1.192885842**	8.03E-06	1.192873769	8.95E-06
22	1.192770119	9.84E-06	**1.192770972**	7.98E-06
23	1.190912932	2.57E-05	**1.190918756**	1.89E-05
24	**1.194264727**	1.43E-05	1.194265925	1.96E-05
25	**1.196114127**	4.01E-05	1.19610454	4.54E-05
26	**1.196157178**	3.55E-05	1.196144906	2.01E-05
27	**1.198333907**	1.53E-05	1.198299596	2.72E-05
28	**1.208037812**	3.46E-05	1.208037196	3.95E-05
29	**1.216811893**	1.43E-05	1.216119425	0.002194361
30	**1.223231667**	1.99E-05	1.222582785	0.00203439

has been found experimentally that PSO methods produce the highest standard deviation of maximum images; this is in contrast to the fireworks algorithm with the enhanced adaptive transfer function for explosion spark generation (FWA-IATFGS), which produces the lowest standard deviation of MR images of the brain. The picture presents the qualitative, i.e. visual, outcomes of brain MRI

Table 3. Mean and standard deviation of NMI over 10 independent runs for two different modalities T_2 and FLAIR

MRI#	FWA-IATFGS		PSO	
	Mean	*Std.*	*Mean*	*Std.*
1	**1.214546512**	2.81E-05	1.214534937	2.36E-05
2	**1.223322795**	1.42E-05	1.213698841	0.024642439
3	**1.221931002**	1.01E-05	1.221930608	9.31E-06
4	**1.203866854**	2.16E-05	1.193168584	0.003779027
5	**1.193180793**	4.34E-05	1.193168584	3.29E-05
6	**1.174204076**	2.31E-05	1.174195948	2.35E-05
7	**1.17758549**	0.000116584	1.17757589	0.000112527
8	**1.172293931**	3.25E-05	1.172066695	0.000407054
9	**1.175726872**	1.86E-05	1.175726019	6.15E-06
10	**1.174362763**	2.85E-05	1.174095185	0.000777148
11	**1.192956195**	9.85E-05	1.192871625	9.78E-05
12	**1.199893702**	0.000305081	1.1988998	0.002937688
13	**1.200141601**	8.38E-05	1.200106794	9.39E-05
14	**1.173056409**	8.72E-05	1.172969542	9.35E-05
15	**1.179888067**	1.36E-05	1.179872075	2.14E-05
16	1.166431	7.16E-05	**1.166464153**	7.38E-05
17	**1.199957336**	1.96E-05	1.199952537	2.30E-05
18	**1.204891678**	2.76E-05	1.204880192	2.24E-05
19	**1.212161516**	2.72E-05	1.210929546	0.003850829
20	**1.212801986**	4.00E-05	1.212794095	5.12E-05
21	**1.187978293**	8.07E-06	1.18797239	8.06E-06
22	**1.191625734**	9.40E-05	1.191617083	0.000132386
23	**1.192152332**	0.000126128	1.192073304	0.000193115
24	1.192009161	1.55E-05	**1.192016886**	1.73E-05
25	**1.192041909**	9.07E-06	1.192034748	4.88E-06
26	1.195556041	1.85E-05	**1.195560621**	1.67E-05
27	**1.162586461**	3.98E-05	1.162547479	7.12E-05
28	**1.157162331**	0.000119019	1.157082927	0.000155548
29	**1.164963947**	0.000178127	1.164706292	0.000860905
30	**1.170947886**	0.000113943	1.170917432	0.000126041

registration using PSO and FWA-IATFGS. It has been seen or can be inferred from the experimental data that the PSO technique is unable to produce a better solution than the FWA-IATFGS when comparing the quantitative and qualitative results of brain MRI registration. This is due to the fact that the

PSO method perpetually experiences early convergence and becomes stuck at the local optimum.

In this study, 30 MR images from both the T_1 and FLAIR modalities are processed through each of the 10 iterations of each approach. Table 2 displays the Mean and standard deviation from 10 separate run. The better outcomes are shown by the typefaces that are bolded. FWA-IATFGS outperforms PSO in the T_1 and FLAIR modality experiments in 24 of 30 MR images, while PSO outperforms FWA-IATFGS in 6 of 30 MR images. This indicates that FWA-IATFGS is more effective in the T_1 and FLAIR modality.

Thirty brain MR images from two additional modalities (T_2 and FLAIR) are subjected to the same experiment over 10 independent runs. In Table 3, we display the Mean and standard deviation over 10 independent runs. The better outcomes are shown by the typefaces that are bolded. Experiments show that FWA-IATFGS outperforms PSO in the T_1 and FLAIR modalities, with the proposed algorithm producing better results for 27 images out of 30 MR images and the PSO technique producing better results for only 3 images of 30 MR images.

3.1 Statistical Analysis

To do a statistical analysis of numerical data. Non-parametric Wilcoxon Signed Ranks Test [19] performed on the mean of 30 brain MR images 10 independent runs across two pairs (T_1, T_2),(T_1, FLAIR) and (T_2, FLAIR) to determine statistical significance. This test has a .01 level of significance. The results of the statistical analysis have been tabulated and can be found in Table 4. This table suggests that FWA-IATFGS is superior to PSO when it comes to registering brain MRIs.

Table 4. Wilcoxon Signed Rank Test Results. R^+: sum of positive ranks, R^-: sum of negative ranks.

Modality	R^+	R^-	Z	p-value
T1-T2	432.00	33.00	−4.103	0.000041
T1-FLAIR	376.00	89.00	−2.952	0.003162
T2-FLAIR	438.00	27.00	−4.226794	0.000024

Figures 1, 2, and 3 show the visual quality of the results of the two approaches of brain MR image registration. Although we have gotten better quantitative results with FWA-IATFGS, it is extremely difficult to visually discern between the registered images produced by the two approaches.

Since PSO likewise experiences premature convergence and becomes caught in local optima, it is clear that it cannot deliver better solutions than FWA-IATFGS.

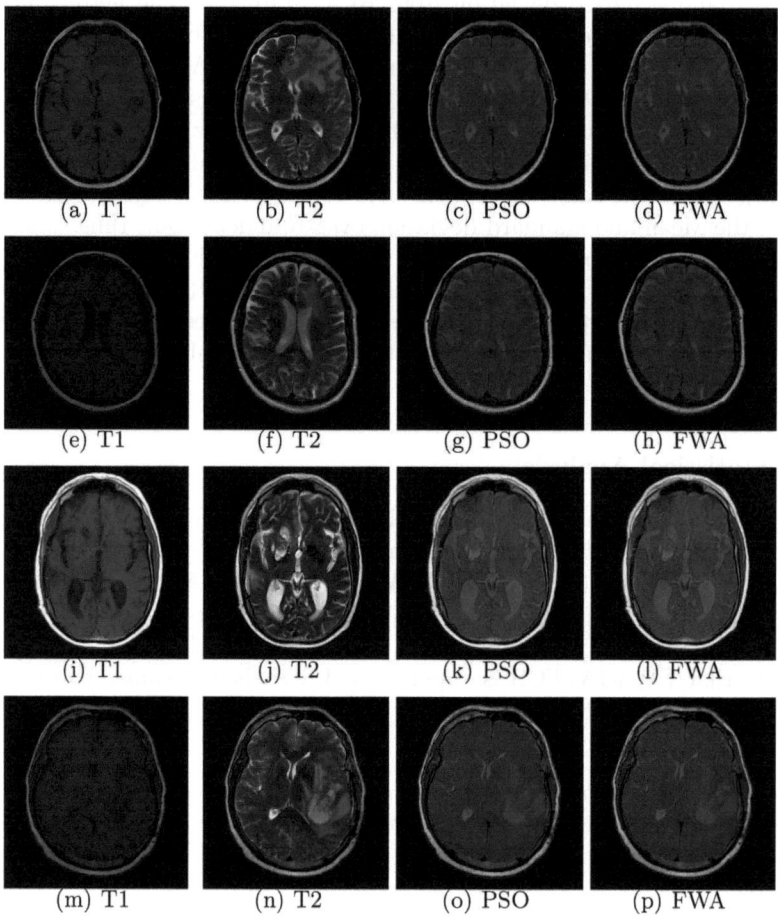

Fig. 1. Registration results of T1 and T2 MR images.

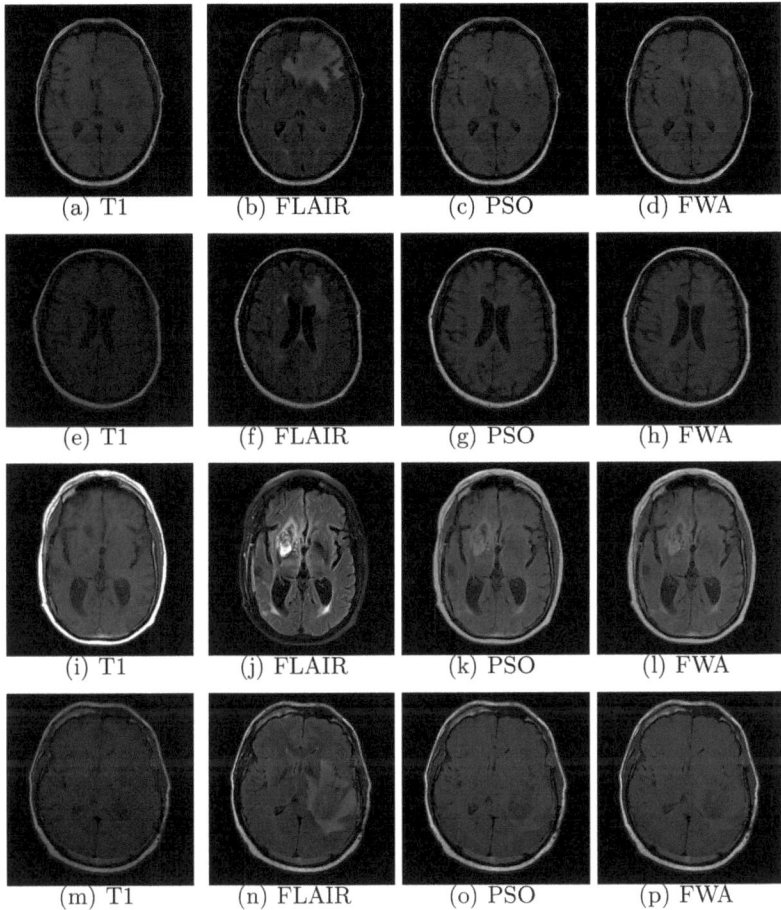

Fig. 2. Registration results of T1 and Flair MR images.

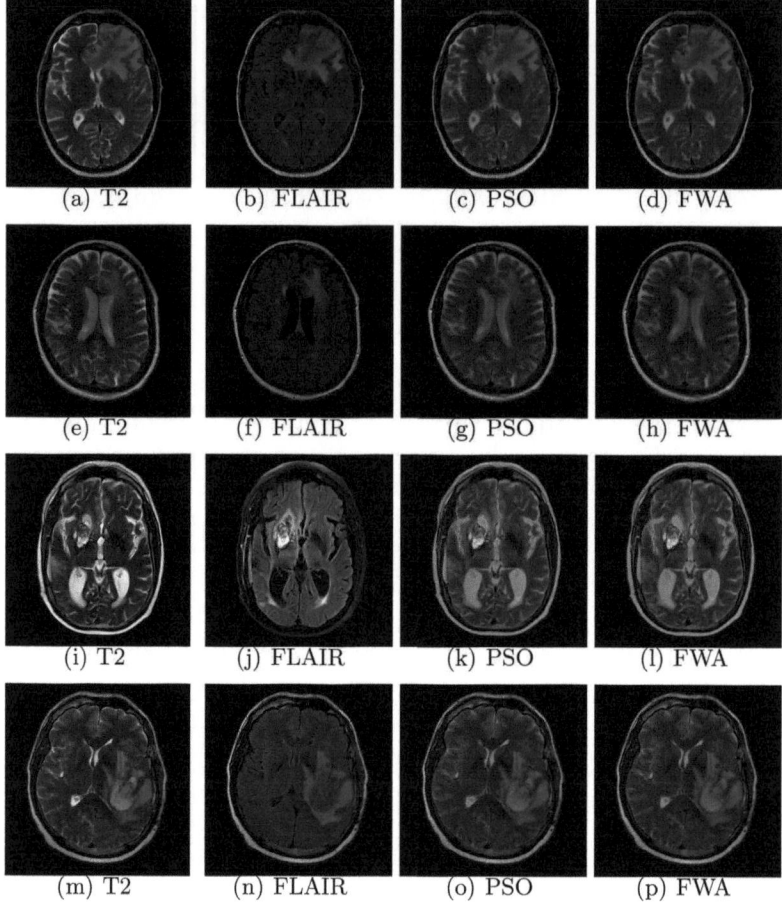

Fig. 3. Registration results of T2 and FLAIR MR images.

4 Conclusion and Future Work

In this work, we suggest employing FWA-IATFGS to register brain MRI scans. The suggested method utilizes FWA-IATFGS to seek out the best transformation parameter for brain MR image registration. The suggested method is evaluated against a popular registration method based on particle swarm optimization (PSO). Comparisons are made between quantitative and qualitative findings. The proposed technique outperforms PSO statistically.

In the future, we hope to incorporate the proposed approach into the brain tumour registration procedure. We also research competing cutting-edge metaheuristic brain MRI registration techniques. The brain MR images used in this work are 2 dimensions. In the future, researchers may potentially think about using the proposed approach to 3D MRI. In addition to brain MRI registration, breast MRI registration is a promising area of research for the suggested method.

References

1. Zitova, B., Flusser, J.: Image registration methods: a survey. Image Vis. Comput. **21**(11), 977–1000 (2003)
2. Hsu, L.-Y., Loew, M.H.: Fully automatic 3D feature-based registration of multi-modality medical images. Image Vis. Comput. **19**(1–2), 75–85 (2001)
3. Mahmoud, H., Masulli, F., Rovetta, S.: Feature-based medical image registration using a fuzzy clustering segmentation approach. In: Peterson, L.E., Masulli, F., Russo, G. (eds.) CIBB 2012. LNCS, vol. 7845, pp. 37–47. Springer, Heidelberg (2013). https://doi.org/10.1007/978-3-642-38342-7_4
4. Gupta, S., Chakarvarti, S., Zaheeruddin, M.: Medical image registration based on fuzzy c-means clustering segmentation approach using SURF. Int. J. Biomed. Eng. Technol. **20**, 33–50 (2016)
5. Glover, F.: Heuristics for integer programming using surrogate constraints. Decis. Sci. **8**(1), 156–166 (1977)
6. Valsecchi, A., Damas, S., Santamaría, J., Marrakchi-Kacem, L.: Intensity-based image registration using scatter search. Artif. Intell. Med. **60**(3), 151–163 (2014)
7. Laguna, M., Marti, R.: Scatter Search: Methodology and Implementations in C, vol. 24. Springer, Cham (2012)
8. Santamaría, J., Cordón, O., Damas, S., Alemán, I., Botella, M.: A scatter search based technique for pair-wise 3D range image registration in forensic anthropology. Soft Comput. **11**(9), 819–828 (2007)
9. Laguna, M., Glover, F., Martı, R.: Advances in Evolutionary Computation: Theory and Applications. Springer, Cham (2003)
10. Eshelman, L.J., Schaffer, J.D.: Real-coded genetic algorithms and interval schemata. In: Foundations of Genetic Algorithms, vol. 2, pp. 187–202. Elsevier (1993)
11. Lozano, M., Herrera, F., Krasnogor, N., Molina, D.: Real-coded memetic algorithms with crossover hill-climbing. Evol. Comput. **12**(3), 273–302 (2004)
12. Bermejo, E., Chica, M., Damas, S., Salcedo-Sanz, S., Cordón, O.: Coral reef optimization with substrate layers for medical image registration. Swarm Evol. Comput. **42**, 138–159 (2018)
13. Salcedo Sanz, S., Del Ser, J., Landa-Torres, I., Gil-López, S., Portilla-Figueras, A.: The coral reefs optimization algorithm: an efficient meta-heuristic for solving hard optimization problems. In: Proceedings of the 15th International Conference on Applied Stochastic Models and Data Analysis (ASMDA2013), pp. 751–758. Mataró (2013)
14. Si, T., Mukhopadhyay, A.: An improved adaptive transfer function for explosion spark generation in fireworks algorithm. Adv. Intell. Syst. Comput. 1154 (2020)
15. Wachowaik, M.P., Smolikova, R, Zurada, J.M., Elmaghraby, A.S.: An approach to multimodal biomedical image registration utilizing particle swarm optimization. IEEE Trans. Evol. Comput. **8**(3) (2004)
16. Tuba, E., Tuba1, M., Dolicanin, E.: Adjusted fireworks algorithm applied to retinal image registration. Stud. Inform. Control, **26**(1) (2017)
17. Schmainda, K., Prah, M.: Data from brain-tumor-progression. the cancer imaging archive. https://doi.org/10.7937/K9/TCIA.2018.15quzvnb
18. Clark, K., et al.: The cancer imaging archive (TCIA): maintaining and operating a public information repository. J. Digit. Imaging **26**, 1045–1057 (2013)
19. Derrac, J., García, S., Molina, D., Herrera, F.: A practical tutorial on the use of non-parametric statistical tests as a methodology for comparing evolutionary and swarm in- intelligence algorithms. Swarm Evol. Comput. **1**, 3–18 (2011)

Quantifying Climate Change Effects on Standard Minimum and Maximum Average Temperature Extremes in Bangladesh: A Machine Learning Regression Analysis from Past to Present

Muhammad Ebrahim Hossain[1], Shahriar Siddique Ayon[1],
Md Saef Ullah Miah[1(✉)], Zahid Hasan Talukder Anik[1],
M. Mostafizur Rahman[2], and Mufti Mahmud[3,4,5]

[1] Department of Computer Science, Faculty of Science and Technology,
American International University-Bangladesh (AIUB), Dhaka 1229, Bangladesh
md.saefullah@gmail.com

[2] Department of Mathematics, Faculty of Science and Technology,
American International University-Bangladesh (AIUB), Dhaka 1229, Bangladesh

[3] Information and Computer Science Department, King Fahd University
of Petroleum and Minerals, Dhahran 31261, Saudi Arabia
mufti.mahmud@kfupm.edu.sa

[4] SDAIA-KFUPM Joint Research Center for AI, King Fahd University of Petroleum and Minerals, Dhahran 31261, Saudi Arabia

[5] Interdisciplinary Research Center for Bio Systems and Machines, King Fahd University of Petroleum and Minerals, Dhahran 31261, Saudi Arabia

Abstract. The impact of climate change on temperature extremes is particularly significant in regions like Bangladesh, and it is a pressing global concern. To quantify the effects of climate change on Bangladesh's standard minimum and maximum average temperature extremes, this study uses machine learning techniques on historical records from 1981 to 2010 with current data from 2022. By utilising information from the Statistical Yearbook Bangladesh 2022, which includes temperature readings from 44 different stations, this study offers a thorough evaluation of temperature fluctuations in various geographic areas. Several machine learning models, including Random Forest, Ridge Regression, Bayesian Ridge Regression, K-Nearest Neighbours Regression, and an Ensemble Model, are applied as part of the methodology. The following evaluation metrics are used: R-squared (R^2), Mean Absolute Percentage Error (MAPE), Root Mean Squared Error (RMSE), Mean Squared Error (MSE), and Root Mean Squared Logarithmic Error (RMSLE). The study's conclusions highlight notable yearly temperature variations and dynamic patterns of climate change in important places like Khulna, Chattogram, Teknaf, and Dhaka. The outcomes show that, compared to other models, the Ensemble Model performs better across evaluation metrics and is the most successful at predicting temperature extremes. Furthermore, comparing the actual and predicted temperatures for a few selected stations reveals significant deviations that underscore Bangladesh's changing climate dynamics. This research enhances our understanding of the impact of climate change on temperature extremes in Bangladesh. This study helps stakeholders, researchers, and policymakers better understand the difficulties brought on by the region's changing climate patterns.

1 Introduction

Bangladesh is a South Asian nation that deals with a wide range of environmental issues, most of which are made worse by the consequences of climate change. Bangladesh's topographical complexity and geographic location make it an ideal place to investigate how climate change affects weather patterns, especially when it comes to standard minimum and maximum average temperature extremes [4,8].

Bangladesh faces pressing socio-economic challenges, rising temperatures, and ecosystem disruption that necessitate quick adaptation measures [18]. This study employs machine learning to gauge climate change effects on Bangladesh's temperature extremes, revealing evolving trends from historical records to current observations and offering key insights into the nation's dynamic climate. Bangladesh, in South Asia, faces a diverse climate influenced by geography [6,10].

This study is driven by the urgent need to comprehend the evolving climate trends in Bangladesh. Focusing on temperature extremes, it aims to unveil nuanced variations in conventional minimum and maximum average temperatures. Using machine learning regression analysis, the study seeks to provide a comprehensive understanding of how climate change has impacted temperature patterns across the nation, extrapolating insights from historical data to current observations for a more informed perspective.

Analyzing climate-driven temperature shifts in Bangladesh is crucial for sectors like infrastructure, health, agriculture, and disaster management [5,9,12,19]. This research offers concise insights for stakeholders and policymakers to develop adaptable strategies in changing climate conditions.

The research methodology utilized in this study is a systematic strategy that includes machine learning regression models and temperature records from 1981 to 2010 derived from dependable data sources. Temperature extremes are analyzed and predicted in Bangladesh using machine learning regression models, including Random Forest Regression, Ridge Regression, Bayesian Ridge Regression, K-Nearest Neighbors Regression and an Ensemble Model.

This research has ramifications that go beyond Bangladesh. Using machine learning techniques for climate analysis provides a reproducible model for comprehending temperature variations and their effects in other sensitive places worldwide as climate change continues to impact regions internationally. The knowledge gained from this research could help shape climate-related decision-making procedures and support proactive steps to mitigate and adapt to the effects of climate change.

2 Literature Review

Khan et al. [14] conducted a comprehensive study assessing the impact of global warming on climate extremes in Bangladesh, a highly vulnerable country to climate change. Using a subset of the Expert Team on Climate Change Detection and Indices (ETCCDI) index set, the study investigated extreme temperature and precipitation trends at warming levels of 1.5 °C, 2 °C and 4 °C. Based on high-resolution regional climate model ensembles, their analysis showed significant increases in temperature rise, extreme rainfall, and maximum rainfall, along with upward and downward shifts in warm and cold indices. The study has limitations due to biased data constraints complex and uncertain climate models, but it still predicts more extreme rainfall and extended dry spells in the northeast and southeast. Challenges include downscaling issues, constrained emission scenarios, and limited variable focus, impacting the study's comprehensiveness and practical relevance.

In recent years, the adoption of machine learning (ML) techniques has surged, particularly in research projects exploring the practical applications of wearable technology and algorithms for gait data analysis [16]. Huntingford et al. [11] categorize these approaches into wearable, ambient, and vision-based methods. Notably, historical trends in climate change have been revealed through ML regression analyses. Climate change is still a challenging scientific issue despite significant advancements in numerical weather forecasting since the 1950s. They proposed machine learning (ML) and artificial intelligence (AI) as tools for climate research, emphasizing their potential for addressing discrepancies in Earth System Models (ESMs). The parameterization of sub-grid processes in ESMs presents difficulties, prompting researchers to look into ML and AI techniques to reduce inter-ESM uncertainty. Despite the advantages, challenges such as the need for high-quality and diverse datasets, as well as the inherent complexity of climate systems, must be taken into account. The complexity of these systems may make it difficult for ML and AI models to accurately depict real-world situations.

Kafy et al. [13] discovered a significant relationship between urban transformations and elevated Land Surface Temperature (LST), posing challenges for environmental engineers and urban planners battling the Surface Urban Heat Island (SUHI) phenomenon. Utilizing the Support Vector Machine (SVM) algorithm and Landsat thermal bands, the study scrutinized Land Use/Land Cover (LULC) variations from 1999 to 2019 due to rapid urbanization. Cellular Automata (CA) machine learning algorithms were used to simulate LULC and seasonal LST scenarios for 2029 and 2039, and the CA model demonstrated excellent accuracy with an overall kappa value of 0.82. MSE and correlation coefficient (R) values of 0.523 and 0.796 in summer and 0.6023 and 0.831 in winter for 2029 and 2039, respectively, were obtained from Artificial Neural Network (ANN) model validation. Simulations predict a notable urban area increase by 9.23% (2029) and 13.59% (2039) compared to 2019, with temperatures exceeding 36 °C. This emphasizes the connection between urbanization and rising LST.

However, due to potential limitations in satellite data quality and uncertainties in climate models, caution is required.

Mahabub et al. [15] (2021) concentrate on the application of machine learning (ML) models for weather forecasting in Bangladesh, a region known for frequent weather changes. Their novel approach entails using ensemble regression algorithms on a raw dataset collected from the Bangladesh Meteorological Division from 2012 to 2018. The dataset includes variables such as wind speed, humidity, temperature, and rainfall from 33 weather stations. The DTR and CatBoost algorithms outperform existing literature metrics using ML-based regression algorithms, according to the study. However, ensemble models for weather prediction face challenges such as a lack of historical data, high computational demands, and uncertainty in representing future climate patterns, which is exacerbated by the dynamic nature of weather systems.

Oyshee et al. [17] advocate integrating machine learning with demand-side management (DSM) strategies for modern grid management amidst rising electricity prices. The study finds strong correlations (0.84, 0.87, 0.89) between meteorological data and a synthesized dataset of Bangladesh's national grid load consumption using the Pearson correlation coefficient. The study finds temperature dependencies and patterns in load consumption using k-Means clustering. Theoretical load shifting potentials are demonstrated by a peak shaving and load shifting algorithm, which produces percentages of 8.83, 9.07, and 8.79 for 2018, 2019, and 2021. Although the paper presents a machine learning model for clustering load and temperature behavior, it also notes limitations in terms of generalization, limited datasets and data quality. It acknowledges possible shortcomings in representing the dynamics of real-world grids, outside influences, interpretability, and viability of widespread adoption. Nevertheless, the research lacks comprehensive validation against alternative models and ignores behavioral and social factors that impact load-shifting strategies' effectiveness.

In order to mitigate climate change and suggest preventive measures, Shams et al. [20] highlight the critical role that weather forecasting plays, particularly in predicting temperatures. The researchers use machine learning techniques to forecast global temperatures based on ten features: aerosols, TSI, MEI, year, month, CH4, N2O, CFC.12, and CFC.11. The relationship between the average global temperature and several variables is investigated using a variety of machine learning regressors, such as Linear Regression (LR), Random Forest (RF), Decision Tree (DT), K-Nearest Neighbour (KNN), Support Vector Machine (SVM), and Cat Boost Regressor (CBR). Notably, the CBR outperformed recent machine learning approaches, yielding impressive results. The Cat Boost Regressor achieved Mean Square Error (MSE), Root Mean Square Error (RMSE), Minimum Absolute Error (MAE), and R^2 determination coefficients of 0.003, 0.054, 0.0036, and 92.40%, respectively. Climate models, on the other hand, face challenges such as limited data quality, generalization issues, stationarity assumptions, and difficulty capturing the complexity of climate systems, introducing uncertainties and potentially ethical concerns in prediction misuse and unintended consequences of policy decisions.

3 Methodology

In this section, we outline the methodology utilized in this study. The proposed methodology encompasses several key steps: data collection, data preprocessing and model selection. Figure 1 provides a graphical representation of the proposed methodology.

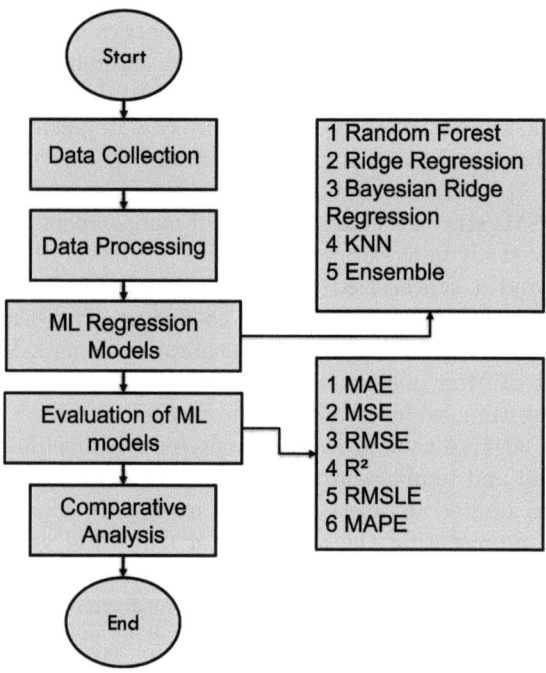

Fig. 1. Overview of the methodology employed in this study for standard minimum and maximum average temperature prediction in Bangladesh.

3.1 Data Collection and Processing

The dataset employed in this study was derived from the Statistical Yearbook Bangladesh 2022, 42nd edition pages 30–34, a comprehensive compilation containing vital information on various aspects of Bangladesh, including land, environment, area, population, agriculture, fishery and more [7]. Specifically, our study focused on the standard minimum and maximum average temperature records for each month spanning 1981–2010. Moreover, an independent dataset was employed for model testing, containing values specifically related to the standard minimum and maximum average temperatures recorded monthly throughout the year 2022. The temperature records are arranged annually and monthly to give a thorough overview. The dataset is noteworthy since it includes 44 distinct stations carefully chosen to reflect regions with larger populations. These stations include prominent places like Dhaka, Chittagong, Cox's Bazar, Rajshahi, Dinajpur, Khulna, Teknaf, and other areas. Including diverse geographical locations ensures a comprehensive representation of temperature variations across Bangladesh. A snapshot of the dataset is provided in Fig. 2. After collecting the data, it was checked for null and missing values. The employed dataset contains no null values and no missing values.

1.26 Monthly Average Maximum Temperature in Bangladesh, 2022

(Celsius)

Station	Jan	Feb	Mar	Apr	May	June	July	Aug	Sep	Oct	Nov	Dec
Dhaka-41923	25.1	27.2	33.9	34.2	33.6	33.2	34.1	34.2	33.3	32.7	31.0	27.4
Tangail-41909	23.8	25.9	33.4	34.2	33.1	33.5	34.1	34.2	33.0	32.4	30.6	26.5
Faridpur-41929	24.3	26.7	33.8	34.5	33.4	33.5	34.5	34.0	33.1	32.2	30.5	27.0
Madaripur-41939	23.8	26.4	33.2	34.5	34.0	33.4	33.8	33.5	32.9	31.6	29.6	26.4
Gopalgonj-41938	24.1	26.8	33.3	34.6	33.4	33.1	33.8	33.4	33.0	31.7	29.5	26.7
Nikli-41902	24.1	25.7	32.9	33.0	32.0	31.3	33.4	33.3	32.6	31.6	30.1	26.1
Mymensingh-41886	24.1	25.7	32.9	33.0	32.0	31.3	33.4	33.3	32.6	31.6	30.1	26.4
Netrokona-41888	24.2	25.1	32.0	32.1	31.9	31.0	33.5	33.7	32.4	32.0	30.4	26.8
Chattogram-41978	24.6	25.0	32.4	31.5	31.2	30.1	33.2	33.7	32.2	31.8	30.6	28.5
Sandwip-41964	26.0	27.9	32.4	33.1	33.2	32.1	32.8	33.1	32.6	32.8	31.5	28.9
Sitakunda-41965	26.4	28.4	33.4	32.6	32.6	31.5	33.3	33.3	32.5	33.2	32.0	29.2
Rangamati-41966	26.8	28.5	33.8	33.1	32.7	31.7	32.7	32.7	33.0	42.9	32.2	28.2
Cumilla-41933	25.9	25.5	34.5	34.8	32.6	31.8	33.2	33.5	32.9	32.9	31.4	28.0
Chandpur-41941	25.4	27.1	32.8	32.9	33.1	31.6	33.7	33.5	33.0	32.8	31.8	27.4
M Court-41953	25.6	27.7	34.1	34.3	33.9	33.1	33.7	33.8	33.1	33.0	31.3	27.1
Feni-41943	24.7	26.8	33.2	33.8	33.4	32.3	34.0	34.0	32.7	31.9	30.6	28.5
Hatiya-41963	26.0	28.5	34.0	33.6	32.8	31.7	33.4	33.2	32.6	32.8	31.8	27.7
Cox's Bazar-41992	25.2	27.4	33.0	33.3	33.0	31.5	33.6	33.7	31.7	32.0	30.5	29.9
Kutubdia-41989	27.2	28.6	32.7	33.5	32.9	31.2	31.8	31.9	31.9	33.0	32.3	29.0
Teknaf-41998	25.8	28.1	31.7	33.1	32.8	32.0	32.2	31.4	32.3	32.7	31.6	30.3
Sylhet-41891	29.0	30.0	33.3	33.6	32.8	31.7	33.0	32.7	31.5	32.3	31.6	27.3
Srimangal-41915	25.9	26.7	33.5	31.9	31.1	29.7	32.0	31.8	33.3	32.1	31.4	28.0
Rajshahi-41895	25.4	26.9	33.2	34.0	32.4	32.0	34.0	34.2	33.6	32.2	31.7	26.8
Ishurdi-41907	23.4	26.0	34.8	36.2	34.1	35.0	33.7	33.9	34.0	33.2	30.4	26.5
Bogura-41883	23.3	25.7	33.9	35.8	33.7	34.4	36.3	34.8	33.7	32.6	30.3	26.7
Badalgachi-41881	23.5	25.5	33.3	33.4	32.9	32.5	35.0	34.4	32.8	32.7	31.0	26.4
Tarash-41897	22.8	24.8	32.7	33.0	32.6	32.4	34.1	33.8	32.6	31.9	30.1	26.0
Rangpur-41859	23.2	25.3	32.1	33.3	33.1	34.0	34.1	34.4	33.5	31.7	30.6	26.5
Dinajpur-41863	23.5	24.5	32.2	30.6	32.1	31.9	34.3	33.9	32.8	32.0	30.1	26.7
Sayedpur-41858	22.2	24.5	32.4	31.7	32.5	32.2	34.8	34.0	32.8	32.3	30.3	27.3
Tetulia-41850	23.3	25.2	33.0	31.4	33.2	32.3	34.6	33.6	33.6	33.2	30.6	26.5
Dimla-41851	23.2	24.1	32.4	30.5	32.1	30.9	35.6	34.7	32.3	31.2	29.8	26.2
Rajarhat-41856	23.0	24.0	31.4	29.7	31.6	30.6	33.8	33.7	32.3	31.4	29.8	26.2
Khulna-41947	23.5	24.0	32.3	29.0	31.0	30.5	33.7	33.6	32.3	31.2	29.2	27.5
Mongla-41958	24.3	27.3	33.7	34.5	34.9	33.7	33.8	33.5	33.3	32.6	30.7	27.6
Satkhira-41946	24.6	27.9	33.9	35.0	34.5	33.8	33.8	33.6	33.3	32.2	30.2	27.0
Jashore-41936	23.8	26.7	32.9	34.4	34.2	34.0	33.8	33.2	32.9	32.0	30.1	27.9
Chuadanga-41926	24.6	27.6	34.0	35.5	34.8	34.8	32.9	32.8	33.8	32.8	30.9	26.6
Kumarkhali-41927	23.3	26.0	33.8	35.4	34.3	34.7	34.6	33.9	33.8	32.8	30.1	26.5
Barishal-41950	23.3	25.9	34.1	34.8	33.3	33.7	34.6	33.9	33.2	32.4	29.9	27.9
Patuakhali-41960	25.3	27.9	33.5	33.9	33.7	33.1	33.8	33.6	32.9	32.4	30.9	27.9
Khepupara-41984	25.2	28.1	33.7	34.2	33.8	33.0	33.2	32.9	32.8	32.3	30.6	28.2
Bhola-41951	25.7	28.3	33.6	33.7	33.7	32.8	32.8	32.9	32.5	32.4	30.5	28.0

Source: Bangladesh Meteorological Department.

Fig. 2. Snapshot of the dataset employed in this study.

3.2 Machine Learning Model Selection

Random Forest Regression. Random Forest Regression is an ensemble learning method that makes accurate predictions by combining the strength of several decision trees. In our study, the Random Forest model excels at capturing nonlinear climate patterns. It aggregates predictions from multiple decision trees, providing a robust and reliable estimation of temperature extremes.

The Random Forest model can be mathematically expressed as follows:

$$\hat{Y} = \frac{1}{n}\sum_{i=1}^{N} T_i \tag{1}$$

where $\hat{Y}$ represents the predicted temperature extreme, N is the total number of decision trees in the ensemble, T_i denotes the predicted temperature extreme from the i-th decision tree.

Ridge Regression. Ridge Regression, a linear regression modification, addresses variability in climate data by including a penalty term in the loss function, improving our study's model resilience. The model is formulated as follows:

$$\hat{Y} = X\beta + \lambda \sum_{j=1}^{p} \beta_j^2 \tag{2}$$

where $\hat{Y}$ represents the predicted temperature extreme, X is the feature matrix, β is the vector of coefficients, λ is the regularization parameter and p is the number of features.

Bayesian Ridge Regression. A probabilistic interpretation of predictions is made possible by Bayesian Ridge Regression, which extends linear regression with a Bayesian framework. Its efficacy in handling multicollinearity makes it well-suited for our study on climate data. The model can be expressed as follows:

$$\begin{aligned}\hat{Y} &= X\beta + \epsilon \\ \beta &\sim \mathcal{N}\left(0, \alpha^{-1}\mathbb{I}\right) \\ \alpha &\sim \gamma(a, b)\end{aligned} \tag{3}$$

where $\hat{Y}$ represents the vector of predicted temperature extremes, X is the feature matrix, β is the vector of coefficients, ϵ is the error term, α is the precision parameter, $\mathcal{N}$ denotes a normal distribution, γ represents a gamma distribution and $\mathbb{I}$ is the identity matrix

K-Nearest Neighbors (KNN) Regression. A non-parametric, instance-based learning technique called K-Nearest Neighbors (KNN) Regression makes predictions about the future based on how close between two data points are. In the context of our study, The following equation describes KNN Regression:

$$\hat{Y} = \frac{1}{K}\sum_{i=1}^{k} Y_i \tag{4}$$

where $\hat{Y}$ represents the predicted temperature extreme, k is the number of nearest neighbors, Y_i denotes the temperature extreme of the i-th nearest neighbor.

Proposed Ensemble Model. The Ensemble Model, which combines Bayesian Ridge Regression and Ridge Regression, provides a thorough quantitative assessment of the impact of climate change on temperature extremes in Bangladesh. Leveraging the strengths of both techniques, it provides nuanced analyses from historical to contemporary records. This amalgamation yields a robust, flexible framework offering valuable insights into evolving climate patterns. The model can be expressed as follows:

$$\hat{Y}_{Ensemble} = \omega.\hat{Y}_{Ridge} + (1-\omega).\hat{Y}_{Bayesian} \quad (5)$$

where $\hat{Y}_{Ensemble}$ represents the predicted temperature extreme by the Ensemble Model, $\hat{Y}_{Ridge}$ is the prediction from the Ridge Regression model, $\hat{Y}_{Bayesian}$ is the prediction from the Bayesian Ridge Regression model, ω is the weight assigned to the Ridge Regression model, with $0 \leq \omega \leq 1$.

3.3 Hyper-parameter Tuning

Upon completing the data processing phase, selecting a suitable machine learning model for temperature prediction relies on analysing previously recorded data. Each candidate model undergoes testing with the selected features to identify the optimal model. The machine learning models used in this study are shown in Table 1 with the associated hyperparameter settings.

Table 1 summarizes the hyper-parameter configurations for this study's five distinct machine learning models. The Random Forest Regressor is characterized by 150 estimators, a maximum depth of 30, a minimum sample split of 2 and a minimum sample leaf of 1. The Ridge Regressor is defined with a default alpha value of 1.0. For the Bayesian Ridge Regressor, the hyperparameters include alpha_1, alpha_2, lambda_1, lambda_2, fit_intercept and verbose. "fit_intercept" (defaulted to True) determines intercept calculation, while "verbose" (set to True) yields detailed output during model fitting for enhanced training insights. The KNN Regressor utilizes 7 neighbours, 'distance' weights, 'auto' algorithm, a leaf size of 30 and a power parameter of 2 for the Minkowski metric. Lastly, the Ensemble Model incorporates alpha, lambda, compute_score, normalize, verbose and fit_intercept parameters. Where "compute_score" (True computes score during fitting) and "normalize" (True enables input feature normalization) are in the Ensemble Model. This extensive collection of hyper-parameter settings is essential for customizing the behavior of each model to the particular needs of the study's climate change analysis.

3.4 Evaluation Matrices

Following the identification of optimal models for this study, the evaluation of their performance is conducted using six metrics: Mean Absolute Error (MAE), Mean Squared Error (MSE), Root Mean Squared Error (RMSE), R-squared (R2), Root Mean Squared Logarithmic Error (RMSLE), and Mean Absolute Percentage Error (MAPE). The equations for these evaluation metrics are detailed below in Eq. 6.

Table 1. Hyper parameter settings for various machine learning models utilized in this study.

Model Name	Hyperperameter Settings
Random Forest	N-estimators = 150 may-depth = 30 min-samples-split = 2 min-samples-leaf = 1
Ridge Regression	alpha = 1.0
Bayesian Ridge Regression	alpha 1 = le-6 alpha 2 = le-6 lambda 1 = le-6 lambda 2 = le-6 fit intercept = True verbose = False
KNN Regression	n-neighbors = 7 weight:distance algorithm:auto leaf-size = 30 p = 2
Ensemble Model	alpha = 1.0 Lambda = 1.0 compute-score = False Normalize = False verbase = False Fit intercept = True

$$MAE = \frac{1}{n}\sum_{i=1}^{n}|y_i - \hat{y}_i|$$

$$MSE = \frac{1}{n}\sum_{i=1}^{n}(y_i - \hat{y}_i)^2$$

$$RMSE = \sqrt{MSE}$$

$$R^2 = 1 - \frac{\sum_{i=1}^{n}(y_i - \hat{y}_i)^2}{\sum_{i=1}^{n}(y_i - \bar{y}_i)^2} \tag{6}$$

$$RMSLE = \sqrt{\frac{1}{n}\sum_{i=1}^{n}\left(log(1+y_i) - log(1+\hat{y}_i)^2\right)}$$

$$MAPE = \frac{1}{n}\sum_{i=1}^{n}\left|\frac{y_i - \hat{y}_i}{y_i}\right| \times 100$$

where, N is the number of samples, y_i is the actual values, $\hat{y}_i$ is the predicted value and $\bar{y}_i$ is the mean of the actual values.

3.5 Experimental Setup

In this study, the main tool for our machine learning model building, implementation and training was the cloud-based platform Google Colab [2]. The utilization of Google Colab's free version afforded us a robust and readily accessible computing environment, thereby enabling the execution of extensive experiments without necessitating substantial computational resources. The research team's ability to easily share code and datasets was made possible by Google Colab's collaborative capabilities, which promoted effective teamwork and increased overall research efficiency. Notably, all code was scripted in Python3 and the machine learning library employed was Scikit Learn [1,3].

4 Result and Discussion

This study utilized diverse modeling approaches, employing various combinations, to explore predictive modeling of standard minimum and maximum average temperatures. The investigation focused on a case study conducted in Bangladesh.

Table 2. Evaluation Metrics for Standard Minimum and Maximum Average Temperature Prediction (MAE, MSE, RMSE, R2, RMSLE, MAPE).

Model Name	MAE	MSE	RMSE	R	RMSLE	MAPE
Random Forest	0.20	0.14	0.37	0.99	0.01	0.88
Bayesian Ridge	0.11	0.02	0.14	1.00	0.00	0.45
KNN Regression	0.88	7.03	2.65	0.65	0.03	4.18
Ridge Regression	0.11	0.02	0.15	1.00	0.00	0.48
Ensemble Model	0.09	0.01	0.12	1.00	0.00	0.37

Within Table 2 comprehensive evaluation of temperature prediction models using metrics like MAE, MSE, RMSE, R2, RMSLE and MAPE, our ensemble model consistently emerges as the superior performer. In MAE, Bayesian Ridge and Ridge Regression score 0.11, while our ensemble model achieves 0.09. For MSE, our ensemble model excels with 0.01, outshining KNN Regression's 7.03. The RMSE showcases the superiority of our ensemble model with a value of 0.12. In R2, KNN Regression and Random Forest score 0.65 and 0.99, respectively, while Ridge Regression, Bayesian Ridge Regression, and our ensemble model all achieve a perfect 1.00. The RMSLE demonstrates the ensemble model's exceptional performance with a score of 0.00. Closing with MAPE, our ensemble model stands out with a score of 0.37, reaffirming its superior accuracy. In summary, the ensemble model consistently outperforms across all metrics, making it the best option for predicting standard minimum and maximum average temperatures.

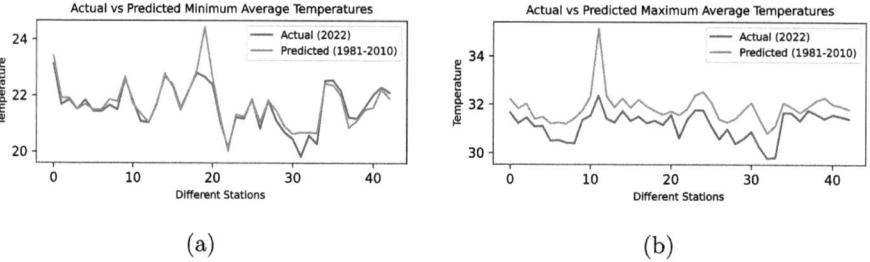

Fig. 3. Annual Comparative Analysis of Actual and Predicted Standard Minimum and Maximum Average Temperatures for 7 Selected Stations Among 44 Locations.

In Fig. 3(a), the representation of standard minimum average temperatures across 44 stations reveals noticeable fluctuations compared to historical records. Similarly, Fig. 3(b) displays standard maximum average temperatures for the same 44 stations, highlighting discernible variations from records.

Table 3. Annual Comparative Analysis of Actual and Predicted Standard Minimum and Maximum Average Temperatures for 7 Selected Stations Among 44 Locations.

Section	Min Avg Temo(Actual)	Min Avg Temo(Predicted)	Max Avg Temo(Actual)	Max Avg Temo(Predicted)
Dhaka	23.13	23.42	31.65	32.21
Chattogram	21.50	21.79	30.40	31.43
Cox's Bazar	22.18	22.16	31.23	31.92
Sylhet	22.39	22.63	31.56	31.7
Rajshahi	20.13	20.03	31.36	31.80
Teknaf	22.67	24.44	31.16	31.58
Khulna	20.28	20.67	29.81	31.12

Table 3 provides a comprehensive overview of annual temperature variations in Bangladesh, emphasizing key stations. Seven key stations has been chosen based on their dense population. Notably, in Dhaka, the observed minimum average temperature of 23.13 differs from the anticipated value of 23.42, and the maximum average temperature of 31.65 contrasts with the expected 32.21. Similar discrepancies are evident in Teknaf, where the observed minimum average temperature of 22.67 deviates from the projected 24.44, indicating a significant disparity. Additionally, in Khulna, the recorded maximum average temperature of 29.81 falls short of the projected 31.12. These variations underscore the annual temperature fluctuations relative to historical data, contributing to discernible shifts in climate patterns. The observed intensification of heat during summer and increased cold during winter aligns with broader climate change trends, where temperature serves as a pivotal factor. Results achieved from this study confirms the role of annual standard minimum and maximum average temperatures in shaping Bangladesh's evolving climate dynamics.

Our study, which extends across a broader time span and incorporates data from more stations compared to a previous analysis [15], highlights the superiority of the proposed ensemble model over baseline machine learning (ML) models. While the previous study achieved moderate accuracy using the CatBoost model, our ensemble model significantly surpassed it in performance, as indicated by substantially lower MAE, MSE, and MAPE values. Our proposed model outperform baseline ML models due to the collective intelligence of multiple models, each capturing different aspects of the underlying data patterns. By aggregating predictions from multiple models, proposed ensemble method mitigate individual model biases and errors, resulting in more accurate and robust predictions. Additionally, the proposed ensemble model offers increased stability and generalization capability, as ensemble models are less susceptible to overfitting compared to single ML models. This advantage of ensemble modeling, coupled with our study's comprehensive data coverage and longer time frame, underscores the effectiveness of ensemble techniques in improving predictive accuracy and providing deeper insights into climate change dynamics in Bangladesh.

5 Conclusion

This study utilizes a robust machine learning regression analysis to quantify the impact of climate change on standard minimum and maximum average temperature extremes in Bangladesh from past to present. A comprehensive assessment across 44 stations reveals significant annual temperature variations, evidenced by deviations in crucial locations such as Dhaka, Chattogram, Teknaf, and Khulna. These observed discrepancies underscore the region's dynamic nature of climate change, exhibiting notable shifts in both summer heat and winter cold.

Our findings emphasize the pivotal role of temperature fluctuations in contributing to broader climate change patterns. This study enhances our understanding of Bangladesh's changing climate dynamics, offering valuable insights for policymakers and researchers to address the challenges posed by climate change in the region. Limitations of the study include potential issues with data quality and availability, as MLRA relies on accurate and up-to-date climate data, which may be subject to errors or gaps. Furthermore, the assumption of stationarity in MLRA may introduce bias due to the non-stationary nature of climate systems, where statistical properties can change over time.

Data and Code Availability. The codes and data employed in this study can be found in the following GitHub repository.https://github.com/ShahriarAyon63/st_min_and_st_max_ave_temperature_predic_Bangladesh.

References

1. 3.12.1 Documentation. https://docs.python.org/3/
2. Google Colaboratory, https://colab.research.google.com/
3. scikit-learn: machine learning in Python — scikit-learn 1.3.2 documentation. https://scikit-learn.org/stable/
4. Ali, A.: Climate change impacts and adaptation assessment in Bangladesh. Climate Res. **12**(2–3), 109–116 (1999)
5. Amin, M.R., Zhang, J., Yang, M.: Effects of climate change on the yield and cropping area of major food crops: a case of bangladesh. Sustainability **7**(1), 898–915 (2015)
6. Azam, M.G., Rahman, M.M.: Assessing spatial vulnerability of Bangladesh to climate change and extremes: a geographic information system approach. Mitig. Adapt. Strat. Glob. Change **27**(6), 38 (2022)
7. BBS: BBS Statistical Yearbook (2023). https://bbs.gov.bd/site/page/29855dc1-f2b4-4dc0-9073-f692361112da/Statistical-Yearbook. Bangladesh Bureau of Statistics
8. Dastagir, M.R.: Modeling recent climate change induced extreme events in Bangladesh: a review. Weather Clim. Extremes **7**, 49–60 (2015)
9. Hashizume, M., Wagatsuma, Y., Hayashi, T., Saha, S.K., Streatfield, K., Yunus, M.: The effect of temperature on mortality in rural Bangladesh–a population-based time-series study. Int. J. Epidemiol. **38**(6), 1689–1697 (2009)
10. Hossain, M.T., Hossain, A., Meem, S.M., Monir, M.F., Miah, M.S.U., Sarwar, T.B.: Impact of COVID-19 lockdowns on air quality in Bangladesh: analysis and AQI forecasting with support vector regression. In: 2023 4th International Conference for Emerging Technology (INCET), pp. 1–6. IEEE (2023)
11. Huntingford, C., Jeffers, E.S., Bonsall, M.B., Christensen, H.M., Lees, T., Yang, H.: Machine learning and artificial intelligence to aid climate change research and preparedness. Environ. Res. Lett. **14**(12), 124007 (2019)
12. Islam, S.S., Haque, M.S., Miah, M.S.U., Sarwar, T.B., Bhowmik, A.: A trend analysis of crimes in Bangladesh. In: Proceedings of the 2nd International Conference on Computing Advancements, p. 501–508. ICCA 2022, Association for Computing Machinery, New York, NY, USA (2022). https://doi.org/10.1145/3542954.3543026
13. Kafy, A.A., et al.: Remote sensing approach to simulate the land use/land cover and seasonal land surface temperature change using machine learning algorithms in a fastest-growing megacity of Bangladesh. Remote Sens. Appl. Soc. Environ. **21**, 100463 (2021)
14. Khan, M.J.U., Islam, A.S., Bala, S.K., Islam, G.T.: Changes in climate extremes over Bangladesh at 1.5 c, 2 c, and 4 c of global warming with high-resolution regional climate modeling. Theoretical and Appl. Climatol. **140**, 1451–1466 (2020)
15. Mahabub, A., Habib, A.-Z.S.B., Mondal, M.R.H., Bharati, S., Podder, P.: Effectiveness of ensemble machine learning algorithms in weather forecasting of bangladesh. In: Abraham, A., Sasaki, H., Rios, R., Gandhi, N., Singh, U., Ma, K. (eds.) IBICA 2020. AISC, vol. 1372, pp. 267–277. Springer, Cham (2021). https://doi.org/10.1007/978-3-030-73603-3_25

16. Mahmud, M., Kaiser, M.S., McGinnity, T.M., Hussain, A.: Deep learning in mining biological data. Cogn. Comput. **13**(1), 1–33 (2021)
17. Oyshee, S.S., Anik, S.R., Chowdhury, M.J.U.K., Kabir, M.A.: Machine learning based load and temperature behavior clustering and peak shifting implementation on Bangladeshi grid data. In: 2023 International Conference on Electrical, Computer and Communication Engineering (ECCE), pp. 1–6. IEEE (2023)
18. Paul, S., Roy, S.: Forecasting the average temperature rise in Bangladesh: a time series analysis. J. Eng. Sci. **11**(1), 83–91 (2020)
19. Sammonds, P., Shamsudduha, M., Ahmed, B.: Climate change driven disaster risks in Bangladesh and its journey towards resilience. J. Br. Acad. **9**(s8), 55–77 (2021)
20. Shams, M.Y., Tarek, Z., Elshewey, A.M., Hany, M., Darwish, A., Hassanien, A.E.: A machine learning-based model for predicting temperature under the effects of climate change. In: The Power of Data: Driving Climate Change with Data Science and Artificial Intelligence Innovations, pp. 61–81. Springer, Cham (2023)

Explainable Machine Learning Strategy to Discover Attributes Accountable for ASD Detection

Arpita Chakraborty[1,2], Jyoti Sekhar Banerjee[1,2(✉)], and Mufti Mahmud[3,4,5]

[1] Department of Computer Science and Engineering (AI & ML), Techno Bengal Institute of Technology, Kolkata, India
tojyoti2001@yahoo.co.in
[2] Cognitive Computing and Brain Informatics Research Group, Nottingham Trent University, Nottingham, UK
[3] Information and Computer Science Department, King Fahd University of Petroleum and Minerals, Dhahran 31261, Saudi Arabia
mufti.mahmud@kfupm.edu.sa
[4] SDAIA-KFUPM Joint Research Center for AI, King Fahd University of Petroleum and Minerals, Dhahran 31261, Saudi Arabia
[5] Interdisciplinary Research Center for Bio Systems and Machines, King Fahd University of Petroleum and Minerals, Dhahran 31261, Saudi Arabia

Abstract. Machine learning is a multidisciplinary study area that makes use of intelligent approaches to identify useful hidden patterns that get used for prediction purpose to enhance deciding ability. Hence, the increasing use of machine learning models in predicting different human illnesses has made it feasible to identify them early by analyzing numerous health and physiological parameters. This reason encouraged us to look more closely at the identification and evaluation of ASD, which is a behavioural disorder that hinders language and communication acquisition, through Machine Learning models. It helps to develop more effective treatment strategies. As it is very difficult for a practitioner to pinpoint the key characteristics that contribute to an accurate ASD prognosis, an automated technique is required. Additionally, it is possible to generate the most influential characteristics for accurately and promptly predicting ASD through our proposed hybrid approach of explainable AI, along with machine learning algorithms. Thus, the suggested framework provides suggestions for expected outcomes along with a more accurate prognosis, which will be a crucial therapeutic help for better and earlier diagnosis of ASD features of child, toddler, adolescent or adult patients with disorder.

Keywords: Explainable machine learning · wearable sensor · stress detection · multimodal dataset · SHAP · Feature Importance

1 Introduction

Previously, diagnosis of patients, classification of diseases and advice of medicines were entirely done by the medical practitioners based on their expertise. ML redefines healthcare by enabling early diagnosis and prediction, personalized treatment, via extensive data analysis as per availability of the abundant structured and unstructured data. Machine learning aims to replicate cognitive processes seen in humans. Basically, the intelligent algorithms of Machine learning, get important insights from data autonomously.

A distinctive combination of genes and neurological connections make the brain the most intricate organ in the body. As it learns, the brain produces additional synaptic connections, complicating processing. The relationship between cognitive development and functional brain circuitry helps explain neurological diseases [1]. Autism is a varied and psychological development disorder caused by faulty brain connections [2].

Autism Spectrum Disorder is a behavioral ailment that disrupts cultural/social reciprocity throughout life. ASD symptoms begin in infancy and last into adulthood [1]. Analyzing repeated behaviours in ASD patients will assist create an early diagnosis method. Age and ability greatly affect ASD sufferers' behaviours. ASD patients often have poor expressive movements, non-responsiveness to hearing, poor eye contact, no pain perception, verbal repetition, and agitation with daily task changes [1]. Autism siblings have a fiftyfold higher risk of ASD than healthy siblings [2]. The prevalence of Autism is about 4–5 times higher in male individuals compared to female ones.

Worldwide, 1 in 160 children are at risk for ASD, according to WHO. Hong Kong, South Korea, and the US have the highest ASD rates. The frequency is every 1 out of 500 and the number of cases is 11,914 year wise in India. The Autism Society of America claims that the rates in the US are growing 10–17% annually. According to the latest CDC estimate, 1 in 54 US children had ASD in 2020, a 10% increase. ASD is one of the rarest disorders, but its prevalence figures are worrying.

Early discovery of ASD symptoms helps reduce its impact, but it cannot be cured. Machine learning (ML) can predict and identify illnesses with high accuracy, offering promise for early ASD screening based on physical and physiological data. ASD is difficult to diagnose and analyze since other mental health issues share symptoms, leading to false positives. Medical professionals may be able to make more informed judgments about early diagnosis if the features of the ML model can clarify why it indicates ASD. It motivated our effort since early identification of ASD would reduce symptoms with prompt treatment, improving patients' and families' lifestyles.

This paper primarily contributes by means of these following ways:

- The unique features of the adult, adolescent, child, and toddler ASD datasets have been examined to identify the most accountable attributes for ASD Detection.
- The authors checked out how well the various classifiers performed when applied to various datasets and found no generalized model for all the datasets. Finally, could justify the performance of the best classifier through graphical presentation by increasing the number of attributes.
- As, Explainable Machine Learning has been employed, detection of ASD is no more a black box approach, rather, justifications of the attributes been used are inferred properly.

This paper is structured in the following order; the related studies on autism screening techniques is provided in Sect. 2, and the features of the dataset utilized for the experiments are described in Sect. 3 along with the suggested framework. In Sect. 4, the Build Model, together with the Training and Testing Models, are given and explored. In Sect. 5, performance measurements and experimental data are provided and reviewed. Section 6 finishes by outlining the findings and potential directions.

2 Relevant Research

To detect and evaluate ASD, several researchers have used a range of machine learning techniques. The main goal of using algorithms based on machine learning on ASD is to increase diagnosis accuracy and shorten detection times, which will allow for faster access to healthcare treatments.

Using RML, i.e., Rules-based Machine Learning to assess ASD symptoms was suggested by Thabtah et al. [2] in their study. They found that RML improves the performance of classifiers. The use of tree-based classifiers allowed Satu et al. to distinguish between typically autistic and normal children in Bangladesh [3]. When it came to feature knowledge of material, Abbas et al. [4] combined the ADI-R and ADOS ML approaches into one assessment to handle issues with scarcity, sparsity, and different definitions. In order to make accurate diagnoses and predictions of ASD, researchers [1–7] used AI methods including, logistic regression (LR), Decision Tree (DT), and Support Vector Machine (SVM) to uncover feature-to-class and feature-to-feature connections. In their analysis of ASD data, Duda et al. [8] employed several classifiers and differentiated ASD from ADHD. When it comes to capturing the numerous elements that determine ASD heterogeneity and phenotype, cluster analysis may be the way to go, according to the authors.

An artificial intelligence (AI) system was suggested by Akter et al. [9] that would utilise sensor data to track the patient's vitals and adapt its learning strategy via engaging games and activities according to the patient's expressions and emotions. Improving machine learning models ability to identify autism was the driving force behind this research. A group of researchers [10] conducted a literature study to ascertain the efficacy of autism screening programmes that are conducted in the community. Screening programmes failed to meet almost all criteria when compared to the most critical concerns about autism. There is no evidence that this programme would have a positive impact, because there are insufficient effective therapies and dependable screening tools. An AI-powered system was introduced by Banna et al. [11] that tracks the patient's vitals using sensor data and adapts its learning strategy to their mood and expressions via engaging games and activities. We provide a hybrid approach to diagnosing Autism Spectrum Disorder (ASD) based on the BRB, i.e., Belief Rule Base and the IoT, i.e., Internet of Things [12–14]. In real-time, this smart technology can gather and categorize data on signs and symptoms from a variety of autistic children. The suggested system outperformed the then-leading expert and fuzzy systems. In this research, an assistive system called C-ASD was introduced for children who had autism spectrum disorder [15]. The primary objective of the addressed approach is to ease the dependence of the children on their parents and other care givers so that they may develop more independence.

A fuzzy logic-based expert system has been created to support the creation of intervention strategies. Several investigations [16–18] examined methodological research papers that suggested utilizing deep ML models to identify neurodegenerative disorders based only on magnetic resonance imaging data. The results show that methods based on deep learning can precisely ascertain the level of chaos. Current challenges are reviewed at the end, along with a few possible directions for further study. Convolutional Neural Networks (CNN), the most popular deep learning technique, were introduced in this research [19] along with its application to distinct brain regions using magnetic resonance imaging, with an emphasis on beginners. It then provides a detailed overview of the techniques' effectiveness along with a numerical assessment of the ones being considered. Mahmud et al. [20] proposed Traditional Markov Model (TMM), which estimates node behavioural trust and data trust, respectively, using weighted-additive approaches and the Adaptive Neuro-Fuzzy Inference System. This allows for an analysis of the trustworthiness of nodes. In contrast to current fuzzy TMMs, the results from NS2 simulator demonstrate accuracy as well as resilience of the claimed TMM in recognizing hostile communicating nodes in the network. A comprehensive review of biological data mining is provided by studies made by Mahmud et al. [21, 22], considering the use of DL, RL, and Deep RL algorithms. Additionally, they contrast the outcomes of DL techniques used to different datasets in a range of application domains, emphasizing open issues in this challenging field of study and talking about potential directions for future growth. People with autism spectrum disorder have communication difficulties and repetitive behaviour as a lifelong developmental issue.

Using real-world health data as input, Payrovnaziri SN et al. [23] constructed a thorough scoping evaluation of explainable AI (XAI) models, classified these approaches into different biomedical uses, found research gaps, and provided recommendations for future studies. The authors concluded that the XAI evaluation was being employed in a medical setting where it did not belong. A big problem remains with reproducibility.

Again, healthcare practitioners are wary of traditional AI algorithms because they believe that a biased or incorrect diagnosis might endanger human life [24]. They thus look for explainability and transparency in the AI model that is used to diagnose illnesses.

3 Proposed Methodology

The prior motive of this research work is to utilize the publicly available ASD data to forecast and categorize new patients into two categories: "patient has ASD" or "patient does not have ASD". Hence, it is basically binary classification challenge to predict if a new adult patient with certain traits has a high risk of developing ASD or not. The suggested approach is depicted in Fig. 1. The steps are like: data pre-processing, training and evaluation of the designated ML model, assessing the output performance, and prediction of ASD, utilizing Explainable AI.

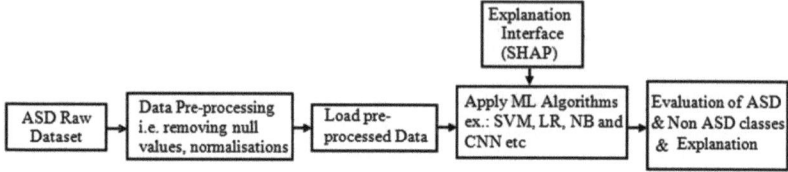

Fig. 1. Stages involved in explaining and prediction of ASD

3.1 Data Collection

Data, which is the most crucial part, usually have been acquired by several researchers/doctors and made available for further use. The dataset acquired for this investigation was gathered from the widely accessible UCI Repository. Dr. Fadi Fayez Thabtah [1, 2] created the Toddler dataset to evaluate autism in young children using the ASD Tests mobile app. Three kinds of datasets were mostly employed in this study. The dataset's comprehensive overview is provided below (Table 1):

Table 1. Collection of ASD Datasets

Sl No	Dataset Name	Source	Questionnaire Type	Attribute Type	No. of Attributes	No. of Instances
1	ASD Screening Data for Adult	UCI Machine Learning Repository [25]	AQ based study	Categorical, continuous and binary	21	704
2	ASD Screening Data for Adolescent	UCI Machine Learning Repository [27]	AQ based study	Categorical, continuous and binary	21	104
3	ASD Screening Data for Children	UCI Machine Learning Repository [26]	AQ based study	Categorical, continuous and binary	21	292
4	ASD Screening Data for Toddler	UCI Machine Learning Repository [26]	AQ based study	Categorical, continuous and binary	21	

3.2 Exploration of Data and Feature Selection

These datasets have twenty properties in common. Each data collection includes ten behavioural characteristics (Q-Chat-10), in addition to other attributes of individuals that have demonstrated utility in the diagnosis of Autism Spectrum Disorder (ASD) in behavioural science. The ASD Test screening program is used to acquire other attributes or features of the dataset. The attributes have been listed below (Table 2):

Table 2. Attributes of ASD Dataset

Sl No	Attribute Name	Attribute Description
1	Age	Age of the patient (in years)
2	Gender	Gender of the patient (M /F)
3	Ethnicity	List of common ethnicities in text format
4	Born with Jaundice	The patient suffered from Jaundice problem by birth
5	Family member with PDD	Whether any immediate family member suffered from Passive Development Disorders (PDD)
6	Who is completing the test	Parents, self, caregiver, medical staff, etc. who is completing the test
7	Country of Residence	The country in which the user lives
8	Used the screening App before	Screening App used by the user before or not
9	Screening method type	Screening test type based on age category
10–19	Questions based on screening method	Answers of 10 questions based on screening method
20	Screening score	Final score obtained based on scoring algorithm of screening method used
21	Class/ASD	ASD trait (No/ Yes)

It is vital to understand that the 'class' variable gets set automatically, according to the score obtained by the user using the ASD Tests program.

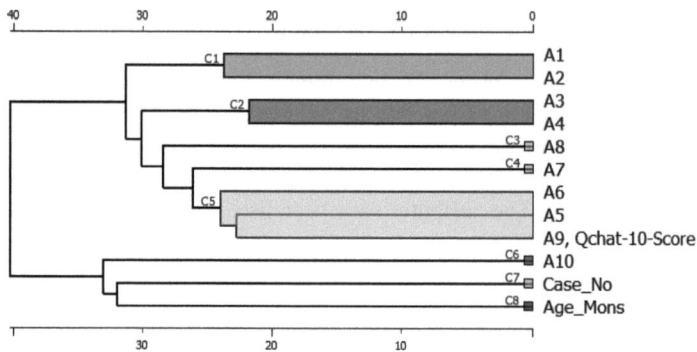

Fig. 2. Hierarchical relationship among the features

The dendrogram depicting the hierarchical connections between the features described in the toddler ASD dataset is shown in Fig. 2.

3.3 Data Pre-Processing

Data preparation before analysis or data preprocessing is the most difficult and tedious aspect of data science, but is one of the most significant steps also. Failure to clean and prepare the data may jeopardize the model and thus the prediction system. To work with practical problems, Data Scientists must constantly use preprocessing methods to make the data more functional. These tasks actually will make it easy to include in machine learning (ML) algorithms, keep things simple to avoid over fitting, and make the model better.

To deal with uncertainties present in data i.e., null values, errors, missing values or unreliable data, different data pre-processing approaches are usually applied, such as finding outliers, data discretization, data reduction (dimension and numerosity reduction), and so on. Usually, imputation technique is used to solve the issue of missing values from the dataset. Thus, through proper pre-processing method, the actual erroneous or incomplete data become accessible.

Inevitably, the data set been used in this correspondence, has a large number of incorrect or missing records. As a result, we need to preprocess our data before utilizing them as input in the following steps:

Step1: Missing records in the dataset are denoted by question marks (?).
Step2: Entries with Question Marks (?) are then transformed as "NAN" (i.e. not a number).
Step3: Any row with missing data is to be removed from the data set.

Thus, the number of occurrences in our Adult data set got reduced from 704 to 609.

After pre-processing task, Attributes of the four different datasets are plotted for better understanding (see Fig. 3).

3.4 Data Visualization

Prior implementing any algorithm, a brief visualization of the ASD data set is carried out utilizing the Seaborn, a popular Python module for the purpose of data analyzing. We start by making box plots that show how the feature "result" is distributed according to "gender" and "relation" (Shown in Fig. 4(a) & (b)). This provides us the first insight into the internal relationships among several characteristics inside our dataset. The red boxplot represents the data distribution for the 'ASD class' i.e., for autistic individuals, whereas the blue boxplot represents the data distribution for non-autistic individuals.

Statistics says, Male patients are more susceptible to ASD than female ones, and plotted in the Fig. 4(a). Again, from Fig. 4(b) it is found that candidates belonging to the family members with ASD are not even susceptible to ASD. Thus, it can be decided that, occurrence of ASD is basically independent of patient's gender and relationship of family members with ASD.

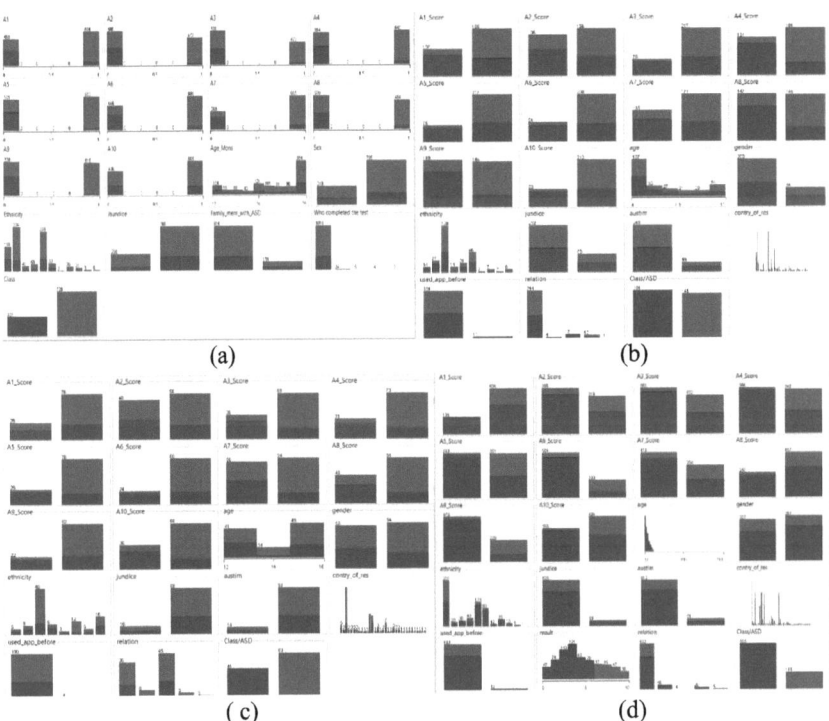

Fig. 3. Histogram plots of different data (a) Toddler, (b) Children (c) Adolescent, (d) Adult

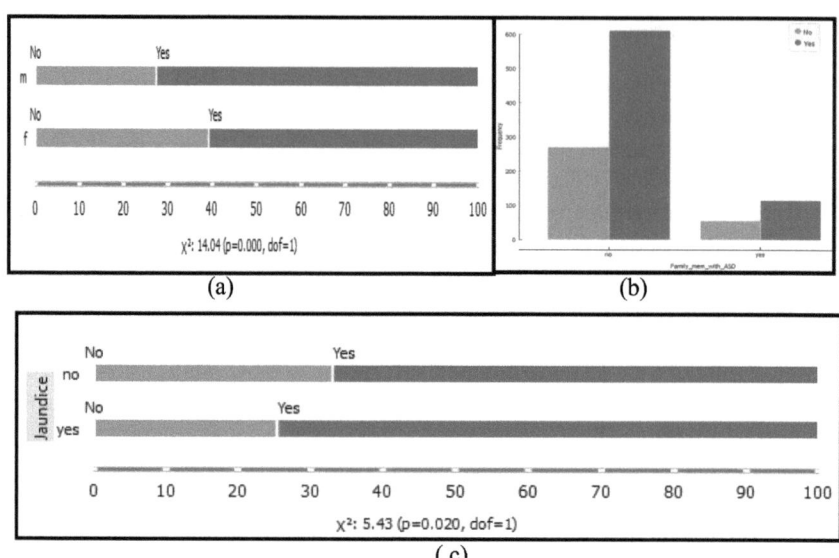

Fig. 4. Probable Impacts and occurrence of ASD (a) Gender, (b) Family member with ASD (c) Jaundice

Figure 4(c) provides the idea that even Jaundice at the time of birth is not responsible for the occurrence of ASD amongst the patients.

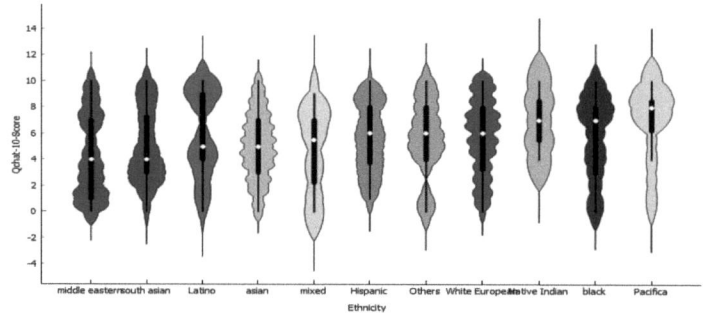

Fig. 5. Probable Impacts and occurrence of ASD: Ethnicity

Again, Fig. 5 provides the idea that the occurrence of ASD amongst the patients is not at all related to the country or species.

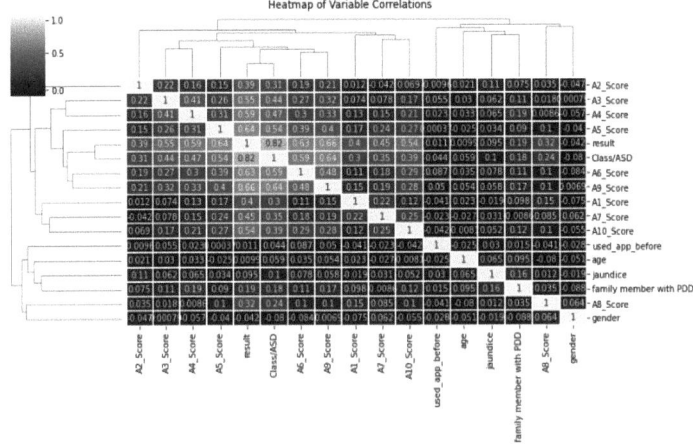

Fig. 6. ASD correlates with features A9, A6, A5 and A4

3.5 Correlation Coefficient

Correlation quantifies the linear association between two or more variables. Correlation allows us to forecast one variable based on another. Correlation is used for feature selection because strong factors have a high correlation with the target variable. Variables should be associated with the goal variable but uncorrelated with each other. One variable may be predicted from the other if two variables are associated. Hence the model only requires knowledge of one, since the second feature does not provide more information. We used Pearson Correlation in this case. From Fig. 6, it's found that ASD correlates with features A9, A6, A5 and A4 (Using Adult Dataset).

4 Build Model

4.1 Training and Testing Model

The whole ASD dataset (Toddler, Children, adolescent and Adult individually) has been split into two halves, having 80:20 ratio for training stage and testing stage respectively. Once again, training data has been divided into two halves for cross-validation. The training dataset is divided into two parts, the validation dataset and the training dataset, having ratio 80:20, correspondingly. The complete training, testing, and validation sets used for the classification process are shown in Fig. 7.

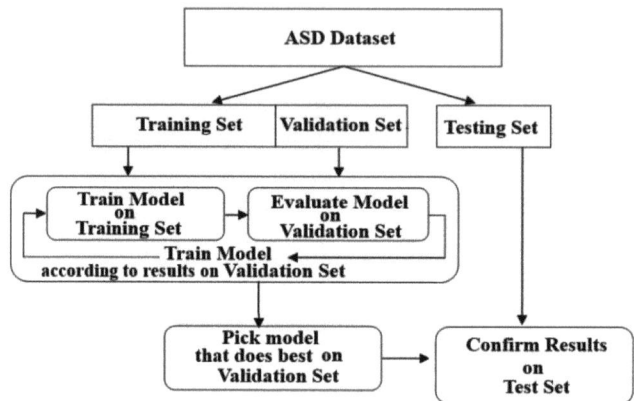

Fig. 7. ASD correlates with A9, A6, A5 and A4 scores

4.2 Comparison of Classifiers' Output

A classifier's performance gets determined in terms of classification accuracy, specificity, AUC, etc.

Performance measurement is essential for determining how effectively a classification model accomplishes a given objective. The performance assessment criteria are employed to assess the classification model's efficacy and execution on the Test dataset. Experimental outcomes of a variety of machine learning algorithm approaches incorporating the selection of all features for ASD screening data involving children, adolescents, and adults have been presented. In order to determine the specificity, sensitivity, and accuracy of the predicted model, each of the twenty-one features is chosen.

Machine learning models were evaluated on the ASD Toddler dataset, achieving an accuracy between 93.1% and 100% while actual data has been utilized. The K-NN algorithm setting K = 5, achieved an accuracy of 93.1%, while Logistic Regression achieved 100% accuracy in predicting the original dataset (see Fig. 8 a).

When evaluating several machine learning methods on a dataset for diagnosing ASD in Children, accuracy ranged from 80.1% to 98.30% utilizing the actual dataset. The K-NN classifier with K = 5 achieved an accuracy of 80.1%. Logistic Regression achieved an accuracy of 98.3% (Fig. 8 b).

When ML (Machine Learning) algorithms got applied on the Adolescent with ASD Diagnosis dataset, revealed an accuracy ranging from 79.8% to 96.2 percent for the initial dataset. The accuracy of the K-NN classifier with K = 5 was the lowest at 80.95%. CNN classifiers generated the most accurate predictions on the original dataset, at 96.2%.

And when applied on Adult dataset, minimum 91.3% accuracy is obtained using SVM algorithm, and maximum 98.3% can be achieved using Logistic Regression model.

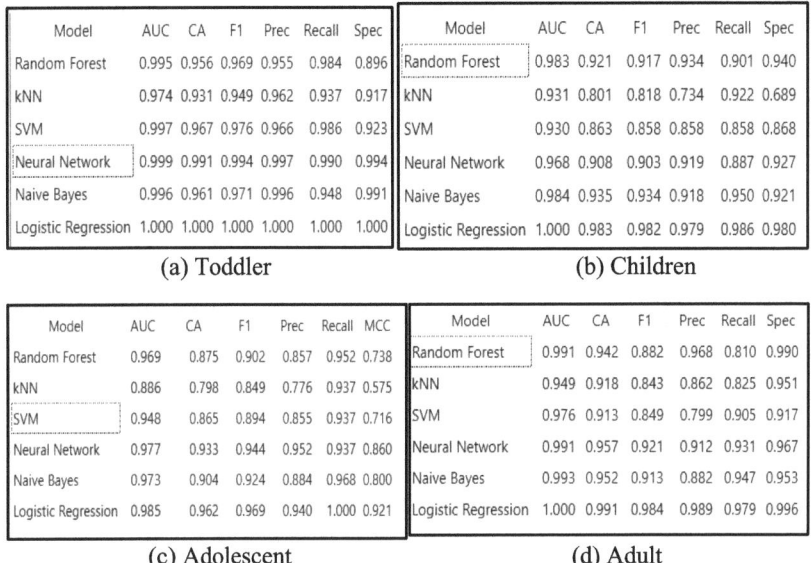

Fig. 8. Performance of Different Classifiers on 4 types of datasets

5 XAI Based Model Predictions

5.1 Explainable Artificial Intelligence

The existing Machine Learning models work in the mode of black box, i.e. it does not infer explicitly how to relate inputs and outputs or what is the mechanism of information flow in the hidden layers. On the contrary, XAI [28–31] offers comprehensibility for tools, models and algorithms. Here, the result may be connected with the input space to identify the distinguishing features of the input. Hence, application of such models in healthcare, provides deep insights of the models and parameters responsible for the prediction of output can be provided easily.

5.2 XAI for Measuring ASD Features Influence

Various approaches, such as SHAP, LIME, etc., may be used to convert a black-box machine learning model with a layered architecture into a white-box model to provide explanations for the machine's decisions. The framework gets trained through the data used for training purpose and later the model can generate prediction using a separate dataset for testing. The authors used Explainable Artificial Intelligence (XAI) to assess how characteristics related to Autism Spectrum Disorder (ASD) impact the classification precision of the framework.

The training data along with the framework are used in explainable AI systems to describe the predictions made with the testing data. As will be discussed in the following part, the major important attributes have been selected and utilized for both model testing and training.

Furthermore, SHAP (SHapley Additive exPlanations) was applied to determine the very important qualities. SHAP is a composite framework designed to interpret predictions by identifying the most crucial attribute necessary for making an informed choice. SHAP incorporates a novel class that encompasses feature significance metrics and a resolution attained by using the most suitable features. SHAP uses shapely values to quantify the effectiveness of any machine learning model, while also considering the fairness aspect from game theory. SHAP provides a paradigm with combined local and global explanations.

5.2.1 Explanation Through Summary Plot

'Summary Plot' highlights which characteristics matter most and the manner in which they impact the forecast for a certain category. Points on the graph represent SHAP values (horizontal axis) for each feature and each data instance (row) in the data. The impact of each feature on the model's output is measured by the SHAP value. Greater feature value has a greater influence on the forecast for the chosen class, according to a larger SHAP value (bigger divergence from the graph's center). Positive SHAP values, which are located at right side from the center, are attributes values that have an influence on the chosen class's prediction. Negative values (points located to the left of the centre) have an unfavorable impact on categorization within this category. The relevance of the attributes have been noted down in the Table 3 for different dataset (Fig. 9).

Explainable Machine Learning Strategy 331

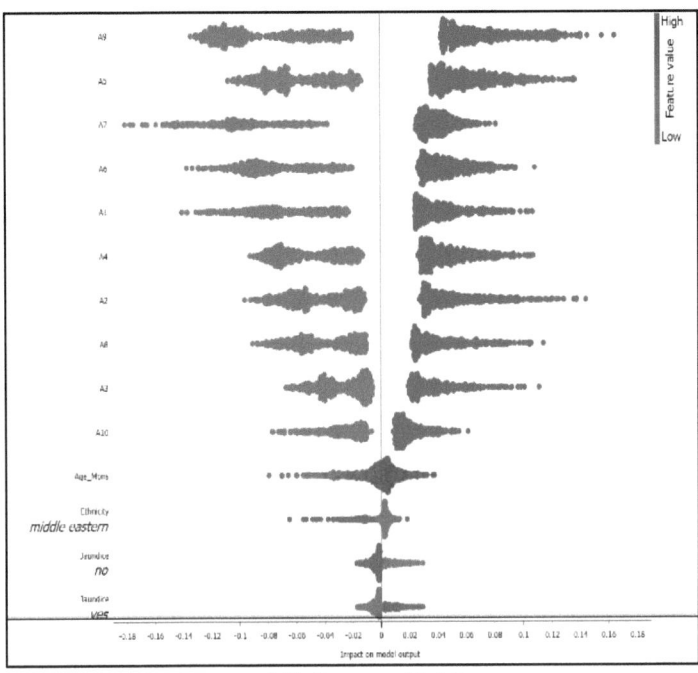

(a)" Category Toddler

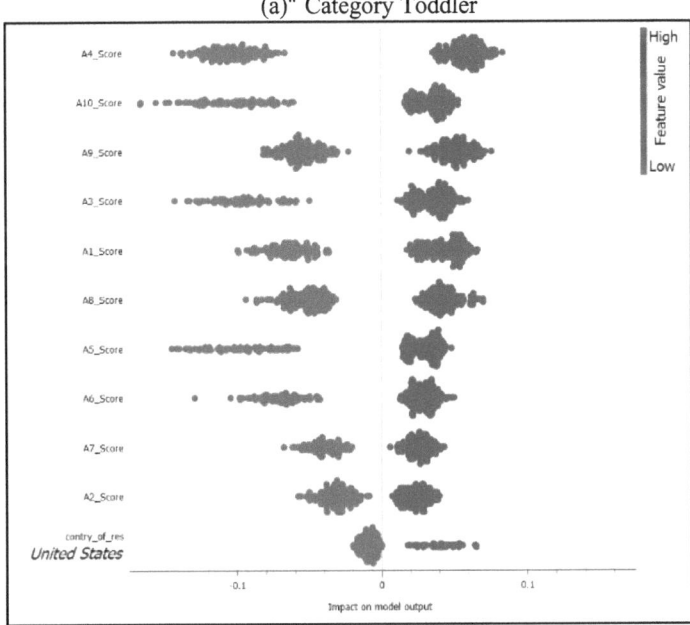

(b)" Category Child

Fig. 9. Output of Summary Plot (For Output Class Yes), for Category (a) Toddler, (b) Children, (c) Adolescent, & (d) Adult

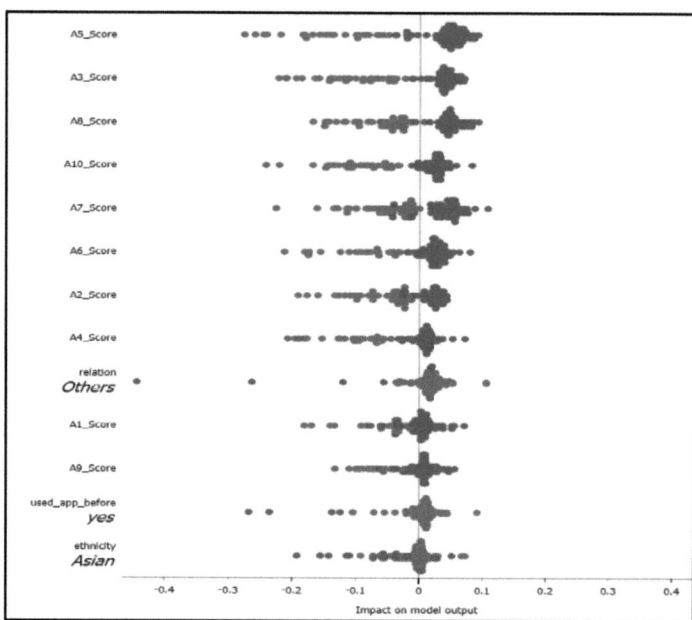

(c) Category Adolescent

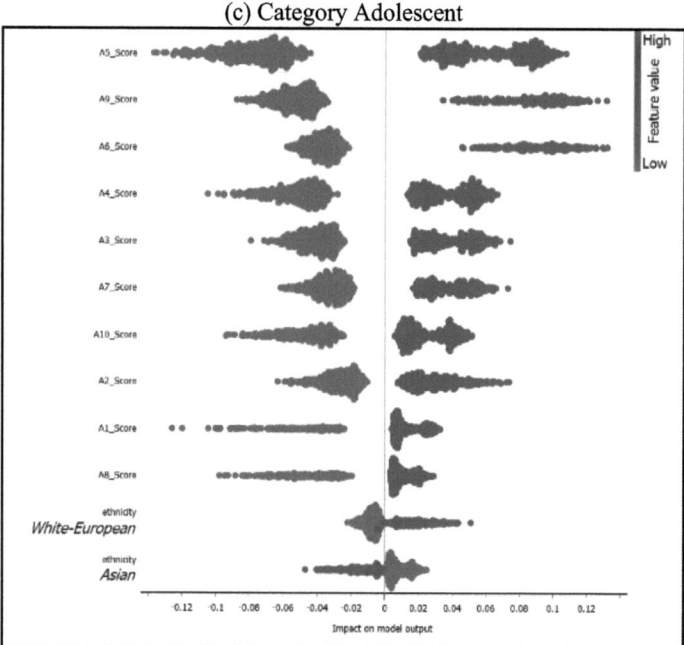

(d) Category Adult

Fig. 9. (*continued*)

These graphical representations display the characteristics that most influence the chosen class's prediction and their relative contributions (towards or against the prediction).

Analyzing the graphs obtained from Summary Plot, it is found that different attributes are responsible for ASD among different age groups like – Toddler, Child, Adolescent and Adult. It has been summarized in the following Table 3. It is found that attributes responsible for ASD amongst Adolescent & Adult age group are mostly same, while for Toddler and children group, these attributes are bit different with few similarities.

Table 3. Accountable Features Selection through Summary plot of XAI Model

	Summary Plot
Toddler	A9,A5,A1,A7,A6, A4,A2,A8,A3,A10
Child	A4,A10,A9,A3,A1,A8,A5,A6
Adolescent	A5,A3,A8,A10,A7, A6,A2,A4
Adult	A5,A9,A6,A4,A3, A7,A10,A2,A1

5.2.2 Feature Engineering

SHAP explainer has already explained the machine learning models and identified the most responsible features for ASD detection. Further, we have used Information Gain and Chi Squared feature selection methods to rank the attributes, which are basically the answers of the questionnaire Q1 to Q10 of the ASD Data set. The ranked attributes have been enlisted in the Table 4 (Fig. 10).

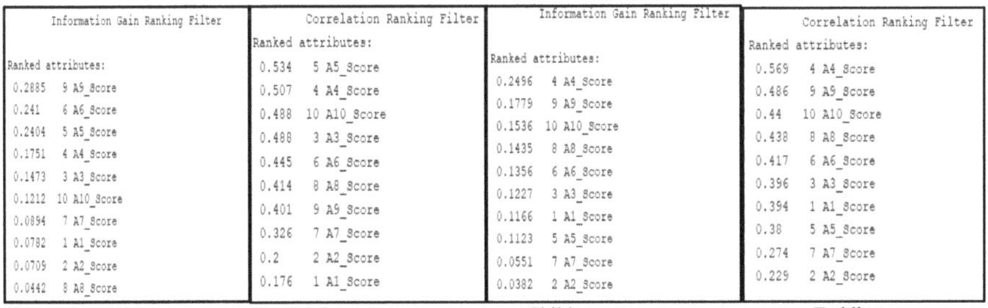

Information Gain Ranking Filter	Correlation Ranking Filter	Information Gain Ranking Filter	Correlation Ranking Filter
Ranked attributes:	Ranked attributes:	Ranked attributes:	Ranked attributes:
0.2885 9 A5_Score	0.534 5 A5_Score	0.2496 4 A4_Score	0.569 4 A4_Score
0.241 6 A6_Score	0.507 4 A4_Score	0.1779 9 A9_Score	0.486 9 A9_Score
0.2404 5 A5_Score	0.488 10 A10_Score	0.1536 10 A10_Score	0.44 10 A10_Score
0.1751 4 A4_Score	0.488 3 A3_Score	0.1435 8 A8_Score	0.438 8 A8_Score
0.1473 3 A3_Score	0.445 6 A6_Score	0.1356 6 A6_Score	0.417 6 A6_Score
0.1212 10 A10_Score	0.414 8 A8_Score	0.1227 3 A3_Score	0.396 3 A3_Score
0.0894 7 A7_Score	0.401 9 A9_Score	0.1166 1 A1_Score	0.394 1 A1_Score
0.0782 1 A1_Score	0.326 7 A7_Score	0.1123 5 A5_Score	0.38 5 A5_Score
0.0709 2 A2_Score	0.2 2 A2_Score	0.0551 7 A7_Score	0.274 7 A7_Score
0.0442 8 A8_Score	0.176 1 A1_Score	0.0382 2 A2_Score	0.229 2 A2_Score
Category: Adult	Adolescent	Child	Toddler

Fig. 10. Ranking of Attributes through Information Gain & Correlation Ranking

Table 4. Features selection through Information Gain & Correlation Ranking

Toddler Data		Child Data		Adolescent Data		Adult Data	
Info Gain Ranking	Correlation Ranking	Info Gain Ranking	Correlation Ranking	Info Gain Ranking	Correlation Ranking	Info Gain Ranking	Correlation Ranking
A4	A4	A4	A4	A5	A5	A9	A9
A9	A9	A9	A9	A4	A4	A6	A6
A10	A10	A10	A10	A3	A10	A5	A5
A8	A8	A8	A8	A10	A3	A4	A4
A6	A6	A6	A6	A6	A6	A3	A3

Comparing Tables 3 and 4, it is seen that the characteristics necessary for ASD identification are quite similar. Table 3 shows qualities from explainable AI, whereas Table 4 shows attributes from two feature selection methods: Info Gain Ranking and Correlation Ranking. The characteristics that provide responses to questions Q1 through Q10 are known to be the Primary Determining variables in ASD cases. We discover that Explainable approaches accurately identify the characteristics responsible for ASD identification. The most important Primary Determining features are summarized in Table 5.

Using SHAP as an explainer, prediction of machine learning model (Random Forest) has been explained here in Table 5. It is vividly found that the set of attributes been selected for a particular age group are justified by human intelligence. As Toddler and Children are unable to express their feelings, mostly their gestures are considered for detection of ASD. On the contrary, ASD symptoms of Adolescent and Adults get identified through their activities, or conversations.

We evaluate the effectiveness of the Random Forest Algorithm, by adjusting attributes count and analysing the F-measure scores accordingly. It has been observed that the F-measure score grows on as the number of attributes got increased. The highest point (such as 1) is attained when we have a total of 21 attributes, as shown in the Fig. 11.

Table 5. Most accountable attributes of ASD Detection

Age Group	ASD Determining Attributes	
Toddler	A9, A5, A1, A7	**A9** Does your child use simple gestures? (e.g. wave goodbye) **A5** Does your child pretend? (e.g. care for dolls, talk on a toy phone) **A1** Does your child look at you when you call his/her name? **A7** If you or someone else in the family is visibly upset, does your child show signs of wanting to comfort them? (e.g. stroking hair, hugging them
Child	A4, A10, A9, A8, A5	**A4** S/he finds it easy to go back and forth between different activities **A10** S/he finds it hard to make new friends **A9** S/he finds it easy to work out what someone is thinking or feeling just by looking at their face **A8** When s/he was in preschool, s/he used to enjoy playing games involving pretending with other children **A5** S/he doesn't know how to keep a conversation going with his/her peers
Adolescent	A5, A3, A10, A4, A8	**A5** S/he doesn't know how to keep a conversation going with his/her peers **A3** In a social group, s/he can easily keep track of several different peoples conversations **A10** S/he finds it hard to make new friends **A4** S/he finds it easy to go back and forth between different activities **A8** S/he finds it difficult to imagine what it would be like to be someone
Adult	A5, A9, A6, A4	**A5** I find it easy to read between the lines when someone is talking to me **A9** I find it easy to work out what someone is thinking or feeling just by looking at their face **A6** I know how to tell if someone listening to me is getting bored **A4** If there is an interruption, s/he can switch back to what s/he was doing very quick

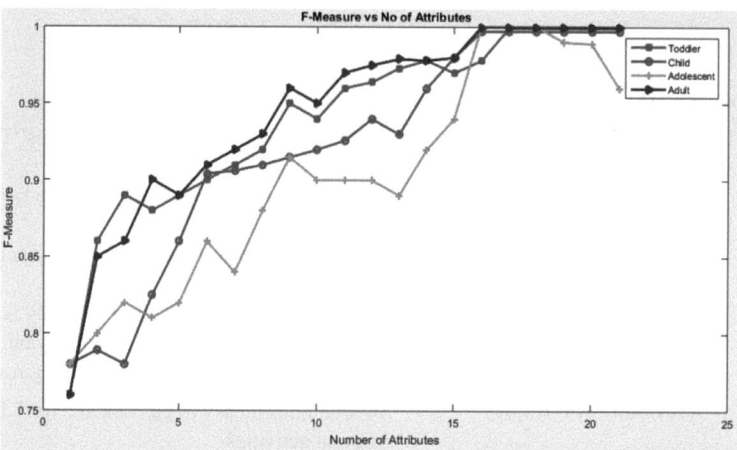

Fig. 11. Random Forest Classifiers Performance over increasing number of attributes for four ASD dataset

6 Conclusion

The autism spectrum disorder prediction framework is essential for identifying autism and aids in prompt diagnosis. In this study, we evaluated prediction models for autism spectrum disorder using several machine learning approaches. The extensive comparison based on common parameters enables the rapid identification of architectural and implementation-related similarities and differences across distinct prediction models. Compared to previous autistic spectrum disorder methodologies, our research is unique because of the comprehensive analysis we provided. This research does not only combined methods for predicting autism spectrum disorders, It also used Explainable Artificial Intelligence (XAI), to explain which attributes are responsible for ASD amongst Toddler, Children. Adolescent and Adult group. With the help of different Machine learning Algorithms along with XAI model, physicians may better assist children and other age groups with ASD by offering customized treatment suggestions. Thus, the research work has turned into more useful for ASD prediction.

References

1. Thabtah, F.: Machine learning in autistic spectrum disorder behavioral research: a review and ways forward. Inform. Health Soc. Care **44**(3), 278–297 (2019)
2. Thabtah, F., Kamalov, F., Rajab, K.: A new computational intelligence approach to detect autistic features for autism screening. Int. J. Med. Informatics **117**, 112–124 (2018)
3. Satu, M.S., Sathi, F.F., Arifen, M.S., Ali, M.H., Moni, M.A.: Early detection of autism by extracting features: A case study in bangladesh. In: Proc. ICREST. pp. 400–405 (2019)
4. Abbas, H., Garberson, F., Glover, E., Wall, D.P.: Machine learning approach for early detection of autism by combining questionnaire and home video screening. J. Am. Med. Inform. Assoc. **25**(8), 1000–1007 (2018)

5. Thabtah, F.: Autism spectrum disorder screening: machine learning adaptation and dsm-5 fulllment. In: Proceedings of the ICMHI'17. pp. 1–6 (2017)
6. Howlader, K.C., Satu, M.S., Barua, A., Moni, M.A.: Mining significant features of diabetes mellitus applying decision trees: a case study in Bangladesh. BioRxiv 481994 (2018)
7. Hossain, M.A., Islam, S.M.S., Quinn, J.M., Huq, F., Moni, M.A.: Machine learning and bioinformatics models to identify gene expression patterns of ovarian cancer associated with disease progression and mortality. J. Biomed. Inform. **100**, 103313 (2019)
8. Duda, M., Ma, R., Haber, N., Wall, D.: Use of machine learning for behavioral distinction of autism and ADHD. Transl. Psychiatry **6**(2), e732–e732 (2016)
9. Akter, T., Khan, M.I., Ali, M.H., Satu, M.S., Uddin, M.J., Moni, M.A.: Improved machine learning based classification model for early autism detection. In: Proceedings of the ICREST, pp. 742–747 (2021)
10. Al-Qabandi, M., Gorter, J.W., Rosenbaum, P.: Early autism detection: are we ready for routine screening? Pediatrics **128**(1), e211–e217 (2011)
11. Al Banna, M.H., Ghosh, T., Taher, K.A., Kaiser, M.S., Mahmud, M.: A monitoring system for patients of autism spectrum disorder using artificial intelligence. In: Proc. Brain Informatics. pp. 251–262 (2020)
12. Alam, M.E., Kaiser, M.S., Hossain, M.S., Andersson, K.: An iot-belief rule base smart system to assess autism. In: Proceedings of the iCEEiCT, pp. 672–676 (2018)
13. Biswas, M., Whaiduzzaman, M.: Efficient mobile cloud computing through computation offloading. Int. J. Adv. Technol. **10**(2) (2018)
14. Akib, A.A.S., Ferdous, M.F., Biswas, M., Khondokar, H.M.: Articial intelligence humanoid bongo robot in bangladesh. In: Proceedings of the ICASERT, pp. 1–6 (2019)
15. Sumi, A. I., Zohora, M. F., Mahjabeen, M., Faria, T. J., Mahmud, M., Kaiser, M.S.: f ASSERT: a fuzzy assistive system for children with autism using Internet of Things. In: Brain Informatics: International Conference, BI 2018, Arlington, TX, USA, December 7–9, 2018, Proceedings 11, pp. 403–412. Springer International Publishing (2018)
16. Noor, M.B.T., Zenia, N.Z., Kaiser, M.S., Mahmud, M., Al Mamun, S.: Detecting neurodegenerative disease from mri: A brief review on a deep learning perspective. In: Proc. Brain Informatics. pp. 115–125. Springer (2019)
17. Ruiz, J., Mahmud, M., Modasshir, M., Kaiser, M.S., Alzheimer's Disease Neuroimaging Initiative, f.t., et al.: 3d densenet ensemble in 4-way classification of alzheimer's disease. In: Proceedings of the Brain Informatics, pp. 85–96 (2020)
18. Deepa, B., Murugappan, M., Sumithra, M., Mahmud, M., Al-Rakhami, M.S.: Pattern descriptors orientation and map rey algorithm based brain pathology classification using hybridized machine learning algorithm. IEEE Access pp. 1–16 (2021)
19. Ali, H.M., Kaiser, M.S., Mahmud, M.: Application of convolutional neural network in segmenting brain regions from MRI data. In: Liang, P., Goel, V., Shan, C. (eds.) Brain Informatics: 12th International Conference, BI 2019, Haikou, China, 13–15 Dec 2019, Proceedings, pp. 136–146. Springer International Publishing, Cham (2019). https://doi.org/10.1007/978-3-030-37078-7_14
20. Mahmud, M., et al.: A brain-inspired trust management model to assure security in a cloud based IoT framework for neuroscience applications. Cogn. Comput. **10**, 864–873 (2018)
21. Mahmud, M., Kaiser, M.S., McGinnity, T.M., Hussain, A.: Deep learning in mining biological data. Cogn. Comput. **13**, 1–33 (2021)
22. Mahmud, M., Kaiser, M.S., Hussain, A., Vassanelli, S.: Applications of deep learning and reinforcement learning to biological data. IEEE Trans. Neural Netw. Learn. Syst. **29**(6), 2063–2079 (2018)
23. Payrovnaziri, S.N., et al.: Explainable artificial intelligence models using real-world electronic health record data: a systematic scoping review. J. Am. Med. Inform. Assoc. **27**(7), 1173–1185 (2020)

24. Shamim Kaiser, M., Mamun, Shamim Al, Mahmud, Mufti, Tania, Marzia Hoque: Healthcare robots to combat COVID-19. In: Santosh, K.C., Joshi, A. (eds.) COVID-19: Prediction, decision-making, and its impacts. LNDECT, vol. 60, pp. 83–97. Springer, Singapore (2021). https://doi.org/10.1007/978-981-15-9682-7_10
25. Thabtah, F.F.: Autistic spectrum disorder screening data for adult. Manukau Inst. Technol. (2017)
26. Thabtah, F.F.: Autistic Spectrum Disorder Screening Data for children (2017)
27. Thabtah, F.F.: Autistic Spectrum Disorder Screening Data for Adolescent, (2017)
28. Banerjee, J.S., Chakraborty, A., Mahmud, M., Kar, U., Lahby, M., Saha, G.: Explainable artificial intelligence (XAI) based analysis of stress among tech workers amidst COVID-19 pandemic. In: Lahby, M., Pilloni, V., Sekhar Banerjee, J., Mahmud, M. (eds.) Advanced AI and Internet of Health Things for Combating Pandemics, pp. 151–174. Springer International Publishing, Cham (2023). https://doi.org/10.1007/978-3-031-28631-5_8
29. Banerjee, J.S., Mahmud, M., Brown, D.: Heart rate variability-based mental stress detection: an explainable machine learning approach. SN Comput. Sci. **4**(2), 176 (2023)
30. Nandan, M., Banerjee, J.S., Chakraborty, A., Sarigiannidis, P.: Unboxing feature engineering with explainable AI (XAI) in diabetes prediction. In: WIN 6.0 2025 Conference Proceedings, Springer (2025) (In Press)
31. Nandan, M., Banerjee, J. S., Chakraborty, A., Sarigiannidis, P.: XAI4Obesity: explainable AI for obesity risk prediction. In: HUMAN 2025 Conference Proceedings, Springer (2025) (In Press)

Short-Term Water Demand Forecasting: A Comparative Study of Deep Learning and Conventional Machine Learning Algorithms

Hakob Grigoryan[✉]

Smart Energy Department, NVISION Systems and Technologies, Barcelona, Spain
hakob.grigoryan@nvision.es

Abstract. Accurate prediction of water consumption and demand is essential for effective resource management and promoting sustainable development, particularly in the face of challenges posed by natural resource scarcity. This paper presents a comparative study between Deep Learning and conventional Machine Learning algorithms for the prediction task of urban water demand. A novel Deep Learning approach combining Autoencoder with Long Short-Term Memory network called AE-LSTM is applied to predict hourly and daily water demand using historical consumption data from households within the Valencia metropolitan area, Spain. The model's performance is evaluated against well-known Machine Learning techniques like Support Vector Machines for Regression (SVR) and Random Forest (RF) using various error metrics, including RMSE, MAE, and POCID. Experimental results demonstrate that the hybrid AE-LSTM model outperforms other techniques for both daily and hourly prediction horizons, establishing it as a reliable method for accurate short-term water demand prediction task. The study concludes that integrating innovative Deep Learning models into water management systems can offer a valuable solution, significantly enhancing effectiveness in addressing the growing global demand for water resources.

Keywords: Water demand prediction · water consumption · Machine Learning · Deep Learning · LSTM · Autoencoder · AE-LSTM · Random Forest · SVM

1 Introduction

Water is a fundamental resource for human life, environment, and economic development [1]. Effective management of water resources is vital for societal wellbeing, impacting health, industry, agriculture, energy, and other sectors [2]. In recent decades, factors like climate change, population growth, industrial development and urbanization have elevated water consumption and exhausted existing resources, leading to a global rise in water scarcity [3]. Addressing these challenges requires a comprehensive approach to water management, emphasizing the critical importance of sustainable practices to balance the increasing water demand with resource preservation for future generations.

Water systems are inherently complicated, comprising of complex networks of infrastructure, technological elements, environmental and socio-economic factors, requiring comprehensive and adaptable management strategies [4]. Water distribution systems are designed to fulfill diverse needs of consumers, ensuring both immediate and long-term requirements. In the design and long-term planning of water infrastructure, variables such as population dynamics, price structure, or climate change are considered. These considerations help to establish new water supplies and enhance existing distribution networks. Conversely, consumption and demand planning, which focuses on periods of less than a year, aims to optimize the operation of water systems and effectively manage consumers' needs considering short-term influencing factors [5]. Overall, an accurate prediction of urban water demand is crucial for effective planning, management, and the optimal operation of water systems.

Short-term water demand prediction serves as a basis for decision-making systems and provides valuable insights into consumption behavior [3]. The methods employed for short-term forecasting tasks can be broadly categorized into linear and non-linear approaches. Linear methods, which include exponential smoothing, autoregressive moving average (ARMA) models, and simple linear regression analysis, utilize either univariate or multivariate methodologies for various regression tasks [6]. These methods are extensively employed to capture and analyze trends by focusing on the statistical characteristics inherent in the data. Short-term water demand, characterized by dynamic fluctuations, is heavily influenced by various external factors. Previous research studies have consistently indicated that while statistical methods are useful in long-term forecasting applications, they tend to exhibit limitations in accurately forecasting short-term water demand when compared to the Machine Learning methods [7, 8]. This underscores the importance of adopting advanced computational approaches to enhance forecasting precision, recognizing the complex dynamics and various influencing factors that impact water usage over time. To address the non-linear nature of water data, we aim to explore various methods discussed in the literature and employ innovative data-driven methodologies for short-term water demand forecasting tasks.

This paper introduces a forecasting framework employing advanced Deep Learning algorithms. Deep Learning is a subset of Machine Learning that leverages multi-layer neural networks to autonomously process extensive raw data, by surpassing the limitations of conventional data-driven techniques [9]. In contrast to traditional Machine Learning with shallow architectures, Deep Learning employs multiple transformations on input data using linear or non-linear techniques, resulting in a complex structure that yields impressive results in various time series analyses and prediction tasks [10]. The presented research aims to develop a hybrid Deep Learning model, named AE-LSTM, which integrates Autoencoders with Long Short-Term Memory networks to predict short-term water demand and directional movements. Through an extensive experimental evaluation using historical urban water consumption data from Spain, the study aims to validate the effectiveness of the proposed methodology. The remainder of this paper is organized as follows: Sect. 2 presents the related work in the field of water management for consumption and demand analysis. Section 3 outlines the methods employed in developing the proposed Deep Learning and Machine Learning prediction models. Section 4 elaborates on the case study and the proposed experimental framework of the comparative study. Section 4 discusses the study and presents the experimental results, while Sect. 5 concludes the research findings.

2 Related Work

Over the last few decades, numerous studies have been undertaken to model and forecast short-term water demand. Traditionally, these methods relied on univariate time series models which were based on the analysis of past historical observations. For example, J. Caiado employed a methodology with Exponential Smoothing, ARIMA, and GARCH models for water demand forecasting, and demonstrated promising results in the forecasting of daily water consumption in Spain [11]. Similarly, Fildes et al. presented two case studies on short-term demand forecasting for water and gas utilities using ARIMA and Exponential Smoothing techniques. Their findings revealed that complex multivariate approaches, incorporating weather effects, outperform extrapolative methods based solely on past historical data [12]. Also, Koo et al. analyzed water demand fluctuation for effective water distribution control, achieving high accuracy in daily water demand prediction task with a multiple ARIMA model, and providing a practical framework for rational water management systems [13]. While linear models offer simplicity and interpretability, their inability to describe the hidden relationships in non-linear data limits their effectiveness and accuracy in capturing the complexities of water data.

To address this non-linear problem, recent studies tend to apply data-driven methodologies for predicting short-term water consumption and demand. The increasing focus on Machine Learning techniques is driven by their recognized capabilities in delivering accurate, tractable, and robust solutions for complex, dynamic, and non-linear real-world challenges [8]. For example, Herrera et al. applied well-known algorithms like ANNs, SVR, Random Forest (RF) to forecast hourly water demand of south-eastern Spanish city. Experimental study revealed the superiority of SVR model against other methods for urban water supply forecasting task [14]. In another study, Pesantez et al. applied several Machine Learning methods for forecasting hourly water demand with smart meter data, revealing that RF and ANNs consistently outperform other models in different scenarios [15]. More comprehensively, Ghalehkhondabi et al. conducted an in-depth literature review of various soft computing methods for water consumption forecasting from 2005 to 2015. They emphasized the potential of these methods in the short-term forecasting task while also addressing the limitations in existing methodologies, highlighting the need for further research [16].

In more recent studies, researchers applied a combination of different methods to predict water demand. For example, Salloom et al. presented a novel Deep Learning model for short-term water demand forecasting using a gated recurrent unit (GRU) combined with K-means algorithm. Their experimental results have shown that the proposed model achieves a 6-fold reduction in model complexity, with a 30% reduction in prediction error [17]. Similarly, Du et al. proposed an LSTM-based model, integrating discrete wavelet transform (DWT) and principal component analysis (PCA), showcasing superior accuracy in demand peak prediction using data from Suzhou, China [18]. Also, Pu et al. introduced a combined model called Wavelet-CNN-LSTM for short-term water demand forecasting task. Their model outperformed other standalone methods in both single-step and multi-step predictions [19]. Fu et al. conducted an extensive literature review on current Deep Learning applications in urban water systems, addressing challenges and emphasizing the transformative potential of these algorithms. Despite highlighting the significant potential in diverse aspects of urban water management, their study underscores that practical applications and measurable benefits of Deep Learning methods in this field remain limited [20]. This emphasizes the necessity for further research to address existing challenges.

3 Methodology

The research presented in this paper conducts a comparative analysis study. The main objective of the study is to evaluate the effectiveness of a hybrid Deep Learning-based system compared to conventional Machine Learning models for the prediction task of short-term water demand. The following sub-sections provide a brief introduction to the computational methods used to build the prediction models employed in the study.

3.1 Autoencoder with Long Short-Term Memory Neural Network (AE-LSTM)

The AE-LSTM model is a hybrid approach combining Autoencoder (AE) with Long Short-Term Memory network (LSTM). It integrates the benefits of unsupervised feature learning of Autoencoders with the ability of capturing temporal dependencies through LSTM models. This combination enhances the model's capability to predict sequences or time-dependent patterns, making it particularly effective for time series data with existing noise. A brief introduction to Autoencoders and LSTM neural networks is provided below.

An Autoencoder is a type of Artificial Neural Network (ANN) used for unsupervised learning. The primary objective of this model is to generate a representation for an input dataset, accomplishing tasks such as dimensionality and noise reduction while ensuring that the restructured data closely resembles the original input data [21]. As depicted in Fig. 1, the Autoencoder model architecture comprises two phases: the encoder and the decoder. The encoder compresses the input data into a lower-dimensional representation, while the decoder reconstructs the input from this condensed form employing non-linear activation function and multiple layers.

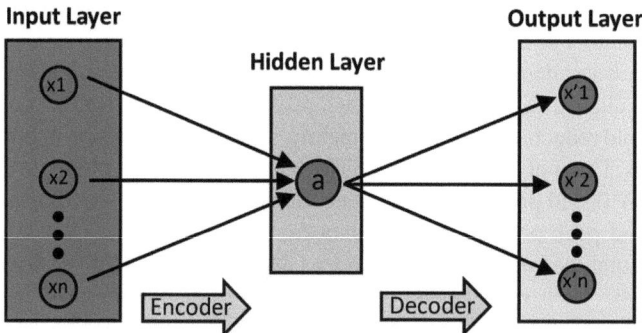

Fig. 1. The architecture of a simple Autoencoder network.

The main objective of the encoder phase is to decrease the dimensions of the input data X using the following equation:

$$Z = \sigma(WX + b) \tag{1}$$

where, W is the weight matrix, b is the bias vector, and σ is the activation function.

The decoder then takes this compressed representation and reconstructs the original data with the following equation:

$$X' = \sigma'(W'Z + b) \tag{2}$$

where, $W\prime$ is the weight matrix for decoding, $b\prime$ is the bias term, and $\sigma\prime$ is the activation function.

Similarly, during the decoding phase, training follows Eq. (2) with the objective of generating output data that closely resembles the original space, achieved through the minimization of the reconstruction error between the two. This involves adjusting the bias, weight, and the activation functions to achieve the desired outcome. The reconstruction error, which quantifies the disparity, can be computed using either a cross-entropy function or the sum of squared errors (SSE). In this study, the sum of squared errors (SSE) is employed to assess this error, as per the following equation:

$$SSE = \sum_{i=1}^{n}(X'_i - X_i)^2 \tag{3}$$

where n represents the number of data points, X_i denotes the original input at index i, and $X\prime_i$ represents the corresponding reconstructed input.

Long Short-Term Memory (LSTM) represents a distinctive variant of Recurrent Neural Network (RNN) architecture, based on the concept of a memory cell capable of preserving its state over time, alongside non-linear gate units that govern the flow of information into and out of the cell [22]. The general architecture of LSTM memory block with a single cell is depicted in Fig. 2.

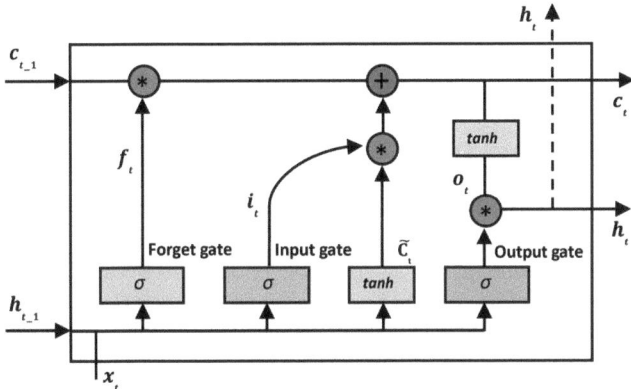

Fig. 2. The structure of the LSTM unit.

Each memory block of LSTM network comprises of one or more self-recurrent memory cells and three multiplicative units: input, output, and forget gates. These gates function as continuous analogs of read, write, and reset operations for each cell. The self-recurrent memory cell plays a critical role in preventing external interference, maintaining the status of the state across different time steps, effectively addressing the vanishing gradient problem. The input gate enables incoming signals to modify the cell state, while the forget and output gates contribute to memory block resetting and determining the next hidden state's value, respectively.

The LSTM model input is represented by the following equation $x = (x_1, x_2 \ldots, x_n)$, where $x_i = R^T$, $i = 1, 2, \ldots, n$; n is the number of input dimensions; T is the time lag; and the output sequence is defined as $y = (y_1, y_2, \ldots, y_n)$.

The forward training process of the LSTM network is formulated through the following equations:

$$f_t = \sigma(W_f \cdot [h_{t-1}, x_t] + b_f) \tag{4}$$

$$i_t = \sigma(W_i [h_{t-1}, x_t] + b_i) \tag{5}$$

$$\widetilde{C_t} = tanh(W_C \cdot [h_{t-1}, x_t] + b_c) \tag{6}$$

$$C_t = f_t * C_{t-1} + i_t \cdot \widetilde{C_t} \tag{7}$$

$$o_t = \sigma(W_0 \cdot [h_{t-1}, x_t] + b_0) \tag{8}$$

$$h_t = o_t * tanh(C_t) \tag{9}$$

where i_t, o_t, f_t denote the activation of the input, output and forget gates, respectively; C_t and h_t denote the activation vector for each cell and memory block, respectively; W and b are the weight parameter and bias term; $\sigma(x)$ and $tanh(x)$ are sigmoid and hyperbolic tangent functions, defined as:

$$\sigma(x) = \frac{1}{1+e^{-x}} \quad \text{and} \quad tanh(x) = \frac{e^x - e^{-x}}{e^x + e^{-x}} \tag{10}$$

3.2 Random Forest (RF) Algorithm

The Random Forest (RF) algorithm is an ensemble learning method developed by Breiman, applicable for both classification and regression problems [23]. It implements classification tasks by constructing an ensemble of decision trees, where each tree independently votes on the class, and the final prediction is determined by majority voting. In regression tasks, RF builds an ensemble of decision trees and predicts the output as the mean of the individual tree predictions (see Fig. 3).

The ensemble learning strategy significantly improves the stability and accuracy of the RF algorithm, providing a robust and accurate regression model capable of effectively

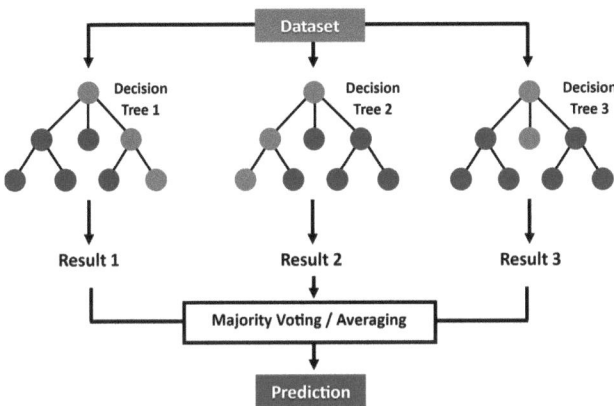

Fig. 3. RF algorithm in action.

handling overfitting problems and minimizing variance. This is achieved through the utilization of the bagging or bootstrap aggregating algorithm during the training phase of RF.

Given a sample data, bagging consistently selects bootstrap samples from the training set and then fits trees using the Gini impurity by the following equation:

$$g(N) = \sum_{i \neq j} P(\omega_i) P(\omega_j) \tag{11}$$

where $P(\omega_i)$ is the proportion of the population with class label i.

Following the training process, the RF model's output is determined by computing the average of the output values from all individual trees, as expressed by the following equation:

$$y = \frac{1}{B} \sum_{b=1}^{B} t_b(x) \tag{12}$$

3.3 Support Vector Machines for Regression (SVR)

Support Vector Machines (SVMs) are a family of robust supervised Machine Learning algorithms based on the early studies of Vapnik and Chervonenkis [24]. Its core concept is to discover a hyperplane with a maximized margin in high-dimensional space, effectively classifying data points into categories based on their position relative to the gap. SVMs for regression, also known as Support Vector Regression (SVR) (see Fig. 4) are designed to solve regression tasks by employing a kernel function.

Given a set of training data $S = \{(x_1, y_1), ..., (x_n, y_n)\}$, where $x_i \epsilon R^d$ is the model's input vector, $y_i \epsilon R$ is the models target output and the goal is to find a regression function $f(x)$ with at most ε deviation from the actual target y_i, while keeping w small for a flatter f.

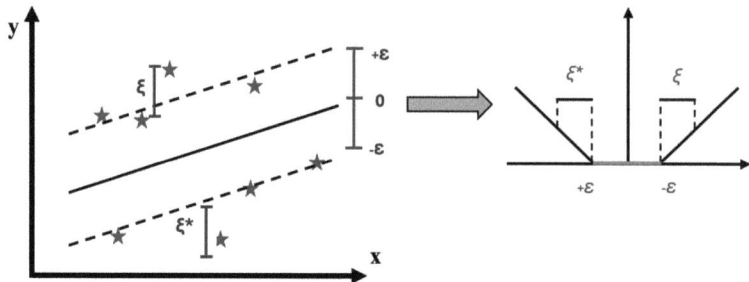

Fig. 4. Support Vector Machines for Regression.

The kernel based SVM discrimination hyperplane is defined by the following equation:

$$f(x) = w\prime \cdot \varphi(x) + b \tag{13}$$

where ω is a weight vector and b is bias, and φ is the feature extractor and n is the number of training data points.

To determine the coefficients w ω ω and b, SVR solves the following optimization problem b b:

$$\begin{aligned}&\text{minimize } \frac{1}{2}w^2 \\ &\text{subject to } \begin{cases} y_i - w^T x_i - b \leq \varepsilon \\ w^T x_i + b - y_i \leq \varepsilon \end{cases}\end{aligned} \tag{14}$$

To handle the feasibility issues, soft margin slack variables ξi ξ_i, ξ_i^* ξ_i, ξ_i^*, $\xi * i$ are introduced to the optimization problem, such that:

$$\begin{aligned}&\text{minimize} \frac{1}{2}w^2 + C\sum_{i=1}^{l}(\xi_i + \xi_i^*) \\ &\text{subject to } \begin{cases} y_i - w^T x_i - b \leq \varepsilon + \xi_i \\ w^T x_i + b - y_i \leq \varepsilon + \xi_i^* \\ \xi_i, \xi_i^* \geq 0 \\ C > 0 \end{cases}\end{aligned} \tag{15}$$

where $\frac{1}{2}w^2$ is a regularization term, C is a regularization constant which controls the trade-off between the empirical risk and regularization term which aim to prevent the overfitting problem.

The presented optimization problem can be solved by introducing Lagrange multipliers, resulting in the general form of the SVM-based regression function:

$$f(x) = \sum_{i=1}^{l}(a_i - \alpha_i^*)K(x_i x) + b \tag{16}$$

where $K(x_i, x_j)$ is the kernel function.

In this research, the widely used Gaussian radial basis function (RBF) kernel is adopted:

$$K(x, x') = exp\left(-\|x - x'\|^2 / 2\sigma^2\right) \tag{17}$$

4 Experiments

Valencia is the third-largest city in Spain, with a population of approximately 800,000 inhabitants. Together with its neighboring municipalities, it forms one of the major urban areas on the European side of the Mediterranean Sea with a combined population of over 1.5 million people. In this research study, water consumption data from the Valencia area has been obtained from the open-source database provided by the SmartH2O project [25].

The experimental dataset contains anonymized data from 334 households collected during the period from May 2015 to April 2017, totaling more than 1,000,000 observations. The raw dataset was thoroughly analyzed using data preprocessing techniques. Different techniques are performed to identify and reduce the irrelevant features present in the dataset and prepare them for the learning algorithms to perform the prediction task.

First, a data normalization step is implemented to standardize the range of different variables to a given scale, aiming to reduce the impact of outliers. This is achieved through the application of a min-max normalization method.

Next, the presence of seasonality in the dataset is analyzed using the Autocorrelation Function (ACF) and Partial Autocorrelation Function (PACF). As presented in Fig. 5, peaks and recurring patterns at specific lags in the ACF plot indicate the existence of seasonality, while significant spikes in the PACF plot provide insights into the duration and direct relationships within the seasonal patterns. Water demand is significantly influenced by human behavior, which varies based on the day of the week. As for instance, during weekdays, water consumption patterns differ from those observed on weekends, and holidays display consumption trends different from regular days.

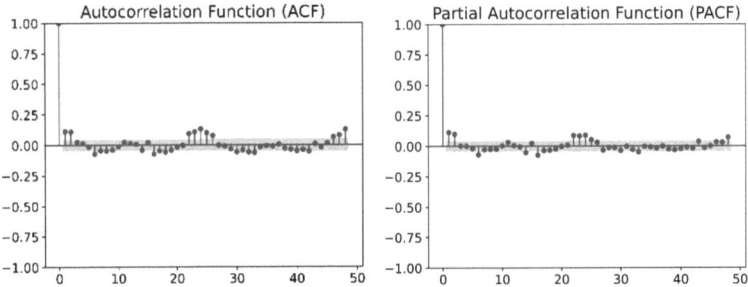

Fig. 5. ACF and PACF functions for hourly water consumption data.

Following those observations, a feature engineering step was implemented considering calendar information. In our model, we categorize days into weekdays, weekends, and holidays, taking into account factors such as the time of day and the month of the year. To enhance the experimental evaluation, we reformatted the original dataset, which originally consisted only of hourly water consumption data, into a daily periodicity, enabling a comprehensive analysis with both interval datasets in our experiments.

In the final stage, the ultimate datasets containing hourly and daily data together with calendar-based information were used as the input of the prediction models. The built models are evaluated considering their forecasting accuracy for water demand values, utilizing metrics such as Root Mean Square Error (RMSE) and Mean Absolute Error (MAE) defined by:

$$MAE = \frac{1}{n} \sum_{i=1}^{n} |A(i) - P(i)| \quad (18)$$

$$RMSE = \sqrt{\frac{1}{n} \sum_{i=1}^{n} (A(i) - P(i))^2} \quad (19)$$

where $A(i)$ is an actual testing sample, $P(i)$ is the prediction result, and n is the total number of testing samples.

Additionally, trend forecasting accuracy is evaluated using the metric called Prediction of Change in Direction (POCID) which measures the percentage of the number of correct decisions related to the changes in direction or trend, defined as:

$$POCID = 100 \times \frac{\sum_{\mu=1}^{N} D\mu}{N} \quad (20)$$

where $D\mu = \begin{cases} 1, & \text{if } (A_{(t+1)} - A_t)(P_{(t+1)} - P_t) > 0 \\ 0, & \text{otherwise} \end{cases}$

Experimental results are discussed in the next section.

5 Results and Discussions

This paper focuses on investigating the short-term forecasting task of urban water demand. The experimental evaluation of different models and scenarios, including the processes of model construction, training, and testing are executed in Python environment using Keras and Scikit-learn libraries dedicated to Deep Learning and statistical analysis. Dataset was standardized and had outliers removed before training. Seasonality in consumption data led to consideration of the calendar effect, separating and labeling holidays, time, and days of the week. The resulting datasets were divided into training and testing sets, with a ratio of approximately 70% for training and 30% for testing.

We constructed three prediction models based on different computational algorithms presented in Sect. 3. For constructing the Deep Learning-based model, the hybrid AE-LSTM model was employed, incorporating LSTM encoder and decoder components specifically designed for sequential data. This architecture utilizes memory cells to excel in learning complex and dynamic input sequences, comprising two LSTM layers in both the encoder and decoder modules. We explored various cases and examined different parameters that influence the accuracy of forecasting results. For model configuration, we utilized the ReLU activation function, mean absolute error (MAE) as the loss function, and the Adam optimizer. Hyperparameters, including the number of hidden units, epochs, and batch size, were set to 64, 100, and 256, respectively. Standard parameters were employed for RF algorithm as proposed in [26]. In SVR, improper parameter selection can easily lead to overfitting problems, making it essential to regulate the model's complexity. This can be solved by tuning the model hyperparameters, for which we adopted K-fold cross-validation to fine-tune the regularization parameter C and the kernel parameter gamma as described in [27].

To thoroughly evaluate each model's capabilities, experiments were carried out on both daily and hourly consumption data, assessing the models for demand prediction values and trends. Comparative results for hourly water demand prediction task using three different models are depicted in Fig. 6. Evaluation results of proposed models using various error metrics are presented in Table 1.

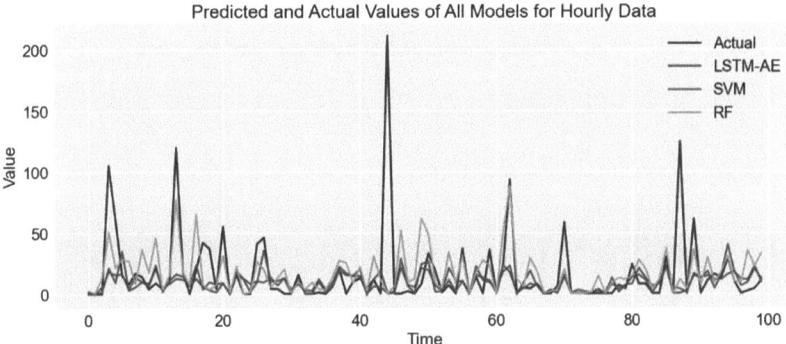

Fig. 6. Actual values versus predicted values in the case of different models using hourly data (household N112).

Table 1. Prediction Results of Proposed Models for Hourly Data.

Model	RMSE	MAE	POCID
AE-LSTM	1.190	0.441	58.24%
SVR	1.250	0.483	55.7%
RF	1.312	0.570	55.4%

Based on the achieved results, the adopted methodology which combines Autoencoders and LSTM improves the accuracy of water demand forecasting. According to the evaluation metrics for hourly data presented in Table 1, AE-LSTM outperforms other models in terms of demand value and trend accuracy. Additionally, based on RMSE, MAE, and POCID measurements, SVR exhibits superior performance compared to the RF model.

Subsequently, Table 2 presents the error metric values obtained for competing models, which are based on Deep Learning and Machine Learning algorithms for daily water consumption data. Additionally, Fig. 7 displays the actual and predicted values of these models.

Table 2. Prediction Results of Proposed Models for Daily Data.

Model	RMSE	MAE	POCID
AE-LSTM	0.770	0.596	60.8%
SVR	0.856	0.687	50%
RF	0.808	0.654	59.6%

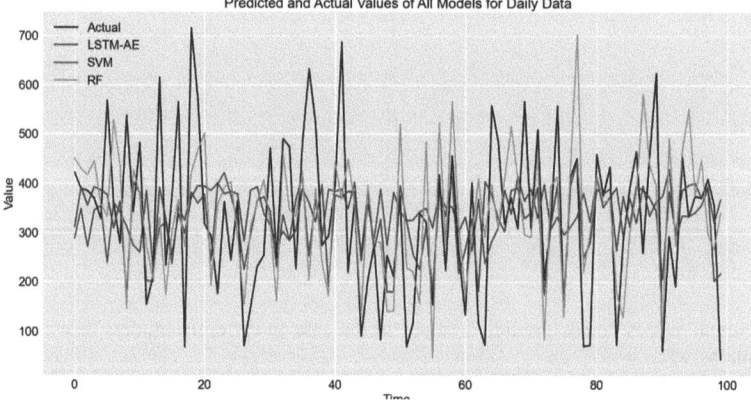

Fig. 7. Actual values versus predicted values in the case of different models using daily data (household N278).

Based on the results presented in Table 2, we observe that the AE-LSTM hybridized model performs best according to all evaluation metrics. The proposed Deep Learning model outperforms other competing models in predicting future water demand values and directional movements, exhibiting comparatively low error rates. The actual versus the predicted values in case of best fitting AE-LSTM model against the original values is presented in Fig. 8.

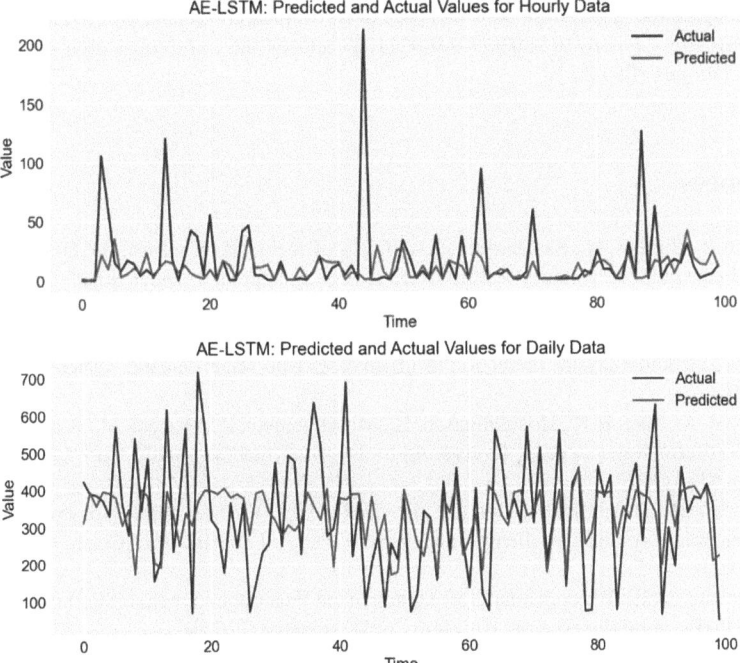

Fig. 8. Actual values versus predicted values in the case of best performing AE-LSTM model using hourly and daily water consumption data.

6 Conclusions

This study underscores the critical importance of accurately predicting short-term water demand in promoting efficient resource management and fostering sustainable development. In a comprehensive comparative analysis focused on water demand prediction, three different frameworks were applied to forecast both hourly and daily water demand using historical consumption data gathered from 334 households in Valencia, Spain. The systematic evaluation of the AE-LSTM model against well-established Machine Learning techniques, including Support Vector Machines for Regression (SVR) and Random Forest (RF) was done in terms of forecasting water demand values and directional movements. Error metrics like RMSE, MAE, and POCID were used to thoroughly analyze the prediction accuracy of each model. The comparative analysis revealed that the forecasting model, integrating Autoencoders with LSTM neural networks, consistently achieves a lower error rate for both daily and hourly water demand predictions (RMSE = 0.77 and MAE = 0.596 for daily data, RMSE = 1.190 and MAE = 0.441 for hourly data) compared to other conventional Machine Learning techniques applied to the same dataset. For the prediction accuracy of demand trends, we achieved 60% and 58.24% accuracy in terms of the POCID metric for daily and hourly data, respectively. The research study concludes that the AE-LSTM hybrid model is a reliable choice for implementing a short-term prediction task, positioning it as a promising candidate for urban water demand modeling.

Acknowledgments. This work was supported by a project CPP2021-008975, funded by MCIN/AEI/https://doi.org/10.13039/501100011033 and by the European Union project called NextGenerationEU/PRTR.

References

1. Leitão, J., Simões, N., Sá Marques, J.A., Gil, P., Ribeiro, B., Cardoso, A.: Detecting urban water consumption patterns: a time-series clustering approach. Water Supply **19**(8), 2323–2329 (2019)
2. Zubaidi, S.L., et al.: Hybridised artificial neural network model with slime mould algorithm: a novel methodology for prediction of urban stochastic water demand. Water **12**(10), 2692 (2020)
3. Niknam, A., Zare, H.K., Hosseininasab, H., Mostafaeipour, A., Herrera, M.: A critical review of short-term water demand forecasting tools—what method should I use? Sustainability **14**(9), 5412 (2022)
4. Bhandari, P., Creighton, D., Gong, J., Boyle, C., Law, K.M.: Evolution of cyber-physical-human water systems: challenges and gaps. Technol. Forecast. Soc. Chang. **191**, 122540 (2023)
5. Kame'enui, A.E.: Water demand forecasting in the Puget Sound region: Short and long-term models (Doctoral dissertation, University of Washington) (2003)
6. Brockwell, P.J., Davis, R.A. (eds.) Introduction to time series and forecasting. New York, NY: Springer New York (2002)
7. Pulido-Calvo, I., Montesinos, P., Roldán, J., Ruiz-Navarro, F.: Linear regressions and neural approaches to water demand forecasting in irrigation districts with telemetry systems. Biosys. Eng. **97**(2), 283–293 (2007)
8. House-Peters, L.A., Chang, H.: Urban water demand modeling: Review of concepts, methods, and organizing principles. Water Resour. Res. **47**(5) (2011)
9. Shinde, P.P., Shah, S.: A review of machine learning and deep learning applications. In 2018 Fourth international conference on computing communication control and automation (ICCUBEA), pp. 1–6. IEEE (2018)
10. Sarker, I.H.: Deep learning: a comprehensive overview on techniques, taxonomy, applications and research directions. SN Comput. Sci. **2**(6), 420 (2021)
11. Caiado, J.: Forecasting water consumption in Spain using univariate time series models (2007)
12. Fildes, R., Randall, A., Stubbs, P.: One day ahead demand forecasting in the utility industries: two case studies. J. Operat. Res. Soc. **48**(1), 15–24 (1997)
13. Koo, J., Koizwui, A., Inakazu, T.: A Study on daily water demand prediction model. J. Korean Soc. Water Wastewater **11**(1), 109–118 (1997)
14. Herrera, M., Torgo, L., Izquierdo, J., Pérez-García, R.: Predictive models for forecasting hourly urban water demand. J. Hydrol. **387**(1–2), 141–150 (2010)
15. Pesantez, J.E., Berglund, E.Z., Kaza, N.: Smart meters data for modeling and forecasting water demand at the user-level. Environ. Model. Softw. **125**, 104633 (2020)
16. Ghalehkhondabi, I., Ardjmand, E., Young, W.A., Weckman, G.R.: Water demand forecasting: review of soft computing methods. Environ. Monit. Assess. **189**, 1–13 (2017)
17. Salloom, T., Kaynak, O., He, W.: A novel deep neural network architecture for real-time water demand forecasting. J. Hydrol. **599**, 126353 (2021)
18. Du, B., Zhou, Q., Guo, J., Guo, S., Wang, L.: Deep learning with long short-term memory neural networks combining wavelet transform and principal component analysis for daily urban water demand forecasting. Expert Syst. Appl. **171**, 114571 (2021)

19. Pu, Z., et al.: A hybrid Wavelet-CNN-LSTM deep learning model for short-term urban water demand forecasting. Front. Environ. Sci. Eng. **17**(2), 22 (2023)
20. Fu, G., Jin, Y., Sun, S., Yuan, Z., Butler, D.: The role of deep learning in urban water management: a critical review. Water Res. **223**, 118973 (2022). https://doi.org/10.1016/j.watres.2022.118973
21. Bank, D., Koenigstein, N., Giryes, R.: Autoencoders. In: Rokach, L., Maimon, O., Shmueli, E. (eds.) Machine Learning for Data Science Handbook: Data Mining and Knowledge Discovery Handbook, pp. 353–374. Springer International Publishing, Cham (2023). https://doi.org/10.1007/978-3-031-24628-9_16
22. Staudemeyer, R.C., Morris, E.R.: Understanding LSTM--a tutorial into long short-term memory recurrent neural networks. arXiv preprint 1909.09586 (2019)
23. Breiman, L.: Random forests. Mach. Learn. **45**(1), 5–32 (2001). https://doi.org/10.1023/A:1010933404324
24. Gunn, S.R.: Support vector machines for classification and regression. ISIS technical report **14**(1), 5–16 (1998)
25. https://zenodo.org/records/556152#.Y_Y8BHbMK5e
26. Grigoryan, H.: Electricity consumption prediction using energy data, Socio-economic and weather indicators. A case study of Spain. In: 2021 9th International Conference on Control, Mechatronics and Automation (ICCMA), pp. 158–164. IEEE (2021)
27. Wang, J.E., Qiao, J.Z.: Parameter selection of svr based on improved k-fold cross validation. Appl. Mech. Mater. **462**, 182–186 (2014)

Improving Crop Yield Prediction Accuracy: A Hybrid Machine Learning Approach

Maharin Afroj[1], S. M. Nuruzzaman Nobel[1], Md Mohsin Kabir[2], M. F. Mridha[3(✉)], and Mufti Mahmud[4,5,6]

[1] Department of Computer Science and Engineering, Bangladesh University of Business and Technology, Dhaka 1216, Bangladesh

[2] Superior Polytechnic School, University of Girona, 17071 Girona, Spain
u1985702@campus.udg.edu

[3] Department of Computer Science, American International University-Bangladesh, Dhaka 1229, Bangladesh
firoz.mridha@aiub.edu

[4] Information and Computer Science Department, King Fahd University of Petroleum and Minerals, Dhahran 31261, Saudi Arabia
mufti.mahmud@kfupm.edu.sa

[5] SDAIA-KFUPM Joint Research Center for AI, King Fahd University of Petroleum and Minerals, Dhahran 31261, Saudi Arabia

[6] Interdisciplinary Research Center for Bio Systems and Machines, King Fahd University of Petroleum and Minerals, Dhahran 31261, Saudi Arabia

Abstract. With the world's growing population and increase in global food demand, improving crop yield is essential to meet this rising need, reduce the impact of food production on the environment, and contribute to the United Nation Sustainable Development Goals 2 (Zero Hunger) and 13 (Climate Action). Harnessing the increasing adoption of Artificial Intelligence in diverse application areas including agriculture, this work utilises the benefits of eXtreme Gradient Boosting (XGBoost), attention mechanism and Support Vector Regression (SVR) in an ensemble for predicting agricultural yields. A remarkable R^2 score of 0.9863, an accuracy of 99.35%, a mean squared error of 97627518.13, and a mean absolute error of 5277.06 are the results of the rigorous evaluation of the ensemble model using 5-fold cross-validation. The cross-validation guarantees generalisability across many datasets and the ensemble's strong performance is credited to its capacity to grasp intricate linkages in agricultural data. These results also indicate the model's ability to outperform the existing methods including recurrent neural networks, random forest and Naive Bayes. Implications for improving agricultural resource management and decision-making may arise from this work, which represents a major step forward in crop output prediction.

Keywords: Agriculture · Crop Prediction · Ensemble approach · Boosting algorithm

1 Introduction

The science of agricultural data analytics and machine learning has become instrumental in addressing critical challenges in the agricultural sector. One such pivotal area is crop yield prediction [3], which plays a central role in global food security and the effective management of agricultural resources. Several datasets have been used to solve this problem because crop output is dependent on a wide range of variables, including soil, weather, fertilizer use, and seed variety [2]. This demonstrates that forecasting agricultural yields involves many complex procedures rather than being a simple process. Even while the yield prediction algorithms in use today can estimate actual yields with reasonable accuracy, there is still room for improvement [4]. Regression techniques are being used to forecast future events and descriptive models are being used to extract meaning from the data and explain past events [5,6]. The nature of an ML model can be categorized as either descriptive or predictive, contingent upon the specific research challenge and the associated research inquiries. Descriptive models are employed to extract knowledge from gathered data and elucidate past events, whilst predictive models are utilized to forecast future outcomes [1].

The effectiveness of agriculture is significantly affected by climate change, which might potentially result in famine or food insecurity. The latter refers to a significant issue in areas that are marked by floods or other weather-induced calamities. Climate factors that impact agricultural productivity include precipitation, temperature of the air, humidity, and sun radiation [9]. Various studies have demonstrated that climate indicators, whether on a global or regional scale, have an impact on agricultural yields and supply and demand for food [10]. According to Damien et al.'s research, the decrease in crop production might be linked to either elevated temperatures or excessive rainfall [11]. Extreme temperature adversely impacts agricultural productivity by causes like elevated rainfall and respiration of crops, as well as heightened insect infestation [9]. The rise in temperature leads to an increase in agricultural water demand, which in turn affects crop yield [9,12,20,25]. To improve their efficacy, artificial neural networks are strong modelling and prediction tools [22]. Regression analysis is a systematic technique that focuses on data analysis for decision-making and problem-solving research purposes [21].

The findings of this study are valuable for both scholars and practitioners seeking to create innovative agricultural yield prediction models. Researchers in this field consider the obstacles to be significant since they enable them to anticipate and address these concerns prior to constructing their own models.

- Suggested an innovative hybrid model that combines leading machine learning techniques, resulting in outstanding accuracy (99.35%) and surpassing the performance of current approaches.
- Expanded the constraints: Utilised the unique capabilities of each model to develop a prediction system that is more reliable and precise.
- Potential for real-world impact: The ability to predict crop yield at an early stage and with high accuracy.

The subsequent sections of the paper are structured in the following manner: Sect. 2 introduces an extensive examination of the existing literature, specifically focusing on several algorithms and their respective applications. Section 3 provides an account of the dataset description and the processes used for preparation and at the end, our proposed model. The analysis and discussion of the results may be found in Sect. 4. Section 5 provides an analysis of the interpreted results.

2 Literature Review

Accurate crop yield forecasts are crucial for high-level decision-makers to make prompt and informed decisions at both national and regional levels. A precise crop yield forecasting model can assist farmers in making informed decisions on crop selection and optimal planting timing. Various methodologies exist for predicting agricultural yields. This review paper has examined the existing research on the application of machine learning in predicting agricultural production. Those publications which are related to our work are discussed in this section. Elavarasan et al. [7] Conducted a comprehensive analysis of literature on machine learning models used for predicting agricultural production by using meteorological factors. The report recommends using a comprehensive approach to identify additional variables that contribute to crop output. Liakos et al. [7] conducted utilising publications that specifically addressed agricultural management, animal management, water management, and soil management. Li, Lecourt, and Bishop conducted a comprehensive evaluation research to ascertain the maturity of fruits to establish the most favourable period for harvesting and predict crop production. Beulah et al. [8] investigated several data mining strategies utilised for predicting agricultural output and determined that utilising data mining techniques may effectively tackle the problem of crop yield prediction. When it comes to predicting crop yields using Deep Learning, hybrid networks and RNN-LSTM networks are the most effective, according to the study by Dharani et al. [13]. Both RNN and LSTM owe their great performance to their storing and feedback loops. They found that such networks can handle agricultural production time-series data better, making them better at generating predictions. To forecast agricultural yields, crops are analysed and categorised according to what Monali et al. [15] suggested. Data mining methods are used to do the classification. Several classification rules, including Naive Bayes and K-Nearest Neighbour, are addressed in this study. The principles that will apply to the dataset utilised in this study have been thoroughly examined and identified [17]. The relationship between forecast accuracy and the prediction itself is investigated by Murynin et al. [16] Yield prediction is accomplished using a linear model. To enhance the prediction accuracy, this model is enhanced with non-linear features. The time interval between the development of the forecast and the time of harvesting has been used to expect the model's accuracy. Using CNN, Villanueva and Salenga [23] created a model that could accurately predict which bitter melon leaves were excellent or poor. Even though the authors of the study stated that their research might estimate crop production, it is extremely challenging to do so using just the classification of excellent and bad leaves. Crop analysis in the research in [26] was done using the Multiple Linear Regression (MLR) approach. Using the decision tree technique and classification, more than 362 datasets are analysed to produce results. In order to predict the kind of soil, the training dataset in this case is divided into three categories: organic, inorganic, and real estate. The results that this system computes are trustworthy and accurate.

3 Methodology

3.1 Dataset Description

The Crop Yield Prediction Dataset [18] utilized in this study focuses on predicting crop yield, a vital aspect of agriculture with significant implications for global food security and climate change mitigation. It integrates various factors, including weather conditions such as rainfall and average temperature, as well as information on pesticide usage. The data sources encompass the Food and Agriculture Organization (FAO) for pesticides and yield information, and the World Data Bank for rainfall and average temperature records. The final dataset, named "Yield_df.csv," results from meticulous processing, including cleaning and merging of the aforementioned components. This dataset serves as a crucial resource for understanding historical crop yield patterns, aiding in agricultural risk management, and facilitating future yield predictions (as shown in Fig. 1) (Table 1).

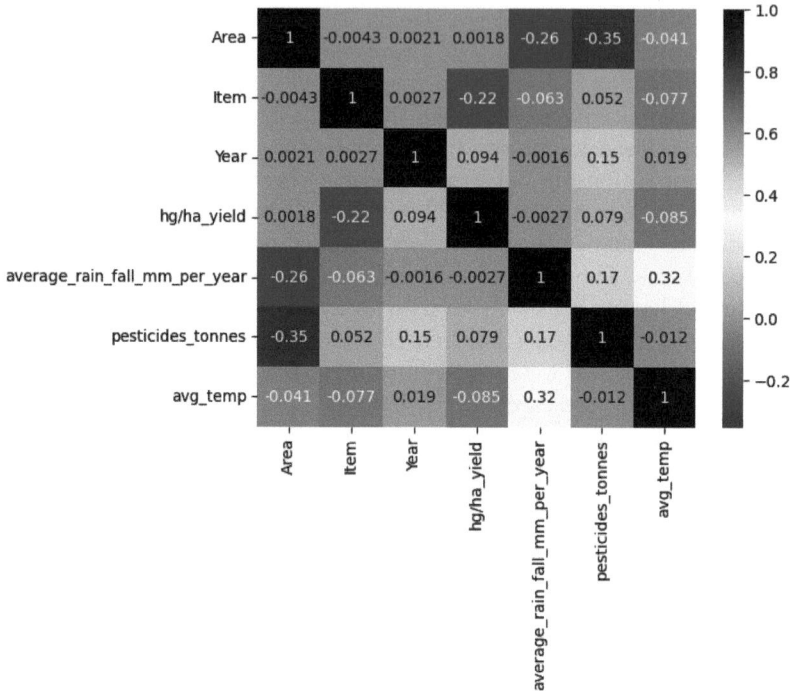

Fig. 1. Correlation matrix

Table 1. Description of Variables in the Dataset

Variable	Description
Area	Country names that plant crops
Item	Types of crops planted
Year	Time of planted crops in years 1990–2013
average_rain_fall_mm_per_year	Average rainfall per year
pesticides_tonnes	Pesticides used in tonnes
avg_temp	Average temperature
hg/ha_yield	Crops yield production value in hectogram per hectare (Hg/Ha)

3.2 Dataset Pre-processing

Within our data preprocessing workflow, we employed a range of advanced approaches to enhance the quality of our dataset. To maintain the initial distribution while scaling values to fit inside a specific range, we employed the Min-Max Scaler. This was particularly beneficial given the diverse sizes and the presence of irregularities in our dataset. The Eq. 1 provided is the Min-max formula, in which m represents the new significance, x represents the initial cell value, xmin represents the minimal value of the column, and xmax indicates the absolute highest value of the column. The Min-Max scaling equation is given by:

$$m = \frac{(x - xmin)}{(xmax - xmin)} \quad (1)$$

Subsequently, the Min-Max Scaling technique was employed to standardize the features into a consistent range in order to account for any possible variations in feature magnitudes. Subsequently, a purposeful partitioning technique was employed to allocate 80% of the dataset for training purposes and the remaining 20% for testing. A subset comprising 10% of the training set was then segregated and reserved for validation purposes. The preprocessing processes discussed in this part lay the foundation for accurate and unbiased model training and assessment, as we strive to forecast heart failure with precision.

3.3 Our Proposed Ensemble Model

A novel hybrid model including machine learning techniques has been devised to overcome the constraints of existing models. The objective of this model is to outperform existing methods in accurately predicting Crop output. The initial step in our proposed methodology involves collecting and integrating the data from the Kaggle data repository. Following that, the second step entails doing data preparation. At this step, missing values have been analysed and replaced, while unnecessarily high values have been modified to fit within a specified range using a min-max scaler to standardise the data. Following the execution of feature selection, we have partitioned the dataset into separate training and testing sets. Ultimately, calculate the assessment matrix and generate forecasts depending on the outcome. The Hybrid model being proposed is depicted in Fig. 3 (Fig. 2).

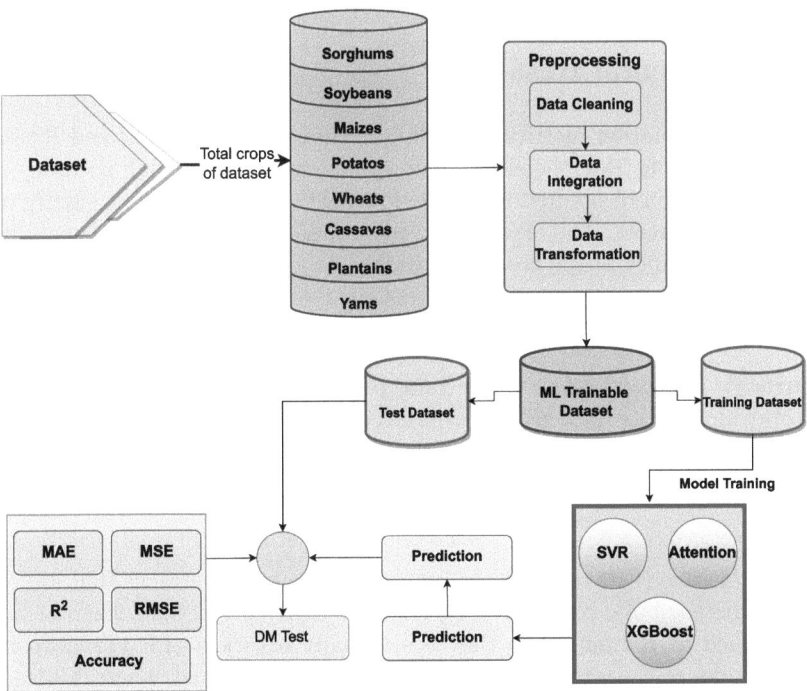

Fig. 2. Proposed Architecture

The model analyses a single dataset including detailed information on 8 different crops. The training data comprises labelled examples, whereas the validation data is utilised for fine-tuning. The test data consists of unique IDs for which forecasts are generated. Pre-processing enhances the quality of the data, while a combination of Attention mechanism, SVR, and XGBoost classifiers improves prediction accuracy. Once the model is trained on the entire dataset, it uses this training to make predictions for the test data. The test data consists of both input characteristics and the corresponding predicted labels. This approach employs a diverse range of classifiers to construct a robust and accurate prediction model. The ensemble approach for crop yield prediction integrates the strengths of three diverse models: XGBoost, an attention mechanism, and Support Vector Regression (SVR). XGBoost is employed for its ability to capture complex relationships in structured data, while the attention mechanism dynamically focuses on relevant elements within the input sequence, particularly beneficial for time-series agricultural data. SVR, known for capturing non-linear patterns, further contributes to the ensemble.

The ensemble combines predictions using weighted averages, with weights optimized during training. Hyperparameter tuning and cross-validation are employed for individual models, and interpretability techniques are considered for insights into model predictions. Regular monitoring, updates with new data, and periodic retraining enhance the ensemble's robustness. This approach aims to provide accurate and context-aware predictions for crop yield, leveraging the complementary strengths of each model in the ensemble.

4 Experimental Result

The chosen evaluation metrics, including accuracy, MSE, MAE, and R^2 score, collectively demonstrate the effectiveness of the model. The high accuracy indicates the precision of predictions, while low MSE and MAE values signify minimal prediction errors. The elevated R^2 score indicates the model's capability to explain the variance in the crop yield data.

4.1 Performance Metrics

Accuracy: Accuracy refers to the ratio of accurately predicted data points to the total number of data points. The accuracy is calculated according to the method shown in Eq. 2.

$$Accuracy = \frac{TP + TN}{TP + TN + FP + FN} \qquad (2)$$

False Positive (FP) refers to the number of recognized attacks that are really normal, whereas False Negative (FN) refers to faulty predictions when instances are identified as normal while they are actually attacked. TP (True Positive) examples refer to cases that are correctly identified as normal, whereas TN (True Negative) instances refer to cases that are correctly classified as attacks.

Mean Squared Error (MSE): MSE is a measure of the average squared difference between the actual and predicted values. It quantifies the average magnitude of errors, giving higher weight to larger errors. A lower MSE indicates a better fit of the model to the data.

$$MSE = \frac{1}{n}\sum_{i=1}^{n}(Y_i - \hat{Y}_i)^2 \quad (3)$$

Mean Absolute Error (MAE): MAE is a metric that calculates the average absolute difference between the actual and predicted values. It provided a measure of the average magnitude of errors, regardless of their direction.

$$MAE = \frac{1}{n}\sum_{i=1}^{n}|Y_i - \hat{Y}_i| \quad (4)$$

Mean Absolute Percentage Error (MAPE): MAPE is a percentage-based metric that measures the average absolute percentage difference between the actual and predicted values. It expresses errors as a percentage of the actual values, providing a relative measure of accuracy. MAPE is used in forecasting and is sensitive to the scale of the data.

$$MAPE = \frac{1}{n}\sum_{i=1}^{n}\left|\frac{Y_i - \hat{Y}_i}{Y_i}\right| \times 100 \quad (5)$$

R-squared (R^2). R-squared is a statistical measure that represents the proportion of the variance in the dependent variable (response) explained by the independent variables (features) in a regression model. It ranges from 0 to 1, where 1 indicates a perfect fit. R-squared is useful for assessing the goodness of fit of a regression model.

$$R^2 = 1 - \frac{\sum_{i=1}^{n}(Y_i - \hat{Y}_i)^2}{\sum_{i=1}^{n}(Y_i - \bar{Y})^2} \quad (6)$$

4.2 Experimental Results

This section presents an examination of the findings obtained from several classification approaches used to predict the existence of Heart Disease.

4.3 Result Analysis and Discussion

The Table 2 displays study findings that compare the efficacy of different machine learning methodologies .

The table provides a comprehensive overview of the performance metrics for various regression models, including Linear Regression, Random Forest, Gradient Boost, XGBoost, KNN, Decision Tree, Bagging Regressor, and a Proposed

Model. Notably, Random Forest and Bagging Regressor demonstrate exceptional accuracy at 98.56% and 98.59%, respectively, coupled with low Mean Squared Error (MSE) and Mean Absolute Error (MAE), indicating robust predictive capabilities. Conversely, Linear Regression and KNN exhibit lower accuracy at 7.37% and 28.82%, respectively, with comparatively higher error metrics, suggesting weaker predictive performance.

Among the models, XGBoost, Decision Tree, and the Proposed Model showcase competitive accuracy at 97.33%, 97.62%, and 99.35%, respectively. These models also demonstrate strong performance in terms of MSE, MAE, and R2 Score, with the Proposed Model standing out with a particularly high R2 Score of 0.9863. These findings suggest that the Proposed Model, alongside XGBoost and Decision Tree, offers a robust alternative to Random Forest and Bagging Regressor, showcasing promising predictive accuracy and overall performance across multiple evaluation metrics (Table 3).

Table 2. Model Evaluation Metrics

Model	Accuracy (%)	MSE	MAE	MAPE	R2_score
Linear Regression	7.37%	6293718529.871188	60955.317749	2.419536	0.073724
Random Forest	98.56%	97654323.573225	3480.841065	0.102571	0.985628
Gradient Boost	83.11%	1147345777.258148	21184.660834	0.596784	0.831140
XGBoost	97.33%	181714671.361342	7341.948649	0.208728	0.973256
KNN	28.82%	4836388296.236208	47716.358935	1.631186	0.288206
Decision Tree	97.62%	161890347.543726	3559.269202	0.096101	0.976174
Bagging Regressor	98.59%	95933983.565644	3450.508398	0.101199	0.985881
Proposed Model	**99.35%**	**97627518.13369368**	**5277.05749351839**	**5102.057493517**	**0.98630941069**

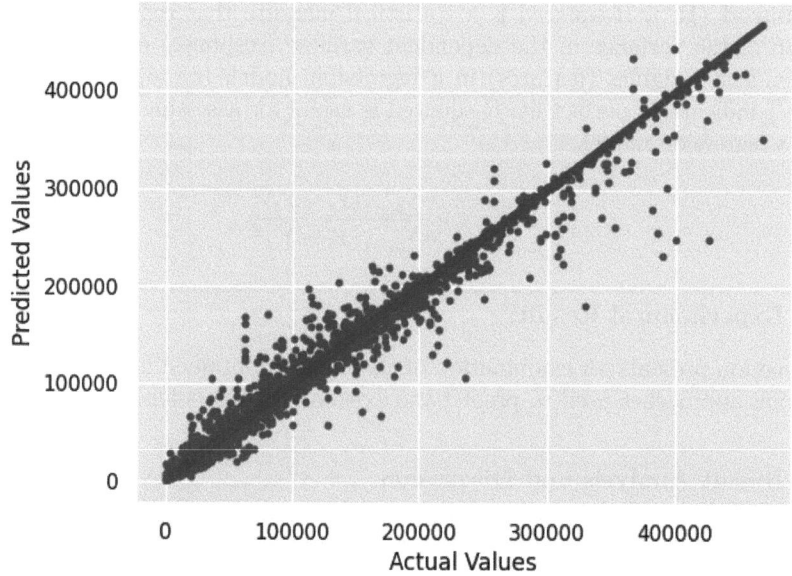

Fig. 3. Proposed Model's Best Fit Line: Regression Analysis Result

K-Fold Validation

The table presented in Table 4 showcases the outcomes of a K-fold cross-validation with K=5. Each row corresponds to a distinct fold in the cross-validation process, while the columns report the training accuracy and test accuracy for each fold. Examining the results provides valuable insights into the model's performance.

Across all folds, the model consistently exhibits robust performance, as evidenced by the minor variations observed in both training and test accuracies. This consistency implies that the model generalizes effectively to diverse subsets of the dataset, suggesting a robust learning capability.

Table 3. Research results about the performance of different machine learning techniques

Authors	Approach	Accuracy
Iniyan et al. [3]	feature engineering-based LSTM	86.3%
Jhajhariaa et al. [6]	Random Forest	96.03%
Hemageetha et al. [19]	Naive Bayes algorithm	77%
Proposed	Hybrid Model()	**99.35%**

Table 4. K-FOLD CROSS VALIDATION

Value of K = 5	Train_acc	Test_acc
Fold = 1	99.04%	98.92%
Fold = 2	99.02%	98.84%
Fold = 3	98.98%	98.98%
Fold = 4	98.98%	99.08%
Fold = 5	98.99%	98.85%

5 Discussion

The proposed ensemble approach for crop yield prediction has demonstrated remarkable performance with an accuracy of 99.35%, a mean squared error (MSE) of 97627518.13, a mean absolute error (MAE) of 5277.06, and an R^2 score of 0.9863, as evaluated through a rigorous 5-fold cross-validation. This impressive accuracy and precision underscore the efficacy of the ensemble, which integrates XGBoost, an attention mechanism, and Support Vector Regression (SVR). The high accuracy and low error metrics suggest that the ensemble effectively captures complex relationships in the agricultural data, enhancing the strengths of each individual model. The 5-fold cross-validation ensures robustness and generalization, addressing concerns related to over-fitting and providing a comprehensive evaluation of the ensemble's performance across diverse subsets of the dataset. In considering the future direction of this work, there are several avenues for enhancement and expansion. Firstly, the ensemble's performance could be further optimized by exploring additional hyperparameter tuning and model architecture adjustments. Fine-tuning the weights assigned to each model in the ensemble may provide opportunities for incremental improvements.

Additionally, incorporating more diverse features, such as advanced weather patterns, soil health indicators, or satellite imagery, could enhance the model's predictive capabilities. Integrating real-time data sources and encouraging advancements in remote sensing technologies may contribute to more accurate and timely predictions, especially in dynamic agricultural environments.

Furthermore, exploring the interpretibility of the ensemble's predictions could provide valuable insights for stakeholders in the agricultural sector. Understanding which features and factors contribute most significantly to the predictions can enhance the model's transparency and facilitate more informed decision-making for farmers and policymakers.

6 Conclusion

Predicting agricultural yields, as well as deciding which crops to cultivate and how to tend to them during their growth, are both aided by machine learning. Studies aimed at predicting agricultural yields have made use of a number of machine learning methods. the presented ensemble approach has achieved outstanding predictive performance in crop yield estimation. Future directions should focus on further refining the model through continuous experimentation with hyperparameters, expanding the feature set, and prioritizing interpretability. This work lays a solid foundation for the application of advanced machine learning techniques in precision agriculture, with the potential to significantly impact agricultural productivity and resource management.

References

1. Alpaydin, E.: Introduction to Machine Learning. MIT press, Cambridge (2020)
2. Xu, X., et al.: Design of an integrated climatic assessment indicator (ICAI) for wheat production: a case study in Jiangsu province, China. Ecol. Ind. **101**, 943–953 (2019)
3. Iniyan, S., Varma, V.A., Naidu, C.T.: Crop yield prediction using machine learning techniques. Adv. Eng. Softw. **175**, 103326 (2023)
4. Filippi, P., et al.: An approach to forecast grain crop yield using multi-layered, multi-farm data sets and machine learning. Precision Agric. **20**(5), 1015–1029 (2019). https://doi.org/10.1007/s11119-018-09628-4
5. Nigam, A., Garg, S., Agrawal, A., Agrawal, P.: Crop yield prediction using machine learning algorithms. In: 2019 Fifth International Conference on Image Information Processing (ICIIP), pp. 125–130. IEEE (2019)
6. Jhajharia, K., Mathur, P., Jain, S., Nijhawan, S.: Crop yield prediction using machine learning and deep learning techniques. Procedia Comput. Sci. **218**(406–417), 12 (2023)

7. Elavarasan, D., Vincent, D.R., Sharma, V., Zomaya, A.Y., Srinivasan, K.: Forecasting yield by integrating agrarian factors and machine learning models: a survey. Comput. Electron. Agric. **155**, 257–282 (2018)
8. Beulah, R.: A survey on different data mining techniques for crop yield prediction. Int. J. Comput. Sci. Eng. **7**(1), 738–744 (2019)
9. Shakoor, U., Saboor, A., Ali, I., Mohsin, A.Q.: Impact of climate change on agriculture: empirical evidence from arid region. Pak. J. Agri. Sci **48**(4), 327–333 (2011)
10. Molden, D., et al.: 4.21-Water availability and its use in agriculture. Treatise on Water Science. Elsevier, Oxford, pp. 707–732 (2011)
11. Shakoor, U., Saboor, A., Ali, I., Mohsin, A.Q.: Impact of climate change on agriculture: empirical evidence from arid region. Pak. J. Agri. Sci **48**(4), 327–333 (2011)
12. Uleberg, E., Hanssen-Bauer, I., van Oort, B., Dalmannsdottir, S.: Impact of climate change on agriculture in Northern Norway and potential strategies for adaptation. Clim. Change **122**, 27–39 (2014)
13. Dharani, M.K., Thamilselvan, R., Natesan, P., Kalaivaani, P.C.D., Santhoshkumar, S.: Review on crop prediction using deep learning techniques. J. Phys: Conf. Ser. **1767**(1), 012026 (2021)
14. Van Klompenburg, T., Kassahun, A., Catal, C.: Crop yield prediction using machine learning: a systematic literature review. Comput. Electron. Agric. **177**, 105709 (2020)
15. Paul, M., Vishwakarma, S.K., Verma, A.: Analysis of soil behavior and prediction of crop yield using data mining approach. Comput. Intell. Commun. Netw. (CICN), 766-771 (2015)
16. Murynin, A., Gorokhovskiy, K., Ignatie, V.: Efficiency of crop yield forecasting depending on the moment of prediction based on large remote sensing data set. http://worldcompproceedings.com/proc/p2013/DMI8036.pdf
17. Elbasi, E., et al.: Crop prediction model using machine learning algorithms. Appl. Sci. **13**(16), 9288 (2023)
18. Patelris. Crop Yield Prediction Dataset. Kaggle. https://www.kaggle.com/datasets/patelris/crop-yield-prediction-dataset
19. Hemageetha, N.: A survey on application of data mining techniques to analyze the soil for agricultural purpose. In: 3rd International Conference on Computing for Sustainable Global Development (INDIACom), pp. 3112–3117 (2016)
20. Manjula, E., Djodiltachoumy, S.: A model for prediction of crop yield. Int. J. Comput. Intell. Inform. **6**(4), 298–305 (2017)
21. Sellam, V., Poovammal, E.: Prediction of crop yield using regression analysis. Indian J. Sci. Technol. **9**(38), 1–5 (2016)
22. Dahikar, S.S., Rode, S.V.: Agricultural crop yield prediction using artificial neural network approach. Int. J. Innovative Res. Electr. Electron. Instrum. Control Eng. **2**(1), 683–686 (2014)
23. Rashid, M., Bari, B.S., Yusup, Y., Kamaruddin, M.A., Khan, N.: A comprehensive review of crop yield prediction using machine learning approaches with special emphasis on palm oil yield prediction. IEEE Access **9**, 63406–63439 (2021)
24. Khaki, S., Wang, L.: Crop yield prediction using deep neural networks. Front. Plant Sci. **10**, 621 (2019)
25. Kamath, P., Patil, P., Shrilatha, S., Sowmya, S.: Crop yield forecasting using data mining. Global Transitions Proc. **2**(2), 402–407 (2021)
26. Piekutowska, M., et al.: The application of multiple linear regression and artificial neural network models for yield prediction of very early potato cultivars before harvest. Agronomy **11**(5), 885 (2021)

PPIoDT: GSO-FL Based Privacy Preserving IoDT Guided Ocean-Wind Aware Ship Trajectory Recommendation

Arnab Hazra[1,2], Debashis De[2(✉)], and Tien Anh Tran[3]

[1] Department of Computer Science and Engineering, Dr. Sudhir Chandra Sur Institute of Technology and Sports Complex, 540 Dum Dum Road, Kolkata 700074, WB, India
[2] Centre of Mobile Cloud Computing, Department of Computer Science and Engineering, Maulana Abul Kalam Azad University of Technology, Nadia, WB, India
debashis.de@makautwb.ac.in
[3] Department of Marine Engineering, Vietnam Maritime University, Haiphong 180000, Vietnam

Abstract. Recently, the Federated Learning (FL) has gained the utmost popularity due to its privacy-preserving intelligent decentralized framework as an alternative to traditional centralized machine learning approaches. The wind disturbances especially in the ocean highly affect the ship trajectories. A drone-guided ship can mitigate wind effects by predicting local weather data without sharing it with the central server in the ocean environment. The drone flights often have privacy-sensitive data that needs a robust framework, especially in disaster, rescue, surveillance, or other various welfare applications. In our work, we have applied the nature-inspired Glowworm Swarm Optimization (GSO) for privacy-preserving Internet of Drone Things (IoDT). We proposed a GSO-FL-based privacy-preserving IoDT-guided ocean-wind aware ship trajectory recommendation model to mitigate real-time wind gust disturbances. The outcome shows the convergence time of the glowworms reduces approximately 17% as compared to other GSO-based models.

Keywords: Glowworm Swarm Optimization · Federated Learning · Internet of Drone Things · Privacy Preserving · Wind Effects

1 Introduction

The international maritime transportation plays a crucial role in promoting the international economic development of each nation in the world nowadays. It is a significant trend to improve the average income of each country, especially for the developing countries. Moreover, the growing number of vessels in the maritime sector and the uncertain factors of navigation environment conditions are the challenges in sailing the safe direction of ships during the navigation routing between the nations in the world [10]. Therefore, the efficient management of maritime transportation is a big challenge in the maritime safety and transportation engineering [3]. The occurrence of ship accidents and maritime risk of ship collision are the keywords in this study to ensure the navigation safety, the route optimization as well as the ship energy efficiency management. The current appearance of Internet of Things (IoT) based models [6] applied to flying vehicles has introduced the Internet of Drone Things (IoDT) [2] paradigm for surveillance, supervision, shipping, and delivery. These IoDT applications for ship movement are the new research trends in the maritime industry. By leveraging IoDT-guided ship movement and FL [9], various wind-mitigated trajectory recommendation methodologies have been proposed to improve ship movement in a real-time windy environment in the ocean [7]. The wind disturbances highly affect ship trajectories to reach to the actual destination. Often ship directions and their destinations have some confidential data to process by centralized ML-based models. Thus, the privacy of these data is a major concern in the ocean environment. Privacy-preserving Federated learning (FL) is one of the solutions where the local private data is not shared with the central federated aggregator for this purpose. For trajectory-recommended energy-efficient optimization, we have used Glowworm Swarm optimization [4,13] as a nature-inspired metaheuristic methodology. In our work, GSO is responsible for local learning to analyze private data collected by the ship. For GSO agents, we have deployed IoDT devices in the search space. Wind gust velocity as a local learning parameter are sent to the global federated server to get the global aggregated wind velocity. The Federated server acts as an aggregator and is responsible for velocity aggregation.

The remainder of this paper is arranged as follows. Section 2 describes the related works of this study. Contributions of our work are discussed in Sect. 3. Section 4 describes our proposed methodology. Results and Analysis of our works are discussed in Sect. 5. Section 6 describes the comparative study with our proposed model. In Sect. 7 we have discussed limitations and future work. Finally, Sect. 8 concludes our paper.

2 Related Works

The modelling of the ship behaviour in the wind and the current impacts are often considered nearby port area. Zhao et al. [15] proposed an impact mechanism to explain the deviation of speed over ground and drift and leeway angle based on the quantified variation of ship size. The regression-based study results on similar type of ships indicating the significant variations between current and wind effects. A ship trajectory generator have been proposed by Ding et al. [5] under interference of wind, waves and current in ocean. This adaptive network-based fuzzy inference system (ANFIS) based model considers wind field, wave field, and current field separately to generate the trajectory in the harsh condition. Wang et al. [11,12] proposed a two-stage model based on FL and optimization methods for prediction of fuel consumption and to optimize the sailing speed of ship. This two-stage model minimizes fuel consumption by 2.5% to 7.5% compared to other existing models. In FedBIP, Zhang et al. [14] proposed a novel FL-based model to predict blade icing. The FedBIP results of outperforms the other existing FL-based models, feature extracting models, and aggregation models. A hybrid model for Stream Flow Estimation has been proposed by Akbulut et al. [1] using various machine learning (ML) based regression techniques in local learning and by combining Federated Learning framework.

3 Contributions

Our GSO-FL based Privacy Preserving IoDT guided Ocean-wind aware Ship Trajectory Recommendation model having the following contributions:

– In this work, we have preserved the location details of the ship despite using a global model to predict wind by covering a large area in the ocean. Location of the ship is updated in real-time and the collection of local data by the ships in continuous intervals helps to achieve higher accuracy of our model. We have found 88.426% accuracy for local learning and 4.08 m/s gust velocity as a global model update.
– The outcome shows the convergence time of the glowworms reduces approximately 17% as compared to other GSO-based models.
– Due to the federated framework, the local data of the ship as well as the IoDT which acts as a supervisor of the ships are not shared with the global aggregator for information security. We have analysed various gust wind parameters and recommended the trajectories of the IoDT guided ships to mitigate the wind effects.

4 Proposed Methodology

We proposed a GSO-FL-based privacy-preserving model for energy-efficient IoDT-guided ocean-wind aware ship trajectory recommendation model to mitigate real-time wind gust disturbances. In our work, $\{s_1, s_2, s_3,...,s_n\}$ are considered to collect local real-time weather data in the ocean. This private data according to position of the ships are sent to IoDT to guide corresponding ships as well as to perform the local learning. Energy-efficient GSO based learning helps ships to find optimized wind mitigated route. IoDT devices are considered as the deployed glowworms in our search space. After getting the local gust velocity from individual IoDT, the server is responsible for velocity aggregation on the local parameters. We train our federated model with the FedAvg method. The global wind velocity is sent to the corresponding IoDT. After that the GSO based wind mitigated trajectory is sent to the corresponding ships. Our proposed privacy Preserving IoDT guided ocean-wind aware ship trajectory recommendation model is shown in Fig. 1.

4.1 Privacy-Preserving Federated Learning

In this work, we have preserved the location details of the ship despite using a global model to predict wind by covering a large area in the ocean. Each ship

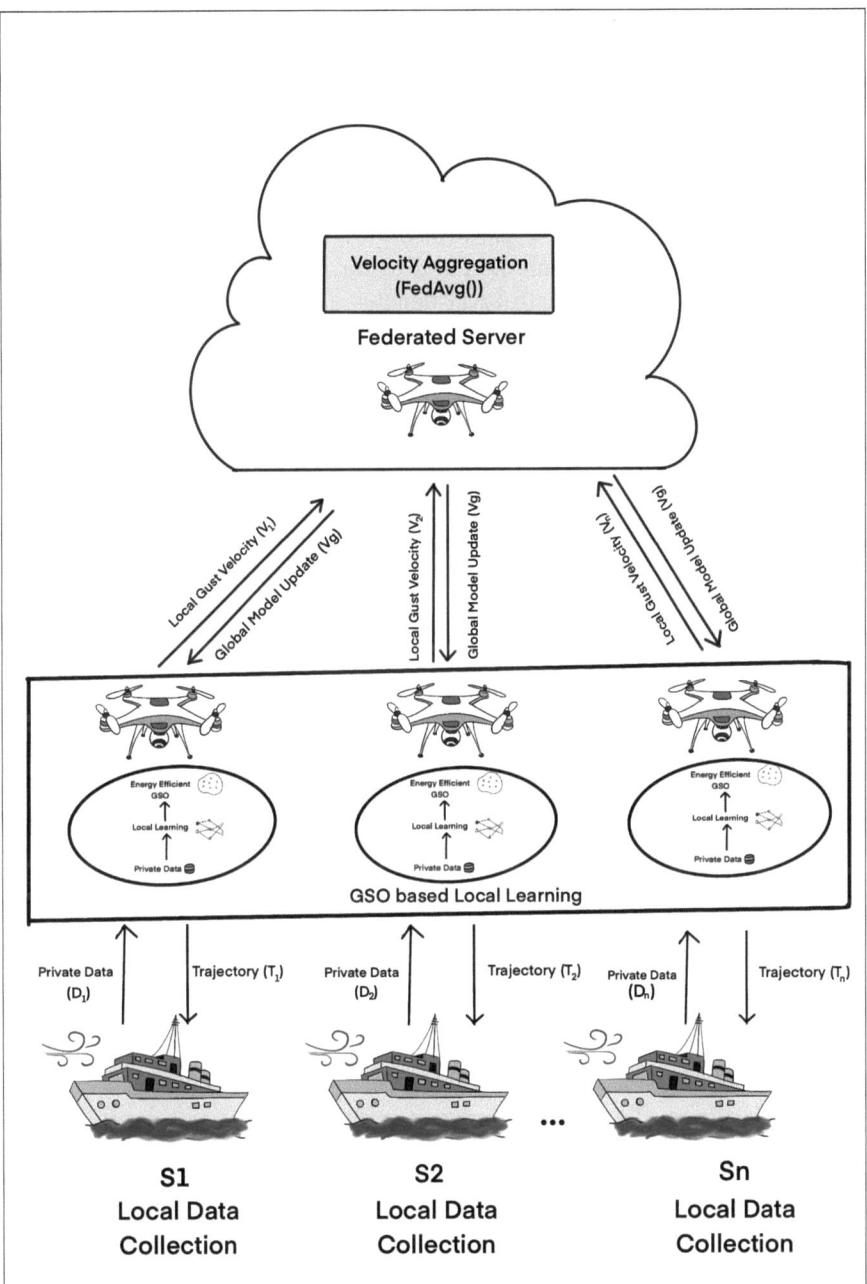

Fig. 1. Proposed model PPIoDT: GSO-FL based privacy preserving IoDT guided ocean-wind aware ship trajectory recommendation.

s_i (where, 1<=i<=n) collects local weather data and sends it to corresponding IoDT with its location details. In local learning, IoDT used private data of the corresponding ship and found the local wind gust velocity of that ship. We have used Linear Regression for our local learning to predict gust wind parameters. Then this local gust velocity information $v_i(t)$ is sent to the global federated server for wind velocity aggregation. Because of the federated framework local parameters and data of the ship as well as the IoDT which acts as a supervisor of the ships are not shared with the global aggregator for information security. For global aggregation, we have performed gust velocity aggregation of output of the local learning. FedAvg method is used for global aggregation and can be expressed as in Eq. ((1)), where $v_g(t)$ denotes global model update i.e., wind velocity, D_i denotes the local dataset, $v_i(t)$ denotes the local gust velocity.

$$v_g(t) = (1/(\sum_{i=1}^{n} D_i)) * \sum_{i=1}^{n} D_i v_i(t) \qquad (1)$$

In our proposed GSO-FL-based model, we have used the root-mean-square error (RMSE) as a loss function. RMSE evaluates the average deviation between predicted values by our methodology with its real values. It estimates how well our proposed model can predict the target wind gust parameter.

4.2 Glowworm Swarm Optimization

In our work, we have used meta-heuristic nature-inspired intelligent method GSO [4] to optimize IoDT guided ship trajectory recommendation for energy efficiency. To optimize multi-modal function, the significant difference between GSO and other optimization methodologies is that adaptive neighborhood in accordance with varying range, the speed of convergence, and can be applied for localization of multiple sources. GSO based learning can be done in the following four steps.

Initial Deployment. Our proposed model starts with a random deployment of IoDT in the search space. Each IoDT is modelled corresponding to one ship in the ocean. This random deployment helps to collect local weather data from various places in our search space.

Luciferin Update. The function value at position of the agent depends on the luciferin update. In the search space, each agent adds a certain quantity to its old luciferin value, which is proportional to the fitness of its current location. In this phase, a smaller quantity of luciferin is subtracted over time for simulation of the luciferin. This rule can be expressed in Eq. (2).

$$lf_i(t) = (1-d) * lf_i(t-1) + e * Y(x_i(t)) \qquad (2)$$

where $lf_i(t)$ is the luciferin amount of glowworm, d is luciferin decay constant, $Y(x_i(t))$ represents the objective function, and e represents the luciferin enhancement constant.

Movement. In movement phase of GSO, a conditional probabilistic mechanism is used. Here, each glowworm decides his own movement toward its adaptive neighbor having a brighter luciferin value. The probability of movement of the glowworm can be expressed in Eq. (3).

$$pr_ij(t) = (lf_j(t) - lf_i(t))/(\sum_{k \in N_i(t)} lf_k(t) - lf_i(t)) \qquad (3)$$

where, $j \in N_i(t)$, $N_i(t) = {j : ed_ij(t) < r_d^i(t); lf_i(t) < lf_j(t)}$ is the set of all neighbors of glowworm, $r_d^i(t)$ is the range of neighbourhood, and $ed_ij(t)$ considered as the Euclidean distance. We assume that in ((2)) glowworm i select a glowworm $j \in N_i(t)$ with $pr_ij(t)$. The discrete-time movement of glowworm is expressed in Eq. (4).

$$x_i(t+1) = x_i(t) + ss((x_j(t) - x_i(t))/(||x_j(t) - x_i(t)||)) \qquad (4)$$

where, $x_i(t)$ and $x_j(t)$ denotes the position of glowworm i and j at t, $||.||$ represents the Euclidean norm operator, and ss is the step size.

Update Neighborhood Range. We assume each glowworm have an adaptive neighborhood range r_d^i, which is bounded by a limited sensor range $r_s (0 < nr_d^i < r_s)$, and is expressed in Eq. (5).

$$nr_d^i(t+1) = minimum(nr_s, maximum{0, nr_d^i(t) + \beta(nn_t - |N_i(t)|)}) \qquad (5)$$

where, nn_t represents the number of neighbours, and β denotes a constant.

4.3 Modelling Wind Effects

In our work, we have considered a gusty wind environment in the ocean. A wind gust is a brief increase in the wind speed in a short period of time. Our GSO-FL based proposed model describes the effect of discrete wind gusts for trajectory recommendation of drone guided ships. The resultant velocity of a discrete wind gust model can be expressed in Eq. (6).

$$V_gw = \begin{cases} 0, & \text{if } l < 0 \\ (v_m/2) * (1 - cos(\pi * l/d_m)), & \text{if } 0 <= l <= d_m \\ v_m, & \text{if } l > d_m \end{cases} \qquad (6)$$

where v_m, d_m, l, and V_gw denote the amplitude of the gust, the length of the gust, the distance travelled, and the resultant velocity respectively. According to the discrete wind gust model, if the gust length lies between 0 and d_m then, the resultant velocity increases rapidly.

4.4 Behaviour Variables of Ship Trajectory

The Speed Over Ground (VSOG) measures the speed of a ship relative to the Earth's surface, considering external effects like wind, current and tides. In our model, we have considered VSOG due to external gust wind and its direction angle θ_w depicted in Fig. 2). In our analysis, ψ, ϕ, and γ denote the ship heading, the course over ground, and the angular deviations due to wind effects respectively. The behavior of the IoDT-guided ship is plotted in the coordinate system O-XY and the IoDT-guided moving ship trajectory is plotted in the $P - x_0 y_0$ coordinate system. When the IoDT-guided ship travels towards the heading direction that means ψ and ϕ are the same, then the angular deviation turns to zero. This situation occurs exactly in two cases. First case is that there is no external effect to affect the ship trajectory. In the second case, the various external environmental impacts on ship behavior compensate with each other, so that the sum of multiple directional impacts is equivalent to zero.

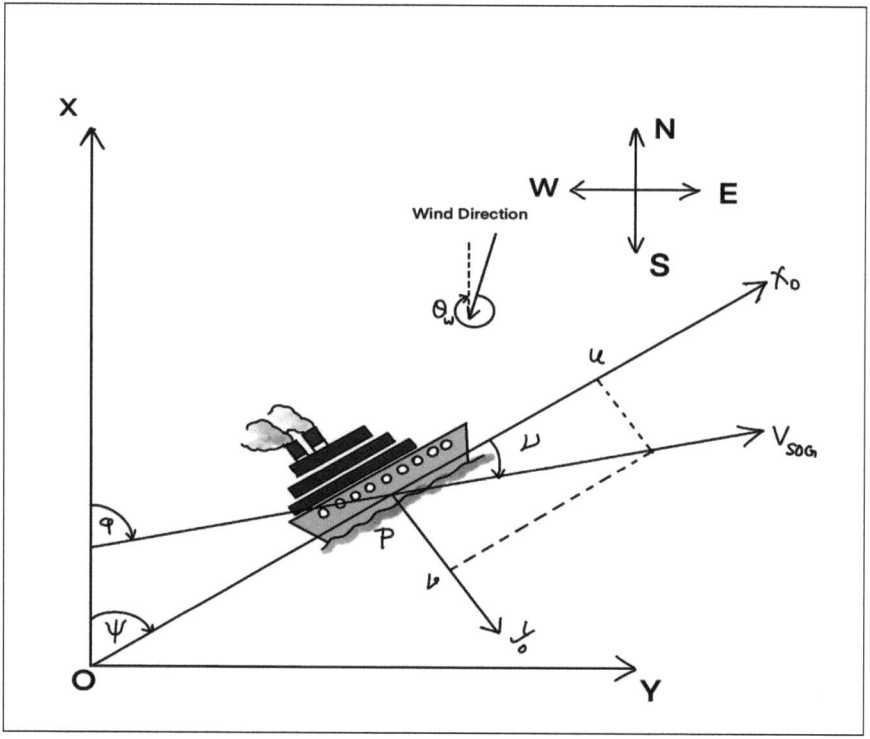

Fig. 2. The behaviour variable of ship trajectory in wind.

5 Results and Analysis

We evaluate the GSO-FL model on a IndianWeatherRepository.csv dataset taken from kaggle.com. This dataset provides real-time weather information for major cities in India having 42 features and 54145 observations. Among all the observations we have selected the nearest 4020 observations for our model. We have also selected 14 relevant features for our local learning. We split this dataset for evaluating our Linear Regression-based local model as the train (70%), and test (30%) after pre-processing. We have found 88.426% accuracy in local learning. For global aggregation we have performed wind gust velocity aggregation of the output of local learning using FedAvg method. The outcome shows 4.08 m/s gust velocity as a global model update. The detailed performance analysis of our proposed model is shown in Table 1.

Table 1. Performance analysis of PPIoDT

Local learning			Global Aggregation
Accuracy (%)	MAE	RMSE	Gust velocity v_g (m/s)
88.426	1.718	2.502	4.08

We have also considered windy.com for real time wind analysis in our model. Figure 3 represents the gust wind, waves, temperature, and the cloudiness of the place having latitude and longitude at 17° 0'0" N and 86°18'30" dated 28th January, 2024.

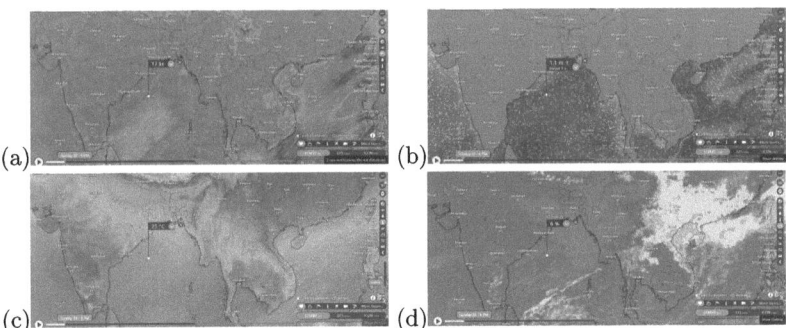

Fig. 3. Real time analysis of (a) gusty wind (b) waves (c) temperature (d) percentage of cloudiness.

In our work we have observed 17 knots (i.e., 8.745 m/s) wind gust, and we have converted it to m/s for our wind analysis. If we consider no wind environment initially, then the increase in wind speed generated by the gust i.e. gust amplitude will be 8.745 m/s. We observed 1.1 m wave, 25 °C with 6% cloudiness in the global position 17°0'0" N and 86°18'30" E. Table 2 shows the observation parameters for our simulation.

Table 2. Observation parameters for simulation

Latitude and Longitude	Wind gust (knot)	Waves(m)	Temperature(°C)	Cloudiness(%)
17°0'0" N and 86°18'30" E	17	1.1	25	6

We have deployed 100 glowworms in the search space and used 300 iterations for our simulation. Furthermore, we have considered luciferin decay constant = 0.4 and luciferin enhancement constant = 0.6 and initial luciferin level = 5 for all the glowworms. Figure 4 shows the trajectory of the glowworms in no-wind effect.

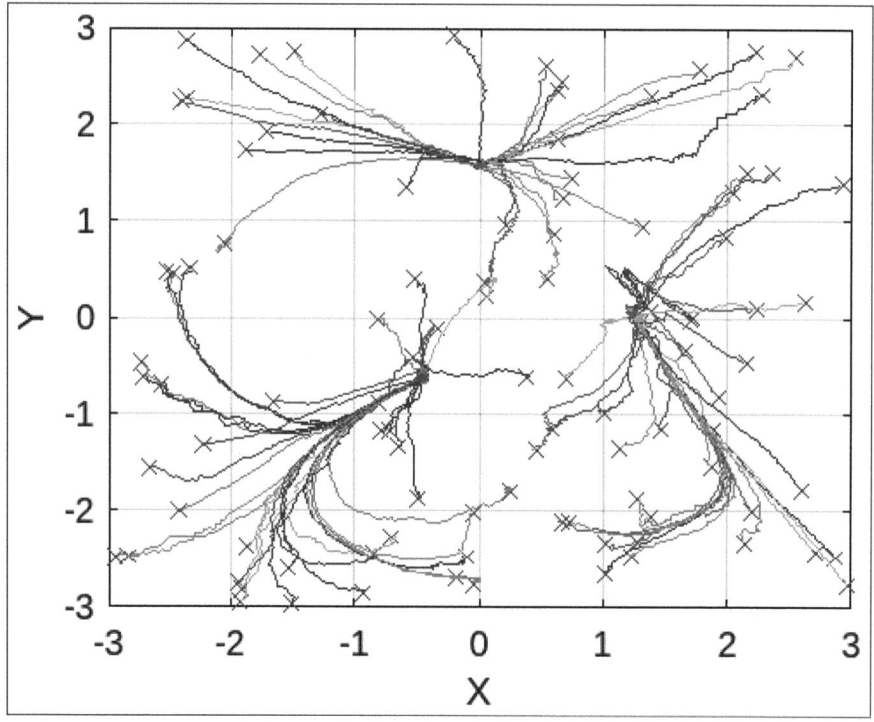

Fig. 4. Trajectory of the glowworms in no-wind effect.

We have applied the observed gust wind i.e., 8.745 m/s and consider the gust length as 10 m to the trajectories of the glowworms to get the recommended trajectories of the glowworms by keeping all other GSO parameters same. Figure 5 shows the recommended trajectory by applying the observed gust wind.

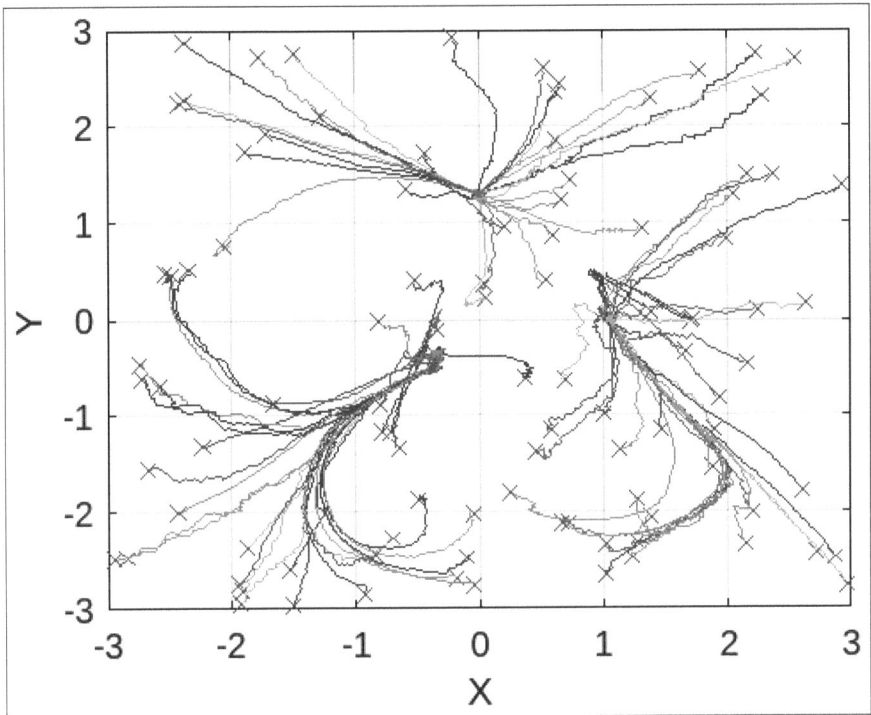

Fig. 5. Recommended trajectory by applying wind gust 8.745 m/s.

We have performed the wind gust analysis of distance versus wind speed having a fixed gust amplitude 8.745 m/s by considering various gust lengths i.e., (5 m, 10 m, 25 m, and 50 m) for the analysis as shown in Fig. 6.

6 Comparative Study

We have compared the convergence time of PPIoDT with other two existing GSO-based models. PPIoDT take 80.24 sec to converge all the glowworms whereas RGSO-UAV [4] takes 96.68 sec and GSO [8] takes 108.56 sec to converge. Table 3 shows the convergence time of our model and other GSO based models. It is observed that PPIoDT reduces at least 17% as compared to other GSO-based models.

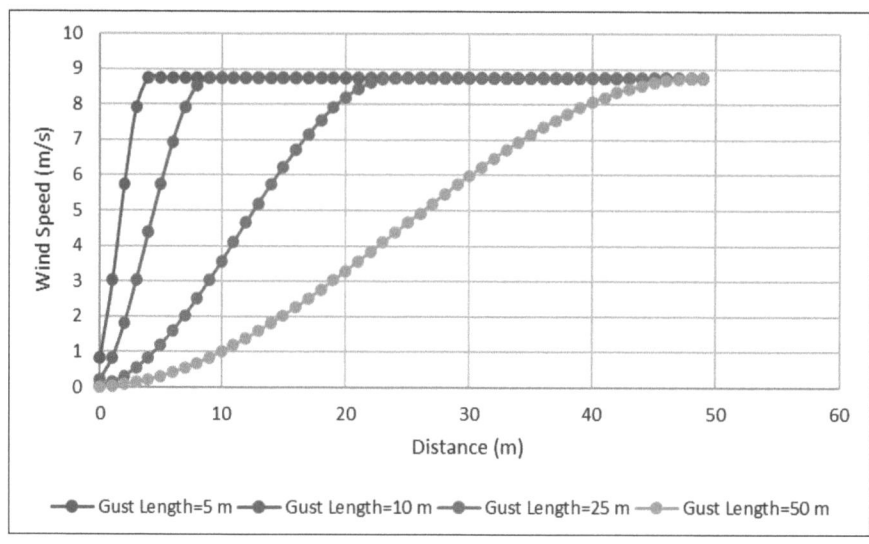

Fig. 6. Wind speed versus distance for a fixed gust amplitude.

Table 3. Comparison on convergence time of PPIoDT with other models

Models	Convergence time (s)
PPIoDT	80.24
RGSO-UAV	96.68
GSO	108.56

Table 4. Comparative study of proposed work with existing works

Working Principles /properties	Impacts of current and wind on ship behaviour based on AIS data [13]	Trajectory Generator of ship under the interference of Wind, Current, and Waves [5]	Federated learning based optimization of green shipping [10]	FL based prediction of Wind Turbine Blade Icing [12]	Hybrid Modelling to estimate stream flow Combining ML and FL [1]	proposed model: PPIoDT
ML-based/ optimization technique used	Regression	ANFIS	Two-stage model for FL and optimization	-	Regression	GSO
Federated learning	✗	✗	✓	✓	✓	✓
Wind effect analysis	✓	✓	✗	✓	✓	✓
Trajectory correction to mitigate wind effect	✓	✓	✗	✗	✗	✓
Privacy preservation	✗	✗	✓	✓	✓	✓
Energy efficient	✗	✗	✓	✗	✗	✓

The comparative study of our proposed work with other existing works with respect to various working principles is shown in Table 4. We have compared with five existing works for our study. Impacts of current and wind current on ship behaviour based on automatic identification systems (AIS) data [15] and trajectory generator of ship under the observation of wind, current and waves disturbances [5] did not consider federated learning, or any other privacy-preserving energy-efficient mechanism. The work in [12] did not consider wind effects on federated framework. FL based prediction of Wind Turbine Blade Icing [14] and Hybrid Modelling to estimate Stream Flow Combining Machine Learning and Federated Learning [1] did not consider any trajectory correction mechanism. Whereas our proposed model considers privacy preserving GSO based federated learning to mitigate gust wind effects on IoDT guided ship movement. We have used GSO for energy efficiency and optimization. For privacy, we have preserved the location details of the ship despite using a global model to predict wind by covering a large area in the ocean using federated learning.

7 Limitations of Study

Although PPIoDT preserves privacy and recommends trajectory of a drone guided ship, still have some limitations. Our proposed model can mitigate wind gust disturbances in the ocean. For this, we have considered discrete wind gust model in our work. Different wind models may result in different trajectories to mitigate it. Furthermore, we have used linear regression in performance analysis of PPIoDT. Other regression based techniques can be applied to get better performance.

8 Conclusion

Use of FL framework adds privacy and security to our proposed IoDT guided Ocean-wind aware Ship Trajectory Recommendation model. We have preserved the location details of the ship despite using a global model to predict wind by covering a large area in the ocean. We have analysed gust wind parameters and recommended the trajectories to mitigate the wind. By leveraging GSO in wind-aware ship trajectory recommendation model guided by IoDT supports optimization perspectives to our work. Our proposed model can mitigate the wind gust having various gust parameters to overcome real-time harsh situations in the ocean environment. Our model reduces the convergence time of the glowworms approximately 17% as compared to other GSO-based models. In future, we will focus on the above-mentioned limitations and will propose a more rigorous model to recommend trajectories of IoDT guided ships in the ocean by mitigating the wind.

References

1. Akbulut, U., Cifci, M.A., Aslan, Z.: Hybrid modeling for stream flow estimation: integrating machine learning and federated learning. Appl. Sci. **13**(18), 10203 (2023)
2. Akram, J., Umair, M., Jhaveri, R.H., Riaz, M.N., Chi, H., Malebary, S.: Chained-drones: Blockchain-based privacy-preserving framework for secure and intelligent service provisioning in internet of drone things. Comput. Electr. Eng. **110**, 108772 (2023)
3. Cao, Y., Wang, X., Yang, Z., Wang, J., Wang, H., Liu, Z.: Research in marine accidents: a bibliometric analysis, systematic review and future directions. Ocean Eng. **284**, 115048 (2023)
4. Chowdhury, A., De, D.: RGSO-UAV: reverse glowworm swarm optimization inspired UAV path-planning in a 3d dynamic environment. Ad Hoc Netw. **140**, 103068 (2023)
5. Ding, X., Bian, H., Ma, H., Wang, R.: Ship trajectory generator under the interference of wind, current and waves. Sensors **22**(23), 9395 (2022)
6. Ghasempour, A.: Internet of things in smart grid: architecture, applications, services, key technologies, and challenges. Inventions **4**(1), 22 (2019)
7. Islam, A., Shin, S.Y.: A digital twin-based drone-assisted secure data aggregation scheme with federated learning in artificial intelligence of things. IEEE Network **37**(2), 278–285 (2023)
8. Pandey, P., Shukla, A., Tiwari, R.: Three-dimensional path planning for unmanned aerial vehicles using glowworm swarm optimization algorithm. Int. J. Syst. Assur. Eng. Manage. **9**, 836–852 (2018)
9. Shvetsov, A.V., et al.: Federated learning meets intelligence reflection surface in drones for enabling 6g networks: challenges and opportunities. IEEE Access (2023)
10. Tran, T.A.: Effects of the uncertain factors impacting on the fuel oil consumption of sea ocean-going vessels based on the hybrid multi criteria decision making method. Ocean Eng. **239**, 109885 (2021)
11. Tran, T.A.: Building the remote surveying system of energy consumption in maritime transportation using internet of things (IoT) technique. In: Handbook of Smart Energy Systems, pp. 1–14. Springer, Cham (2022)
12. Wang, H., Yan, R., Au, M.H., Wang, S., Jin, Y.J.: Federated learning for green shipping optimization and management. Adv. Eng. Inform. **56**, 101994 (2023)
13. Yadav, K., Al-Dhlan, K.A.: Performance evaluation using hybrid glowworm swarm-pareto optimization in the smart communication system. Comput. Electr. Eng. **103**, 108313 (2022)
14. Zhang, D., et al.: Fedbip: a federated learning based model for wind turbine blade icing prediction. IEEE Trans. Instrum. Meas. (2023)
15. Zhou, Y., Daamen, W., Vellinga, T., Hoogendoorn, S.P.: Impacts of wind and current on ship behavior in ports and waterways: a quantitative analysis based on AIS data. Ocean Eng. **213**, 107774 (2020)

Multiple Linear Regression Based Multipath Green Routing for Internet of Vehicular Things in Smart Cities

Sushovan Khatua[1(✉)], Samarjit Roy[2], and Debashis De[1]

[1] Department of Computer Science and Engineering, Maulana Abul Kalam Azad University of Technology, West Bengal, Simhat, Haringhata, Nadia 741249, West Bengal, India
sushovankhatua79@gmail.com
[2] School of Computing and Information Technology, Eastern International University, Thu Dau Mot City, Binh Duong Province, Vietnam
samarjit.roy@ieee.org

Abstract. The increasing integration of smart technologies in urban environments has led to the emergence of Smart Cities, where the Internet of Things (IoT) plays a pivotal role in enhancing the efficiency of various systems. These systems' critical component is the Internet of Vehicular Things (IoVT), which leverages connected vehicles to optimize transportation networks. In pursuing sustainable urban mobility, this study proposes a Machine Learning (ML) based approach for optimizing green routing within the IoVT framework. The primary objective is to develop a sophisticated routing algorithm that considers real-time traffic conditions and environmental impact to minimize carbon emissions and energy consumption. Based on historical and current data, the proposed model harnesses multiple linear regression to predict carbon emission for optimized routes. The ML model dynamically adjusts routing decisions based on minimum carbon emission-enabled routes by continuously updating its knowledge, considering factors such as traffic congestion, vehicle types, and emission levels. The research contributes to the growing field of green transportation by providing a scalable and adaptable solution for optimizing vehicular routes in Smart Cities containing minimum carbon emissions. Using Multiple linear regression to predict carbon emission of a road, our model contains 82.14% accuracy. ML algorithms empower the system to make informed decisions, promoting energy-efficient and environmentally friendly transportation.

Keywords: IoV · Intelligent Routing · Carbon Emission · Multiple Linear Regression

1 Introduction

As the world's urban population is expected to reach 66–70% by 2050, cities will face unprecedented challenges in managing their environments, resources, and security. To address these challenges, many countries are developing smart city [7] initiatives that use technology to optimize resource use and reduce environmental impact. In intelligent transportation, Artificial intelligence (AI) [5], machine learning (ML) [1]. Deep reinforcement learning (DRL) are playing an increasingly important role, and these technologies are being used to develop new ways to smart cities. Energy generation, management, and consumption are also essential for smart cities. Big data analytics is used to improve the efficiency and reliability of smart grids, which are the electrical grids that power our cities. Finding the shortest path [14] between two locations within road networks poses a significant challenge in vehicle routing and the smart city's broader transportation, distribution, and logistics industry. The selection of an appropriate route planning algorithm from the multitude proposed in the literature is a critical consideration in various transportation applications involving real road networks [15]. This complexity arises because dynamic parameters, such as traffic congestion, random incidents, and weather conditions, can substantially impact the efficiency of the applied machine learning (ML) model within these networks. Consequently, ML learning automatically must be extended to accommodate these dynamic factors, ensuring the adaptation of the shortest path. This paper [6] integrates mobile edge computing, vehicular ad-hoc networks, and social networks to propose an emerging path planning schema named Social Vehicular Edge Computing (SoVEC). Intelligent Transportation Systems (ITS) [4] commonly employ car navigation systems as their flagship applications. These systems leverage Global Positioning System (GPS) data and digital road map databases to furnish information about traffic conditions in tourist locations and recommend optimal routes to destinations. To fully exploit the advantages of car navigation systems, the software components must operate in real-time or dynamic network environments where road conditions change over time. Algorithms applied in dynamic road networks must react to these changes, updating the selected route to maintain optimal properties under new conditions. Carbon emissions are essential in smart cities because they are intricately linked to environmental health, public well-being, resource efficiency, and the overall sustainability of urban areas. Addressing carbon emissions aligns with the broader goals of creating resilient, livable, and environmentally friendly cities.

In Fig. 1 visualizes the interconnected components of the Machine Learning-based Optimizing Green Routing system in Smart Cities. Connected vehicles contribute data to the system, enabling adaptive and eco-friendly routing decisions through machine learning and smart city infrastructure integration.

1.1 Motivation and Contribution

Managing and reducing carbon emissions is crucial for addressing climate change, protecting the environment, ensuring air quality and human health, and promoting a sustainable and resilient future. The urgency of modern urbanization's environmental and sustainability concerns must be addressed, which drives the inspiration behind our effort. Problems like traffic congestion, carbon emissions, air pollution, and energy consumption also increase with the size of cities, significantly affecting the standard of living for those who live there. The emergence of Smart Cities presents a chance to rethink and improve transport systems, specifically by applying cutting-edge technologies like the Internet of Vehicles (IoVT). In multipath, there is more than one route connecting one location to another.

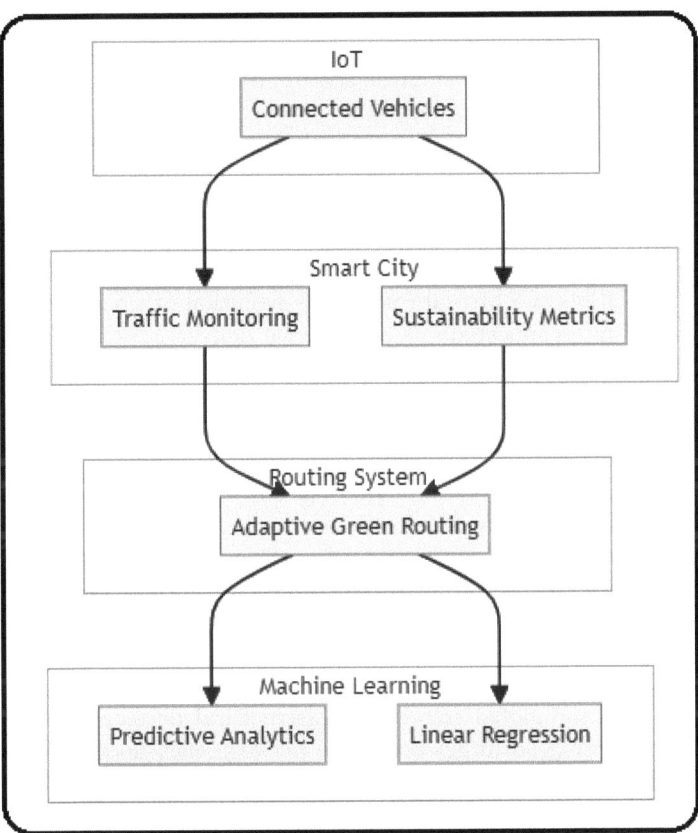

Fig. 1. Proposed framework for analysing ML-based Multipath Green Routing for IoVT. (Color figure online)

The primary contribution of this work lies in developing and applying a sophisticated ML-based green routing system within the IoVT framework. Integrating predictive analytics used in multiple linear regression, this machine learning model allows the system to continually learn and adapt, making informed routing decisions and prioritizing minimizing carbon emissions and energy consumption. This adaptability distinguishes the proposed system from conventional multipath routing methods, offering a more responsive and sustainable solution for urban transportation.

2 Literature Survey

Cities are currently grappling with intricate challenges associated with socio-economic development and improving quality of life. The term "smart city" has emerged as a strategic response to address these multifaceted challenges. The foundational elements of urban development in smart cities are rooted in Internet and broadband network technologies [11], which serve as the backbone for providing various e-services. Smart cities fundamentally rely on Internet technology, facilitating seamless access and interaction with diverse devices. Examples include cameras for video surveillance, sensors monitoring air pollution, actuators, and devices for traffic monitoring.

The accessibility to the Internet not only enables real-time connectivity [3] but also fosters the development of a myriad of applications capable of harnessing the vast volume of data generated by these devices. This proliferation of data gives rise to the creation of innovative services for the benefit of citizens, businesses, and public administration alike. Therefore, the integration of Internet technology [2] plays a pivotal role in the evolution of smart cities, ushering in a new era of interconnectedness and service delivery. Numerous algorithms addressing travel route selection have been published, each with its distinct characteristics. The Dijkstra algorithm, while straightforward, operates by identifying the shortest path on a road map. Although simple to implement, its drawback lies in its computational intensity, resulting in slow performance due to an extensive number of numerical operations. Recognized as an optimal algorithm within the labeling method category, Dijkstra offers accuracy but at the expense of efficiency [9]. The derivation of Dijkstra's approach introduces a heuristic function to optimize route exploration. This algorithm substantially reduces computational operations by leveraging heuristic insights, enhancing operational speed [13].

The author employing a multipath [10] approach in a routing model aligns more closely with the global trend of infrastructural development. In light of the various connecting pathways accessible between each node, empirical studies indicate that this strategy yields superior outcomes compared to a singular path between nodes in a two-dimensional (2D) framework. In this paper [12], the author tackles the issue of eco-friendly communication in 6G-enabled extensive Internet of Things (IoT) devices by adopting a cluster-based data dissemination approach in the network. The author introduces an innovative Hybrid Whale-Spotted Hyena Optimization (HWSHO) algorithm, synthesizing the Whale Optimizer Algorithm (WOA) with the exploitation capabilities of the Spotted Hyena Optimizer (SHO).

Algorithm 1. Optimal Path Selection based on Carbon Emissions

Input: Graph G representing the road network, Start node s, End node t
Output: Optimal path from s to t based on carbon emissions

1 Initialize empty priority queue PQ
 Initialize distance array $dist[]$ with ∞ for all nodes
 Initialize carbon emission array $emission[]$ with 0 for all nodes
 Set $dist[s] \leftarrow 0$ and $emission[s] \leftarrow 0$
 Insert $(s, 0)$ into PQ

2 **while** PQ is not empty **do**
3 $(u, d) \leftarrow$ extract minimum element from PQ
4 **foreach** neighbor v of u **do**
5   $w \leftarrow$ weight of edge (u, v) $e \leftarrow$ carbon emission of edge (u, v)
6   **if** $dist[u] + w < dist[v]$ **then**
7    $dist[v] \leftarrow dist[u] + w$ $emission[v] \leftarrow emission[u] + e$ Insert $(v, dist[v])$ into PQ
8   **end**
9 **end**
10 **end**
11 Reconstruct the optimal path from s to t using $dist[]$ and $emission[]$

This article [8] critically examines established annual-based carbon accounting methodologies, emphasizing emerging real-time carbon emission technologies and their prevailing application trends. Additionally, a framework for the latest near-real-time carbon emission accounting technology, poised for widespread adoption, is introduced.

This Algorithm 1 is used for emphasizing emerging real-time carbon emissions when the vehicle is traversing from one node to another and containing the minimum carbon emission enabled route. Finding the shortest path in a graph with weighted (minimum carbon emission) edges. The weight of each edge represents the travel time or distance, and the carbon emission of each edge is taken into account during the path selection process based on machine learning. The priority queue efficiently selects the node with the minimum distance at each step that contains the minimum carbon emission-enabled route. The algorithm outputs the optimal path from the start node s to the end node t based on travel distance and carbon emissions.

3 Proposed Model

The optimal route planning in the Internet of Vehicles (IoV) focusing on minimizing carbon emissions involves various factors.

Let:

V = Set of vehicles
R = Set of road segments
E = Set of edges representing connections between road segments
$\text{dist}(i, j, r)$ = Distance between road segments i to j via r^{th} route
$\text{emission}(i, j, r)$ = Carbon emission from road segment i to j via r^{th} route

Decision Variables:

x_{ijr} The connection between road segments one location to another i to j via r^{th} route

Objective Function:

$$\text{Minimize} \sum_{i \in R} \sum_{j \in R} \text{emission}(i, j, r) \cdot \text{dist}(i, j, r) \cdot x_{ijr} \quad (1)$$

Constraints:

$$\sum_{j \in R} x_{ijr} = 1, \quad \forall i \in R \quad (2)$$

$$\sum_{i \in R} x_{ijr} = 1, \quad \forall j \in R \quad (3)$$

$$\sum_{i \in S} \sum_{j \in S} x_{ijr} \leq |S| - 1, \quad \forall S \subset R, 2 \leq |S| \leq |R| - 1 \quad (4)$$

In Eq. 1 minimizing the total carbon emissions. Each road segment is visited precisely once in Eq. 2. Each road segment is left once in Eq. 3. In Eq. 4 No sub-tours are allowed in the path.

This model represents the road network as a graph, where R is the set of road segments, and E means the connections between road segments. The decision variable x_{ij} is binary and indicates whether there is a connection between road segments i and j. The objective function aims to minimize the total carbon emissions based on the distance traveled. Constraints ensure that each road segment is visited and left exactly once, preventing sub-tours in the solution.

3.1 Result and Discussion

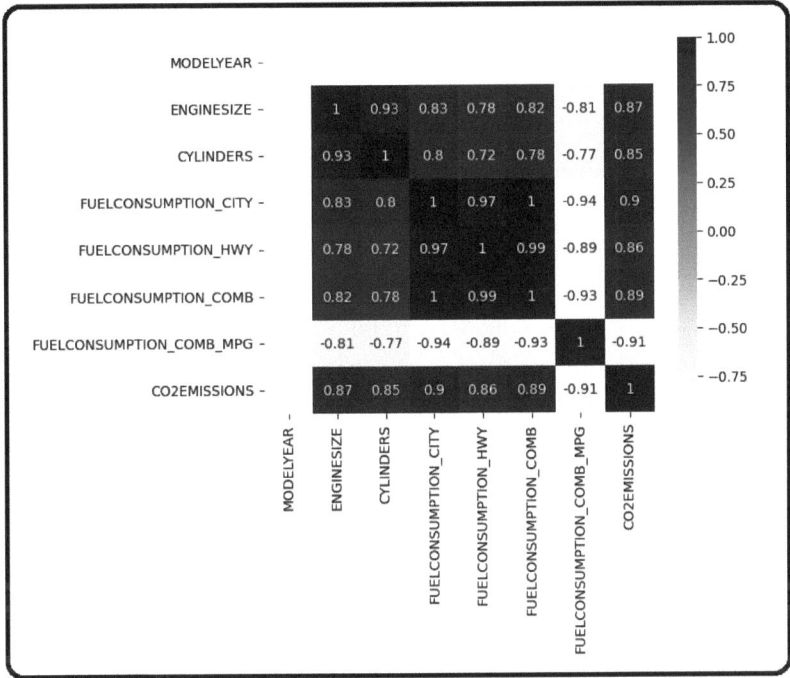

Fig. 2. Hitmap of the dataset

In Fig. 2 shows the heatmap of the particular dataset. The dataset contains the attribute modelyear make, model, vehicleclass, enginesize, cylinders, transmission, fueltype, fuelconsumption city, fuelconsumption hwy, fuelconsumption comb, fuelconsumption comb mpg, co2emissions. After prepossessing the data, we take the most influential of the five parameters that enhance the accuracy of the system's performance. It fits the multiple linear regression model, which provides an accuracy of 84.12%.

$$Y = \beta_0 + \beta_1 X + \varepsilon$$

where:
Y is the response variable, X is the predictor variable, β_0 is the intercept, β_1 is the slope, ε is the error term. The goal of multiple linear regression is to estimate the values of β_0 and β_1 that minimize the sum of squared errors (residuals) between the predicted values ($\hat{Y}$) and the actual values (Y). The estimated regression equation is given by:

$$\hat{Y} = \hat{\beta}_0 + \hat{\beta}_1 X$$

where:

$\hat{Y}$ is the predicted response variable,, $\hat{\beta}_0$ is the estimated intercept,, $\hat{\beta}_1$ is the estimated slope.

The estimated coefficients ($\hat{\beta}_0$ and $\hat{\beta}_1$) are obtained through the method of least squares.

Table 1. Minimum Carbon emission bases optimal path planning

Model Objective	multipath	singlepath (1st path)
path	0(2) -6(0)- 8(1)- 7(1)- 5(0)- 2(1)-9(0)- 1(0)- 3(1)- 4(2)-0	0(0)-6(0)-7(0)-9(0) -8(0)-4(0)-5(0) -3(0)-1(0)-2(0)-0
travel distance (km)	191	203
travel cost (INR)	1791	1815
travel time (minute)	1095	1146
additional time (minute)	301	311
total time (minute)	1396	1457
Total Carbon Emission	2974	3019

In Table 1, the optimal result path for multipath 0(2) -6(0)- 8(1)- 7(1)- 5(0)- 2(1)-9(0)- 1(0)- 3(1)- 4(2)-0 and singlepath 0(0)-6(0)-7(0)-9(0)-8(0)-4(0)-5(0)- 3(0)-1(0)-2(0)-0. Here, we are taking ten nodes, including the depot. Every path starts with the depot 0. In multipath, the result node $0(2) - 6(0)$ represents the Node 0 to node 6 via 2nd route and continuously so on, and which route will taken means 0th node via 2th route in multipath. In singlepath, every route is 0th route. Here, we consider total travel distance, travel cost, travel time, additional time of every node, and carbon emissions. This is the optimal path result. In Fig. 3 shows the result comparison among multipath results better than a singlepath.

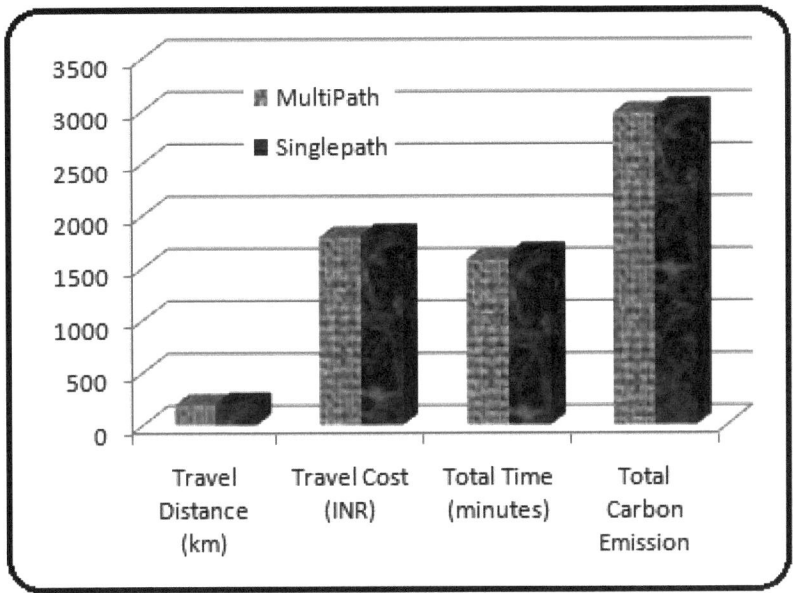

Fig. 3. Result comparing multipath and singlepath

4 Conclusion

In the implementing a Machine Learning-based Multipath Green Routing system for the Internet of Vehicular Things (IoVT) in Smart Cities holds significant promise. The study focused on optimizing vehicle routes by incorporating machine learning algorithms to minimize carbon emissions, considering the dynamic nature of traffic and environmental conditions. The results indicated that the proposed system effectively reduced carbon emissions and travel time and improved the overall efficiency of vehicular routes. Integrating machine learning models and real-time data from the Internet of Things (IoT) demonstrated the system's adaptability to changing traffic patterns and environmental factors. The multipath approach provided resilience to unexpected events and congestion, contributing to a more robust and sustainable transportation network in smart cities. Machine learning provides a powerful toolset for optimizing multipath green routing by leveraging data-driven insights, predictive modeling, adaptive decision-making, and optimization techniques to minimize energy consumption and environmental impact while maintaining efficient transportation or networking operations. The future of this paper is the development of more sophisticated machine learning algorithms that can better capture the complex dynamics of IoV networks and adapt carbon emissions to changing traffic patterns. Integration of reinforcement learning to proactively learn from its interactions with the environment and make optimal routing decisions in real-time. When selecting routing paths, consider factors beyond energy efficiency, such as security and privacy. Development of standardized protocols for this paper to facilitate interoperability between network providers and vehicle manufacturers.

References

1. Barua, L., Zou, B., Zhou, Y.: Machine learning for international freight transportation management: a comprehensive review. Res. Transp. Bus. Manage. **34**, 100453 (2020)
2. Dana, L.-P., Salamzadeh, A., Hadizadeh, M., Heydari, G., Shamsoddin, S.: Urban entrepreneurship and sustainable businesses in smart cities: exploring the role of digital technologies. Sustain. Technol. Entrepreneurship **1**(2), 100016 (2022)
3. Dolgui, A., Ivanov, D.: 5g in digital supply chain and operations management: fostering flexibility, end-to-end connectivity and real-time visibility through internet-of-everything. Int. J. Prod. Res. **60**(2), 442–451 (2022)
4. Gohar, A., Nencioni, G.: The role of 5g technologies in a smart city: the case for intelligent transportation system. Sustainability **13**(9), 5188 (2021)
5. Lakshmi Shankar Iyer: Ai enabled applications towards intelligent transportation. Transp. Eng. **5**, 100083 (2021)
6. Khatua, S., Mukherjee, A., De, D.: SoVEC: social vehicular edge computing-based optimum route selection. Veh. Commun. 100764 (2024)
7. Kirimtat, A., Krejcar, O., Kertesz, A., Fatih Tasgetiren, M.: Future trends and current state of smart city concepts: a survey. IEEE Access **8**, 86448–86467 (2020)
8. Liu, Z., et al.: Near-real-time carbon emission accounting technology toward carbon neutrality. Engineering **14**, 44–51 (2022)
9. Luo, M., Hou, X., Yang, J.: Surface optimal path planning using an extended dijkstra algorithm. IEEE Access **8**, 147827–147838 (2020)
10. Maji, S., Maity, S., Giri, D., Castillo, O., Maiti, M.: A multi-path delivery system with random refusal against online booking using type-2 fuzzy logic-based fireworks algorithm. Decis. Anal. J. **6**, 100151 (2023)
11. Paredes-Páliz, D.F., Royo, G., Aznar, F., Aldea, C., Celma, S.: Radio over fiber: an alternative broadband network technology for IoT. Electronics **9**(11), 1785 (2020)
12. Verma, S., Kaur, S., Khan, M.A., Sehdev, P.S.: Toward green communication in 6g-enabled massive internet of things. IEEE Internet Things J. **8**(7), 5408–5415 (2020)
13. Yang, N., Han, L., Xiang, C., Liu, H., Ma, T., Ruan, S.: Real-time energy management for a hybrid electric vehicle based on heuristic search. IEEE Trans. Veh. Technol. **71**(12), 12635–12647 (2022)
14. Yang, Z., Xia, H., Su, F., Zhao, J., Feng, F.: Application of genetic algorithm in modeling of shortest path problem. In: 2020 Chinese Automation Congress (CAC), pp. 3447–3450. IEEE (2020)
15. Zhang, D., Wallace, S.W., Guo, Z., Dong, Y., Kaut, M.: On scenario construction for stochastic shortest path problems in real road networks. Transp. Res. Part E: Logistics Transp. Rev. **152**, 102410 (2021)

FemCrop: A Femtocell-Based Edge-Cloud Frame-Work for Crop Yield Prediction Using Deep Learning

Tanushree Dey[1], Somnath Bera[1], Anwesha Mukherjee[2](✉)[iD], Samarjit Roy[3][iD], and Debashis De[1][iD]

[1] Centre of Mobile Cloud Computing, Department of Computer Science and Engineering, Maulana Abul Kalam Azad University of Technology, West Bengal, NH-12, Simhat, Haringhata, Nadia 741249, West Bengal, India
[2] Department of Computer Science, Mahishadal Raj College, Mahishadal, Purba Medinipur 721628, West Bengal, India
anweshamukherjee2011@gmail.com
[3] School of Computing and Information Technology, Eastern International University, Nam Ky Khoi Nghia Street, Hoa Phu Ward, Thu Dau Mot City, Binh Duong Province, Vietnam
samarjit.roy@ieee.org

Abstract. Crop recommendation is one of the substantial research areas of Agriculture 5.0. In conventional IoT-based crop recommendation systems, the information storage and analysis happen inside the cloud that has several shortcomings such as connection interruption, high latency, huge overhead on the cloud, etc.. To overcome these issues, this paper proposes a crop yield prediction system FemCrop based on femtocell, edge computing, and deep learning. The femtocell is a low-power base station that serves an intermediary device in FemCrop for facilitating seamless data transmission between IoT devices and the edge server by enhancing signal strength. The edge server utilizes sophisticated deep-learning methods to analyze data and produce recommended outcomes that are sent to the cloud. Users can access these predicted outcomes from the cloud for selection regarding appropriate crop. The outcomes indicate that FemCrop achieves ∼99% prediction accuracy, and reduces ∼30% latency and ∼10% energy consumption than the conventional edge-cloud system.

Keywords: Femtocell · Crop yield prediction · Deep learning · Latency · Energy

1 Introduction

The incorporation of the Internet of Things (IoT) into agriculture has introduced Internet of Agricultural Things (IoAT) [1], transforming the methods of data gathering, analyzing, and making decisions to maximize crop yield and improve the long-term viability of agricultural practices. The modernization of agricultural practices owes much to the amalgamation of traditional methodologies with cutting-edge technologies like IoT, cloud computing, and machine learning. A wide range of factors, including organic, economic, and seasonal dynamics significantly impacts agricultural production. Environmental factors, including soil composition, climate conditions, water availability, temperature changes, rainfall patterns, vegetative indices, and nutrient levels, have a significant influence on crop yields. Traditionally, the process of gathering data in agricultural environments mainly depends on human effort, resulting in a small number of data points that have less than ideal precision and accuracy. To overcome, these issues IoT is integrated with agriculture, where the IoT sensors continuously accumulate real-time agricultural data [2,3]. After the analysis of the collected data, the farmers can obtain a legendary under-standing of the complex dynamics of crop development and environmental factors in agricultural areas. In conventional IoT-based systems, the data analytics takes place inside the cloud server. However, the information transmission from the IoT devices to the cloud is a challenge owing to poor signal strength at the rural regions containing the agricultural lands. Further, the entire data transmission to the cloud for analysis increases latency, network traffic, etc. The use of edge computing overcomes the issue by bringing computing and storage facilities at the network edge [4]. The edge servers are usually attached with the large cell base stations (macrocell/microcell) [5], and the edge servers are connected with the cloud. However, the transfer of data from IoT devices to the edge server is hampered by inadequate network connectivity. For providing good signal strength the use of femtocells are well-known [6]. The use of femtocell as an intermediate device between the IoT devices and edge server, can deal with the network connectivity issue. Inside the edge server, data is analyzed and predictive algorithms are taught to effectively anticipate crop yields. In this paper, we explore the use of femtocells and deep learning for crop yield prediction and recommendation in IoAT. The femtocells can play a decisive role in enabling the smooth transfer of data gathered by IoT sensors to the edge server for data processing. Utilizing femtocell technology can allow effective data transmission, facilitating prompt analysis and model creation utilizing advanced techniques like Long Short-Term Memory (LSTM) [7] and Gated Recurrent Unit (GRU) networks. GRU [8] is a recurrent neural network (RNN) architecture that aims at several challenges of traditional RNNs, particularly in capturing long-term dependencies while mitigating the vanishing gradient problem. The combination of femtocell-enabled data transmission, edge server-based data processing, and cloud connectivity highlights the significant impact that current agricultural technologies can have on revolutionizing crop management practices.

1.1 Motivations and Contributions

Rural agricultural fields frequently face challenges like poor signal strength due to insufficient cellular base station coverage and a lack Wi-Fi connectivity. Hence, the transmission of sensor data to the cloud presents a notable obstacle. Edge computing expands network resources to the periphery, however, interruptions in connectivity with base stations hinder the ability to reach the edge server in the traditional edge-cloud model. The objective of this work is to propose a crop yield prediction system that will conquer these challenges. To achieve this goal, the contributions of this paper are:

- A *Fem*tocell and deep learning-based *Crop* yield prediction system (*Fem-Crop*) is proposed, where IoT devices collect soil and environmental data, and send to the femtocell. The femtocell transmit the data to the edge server attached to the macrocell/microcell base station. The edge server processes the data and sends the suitable crop recommendation result to the cloud. From the cloud the user access the recommended results anytime, anywhere using his/her mobile device.
- For data analysis LSTM and GRU are used. The crop yield prediction accuracy for FemCrop is measured, and compared with the existing systems. The latency and energy consumption for FemCrop are measured and compared with the conventional edge-cloud and cloud-only systems.

We arrange the rest of the paper as follows. Section 2 presents the related works. Section 3 illustrates the proposed methodology. Section 4 analyses the performance of the proposed system. Section 5 concludes the paper.

2 Related Works

Machine learning (ML) and Deep Learning (DL) algorithms were utilized for crop yield prediction to improve agricultural productivity. An extensive literature review is conducted to gain a thorough understanding of the use of ML and DL in predicting crop yields.

2.1 Use of ML

ML focuses on predicting future outcomes rather than trying to understand the underlying mechanical processes [9]. ML applications are extensively utilized to handle many problems that people often struggle with or require significant effort to resolve. In [10], mustard crop yield prediction was performed by analyzing the soil data using five ML methods. Both the K-Nearest Neighbours (KNN) algorithm and Artificial Neural Network (ANN) were identified as viable methods for predicting mustard crop yield. Weather and soil factors' related data are acquired and studied to improve agricultural productivity [11]. Using K-means classification the dataset was classified to identify the optimal mix of precipitation and temperature to improve crop yield [12]. A Deep Recurrent Q-Network model was developed to predict crop yield [3]. For better crop yield prediction, an enhanced variant of the Deep Recurrent Q-Network Support Vector Machine algorithm was proposed in [13]. A new approach was introduced in [14] by utilizing Wireless Sensor Networks (WSNs) to pinpoint the best areas for growing particular crops like Kidney Beans, Pomegranate, and Apple. The system utilized WSNs to collect real-time environmental data. The system's objective was to identify areas with optimal circumstances for cultivating specific crops through data analysis. An analysis of Artificial Intelligence (AI)-driven precision farming was presented in [15] with a cloud-based ML-powered crop recommendation system designed to help farmers regarding the suitable crop to harvest. The use of Random Forest (RF), Extreme Gradient Boosting (XGBoost), Decision Tree (DT), KNN, and Support Vector Machine (SVM), was demonstrated in [15]. In [16], ML and edge computing were used for crop recommendation.

2.2 Use of DL

A multi-parametric deep neural network (DNN) was suggested as a means to simulate the effects of variations in temperature, soil, and climate attributes, with the aim of forecasting crop yield [17]. By using prior knowledge of several functional forms associated with agricultural productivity, the multi-parametric DNN demonstrated superior statistical efficiency compared to the DNN. In [18], a novel approach using DNNs was proposed to leverage traditional models. Deep learning models were created in [19] to evaluate the performance of underlying algorithms across several performance metrics. The algorithms assessed in the study included the XGBoost, Convolutional Neural Networks (CNN)-DNN, CNN-XGBoost, CNN-RNN, and CNN-LSTM. The Red Fox Optimization with Ensemble Recurrent Neural Network for Crop Recommendation and Yield Prediction (RFOERNN-CRYP) model was developed in [20]. The RFOERNN-CRYP model utilized an ensemble learning approach with three distinct DL models (LSTM, BiLSTM, and GRU) to achieve improved prediction accuracy compared to individual classifier models. Though several crop yield prediction approaches exist, the response latency and energy consumption were not highlighted much. In the present work, we propose a femtocell and DL-based approach that will provide crop yield prediction at high accuracy, low latency, and low energy consumption.

3 FemCrop: Proposed Framework

FemCrop contains the following components: IoAT devices equipped with sensors and microcontrollers, femtocell, edge server, and cloud. These components are mathematically defined as follows.

- A sensor node (ψ) is represented as a three tuple $\psi =< \psi_{id}, \psi_o, \psi_s >$, where ψ_{id} presents the ID of the sensor, ψ_o presents the respective object, and ψ_s presents the sensor status i.e., active or not.
- A microcontroller (μ) is defined as a two tuple as follows: $\mu =< \mu_{id}, \mu_s, \mu_{con} >$, where μ_{id}, μ_s, and μ_{con} denotes the microcontroller ID, its status i.e., active or not, and its configuration in terms of memory, processing ability, etc., respectively.

- A femtocell (ϕ) is defined as a three tuple as follows: $\phi =< \phi_{id}, \phi_s, \phi_{con} >$, where ϕ_{id}, ϕ_s, and ϕ_{con} denotes femtocell ID, its status i.e., active or not, and its configuration in terms of memory, processing ability, storage capacity, etc., respectively.
- An edge server (ϵ) is defined as a two tuple as follows: $\epsilon =< \epsilon_{id}, \epsilon_{con} >$, where ϵ_{id} and ϵ_{con} denotes edge server ID and its configuration in terms of memory, processing ability, storage capacity, etc., respectively.
- An instance of cloud computing (ζ) is represented as a two tuple as follows: $\zeta =< \zeta_{id}, \zeta_p >$, where ζ_{id} presents the cloud computing instance ID, and ζ_p the set contains processing unit IDs of the required respective cloud servers.

3.1 Working Model of FemCrop

The three-tier architecture of FemCrop is presented in Fig. 1, where tier-I contains sensors and microcontroller, tier-II contains femtocell and edge server, and tier-III contains cloud. The working procedure of FemCrop is stated as follows.

1. IoAT sensor nodes are deployed to collect the soil and environmental data. In FemCrop, pH sensors, NPK (Nitrogen (N), Phosphorous (P), and Potassium (K)) sensors, air temperature and humidity sensors are used. The sensor nodes collect respective object status and transmit it to an interfaced microcontroller.
2. The microcontroller receives data from the linked sensors and transmits it to the femtocell, with which it is connected. The enterprise femtocell has a coverage area of 100–150 m. One or several femtocells are deployed within agricultural fields, customized to match the size of the land area being harvested. The femtocells serve as the intermediate nodes for smooth data transmission from the IoT devices to the edge server.
3. The femtocell receives data from the microcontroller, pre-processes the data, and transmits it to the edge server attached to the nearby macrocell/microcell base station.
4. The edge server receives soil and environmental data from the femtocell, and obtains weather-related data of the respective region from the cloud. The edge server utilizes both LSTM and GRU to assess the soil data, environmental data, and weather-related data, and subsequently transmits the recommendation outcomes to the cloud. The user accesses the outcomes from the cloud anytime, anywhere using his/her mobile device.

There are several advantages of femtocell such as low-power, security, good signal strength, etc. The femtocell is a low-power cellular base station that transmits data through a security tunnel to maintain data integrity and confidentiality. Thus, in FemCrop secure transmission of data to the edge server is performed. Further, due to low power transmission, energy efficiency is achieved. By processing data within the edge server, it minimizes the need for extensive transfer of information to the cloud, resulting in less data traffic and packet loss.

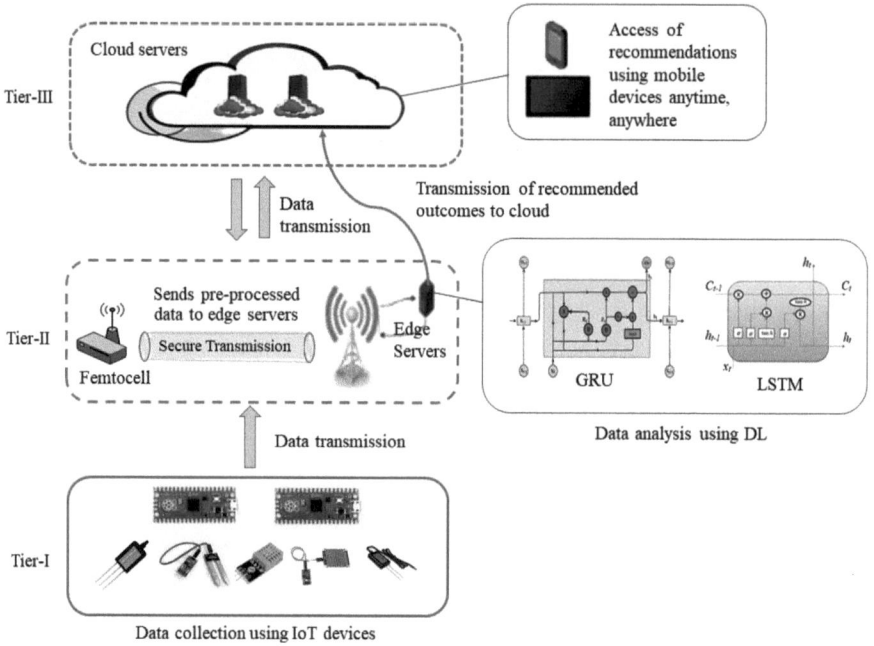

Fig. 1. Three-tier architecture of FemCrop.

3.2 Data Analysis Using LSTM and GRU

In the proposed framework, LSTM and GRU are employed to predict the crop yield of a land-based on sensor data and weather-related information. LSTM networks excel at retaining information over extended periods, enabling them to learn long-term dependencies. At the core of LSTM architecture the cell state lies that is crucial for its memory function. LSTM is structured in a chain-like manner, incorporating four neural networks called gates and various memory blocks known as cells. Despite its strengths, a notable drawback of standard LSTM models is their tendency to overlook future context, which is essential for accurately classifying long-period occurrences. In LSTM, a sigmoid function is employed to decide what information to retain or discard. This decision is based on the combined input and hidden state of the previous time step, forming what is known as the forget gate. The forget gate is represented by Eq. (1) as follows:

$$f_t = \sigma(w_t h_{t-1} + w_t x_t + b_f) \qquad (1)$$

where w_t is weight at time t, h_{t-1} defines hidden state at time $(t-1)$, x_t defines current input at time t, and b_f denotes bias of the forget gate. The subsequent step is to determine what new data will be added to the cell state. This is done in two parts. Firstly, an input gate (i_t) in a sigmoid layer decides which value to change. Secondly, a tanh function makes a vector of new candidate gate value c_t. The state will then be updated by adding these two values. The equations are as follows:

$$i_t = \sigma(w_i h_{t-1} + w_i x_t + b_i) \tag{2}$$

$$c_t = \tanh(w_c h_{t-1} + w_c x_t + b_c) \tag{3}$$

where the weight of the input gate is denoted as w_i, b_i denotes the bias of the input gate, w_c is mentioned as the weight of the candidate gate, and b_c denotes the bias of the candidate gate. The old cell state C_{t-1} is updated to the new cell state C_t by the calculated value of f_t, i_t, and c_t. The new cell state is presented by Eq. (4) as follows:

$$C_t = (i_t * c_t) + (f_t * C_{t-1}) \tag{4}$$

Eventually, the output is resolved depending on the cell state and filtered using an output gate. The output gate, determined by a sigmoid function, decides which parts of the cell state contribute to the output. The new cell state is then passed through a hyperbolic tangent function and multiplied by the output of the sigmoid function to determine the information carried by the hidden state. The new cell state and hidden state are then carried forward to the next time step. The equations of O_t and h_t are presented by Eqs. (5) and (6) respectively, as follows:

$$O_t = \sigma(h_{t-1} + w_O x_t + b_O) \tag{5}$$

$$h_t = O_t * \tanh(C_t) \tag{6}$$

where x_t defines current input at time t, h_t defines hidden state at time t, h_{t-1} defines hidden state at the previous time $(t-1)$, b_O is the bias, C_t defines memory or cell state, w_O is the initial weight, and O_t defines output gate. The weight values (w_i, w_c, w_O) are updated during the training of LSTM.

GRU is another type of RNN architecture that simplifies the LSTM by merging the cell state and hidden state, and reducing the number of gates. It integrates the forget and input gates into a single"update gate", and merges the cell state and hidden state into a single vector. The key components of a GRU cell are:

- Update Gate (z): It controls how much of the past information should be sent along to the future, and it is represented by Eq. (7) as follows.

$$z_t = \sigma(w_z h_{t-1} + w_z x_t + b_z) \tag{7}$$

- Reset Gate (r): It controls how much of the past information should be forgotten, and it is expressed by Eq. (8) as follows.

$$r_t = \sigma(w_r h_{t-1} + w_r x_t + b_r) \tag{8}$$

The candidate hidden state is represented by Eq. (9) as follows.

$$v_t = \tanh(w_h r_t h_{t-1} + w_h x_t + b_h) \tag{9}$$

The hidden state at time t is represented by Eq. (10) as follows.

$$h_t = (1 - z_t)h_{t-1} + z_t v_t \tag{10}$$

In Sect. 4, the performance of LSTM and GRU in data analysis is assessed based on accuracy, precision, recall, and F1-Score. Let assume α_1, α_2, α_3, and α_4 denotes true positive, true negative, false positive, and false negative predicted values respectively. The accuracy is expressed as: $(\alpha_1 + \alpha_2)/(\alpha_1 + \alpha_2 + \alpha_3 + \alpha_4)$. The precision is expressed as: $\alpha_1/(\alpha_1 + \alpha_3)$. The recall is expressed as: $\alpha_1/(\alpha_1 + \alpha_4)$. The F1-score is represented as $(2 * \frac{\alpha_1}{\alpha_1+\alpha_3} * \frac{\alpha_1}{\alpha_1+\alpha_4})/(\frac{\alpha_1}{\alpha_1+\alpha_3} + \frac{\alpha_1}{\alpha_1+\alpha_4})$.

3.3 Latency and Energy Consumption

To determine the latency for FemCrop, the data transmission latency from the microcontroller to the femtocell, from femtocell to the edge server, and from the edge server to the cloud (outcome) is considered. The data transmission latency from node a to node b is presented as: $T_{ab} = (1 + \theta_{ab}) * (\frac{\delta_{ab}}{\rho_{ab}})$, where θ_{ab} is failure rate of communication link, ρ_{ab} is the data transmission rate, and δ_{ab} is the data amount. If the data transmission latency from microcontroller to the femtocell is $T_{\mu\phi}$, from the femtocell to the edge server is $T_{\phi\epsilon}$, and from the edge server to the cloud is $T_{\epsilon\zeta}$, the data transmission latency for FemCrop is given by Eq. (11) as follows:

$$T_{tr} = T_{\mu\phi} + T_{\phi\epsilon} + T_{\epsilon\zeta} \tag{11}$$

The data filtering takes place inside the microcontroller, the data preprocessing takes place inside the femtocell, and finally edge server analyzes the data using LSTM and GRU. Therefore, the data processing latency for microcontroller, femtocell, and edge server are considered. The processing latency for a node a is given as: $T_a = \frac{\delta_a}{\rho_a}$, where δ_a is the data amount and ρ_a is the data processing rate. If the processing latency for microcontroller is T_μ, for femtocell is T_ϕ, and for edge server is T_ϵ, the data processing latency for FemCrop is given by Eq. (12) as follows:

$$T_{pr} = T_\mu + T_\phi + T_\epsilon \tag{12}$$

The latency for FemCrop is then given by Eq. (13) as follows:

$$T = T_{tr} + T_{pr} \tag{13}$$

The energy consumption of the FemCrop is given as the sum of the energy consumption of the sensors for data collection and transmission, microcontroller for data transmission and processing, femtocell for data transmission and processing, and edge server for data transmission and processing (analysis). Let assume the energy consumption of the sensors for data collection and transmission is E_ψ, the energy consumption of the microcontroller for data transmission and processing is E_μ, the energy consumption of the femtocell for data transmission and processing is E_ϕ, and the energy consumption of the edge server for data transmission and processing is E_ϵ. Then, the energy consumption of the FemCrop is given by Eq. (14) as follows:

$$E = E_\psi + E_\mu + E_\phi + E_\epsilon \qquad (14)$$

In Sect. 4, the latency and energy consumption of FemCrop are measured and compared with the conventional edge-cloud and cloud-only systems.

4 Performance Analysis of FemCrop

The performance of FemCrop is evaluated in terms of prediction accuracy, latency, and energy consumption. LSTM and GRU are used to predict crop yields from the input dataset[1]. The soil, environmental, and weather factors (levels of pH, N, P, K in the soil, humidity, temperature, rainfall), and the crop, are considered in the input dataset containing 2200 samples. There are twenty two crops, which are considered as 22 classes. 1. Jute, 2. Rice, 3. Coffee, 4. Cotton, 5. Coconut, 6. Papaya, 7. Orange, 8. Banana, 9. Mango, 10. Grapes, 11. Watermelon, 12. Muskmelon, 13. Apple, 14. Pomegranate, 15. Lentil, 16. Blackgram, 17. Mungbean, 18. Mothbeans, 19. Pigeon-peas, 20. Kidneybeans, 21. Chickpea, and 22. Maize. The accuracy, precision, recall, and F1-score while using LSTM and GRU in FemCrop, are measured, and presented in Fig. 2. As observed from Fig. 2, LSTM achieves better prediction accuracy, precision, recall, and F1-score values than the GRU.

Comparison with Existing Crop Yield Prediction Methods: The FemCrop is compared with three existing crop yield prediction strategies in Table 1. In [14], KNN achieved 92.62% accuracy. In [15], RF, KNN, DT, XGBoost, and SVM, were used, and RF achieved the highest accuracy of 97.18%. In [20], LSTM, Bi-LSTM, and GRU were used, and achieved an accuracy of 98.45%. In the proposed work FemCrop, LSTM and GRU are used, and LSTM achieved the highest accuracy of 99%, which is higher than [14,15,20]. The FemCrop also outperforms the existing strategies in terms of precision, recall, and F1-score. Further, the existing works did not measure the latency and energy consumption, which we have measured in our work.

---

[1] https://www.kaggle.com/datasets/atharvaingle/crop-recommendation-dataset.

Table 1. Comparison of FemCrop with existing crop-yield prediction approaches

Work	Classifier used	Use of edge	Accuracy	Precision	Recall	F1-score	Latency	Energy consumption
Cruz et al. [14]	KNN	No	92.62%	96.74%	92.62%	95.46%	Not measured	Not measured
Thilakarathne et al. [15]	RF(Highest accuracy), KNN, DT, XGBoost, SVM	No	97.18%	97%	97%	97%	Not measured	Not measured
Gopi et al. [20]	LSTM, Bi-LSTM, GRU	No	98.45%	98.51%	98.45%	98.46%	Not measured	Not measured
Femcrop (Proposed framework),	LSTM, (Highest accuracy) GRU	Yes	99% (LSTM), 98% (GRU)	98.9% (LSTM), 98.18% (GRU)	99.18% (LSTM), 98% (GRU)	99% (LSTM), 98% (GRU)	1.65 S (LSTM), 1.74 S (GRU)	2.66 KJ (LSTM), 2.7 KJ (GRU)

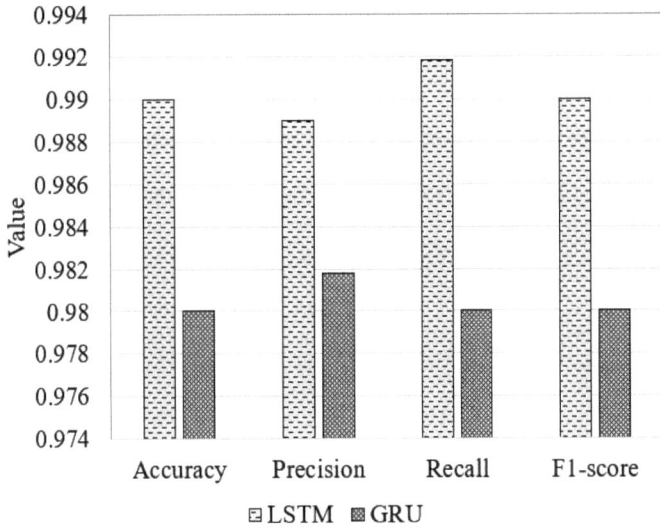

Fig. 2. Comparison of performance of LSTM and GRU in FemCrop.

The latency and energy consumption of FemCrop are measured and compared with the conventional edge-cloud and cloud-only systems in Fig. 3 and Fig. 4 respectively. As in FemCrop LSTM and GRU are used, we have considered both while measured the latency and energy consumption. The latency is measured in seconds and energy consumption is measured in Kilo Joule (KJ). The results demonstrate that FemCrop achieves ∼30% (∼32% in LSTM, ∼30% in GRU) and ∼47% (∼48% in LSTM, ∼47% in GRU) reduction in latency than the conventional edge-cloud and cloud-only systems respectively. The results also demonstrate that FemCrop achieves ∼10% (∼10% in LSTM, ∼10% in GRU) and ∼18% (∼19% in LSTM, ∼18% in GRU) reduction in energy consumption than the conventional edge-cloud and cloud-only systems respectively.

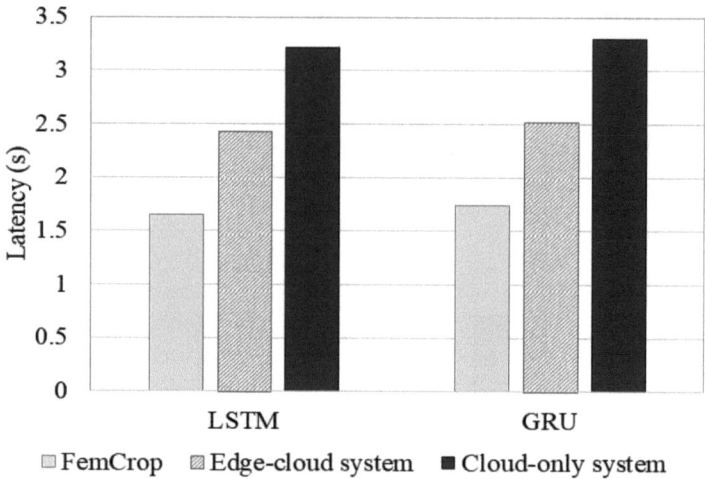

Fig. 3. Latency in FemCrop, edge-cloud, and cloud-only systems.

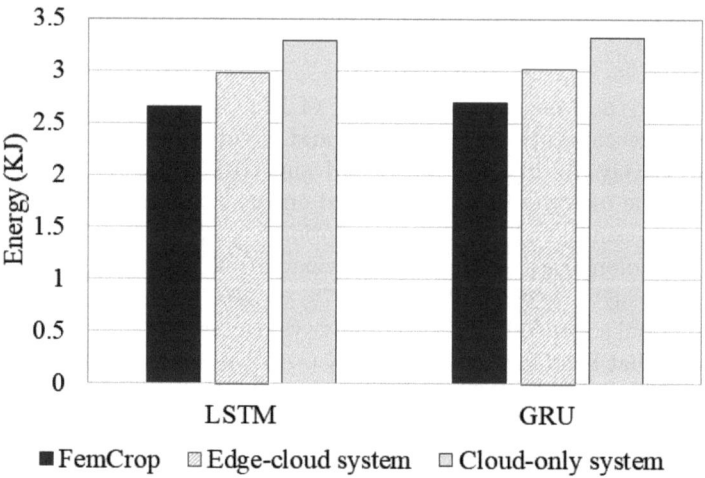

Fig. 4. Energy consumption of FemCrop, edge-cloud, and cloud-only systems.

5 Conclusion

In this paper, a femtocell-based crop yield prediction system referred to as Fem-Crop has been proposed using edge computing and deep learning. The femtocells are allocated at the agricultural fields to provide better signal strength in those areas. The IoT devices send the collected soil and environmental data to the femtocell. The femtocell after pre-processing sends the data to the edge server attached to the large cell base station. The femtocell performs data transmission through a security tunnel to maintain data confidentiality and integrity. The edge server performs data analysis using deep learning-based approaches LSTM and GRU, and sends the recommended outcomes to the cloud. The user can access the outcomes anytime, anywhere using his/her mobile device. The results present that the proposed framework achieves ∼99% prediction accuracy which is higher than the existing approaches. The results also present that FemCrop reduces ∼30% latency and ∼10% energy consumption than the conventional edge-cloud system, and reduces ∼47% latency and ∼18% energy consumption compared to the cloud-only system. Federated learning-based crop recommendation is a future research scope of this work.

References

1. Javaid, N.: Integration of context awareness in internet of agricultural things. ICT Express **9**(2), 189–196 (2023)
2. Van Klompenburg, T., Kassahun, A., Catal, C.: Crop yield prediction using machine learning: a systematic literature review. Comput. Electron. Agric. **177**, 105709 (2020)
3. Elavarasan, D., Vincent, P.M.D.: Crop yield prediction using deep reinforcement learning model for sustainable agrarian applications. IEEE Access **8**, 86886–86901 (2020)
4. Mukherjee, A., De, D., Ghosh, S.K., Buyya, R.: Mobile Edge Computing. Springer, Hidelberg (2021)
5. Mukherjee, A., Deb, P., De, D.: LFMTCN: a green ultra-dense multi-tier small cell network using leader-follower strategy. Wireless Pers. Commun. **110**, 275–289 (2020)
6. Sathya, V., Kala, S.M., Naidu, K.: Heterogenous networks: from small cells to 5G NR-U. Wirel. Pers. Commun. **128**(4), 2779–2810 (2023)
7. Rani, S., Mishra, A.K., Kataria, A., Mallik, S., Qin, H.: Machine learning-based optimal crop selection system in smart agriculture. Sci. Rep. **13**(1), 15997 (2023)
8. Jingxin, Yu., Zhang, X., Linlin, X., Dong, J., Zhangzhong, L.: A hybrid CNN-GRU model for predicting soil moisture in maize root zone. Agric. Water Manag. **245**, 106649 (2021)
9. Crane-Droesch, A.: Machine learning methods for crop yield prediction and climate change impact assessment in agriculture. Environ. Res. Lett. **13**(11), 114003 (2018)
10. Pandith, V., Kour, H., Singh, S., Manhas, J., Sharma, V.: Performance evaluation of machine learning techniques for mustard crop yield prediction from soil analysis. J. Sci. Res. **64**(2), 394–398 (2020)
11. Gupta, R., et al.: WB-CPI: weather based crop prediction in India using big data analytics. IEEE Access **9**, 137869–137885 (2021)
12. Babatunde, G., Emmanuel, A.A., Oluwaseun, O.R., Bunmi, O.B., Precious, A.E.: Impact of climatic change on agricultural product yield using k-means and multiple linear regressions. Int. J. Educ. Manag. Eng. (IJEME) **9**(3), 16–26 (2019)
13. Jayakumar, D., Srinivasan, S., Prithi, P., Vemula, S., Sri, N.: Application of machine learning on crop yield prediction in agriculture enforcement. Revista Geintec-gestao Inovacao e Tecnologias **11**(2), 2142–2155 (2021)
14. Cruz, M., Mafra, S., Teixeira, E.: An IoT crop recommendation system with k-nn and lora for precision farming (2022)
15. Thilakarathne, N.N., Bakar, M.S.A., Abas, P.E., Yassin, H.: A cloud enabled crop recommendation platform for machine learning-driven precision farming. Sensors **22**(16), 6299 (2022)

16. Bera, S., Dey, T., Mukherjee, A., Buyya, R.: E-cropreco: a dew-edge-based multi-parametric crop recommendation framework for internet of agricultural things. J. Supercomput. 1–35 (2023)
17. Kalaiarasi, E., Anbarasi, A.: Crop yield prediction using multi-parametric deep neural networks. Indian J. Sci. Technol. **14**(2), 131–140 (2021)
18. Sucharitha, Y., Reddy, P.C.S., Chitti, T.N.: Deep learning based framework for crop yield prediction. In: AIP Conference Proceedings, vol. 2548. AIP Publishing (2023)
19. Oikonomidis, A., Catal, C., Kassahun, A.: Hybrid deep learning-based models for crop yield prediction. Appl. Artif. Intell. **36**(1), 2031822 (2022)
20. Gopi, P.S.S., Karthikeyan, M.: Red fox optimization with ensemble recurrent neural network for crop recommendation and yield prediction model. Multimedia Tools Appl. 1–21 (2023)

Detection of Ransomware Attacks Using Federated Learning Based on the CNN Model

Hong Nhung Nguyen[1(✉)], Ha Thanh Nguyen[2], and Damien Lescos[3]

[1] Gachon University, Seongnam, South Korea
`nhungnguyen.uet@gmail.com`
[2] National Institute of Informatics, Tokyo, Japan
`nguyenhathanh@nii.ac.jp`
[3] Sitin Clound, Chéraute, France
`damien.lescos@sitincloud.com`

Abstract. Computing is still under a significant threat from ransomware, which necessitates prompt action to prevent it. Ransomware attacks can have a negative impact on how smart grids, particularly digital substations. In addition to examining a ransomware detection method using artificial intelligence (AI), this paper offers a ransomware attack modeling technique that targets the disrupted operation of a digital substation. The first, binary data is transformed into image data and fed into the convolution neural network model using federated learning. The experimental findings demonstrate that the suggested technique detects ransomware with a high accuracy rate.

Keywords: Ransomeware attack · Cyber Security · Deep Learning

1 Introduction

Nowadays, cyber threats are one of the costliest losses an institution can encounter. Ransomware is malware that threatens to publish the victim's data or block access to it unless a ransom is paid. It became popular in the early 2010s, and its use has been overgrown. Ransomware attacks have been increasing in number and sophistication in recent years. WannaCry, for example, was a ransomware worm that spread rapidly across the world in May 2017, affecting more than 230,000 computers in 150 countries.

With the development of federated learning techniques, it becomes possible to train machine learning models on data that is distributed across different devices or organizations. The federated learning approach has the potential to be used in training models for detecting ransomware. The reason is that, in a federated learning setting, each data owner keeps its data locally and only shares model updates with a central server. Therefore, the data never leaves the owner's premises, which alleviates privacy concerns.

A convolutional neural network (CNN) is a type of deep learning neural network that is generally used for image classification and recognition. It has been shown to be effective in various types of image classification tasks [2,3,6,7,11,13–15,18,19]. An idea comes to using the CNN model to classify ransomware attacks. The advantages of using the CNN model are that it can automatically learn features from data and that it is robust to data variability. In addition, it also allows the representation of the data in a more compact and efficient way. The paper first preprocesses the data into images and then uses the CNN model to learn and classify the data. The proposed method has the advantage of being privacy-preserving because the data never leaves the data owner's premises. By experimenting, we found that our proposed model is more accurate than several traditional methods in the literature.

There are several methods proposed in the literature for detecting ransomware. Takeuchi [16] proposed a detection method using support vector machines (SVMs). The key idea is to trace the API call when the ransomware is executing. With this approach, the authors can detect unseen ransomware by the similarity of API calls between samples. Another approach proposed by Arabo et al. is to monitor the behavior of the ransomware process. The key idea is to monitor the process behavior to detect ransomware. In this approach, the authors look into the key process usages to detect ransomware. They also include the analysis of DLLs and system calls.

However, the ransomware detection methods proposed in the literature have several limitations. First, many of them require the use of static features, which may be hard to collect, especially on obfuscated and metamorphic binaries. Second, many of them require the use of dynamic features, which means that they require the execution of the ransomware for analysis. As a result, we may want some approximate static features that can be used to detect ransomware.

2 Background

In this section, some key concepts related to Machine learning and cyber security are discussed in order to understand and appreciate the novelties of the proposed approach.

2.1 Machine Learning

Currently, we can apply machine learning to solve issues in the real world such as autonomous driver, healthcare [12] and cyber security [8].

Using the technique of machine learning (ML), which is a type of artificial intelligence (AI), software programs can make predictions more accurately with having to be explicitly trained to do so [5]. As shown in Fig. 1, In the paradigm of symbolic AI known as classical programming, humans input rules (a program) and data to be processed in accordance with these rules, and the results are replies. With machine learning, humans input data along with the predictions

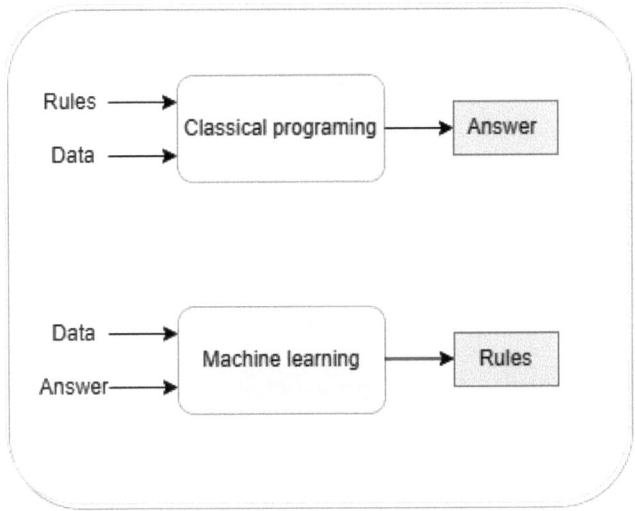

Fig. 1. Machine learning: a new programming paradigm

made from the data, and the rules are produced as a result. Then, using new data, these rules can be employed to develop new results [17].

In order to estimate new target values, machine learning algorithms use existing data as input. The research on machine learning is divided into the following categories:

- Supervise learning Supervised learning is a staple of many machine learning problems. It involves learning any input for which we already know the target or labels. The applications of near-complete deep learning are usually aimed at: object recognition, voice recognition, image classification, and supervised machine learning. Most of these include two problems, namely classification and regression problems. It can also be extended to several issues such as sequence generation, syntax tree prediction, object detection, and image segmentation. Some famous criteria of supervised learning are face recognition and spam detection
- Unsupervised learning Unsupervised learning involves learning data without labels. It is usually aimed at, for example, visualizing data or reducing data noise. Unsupervised learning mainly analyzes the data and is often necessary to understand the data better before solving machine learning problems. In fact, dimensional reduction or clustering are well-known algorithms in unsupervised machine learning.
- Semi-supervised Learning Semi-supervised learning is a machine learning technique that involves training using a small amount of labeled data and a large amount of unlabeled data. When unlabeled data is combined with a modest bit of labeled data, learning accuracy can be significantly improved. An expert human or a physical experiment is frequently required for collecting

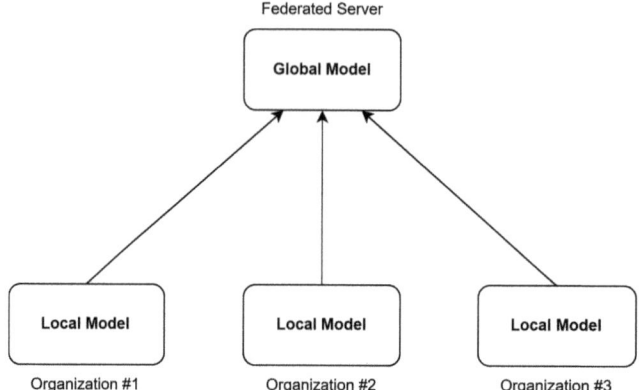

Fig. 2. Federated Learning

the data labels for the training task. Therefore, the cost of labeling may be prohibitive. As a result, the application of semi-supervised machine learning has a lot of potentials.
– Reinforcement learning
It was long overlooked, but this branch of learning was recently noticed when Google DeepMind successfully applied it to learning to play the game of Go. In reinforcement learning, an actor receives information about its environment and chooses actions that maximize the reward. For example, a neural network idles into an electromagnetic game screen and outputs in-game actions to maximize its score which can be trained through reinforcement learning. Reinforcement learning is a relatively new field of research and has not had significant practical success outside of games. However, we expect reinforcement learning to be widely applied in many fields. such as self-driving cars, robotics, resource management, and education.

Federated Learning, a new machine learning technique, is a form of collaborative learning in which multiple machines train a shared model by sharing local models with each other. The objective of federated learning is to enable the use of collective intelligence to enable all devices to learn a shared model directly from user data and improve the accuracy of individual devices. Federated learning is a type of conventional machine learning that is distributed and decentralized, so it can be used when users do not have to share their data with a central server due to privacy and security concerns.

As in Fig. 2, the local models update the global model in federated learning. The advantage of this method is that the training data is not exposed, and the data privacy is protected. Besides, this technique can be used in many distributed data situations, such as smart health, educational technology, and social networking.

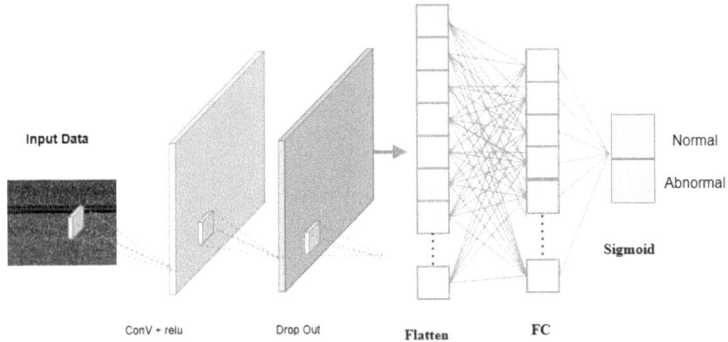

Fig. 3. Structure of CNN model

2.2 Deep Learning

Deep learning is a subset of machine learning in which neural networks automatically extract and process data representation. Deep learning can be used to process data in many ways. For example, deep learning can be used to process unordered text data, images, time-series data, and structured data such as relational databases. Deep learning can be used to extract high-level feature representations from data automatically. Deep learning can also be used to learn complex functions from data.

Feed-forward neural network is the most basic type of neural network. Feed-forward neural networks consist of a series of layers of neurons. The first layer of neurons receives the input data, and each subsequent layer accepts the previous layer's output as input. The last layer produces the output of the neural network.

Recurrent neural networks [4,9,10] are a type of neural network that is used to model time series data or data that has a sequential nature. In recurrent neural networks, the output of the current layer is fed back to the input of the next layer. This feedback connection allows the recurrent neural network to model the temporal dependence of the input data.

Convolutional neural networks are a type of neural network that originally is used to model data that has a spatial structure. Convolutional neural networks are composed of layers of neurons that are arranged in a three-dimensional grid. In convolutional neural networks, the neurons in each layer are connected to a small region of the previous layer. This connection pattern allows convolutional neural networks to model the spatial structure of the input data.

3 Proposed Method

We propose a deep learning model that can classify the given input image according to its class type. We also want to ensure the proposed deep learning model (CNN) can learn the weights and the images properly. We have made presumptions about the techniques we have implemented, and through this section, we want to justify and analyze our approach to this problem more.

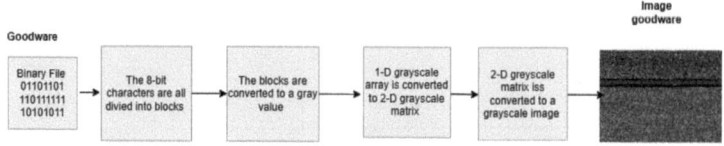

Fig. 4. Data Processing

3.1 Input for the CNN Model

Data Collection. We initially obtained a vast collection of about 30.000 PE ransomware binaries from *virusshare.com*, collected over the period 2010 to 2017.

Research on the Darknet also provided us with the most recent samples, known for damages caused to vital organisations (for example, the gang behind *Lockbit 3.0* leaked its competitors products).

Ransomware binaries tend to be small and written in low level languages, with notable exceptions (GoLang is trendy among hackers and its runtime creates heavy binaries, even after having been compressed with UPX). That's why about 600 negative examples come from $C:\backslash Windows\backslash System32$ as they are small low-level binaries.

The Windows Application Store was used to provide about 2400 others negative examples.

To balance the dataset classes, we keep the 3000 most recent ransomware binaries. Finally, the dataset consists of 3000 positive (malicious) and 3000 negative (benign) examples, in the same order of magnitude as other studies.

We decide to ignore potential variants among ransomware samples as it would be difficult, if not impossible, to comment on the differences and gains in function that distinguish them.

Transforming Binaries into Images. Firstly, we collect software from the window files, then convert data into image format, as shown in Figure a. The grey image has a size of 300×300 in height and width. The process of converting data into image format is shown in Fig. 4.

Examples of common and unusual binaries images are shown in Fig. 5. Ransomware binaries images often show particular patterns that may be discovered by machine learning models:

- Obfuscation methods may alter the binary sections in a recognizable way (like big sections with high entropy due to the payload being compressed),
- They behaviour are not so diverse (encrypt files, send them over the network for double-extortion, display instructions about the ransom payment). This is clearly reflected in their structure.

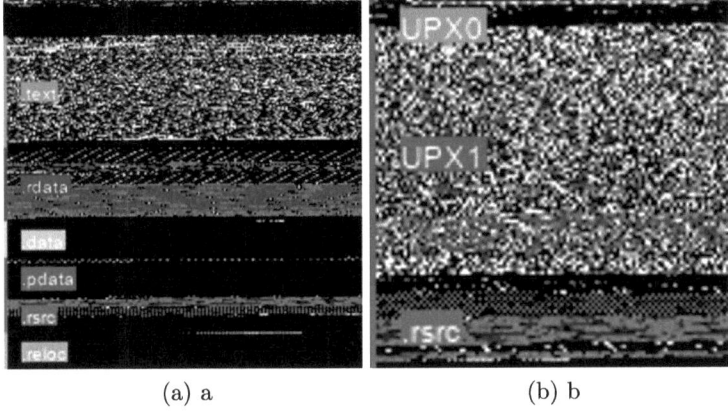

Fig. 5. Benign binary data (a); Unusual binary (b)

3.2 Proposed CNN Model for Classification

A Convolutional Neural Network Model is developed to classify the two classes. The CNN has a total of 3 hidden layers with 1 convolution layers, 1 Dropt Out layer and two fully connected layers. The final output layer is two classes, a classification layer with Sigmoid activation. The structure of CNN is shown in Fig. 3, which contains a combination of convolutional layers, Dropout layer to prevent overfitting, rectified linear unit (ReLU) activation layers, Fully connected layers and an output layer. The output feature map of each convolution in the three layers is applied to the ReLU activation function in the network [1]. The ReLU function is defined

$$f(z^k) = \max\{0, z^k\} = \begin{cases} z^k, z^k \geq 0 \\ 0, else, \end{cases} \tag{1}$$

where z^k is element of outputs in kth convolutional layer.

The feature map is converted from a 2-dimensional matrix into a single vector. The Fully-connected layer is applied in the final convolutional layer with sigmoid activation function as shown:

$$Z = [z_1, ..., z_m]^T = \sigma(h) \tag{2}$$

where z_m is the predicted fault type in the mth category in the M classes, $h = [h_1, ..., h_m]^T$ where $\sigma(h)$ is the sigmoid function, which is defined as:

$$z_m = [\sigma(h)]_m = \frac{e^{h_m}}{\sum_{j=1}^{M} e^{h_j}}, \tag{3}$$

We conducted grid search experiments with different parameters to adjust our model to achieve the other optimized hyperparameters, such as the number of epochs, batch size, and learning rate. The CNN model structure of the proposed architecture in our work is detailed in Table 1 which contains name layers, output shapes, activation function, kernel number and padding.

Table 1. Overview of the Proposed Network Architecture

No	Layer type	Kernel size/Stride	Kernel number	Output size	Padding
1	Convolution + Relu	3 × 3/1	32	300 × 300 × 32	same
2	Drop out	-	-	300 × 300 × 32	-
3	Flatten layer	-	4	2,880,000	same
4	Dense	-	2	-	

3.3 Federated Learning Using CNN Model

The reason that a CNN model is used to implement federated learning is that CNN models can extract useful features and learn representations from images. In the federated learning task, the CNN model is trained using the clients' local data. After the CNN model is trained locally, the weight of the model is aggregated to update the global model. Assume that there are three people using computers: Bob, Alice and Sue. Our ultimate goal is to train a global model that can detect ransomware on Bob, Alice, and Sue computers. However, the data that Bob, Alice, and Sue have is different. Bob may have a collection of ransomware images that Alice and Sue do not have. He may not want to share them. Besides, the data may contain sensitive and private information. For example, the file name or the path of the file may contain personal information. Because of the above reason, a federated learning task is needed to train the global model.

3.4 Experiments

Results with CNN Model. In order to detect ransomware attacks, the CNN model needs to be trained with the prepared data. In this simulation experiment process, to achieve accurate results, image classification is the main result. The proposed CNN models are described as learning a target function that maps input variables to an output variable. This is a general learning task where predictions of the events will be executed using given examples of input variables. Therefore, the CNN will learn based on the input data. There are two classes: normal and ransomware data, which includes more than 100 images in each category.

Each class is assumed to be 0 and 1, corresponding to the normal and ransomware data. Then, we divided the data into three parts: 80% for training, 10%

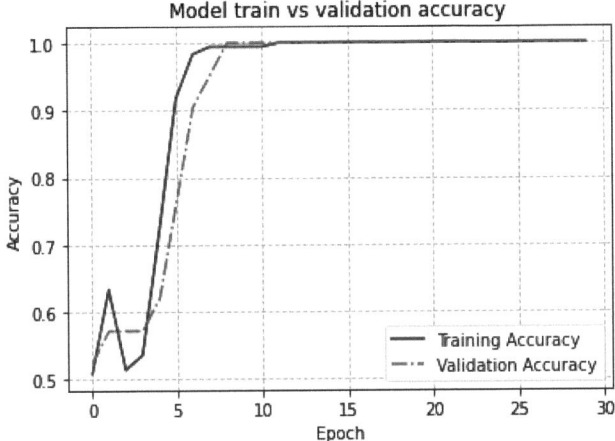

Fig. 6. Traning and validation accuracy

for validation and 10% for testing. In the training phase, the optimization step was set to obtain the optimized hyper parameters corresponding to the layer type, batch size, and a number of filter sizes. The mini batch size is set as 64, the learning rate is set as 0.006, and the epoch is 10 for the training model.

There are two classes of data: normal and ransomware data. The dataset in the experiments is shown in Table 2 together with the amount of data. The dataset was composed of a total of 6,000 samples that contain the two considered categories of "normal" and ransomeware.

Table 2. Experimental Dataset

Type of data	Normal (0)	Ransomeware (1)
Number of sample	3000	3000

Each class is assumed to be 0 and 1, corresponding to the normal and ransomware data. Then, we divided the data into three parts: 80% for training, 10% for validation and 10% for testing. In the training phase, the optimization step was set to obtain the optimized hyper parameters corresponding to the layer type, batch size, and a number of filter sizes. The mini batch size is set as 64, the learning rate is set as 0.006, and the epoch is 10 for the training model.

Figure 6 illustrates the training accuracy and validation accuracy over epoch number for the classification. In the initial stage, we observe that our model has a performance decrease on the training set. This is due to the initial training will only perform a simple approximation of the model. After about 4 epochs, the model's performance increases in both training set and the validation set. The training accuracy and the validation accuracy were increased and converged to 100%.

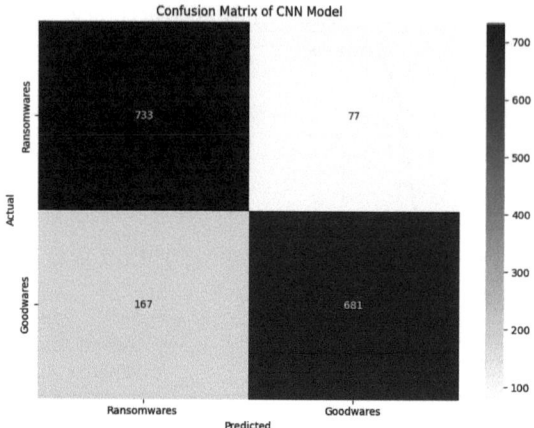

Fig. 7. Confusion matrix of CNN model

After training the prepared dataset with the CNN model, we evaluated the performance classification with the testing dataset. Figure 7 presents the confusion matrix of CNN model when predicting on the testing dataset. These results validate that the proposed CNN can successfully identify cyber-attacks with high accuracy based on the image feature.

CNN Model Using Federated Learning. The purpose of federated learning is not to increase accuracy but to increase data privacy and solve the problem of data decentralization, so in this experiment, we simulate training data on different servers. Considering a real-world scenario where the training data for ransomware attacks is on three different servers, this data is the combination of user behavior data and the data generated by the malware itself. To train a model that is more robust to ransomware detection, data from all three servers have to be used to train the model. However, data from each server is sensitive and should not be shared with other servers. So the federated learning concept can be used to train a model that is more robust to ransomware detection. In federated learning, the model is trained on each server with its own data and then the weights of the model are shared with the other servers. In this way, the data remains private.

We performed comprehensive federated learning experiments with different parameters to adjust the CNN model to achieve the other optimized hyperparameters, such as the number of clients, the number of epochs, batch size, and the learning rate. At the end of the turning process, we have a combination of the parameter as shown in Table 4.

Table 3 shows the precision, recall, and F1-score for the CNN model using federated learning. For precision and recall, the detection scores for normal and Ransomeware attacks achieved identical scores of 92% and 100%, respectively. Similarly, recall scores of 100% and 92%, respectively, are obtained for the normal and Ransomeware attacks. The F1-Score is 96%, which proves the effectiveness of the proposed CNN model using Federated learning.

Table 3. Classification Report of Federated Learning

Classes	Precision	Recall	F1 score
Goodware	81%	90%	86%
Ransomeward	90%	80%	85%

Table 4. Hyperparameter Federated learning

Hyperparameter	Value
Method	"tff_training"
Number of clients	3
NUM_ROUNDS	30
NUM_EPOCHS	30
BATCH_SIZE	64

Discussions. Although the experimental results show some positive results, there are some limitations to our experimental setup. First, the size of our dataset is relatively small. This limitation may lead to overemphasizing the robustness of our federated learning algorithm. Future work will consider a larger dataset. Second, our dataset is mostly equally distributed among clients. However, the data is distributed unequally among clients in the real world. We will consider this case in future work. Third, our experiment can easily split the data into two separate labels, normal and abnormal. However, real-world data may be far more complex and have more classes. We will also consider this case in future work. Also, there is a high risk to learn two important bias. Ransomware binaries are often quite small and zipped by UPX to escape signature based detection. That's why we have to be particularly careful when creating the learning dataset.

4 Conclusions

The proposed system can classify normal and ransomware attacks with high efficiency. The Proposed CNN Model has been tested with a variety of federated learning techniques and the attention of the CNN has been visualized for a better understanding of the classification decisions made by the model to differentiate. Moreover, there has been a detailed analysis done for different Federated learning training techniques for the model and further, the model layers and training parameters can be tweaked to improve and make it more robust.

References

1. Agarap, A.F.: Deep learning using rectified linear units (relu). arXiv preprint arXiv:1803.08375 (2018)
2. Ali, H.M., Kaiser, M.S., Mahmud, M.: Application of convolutional neural network in segmenting brain regions from MRI data. In: International Conference on Brain Informatics, pp. 136–146. Springer, Cham (2019)
3. Bhadra, R., Singh, P.K., Mahmud, M.: Hyepiseid: a hybrid convolutional neural network and gated recurrent unit model for epileptic seizure detection from electroencephalogram signals. Brain Inform. **11**(1), 21 (2024)
4. Cho, K., et al.: Learning phrase representations using RNN encoder-decoder for statistical machine translation. arXiv preprint arXiv:1406.1078 (2014)
5. Chollet, F.: Deep Learning with Python, 1st edn. Manning Publications Co., New York (2017)
6. Fabietti, M., et al.: Adaptation of convolutional neural networks for multi-channel artifact detection in chronically recorded local field potentials. In: 2020 IEEE Symposium Series on Computational Intelligence (SSCI), pp. 1607–1613 (2021). https://doi.org/10.1109/SSCI47803.2020.9308415
7. Hajamohideen, F., et al.: Four-way classification of Alzheimer's disease using deep siamese convolutional neural network with triplet-loss function. Brain Informatics **10**(1), 1–13 (2023)
8. Hnamte, V., Nhung-Nguyen, H., Hussain, J., Hwa-Kim, Y.: A novel two-stage deep learning model for network intrusion detection: LSTM-AE. IEEE Access **11**, 37131–37148 (2023). https://doi.org/10.1109/ACCESS.2023.3266979
9. Hochreiter, S., Schmidhuber, J.: Long short-term memory. Neural Comput. **9**(8), 1735–1780 (1997)
10. John, J.H.: Neural network and physical systems with emergent collective computational abilities. Proc. Natl. Acad. Sci. U.S.A. **79**, 2554–2558 (1982)
11. Mammoottil, M.J., Kulangara, L.J., Cherian, A.S., Mohandas, P., Hasikin, K., Mahmud, M.: Detection of breast cancer from five-view thermal images using convolutional neural networks. J. Healthc. Eng. **2022**(1), 4295221 (2022)
12. Nguyen, H.N., Lee, S., Nguyen, T.T., Kim, Y.H.: One-shot learning-based driver's head movement identification using a millimetre-wave radar sensor. IET Radar, Sonar Navig. **16**(5), 825–836 (2022). https://doi.org/10.1049/rsn2.12223, https://ietresearch.onlinelibrary.wiley.com/doi/abs/10.1049/rsn2.12223
13. Shaffi, N., Hajamohideen, F., Mahmud, M., Abdesselam, A., Subramanian, K., Sariri, A.A.: Triplet-loss based siamese convolutional neural network for 4-way classification of alzheimer's disease. In: International Conference on Brain Informatics, pp. 277–287. Springer, Cham (2022)
14. Singh, R., Mahmud, M., Yovera, L.: Classification of first trimester ultrasound images using deep convolutional neural network. In: Mahmud, M., Kaiser, M.S., Kasabov, N., Iftekharuddin, K., Zhong, N. (eds.) AII 2021. CCIS, vol. 1435, pp. 92–105. Springer, Cham (2021). https://doi.org/10.1007/978-3-030-82269-9_8
15. Sutton, S., Mahmud, M., Singh, R., Yovera, L.: Identification of crown and rump in first-trimester ultrasound images using deep convolutional neural network. In: International Conference on Applied Intelligence and Informatics, pp. 231–247. Springer, Cham (2022)
16. Takeuchi, Y., Sakai, K., Fukumoto, S.: Detecting ransomware using support vector machines. In: Workshop Proceedings of the 47th International Conference on Parallel Processing. ICPP Workshops 2018, Association for Computing Machinery, New York, NY, USA (2018). https://doi.org/10.1145/3229710.3229726

17. Trask, A.W.: Grokking Deep Learning, 1st edn. Manning Publications Co., New York (2019)
18. Wadhera, T., Mahmud, M.: Computing hierarchical complexity of the brain from electroencephalogram signals: a graph convolutional network-based approach. In: 2022 International Joint Conference on Neural Networks (IJCNN), pp. 1–6. IEEE (2022)
19. Wadhera, T., Mahmud, M., Brown, D.J.: A deep concatenated convolutional neural network-based method to classify autism. In: International Conference on Neural Information Processing, pp. 446–458. Springer, Singapore (2022)

Author Index

A
Acharya, Suman 33, 78
Afroj, Maharin 354
Altahan, Abeer 173
Amisha, S. 223
Anik, Zahid Hasan Talukder 304
Anusha, 223
Ayon, Shahriar Siddique 304

B
Badilles, Frandy P. 99
Banerjee, Jyoti Sekhar 318
Batayola, Ferdinand F. 3, 99
Bera, Somnath 389
Bhattacharjya, Kamalika 236
Brown, David J. 141

C
Chakraborty, Arpita 318
Chakraborty, Chinmay 258
Chamarthy, Murthy 199
Chatterjee, Souvik 114
Chattopadhyay, Tanushyam 199

D
Das, Subhranil 163
Dasgupta, Jija 199
De, Debashis 114, 236, 366, 379, 389
Dey, Nilanjan 114
Dey, Tanushree 389

F
Fanani, Ahmad Zainul 90

G
Galimba, John Loey T. 3
Grigoryan, Hakob 339
Guerrache, Faiza 141
Gurjarand, Aruna 49

H
Hasson, Saad Talib 173
Hazra, Arnab 366
Hossain, Muhammad Ebrahim 304

I
Isa, Nor Ashidi Mat 18

J
Jueco, Jayson C. 3, 99
Jumawan, John Cliff A. 99

K
Kabir, Md Mohsin 354
Khatua, Sushovan 379
Kumari, Rashmi 163

L
Lescos, Damien 403
Leukkunen, Jere 208

M
Mahmud, Mufti 60, 141, 186, 304, 318, 354
Maity, Sourajit 186
Majhi, Bablu Kumar 33, 78
Mansoor, Wathiq 49
Miah, Md Saef Ullah 304
Mohammed Ridha, Ali 18
Mridha, M. F. 354
Mukherjee, Anwesha 389
Mukhrjee, Amartya 114
Muljono 90

N
Narvios, Wilen Melsedec O. 3, 99
Nayak, Somen 33, 78, 275, 289
Nguyen, Ha Thanh 403
Nguyen, Hong Nhung 403

Noersasongko, Edi 90
Nurchim 90
Nuruzzaman Nobel, S. M. 354

O
Onipa, Arcel N. 3
Oussalah, Mourad 208

P
Padmashree, G. 223, 246
Panaguiton, Angel Faith M. 3
Panthakkan, Alavikunhu 49
Parikh, Satyen 49
Patel, Hardik 49
Patel, Jagruti 49
Poojary, Sakshi S. 246

R
Radaza, Marvin A. 3, 99
Rahman, M. Mostafizur 304

Rathore, Pramod Singh 124
Roy, Samarjit 379, 389

S
Sarkar, Achyuth 33, 78, 275, 289
Sarkar, Mrinal Kanti 124, 258
Sarkar, Ram 186
Shenoy, B. Mahima 246
Singh, Pawan Kumar 186
Singh, Raghwendra Kishore 163
Srivastava, Shobhit 258

T
Tawfik, Ayman 18
Tran, Tien Anh 366
Tulipas, Riza A. 99

W
Wang, Xiaowen 208

Z
Zouari, Farouk 60

MIX
Papier aus verantwortungsvollen Quellen
Paper from responsible sources
FSC® C105338

If you have any concerns about our products,
you can contact us on
ProductSafety@springernature.com

In case Publisher is established outside the EU,
the EU authorized representative is:
**Springer Nature Customer Service Center GmbH
Europaplatz 3, 69115 Heidelberg, Germany**

Printed by Libri Plureos GmbH
in Hamburg, Germany